Wellbeing, Recovery and Mental Health

Wellbeing, Recovery and Mental Health

Edited by

Mike Slade
Professor of Mental Health Recovery and Social Inclusion, Institute of Mental Health, School of Health Sciences, University of Nottingham, United Kingdom

Lindsay G. Oades
Associate Professor of Positive Psychology, Centre for Positive Psychology, Melbourne Graduate School of Education, University of Melbourne, Australia

Aaron Jarden
Senior Lecturer in Psychology and Research Officer at the Human Potential Centre, Auckland University of Technology, Auckland, New Zealand

CAMBRIDGE
UNIVERSITY PRESS

CAMBRIDGE
UNIVERSITY PRESS

University Printing House, Cambridge CB2 8BS, United Kingdom

One Liberty Plaza, 20th Floor, New York, NY 10006, USA

477 Williamstown Road, Port Melbourne, VIC 3207, Australia

4843/24, 2nd Floor, Ansari Road, Daryaganj, Delhi - 110002, India

79 Anson Road, #06-04/06, Singapore 079906

Cambridge University Press is part of the University of Cambridge.

It furthers the University's mission by disseminating knowledge in the pursuit of education, learning and research at the highest international levels of excellence.

www.cambridge.org
Information on this title: www.cambridge.org/9781107543058

© Cambridge University Press 2017

First published 2017

Printed in the United States of America by Sheridan Books, Inc.

A catalogue record for this publication is available from the British Library.

Library of Congress Cataloguing in Publication data
Names: Slade, Mike, editor. | Oades, Lindsay G., editor. | Jarden, Aaron, editor.
Title: Wellbeing, recovery and mental health / edited by Mike Slade, Lindsay Oades, Aaron Jarden.
Description: Cambridge ; New York : Cambridge University Press, 2016. | Includes bibliographical references and index.
Identifiers: LCCN 2016021863 | ISBN 9781107543058 (paperback)
Subjects: | MESH: Personal Satisfaction | Psychotherapy – methods | Happiness | Mental Disorders – therapy | Psychiatric Rehabilitation – methods
Classification: LCC RC480 | NLM WM 420 | DDC 616.89/14 – dc23
LC record available at https://lccn.loc.gov/2016021863

ISBN 978-1-107-54305-8 Paperback

Contents

Contributors

Amanda Allisey
Deakin Business School, Deakin University, Melbourne, Victoria, Australia

Alice Arch
Melbourne Graduate School of Education, University of Melbourne, Parkville, Victoria, Australia

Nidhi Badiyani
mHealth for Mental Health Program, Geisel School of Medicine at Dartmouth College, Hanover, New Hampshire, US

Dror Ben-Zeev
mHealth for Mental Health Program, Geisel School of Medicine at Dartmouth College, Hanover, New Hampshire, US

Tony Coggins
Head of Mental Health Promotion, South London and Maudsley NHS Foundation Trust, London, UK

Alice Cotton
Melbourne Graduate School of Education, University of Melbourne, Parkville, Victoria, Australia

Justin C. Coulson
Centre for Positive Psychology, Melbourne Graduate School of Education, University of Melbourne, Melbourne, Victoria, Australia

Trevor P. Crowe
Illawarra Institute for Mental Health, School of Psychology, University of Wollongong, Wollongong, New South Wales, Australia

Frank P. Deane
Illawarra Institute for Mental Health, School of Psychology, University of Wollongong, Wollongong, New South Wales, Australia

Deborah Delman
Executive Director, The Transformation Center, Roxbury, Massachusetts, US

Jonathan Delman
Systems and Psychosocial Advances Research Center (SPARC), Department of Psychiatry, University of Massachusetts Medical School, Worcester, Massachusetts, US

Ross Gordon
Senior Lecturer in Marketing, Department of Marketing and Management, Macquarie University, Sydney, New South Wales, Australia

Kristen Hamling
Faculty of Health and Environmental Sciences, Auckland University of Technology, Auckland, New Zealand

Ryan N. Howes
University of Toronto Scarborough, Toronto, Ontario, Canada

Aaron Jarden
Senior Lecturer in Psychology and Research Officer at the Human Potential Centre, Auckland University of Technology, Auckland, New Zealand

Rebecca Jarden
Lecturer in Nursing, School of Clinical Sciences, Auckland University of Technology, Auckland, New Zealand

Corey L. M. Keyes
Department of Sociology, Emory University, Atlanta, Georgia, US

Anthony D. LaMontagne
Centre for Population Health Research, School of Health & Social Development, Deakin University, Melbourne, Victoria, Australia

Ruth Louden
University of Toronto Scarborough,
Toronto, Ontario, Canada

Jane McGregor
Independent education researcher

Pawel D. Mankiewicz
National Health Service, North-East
London NHS Foundation Trust, Early
Intervention in Psychosis, London, UK

Chris C. Martin
Department of Sociology, Emory
University, Atlanta, Georgia, US

Sara Meddings
Consultant Clinical Psychologist, Sussex
Partnership NHS Foundation Trust,
Horsham, UK

Allison J. Milner
Centre for Population Health Research,
School of Health & Social Development,
Deakin University, Melbourne, Victoria,
Australia, and Centre for Health Equity,
School of Population and Global Health,
University of Melbourne, Melbourne,
Victoria, Australia

Lara Mossman
Centre for Positive Psychology, Melbourne
Graduate School of Education, University
of Melbourne, Melbourne, Victoria,
Australia

Mohammad-Reza Namazi-Rad
Senior Honorary Research Fellow,
University of Wollongong, Wollongong,
New South Wales, Australia

Christopher P. Niemiec
Senior Lecturer and Research Associate,
Department of Clinical and Social Sciences
in Psychology, University of Rochester,
Rochester, New York, US

Andrew Noblet
Deakin Business School, Deakin
University, Melbourne, Victoria,
Australia

Lindsay G. Oades
Associate Professor of Positive Psychology,
Centre for Positive Psychology, Melbourne
Graduate School of Education, University
of Melbourne, Melbourne, Victoria,
Australia

Kathryn Page
Deakin Population Health Strategic
Research Centre, School of Health &
Social Development, Deakin University,
Melbourne, Victoria, Australia

Pascal Perez
Professor and Director, SMART
Infrastructure Facility, University of
Wollongong, Wollongong, New South
Wales, Australia

Tayyab Rashid
Health & Wellness Centre, University of
Toronto Scarborough, Toronto, Ontario,
Canada

Julia C. Renton
National Health Service, South Essex
Partnership University NHS Foundation
Trust, Dunstable, UK

Simon Riches
Institute of Psychiatry, King's College
London, London, UK

Waldo Roeg
Peer Recovery Trainer, Central and North
West London NHS Foundation Trust,
London, UK

Reuben Rusk
Melbourne Graduate School of Education,
University of Melbourne, Melbourne,
Victoria, Australia

Beate Schrank
Division of Social Psychiatry, Department
of Psychiatry and Psychotherapy, Medical
University of Vienna, Vienna, Austria

Geoff Shepherd
Senior Consultant, ImROC Programme,
Centre for Mental Health, London, UK

Mike Slade
Professor of Mental Health Recovery
and Social Inclusion, Institute of Mental
Health, School of Health Sciences,
University of Nottingham, UK

Gordon B. Spence
Senior Lecturer, University of Wollongong,
Wollongong, New South Wales, Australia

Michael F. Steger
Director of the Center for Meaning and
Purpose, Department of Psychology,
Colorado State University, Fort Collins,
Colorado, USA, and North-West
University, Vanderbijlpark, Gauteng,
South Africa

Sarah Stewart-Brown
Professor, Warwick Medical School,
University of Warwick, Coventry, UK

Jessie Sun
Melbourne School of Psychological
Sciences, University of Melbourne,
Melbourne, Victoria, Australia

Samson Tse
Associate Dean (Undergraduate
Education), Faculty of Social Sciences and
Professor of Mental Health, Department
of Social Work and Social Administration,
The University of Hong Kong, Hong Kong

Genevieve Wallace
King's College London, London, UK

Lea Waters
Professor and Gerry Higgins Chair in
Positive Psychology, Melbourne Graduate
School of Education, University of
Melbourne, Melbourne, Victoria, Australia

Dan Weijers
Lecturer in Philosophy, School of Social
Sciences, University of Waikato, Hamilton,
New Zealand

Foreword

"Doctor, I hope you can cure what I have."

"Mister, I hope you have what I can cure."

When I started out as a therapist forty years ago, it was common for my patients to tell me, "I just want to be happy." I replied, "You mean you want to get rid of depression."

Back then we did not have the tools for building well-being and, blinded by Freud and Schopenhauer (who taught that the best humans can ever do is to minimize their own misery), I had not even become aware of the difference. What I had was only the tools for relieving depression. But every person, every patient "just wants to be happy," and this legitimate goal combines relieving suffering and building well-being. Cure, to my way of thinking, uses the entire arsenal for minimizing misery – drugs and psychotherapy – and combines these with positive psychology. Further, being happy is every person's birthright.

And importantly for this volume, learning well-being may circle back and ameliorate misery.

The dirty little secret of biological psychiatry and of clinical psychology is that they both have given up the notion of cure. Cure takes too long, if it can be done at all, and only brief treatment is reimbursed by insurance companies. So therapy and drugs are now entirely about short-term crisis management and about dispensing cosmetic treatments. But progress has come to a dead end at symptom relief. There are no curative drugs, and no drug is in development that I know of that aims at cure. I am by no means a Freudian, but one thing that I think was exemplary about Freud is that he was after cure. Freud wanted a psychotherapy that worked like an antibiotic – killing the bacteria. Freud's talking cure was an attempt to cure patients by ridding them of symptoms forever using insight and catharsis. The decline of the Freudian influence, but much more importantly the stringencies of managed care, has seduced psychology and psychiatry into working only on symptom relief and not on cure.

I've spent a good part of my life measuring the effects of psychotherapy and of drugs, and here's another dirty little secret: almost always the effects are what is technically called "small." Depression is typical. Consider two treatments that are certified by vast literatures to "work": cognitive therapy of depression and selective serotonin reuptake inhibitors (SSRIs, e.g. Prozac). Taking an average over the entire huge literature, for each you get a 65% relief rate, accompanied by a placebo effect that ranges from 45% to 55%. This 65% rate crops up over and over, whether you're looking at percentage of patients or at percentage of relief of symptoms within patients. I call this problem "the 65% barrier."

Why is there a 65% barrier and why are the effects so small?

From the first day I took up skiing until five years later when I quit, I was always fighting the mountain. Skiing was never easy. Every form of psychotherapy I know, every exercise, is a "fighting the mountain" intervention. In other words, these therapies are not self-reinforcing and so they fail to maintain themselves. In general, therapeutic techniques all share the property of being difficult to do, no fun at all, and so they are difficult to incorporate into your life. In fact, the way we measure how efficacious therapies are is by how long they last before they "melt" once treatment ends. Every single drug has exactly the same property: once you stop taking the drug you are back to square one, and recurrence and relapse are the rule.

Many of the positive interventions you will read about in this volume are, in contrast, self-maintaining – they are fun.

In the therapeutic century we've just lived through, the therapist's job was to minimize negative emotion: to dispense drugs or psychological interventions that make people less anxious, angry, or depressed. There is another, more realistic approach to dysphoria, however: learning to function well even if you are sad or anxious or angry – in other words, *dealing with it*.

This posture emerges from the most important (and most politically uncongenial) research finding in the field of personality of the last quarter of the 20th century. This rock-solid finding disillusioned an entire generation of environmentalist researchers (me included), but it is true that most personality traits are highly heritable, and dysphorias often stem from these personality traits. Strong biological underpinnings predispose some of us to sadness, anxiety, and anger. Therapists can modify these emotions but only within limits.

What can a therapist do if the heritability of dysphoria is one cause of the 65% barrier? Oddly enough, therapists can use information from the way that snipers are trained. (I'm not endorsing sniping, by the way; I only want to describe how training is done.) It takes about 24 hours for a sniper to get into position. And then it can take another 36 hours to get off the shot. This means that snipers typically haven't slept for two days before they shoot. They're dead tired. Now, let's say the army went to a psychotherapist and asked how she would train a sniper. She would use wake-up drugs or psychological interventions that relieve sleepiness (a rubber band on the wrist snapping you into temporary alertness).

That is not how snipers are trained, however. To train them, you keep them up for three days, and you have them practice shooting when they are dead tired. That is, you teach snipers to *deal* with the negative state they're in: to function well in the presence of fatigue.

The modifiability of negative emotions and negative personality traits has very strong biological limits, and the best you can ever do with the cosmetic approach is to get patients to live in the best part of their set range of depression or anxiety or anger. Think about Abraham Lincoln and Winston Churchill, two severe unipolar depressives. They were both enormously well-functioning human beings who dealt with their "black dog" and their suicidal thoughts (Lincoln likely tried to kill himself in January 1841). Both learned to function extremely well even when they were massively depressed. So one thing that clinical psychology needs to develop in light of the heritable stubbornness of human pathologies is a psychology of "dealing with it." We need to tell our patients, "Look, the truth is that many days – no matter how successful we are in therapy – you will wake up blue and hopeless. Your job is not only to fight these feelings but also to live heroically: functioning well even when you are very sad."

This volume discusses a new approach to cure that goes beyond this realism.

It is possible that the positive interventions may break through the 65% barrier and move psychotherapy beyond cosmetic symptom relief toward cure.

Psychotherapy and drugs as they now are used are half-baked. At their very, very best they remove the internal disabling conditions of life. *Removing* the disabling conditions, however, is not remotely the same as *building* the enabling conditions of life. If we want to flourish and to have well-being, we must indeed minimize our misery, but in addition we must have positive emotion, meaning, accomplishment, and positive relationships.

The skills of flourishing – of having positive emotion, meaning, good work, and positive relationships – are something over and above the skills of minimizing suffering. These skills are documented to build well-being, and they also may act to relieve psychopathology itself. This volume tells their story.

Martin Seligman

Chapter

1

Why Wellbeing and Recovery?

Mike Slade, Lindsay G. Oades and Aaron Jarden

This book brings together two bodies of knowledge.

What Is Wellbeing?

The first body of knowledge is concerned with 'a good life' – understanding what makes life worth living. Research into this topic is variously labelled as wellbeing, mental capital, positive psychology or positive mental health. These academic disciplines have a long tradition, certainly dating back at least 2,000 years to Aristotle's concept of eudaemonia – 'human flourishing'. However, as a scientific endeavour it has gained traction in the last two decades, in particular with the advent of the emerging field of positive psychology (Rusk, 2013).

Several theories have attempted to define and characterise key aspects of wellbeing. Self-determination theory, for example, emphasises the role of personal autonomy, competence and relatedness to others and the mechanisms by which meeting these requirements leads to autonomous motivation (Ryan, 2000). In contrast, the 'PERMA' theory of wellbeing asserts that five key areas constitute wellbeing: positive emotions, engagement, positive relationships, meaning and accomplishment (Seligman, 2011). The Foresight Report (subtitled 'making the most of ourselves in the 21st century') summarised the best available evidence on improving mental capital and wellbeing (Foresight Mental Capital Wellbeing Project, 2008). Its key messages were summarised by the New Economics Foundation as Five Ways to Wellbeing: connect, be active, keep learning, give to others and take notice (Aked, 2008).

Positive interventions demonstrate evidence of effectiveness: meta-analyses show that positive interventions have effect sizes around 0.3 (Bolier et al., 2013; Sin and Lyubomirsky, 2009), as outlined in Chapter 2. Wellbeing research has been increasingly widely applied, for example in organisations (Page, 2009) and in positive education frameworks for schools (Norrish, 2013). Governments are investing in positive assessment; for example, protective factors against trauma identified in wellbeing research inform the US$125m Comprehensive Soldier Fitness program in the US Army. Finally, wellbeing research has been applied to health settings, through positive neuroscience (http://www.posneuroscience.org), positive psychotherapy (Rashid and Seligman, 2013) and positive clinical psychology (Wood, 2010).

At the national level, the United Kingdom now has a Measuring National Well-Being Programme, run by the Office of National Statistics. The programme aims to produce accepted and trusted measures of the wellbeing of the nation – how the United Kingdom as a whole is doing. Population-level annual survey data are used to investigate how wellbeing is connected with relationships (Randall, 2015), social capital (Siegler, 2015) and many other areas

Wellbeing, Recovery and Mental Health, ed. Mike Slade, Lindsay Oades and Aaron Jarden.
Published by Cambridge University Press. © Mike Slade, Lindsay Oades and Aaron Jarden 2017

of life (http://www.ons.gov.uk/ons/guide-method/user-guidance/well-being/publications/index.html). This allows international comparison of wellbeing indicators (Randall, 2014).

What Is Recovery?

The second body of knowledge is concerned with recovery in the context of mental illness. The notion of recovery has a long history in mental health services, traditionally understood as a 'return to normal'. A typical definition is that recovery involves full symptom remission, full- or part-time work/education, independent living without supervision by informal caregivers, and having friends with whom activities can be shared, all sustained for a period of at least two years (Libermann and Kopelowicz, 2002). However, in the past two or three decades a new understanding has emerged, which challenges the view that recovery involves a return to symptom-free normality. People personally affected by mental illness have become increasingly vocal in communicating what helps in moving beyond the role of 'patient'. Recovery has been defined as 'a deeply personal, unique process of changing one's attitudes, values, feelings, goals, skills, and/or roles' and 'a way of living a satisfying, hopeful, and contributing life even within the limitations caused by illness' (Anthony, 1993).

The new understanding of recovery therefore places far greater emphasis on subjective experience, and is the meaning of recovery which is used in this book.

Implementing Recovery Is Challenging

The recovery approach has captured the policy ground internationally, as outlined in Chapter 3. Despite the international policy consensus, it has proved challenging to develop a recovery orientation in mental health services which gives primacy to the individual's understanding (Davidson et al., 2006). This is partly because the development of an empirical science of recovery lags behind policy. This mismatch is decreasing, as discussed in Chapter 3.

However, we believe that another reason that translating recovery policy into clinical reality has proved problematic is that a recovery approach remains embedded in a clinical perspective. However described, recovery is defined in relation to illness. This inadvertently reinforces a view of otherness – that even in a recovery-oriented mental health system, people with mental health problems remain different from other people. The empirical evidence supports this concern. Globally, high levels of experienced and anticipated discrimination are identified by people living with schizophrenia (Thornicroft et al., 2009) and other diagnoses, such as depression (Lasalvia et al., 2013). Stigmatising views are also present, and persistent, in health professionals (Henderson, 2014). Despite modest decreases in stigmatising attitudes in the wider community following national anti-stigma campaigns (Evans-Lacko, 2014), stigma in mental health staff and service users remains high.

Stigma creates problems. For staff, even those working to support recovery, it is hard to let go of the assumption that their need is primarily to deal with illness, that is to do things, ideally *with* but if necessary *to*, the service user. Care planning therefore involves actions primarily by staff, not service users (Gilburt et al., 2013). Illness-specific interventions are developed for everyday problems, such as social skills training for people wanting a relationship, or Individual Placement and Support for people wanting a job (Slade, 2012). Strengths of individuals are far less visible than deficits, so specific interventions are developed to assess (Rashid and Ostermann, 2009), amplify (Oades and Anderson, 2012) and orient services (Rapp and Goscha, 2006) to strengths. People living with mental illness continue to live in social spaces defined by their illnesses, albeit the previous physical institution has been replaced by a 'virtual' institution (Priebe et al., 2005). A mental illness remains an 'engulfing' or 'enmeshing' identity.

The Intersection between Recovery and Wellbeing

The focus of this book is on the overlap between these two bodies of knowledge.

Wellbeing and the positive psychology literature have focussed on *living well*. Traditional mental health services have focussed on *getting rid of illness*. The overlap is very limited, because illness-oriented clinical discourse is irrelevant to the concerns of most people (who do not have an illness to 'get rid of'). The recovery approach, by contrast, focuses on *living well with illness*. The emerging scientific evidence about recovery therefore has implications for wellbeing in the wider community, and wellbeing research applies to people with mental illness.

The integration of ideas from these two disciplines is not entirely novel. The established and empirically validated two-factor model of mental illness and mental health is outlined in Chapter 8. The use of positive psychology research to support psychological recovery is described in Chapter 9. The aim of this interdisciplinary book is to enhance this rapprochement between these two bodies of knowledge, by

1. identifying the points of connection, where similar if differently named concepts have emerged within both disciplines;
2. using analogical reasoning to extend thinking, in other words, to speculate how a research finding about wellbeing in the general population may also apply to people recovering with mental illness, and how a research finding about recovery may have wider societal relevance.

One benefit of the scientific method is that ideas are made explicit, and hence amenable to debate. To illuminate some of the challenges arising from the use of academic knowledge to help people to live as well as possible, we outline some of the emerging criticisms of recovery.

Critiques of Recovery

A summary of international best practice in supporting recovery (described further in Chapter 3) identified four domains: supporting personally defined recovery; working relationships; organisational commitment; and promoting citizenship. The first three domains are being actively addressed. However, progress in the fourth domain remains elusive. Promoting citizenship involves living a life *beyond* illness, as a productive and contributing member of society. It overlaps with ideas around social inclusion (the term used in Europe and Australasia) and community integration (the term used in North America).

Critics of the recovery movement make the point that recovery as currently operationalised within mental health systems has several problems. It ignores issues of power (Morrow, 2012). It is political, maintaining neoliberalism (Braslow, 2013) and allowing continued denial of fundamental human rights (Forrest, 2014). Overall, recovery as a social justice movement has been hijacked by the mental health system (Mental Health "Recovery" Study Working Group, 2009).

This has led some commentators to link recovery with other struggles for power within society. In a wide-ranging book, Larry Davidson and colleagues show how recovery is linked to other social movements (Davidson et al., 2010). A recovery approach involves fundamental changes in power, and thus links with other forms of identity politics (Slade, 2009). It involves a changed role for mental health professionals, from providers of treatment to political activists (Slade, 2010). However, power is rarely if ever given to groups – it is taken, through collective identity and empowerment. Historical examples include addressing racial segregation in the United States, obtaining voting rights for women in the United Kingdom and upholding rights for indigenous people in New Zealand and Australia. In relation to the mental health system, it is noteworthy that homosexuality ceased in 1974 to be classified as a mental illness not because of new scientific evidence, but because of protesters picketing the American Psychiatric Association's annual conventions.

Bill Anthony, in characterising the various approaches to defining and understanding recovery, proposed that they are united in their focus away from illness and towards personhood – his grandly named Transcendent Principle of Personhood summarised this as "People with severe mental illness are people" (Anthony, 2004). We have yet to witness the revolutionary phase of seeing people like us rather than people living with illness.

One approach to supporting this revolution is to envisage what it might look like. We believe that a mental health system that was fully supporting recovery would look different in language, assumptions, theory base and working practices. It would have a natural focus on strengths. The focus of worker actions would naturally be around the person's goals – there would be no need for specific technologies to support patient-centred care. Just as much attention would be given to society as to the individual, so rights, entitlements and responsibilities would be the common discourse, rather than management, treatment and risk. The organisation would be focussed on supporting access to mainstream solutions to everyday problems, with treatments provided as a means, not an end. The consumer would be in charge, deciding whether to use different types of support – so services would need to be customer-focussed to survive.

This might seem a far-off goal, but we are optimistic. Just as the idea that homosexuality could be just part of the rich tapestry of life must have seemed a distant dream fifty or a hundred years ago, so we envisage a society in which mental health problems are an acceptable and in some ways valued part of human experience. People will need help and support, either intermittently or continuously, but their mental health experience no more defines them than their sexuality, gender, personality or any other aspect of their identity.

Aims of the Book

This book has two aims. The mental health system is in the process of developing a deep understanding of recovery. The developing scientific evidence base of new technologies and approaches to support recovery has wider societal applicability. For example, the empirical evidence of benefit from the peer support worker role in mental health services has implications for other marginalised groups within society. The first aim of this book is to apply insights from recovery to the wider society.

The second aim is to consider what a mental health system would look like which started with the assumption that people with mental health problems are fundamentally like anyone else in society, with the same aspirations and goals. We believe that insights from wellbeing research – what everyone else needs for a 'good life' – are equally relevant to people with mental health problems. The aim is therefore to bring insights from wider research into the mental health system, by considering how mental health services should change if their goal is to support wellbeing.

The book is intended for an international readership. It will be of specific interest to two groups. Mental health service users, caregivers, workers and researchers will develop a better understanding of how wellbeing research can and should impact on clinical practice. Policy makers, researchers and community development stakeholders will develop a better understanding of how the methods of health services research illuminate some of the processes by which people with mental illness – and, by extension, other marginalised groups in society – can be supported to have lives worth living.

The book has three sections. In Section 1, contributors outline relevant theoretical foundations and conceptual frameworks for recovery and wellbeing. As noted, these are currently somewhat separate, so Section 1 makes linkages. In Section 2, contributors identify what mental health services might look like if wellbeing research is drawn in. In Section 3, contributors describe the implications of recovery and wellbeing research and related practises for the wider society.

References

Aked, J., Marks, N., Cordon, C., & Thompson, S. (2008). *Five ways to wellbeing: The evidence*. London, UK: New Economics Foundation.

Anthony, W. (2004). The principle of personhood: The field's transcendent principle. *Psychiatric Rehabilitation Journal*, 27, 205.

Anthony, W. A. (1993). Recovery from mental illness: The guiding vision of the mental health system in the 1990s. *Psychosocial Rehabilitation Journal*, 16, 11–23.

Bolier, L., Haverman, M., Westerhof, G., Riper, H., Smit, F., & Bohlmeijer, E. (2013). Positive psychology interventions: A meta-analysis of randomized controlled studies. *BMC Public Health*, 13–119.

Braslow, J. (2013). The manufacture of recovery. *Annual Review of Clinical Psychology*, 9, 781–809.

Davidson, L., O'Connell, M., Tondora, J., Styron, T., & Kangas, K. (2006). The top ten concerns about recovery encountered in mental health system transformation. *Psychiatric Services*, 57 640–645.

Davidson, L., Rakfeldt, J., & Strauss, J. (2010). *The roots of the recovery movement in psychiatry*. Chichester, UK: Wiley-Blackwell.

Evans-Lacko, S., Corker, E., Williams, P., Henderson, C., & Thornicroft, G. (2014). Effect of the Time to Change anti-stigma campaign on trends in mental-illness-related public stigma among the English population in 2003–13: An analysis of survey data. *Lancet Psychiatry*, 1, 121–128.

Foresight Mental Capital Wellbeing Project (2008). *Mental capital and wellbeing: Making the most of ourselves in the 21st century* (Final Project Report). London, UK: Government Office for Science.

Forrest, R. (2014). The implications of adopting a human rights approach to recovery in practice. *Mental Health Practice*, 17, 29–33.

Gilburt, H., Slade, M., Bird, V., Oduola, S., & Craig, T. K. (2013). Promoting recovery-oriented practice in mental health services: A quasi-experimental mixed-methods study. *BMC Psychiatry*, 13, 167.

Henderson, C., Noblett, J., Parke, H., Clement, S., Caffrey, A., Gale-Grant, O., et al. (2014). Mental health-related stigma in health care and mental health-care settings. *Lancet Psychiatry*, 1, 467–482.

Lasalvia, A., Zoppei, S., Van Bortel, T., Bonetto, C., Cristofalo, D., Wahlbeck, K., et al. (2013). Global pattern of experienced and anticipated discrimination reported by people with major depressive disorder: A cross-sectional survey. *Lancet*, 381, 55–62.

Libermann, R. P., & Kopelowicz, A. (2002). Recovery from schizophrenia: A challenge for the 21st century. *International Review of Psychiatry*, 14, 242–255.

Mental Health "Recovery" Study Working Group (2009). *Mental health "recovery": Users and refusers*. Toronto, Ontario: Wellesley Institute.

Morrow, M., & Weisser, J. (2012). Towards a social justice framework of mental health recovery. *Studies in Social Justice*, 6, 27–43.

Norrish, J., Williams, P., O'Connor, M., & Robinson, J. (2013). An applied framework for positive education. *International Journal of Wellbeing*, 3, 147–161.

Oades, L. G., & Anderson, J. (2012). Recovery in Australia: Marshalling strengths and living values. *International Review of Psychiatry*, 24, 5–10.

Page, K., & Vella-Brodrick, D. (2009). The 'what', 'why' and 'how' of employee well-being: A new model. *Social Indicators Research*, 90, 441–458.

Priebe, S., Badesconyi, A., Fioritti, A., Hansson, L., Kilian, R., Torres-Gonzales, F., et al. (2005). Reinstitutionalisation in mental health care: Comparison of data on service provision from six European countries. *BMJ*, 330, 123–126.

Randall, C. (2015). *Measuring national well-being: Our relationships, 2015*. London, UK: Office for National Statistics.

Randall, C., & Corp, A. (2014). *Measuring national well-being: European comparisons, 2014*. London, UK: Office for National Statistics.

Rapp, C., & Goscha, R. J. (2006). *The strengths model: Case management with people with psychiatric disabilities* (2nd ed.). New York, NY: Oxford University Press.

Rashid, T., & Ostermann, R. F. (2009). Strength-based assessment in clinical practice. *Journal of Clinical Psychology*, 65, 488–498.

Rashid, T., & Seligman, M. E. (2013). Positive psychotherapy. In Wedding, D. & Corsini, R. J. (Eds.), *Current Psychotherapies* (pp. 98–110). Belmont, CA: Cengage.

Rusk, R., & Waters, L. (2013). Tracing the size, reach, impact and breadth of positive psychology. *Journal of Positive Psychology*, 8, 207–222.

Ryan, R., & Decl, E. (2000). Self-determination theory and the facilitation of intrinsic motivation, social development and well-being. *American Psychologist*, 55, 68–78.

Seligman, M. (2011). *Flourish*, London, Nicholas Brealy Publishing.

Siegler, V. (2015). *Measuring national well-being – An analysis of social capital in the UK*. London, UK: Office for National Statistics.

Sin, N. L., & Lyubomirsky, S. (2009). Enhancing well-being and alleviating depressive symptoms with positive psychology interventions: A practice-friendly meta-analysis. *Journal of Clinical Psychology*, 65, 467–487.

Slade, M. (2009). *Personal Recovery and Mental Illness*, Cambridge, UK: Cambridge University Press.

Slade, M. (2010). Mental illness and well-being: The central importance of positive psychology and recovery approaches. *BMC Health Services Research*, 10, 26.

Slade, M. (2012). Everyday solutions for everyday problems: How mental health systems can support recovery. *Psychiatric Services*, 63, 702–704.

Thornicroft, G., Brohan, E., Rose, D., Sartorius, N., Leese, M., & Group, I. S. (2009). Global pattern of experienced and anticipated discrimination against people with schizophrenia: A cross-sectional survey. *Lancet*, 9661, 408–415.

Wood, A., & Tarrier, N. (2010). Positive clinical psychology: A new vision and strategy for integrated research and practice. *Clinical Psychology Review*, 30, 819–829.

Chapter

The Science of Wellbeing and Positive Psychology

Lindsay G. Oades and Lara Mossman

The seemingly innocuous question "What is wellbeing?" easily leads to passionate debates and much conceptual confusion. This chapter first provides some signposts for a definition of wellbeing. Sound definition of the construct is essential to the measurement of wellbeing and the growth of the science of wellbeing. The emergence of the science of positive psychology and its application through positive psychology interventions (i.e. strategies to increase wellbeing) have created new opportunities to develop wellbeing in individuals, organizations and communities. After positive psychology is defined, key theories of wellbeing and positive psychology are summarized. An overview of key research evidence from positive psychology interventions is then provided. This overview is intended not as an exhaustive review, but rather as a sample to enable readers to explore the fertile interface of the science of wellbeing and positive psychology with the literature and experience of recovery.

What Is Wellbeing?

Responses to the question *What is wellbeing?* vary greatly depending on whether it is a lay person, health practitioner, person with lived experience of illness, economist, philosopher, psychologist or sociologist answering the question. Lay persons or persons unfamiliar with defining concepts or constructs commonly give examples of situations or experiences that lead to wellbeing, such as having good friends or a good job. A philosophical definition is commonly brief and coherent, but may lack the precision that a scientist is seeking. One philosophical example is the following definition: how well someone's life is going for them (Crisp, 2014).

Philosophers have been arguing over and defining wellbeing for many centuries. Economists have been doing so for over one hundred years. Psychologists and wellbeing scientists are relatively new to this arena. Although recognizing the contributions to this area from philosophers (e.g. the distinction between hedonic and eudaemonic wellbeing) and economists (e.g. the distinction between evaluative and experienced wellbeing), this chapter focuses primarily on empirical attempts to define, measure and increase wellbeing, with particular focus on positive psychology and its related interventions.

In attempting to define wellbeing it is useful to consider several questions from the outset:

1. What is the level of analysis? for example: individual, group, organization, society
2. What domain is being discussed? for example: physical, mental, social
3. Is it to be defined subjectively or objectively?
4. Does it necessarily require the presence of positive attributes? in other words, is it more than the absence of negative attributes such as symptoms of illness?

Wellbeing, Recovery and Mental Health, ed. Mike Slade, Lindsay Oades and Aaron Jarden.
Published by Cambridge University Press. © Mike Slade, Lindsay Oades and Aaron Jarden 2017

5. Is wellbeing multifaceted (multidimensional)?
6. How is it different from health?

Clarity regarding these six questions makes it is easier to locate one's position within the contested space of wellbeing constructs. Table 2.1 summarizes some key examples of contemporary wellbeing constructs in wellbeing science and positive psychology. Such constructs underpin the emerging health and wellbeing outcome measurement in health and human services. In reading Table 2.1, it is useful to examine the difference between hedonic and eudaemonic assumptions in terms of defining wellbeing. Shorthand definitions often combine these two approaches in phrases such as *"feeling good and functioning well"* (see Huppert and So, 2013).

Table 2.1 Scientific Constructs of Wellbeing

Wellbeing construct	Definition	Reference
Hedonic wellbeing	"focuses on happiness and defines wellbeing in terms of pleasure attainment and pain avoidance""the predominant view among hedonic psychologists is that wellbeing consists of subjective happiness and concerns the experience of pleasure versus displeasure broadly construed to include all judgments about the good/bad elements of life. Happiness is thus not reducible to physical hedonism, for it can be derived from attainment of goals or valued outcomes in varied realms"	Ryan and Deci (2001b, p. 141)
Eudaemonic wellbeing	"The eudaimonic perspective of wellbeing – based on Aristotle's view that true happiness comes from doing what is worth doing – focuses on meaning and self-realization, and defines wellbeing largely in terms of ways of thought and behavior that provide fulfillment"	Gale et al. (2013, p. 687)
Wellbeing	"refers to optimal psychological experience and functioning""Ryff and Keyes (1995) … spoke of psychological well-being (PWB) as distinct from SWB and presented a multidimensional approach to the measurement of PWB that taps six distinct aspects of human actualization: autonomy, personal growth, self-acceptance, life purpose, mastery, and positive relatedness. These six constructs define PWB both theoretically and operationally and they specify what promotes emotional and physical health"	Deci and Ryan (2008, p. 1) Ryan and Deci (2001b, p. 146)

Table 2.1 *(cont.)*

Wellbeing construct	Definition	Reference
Psychological wellbeing	"Each dimension of PWB articulates different challenges individuals encounter as they strive to function positively (Ryff, 1989a; Ryff and Keyes, 1995). That is, people attempt to feel good about themselves even while aware of their own limitations (self-acceptance). They also seek to develop and maintain warm and trusting interpersonal relationships (positive relations with others) and to shape their environment so as to meet personal needs and desires (environmental mastery). In sustaining individuality within a larger social context, people also seek a sense [of] self-determination and personal authority (autonomy). A vital endeavor is to find meaning in one's efforts and challenges (purpose in life). Lastly, making the most of one's talents and capacities (personal growth) is central to PWB."	Keyes et al. (2002, p. 1008)
Subjective wellbeing	"As an operational definition, SWB is most often interpreted to mean experiencing a high level of positive affect, a low level of negative affect, and a high degree of satisfaction with one's life …The concept of SWB, assessed in this way, has frequently been used interchangeably with 'happiness'. Thus, maximizing one's well-being has been viewed as maximizing one's feelings of happiness."	Deci and Ryan (2008, p. 1)
Wellbeing	"In 2 large samples, results supported the proposed latent structures of hedonic, eudaimonic and social well-being and indicated that the various components of well-being could be represented most parsimoniously with 3 oblique second-order constructs of hedonic, eudaimonic, and social well-being."	Gallagher et al. (2009, p. 1025)
Social wellbeing	"Keyes (1998) conceived of a five-component model of social well-being: social integration, social contribution, social coherence, social actualization, and social acceptance. These five elements, taken together, indicate whether and to what degree individuals are overcoming social challenges and are functioning well in their social world (alongside neighbors, coworkers, and fellow world citizens)."	Gallagher et al. (2009, p. 1027)

(cont.)

Table 2.1 (cont.)

Wellbeing construct	Definition	Reference
Mental health	"a syndrome of symptoms of positive feelings and positive functioning in life"	Keyes (2002, p. 207)
Flourishing	"high levels of wellbeing" "To be *flourishing* in life, individuals must exhibit a high level (high = upper tertile) on one of the two measures of emotional well-being and high levels on six of the 11 scales of positive functioning"	Hone et al. (2014, p. 62) Keyes (2002, p. 210)
Life satisfaction	"Life satisfaction, according to Campbell et al. (1976), reflects individuals' perceived distance from their aspirations … satisfaction is a judgmental, long-term assessment of one's life"	Keyes et al. (2002, pp. 1007–1008)
Happiness	"according to Bradburn (1969), results from a balance between positive affect and negative affect … happiness is a reflection of pleasant and unpleasant affects in one's immediate experience"	Keyes et al. (2002, p. 1008)
Optimal wellbeing	"high subjective wellbeing and psychological wellbeing"	Keyes et al. (2002, p. 1007)
Happiness	"In the first version of his theory, Seligman (2002) claimed that 'happiness' was composed of three subjective facets: positive emotion, engagement, and meaning. Happiness was therefore achievable by pursuing one or more of these facets. As a result, individuals low in one aspect could still be 'happy' if they nurtured other components."	Forgeard et al. (2011, p. 96)
Wellbeing	"wellbeing consists of the nurturing of one or more of the five following elements: Positive emotion, Engagement, Relationships, Meaning, and Accomplishment (abbreviated as the acronym PERMA). These five elements are the best approximation of what humans pursue *for their own sake*"	Forgeard et al. (2011, p. 96)
Positive wellbeing	"we identified the positive pole of each symptom dimension. This resulted in ten features representing positive aspects of mental functioning: competence, emotional stability, engagement, meaning, optimism, positive emotion, positive relationship, resilience, self-esteem, and vitality … it includes both hedonic and eudaimonic components; that is, both positive feeling and positive functioning."	Huppert and So (2013, p. 849)

What Is Positive Psychology?

While the origin of the term 'positive psychology' can be traced back to Abraham Maslow's 1954 book, *Motivation and Personality* (Maslow, 1970; Snyder et al., 2011), it was many years before positive psychology as an academic field was born: a vision that included steering psychology back toward what makes life worth living, toward courage, generosity, creativity, joy, gratitude (Csikszentmihalyi and Nakamura, 2011). The founders of positive psychology recognized that traditional psychology had become predominantly weakness-oriented: an approach that had succeeded in alleviating many forms of human suffering but had failed at capturing the whole human picture (Snyder et al., 2011). The timing was ripe to address this imbalance issue. In the months that followed, Martin Seligman became the President of the American Psychological Association (APA), enabling him to pioneer the new field of positive psychology. He identified two "neglected missions" of psychology (Seligman, 1998, p. 2). The first was building human strength and making people more productive. The second was the nurturing of genius, the generation of high human potential (Compton and Hoffman, 2013; Seligman, 1998). Seligman saw this new field as combining scientific and applied approaches. He called for a mass of research on human strength and virtue. So 1998, therefore, marked the beginning of a seismic shift in psychology (Rusk and Waters, 2013b) and the birth of the field of positive psychology.

In their seminal paper, *Positive Psychology: An Introduction*, Seligman and Csikszentmihalyi (2000) outlined the purpose of the new field: the research and development of the factors that enable flourishing at individual, community and societal levels. The field's scope included three levels of research: the subjective level, the individual level and the group level. Research at the *subjective level* included valued subjective experiences and was broken down into past, present and future constructs: the past involving wellbeing, contentment and satisfaction; the present involving flow and happiness; and the future involving hope and optimism. The *individual level* called for research into individual traits that are positive, such as character strengths (including those that guide our interactions with others), talent and the capacity for vocation. Last, the *group level* comprised research into "civic virtues and the institutions that move individuals towards better citizenship: responsibility, nurturance, altruism, civility, moderation, tolerance and work ethic" (Seligman and Csikszentmihalyi, 2000, p. 5). Positive psychology thus emerged as the scientific study of positive human functioning and flourishing intrapersonally (e.g. biologically, emotionally, cognitively), interpersonally (e.g. relationally) and collectively (e.g. institutionally, culturally and globally) (Crompton and Hoffman, 2013; Seligman and Csikszentmihalyi, 2000).

In the 15 or so years since the inception of positive psychology, a number of themes have surfaced, such as altruism, accomplishment, appreciation of beauty and excellence, authenticity, best possible selves, character strengths, coaching, compassion, courage, coping, creativity, curiosity, emotional intelligence, empathy, flow, forgiveness, goal setting, gratitude, grit, happiness, hope, humour, kindness, leadership, love, meaning, meditation, mindfulness, motivation, optimism, performance, perseverance, positive emotions, positive relationships, post-traumatic growth, psychological capital, purpose, resilience, savoring, self-efficacy, self-regulation, spirituality, the good life, virtues, wisdom and zest. Many of the themes studied have their origins outside of the field of positive psychology. However, Rusk and Waters (2013b) looked at the breadth of the field and found that approximately a third of the positive-psychology-related terms they studied were new to the field since 1999. Therefore, it seems that positive psychology is largely exploring existing constructs, but through a fresh lens. In addition to the breadth, they also found that the size, reach and impact of the field had grown substantially since its founding. This growth has generated new sub–fields focused on the application of the science, such as positive education (Norrish 2015; Norrish et al., 2013) or positive organizational behavior and positive organizational scholarship (Wright and Quick, 2009).

As the science disseminates, there are some issues that arise by virtue of the immaturity of the field. While the breadth of research undertaken is substantial (Rusk and Waters, 2013b), there is tension between the depth of research and the desire for real-world application. A number of single studies have shown promising findings, but more research that replicates them across a range of populations and contexts is required: whom do interventions work for and under what conditions (i.e. effectiveness rather than efficacy: see Hone et al., 2015)? More longitudinal studies are required, too. As the field matures, longitudinal studies will be conducted. In the meantime, positive psychology researchers are reminded to adhere to rigorous scientific standards (Snyder et al., 2011) such as those of meta-analysis and randomized control trials (Vella-Brodrick, 2013). Paradoxically, while positive psychology offers itself as the antidote to the negativity bias of psychology as usual, it must not fall prey to focusing solely on the good in the world. Good science looks at the whole picture (Snyder et al., 2011). As the field works toward this, those working with the application of positive psychology must ensure that they are conscientious consumers of the science, and as such new journals focusing specifically on these issues are emerging (e.g. the *International Journal of Applied Positive Psychology*, which will launch in 2016). It is with this in mind that we move to the key theories and evidence.

What Are Some Key Theories within Wellbeing and Positive Psychology Research?

There is a well-established suite of theories relating to wellbeing and key areas of positive psychology. Table 2.2 provides a sample of some of the key theories, which include emotions, attentional states, cognition, motivation, goal striving and relationships.

What Is the Evidence Base?

The evidence base underpinning the field of positive psychology is small but rapidly growing (Rusk and Waters, 2013) and can be broken down into cross-sectional studies and causal studies. Cross-sectional studies look at associations between variables (e.g. are happier people healthier?), and causal studies look at what impacts wellbeing over time (i.e. does marriage increase wellbeing?). Both types of studies can lead to inferences about what leads to or predicts wellbeing, with causal studies providing strong evidence.

As an example of a cross-sectional study, Waugh and Fredrickson (2006) found that in a group of students increased assimilation and understanding of their roommates was associated with higher levels of positive emotion. The caution with these types of cross-sectional studies is that it is not clear or conclusive if A leads to B, of if B leads to A, or if some other variable mediates the relationship – for example, if higher positive emotion leads to greater understanding of roommates, or if greater understanding of roommates leads to higher positive emotion. As some further examples of this type of research, Fredrickson and Levenson (1998) found that positive emotions can help people cope with physiological responses to negative emotions, and in a large meta-analysis, Lyubomirsky et al. (2005) found that people

Table 2.2 Key Theories of Wellbeing and Positive Psychology

Theory	Key proposition	Key researcher
Broaden-and-build theory	Positive emotions *broaden* awareness and over time enable the *building* of resources.	Fredrickson
Flow theory	Flow is focused motivation involving single-minded immersion in an appropriately challenging goal-based activity.	Csikszentmihalyi
Hope theory	Hope is perceived ability to produce pathways to achieve desired goals and motivation to use those pathways.	Snyder
Psychological wellbeing	Psychological wellbeing involves not only the absence of illness, but the presence of something positive: growth, positive relationships, autonomy, purpose and environmental mastery.	Ryff & Keyes
Self-determination theory	There are different types of motivation for activities, ranging from those that feel intrinsic to those that feel extrinsic. Conditions will meet our psychological needs differently through our sense of autonomy, competence and relatedness. In turn this impacts our quality of motivation.	Deci & Ryan
Strengths theories	Individuals have personal strengths that can be measured reliably across cultures.	Peterson/Seligman Linley
Wellbeing (PERMA) theory	Wellbeing can be achieved through five key pathways: positive emotions, engagement, positive relationships, meaning and accomplishment.	Seligman

with higher levels of positive emotion were more successful across many life domains such as work, relationships and health.

As an example of a causal study, Lyubomirsky et al. (2005) examined the results of experimental studies and found that increasing people's positive emotions had the effect of making them better at conflict resolution and more social. They also found in their meta-analysis, which included longitudinal studies, that happiness does lead to better relationship and work outcomes. As examples of evidence they cited findings that increases in happiness lead to greater creativity, productivity and quality of work, and income (Estrada et al., 1994) and to stronger social support and an increased likelihood of marriage (Harker and Keltner, 2001), that subjective wellbeing impacts mental and physical health (Pressman and Cohen, 2005) and leads to healthier immune function (Davidson et al., 2003), and that happier people even live longer.

Furthermore, what both this cross-sectional and causal research suggest is that positive emotions can and do have impacts beyond individuals to their close connections.

What Is the Evidence for Positive Psychology Interventions?

Sin and Lyubomirsky (2009) define positive psychology interventions (PPIs) as "treatment methods or intentional activities aimed at cultivating positive feelings, positive behaviours, or positive cognitions." Their meta-analysis found that PPIs are effective at increasing wellbeing and decreasing depression, but the effect sizes were moderate and should be

Table 2.3 Efficacy of Positive Psychology Interventions (PPIs)

Intervention	Efficacy	Participants	Measures
Best possible selves (BPS; including you at your best) *(involves writing about oneself at one's best in all domains of one's life)*	You at your best led to gains in happiness and decreased depression immediately postintervention (Seligman et al., 2005).	Adults (range = 35–54 years) recruited via the Internet	Center for Epidemiological Studies – Depression Scale (CES-D) symptom survey; 20-item Steen Happiness Index (SHI)
	BPS has been shown to lead to greater increases in positive affect and self-concordant motivation as compared with counting blessings and control groups. It has also led to immediate decreases in negative affect (Sheldon and Lyubomirsky, 2006).	University students	Positive and Negative Affect Schedule (PANAS); Self-Concordant Motivation (SCM); exercise performance, for example, how frequently exercise was practiced
	The BPS condition was found to be more effective at increasing optimism than the control condition (Peters et al., 2010).	Swedish university students (mean age = 29.6 years, range 21–50)	Dispositional optimism, the Life Orientation Test (LOT); extraversion and neuroticism measured by two subscales of the Eysenck Personality Questionnaire Revised Short Form (EPQ-RSS); short form of the Positive and Negative Affect Schedule (PANAS)
Forgiveness	Forgiveness interventions have been used with a broad range of clinical clients, with foundational research occurring before positive psychology. Combined with gratitude and life memories in an intervention, forgiveness has been found to help increase subjective well-being and quality of life (Ramírez et al., 2014).	Older adults (mean = 71.18 years; range 60–93 years)	Spanish versions of the State and Trait Anxiety Inventory (STAI); Beck Depression Inventory (BDI); Autobiographical Memory Test (AMT); Mini-cognitive Exam (Mini-Examen Cognoscitivo [MEC]; Life Satisfaction Scale (LSS); Subjective Happiness Scale

Gratitude	Gratitude visits have been shown to lead to gains in happiness and decreased depression in adults immediately postintervention and up to 1 month postintervention (Seligman et al., 2005).	Adults (range = 35–54 years) recruited via the Internet	Center for Epidemiological Studies – Depression Scale (CES-D) symptom survey; 20-item Steen Happiness Index (SHI)
(including gratitude visit; gratitude letters; noticing good things; recording good things; counting blessings)	Youth low in positive affect have reported high levels of gratitude (compared to the control group) and positive affect immediately after the gratitude letter/journal intervention, and positive affect at 2 months' follow-up (Froh et al., 2009).	Students (mean age = 12.74 years, range = 8–19 years)	Gratitude Adjective Checklist (GAC); Positive and Negative Affect Scale – Children (PANAS-C)
	Counting blessings participants in the gratitude condition have reported improved wellbeing as measured by optimistic appraisal of life, increased exercise, decreased reporting of physical symptoms and increased positive affect (Emmons and McCullough, 2003).	Undergraduate students plus adults with either congenital or adult-onset neuromuscular disease (mean age = 49 years, range = 22–77 years)	A weekly form included ratings of mood, physical symptoms, reactions to social support received, estimated amount of time spent exercising, and two global life appraisal questions
	Counting blessings has also been shown to lead to immediate decreases in negative affect (Sheldon and Lyubomirsky, 2006).	University students	Positive and Negative Affect Schedule (PANAS); Self-Concordant Motivation (SCM); exercise performance, for example, how frequently exercise was practiced
	In a double-blind randomized controlled trial Cheng et al. (2015) found lower depressive symptoms and a reduction in perceived stress for a gratitude condition.	Full-time Chinese professional healthcare practitioners	Chinese version of the 10-item version of the Center for Epidemiologic Studies-Depression Scale (CES-D); Chinese version of the 10-item Perceived Stress Scale

(cont.)

Table 2.3 (cont.)

Intervention	Efficacy	Participants	Measures
	Kerr et al. (2015) reliably cultivated the emotional experience of gratitude in a two-week intervention with a clinical sample on a waiting list for outpatient psychological treatment.	Adults (mean age = 43 years, range 19–67) seeking individual psychological treatment.	Participants rated intensity of gratitude or kindness felt; a version of the Positive and Negative Affect Schedule; the Purpose in Life test (PIL); Outcome Questionnaire-45.2 (OQ-45); the Depression Anxiety and Stress Scale (DASS-21). Participants also rated how connected they felt with others.
	Three good things led to gains in happiness and decreased depression immediately postintervention as well as increases for up to 6 months postintervention in comparison with the placebo control group (Seligman et al., 2005). Some researchers may consider three good things as savoring rather than gratitude.	Adults (range = 35–54 years) recruited via the Internet	Center for Epidemiological Studies – Depression Scale (CES-D) symptom survey; 20-item Steen Happiness Index (SHI)
	Sergeant and Mongrain (2011) found that a gratitude condition where participants identify five good things over the course of a day led to increased reported happiness over time in comparison to the control group. Self-critics reported the most favorable outcomes if they were assigned to the gratitude condition. Needy individuals did not benefit from the intervention and even decreased with regards to self-esteem (Sergeant and Mongrain, 2011).	Volunteer adults (mean age = 34 years, range = 18–72 years)	Centre for Epidemiological Studies – Depression Scale, Depressive Experiences Questionnaire, Gratitude Questionnaire-6, measure of physical symptoms, Rosenberg Self-Esteem Scale, Steen Happiness Index

Hope	Hope interventions have led to improvements from pre to postintervention for agency hope (but not pathways hope), anxiety, self-esteem and purpose in life (Cheavens et al., 2006).	Adults recruited from the community through advertisements in the local newspaper (mean age = 49 years old, range = 32–64)	The State Hope Scale; Center for Epidemiologie Studies – Depression Scale (CES-D); State-Trait Anxiety Inventory (STAI) Form Y; Index of Self-Esteem (ISE); Purpose In Life Test (PIL)
Mindfulness (defined as "the awareness that emerges through paying attention on purpose, in the present moment, and nonjudgmentally to the unfolding of experience moment by moment" (Kabat-Zinn, 2003, p. 2)	Huppert and Johnson (2010) found a positive relationship between the amount of time adolescent boys spent practicing mindfulness and improvements in both psychological wellbeing and mindfulness.	Adolescent boys (range 14–15 years).	Cognitive and Affective Mindfulness Scale – Revised (CAMS-R); Ego-Resiliency Scale (ERS); Warwick–Edinburgh Mental Well-being Scale (WEMWBS); Big Five personality dimensions were measured using the Ten-Item Personality Inventory (TIPI). At follow-up, participants in the mindfulness condition were also asked a series of questions such as the number of times they had practiced mindfulness outside of class, how helpful they found it and whether they thought they would continue to practice mindfulness.
	Jha et al. (2010) found improvements in positive affect for participants with higher levels of mindfulness training. Due to limitations of sampling, this was not a randomized study design.	Adult participants included three groups: military control (MC) group; civilian control (CC) group; mindfulness and mindfulness training group (MT)	The Positive and Negative Affect Schedule (PANAS). Working memory capacity (WMC) was also tested through an automated test.

(cont.)

Table 2.3 (cont.)

Intervention	Efficacy	Participants	Measures
Music (listening to three or four uplifting songs of participant's choosing each day)	Participants reported greater increases in happiness over time than the control group (Sergeant and Mongrain, 2011).	Volunteer adults (mean age = 34 years, range = 18–72 years)	Centre for Epidemiological Studies – Depression Scale, Depressive Experiences Questionnaire, Gratitude Questionnaire-6, measure of physical symptoms, Rosenberg Self-Esteem Scale, Steen Happiness Index
Positive psychotherapy (PPT) (includes a combination of gratitude visit, three good things in life, you at your best, using signature strengths in a new way, identifying signature strengths)	Seligman et al. (2006) tested the efficacy of PPT in two studies. In the first study, PPT was delivered to groups of university students with mild to moderate depression. This significantly decreased levels of depression through 1-year follow-up as compared with the control group. In the second study, PPT delivered to outpatients with unipolar depression produced higher remission rates than did treatment as usual or treatment as usual plus medication. The findings of these studies suggest that exercises that explicitly increase positive emotion, engagement and meaning may be useful in treating depression.	Study One: mild to moderate depressive symptoms. Study Two: major depressive disorder (MDD; unipolar depression).	Study One: Beck Depression Inventory–II (BDI); Satisfaction with Life Scale (SWLS); Study Two: Zung Self-Rating Scale (ZSRS); Hamilton Rating Scale for Depression (HRSD); Outcome Questionnaire (OQ); DSM–IV's Global Assessment of Functioning (GAF). Happiness and wellbeing were assessed using and by the Satisfaction with Life Scale (SWLS) and the Positive Psychotherapy Inventory (PPTI), a 21-item PPT outcome measure created and validated by the study researchers.
Savoring (savoring can be past-focused (reminiscing about positive experiences), present-focused (savoring the moment) or future-focused (anticipating positive experiences yet to come) (Smith et al., 2014)	Preference for undertaking PPI is positively related to adherence to the activity. The savoring exercise produced statistically significant increases in happiness and decreases in depression. Those who preferred active constructive responding also preferred savoring (Schueller, 2010).	Participants were visitors to a university research Internet portal. 329 were assigned to savoring (average age = 53.5).	The Authentic Happiness Inventory (AHI); the Center for Epidemiologic Studies Depression Scale (CES-D).

| Self-compassionate writing | Negative mood induced. Randomly allocated to write about a negative event in either a self-compassionate or an emotionally expressive way. Self-compassionate writing has been shown to significantly predict improved mood compared with the control group (Odou and Brinker, 2014a). | Undergraduate (mostly first-year) psychology students (mean age = 20.9, range = 17–59): 3.7% reported a past diagnosis, and 3.7% reported a current diagnosis of depression. | The Self-Compassion Scale (SCS); Ruminative Thought Style Scale (RTS); Positive and Negative Affect Schedule (PANAS); 100mm Visual Analogue Scale (VAS) |
| | Participants writing self-compassionately experienced increased positive affect and reduced negative affect; high ruminators experienced greater reduction of sadness than low ruminators (Odou and Brinker, 2014b). | Undergraduate students (mean = 21.3, range = 17–57 years): 14% of participants had a past diagnosis of depression while 2% reported having a current diagnosis. | The Self-Compassion Scale (SCS); Ruminative Thought Style Scale (RTS); The Positive and Negative Affect Schedule (PANAS); 100mm Visual Analogue Scale (VAS). |

treated with a level of caution. They found four factors that heighten the efficacy of PPIs: high levels of depression; increased age; individual interventions (rather than group interventions); and longer interventions. There is some debate as to whether participants should be matched to interventions based on a person–activity fit or not. For example, participant preference for undertaking a PPI has been positively related to commitment to adhere to the activity (Schueller, 2010), and matching participants to an intervention that was based on an orientation to happiness that differed from their dominant orientation was effective at enhancing wellbeing (Giannopoulos and Vella-Brodrick, 2011).

However, Schueller (2011) found no significant difference between participants assigned to activities based on preference and those randomly assigned to activities. PPIs have been used in studies specifically targeting clinical participants, such as positive psychotherapy (PPT; Seligman et al., 2006; see Chapter 11) and in nonclinical studies. However, regardless of the population, many study designs include pre- and post-test measures of depression and/or negative affect as well as measures of positive functioning.

Typically, studies include a broader range of measures, such as stress (Cheng et al., 2015); state and trait anxiety (Cheavens et al., 2006); ruminative thinking (Odou and Brinker, 2014a); self-esteem (Sergeant and Mongrain, 2011); Big Five personality (Huppert and Johnson, 2010); working memory capacity (Jha et al., 2010); physical symptoms (Emmons and McCullough, 2003; Sergeant and Mongrain, 2011); and self-compassion (Odou and Brinker, 2014a, 2014b).

Table 2.3 includes examples of the efficacy of PPIs. It should be noted that many constructs explored in PPIs have their origins outside positive psychology, such as gratitude, forgiveness and mindfulness. While positive psychology cannot lay claim to these concepts, its role does include an understanding of their function in building human strength and generating high human potential.

Conclusion

In this chapter we introduced key definitions relating to wellbeing and highlighted ways to approach this contested domain. After a summary of some key theories within the science of wellbeing and positive psychology, a brief overview of recent empirical evidence for positive psychology interventions (PPIs) was provided. Key debates continue about evidence from clinical compared with nonclinical populations, adding emphasis to the usefulness of cross- [?] fertilization between wellbeing research and research in mental health recovery.

References

Cheavens, J. S., Feldman, D. B., Gum, A., Scott, T. M., & Snyder, C. R. (2006). Hope therapy in a community sample: A pilot investigation. *Social Indicators Research*, 77, 61–86.

Cheng, S-T., Tsu, P. K., & Lam, J. H. M. (2015). Improving mental health in health care practitioners: Randomized controlled trial of a gratitude intervention. *Journal of Consulting and Clinical Psychology*, 83(1), 177–186.

Crisp, R. (2014). Well-being. In Zalta, E. N. (Ed.), *The Stanford Encyclopedia of Philosophy* (Winter 2014 ed.). Available at http://plato.stanford.edu/archives/win2014/entries/well-being/.

Crompton, W. C., & Hoffman, E. (2013). *Positive psychology: The science of happiness and flourishing.* Belmont, CA: Wadsworth, Cengage Learning.

Csikszentmihalyi, M., & Nakamura, J. (2011). Positive psychology: Where did it come from, where is it going? In Sheldon, K. M., Kashdan, T. B., & Steger, M. F. (ch. 1). *Designing positive psychology: Taking stock and moving forward.* New York, NY: Oxford University Press.

Davidson, R. J., Kabat-Zinn, J., Schumacker, J., Rosenkranz, M., Muller, D., Sontorelli, S. F., et al. (2003). Alterations in brain and immune function produced by mindfulness meditation. *Psychosomatic Medicine*, 65, 564–570.

Deci, E. L., & Ryan, R. M. (2008). Hedonia, eudaimonia and well-being: An introduction. doi:10.1007/s10902–006–9018–1.

Diener, E., & Chan, M. Y. (2011). Happy people live longer: Subjective well-being contributes to health and longevity. *Applied Psychology: Health and Well-Being*, 3(1), 1–43, doi:10.1111/j.1758–0854.2010.01045.x.

Emmons, R. A., & McCullough, M. E. (2003). Counting blessings versus burdens: An experimental investigation of gratitude and SWB in daily life. *Journal of Personality and Social Psychology*, 84, 377–389.

Estrada, C., Isen, A. M., & Young, M. J. (1994). Positive affect influences creative problem solving and reported source of practice satisfaction in physicians. *Motivation and Emotion*, 18, 285–299.

Forgeard, M. J. C., Jayawickreme, E., Kern, M., & Seligman, M. E. P. (2011). Doing the right thing: Measuring wellbeing for public policy. *International Journal of Wellbeing*, 1(1), 79–106, doi:10.5502/ijw.v1i1.15.

Fredrickson, B. L., & Levenson, R. W. (1998). Positive emotions speed recovery from the cardiovascular sequelae of negative emotions. *Cognition and Emotion*, 12, 191–220.

Froh, J. J., Kashdan, T. B., Ozimkowsk, K. M., & Miller, N. (2009). Who benefits the most from a gratitude intervention in children and adolescents? Examining positive affect as a moderator. *Journal of Positive Psychology*, 4, 408–422.

Gale, C. R., Booth, T., Mõttus, R., Kuh, D., & Deary, I. J. (2009) Neuroticism and extraversion in youth predict mental wellbeing and life satisfaction 40 years later: The hierarchical structure of well-being. *Journal of Personality* 77(4), 1025–1050, doi:10.1111/j.1467–6494.2009.00573.x.

Giannopoulos, V. L., & Vella-Brodrick, D. A. (2011). Effects of positive interventions and orientations to happiness on subjective well-being. *Journal of Positive Psychology*, 6, 95–105.

Harker, L., & Keltner, D. (2001). Expressions of positive emotions in women's college yearbook pictures and their relationship to personality and life outcomes across adulthood. *Journal of Personality and Social Psychology*, 80, 112–124.

Hone, L., Jarden, A., & Schofield, G. (2015). An evaluation of positive psychology intervention effectiveness trials using the re-aim framework: A practice-friendly review. *Journal of Positive Psychology*, 10(4), 303–322.

Hone, L. C., Jarden, A., Schofield, G. M., & Duncan, S. (2014). Measuring flourishing: The impact of operational definitions on the prevalence of high levels of wellbeing. *International Journal of Wellbeing*, 4(1), 62–90, doi:10.5502/ijw.v4i1.4.

Huppert, F. A., & Johnson, D. M. (2010). A controlled trial of mindfulness training in schools: The importance of practice for an impact on well-being. *Journal of Positive Psychology*, 5, 264–274.

Huppert, F. A., & So, T. T. C. (2013). Flourishing across Europe: Application of a new conceptual framework for defining well-being. *Social Indicators Resource*, 110(3), 837–861.

International Positive Psychology Association (2015, October 6). About IPPA. Available at http://www.ippanetwork.org/about/.

Jha, A. P., Stanley, E. A., Kiyonaga, A., Wong, L., & Gelfand, L. (2010). Examining the protective effects of mindfulness training on working capacity and affective experience. *Emotion*, 10, 54–64.

Kabat-Zinn, J. (2003). Mindfulness-based interventions in context: Past, present, and future. *Clinical Psychology: Science and Practice*, 10, 144–156.

Kerr, S. L., O'Donovan, A., & Pepping, C. A. (2015). Can gratitude and kindness interventions enhance well-being in a clinical sample? *Journal of Happiness Studies*, 16, 17–36.

Keyes, C. L. M. (2002). The mental health continuum: From languishing to flourishing in life. *Journal of Health and Social Research*, 43, 207–222.

Keyes, C. L. M., Shmotkin, D., & Ryff, C. D. (2002). Optimizing well-being: The empirical encounter of two traditions. *Journal of Personality and Social Psychology*, 82(6), 1007–1022, doi:10.1037//0022–3514.82.6.1007.

Lyubomirsky, S., King, L., & Diener, E. (2005). The benefits of frequent positive affect: Does happiness lead to success? *Psychological Bulletin*, 131(6), 803–855, doi:10.1037/0033–2909.131.6.803.

Maslow, A. H. (1970). *Motivation and personality*. New York, NY: Harper & Row.

Norrish, J. M. (2015). *Positive education: The Geelong Grammar School journey*. Oxford, UK: Oxford University Press.

Norrish, J. M., Williams, P., O'Connor, M., & Robinson, J. (2013). An applied framework for positive education. *International Journal of Wellbeing*, 3(2), 147–161, doi:10.5502/ijw.v3i2.2.

Odou, N., & Brinker, J. (2014a). Exploring the relationship between rumination, self-compassion, and mood. *Self and Identity*, 13(4), 449–459, doi:10.1080/15298868.2013.840332.

Odou, N., & Brinker, J. (2014b). Self-compassion, a better alternative to rumination than distraction as a response to negative mood. *Journal of Positive Psychology*, 1–11, doi:10.1080/17439760.2014.9 67800.

Otake, K., Shimai, S., Tanaka-Matsumi, J., Otsui, K., & Fredrickson, B. L. (2006). Happy people become happier through kindness: A counting kindness intervention. *Journal of Happiness Studies*, 7, 361–375.

Peters, M. L., Flink. I. K., Boersma, K., & Linton, S. J. (2010). Manipulating optimism: Can mental imagining a best possible self be used to increase positive future expectancies? *Journal of Positive Psychology*, 5, 204–211.

Pressman, S. D., & Cohen, S. (2005). Does positive affect influence health? *Psychological Bulletin*, 131, 925–971.

Ramírez, E., Ortega, A. R., Chamorro, A., & Colmenero, J. M. (2014). A program of positive intervention in the elderly: Memories, gratitude and forgiveness. *Aging & Mental Health*, 18(4), 463–470, doi:10.1080/13607863.2013.856858.

Rusk, R. D., & Waters, L. E. (2013). Tracing the size, reach, impact, and breadth of positive psychology. *Journal of Positive Psychology*, 8(3), 207–221, doi:10.1080/17439760.2013.777766.

Ryan, R. M., & Deci, E. L. (2000). Self-Determination Theory and the facilitation of intrinsic motivation, social development, and well-being. *American Psychologist*, 55(1), 68–78, doi:10.1037110003–066X.55.1.68.

Ryan, R. M., & Deci, E. L. (2001a). Hedonia, eudaimonia, and well-being: An introduction. *Journal of Happiness Studies*, 9, 1–11, doi:10.1007/s10902–006–9018–1.

Ryan, R. M., & Deci, E. L. (2001b). On happiness and human potentials: A review of research on hedonic and eudaimonic well-being. *Annual Review of Psychology*, 52, 141–166.

Ryff, C. D. (1989). Happiness is everything, or is it? Explorations on the meaning of psychological wellbeing. *Journal of Personality and Social Psychology*. 57(6), 1069–1081.

Ryff, C. D. (1995). Psychological well-being in adult life. *Current Directions in Psychological Science*, 4(4), 99–104.

Ryff, C. D., & Keyes, C. L. M. (1995). The structure of psychological well-being revisited. *Journal of Personality and Social Psychology*, 69(4), 719–727.

Seligman, M. E. P. (1998). Building human strength: Psychology's forgotten mission. *APA Monitor*, 29(1), 2.

Seligman, M. E. P. (2002). *Authentic happiness*. New York, NY: Free Press.

Seligman, M. E. P., & Csikszentmihalyi, M. (2000). Positive psychology: An introduction. *American Psychologist*, 55, 5–14.

Seligman, M. E. P., Rashid, T., & Parks, A. C. (2006). Positive psychotherapy. *American Psychologist*, 61, 774–788.

Seligman, M. E. P., Steen, T., Park, N., & Peterson, C. (2005). Positive psychology progress: Empirical validation of interventions. *American Psychologist*, 60(5), 410–421, doi:10.1037/0003–066X.60.5.410.

Sergeant, S., & Mongrain, M. (2011). Are positive psychology exercises helpful for people with depressive personality styles? *Journal of Positive Psychology*, 6, 260–272.

Sheldon, K. M., & Lyubomirsky, S. (2006). How to increase and sustain positive emotion: The effect of expressing gratitude and visualising best possible selves. *Journal of Positive Psychology*, 1, 73–82.

Shueller, S. M. (2010). Preferences for positive psychology exercises. *Journal of Positive Psychology*, 5, 192–203.

Shueller, S. M. (2011). To each his own well-being boosting intervention: Using preference to guide selection. *Journal of Positive Psychology*, 6, 300–313.

Sin, N. L., & Lyubomirsky, S. (2009). Enhancing well-being and alleviating depressive symptoms with positive psychology interventions: A practice-friendly meta-analysis. *Journal of Clinical Psychology: In Session*, 65(5), 467–487, doi:10.1002/jclp.20593.

Snyder, C. R. (2002). Hope theory: Rainbows in the mind. *Psychological Inquiry*, 13(4), 249–275.

Snyder, C. R., Lopez, S. J., & Pedrotti, J. T. (2011). *Positive psychology: The scientific and practical explorations of human strengths* (2nd ed.). Los Angeles, CA: Sage.

Steger, M. F., Shigehiro, O., & Kashdan, T. B. (2009). Meaning in life across the life span: Levels and correlates of meaning in life from emerging adulthood to older adulthood. *Journal of Positive Psychology*, 4, 43–52.

Tennant, R., Hiller, L., Fishwick, R., Platt, S., Joseph, S., Weich, S., et al. (2007). The Warwick–Edinburgh Mental Well-Being Scale (WEMWBS): Development and UK validation. *Health and Quality of Life Outcomes*, 5 (63). doi:10.1186/1477-7525-5-63.

Tugade, M. M., & Fredrickson, B. L. (2004). Resilient individuals use positive emotions to bounce back from negative emotional experiences. *Journal of Personality and Social Psychology*, 86(2), 320–333.

Vella-Brodrick, D. A. (2013). Positive psychology interventions: Research evidence, practical utility, and future steps. In Keyes, C. L.M. (ch. 15). *Mental Well-Being: International Contributions to the Study of Positive Mental Health*. Dordrecht, the Netherlands, Springer.

Waters, L. (2011). A review of school-based positive psychology interventions. *Australian Educational and Developmental Psychologist*, 28(2), 75–90, doi:10.1375/aedp.28.2.75.

Waugh, C. E., & Fredrickson, B. L. (2006). Nice to know you: Positive emotions, self-other overlap, and complex understanding in the formation of a new relationship. *Journal of Positive Psychology*, 1, 93–106.

Williams, S., & Shiaw, W. T. (1999). Mood and organizational citizenship behavior: The effects of positive affect on employee organizational citizenship behavior intentions. *Journal of Psychology*, 133, 656–668.

Wright, T. A., & Quick, J. C. (2009). The emerging positive agenda in organizations: Greater than a trickle, but not yet a deluge. *Journal of Organizational Behavior*, 30, 147–159.

Chapter 3

Recovery and Mental Health

Mike Slade and Genevieve Wallace

Introduction

The term 'recovery' has become widely used in mental health systems internationally. Empirical (Resnick et al., 2005) and conceptual (Whitley and Drake, 2010) approaches have been used to differentiate aspects of recovery. However, it can be most useful to consider two contrasting understandings: clinical recovery, meaning recovery from mental health difficulties, and personal recovery, meaning recovery with mental health difficulties (Slade, 2009b). Both meanings are underpinned by sets of values and create role expectations for mental health professionals and for people using mental health services. The distinction between the two meanings reflects a debate about the core purpose of mental health systems.

Meaning 1: Clinical Recovery

Clinical recovery has emerged from professional-led research and practice, and has four key features:

1. It is an outcome or a state, generally dichotomous – a person is either 'in recovery' or 'not in recovery'.
2. It is observable – in clinical language, it is objective, not subjective.
3. It is rated by the expert clinician, not the patient.
4. The definition of recovery does not vary between individuals.

Various definitions of recovery have been proposed by mental health professionals. A widely used definition is that recovery comprises full symptom remission, full- or part-time work or education, independent living without supervision by informal caregivers, and having friends with whom activities can be shared, all sustained for a period of two years (Libermann and Kopelowicz, 2002).

The definition of clinical recovery does not vary across individuals, which means it is relatively easy to define, measure and investigate in empirical studies. A review of all epidemiological prevalence studies in schizophrenia assessing recovery over more than a 20-year follow-up period indicated that rates of clinical recovery in excess of 50% are the norm (Slade et al., 2008).

However, deep assumptions about normality are embedded in clinical recovery:

> This kind of definition begs several questions that need to be addressed to come up with an understanding of recovery as outcome: How many goals must be achieved to be considered recovered? For that matter, how much life success is considered "normal"?
>
> (Ralph and Corrigan, 2005) (p. 5)

Wellbeing, Recovery and Mental Health, ed. Mike Slade, Lindsay Oades and Aaron Jarden.
Published by Cambridge University Press. © Mike Slade, Lindsay Oades and Aaron Jarden 2017

A different understanding of recovery has emerged from the mental health service user and survivor movement. This can be called personal recovery.

Meaning 2: Personal Recovery

In contrast to clinical recovery, personal recovery

1. is a process or a continuum
2. is subjectively defined by the person him- or herself
3. is 'rated' by the person experiencing the mental health difficulties, who is considered the expert on his or her recovery
4. means different things to different people, although there are aspects that many people share

Personal recovery has a different focus than clinical recovery, for example in emphasising the centrality of hope, identity, meaning and personal responsibility (Andresen et al., 2003). The most widely cited definition, which underpins most recovery policy internationally, is by Bill Anthony:

> Recovery is a deeply personal, unique process of changing one's attitudes, values, feelings, goals, skills, and/or roles. It is a way of living a satisfying, hopeful, and contributing life even within the limitations caused by illness. Recovery involves the development of new meaning and purpose in one's life as one grows beyond the catastrophic effects of mental illness.
>
> (Anthony, 1993)

Since recovery has a personal meaning for each individual, it can be difficult to find a shared definition. In a Delphi study with 381 participants, all of whom had personal experience of psychosis, the largest number of participants agreed on the statements 'recovery is the achievement of a personally acceptable quality of life' and 'recovery is feeling better about yourself' (Law and Morrison, 2014).

This distinction between the different understandings of recovery has been characterised in different ways: recovery 'from' versus recovery 'in' (Davidson et al., 2008); scientific versus consumer models of recovery (Bellack, 2006); clinical recovery versus personal recovery (Slade, 2009a) or versus social recovery (Secker et al., 2002).

It is this second understanding of recovery – perhaps most commonly called personal recovery – which is meant when policies or services refer to supporting recovery, using a 'recovery approach' or being based on a 'recovery model'. This is the meaning of recovery used in the remainder of this chapter.

Recovery and Policy

A recovery orientation is embedded in national mental health policy in many countries across the Anglophone world (Department of Health and Ageing, 2009, Mental Health Commission of Canada, 2012, Department of Health Social Services and Public Safety (Northern Ireland), 2010, New Freedom Commission on Mental Health, 2003, HM Government, 2011) and elsewhere (Slade et al., 2012a, Olij, 2009).

At least rhetorically, recovery has also been embraced by professional groups. In England, for example, the principles of recovery have been adopted in clinical psychology (Cooke, 2014), mental health nursing (Department of Health, 2006), occupational therapy (College of Occupational Therapists, 2006), psychiatry (Care Services Improvement Partnership, 2007) and social work (Allen, 2014). Perhaps the most influential professional group internationally is psychiatry in the United States, which has also embraced the term (American Psychiatric Association, 2005).

A Conceptual Framework for Personal Recovery

To provide a framework to inform understanding of how personal recovery can be defined and measured and the process by which it can take place, a systematic review was undertaken to collate and synthesise published frameworks and models of recovery (Leamy et al., 2011). A total of 97 papers from 13 different countries which offered new conceptualisations of recovery were identified, based on 366 reviewed papers. Narrative synthesis (Popay et al., 2006) was used to develop a conceptual framework. The synthesis was subsequently shown to be applicable across Western cultures (Slade et al., 2012b) and consistent with the understanding of recovery held by current mental health service users (Bird, 2014c).

The narrative synthesis identified

1. Thirteen characteristics of the recovery journey, for example, recovery is an active process, individual and unique process, nonlinear process, recovery is a struggle, recovery is a life-changing experience, recovery is possible without cure. These help in understanding the subjective experience of recovery.

2. Thirteen published stage models of recovery, all of which can be mapped to the Transtheoretical Model of Change (Prochaska and DiClemente, 1982). These describe how distinct stages of recovery can be differentiated.

3. Five overarching recovery processes comprising connectedness, hope and optimism about the future, identity, meaning in life and empowerment (giving the acronym CHIME). The CHIME framework has proved useful as a focus for understanding recovery (Wyder, 2014) and in identifying how mental health workers can support recovery (Eriksen, 2014).

The CHIME framework can inform the development of new interventions. There is empirical evidence for interventions addressing each of these five domains.

Connectedness

Despite the many policies (South Australian Social Inclusion Board, 2007) and books (Boardman et al., 2010) highlighting the importance of social inclusion, empirical research into interventions which improve connectedness is limited (Tew, 2012). The strongest evidence base relates to employment and meaningful activities (Crowther et al., 2001), with the Individual Placement and Support model (Killackey et al., 2008) showing particular promise. There is some evidence for interventions to support relationships with others, including for example the beneficial impact of meeting other people with personal experience of mental health problems – either through their employment as peer support workers within the mental health system (Repper and Carter, 2011) or (with weaker evidence) through mutual self-help groups (Slade, 2009b). A number of national anti-stigma campaigns have been undertaken internationally, using three broad approaches: educational lectures and information, video-based media and social contact with individuals with lived experience. A review of such interventions indicated that direct social contact with people with mental health problems was the most effective method of changing attitudes towards mental health problems (Clement, 2011), and the first empirical evidence of a shift in societal attitudes following a national campaign is emerging (Henderson et al., 2012).

Hope and Optimism

A systematic review of candidate interventions for fostering hope identified promising interventions including collaborative illness management strategies, fostering positive relationships, peer support and support for setting and attaining realistic personally valued goals (Schrank et al., 2012). A specific approach is Wellness Recovery Action Planning (WRAP), which is an evidence-based strategy used internationally to promote wellness and recovery through the development of coping strategies (Copeland, 1999). WRAP stands out as an intervention which has been widely evaluated using both randomised and nonrandomised designs. Positive outcomes include increased hopefulness (Barbic et al., 2009; Cook, 2011; Fukui et al., 2011), among others. Receiving peer support from peer support workers or mentors who have themselves experienced mental health difficulties has also been shown to increase hopefulness when compared with treatment as usual, with additional recovery benefits noted for the peer workers themselves (Davidson, 2012).

Identity

Interventions to support the development and maintenance of a positive identity are lacking. Approaches which are worth developing as intervention technologies include life-story work, Tree of Life and narrative therapy. For example, life-story work aims to help individuals develop their personal narratives and has been shown to be effective in people with dementia (Subramaniam and Woods, 2012). A key challenge for future research will be developing interventions which are sensitive to nonindividualistic expressions of identity – an emphasis on collective identity is one way in which the experience of recovery differs for individuals from BME communities (Leamy et al., 2011). Finally, symptom severity is linked to the integrity of the person's narrative (Lysaker et al., 2012), so evidence-based interventions which directly address symptoms may also contribute to the development of a more positive identity.

Meaning and Purpose

Meaning and purpose in life find expression in many ways, but one key aspect is through spirituality and religion. Unfortunately, these domains are not only deprioritised but often actively excluded from clinical discourse. For example, an intervention involving spiritual assessment by psychiatrists showed benefits for service users but low acceptance by participating psychiatrists (Huguelet et al., 2011). Other professional groups are more amenable to spirituality discussions (Post and Wade, 2009), and the approach is starting to be incorporated into psychological therapies (Hathaway and Tan, 2009).

More generally, a sense of purpose can be gained from amplifying strengths (Gander, 2012), for example by setting and working towards personally valued goals. Staff can have an important role in supporting this process, and giving staff goal-setting training improves the quality of the goal plans they are able to support. Additionally, supporting people in becoming aware of their values, and linking these with their goals, can ensure that goals are intrinsically meaningful to the individual (Clarke et al., 2009).

Empowerment

Several interventions have been developed which target personal responsibility and control, including advance directives (Swanson et al., 2006), joint crisis plans (Henderson et al.,

2004) and shared decision making (Drake and Deegan, 2009). A specific well-evaluated and widely used approach is the strengths model of case management, which focuses on the relationships between staff and consumers, prioritises strengths over deficits, is consumer-led and actively promotes resource acquisition through advocacy (Rapp and Goscha, 2006). Evaluations have included randomised controlled trials and quasi-experimental designs, and have shown a range of positive outcomes including reduced hospitalisation, increased social support, goal setting and goal attainment.

As well as supporting people in taking a more active role in their own recovery, empowerment can also be supported by involvement in the development, delivery and evaluation of mental health services. Mental health services internationally are increasingly involving people with personal experience of mental health problems in the recruitment and training of staff, in service development, in the workforce (Tait and Lester, 2005), in mental health service research and evaluation and in policy making (Callard and Rose, 2012). Examples of some of these initiatives are given in Chapters 14, 15 and 16. Despite many challenges associated with achieving meaningful involvement and partnership, the subjective ability to exercise greater choice and control has been reported by involved service users (Omeni et al., 2014),

Positive psychology interventions, such as positive psychotherapy (Seligman et al., 2006), also identify and amplify an individual's capabilities and resources through the therapeutic process, with the aim of developing positive mental health including resilience and uplifting emotional experiences. These interventions can be provided on line, and benefits have been shown for depressive symptomatology (Lopez and Edwards, 2008), reduced service use (Duckworth et al., 2005) and self-rated happiness (Seligman et al., 2005). The modification and evaluation of positive psychology interventions for psychosis are described in Chapters 6 and 12 respectively.

How Mental Health Services Can Support Recovery

Although guidance on recovery-oriented practice exists, there remains a lack of clarity regarding best practice (Lakeman, 2010). An empirically based framework to guide recovery practice was therefore developed to address this knowledge gap (Le Boutillier et al., 2011). The practice framework was developed by analysing 30 documents from six countries (Denmark, England, New Zealand, Republic of Ireland, Scotland, United States of America) detailing international practice guidance on supporting recovery. Inductive thematic analysis was used to systematically identify and synthesise the range and diversity of the key concepts of recovery-oriented practice identified in the reviewed documents. Interpretive analysis was then undertaken to organise the themes into practice domains.

Four overarching levels of practice emerged from the synthesis: supporting personally defined recovery; working relationship; organisational commitment and promoting citizenship. Each practice domain is as important as the next, and there is no hierarchical order. The first two domains involve the content and process of care, and are being actively addressed in person-centred approaches (Tondora, 2014) and through emergent technologies such as the Collaborative Recovery Model (Crowe et al., 2006) described in Chapter 9. The third domain is being addressed through national transformation programmes, such as ImROC in England (NHS Confederation Mental Health Network, 2012), Partners in Recovery in Australia (Australian Government, 2012) and Recovery to Practice in the United States (http://www.samhsa.gov/recoverytopractice/). This has led to the development of new ways of providing support, such as Recovery Colleges (Perkins, 2012). Progress on the fourth domain of promoting citizenship, as noted in Chapter 1, is much more limited.

A recent review identified ten evidence-based approaches to supporting recovery (Slade, 2014). The evidence base for recovery-supporting interventions is increasingly robust. As an example, the REFOCUS intervention is a manualised transdiagnostic team-level intervention to improve mental health service support for recovery (Bird et al., 2011). It comprises a one-year whole-team intervention aiming to impact team and individual staff values (which can be conflicting) (Le Boutillier, 2015), recovery-related knowledge, skills and behaviour and staff–patient relationships. The intervention has two components: behavioural and interpersonal. The behavioural component comprises three desired behaviours by staff, called working practices (WPs). WP1 is Understanding Values and Treatment Preferences and involves focussing on the patient's values and identity beyond being a patient and placing these preferences at the centre of care planning. WP2 is Assessing Strengths and involves using a standardised assessment of personal and social strengths to identify existing and potential resources the patient can build on. WP3 is Supporting Goal-striving and involves orienting clinical care around goals valued by the patient. These working practices are undertaken in the context of the interpersonal component, called recovery-promoting relationships, which included training staff to use coaching skills in interactions with patients (Grey, 2014) and undertaking a partnership project, in which staff and patients from the same team take on a joint and nonclinical task, co-produced between staff and patients.

The development of the REFOCUS intervention was informed by primary research and secondary systematic reviews addressing knowledge gaps (Slade, 2015b). The REFOCUS intervention targets the supporting recovery and working relationships practice domains of the practice framework outlined earlier (Le Boutillier et al., 2011). The CHIME framework, also described earlier, provides the focus for intervention and evaluation (Leamy et al., 2011). A systematic review of strengths measures identified the best measure to use in WP2 (Strengths Assessment) (Bird, 2012). The optimal primary outcome for the trial of REFOCUS was based on a systematic review of recovery measures (Shanks et al., 2013). A separate systematic review of recovery support measures concluded that no existing measure was suitable (Williams et al., 2012), so a new measure of recovery support based on the CHIME framework and called INSPIRE was developed and psychometrically evaluated(Williams, 2015). A grounded theory of staff experiences of supporting recovery was developed (Le Boutillier, 2015) to understand staff perspectives. A new measure of feasibility based on implementation science research was developed to maximise implementation (Bird, 2014a). Innovative approaches to individualising trial endpoint measurement were evaluated (Pesola, 2015). In line with best scientific practice (Craig et al., 2008), a testable model (Bird et al., 2011) and trial protocol (Slade et al., 2011) were published in advance of the evaluation.

The results of the randomised controlled trial (ISRCTN02507940) involving 403 service users from 27 community-based adult mental health teams indicated that the intervention was effective at improving recovery when adequately implemented (Slade, 2015a), and implementation challenges were explored in process evaluation (Leamy, 2014). An unpublished thematic analysis of interviews conducted with people who had received the REFOCUS intervention indicated that a working relationship that is collaborative, in which the staff member demonstrates 'genuine' interest in the individual, was felt to support recovery. Participants highlighted that recovery-supporting tools exploring strengths, goals and values and treatment preferences could support personal recovery by helping the person feel more hopeful and empowered, with a more positive sense of identity. However, they also highlighted that the tools must be used collaboratively and the resulting information used to inform care planning, with a need to avoid attempts to 'do' recovery 'to' service users by focusing on the development of hope-inspiring, power-balanced relationships. These findings are in line with a previous qualitative study in which service users were asked how professionals could support them in their recovery process (Borg and Kristiansen, 2004). The value of professionals who conveyed hope, shared power, were available when needed, were open regarding the diversity in what helps and were willing to stretch the boundaries of what is considered the 'professional' role was highlighted. The REFOCUS intervention manual was updated based on these findings (Bird, 2014b).

Other approaches with a strong evidence base include peer support workers (Pitt et al., 2013), advance directives (Swanson et al., 2006), wellness recovery action planning (Jonikas et al., 2013), and individual placement and support (Grove, 2009). Additionally, recovery colleges (described in Chapter 16) (Perkins, 2012) and trialogues (Amering, 2012) are also widely used to support recovery.

The development of an empirical evidence base for supporting recovery indicates strong overlap with wellbeing research. Points of linkage include the emphasis on connection, the importance of developing a layered and resilient identity, the focus on strengths amplification rather than deficit amelioration and the need to contribute as well as receive. Recovery research is being influenced by wellbeing, for example, in the emphasis in the REFOCUS intervention on coaching to support goal striving. Similarly, emergent findings about the importance of lived experience as a source of knowledge in the context of recovery can inform approaches to increasing wider societal wellbeing. In the longer term, it may be that recovery – which is inextricably linked to illness – becomes redundant as services orient around the goal of supporting wellbeing in people living with mental health problems.

References

Allen, R. (2014). *The role of the social worker in adult mental health services*. London, UK: College of Social Work.

American Psychiatric Association (2005). *Position statement on the use of the concept of recovery*. Washington, DC: American Psychiatric Association.

Amering, M., Mikus, M., & Steffen, S. (2012). Recovery in Austria: Mental health trialogue. *International Review of Psychiatry*, 24, 11–18.

Andresen, R., Oades, L., & Caputi, P. (2003). The experience of recovery from schizophrenia: Towards an empirically-validated stage model. *Australian and New Zealand Journal of Psychiatry*, 37, 586–594.

Anthony, W. A. (1993). Recovery from mental illness: The guiding vision of the mental health system in the 1990s. *Psychosocial Rehabilitation Journal*, 16, 11–23.

Australian Government (2012). *Partners in recovery: Coordinated support and flexible funding for people with severe, persistent mental illness and complex needs initiative*. Canberra, Australia: Department of Health and Ageing.

Barbic, S., Krupa, T., & Armstrong, I. (2009). A randomized controlled trial of the effectiveness of a modified recovery workbook program: Preliminary findings. *Psychiatric Services*, 60, 491–497.

Bellack, A. (2006). Scientific and consumer models of recovery in schizophrenia: concordance, contrasts, and implications. *Schizophrenia Bulletin*, 32, 432–442.

Bird, V., Le Boutillier, C., Leamy, M., Larsen, J., Oades, L., Williams, J., et al. (2012). Assessing the strengths of mental health service users – Systematic review. *Psychological Assessment*, 24, 1024–1033.

Bird, V., Le Boutillier, C., Leamy, M., Williams, J., Bradstreet, S., & Slade, M. (2014a). Evaluating the feasibility of complex interventions in mental health services: Standardised measure and reporting guidelines. *British Journal of Psychiatry*, 204, 316–321.

Bird, V., Leamy, M., Le Boutillier, C., Williams, J., & Slade, M. (2011). *REFOCUS: Promoting recovery in community mental health services*. London, UK: Rethink (researchintorecovery.com/refocus).

Bird, V., Leamy, M., Le Boutillier, C., Williams, J., & Slade, M. (2014b). *REFOCUS (second ed.): Promoting recovery in mental health services*. London, UK: Rethink Mental Illness.

Bird, V., Leamy, M., Tew, J., Le Boutillier, C., Williams, J., & Slade, M. (2014c). Fit for purpose? Validation of the conceptual framework of personal recovery with current mental health service users. *Australian and New Zealand Journal of Psychiatry*, 48, 644–653.

Boardman, J., Currie, A., Killaspy, H., & Mezey, G. (2010). *Social inclusion and mental health*. London, UK: RCPsychPublications.

Borg, M., & Kristiansen, K. (2004). Recovery-oriented professionals: Helping relationships in mental health services. *Journal of Mental Health*, 13, 493–505.

Callard, F., & Rose, D. (2012). The mental health strategy for Europe: Why service user leadership in research is indispensable. *Journal of Mental Health*, 21, 219–226.

Care Services Improvement Partnership, R. C. O. P., Social Care Institute for Excellence, (2007). *A common purpose: Recovery in future mental health services*. Leeds, UK: Care Services Improvement Partnership.

Clarke, S., Crowe, T., Oades, L., & Deane, F. (2009). Do goal setting interventions improve the quality of goals in mental health services? *Psychiatric Rehabilitation Journal*, 32, 292–299.

Clement, S., Lassman, F., Barley, E., Evans-Lacko, S., Williams, P., Pagdin, R., et al. (2011). Mass media interventions for reducing mental health-health related stigma (Protocol). *Cochrane Database of Systematic Reviews*, 12.

College of Occupational Therapists (2006) *Recovering ordinary lives: The strategy for occupational therapy in mental health services 2007-2017*. London, UK: College of Occupational Therapists.

Cook, J. A. (2011). Peer-delivered wellness recovery services: From evidence to widespread implementation. *Psychiatric Rehabilitation Journal*, 35, 87–9.

Cooke, A., Basset, T., Bentall, R., Boyle, M., Cupitt, C., Dillon, J., et al. (2014). *Understanding psychosis and schizophrenia*. London, UK: British Psychological Society.

Copeland, M. E. (1999). *Wellness recovery action plan*. Brattleboro, VT: Peach Press.

Craig, P., Dieppe, P., Macintyre, S., Michie, S., Nazareth, I., & Petticrew, M. (2008). Developing and evaluating complex interventions: The new Medical Research Council guidance. *BMJ*, 337, a1655.

Crowe, T., Deane, F., Oades, L. G., Caputi, P., & Morland, K. G. (2006). Effectiveness of a collaborative recovery training program in Australia in promoting positive views about recovery. *Psychiatric Services*, 57 1497–1500.

Crowther, R. E., Marshall, M., Bond, G. R., et al. (2001). Vocational rehabilitation for people with severe mental illness. *Cochrane Database of Systematic Reviews*, 1–55.

Davidson, L., Bellamy, C., Guy, K., & Miller, R. (2012). Peer support among persons with severe mental illnesses: A review of evidence and experience. *World Psychiatry*, 11, 123–128.

Davidson, L., Schmutte, T., Dinzeo, T., & Andres-Hyman, R. (2008). Remission and recovery in schizophrenia: Practitioner and patient perspectives. *Schizophrenia Bulletin*, 34, 5–8.

Department of Health (2006) *From values to action: The chief nursing officer's review of mental health nursing*. London, UK: HMSO.

Department of Health and Ageing (2009) *Fourth National Mental Health Plan: An agenda for collaborative government action in mental health 2009-2014*. Canberra, Australia: Commonwealth of Australia.

Department of Health Social Services and Public Safety (Northern Ireland) (2010). *Service Framework for Mental Health and Wellbeing*. Belfast, UK: DHSSPS (NI).

Drake, R. E., & Deegan, P. E. (2009). Shared decision making is an ethical imperative. *Psychiatric Services*, 60, 1007.

Duckworth, L. A., Steen, T. A., & Seligman, M. E. (2005). Positive psychology in clinical practice. *Annual Review of Clinical Psychology*, 1, 629–651.

Eriksen, K., Arman, M., Davidson, L., Sundfør, B., & Karlsson, B. (2014). Challenges in relating to mental health professionals: Perspectives of persons with severe mental illness. *International Journal of Mental Health Nursing*, 23, 110–117.

Fukui, S., Starnino, V. R., Susana, M., Davidson, L. J., Cook, K., Rapp, C. A., et al. (2011). Effect of Wellness Recovery Action Plan (WRAP) participation on psychiatric symptoms, sense of hope, and recovery. *Psychiatric Rehabilitation Journal*, 34, 214–22.

Gander, F., Proyer, R., Ruch, W., & Wyss, T. (2012). Strength-based positive interventions: further evidence for their potential in enhancing wellbeing and alleviating depression. *Journal of Happiness Studies*, 14, 1241–1259.

Grey, B., Bailey, S., Leamy, M., & Slade, M. (2014). *REFOCUS coaching conversations for recovery. Participant manual*. London, UK: Slam Partners.

Grove, B., Locket, H., Shepherd, G., Bacon, J., & Rinaldi, M. (2009). *Doing what works – Individual placement and support into employment*. London, UK: Sainsbury Centre for Mental Health.

Hathaway, W., & Tan, E. (2009). Religiously oriented mindfulness-based cognitive therapy. *Journal of Clinical Psychology*, 65, 158–171.

Henderson, C., Corker, E., Lewis-Holmes, E., Hamilton, S., Flach, C., Rose, D., et al. (2012). England's Time to Change antistigma campaign: One-year outcomes of service user-rated experiences of discrimination. *Psychiatric Services*, 63, 451–7.

Henderson, C., Flood, C., Leese, M., Thornicroft, G., Sutherby, K., & Szmukler, G. (2004). Effect of joint crisis plans on use of compulsory treatment in psychiatry: Single blind randomised controlled trial. *BMJ*, 329 136–140.

HM Government (2011). *No health without mental health. Delivering better mental health outcomes for people of all ages*. London, UK: Department of Health.

Huguelet, P., Mohr, S., Betrisey, C., Borras, L., Gillieron, C., Marie, A. M., et al. (2011). A randomized trial of spiritual assessment of outpatients with schizophrenia: Patients' and clinicians' experience. *Psychiatric Services*, 62, 79–86.

Jonikas, J. A., Grey, D. D., Copeland, M. E., Razzano, L. A., Hamilton, M. M., Floyd, C. B., et al. (2013). Improving propensity for patient self-advocacy through wellness recovery action planning: Results of a randomized controlled trial. *Community Mental Health Journal*, 49, 260–269.

Killackey, E., Jackson, H., & McGorry, P. D. (2008). Vocational intervention in first-episode psychosis: Individual placement and support v. treatment as usual. *British Journal of Psychiatry*, 193, 114–120.

Lakeman, R. (2010). Mental health recovery competencies for mental health workers: A Delphi study. *Journal of Mental Health*, 19, 62–74.

Law, H., & Morrison, A. P. (2014). Recovery in psychosis: A Delphi study with experts by experience. *Schizophrenia Bulletin*, sbu047.

Le Boutillier, C., Leamy, M., Bird, V. J., Davidson, L., Williams, J., & Slade, M. (2011). What does recovery mean in practice? A qualitative analysis of international recovery-oriented practice guidance. *Psychiatric Services*, 62, 1470–1476.

Le Boutillier, C., Slade, M., Lawrence, V., Bird, V., Chandler, R., Farkas, M., et al. (2015). Competing priorities: Staff perspectives on supporting recovery. *Administration and Policy in Mental Health and Mental Health Services Research*, 42, 429–438.

Leamy, M., Bird, V., Le Boutillier, C., Williams, J., & Slade, M. (2011). A conceptual framework for personal recovery in mental health: Systematic review and narrative synthesis. *British Journal of Psychiatry*, 199, 445–452.

Leamy, M., Clarke, E., Le Boutillier, C., Bird, V., Janosik, M., Sabas, K., et al. (2014). Implementing a complex intervention to support personal recovery: A qualitative study nested within a cluster randomised controlled trial. *PLoS ONE*, 9, e97091.

Libermann, R. P., & Kopelowicz, A. (2002). Recovery from schizophrenia: A challenge for the 21st century. *International Review of Psychiatry*, 14, 242–255.

Lopez, S. J., & Edwards, L. M. (2008). The interface of counseling psychology and positive psychology: Assessing and promoting strengths. In Brown, S. D., & Lent, R. W. (Eds.), *Handbook of Counseling Psychology* (fourth ed., pp. 86–99). Hoboken, NJ: John Wiley and Sons.

Lysaker, P. H., Erikson, M., Macapagal, K. R., Tunze, C., Gilmore, E., & Ringer, J. M. (2012). Development of personal narratives as a mediator of the impact of deficits in social cognition and social withdrawal on negative symptoms in schizophrenia. *Journal of Nervous and Mental Disease,* 200, 290–5.

Mental Health Commission of Canada (2012). *Changing directions, changing lives: The mental health strategy for Canada.* Calgary, Alberta: Mental Health Commission of Canada.

New Freedom Commission on Mental Health (2003). *Achieving the promise: Transforming mental health care in America. Final report.* Rockville, MD: Department of Health and Human Services.

NHS Confederation Mental Health Network (2012). *Supporting recovery in mental health.* London, UK: NHS Confederation.

Olij, L., & De Haan, E. (2009). *Naar herstel en gelijkwaardig burgerschap [Restoring dignity and equal citizenship].* Amsterdam, the Netherlands: GGZ Nederland.

Omeni, E., Barnes, M., MacDonald, D., Crawford, M., & Rose, D. (2014). Service user involvement: Impact and participation: A survey of service user and staff perspectives. *BMC Health Services Research,* 14, 491.

Perkins, R., Repper, J., Rinaldi, M., & Brown, H. (2012). *ImROC 1. Recovery colleges.* London, UK: Centre for Mental Health.

Pesola, F., Williams, J., Bird, V., Freidl, M., Le Boutillier, C., Leamy, M., et al. (2015). Development and evaluation of an Individualised Outcome Measure (IOM) for randomised controlled trials in mental health. *International Journal of Methods in Psychiatric Research,* 24, 257–265.

Pitt, V., Lowe, D., Hill, S., Prictor, M., Hetrick, S. E., Ryan, R., et al. (2013). Consumer-providers of care for adult clients of statutory mental health services. *Cochrane Database of Systematic Reviews.*

Popay, J., Roberts, H., Sowden, A., Petticrew, M., Arai, L., Rodgers, M., et al. (2006). *Guidance on the conduct of narrative synthesis in systematic reviews. Results of an ESRC funded research project.* Lancaster, UK: University of Lancaster.

Post, B. C., & Wade, N. G. (2009). Religion and spirituality in psychotherapy: A practice-friendly review of research. *Journal of Clinical Psychology,* 65, 131–146.

Prochaska, J. O., & Diclemente, C. C. (1982). Transtheoretical therapy: Toward a more integrative model of change. *Psychotherapy: Theory, Research and Practice,* 19, 276–288.

Ralph, R. O., & Corrigan, P. W. (2005). *Recovery in mental illness. Broadening our understanding of wellness.* Washington, DC: American Psychological Association.

Rapp, C., & Goscha, R. J. (2006). *The strengths model: Case management with people with psychiatric disabilities* (2nd ed.). New York, NY: Oxford University Press.

Repper, J., & Carter, T. (2011). A review of the literature on peer support in mental health services. *Journal of Mental Health,* 20, 392–411.

Resnick, S. G., Fontana, A., Lehman, A., & Rosenheck, R. A. (2005). An empirical conceptualization of the recovery orientation. *Schizophrenia Research,* 75, 119–128.

SChrank, B., Bird, V., Rudnick, A., & Slade, M. (2012). Determinants, self-management strategies and interventions for hope in people with mental disorders: Systematic search and narrative review. *Social Science and Medicine,* 74, 554–564.

Secker, J., Membrey, H., Grove, B., & Seebohm, P. (2002). Recovering from illness or recovering your life? Implications of clinical versus social models of recovery from mental health problems for employment support services. *Disability & Society,* 17, 403–418.

Seligman, M., Rashid, T., & Parks, A. C. (2006). Positive psychotherapy. *American Psychologist,* 61, 774–788.

Seligman, M. E. P., Steen, T. A., Park, N., & Peterson, C. (2005). Positive psychology progress: Empirical validation of interventions. *Tidsskrift for Norsk Psykologforening,* 42, 874–884.

Shanks, V., Williams, J., Leamy, M., Bird, V. J., Le Boutillier, C., & Slade, M. (2013). Measures of personal recovery: A systematic review. *Psychiatric Services,* 64, 974–980.

Slade, M. (2009a). *Personal recovery and mental illness.* Cambridge, UK: Cambridge University Press.

Slade, M. (2009b). *Personal recovery and mental illness. A guide for mental health professionals.* Cambridge, UK: Cambridge University Press.

Slade, M., Adams, N., & O'Hagan, M. (2012a). Recovery: Past progress and future challenges. *International Review of Psychiatry*, 24, 1–4.

Slade, M., Amering, M., & Oades, L. (2008). Recovery: An international perspective. *Epidemiologia e Psichiatria Sociale*, 17, 128–137.

Slade, M., Amering, M., Farkas, M., Hamilton, B., O'Hagan, M., Panther, G., et al. (2014). Uses and abuses of recovery: Implementing recovery-oriented practices in mental health systems. *World Psychiatry*, 13, 12–20.

Slade, M., Bird, V., Le Boutillier, C., Williams, J., McCrone, P., & Leamy, M. (2011). REFOCUS trial: Protocol for a cluster randomised controlled trial of a pro-recovery intervention within community based mental health teams. *BMC Psychiatry*, 11, 185.

Slade, M., Bird, V., Clarke, E., Le Boutillier, C., McCrone, P., MacPherson, R., et al. (2015a). Supporting recovery in patients with psychosis using adult mental health teams (REFOCUS): A multi-site cluster randomised controlled trial. *Lancet Psychiatry*, 2, 503–514.

Slade, M., Bird, V., Le Boutillier, C., Grey, B., Larsen, J., Leamy, M., et al. (2015b). Development of the REFOCUS intervention to increase mental health team support for personal recovery. *British Journal of Psychiatry*, 207, 544–550.

Slade, M., Leamy, M., Bacon, F., Janosik, M., Le Boutillier, C., Williams, J., et al. (2012b). International differences in understanding recovery: Systematic review. *Epidemiology and Psychiatric Sciences*, 21, 353–364.

South Australian Social Inclusion Board (2007). *Stepping up: A social inclusion action plan for mental health reform 2007–2012*. Adelaide, Australia: Government of South Australia.

Subramaniam, P., & Woods, B. (2012). The impact of individual reminiscence therapy for people with dementia: Systematic review. *Expert Review of Neurotherapeutics*, 12, 545–555.

Swanson, J., Swartz, M., Ferron, J., Elbogen, E. B., Wagner, H., McCauley, B., et al. (2006). Facilitated psychiatric advance directives: A randomized trial of an intervention to foster advance treatment planning among persons with severe mental illness. *American Journal of Psychiatry*, 163, 1943–1951.

Tait, L., & Lester, H. (2005). Encouraging user involvement in mental health services. *Advances in Psychiatric Treatment*, 11, 168–175.

Tew, J., Ramon, S., Slade, M., Bird, V., Melton, J., & Le Boutillier, C. (2012). Social factors and recovery from mental health difficulties: A review of the evidence. *British Journal of Social Work*, 42, 443–460.

Tondora, J., Miller, R., Slade, M., & Davidson, L. (2014). *Partnering for recovery in mental health: A practical guide to person-centered planning*. Chichester, UK: Wiley-Blackwell.

Whitley, R., & Drake, R. (2010). Recovery: A dimensional approach. *Psychiatric Services*, 61, 1248–1250.

Williams, J., Leamy, M., Bird, V., Harding, C., Larsen, J., Le Boutillier, C., et al. (2012). Measures of the recovery orientation of mental health services: Systematic review. *Social Psychiatry and Psychiatric Epidemiology*, 47, 1827–1835.

Williams, J., Leamy, M., Bird, V., Le Boutillier, C., Norton, S., Pesola, F., et al. (2015). Development and evaluation of a measure to identify mental health service support for recovery (INSPIRE). *Social Psychiatry and Psychiatric Epidemiology*, 50, 777–786.

Wyder, M., & Bland, R. (2014). The recovery framework as a way of understanding families' responses to mental illness: Balancing different needs and recovery journeys. *Australian Social Work*, 67, 179–196.

Chapter

4

Wellbeing Policy
An Overview

Dan Weijers and Aaron Jarden

Introduction[1]

Wellbeing – or the prudential good life – refers to how well someone's life is going *for him or her* (Crisp, 2014). Increasingly, awareness of the limitations of traditional economic indicators has led researchers to call for scientific measures of wellbeing to augment traditional measures (Diener et al., 2009; Diener and Seligman, 2004; Layard, 2005). The main problem with measures of per capita production, income and wealth is that they do not attribute direct value to many factors widely viewed as essential to high wellbeing, including relationships, health and happiness (Helliwell, 2006). In light of this problem and the attendant research, national governments and multinational organisations are investigating new measures of wellbeing to inform policy making (Diener, 2009; Stiglitz et al., 2009). Over the last decade, many of these new measures have been incorporated into various policymaking processes (see Diener et al., 2009). Within this movement toward new measures of wellbeing, some researchers are calling for the importance of mental health to be recognized by including various measures of mental health in any collection of key policy outcomes (e.g. Bok, 2010; Layard, 2005; Layard and Clark, 2014).

To pave the way for a focus on wellbeing policy in the context of mental health and recovery specifically (e.g. see Jarden, Jarden & Oades, this volume), this chapter briefly reviews the history of this debate, the current challenges of using measures of wellbeing and mental health for policy making, and some of the possibilities for meeting these challenges. We conclude that, with public backing, it would be appropriate for governments to measure mental health and wellbeing, and for the resultant data to inform policy making generally, and specifically as it relates to mental health.

Why Measure Wellbeing, Mental Health, and Recovery?

The limits of Gross Domestic Product (GDP) and Gross National Product (GNP) have been discussed by economists and many others for quite some time (Diener et al., 2009). Economic historians would point out that most of these perceived limitations are caused by the more recent use of these measures as general gauges of societal progress, rather than as a tool to assess the rate of economic growth (England, 1998). The limitations of GDP and

---

[1] This chapter is based on an earlier paper by the same authors, "The science of happiness for policymakers: An overview," published in the *Journal of Social Research & Policy*, Volume 4, Issue 2, 2013. We thank the editor of the *JSR&P* for allowing us to reproduce some material here.

Wellbeing, Recovery and Mental Health, ed. Mike Slade, Lindsay Oades and Aaron Jarden.
Published by Cambridge University Press. © Mike Slade, Lindsay Oades and Aaron Jarden 2017

GNP as general measures of progress were perhaps most passionately espoused by Robert F. Kennedy in his speech at the University of Kansas in 1968:

> Too much and for too long, we seemed to have surrendered personal excellence and community values in the mere accumulation of material things. Our Gross National Product, now, is over $800 billion dollars a year, but that Gross National Product – if we judge the United States of America by that – that Gross National Product counts air pollution and cigarette advertising and ambulances to clear our highways of carnage. It counts special locks for our doors and the jails for the people who break them. It counts the destruction of the redwood and the loss of our natural wonder in chaotic sprawl. It counts napalm and counts nuclear warheads and armored cars for the police to fight the riots in our cities. It counts … the television programs, which glorify violence in order to sell toys to our children. Yet the gross national product does not allow for the health of our children, the quality of their education or the joy of their play. It does not include the beauty of our poetry or the strength of our marriages, the intelligence of our public debate or the integrity of our public officials. It measures neither our wit nor our courage, neither our wisdom nor our learning, neither our compassion nor our devotion to our country; it measures everything, in short, except that which makes life worthwhile. And it can tell us everything about America except why we are proud that we are Americans.
>
> (Kennedy, 1968)

The message was clear; there are many things that we value highly that are not captured by GDP and GNP. In response to this and other shortcomings of the existing economic indicators, researchers, national statisticians, and several nongovernmental organisations began to investigate and measure other policy goals, including human, social, and environmental capital (Carneiro and Heckman, 2003). In addition to broadening and refining the existing range of economic measures, these initiatives led to the collection of data related to individual wellbeing, quality of life, and happiness (Michalos, 2011). Academics from several disciplines and various countries, and some civil servants, have been increasingly pushing for these new measures of wellbeing to play more important roles in policy making (e.g. Bok, 2010; Layard, 2005; Stoll et al., 2012). Over the last few years, politicians have also become engaged. For example, in 2008, French President Nicolas Sarkozy chartered the Commission on the Measurement of Economic Performance and Social Progress. The Commission, headed by Nobel-winning economist Joseph Stiglitz, advised that their report

> … is addressed, first of all, to political leaders. In this time of crises, when new political narratives are necessary to identify where our societies should go, the report advocates a shift of emphasis from a "production-oriented" measurement system to one focused on the well-being of current and future generations, in other words, toward broader measures of social progress.
>
> (Stiglitz et al., 2009, p. 10)

Shortly afterward the British Prime Minister, David Cameron, announced the investigation and subsequent measurement of wellbeing by the British government:

> [F]rom April next year, we'll start measuring our progress as a country, not just by how our economy is growing, but by how our lives are improving; not just by our standard of living, but by our quality of life.
>
> (Cameron, 2010)

However, it may yet transpire that supranational organisations, such as the United Nations (UN) and the Organisation for Economic Cooperation and Development (OECD), may end up leading the way in promoting the use of broader measures of wellbeing in policy making. For example, in April 2012, the UN General Assembly held a high-level meeting in New York on Happiness and Wellbeing: Defining a New Economic Paradigm. Importantly, the agenda for this meeting included the use of measures of subjective wellbeing (for which individuals are asked to report on how well they think their lives are going). Indeed, the *World Happiness Report*, which was commissioned for the meeting, contained a chapter on "The state of world happiness" that relies exclusively on research using measures of subjective wellbeing because "they capture best how people rate the quality of their lives" (Helliwell and Wang, 2012, p.11).

The assessment of subjective wellbeing is probably the most contentious issue in the wider debate about the new measures of societal progress. For example, Cameron's announcement that the UK government would begin collecting data on subjective wellbeing received mixed reviews (Cohen, 2011; Fitzpatrick, 2011; Vaillant, 2011). However, even major traditional economic organisations are beginning to stress the importance of subjective wellbeing. For example, the OECD (2013) has identified measures of subjective wellbeing (e.g. self-reported overall satisfaction with life) as essential for a complete understanding of wellbeing.

Lord Richard Layard, one of the most prominent proponents of the use of measures of subjective wellbeing, recommended that "quality of life, as people experience it, ought to be a key measure of progress and a central objective for any government" (Layard, 2011). Positions similar to Layard's are held by individuals such as Derek Bok (2010), Ed Diener (2011), and Bruno Frey (2008). Layard has argued that measures of subjective wellbeing should be the main yardstick for public policy because happiness is the most important goal in life for most of us (Layard, 2005). Happiness is "what people want for their children and for their fellow citizens" and thereby "the greatest happiness of all" deserves to be the ultimate goal of governments and policy makers (Layard, 2005, pp. 124–125). Layard understands happiness as meaning "feeling good – enjoying life and wanting the feeling to be maintained" (2005, p. 12) and believes that the emerging field of wellbeing science has come far enough to accurately measure this kind of happiness using subjective survey questions. Thus, according to Layard, we should be using data from subjective survey measures of happiness and wellbeing to inform policy making. However, the use of subjective measures of happiness and wellbeing as the only or ultimate criterion to assess specific policies or progress in general has been criticised by philosophers and economists on many grounds (e.g. Diener and Scollon, 2003; Frey and Stutzer, 2007).

In addition, several scholars have argued that happiness is understood differently by different individuals and in different cultures (Joshanloo, 2014; Thin, 2012), and also that happiness is not always viewed as positive (Joshanloo and Weijers, 2014). However, while several researchers have concerns about happiness being the supreme aim of public policy, or even *an* aim of policy at all in some cultures, happiness as an aim of public policy in Western cultures seems to be fairly well supported (e.g. Bok, 2010; Diener, 2006, 2011; Diener and Scollon, 2003; Frey, 2008; Frey and Stutzer, 2007). If the citizenry of a democratic state demand that its government include subjective wellbeing as one of its overarching goals, then there is reason for policy makers to investigate measuring happiness and other subjective reports of the good life, and then use the resulting data as one of a set of guides for public policy. While citizens demanding that their government measure their subjective wellbeing might seem unlikely, a 2005 BBC opinion poll, which asked whether the government's main objective should be the "greatest happiness" or the "greatest wealth," returned a clear verdict, with 81% reporting that happiness should be the main goal (Easton, 2006). This result resembles a poll taken on *The Economist*'s website in 2011 during a debate between Richard Layard and Paul Ormerod, in which the motion "new measures of economic and social progress are needed for the 21st-century economy" (using happiness science to inform policy making was the focus of the debate) received 83% of the support of the online audience. If these results are representative of popular opinion, then, in democracies at least, the practicality of measuring happiness for policy making should be investigated. Furthermore, since happiness is usually understood as being a subjective state (Layard, 2005), the practicality and processes of measuring subjective wellbeing for policy making should be investigated.

A closer look at the more detailed works by the researchers discussed above reveals a near-uniform preference for focusing initial subjective-wellbeing-related policy interventions on those with the worst subjective wellbeing. In most cases, the general argument in favour of focusing on those already worst off is that the gains are more easily achievable, and that it seems inhumane to help fairly happy people become very happy when others are suffering (Bok, 2010; Layard, 2005; Layard and Clark, 2014). Layard and Clark (2014) detail the great disparity in how much the UK government spends on physical health care compared with mental health care. They make a convincing case for modest increases in mental health spending making a big difference in the quality of life of thousands of unhappy people. In particular, they argue that getting the right help to people with mental illnesses could enable them to recover and live much more fulfilling lives and be more productive members of society. Thus policies targeted at mental health and recovery initiatives more than pay for themselves when broader range policy goals are considered.

An Overview of Measuring Subjective Wellbeing, Mental Health and Recovery

Whether the use of measures of mental health and happiness for policy making should be pursued depends not only on how important mental health and happiness are to people, but also on whether they can be efficiently and accurately measured. Of all the new methods for measuring happiness, only survey questions are currently practical on scales large enough to be useful for public policy. For example, survey questions asking for respondents' judgments about how happy or satisfied they are with their lives can be quickly and cheaply disseminated via online survey technology. Furthermore, the use of online surveys enables respondents' answers to be formatted into usable data quickly. In contrast, collecting wellbeing data with behavioral measures, such as expert observations, tracking devices, or neuroimaging techniques, is likely to be prohibitively expensive and time-consuming. It is also unclear if any of these more objective measures are better at capturing how happy people are than simply asking them (Layard, 2005).

Subjective measures of wellbeing can be global or domain-specific. Global measures aim to assess respondents' judgments of their lives as a whole, while domain-specific measures target aspects of respondents' lives, such as their work lives, family lives, health, or finances. Although domain-specific measures have their uses (see Huppert et al., 2009), the focus in this chapter is on global measures because they provide a better approximation to the terms 'happiness' and 'wellbeing' as they are normally understood, and also usefully generalize across various states of mental health by way of individuals' subjective experience.

There are a wide range of global subjective wellbeing questions (Diener, 2009), but most are subtle variants of general questions about happiness or satisfaction with life. For example, the United States' General Social Survey asks, "Taken all together, how would you say things are these days? Would you say that you are very happy, pretty happy, or not too happy?" (Kahneman and Krueger, 2006, p. 6). The World Values Survey asks, "All things considered, how satisfied are you with your life as a whole these days?" and uses a response scale ranging from "1 (not at all satisfied)" to "10 (very satisfied)" (Ingleheart et al., 2008). The subtle variations on these questions usually amount to changing the number of available points on the response scale, or slightly adjusting the wording of the question (e.g. "in general," "all things considered"). For example, the World Values Survey also asks the following question about happiness: "Taking all things together, would you say you are ... Very happy ... Rather happy ... Not very happy ... Not at all happy" using a four-point response scale.

Global subjective wellbeing questions elicit responses that are biased by aspects such as contextual factors, the specific wording of questions, the order and type of preceding questions, and respondents' current moods (see OECD, 2013). Experiments have shown that contextual factors, such as the weather (Schwarz and Clore, 1983) or unexpectedly finding a dime (Schwarz, 1987), significantly affect how satisfied participants reported being with their lives. Experiments on the variability of self-reported satisfaction with life within individuals have demonstrated that people's reported satisfaction with life as a whole can change over a period of a few weeks (Kahneman and Krueger, 2006; OECD, 2013).

However, large representative samples and careful psychometric survey creation can avoid or mitigate these issues. Indeed, many of these potential biases can be avoided because they are random biases, which tend to affect different people at different times. Therefore, by conducting surveys on large representative samples (e.g. $n = 10,000+$: The Sovereign New Zealand Wellbeing Index, Jarden et al., 2013), the impact of random bias tends to cancel itself out (the law of averages) and is thereby considerably reduced. In this way, sampling can eliminate the potential bias associated with personal variations in mood and localized variation in important events (e.g. sports teams winning or variations in the weather). The effects of recent events and participants' current moods can also be reduced by using a battery of questions about satisfaction with life, such as the Satisfaction with Life Scale (Diener et al., 1985), instead of just one question (Lucas et al., 1996). To prevent the small but robust effects that specific questions have on subsequent responses to the more global questions, researchers usually put global questions first on their surveys (Schimmack and Oishi, 2005). Measures that span both mental health and wellbeing, such as the Mental Health Continuum – Short Form (Keyes, 2005) and the Warwick-Edinburgh Mental Well-Being Scale (Tennant, Hiller, Fishwick, Platt, Joseph, Weich, et al., 2007), have also been developed.

Challenges in Using Measures of Subjective Wellbeing to Inform Policy Making

Many criticisms have been leveled at the use of wellbeing science to inform policy. Three of the most pertinent criticisms will be briefly discussed here: that survey measures of happiness and wellbeing are too insensitive to be useful, that we cannot know what measures of happiness and wellbeing are really measuring, and that the wrong kind of happiness and wellbeing is being measured.

Are Happiness and Wellbeing Scales Insensitive?

Johns and Ormerod (2008) claim that time series happiness data are insensitive. Put simply, if time series happiness data are insensitive, then the happiness scores will not change enough in response to environmental changes for us to be 95% confident that the small changes in the happiness scores are not simply a product of chance. While insensitivity is a problem for many measures of happiness, it is not an insurmountable one. The argument for the insensitivity of time series happiness data that Johns and Ormerod put forward is based on a discussion of one measure of happiness with a three-point response scale. This particular selection is somewhat misleading because most recent and contemporary happiness questions have larger response scales. Indeed, many of the subjective wellbeing scales currently in use have ten or eleven response options – for example, the life satisfaction question from the World Values Survey (question V22), the wellbeing questions used in the Gallup World Poll (Gallup Inc., 2008), or the questions in Work on Wellbeing (Work on Wellbeing, 2015). Moreover, as the OECD report and guidelines (OECD, 2013) indicate, the trend is to larger and more discriminant response scales (e.g., the OECD recommends that national statistical offices use 0–10 scales, with 0 representing an absence of the construct measured rather than the opposite of the construct – allowing even further discrimination of variables, and thus increased sensitivity). Even if there were not a trend toward more discriminant scales, researchers have routinely discovered statistically significant changes in time series happiness data even over short periods of time, and even in Johns and Ormerod's home nation of the United Kingdom (e.g. Ingleheart et al., 2008).

Therefore, although worries about the insensitivity of happiness measures are not completely unfounded, they do not provide a good reason to avoid using time series happiness data to guide policy. Indeed, many time series happiness studies can be useful for policy making in several ways (Frey, 2008). For example, careful comparison of survey data from similar nations, or other groups, where policy change has occurred in some groups but not others, can help to evaluate the effects of policy change on reported wellbeing (Turton, 2009).

Do Measures of Happiness and Wellbeing Really Assess Happiness and Wellbeing?

There are currently a number of different methods that are claimed to be measures of happiness and wellbeing (Lopez and Snyder, 2003). These include brain scans (neuroimaging), daily reports of feelings, the opinions of participants' friends or colleagues, the opinion of an expert, the amount of time participants smile and, most commonly, survey questions (Lopez and Snyder, 2003; Weijers, 2010). Importantly, there are a range of survey questions about happiness and wellbeing, many of which are worded very differently. Some ask about positive and negative feelings, satisfaction with life, whether you would change anything about your life and, of course, happiness. The results of these diverse survey measures tend to correlate with one another and the nonsubjective measures just mentioned (Layard 2005). Kroll (2010), Layard (2005), and Bok (2010) all argue that these correlations should encourage us to have faith in the validity of subjective measures of wellbeing. Indeed, the high significance of these correlations does provide good evidence that answers to survey questions about happiness and wellbeing are related to the relevant nonsubjective assessments. However, since the correlations are also never close to being large, we also have good evidence that the various measures are not assessing the same phenomenon (Weijers, 2010). So the most reasonable answer to the question heading this subsection is that measures of happiness and wellbeing really do assess happiness and wellbeing, but with each measure assessing a related but different conception of happiness and wellbeing. Simply being clear about which measures (and related conceptions) are being used pretty well resolves this problem for policy makers. However, this solution also highlights our next problem.

How Do We Know If We Are Measuring the Right Kind of Happiness and Wellbeing?

It is well known by happiness researchers that the various questions in wellbeing surveys are not tracking the same phenomena (Dodge et al., 2012). Indeed, many social scientists and philosophers recognize that the different kinds of questions used in subjective wellbeing surveys often endorse one particular theory of wellbeing (e.g. Feldman, 2010; McDowell, 2010). Do these differences matter if the measures are assessing something that is obviously good? We suggest that for policy-relevant research, yes, they do (or at least they may, depending on the details).

What if findings based on different measures of wellbeing imply different policies? This is not just a theoretical problem, as many seemingly contradictory results from wellbeing science show. For example, Diener et al. (2010) provided evidence that the more a measure of subjective wellbeing asks about the respondents' emotional lives, and the less it encourages them to engage in cognitive deliberation about how satisfied they are with their lives compared with what they might have been, the smaller and less significant the relationship between increases in income and increases in subjective wellbeing becomes. So, in this case, the choice of a subjective wellbeing measure might affect policy decisions about income redistribution.

How ought the problem of apparently contradictory findings from the science of wellbeing to be resolved? First, researchers should avoid generalizing findings from different measures of wellbeing, unless those questions have been shown to track the same phenomena in the same circumstances in other studies. Second, policy makers should always refer to the original research papers, and even the survey questions themselves, if the researchers have not made the phenomena obvious (Weijers, 2010). Having found that the contradictory wellbeing science findings are based on the use of different measures of wellbeing, what should a policy maker do? Discovery of such a conflict illuminates the fundamental problem policy makers intent on using wellbeing science face, which is, "Which question or questions about subjective wellbeing are the most appropriate basis for policy making?"

Policy makers should not expect to have to answer this question by themselves. Philosophers have debated the merits of various theories of wellbeing for at least two thousand years (Weijers, 2010), and social scientists have been debating which measures of wellbeing are the most valid, reliable, and representative of the best philosophical theories of wellbeing (Huppert et al., 2009; McDowell, 2010). Unfortunately, there is still no agreement between academics on which question about subjective wellbeing is the most appropriate basis for policy making. However, there are many candidates whose advantages and disadvantages have been discussed at length (e.g. Helliwell and Wang, 2012; Huppert et al., 2009), and new proposals about how to resolve this issue continue to emerge (Forgeard et al., 2011; Taylor, 2015). This academic knowledge needs to be discussed widely to engender public debate about what makes people's lives go well for them and the proper aims of government. A populace that is informed about what makes citizens' lives go well for them will be able to exercise its democratic rights to lobby (and perhaps vote) for its members' preferred conception of wellbeing (Weijers, 2010). When this occurs, policy makers can work with social scientists to ensure that appropriate measures of wellbeing are used to guide public policy. This approach will allow happiness researchers to be confident that they are producing findings that are relevant for policy making, and policy makers to benefit fully from happiness science.

These potential problems just discussed for subjective measures of happiness and well-being apply equally to general measures of mental health. If subjective measures of mental health are not sensitive enough to external factors, or if they do not capture the elements that are widely viewed as essential to mental health, then they will not be useful to policy makers. However, the solutions discussed above also apply in equal measure. Perhaps most importantly, researchers have demonstrated how a subjective wellbeing approach can create policy-friendly information (Fujiwara and Campbell, 2011), including information on mental health issues (Fujiwara and Dolan, 2014).

What Roles Should Mental Health, Happiness, and Wellbeing Play in Policy Making?

In any democratic society, citizens should decide what conceptions of mental health, happiness, or wellbeing are important and the extent of the roles any such conceptions should play in policy making. In order to educate citizens and encourage effective evidence-based policy making, academics and top-level civil servants need to better clarify the various conceptions of mental health, happiness, and wellbeing and whether we can accurately and efficiently measure them. After these issues have been clarified, the circumstances and policies that affect mental health, happiness, or wellbeing (as defined in each case) should be investigated to help better understand where each concept fits in the economic, political, and cultural landscape and also to promote public debate on the relevant merits of certain kinds of happiness and mental health. Initial steps have been taken to provide sketches of what public policies based on happiness research might look like at the local (Rablen, 2012), national (Bok, 2010; Di Tella and MacCulloch, 2006; Dolan and White, 2007) and international levels (Di Tella and MacCulloch, 2006), but specific and thoroughly justified recommendations are only just beginning to emerge. Philosophers, psychologists, economists, statisticians, political scientists, and policy makers should work together collaboratively on this important endeavor in order to pool their collective expertise and progress most effectively. The conference series "Wellbeing and Public Policy" by Morrison, Weijers and Jarden (Morrison and Weijers, 2012), which began in 2012, is one such collaborative effort.

Mental health, happiness, and wellbeing are clearly important values. However, the scope and depth of the roles of these values in public policy are ultimately in the hands of governments and citizens around the world. One of the goals of this book is to provide rigorous and contemporary scientific findings about what we can and might be able to do to enhance the mental health and wellbeing of various subgroups and populations. We hope that this information will be used to inform future policies that enhance people's mental health and wellbeing.

References

Bok, D. (2010). *The politics of happiness: What governments can learn from the new research on well-being.* Princeton, NJ: Princeton University Press.

Cameron, D. (2010). A transcript of a speech given by the Prime Minister on wellbeing on 25 November 2010. Available at http://www.number10.gov.uk/news/pm-speech-on-well-being/.

Carneiro, P., & Heckman, J. J. (2003). Human capital policy. In Heckman, J. J., & Krueger, A. (Eds.), *Inequality in America: What Role for Human Capital Policies?* Cambridge, MA: MIT Press.

Cohen, R. (2011). The happynomics of life. New York Times, 12 March 2011.

Crisp, R. (2014). Well-being. In Zalta, E. N. (Ed.), *The Stanford Encyclopedia of Philosophy* (Winter 2014 ed.). Available at plato.stanford.edu/archives/win2014/entries/well-being/.

Diener, E. (2006). Guidelines for national indicators of subjective well-being and ill-being. *Applied Research in Quality of Life*, 1, 151–157.

Diener, E. (2009). *Assessing well-being: The collected works of Ed Diener*. Dordrecht: Springer.

Diener, E. (2011). Happiness, *Economist* debates. The Economist, 18 May 2011. Available at http://www.economist.com/debate/days/view/702.

Diener, E., Emmons, R. A., Larsen, R. J., & Griffin, S. (1985). The Satisfaction with Life Scale. *Journal of Personality Assessment*, 49, 71–75.

Diener, E., Kahneman, D., Tov, W., & Arora, R. (2010). Income's differential impact on judgments of life versus affective well-being. In Diener, E., Kahneman, D. & Helliwell, J. F. (Eds.), *International Differences in Well-Being* (pp. 3–15). New York, NY: Oxford University Press.

Diener, E., Lucas, R. E., Schimmack, U., & Helliwell, J. F. (2009). *Well-being for public policy*. Oxford, UK: Oxford University Press.

Diener, E., & Scollon, C. (2003). Subjective well-being is desirable, but not the summum bonum. Unpublished manuscript. Presented at the University of Minnesota Workshop on Well-Being. Available at http://scholar.googleusercontent.com/scholar?q=cache:2gjgl65fdpQJ:scholar.google.com/&hl=en&as_sdt=0,5.

Diener, E. & Seligman, M. E. P. (2004). Beyond money: Toward an economy of wellbeing. *Psychological Science in the Public Interest*, 5, 1–31.

Di Tella, R., & MacCulloch, R. (2006). Some uses of happiness data in economics. *Journal of Economic Perspectives*, 20(1): 25–46.

Dodge, R., Daly, A. P., Huyton, J., & Sanders, L. D. (2012). The challenge of defining wellbeing. *International Journal of Wellbeing*, 2(3), 222–235.

Dolan, P., Peasgood, T., & White, M. (2008). Do we really know what makes us happy? A review of the economic literature on the factors associated with subjective well-being. *Journal of Economic Psychology*, 29, 94–122.

Dolan, P., & White, M. P. (2007). How can measures of subjective well-being be used to inform public policy? *Perspectives on Psychological Science*, 2(1), 71–85.

Easton, M. (2006). Britain's happiness in decline, BBC News, 2 May 2006. Available at http://news.bbc.co.uk/2/hi/programmes/happiness_formula/4771908.stm.

England, R. W. (1998). Alternatives to Gross Domestic Product: A critical survey. In Ackerman, F., Kiron, D., Goodwin, N., Harris, J., & Gallagher, K. P. (Eds.), *Human Wellbeing and Economic Goals* (vol. 3, pp. 373–402). Island Press.

Feldman, F. (2010). *What is this thing called happiness?* Oxford, UK: Clarendon Press.

Fitzpatrick, M. (2011). Mad men take over the coalition. *British Journal of General Practice*, 61(582), 71.

Forgeard, M. J. C., Jayawickreme, E., Kern, M., & Seligman, M. E. P. (2011). Doing the right thing: Measuring wellbeing for public policy. *International Journal of Wellbeing*, 1(1), 79–106. doi:10.5502/ijw.v1i1.15.

Frey, B. S. (2008). *Happiness: A revolution in economics*. Cambridge, MA: MIT Press.

Frey, B. S., & Stutzer, A. (2002). What can economists learn from happiness research? *Journal of Economic Literature*, 40(2), 402–435.

Frey, B. S., & Stutzer, A. (2007). Should national happiness be maximized? Institute for Empirical Research in Economics, University of Zürich, working paper 306, March 2007. Available at http://www.iew.uzh.ch/wp/iewwp306.pdf.

Fujiwara, D., & Campbell, R. (2011). Valuation techniques for social cost-benefit analysis: Stated preference, revealed preference and subjective well-being approaches. HM Treasury Green Book Discussion Paper. Available at https://www.gov.uk/government/publications/valuation-techniques-for-social-cost-benefit-analysis.

Fujiwara, D., & Dolan, P. (2014). Valuing mental health: How a subjective wellbeing approach can show just how much it matters. UK Council for Psychotherapy, January 2014, 1–20.

Gallup Inc. (2008). *World Poll questions*. Washington, DC: Gallup Inc. Available at http://media.gallup.com/dataviz/www/WP_Questions_WHITE.pdf.

Helliwell, J. F. (2006). Well-being, social capital and public policy: What's new? *Economic Journal*, 116(510), C34–C45.

Helliwell, J. F., & Wang, S. (2012). The state of world happiness. In Sachs, J., Helliwell, J. F., & Layard, R. (Eds.), World Happiness Report. Commissioned for the United Nations. Available at http:// www.earth.columbia.edu/sitefiles/file/Sachs%20Writing/2012/World%20Happiness%20Report .pdf (accessed 4 September 2013).

Huppert, F. A., Marks, N., Clark, A., Siegrist, J., Stutzer, A., Vittersø, J., et al. (2009). Measuring well-being across Europe: Description of the ESS well-being module and preliminary findings. *Social Indicators Research*, 91(3), 301–315.

Ingleheart, R., Foa, R., Peterson, C., & Welzel, C. (2008). Development, freedom, and rising happiness: A global perspective (1981–2007). *Perspectives on Psychological Science*, 3(4), 264–285.

Jarden, A., MacKay, L., White, K., Schofield, G., Duncan, S., Williden, M., et al. (2013). The Sovereign New Zealand Wellbeing Index. *Psychology Aotearoa*, 5(1), pp. 22–27.

Johns, H., & Ormerod, P. (2008). The unhappy thing about happiness studies. *Real-World Economics Review*, 46, 139–146.

Joshanloo, M. (2014). Eastern conceptualizations of happiness: Fundamental differences with Western views. *Journal of Happiness Studies*, 15(2): 475–493.

Joshanloo, Mohsen, & Weijers, Dan (2014). Aversion to happiness across cultures: A review of where and why people are averse to happiness. *Journal of Happiness Studies*, 15(3): 717–735.

Kahneman, D., & Krueger, A. B. (2006). Developments in the measurement of subjective well-being. *Journal of Economic Perspectives*, 20(1), 3–24.

Kennedy, R. F. (1968). Speech at University of Kansas, March 18. Transcript available at http://www .glaserprogress.org/program_areas/pdf/Remarks_of_Robert_F_Kennedy.pdf.

Keyes, C. L. M. (2005). Mental illness and/or mental health? Investigating axioms of the complete state model of health. *Journal of Consulting and Clinical Psychology*, 73, 539–548.

Kroll, C. (2010). Social democracy and happiness. *Social Europe Journal*. Available at http://www .social-europe.eu/2010/01/social-democracy-and-happiness/.

Layard, R. (2005). *Happiness: Lessons from a new science*. London, UK: Penguin.

Layard, R. (2011). Happiness, *Economist* debates. The Economist, 17 May 2011. Available at http:// www.economist.com/debate/days/view/698.

Layard, R., & Clark, D. (2014). *Thrive: The power of evidence-based psychological therapies*. London, UK: Penguin.

Lopez, S. J., & Snyder, C. R. (Eds.) (2003). *Positive psychological assessment: A handbook of models and measures*. Washington, DC: American Psychological Association.

Lucas, R. E., Diener, E., & Suh, E. M. (1996). Discriminant validity of well-being measures. *Journal of Personality and Social Psychology*, 71(3), 616–28.

McDowell, I. (2010). Measures of self-perceived well-being. *Journal of psychosomatic research*, 69(1), 69–79.

Michalos, A. C. (2011). What did Stiglitz, Sen and Fitoussi get right and what did they get wrong? *Social Indicators Research*, 102, 117–129.

Morrison, P. S., & Weijers, D. (2012). Wellbeing in Wellington: A report on the June 2012 Wellbeing and Public Policy Conference. *Policy Quarterly*, 8(4), 51–55.

OECD (Organisation for Economic Cooperation and Development). (2013). Your Better Life Index: Executive summary. Organisation for Economic Cooperation and Development. Available at http://oecdbetterlifeindex.org/wpsystem/wp-content/uploads/2012/02/YourBetterLifeIndex_ ExecutiveSummary3.pdf

Rablen, M. D. (2012). The promotion of local wellbeing: A primer for policymakers. *Local Economy*, 27(3), 297–314.

Schimmack, U., & Oishi, S. (2005). The influence of chronically and temporarily accessible information on life satisfaction judgments. *Journal of Personality and Social Psychology*, 89(3), 395–406.

Schwarz, N. (1987). *Stimmung als information* [Mood as information]. Heidelberg, Germany: Springer Verlag.

Schwarz, N., & Clore, G. L. (1983). Mood, misattribution, and judgments of well-being: Informative and directive functions of affective states. *Journal of Personality and Social Psychology*, 45(3), 513–23.

Stiglitz, J. E., Sen, A., & Fitoussi, J. P. (Eds.) (2009). *Report by the Commission on the Measurement of Economic Performance and Social Progress*. Paris: Commission on the Measurement of Economic Performance and Social Progress.

Stoll, L., Michaelson, J., & Seaford, C. (2012). *Well-being evidence for policy: A review*. London, UK: New Economics Foundation. Available at http://scholar.google.co.nz/scholar?q=%22Well-being+evidence+for+policy%3A+A+review%22&btnG=&hl=en&as_sdt=1%2C5.

Taylor, T. E. (2015). The markers of wellbeing: A basis for a theory-neutral approach. *International Journal of Wellbeing*, 5, 79–80.

Tennant, R., Hiller, L., Fishwick, R., Platt, S., Joseph, S., Weich, S., et al. (2007). The Warwick–Edinburgh mental well-being scale (WEMWBS): Development and UK validation. *Health and Quality of Life Outcomes*, 5(1), 63. doi:101186/1477-7252-5-63.

Thin, N. (2012). Counting and recounting happiness and culture: On happiness surveys and prudential ethnobiography. *International Journal of Wellbeing*, 2(4), 313–332.

Turton, D. (2009). The real dirt on happiness studies: A reply to "The unhappy thing about happiness economics." *Real-World Economics Review*, 49, 83–89.

Vaillant, G. (2011). The happiness effect. *Bulletin of the World Health Organization*, 89(4), 246–247. Available at http://www.scielosp.org/scielo.php?script=sci_arttext&pid=S0042-96862011000400005&lng=en&tlng=en. 10.1590/S0042-96862011000400005.

Weijers, D. (2010). A warning to policy-makers: What exactly is well-being anyway? *Social Europe Journal*. Available at http://www.social-europe.eu/2010/09/a-warning-to-policy-makers-what-exactly-is-well-being-anyway/.

Work on Wellbeing. (2015). Available at http://www.workonwellbeing.com.

Positive Psychology and Severe Mental Ill Health
Strengths-Based Cognitive–Behavioural Interventions in Psychosis

Pawel D. Mankiewicz and Julia C. Renton

Introduction

Although little has been written about the impact of positive psychology within psychosis, this perspective has the potential to enable recovery across a range of domains for those who have experienced or are experiencing a psychotic episode. Within the field of clinical psychology, the neglect of subjective wellbeing (SWB) might be explained by the field's long-established focus on the more severe, complex and enduring forms of psychological difficulties, which in practice often entails addressing problems and reducing distress rather than promoting happiness (Conway and MacLeod, 2002). Although examples of studies describing successfully implemented interventions and their positive impact on the wellbeing of people with psychosis have been available in the clinical literature, Braehler and Harper (2008) still report that the quality of life of those diagnosed with schizophrenia remains low.

Yet, more than two decades ago, Romme and Escher (1993) proposed that rehabilitation of people with psychosis should focus on enhancing all fundamental aptitudes in their lives. Similarly, Chadwick (1997) demonstrated that such individuals have virtues as well as deficits, and psychological interventions needed to focus on these strengths in order to increase the dignity and SWB of those with psychosis. Cognitive models of psychosis have focussed on understanding individual presentation and the experience of symptomatology rather than diagnostic criteria. This gives the advantage of understanding difficulties from an individualised perspective and tailoring treatment approaches around this. However, as Chadwick describes, such models need to be further elaborated to encompass the development of SWB alongside the alleviation of problematic symptomatology. Given the historic endorsement of the disease paradigm of emotional difficulties and neglect of individual virtues in clinical psychology, it appears important for clinicians working within the specialism of severe and complex mental ill-health to recognise how applied positive psychology may be utilised with their clients, and how this discipline may inform the development of positive clinical practice aimed at supporting and increasing their clients' life satisfaction.

In this chapter we will initially review the existing research literature that informs the development of positive psychological practice in psychosis, with particular consideration given to evidence-based cognitive-behavioural therapy. Second, with the use of case

Wellbeing, Recovery and Mental Health, ed. Mike Slade, Lindsay Oades and Aaron Jarden.
Published by Cambridge University Press. © Mike Slade, Lindsay Oades and Aaron Jarden 2017

examples, we will illustrate the utilisation of positive cognitive-behavioural interventions as applied with clients with psychosis in our clinical practice.

Subjective Wellbeing in Psychosis

To address the apparent absence of research literature addressing SWB among people with psychosis, Mankiewicz et al. (2013a) conducted a clinical study in which they examined the utilisation of SWB measures among individuals with active experiences of hallucinations and paranoia. The authors demonstrated that SWB measures could be effectively and reliably administered with individuals with active psychoses, including those in acute mental health wards. Interestingly, the sample's mean for the affective component of SWB, that is, positive affect, approximated the levels established in the general population, indicating that the participants exhibited average levels of positive affect. Thus, contrary to the negative inferences derived from the disease paradigm of schizophrenia, the participants exhibited levels of positive affect typical for the universal nonclinical average.

Mankiewicz et al. (2013b) investigated levels of psychological distress and examined how experiences of psychosis affected their cognitive component of SWB, that is, satisfaction with life. They found that the effects that experiences of psychosis, such as paranoid beliefs, had on individual life satisfaction were mediated by the levels of individual emotional distress. In particular, mediational analysis of data demonstrated that depression acted as a dominant mediator in the association between the experiences of psychosis and satisfaction with life.

Based on the outcomes of their research, Mankiewicz et al. (2013b) proposed a number of conclusions to inform positive psychological practice with psychosis. The authors suggested that psychosis did not equal unhappiness and that the levels of SWB among people with psychosis appeared largely similar to the levels typical for the general population. Moreover, the range of sample scores demonstrated that such individuals could experience joy and be satisfied with their lives. Hence, contrary to the traditional deficit-oriented portrayal of psychosis, empirical data supported the argument that individuals with such experiences are able to report levels of SWB similar to those in the general population.

It was also concluded that psychosis did not exempt individuals from positive mood set points. In their positive mood set-point theory, Diener and Diener (1996) proposed that there is a positive, rather than neutral, baseline for affect in human beings, which has significant adaptive, evolutionary, motivational, social, learning and intrinsic functions. Although the exact set point varies among individuals depending on a person's socialisation and temperament, for most people it remains in the positive range. Since the general levels of positive affect in psychosis were demonstrated to be similar to those reported in the general population, experiences of psychosis did not appear to automatically disturb positive mood set points among individuals diagnosed with paranoid schizophrenia.

Furthermore, Mankiewicz et al. concluded that psychosis did not indiscriminately reduce satisfaction with life. They suggested that experiences of psychosis would indirectly affect individual life satisfaction through their influence on depression levels. The findings remained consistent with a cognitive model of depression, in which negative and self-defeating cognitions are unconditional and overgeneralised, and thus affect perception of one's whole life (Gilbert, 2009).

Finally, it was suggested that psychosis did not immobilize adaptive mechanisms of SWB. The positive affect levels among individuals with psychosis were similar to those reported in the general population. Findings of stable levels of positive affect, despite clearly elevated experiences of psychological distress, showed that average satisfaction with life was only slightly lowered in comparison with general population trends. In his dynamic equilibrium theory of happiness, Headey (2006) hypothesised that both positive and negative major life events are typically habituated to and people soon return to their usual individually set equilibrium states of SWB. Thus, on most occasions after major negative life events, the initially increased levels of psychological distress and reduced levels of positive affect would eventually return to their idiosyncratic base levels, reinstating an equilibrium in individual SWB. Empirical data produced by Mankiewicz et al. (2013b) indicated that individuals diagnosed with paranoid schizophrenia were also able to habituate to such disconcerting experiences as onset of psychosis, acute episodes of paranoia and hearing voices or admissions to inpatient wards, and with time returned to their individual SWB equilibrium states.

Towards Positive Interventions in Psychosis

Numerous analyses of current evidence in the specialism of psychological interventions for psychosis demonstrated the effectiveness of cognitive-behavioural therapy for psychosis (CBTp). In their meta-analytical evaluation of controlled research and qualitative reviews, Roth and Fonagy (2005) presented numerous studies with favourable outcomes. CBTp has been supported by affirmative results of case studies (e.g. Hagen and Nordahl, 2008) and randomised control trials (e.g. Farhall et al., 2009).

In the past two decades, the idea that experiences of psychosis could be understood in a similar way to other psychological difficulties has been growing and has initiated a fundamental change in the culture of mental health services (Hayward et al., 2005). The existing evidence suggests that even very healthy individuals may hear voices, which argues against treating hallucinations on their own as symptoms of psychopathology (Romme and Escher, 1993). Thus, Dunn (2002) proposed that CBTp should not primarily focus on targeting the presence of hallucinations or delusions, but should rather address the emotional distress that affects individuals' wellbeing and increase the persons' ability and identify their strengths to cope with such experiences.

Yet can a range of cognitive-behavioural interventions be employed within a positive therapeutic framework? And, if so, what criteria would need to be met to ensure that the delivered cognitive-based therapy was indeed positive in its nature? Such enquiries were explored by Weiss and Knoster (2008), who argued that such therapy needed to move away from the traditional utilisation of mechanistic interventions and become person-based. Subsequently, those authors proposed that in order for a therapeutic model to meet criteria of positive psychological intervention it must allow the client opportunity to express opinions and exert a level of control over his or her life through meaningful choices, help the person to identify fundamental needs, positively influence the client's quality of life, consider the person's immediate and wider environment, and help him or her minimise the likelihood of future crises.

Lopez and Kerr (2006) emphasised that positive therapy practice needs to be based on core values of shared therapeutic goals, collaborative work and reciprocally attainable results. In such intervention, the importance of a therapeutic alliance needs to be explicitly acknowledged and prioritised. Similarly, Weiss and Knoster (2008) argued that positive behavioural approaches ought to be overtly based on therapeutic collaboration (versus authoritarian control) and functionally focused on illumination, that is understanding the meanings and purposes of individuals' behaviour from their subjective perspective, rather than exclusively on elimination, that is extinguishing unhelpful behaviours.

Even earlier, Keyes and Lopez (2002) proposed that positive treatments were those that had the objectives of building upon a person's existing strengths and eliminating barriers to personal growth. Once more, the major importance of integration of the positive (promoting wellbeing) and negative (addressing signs of psychological distress) was highlighted. The authors emphasised that such therapies do not differ from traditional models in their content, but rather in their explicit focus. Thus, for instance, research studies reviewed by Thompson (2002) demonstrated how a range of conventional cognitive-behavioural interventions (such as goal setting, cognitive restructuring, stress reduction, problem-solving skills, positive mental imagery and self-instruction training) were effectively employed to increase individuals' subjective quality of life.

Subsequently, Fava and Ruini (2003) proposed that wellbeing-oriented psychological interventions should be integrated with traditional approaches and delivered after a range of problematic cognitions and behaviours had been addressed. Also, Frish (2006) demonstrated that traditional cognitive-behavioural therapy could be successfully combined with positive psychology principles and utilised across a wide spectrum of mental health needs. Both models explicitly address unhelpful cognitions, maladaptive relationships, difficult emotions and dysfunctional behaviours through numerous cognitive and behavioural therapeutic strategies, yet complement the traditional cognitive-behavioural approach with an integrated wellbeing component.

An intervention based on such integrative principles was investigated by Seligman et al. (2006), who studied the effectiveness of positive psychotherapeutic input in alleviating depression. The treatment, derived from the traditional cognitive-behavioural approach, integrated interventions focusing on negative and positive experiences and incorporated both cognitive techniques and behavioural tasks. The authors demonstrated that the treatment led to considerable symptomatic relief, even among severely depressed clients. The effect sizes were moderate to large. Similarly, the effectiveness of cognitive therapy based on the notions of positive psychology was investigated by Padash et al. (2012). The delivered intervention considerably increased individuals' SWB with particular gains in life satisfaction, in spite of various psychological problems, such as depression.

Positive Therapeutic Framework and CBTp

Interventions informed by applied positive psychology provide an alternative approach that complements the traditional deficit-based stance. In other words, positive therapists may offer a range of strengths-based interventions that promote individual SWB and buffer against mental ill health (Joseph and Linley, 2006). Considering the discussed principles of positive cognitive-behavioural therapies, it appears that CBTp may potentially be delivered within the positive therapeutic framework.

The crucial importance of adopting a person-centred stance towards the therapeutic relationship and processes in positive therapies was emphasised by Joseph and Linley (2006). As argued by the authors, in positive psychological practice, despite initial focus on alleviating distressing symptoms, the clients ought to be supported in finding outlets and expression for their directional tendencies that are congruent with their intrinsic values. Such a positive shift in the therapeutic focus would provide an empowering alternative to the disease model of mental illness, and thus appears particularly important for those with severe, complex and enduring psychological needs.

In 1996, Chadwick, Birchwood and Trower predicted that although CBTp had initially helped clinicians to move away from the medical constructs of schizophrenia and liberated psychological research and practice, it would one day need to step beyond its symptom focus and turn towards ordinary human psychology, that is, psychology of the person. Subsequently, Chadwick (2006) proposed that CBTp ought to return to the core values of cognitive-behavioural practice and launched the person-based CBTp. The therapy's methodological principles were defined as follows: interventions would initially address clients' emotional distress; a cognitive mediational model of distress would be used for formulation purposes to enhance individuals' understanding of their experiences; continuity between psychotic and nonpsychotic experiences would be explicitly assumed, to destigmatise clients' experiences and reinstate hope; individual links would be established between delusional beliefs and personal concerns; individually constructed realities would be elicited; and interventions would be based on a collaborative therapeutic relationship and employed as a conceptual rather than manualised process, thus empowering clients to achieve their personal goals.

As emphasised by Waddington (2002), a collaborative therapeutic relationship in cognitive-behavioural interventions entails that a client is encouraged to disagree with a therapist on any matter discussed. The empowering therapeutic alliance in person-based CBTp was argued by Mankiewicz (2013) as central in establishing rapport with often socially stigmatised and excluded individuals. In such relationships, therapists would aim to engage with the subjective values and beliefs of their clients, build an empathic and respectful understanding of their accounts as valid in their own terms and investigate their clients' perceptions without assuming the superiority of any particular way of experiencing and knowing.

Strengths-Based CBTp: Clinical Applications

As discussed earlier in this chapter, empirical research clearly suggests that people with psychosis are able to experience reasonable levels of SWB even when significant levels of positive symptoms of psychosis remain. Furthermore, CBTp approaches can be personalised and focussed on SWB, and that collaborative is central to its application and process.

In considering the application of positive psychology to those with psychosis, it is helpful to consider three main clinical groups within the spectrum of psychotic presentation in order to adapt the application of positive psychology to these groups:

Clinical group 1 – Those who have experienced a psychotic episode but have responded well to traditional CBTp, have few or no residual psychotic symptoms and appear to be in the process of returning to previous levels of functioning.

Clinical group 2 – Those who have experienced a psychotic episode and have responded to traditional CBTp but whose levels of SWB remain low.

Clinical group 3 – Those who have experienced a significant psychotic episode and who either have not responded to traditional CBTp or are not interested or able at the current time to utilise it to examine the beliefs which are central to their psychosis.

It is important to note that within all these groups, positive psychology has a strong role in relapse prevention as well as the improvement of SWB. In this chapter, we present each subgroup alongside an illustrative case example of how positive cognitive and behavioural interventions can enhance subjective wellbeing.

Clinical Group 1

Let's begin with those who have experienced a psychotic episode but have responded well to traditional CBTp and have few or no residual psychotic symptoms. In such cases, as mentioned previously, cognitive therapists can augment traditional CBTp with a range of strengths-based positive interventions that promote individual SWB and buffer against mental ill health. In the following case, we demonstrate how positive interventions have enabled a client to redefine a range of unhelpful and dysfunctional self-beliefs into more positive, functional and reality-based ones. The employed interventions focused on the development of the client's awareness of own goals and achievements and an augmentation of practical skills to collect evidential data supporting positive self-appraisals. The critical significance of cognitive restructuring and simultaneous facilitation of positive behavioural adjustments in psychosis was described in detail by Mankiewicz and Turner (2014).

Sonya (21) had spent the last two years travelling around Asia and Australia. She then returned to take up a place studying sociology at university. Despite having spent the last two years travelling, Sonya struggled to connect with her flatmates, course peers and academic program. She stopped attending the course, started staying in her room and began smoking marijuana heavily. In March, she was called to a meeting with her academic tutors who gave her an opportunity to engage with the course with some additional support and tutoring. Sonya failed to attend for the rest of the academic year and in June she was asked to leave the course. Sonya returned to her parents' home (where she had not lived for 3 years) and continued to be socially isolated. She did not reconnect with school friends despite her parents' encouragement and continued smoking for much of the day. Sonya began to hear voices telling her that she was a 'waster', 'useless' and a 'sponger'. She started thinking that the police were watching her and wanting to set her up for a crime she had not committed. Sonya refused to leave the house and closed all the curtains in the house, becoming highly agitated if either of her parents tried to open them.

Eventually, Sonya's mum called the GP requesting a visit at home as Sonya refused to leave the house. The GP was able to persuade Sonya to engage with the early intervention team.

Although she refused to take medication, she was referred straight away to the psychologist within the team and began cognitive therapy. Sonya and her therapist began to explore alternative understandings of her voices and began to formulate how her distressing explanations made her review all her experiences in a way which confirmed her beliefs about the police. She began to question her own beliefs and engaged in a range of experiments which led her to leave the house and to make contact with old friends. Eventually, Sonya no longer believed that the police were watching her and although she was still occasionally hearing voices, she understood these as an anomalous experience which was the result of drug use and stress. She stopped using marijuana and applied to restart her university course the next September.

In therapy, Sonya identified that a range of core beliefs regarding her appraisal of herself as useless, unappealing and unlikeable had contributed to her burgeoning social anxiety, her social withdrawal and ultimately her psychosis. Within her initial psychology sessions, work was done to identify the troubling core beliefs, to use a range of historical and present-day information to challenge these beliefs and to set up a series of experiments to test the new beliefs in practice. Behavioural testing of the restructured beliefs in practice constituted a positive intervention, as it contributed to the development of higher believability associated with the new strengths-focused appraisals. Sonya was happy with her new beliefs and described that whilst her conviction levels in session were high for these beliefs (around 80%), that between sessions and on thoughts of ending psychology, she struggled to maintain this conviction and found it falling to 30–40%. The therapist discussed with Sonya the use of a positive data log, which could be used in an ongoing manner to continue to search for and store information consistent with her new emerging positive beliefs.

The beliefs that Sonya and her therapist had developed as an alternative to her unhelpful core beliefs were as follows: I am useful, I am appealing and I am likeable. As shown in Table 5.1, Sonya and

Table 5.1 Sonya's Alternative, Helpful Beliefs

Alternative, helpful belief	Descriptive subbeliefs
I am useful.	I am a useful friend, I am useful at work, I'm useful to my family.
I am appealing.	I am interesting, people like to talk to me, I am attractive.
I am likeable.	People like to talk to me, people enjoy my company, I am friendly.

her therapist decided that they would create a subset of more descriptive and more detailed statements enabling her ability to collate evidence supporting these new beliefs.

Sonya discussed that whilst she was adept at technology, she had always enjoyed keeping paper records and had utilised a diary when she was younger. She discussed that she would like to keep this record in a physical journal which she would be able to keep with her at all times. Sonya bought herself a tan leather bound book and a fountain pen, which she felt would help ensure that this record had a status for her and that she could continue to 'feel proud' of her achievements. She began to keep a log detailing all the day's achievements and considering if they fell within any subcategory of her restructured beliefs. Table 5.2 illustrates an extract from her diary. Sonya decided that she would like to review her daily events each evening at a set time and would do this between 9 and 10 (unless she was out).

Table 5.2 Sonya's Diary

Date: Wednesday, 16 April.	
New core belief: *I am likeable.*	
New helpful beliefs:	**Evidence:**
People like to talk to me.	Lucy phoned me out of the blue and invited me to the cinema. Kerry finished with her boyfriend and asked if I would come round and cheer her up. Kerry described me as 'a good listener'.
People enjoy my company.	I got three invites to different 21st birthday parties this week. Lucy said she really enjoyed our night at the cinema. Kerry said I was good to hang out with.
I am friendly.	Lucy's friend Stacy told her that she thought I was really friendly and would like to join us next time we went out. Peter asked if I would be prepared to help out at weekends in the bar he works at. He said he thought the customers would really like me. No one knows how anxious I am in company; they just think I am friendly.

Sonya and her therapist decided that she would continue to keep this record for at least six months, and agreed that continuing to fully embed her chosen positive beliefs about herself would enable her to develop resilience for stressful times ahead which she thought that her return to university might bring. Sonya felt that many of her difficulties had come from social anxieties which she had managed for years. This had been kept in check whilst she had a few close friends throughout schooling, but had been further triggered during her travels and changeable peer group. Sonya realised that over the two years she had spent travelling, she had isolated herself more and more with each month. This realisation allowed Sonya to outline a series of social goals for her university years and to develop a checklist to spot a need to isolate herself early and to use her strengths-based therapeutic techniques to reengage with her goals.

Alongside this, Sonya agreed to continue to engage in a range of activities which would enable her to gather evidence which could support 'I am useful, appealing and likeable', agreeing that her old practice of staying in her bedroom alone allowed no scope for gathering any evidence, either in support of the old or of the new beliefs.

Clinical Group 2

As proposed earlier, the second group of clients consists of those who have experienced a psychotic episode and responded to traditional CBTp, but whose level of subjective well-being remains low. In such cases, cognitive therapists should use positive interventions to empower their clients to find individual ways to alleviate their distress and promote their optimal functioning based on an individualised understanding of their difficulties. A clinical case example of a successful delivery of positive interventions to a client with enduring psychosis was reported almost two decades ago by Csikszentmihalyi (1997). Csikszentmihalyi's experience sampling method was used with a female client, after more than a decade of her continuous inpatient hospitalization, to identify a range of joy-inducing activities. Subsequently, such activities (e.g. taking care of fingernails) were supported with further input encouraging the development of personal competencies (e.g. participation in a professional manicurist training course) to ensure the frequency of positive experiences. As a result, despite preceding unresponsiveness to medical and pharmacological treatments, the person was discharged to the community and within a year became self-sufficient. Similarly, in the following case, we demonstrate how an implementation of various cognitive-behavioural strategies enabled our client to identify own strengths and goals, and to operationalise particular steps to pursue enjoyable activities and satisfaction with life.

Michal (27) came over from Poland when he was 17 in order to find work in the UK. He originally came to live with his cousin but soon found work and took on a flat, TV contract, telephone and other commitments. However, Michal suffered from Crohn's (a chronic gastrointestinal condition), which meant that he had a poor work attendance record, and as a result, his contract was not renewed. Michal was unable to find more work and began to borrow money from unscrupulous lenders in order to meet the requirements of his financial obligations.

In desperation, Michal went back to Poland to try to seek work, but became paranoid that people were following him, watching his every move and intervening to stop him getting work. He moved back to England but instead of stopping, his concerns intensified and he became preoccupied that helicopters were beaming lasers onto his head. He started to wrap his head in silver foil under a cycling helmet to help him with the rays. Michal became so paranoid about his neighbours that he moved out of his flat, preferring to remain homeless and able to move around on a daily basis. He lost contact with his family.

Michal came into contact with services when a night shelter set up to deal with the cold spell over Christmas asked him questions about his helmet. He had shown them the silver foil and explained to them about the lasers. The staff at the shelter had asked him if he would like to have contact with mental health services and Michal agreed and engaged with his local CMHT. They arranged for Michal to secure a tenancy and gain benefits. They also referred him for cognitive therapy. Michal engaged well with therapy and agreed to work on his fears about the lasers. As a result, Michal began to experiment with leaving his helmet at home and appeared rather certain that he was no longer the focus of the lasers, although he remained nervous when helicopters flew overhead. However, Michal continued to be suspicious of the motives of others and remained isolated, lonely and bored. He told the team that although he now has somewhere to live, he feels sadder and lonelier than before.

For Michal, the shift to an emphasis on positive psychology was collaboratively encouraged in order to allow reflection on constructive social interaction, purpose and values and to identify those activities which he found intrinsically motivating and flow-inducing. Whilst therapy had been helpful in reducing his conviction in his unhelpful beliefs, and whilst these beliefs had not been completely alleviated, it was agreed that further work on these areas would not add to Michal's wellbeing at the current time. Rather, the shift of focus to look at what he needed in the interpersonal and achievement-oriented domains appeared more important at the current time. Michal began to work with his therapist in beginning to set positive goals for his future. These goals focussed around what he needed in order to feel happy and included, rather than continuing to focus on his experience of paranoia or other anomalous experiences. On questioning, Michal was able to elaborate on his sadness and loneliness but unable to begin to think about what he wanted to aim for.

Therefore, therapy assisted him in working out what positive goals he wanted to set for himself. Whilst he struggled within the context of the present, therapy enabled him to think about what he would like life to look like in 5 years' time. When this context for planning was proposed, Michal was better able to engage, stating that 'this takes the pressure off'. Therapy used positive imagery to help Michal to develop a clear perspective on how he would like life to develop. This was then used to work backwards and develop a series of stages with particular operational steps to aid in the facilitation of his goals. As shown in Table 5.3, Michal was assisted in developing a timeline which consisted of particular steps he would need to undertake in order to introduce positive changes in his life.

Table 5.3 Michal's Timeline

1 month	6 months	1 year	2 years	5 years
Join a gym and a boxing class (gain confidence and make friends). Contact Citizen Advice Bureau for financial advice.	Commence English course at local college. Join recovery college at local trust and learn how to manage finances.	Find and begin volunteer work.	Take driving lessons. Apply for jobs and attend interviews. Start dating.	Live with a girlfriend or a flatmate. Work full time. Have a dog. Exercise regularly and maintain fitness levels. Have 3 or 4 good friends and meet with them regularly.

Clinical Group 3

The final group of clients for whom positive interventions are argued to be beneficial consists of those who have experienced a significant psychotic episode and who either have not responded to traditional CBTp or are not interested or able at the current time to utilise this to examine those beliefs which are central to their psychosis. For this group, cognitive therapists should utilise positive psychology to address the emotional distress that affects their clients' wellbeing, and to work with them to help increase their ability to identify and augment their strengths to cope with such experiences. For clinicians supporting such clients, a cognitive formulation can help them to shift their experiences from focussing on the 'pathological syndrome' to working with the distress and decrease in subjective wellbeing that this difficulty engenders (Mankiewicz, 2013). In the case below, we illustrate how an employment of positive cognitive interventions, such as guided positive imagery, helped our client to utilise her strengths in the facilitation of own goals and development of functional social skills, despite residual symptoms of enduring psychosis.

Carol (45) has a long history of psychosis dating back to her early teens. She disclosed a considerably disrupted childhood with frequent moves in and out of care and significant physical and sexual abuse. Carol believes that the devil is using her to mete out punishment for the wrongdoing in the world. She hears the voice of God and the devil constantly discussing what she does and what is going on around her and has been in trouble with the police for harassing local shopkeepers for what she describes as 'working for the dark side'. Carol has lived in supported housing for the last 20 years and is supported by the assertive outreach team. During this period, the team have promoted various trials at independent living, but none of these succeeded. Attempts to discuss her concerns regarding the devil are dismissed by Carol stating that she is not interested in talking about this.

It appeared that Carol had not developed a clear awareness of her fundamental needs and what would need to happen to improve her quality of life. Rather than making specific suggestions, a positive psychology approach would focus on giving her the opportunity to express opinions and exert life control. Whilst Carol has shown difficulties in decision making throughout her life, a structured and stepwise approach to this with a clear explanation of process could enable her to move to making more significant decisions over time. After much discussion, Carol agreed that she would engage with psychology as long they would not discuss her concerns about the devil. Carol and her therapist began by trying to help Carol work out a range of valuable goals that could have a positive impact on her life. Due to her unconventional lifestyle, Carol really struggled with this and was unable to come up with any life changes that she thought would be worth striving for. At this point, Carol and her therapist agreed to set a range of alternative changes and to utilise imagery to help Carol help identify whether any of the suggested changes would be of value to her. They agreed to start with a range of unrealistic options to interject some humour into the sessions whilst getting them used to the imagery. Carol surprised herself by being able to utilise this therapeutic medium and really enjoyed her session talking about what she might aim for. At the next session, Carol and her therapist began to develop a range of possible, more realistic goals, using imagery to 'try them on for size'. Carol decided that she would like to work on the following goals: to paint her bedroom, to take singing lessons, to find someone to go for a pizza with once a week, to see if social services could help her find out about any of her biological siblings, and to buy new clothes and look 'normal'.

Once Carol and her therapist had set her goals, they began to prioritise these and set the steps by which Carol would begin to meet these. Carol and her therapist decided to start with the goal of buying new clothes. Carol had not bought clothes for over 20 years and was wearing an array of old men's clothes tied by a belt around her waist. These clothes had been amassed from various hostels she had stayed in over the years. Carol and her therapist worked to put these into manageable stages and to develop an action plan (Table 5.4).

Table 5.4 Carol's Initial Goal and Action Plan

Goal 1: Buy new clothes.	
Step 1	To get catalogues from Matalan (this was somewhere that Carol had bought clothes from before and had liked them very much).
Step 2	To go through the catalogues with her support worker deciding which she liked and whether they were appropriate for her.
Step 3	To see whether she was able to afford the outfit that she had chosen.
Step 4	To go to Matalan, try the clothes on and see if she liked them.
Step 5	To buy the clothes.

Table 5.5 Carol's Predicted Difficulties in Achieving Her Goal and Helpful Problem-Solving Strategies

Problem	Options	Advantages of option	Disadvantages of option	Option chosen	What happened
Might be too embarrassed to walk into the store	Ask care co-ordinator to come with me	It will keep me calm	She'll think I'm stupid for asking		
	Go when it's quiet Go when it's very busy	Able to ask for help	People might look at me		
	Put on a hat	Be unnoticed	Won't be able to find what I need		
	Have a drink before I go	Feel hidden Won't care what others think	People might think I'm odd		
			Will give up, get upset and leave		
Might not fit into the changing room	See if they have a bigger one	This will help	Might be busy		
	Ask if there is a disabled changing room	This will be bigger	Might not let me use it		
	Try and wear less clothes when I go	Will be less to take off	Will feel weird		
Don't know what size I am	Take a lot of different sizes into the changing room	One will fit	Confusing and might freak me out		
	See if I can ask someone in the local charity shop what size they think I am	Lady down the road works in Oxfam	She might not know		

Carol found this very difficult as she was concerned that staff in Matalan would laugh at her and turn her away. Carol and her therapist used guided imagery to help her practice walking into the store, asking for help and removing her own many layers of clothing in the changing room. Carol identified a number of difficulties which she felt would get in the way of her completing this task. As a result of this, Carol, her therapist and her care coordinator created a list of helpful problem-solving strategies, as illustrated in Table 5.5.

Conclusion

For Sonya, Michal and Carol, the use of positive psychological interventions enabled therapeutic intervention to proceed far beyond the scope of symptom alleviation. Rather, it aimed to capitalise on symptom improvement where it did exist and to continue to help individuals move to functional and emotional wellbeing. Where traditional therapies do not lead to symptomatic improvement in psychosis, positive psychology hosts an important reminder that this is not the only way in which psychological therapies have merit. The goals of improvement in SWB have merit in themselves, in addition to often having the sequelae of further symptomatic relief.

This leads us to raise the following question: Are mental health services, including clinical psychology, too symptom-focussed? Is SWB ignored? Do services have a range of interventions available to them when 'traditional psychological interventions' fail to make the required symptomatic changes or fail to make the necessary lifestyle and emotional changes that are required for someone to lead a happy and fulfilled life? Based on our clinical experiences, we propose that, in the specialism of severe, complex and enduring mental ill-health, particularly psychosis, CBTp combined with a range of positive psychology interventions may provide a helpful platform from which to begin further individualised interventions focussed not only on amelioration of psychotic experiences but on enabling the improvement of all aspects of subjective, interpersonal and social recovery.

In conclusion, for clinicians working within the specialism of complex and severe mental ill health, it is important to remember that therapeutic interventions should habitually include a variety of deficits- and strengths-based techniques. We hope that therapists trained in a person-based cognitive therapy will inevitably consider the full range of factors involved in their clients' subjective wellbeing. However, it appears that, regrettably, the move away from formulation-focussed cognitive therapy towards manualised CBT interventions somewhat precludes such a holistic, and thus positive, perspective.

References

Chadwick, P. (2006). *Person-based cognitive therapy for distressing psychosis*. Chichester, UK: Wiley.

Chadwick, P., Birchwood, M., & Trower, P. (1996). *Cognitive therapy for delusions, voices and paranoia*. Chichester, UK: Wiley.

Chadwick, P. K. (1997). *Schizophrenia. The positive perspective*. New York, NY: Brunner-Routledge.

Conway, C., & MacLeod, A. (2002). Well-being. Its importance in clinical practice and research. *Clinical Psychology*, 16, 26–29.

Csikszentmihalyi, M. (1997). *Finding flow. The psychology of engagement with everyday life*. New York, NY: Perseus Books Group.

Diener, E., & Diener, C. (1996). Most people are happy. *Psychological Science*, 7, 181–185.

Dunn, H. (2002). Cognitive therapy for psychosis. Emphasising engagement. In Morrison, A. P. (Ed.), *A Casebook of Cognitive Therapy for Psychosis* (pp. 37–58). London, UK: Routledge.

Farhall, J., Freeman, N. C., Shawyer, F., & Trauer, T. (2009). An effectiveness trial of cognitive-behaviour therapy in a representative sample of outpatients with psychosis. *British Journal of Clinical Psychology*, 48, 47–62.

Fava, G. A., & Ruini, C. (2003). Development and characteristics of a well-being psychotherapeutic strategy. Well-being therapy. *Journal of Behavior Therapy and Experimental Psychiatry*, 34, 45–63.

Frish, M. B. (2006). *Quality of life therapy. Applying a life satisfaction approach to positive psychology and cognitive therapy*. Hoboken, NJ: John Wiley & Sons.

Gilbert, P. (2009). *Overcoming depression. A self-help guide using cognitive-behavioural techniques* (3rd ed.). London, UK: Robinson.

Hagen, R., & Nordahl, H. M. (2008). Behavioural experiments in the treatment of paranoid schizophrenia. A single case study. *Cognitive and Behavioral Practice*, 15, 296–305.

Hayward, M., Blank, A., & Cooke, A. (2005). A fresh approach to psychosis. Revisited. *Clinical Psychology Forum*, 152, 17–19.

Headey, B. (2006). Happiness. Revisiting set-point theory and dynamic equilibrium theory to account for long term change. *Discussion Papers*, 607, 1–18.

Joseph, S., & Linley, P. A. (2006). *Positive therapy. A meta-theory for positive psychological practice.* London, UK: Routledge.

Keyes, C. L. M., & Lopez, S. J. (2002). Toward a science of mental health. Positive directions in diagnosis and interventions. In Snyder, C. R., & Lopez, S. J. (Eds.), *Handbook of Positive Psychology* (pp. 45–59). New York, NY: Oxford University Press.

Lopez, S. J., & Kerr, B. A. (2006). An open approach to creating positive psychological practice. A comment on Wong's strengths-centred therapy. *Psychotherapy: Theory, Research, Practice, Training,* 43, 147–150.

Mankiewicz, P. D. (2013). Cognitive-behavioural symptom-oriented understanding of psychosis. Abandoning the disease paradigm of schizophrenia. *Counselling Psychology Review,* 28, 53–63.

Mankiewicz, P. D., Gresswell, D. M., & Turner, C. (2013a). Happiness in severe mental illness. Exploring subjective wellbeing of individuals with psychosis and encouraging socially inclusive multidisciplinary practice. *Mental Health and Social Inclusion,* 17, 27–34.

Mankiewicz, P. D., Gresswell, D. M., & Turner, C. (2013b). Subjective wellbeing in psychosis. Mediating effects of psychological distress on happiness levels amongst individuals diagnosed with paranoid schizophrenia. *International Journal of Wellbeing,* 3, 35–59.

Mankiewicz, P. D., & Turner, C. (2014). Cognitive restructuring and graded behavioural exposure for delusional appraisals of auditory hallucinations and comorbid anxiety in paranoid schizophrenia. *Case Reports in Psychiatry,* 14, 1–8.

Padash, Z., Dehnavi, S. R., & Botlani, S. (2012). The study of efficacy of cognitive therapy based on positive psychology on subjective wellbeing. *International Journal of Business and Social Science,* 3, 202–207.

Romme, M., & Escher, S. (Eds.) (1993). *Accepting voices.* London, UK: Mind Publications.

Roth, A., & Fonagy, P. (2005). *What works for whom? A critical overview of psychotherapy research* (2nd ed.). New York, NY: The Guilford Press.

Seligman, M. E. P., Rashid, T., & Parks, A. C. (2006). Positive psychotherapy. *American Psychologist,* 61, 774–788.

Thompson, S. C. (2002). The role of personal control in adaptive functioning. In Snyder, C. R., & Lopez, S. J. (Eds.), *Handbook of positive psychology* (pp. 202–213). New York, NY: Oxford University Press.

Waddington, L. (2002). The therapy relationship in cognitive therapy. A review. *Behavioural and Cognitive Psychotherapy,* 30, 179–191.

Weiss, N. R., & Knoster, T. (2008). It may be nonaversive, but is it a positive approach? Relevant questions to ask throughout the process of behavioural assessment and intervention. *Journal of Positive Behavior Interventions,* 10, 72–78.

Conceptual Framework for Wellbeing in Psychosis

Mike Slade and Beate Schrank

Introduction

The term *wellbeing* has become popular in the political arena in recent years, and its relevance to mental health systems is becoming evident. At least four academic phases of wellbeing conceptualisation and measurement can be identified (Schrank et al., 2013). Economic concepts frame wellbeing in terms of national wealth, social determinants, development and general quality of life. Medical concepts of wellbeing frame it in relation to disorder and illness, in other words health-related quality of life. Psychological approaches view wellbeing in terms of subjective and mental concepts, ranging from positive affect to lifespan development and self-actualisation. Finally, integrative concepts are evolving and are informed by economic, medical and psychological phases. Throughout these phases, the notion of wellbeing has shifted from a collectivist concept with objective measures to being conceived in individualistic terms, with subjective measures and a distinct focus on positive psychology and recovery research.

The transition from objectivity to subjectivity has led to wellbeing becoming a key concept in mental health. In particular, wellbeing is also a central component of recovery from mental illness (Slade, 2010). Its importance is further supported by research showing an association between wellbeing and improved functioning, increased resilience and life satisfaction (Fredrickson, 2002) and suggesting its protective value against the onset or recurrence of mental illness (Schueller and Parks, 2012).

So far, wellbeing research has focused on a variety of groups, including the general population across the life span (Hatch, 2010), and on physical health problems such as cancer (Schwarzer, 2006) and HIV/AIDS (Mak, 2007). There have been calls for a stronger focus on wellbeing in mental health systems (Hanlon and Carlisle, 2008), especially in relation to supporting recovery (Resnick and Rosenheck, 2006). However, the concept of wellbeing is not yet well defined, especially in relation to people with severe mental illnesses such as psychosis (Wissing, 2002).

In this chapter, we describe two interlinked studies which together provide a defensible empirical foundation for wellbeing research in psychosis. Both studies were funded by Guy's & St Thomas' Charity, and fuller reports of both studies have been published. The first study was a systematic review to develop a conceptual understanding of wellbeing (Schrank, 2013). The second study used a qualitative design to develop a framework for characterising how wellbeing changes in people experiencing psychosis (Schrank, 2014).

Wellbeing, Recovery and Mental Health, ed. Mike Slade, Lindsay Oades and Aaron Jarden.
Published by Cambridge University Press. © Mike Slade, Lindsay Oades and Aaron Jarden 2017

Conceptual Framework for Wellbeing in Psychosis

We undertook a systematic review to characterise the evidence base relating to wellbeing in people with psychosis (Schrank, 2013). The objectives were (1) to understand how wellbeing is measured in high-quality research studies involving people with psychosis and (2) to develop an organising conceptual framework for wellbeing as used in these studies.

Method

We included randomised and nonrandomised intervention studies investigating the effects of intervention compared with control on service users' wellbeing as the primary or secondary outcome, available in full text in English or German. Inclusion criteria for participants were (i) age 16–65 years; (ii) past or present diagnosis of a psychotic illness based on ICD-10 or DSM-IV or at least 70% in a mixed diagnosis sample (interpreted to be overinclusive when the diagnostic description was unclear); and (iii) use or having used mental health services.

Five sources of data were searched from inception to May 2012. Bibliographic databases (EMBASE, MEDLINE, PsycINFO, British Nursing Index and Archive, Applied Social Sciences Index and Abstracts, British Humanities Index, Sociological Abstracts, Social Services Abstracts, International Bibliography of Social Sciences, CINAHL and Cochrane) were searched using variants of 'wellbeing' AND 'severe mental illness'. We also reviewed tables of contents from journals (*British Journal of Wellbeing*, *Journal of Positive Psychology*, *Psychiatric Rehabilitation Journal*) and special issues, searched the Grey Literature Network Service and charity websites (Mental Health Foundation, New Economic Foundation, Young Foundation, Mind, Rethink), consulted eight experts, and hand-searched reference lists of all included studies and of relevant reviews, opinion papers and guidelines.

The first 200 studies were independently rated for inclusion by two reviewers (BS, VB), achieving a concordance rate of 0.98. Disagreement was resolved by consensus. The remaining 19,137 studies were appraised by one review author (BS). Data were extracted into an Excel spreadsheet developed for a previous systematic review with narrative synthesis (Schrank et al., 2008).

To meet Objective 1 (measurement of wellbeing), we descriptively listed the measures and counted the retrieved studies in which they were used. After constructing the conceptual framework, we used vote counting to assess how frequently the individual framework dimensions were included in the measures used.

To meet Objective 2 (conceptual framework), we used a modified narrative synthesis approach (Popay et al., 2006), taking measures of wellbeing from included studies as the units of data. We used the three domains of wellbeing and its determinants proposed by the UK Office for National Statistics (individual feeling of wellbeing, factors directly affecting individual wellbeing and more contextual domains) as the initial organising framework (Beaumont, 2011). We plotted the measures according to the ONS domains, detected common components across the scales and grouped them into higher-order constructs. In an iterative process, the broad groups were repeatedly split into different categories and regrouped.

Results

Study selection is shown in Figure 6.1.

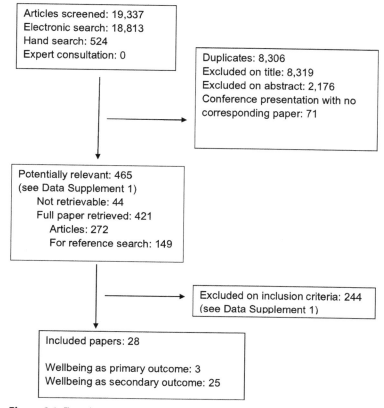

Figure 6.1 Flow diagram of studies included in the review.

Objective 1: Measurement of Wellbeing

The search resulted in 28 eligible articles. These used 20 measures to assess wellbeing, described in Table 6.1.

Objective 2: Conceptual Framework of Wellbeing in Psychosis

The analysis of the measures' content resulted in a conceptual framework of wellbeing that spans five domains: (i) nonobservable; (ii) observable; (iii) proximal; (iv) distal; and (v) self-defined. These domains can be understood as four layers of proximity to the person and one additional self-defined dimension.

The *nonobservable* domain refers to intrapsychic phenomena such as self-perception, mood tone or meaning and purpose in life, which are not readily visible from outside. The *observable* domain comprises aspects of a person that are exhibited to the outside world, such as environmental mastery, resolution or physical health. The *proximal* domain describes factors which directly and immediately affect the individual. It includes what a person has or does, such as various kinds of relationships, finances or occupation. Finally, the *distal* domain encompasses contextual factors which are not under a person's immediate influence, such as the wider environment or access to services.

Table 6.1 Description of Wellbeing Measures with Number of Studies Included in the Review Using Them as Primary or Secondary Outcome Measures

Scale name	Brief description of constituent factors and domains	Established psychometric properties	Primary outcome measure (*N* studies)	Secondary outcome measure (*N* studies)
Subjective Satisfaction with Life Scale (SSLS)	Four domains: living situation, social relationships, work, self and present life.	Yes	0	2
WHOQOL-BREF	Four dimensions: psychological wellbeing (or health), physical health, social relationships, environment; plus overall quality of life.	Yes	0	2
Lancashire Quality of Life Profile (LQoLP)	Eight life domains: work, leisure, social involvement, finances, living situation, legal and safety, health, family relations; plus general wellbeing.	Yes	0	1
Yu Quality of Life for Mental Illness Scale	Eight factors: life satisfaction, autonomy, health maintenance, family support, function, social activity, physical health, psychological wellbeing.	No	0	1
Short Form (SF)	Six or eight factors depending on version: physical functioning, role limitations due to physical health problems, bodily pain, social functioning, general mental health, role limitations because of emotional problems, vitality, health perception.	Yes	0	1
Manchester Assessment of Quality of Life (MANSA)	Eight life domains: job, finances, friendships, leisure activities, accommodation, safety, physical health, mental health; plus general life satisfaction.	Yes	0	1
Lehman Quality of Life Interview (LQOL)	Eight life domains: living situation, family, social relations, leisure, work, safety, finances, physical health; plus general life satisfaction.	Yes	0	4
Quality of Life Enjoyment and Satisfaction Questionnaire (Q-LES-Q)	Five life domains: physical health, subjective feelings, leisure time activities, social relationships, general activities; plus overall life satisfaction.	Yes	0	2

Table 6.1 *(cont.)*

Scale name	Brief description of constituent factors and domains	Established psychometric properties	Primary outcome measure (*N* studies)	Secondary outcome measure (*N* studies)
Subjective Wellbeing under Neuroleptics Scale (SWN)	Five subscales: emotional regulation, mental functioning, self-control, social integration, physical functioning.	Yes	0	2
Psychological General Wellbeing Index (PGWI)	Six affective states equal six subscales: anxiety, depressed mood, positive wellbeing, self-control, general health, vitality.	Yes	0	2
Social Adjustment Scale II (SAS-II)	Eight subscales: work role, household role, parental role, external family role, conjugal and nonconjugal sexual roles, romantic involvement, social and leisure activities, personal wellbeing.	Yes	0	1
Ryff's Scales of Psychological Wellbeing (RSPW)	Six factors in the original scale (shorter version partly differs): environmental mastery, personal growth, self-acceptance, autonomy, purpose in life, positive relations with others.	Yes	0	2
Scale for the Assessment of Wellbeing (SAWB)	No subdimension, scale asks for 56 pairs of opposite feelings/mental states.	Yes	0	1
Snaith-Hamilton Pleasure Scale (SHPS)	Four domains: interest/pastimes, social interaction, sensory experience, food/drink.	Yes	1	0
Personal Wellbeing Index (PWI)	Eight life domains: standard of living, health, achievement in life, personal relationships, personal safety, community-connectedness, future security, spirituality.	Yes	0	2
Life Satisfaction Index (LSI)	Five components: zest, resolution and fortitude, congruence among desired and achieved goals, a positive self-concept, mood tone.	Yes	0	1

(cont.)

Table 6.1 *(cont.)*

Scale name	Brief description of constituent factors and domains	Established psychometric properties	Primary outcome measure (*N* studies)	Secondary outcome measure (*N* studies)
Subjective Exercise Experiences Scale (SEES)	Three subscales: psychological distress, subjective positive wellbeing, fatigue.	Yes	2	0
Quality of Life Inventory (QOLI)	Satisfaction in eight areas: self-esteem, health, friends, relatives, money, work, play, love.	Yes	0	1
General life satisfaction (LS)	Single question	N.A.	0	1
Enjoyment (ENJ)	Single question	N.A.	0	1

In addition, some measures included a broad general question on overall wellbeing or overall life satisfaction, which we defined as a separate *self-defined* domain.

Table 6.2 shows the framework of wellbeing in psychosis resulting from our analysis in comparison with the generic framework of national wellbeing.

The ONS framework of national wellbeing addresses the whole of society (Beaumont, 2011). In contrast, the framework of wellbeing modified for psychosis focuses on the individual. Consequently, it places stronger emphasis on individual dimensions while distal dimensions such as environment are less prominent.

Table 6.3 displays the scales used to measure wellbeing in the included studies according to their coverage of the conceptual framework of wellbeing in psychosis.

Of the measures in the table, 15 included 14 proximal, 15 observable, and 14 nonobservable dimensions. Distal dimensions were mentioned only once, and self-defined wellbeing was asked for in nine scales. The emphasis placed on the addressed domains varied between the measures.

Discussion

This review characterised the evidence base relating to wellbeing in people with psychosis. The results offer detailed insight into the use of the concept of wellbeing in intervention research involving people with psychosis, as well as explicit practical suggestions for a potential way forward in this scientific area.

In relation to Objective 1 (measurement of wellbeing), the 28 studies included in our analysis used 20 different scales to assess wellbeing. These scales covered a wide range of conceptual backgrounds. Although there is consensus that wellbeing is multidimensional in nature, there was no single agreed-upon definition or framework for wellbeing, and authors did usually not state why they chose a specific scale. This confirms the impression of wellbeing as an ill-defined concept. The most prominent conceptual overlap was found between wellbeing and health-related quality of life (HRQOL), although the decisions by authors about whether to describe their scales as measures of HRQOL or of wellbeing appeared to be arbitrary and were usually not justified. It is also interesting that none of

Table 6.2 Generic ONS Framework Modified for Psychosis

ONS conceptual framework	Modified conceptual framework	Example domains
More contextual domains	**Domain 1: Distal**	
1. Natural environment	1. The environment	Area of residence, access to services, access to transport
2. The economy		
3. Governance		
Factors directly affecting individual wellbeing	**Domain 2: Proximal**	
1. Relationships	1. Connectedness	
	– general social connection	Social activity, relationships, social functioning, community, integration
	– family connection	Family relations, family support, parental role, relationship with children and relatives
	– emotional connection	Friendships, emotional ties
	– romantic connection	Sexual roles, romantic involvement, love relationship
2. What we do	2. Activities	
	– general activity	Usual activities, daily activities
	– professional activity	Work, job, professional role
	– leisure activity	Leisure time activities, recreation
3. Where we live	3. Living conditions	
	– housing situation	Living situation, standard of living, accommodation, immediate neighbourhood
	– financial situation	Finances, economic function
	– safety	Legal security, safety, personal safety
4. Personal finance	4. Mobility	
	Domain 3: Observable	
5. Health – mental and physical	1. Health – mental and physical	
	– physical health and functioning	Physical health, physical activity, physical functioning
	– physical self-care	Attention to physical health and care, self-care, health maintenance
	– general mental health and functioning	Mental functioning, cognition, concentration, role limitations due to emotional problems

Table 6.2 *(cont.)*

ONS conceptual framework	Modified conceptual framework	Example domains
	2. Participation	Learning, creativity, helping others, civic action
	3. Autonomy	Freedom, autonomy, environmental mastery
	4. Success	Achievement in life, desired and achieved goals, resolution, fortitude
	Domain 4: Nonobservable	
	1. Bodily feelings/vitality	
	– negative feelings	Fatigue, tiredness, apathy, exhaustion
	– positive feelings	Energy, pep, vitality, zest
	2. Affect, mood tone	
	– negative affect	Depression, anxiety, sadness, despair, anger
	– positive affect	Feeling peaceful, happy, strong, great, terrific
	– emotional regulation	
	3. Self-perception	Satisfaction with self, self-acceptance, self-concept, self-regard
	4. Self-control	Self-control, behavioural emotional control
	5. Life perspective	Meaning, purpose, spirituality, philosophy of life
Individual wellbeing	**Domain 5: Self-defined**	
1. People's own assessment of their own wellbeing	1. Overall wellbeing	
	2. Overall life satisfaction	

the four main theories of wellbeing and flourishing include health as a central component (Hone, 2014). This ambiguity reflects academic debates as to how far wellbeing, HRQOL and other related constructs overlap or include each other (Spiro, 2000).

In relation to Objective 2 (conceptual framework), our conceptual framework identifies five dimensions of wellbeing. The nonobservable, observable, proximal, and distal domains are conceptualised as layers of proximity to the person, ranging from intrapsychic to contextual factors. In addition, the self-defined domain is based on the individual assessment of general overall wellbeing. Assessment of overall wellbeing or life satisfaction has been theorised to require respondents to reflect on their overall state of life, including as many domains or components as are relevant to the individual (Cummins, 1998). Global ratings are thought to reflect a subjective valuation, since different areas of life may be valued differently by different individuals (Diener, 1985). Such personally relevant factors do not necessarily overlap with a given scale's explicitly mentioned

Table 6.3 Scales Used to Measure Wellbeing in the Included Studies and Their Coverage of Domains of the Applied Conceptual Framework of Wellbeing in Psychosis

Scale Name	Coverage of conceptual framework domains				
	Distal	Proximal	Observable	Nonobservable	Self-defined
WHOQOL-BREF	X	X	X	X	X
Yu quality of life for mental illness scale (YuQoL)	X	X	X	X	
Short Form (SF)	X	X	X	X	
Quality of Life Enjoyment and Satisfaction Questionnaire (Q-LES-Q)	X	X	X	X	
Lancashire Quality of Life Profile (LQoLP)	X	X		X	
Lehman Quality of Life Interview (LQOL)	X	X		X	
Social Adjustment Scale II (SAS-II)	X	X		X	
Ryff's scales of psychological wellbeing (RSPW)	X	X	X		
Subjective Wellbeing under Neuroleptics Scale (SWN)	X	X	X		
Quality of Life Inventory (QOLI)	X	X	X		
Subjective Satisfaction with Life Scale (SSLS)	X		X	X	
Personal Wellbeing Index (PWI)	X	X			
Manchester Assessment of Quality of Life (MANSA)	X	X			
Snaith–Hamilton Pleasure Scale (SHPS)	X		X		
Scale for the Assessment of Wellbeing (SAWB)		X	X		
Life Satisfaction Index (LSI)		X	X		
Psychological General Wellbeing Index (PGWI)		X	X		
Single question on enjoyment (ENJ)			X		
Subjective Exercise Experiences Scale (SEES)			X		
Single question on general life satisfaction (LS)					X

dimensions, and an individual's personal view of what wellbeing means may be different to any aggregate framework.

The proposed conceptual framework of wellbeing in psychosis differs from the generic framework of national wellbeing developed by the ONS. Issues of inequality and social justice are not captured in the framework of wellbeing in psychosis. Instead, the framework places stronger emphasis on individual rather than societal factors and refers to a number of specific dimensions that may be particularly relevant to people with psychosis, such as mental health and functioning, but also participation, autonomy, self-perception or self-control. In the ONS framework, the domain of individual wellbeing represents the subjective part of the concept. In contrast, the new conceptual framework includes subjective experience more pervasively. The new 'self-defined' domain adds an additional level of subjectivity, in that it captures a person's overall intuitive understanding of wellbeing.

So, to summarise, our systematic review of studies on psychosis showed that 'wellbeing' was used within a range of theoretical perspectives, with an unclear distinction from concepts such as health-related quality of life, mental health, affect, life satisfaction, social adjustment, and other psychological conceptualisations (Schrank, 2013). Interventions to increase wellbeing in psychosis were highly diverse and not based on a coherent framework of wellbeing. The systematic review developed a static framework of wellbeing, based on the measurement of wellbeing in research involving people with psychosis. This static framework differentiates four domains of factors relevant to wellbeing: observable (visible behaviours and characteristics); nonobservable (internal emotional and cognitive processes); proximal (factors under partial individual control in the immediate physical and social environment); and distal (factors beyond individual influence, in the more distant environment), as well as a separate rating of individual overall self-defined wellbeing.

The framework offers an empirically defensible organising structure for wellbeing research in psychosis but does not illuminate the processes by which wellbeing is experienced or modified in this client group. This is important, because understanding processes of change will identify the most promising target points for evidence-based interventions.

Understanding Wellbeing Changes in Psychosis

We therefore undertook a linked qualitative study to understand the processes involved in wellbeing change in psychosis (Schrank, 2014). The objectives were (3) to validate the static framework of wellbeing by applying it to a second data source for triangulation and (4) to develop a dynamic framework of wellbeing to describe the process of changes involved in wellbeing.

A convenience sample of individuals with psychosis was recruited from community mental health teams in London in October and November 2012. Recruitment was conducted with the goal of theoretical saturation (Willig, 2008). Inclusion criteria were age 18–65 years, a diagnosis of psychosis, using or having used mental health services, sufficient fluency in English, and ability to give informed consent. One researcher conducted all interviews, using a topic guide asking about the personal experience of wellbeing and its improvement. Participants were invited for a reinterview to validate the emergent dynamic framework. Interviews were audiorecorded, transcribed, and anonymised.

Transcripts were coded using NVivo9. We applied thematic analysis using a combination of inductive and theoretically driven techniques (Braun and Clarke, 2006). Analytical rigour was enhanced using techniques taken from grounded theory, including iterative inductive coding, line-by-line coding, constant comparison, the use of memos throughout the analysis process and the use of summary tables to organise clusters of topics for each participant (Willig, 2008).

A total of 23 participants were interviewed, of whom 13 agreed to be reinterviewed. Characteristics of participants are shown in Table 6.4.

Objective 3: Validation of the Static Framework of Wellbeing

The coding framework for influences on transition to an enhanced sense of self is shown in column 2 of Table 6.5. The respondent validation identified no changes in the results.

Table 6.4 Sociodemographic and Clinical Characteristics of Participants (*n* = 23)

Age (mean years, SD)	**44.6**	**9.3**
Gender male (*n*, %)	**15**	**65.2**
Time since first illness onset (mean years, SD)*	16.5	10.5
Self-reported diagnosis (*n*, %)		
Schizophrenia	15	65.2
Psychosis	2	8.7
Schizoaffective disorder/bipolar psychosis	2	8.7
Depression	2	8.7
Nervous breakdown	1	4.3
No mental health problems	1	4.3

* Two participants excluded due to invalid response

Table 6.5 Coding Framework for Wellbeing

Category 1: Determinants of current sense of self	Category 2: Influences on transition to enhanced sense of self	Category 3: Indicators of enhanced sense of self
1.1 Personality	2.1 Nonobservable influences	3.1 Good feelings
Character traits	Attitudes	3.2 Symptom relief
Personal values	Future thinking	3.3 Connectedness
Strengths	Reflection	3.4 Hope and optimism
Interests	2.2 Observable influences	3.5 Self-worth
1.2 Memories	Social interactions	3.6 Empowerment
Good memories	Support-seeking	3.7 Meaning and orientation
Bad memories	Self-care	
1.3 Health	Having a treat	
Mental health	Kindness	
Physical health	Spiritual practise	
	Engaging in activities	
	2.3 Proximal influences	
	Basic needs	
	Relationships	
	Mental health services and staff	
	Antipsychotic medication	
	Psychotherapy	
	2.4 Distal influences	
	Societal values	
	Economy	
	Environment	

The four elements of the static framework (nonobservable, observable, proximal and distal) provided an adequate organising framework to allow full categorisation of the influences on the transition to an enhanced sense of self identified by participants. This transition represents a process of enhancing wellbeing, providing independent validation of the static framework.

Objective 4: Development of a Dynamic Framework of Wellbeing

Participants described wellbeing as a desirable state which needed active input to be achieved and also to be maintained. Wellbeing was tied to participants' sense of self and involved transition from a current sense of self, described as deficient at least in some of its aspects, towards an enhanced sense of self. The attainment of this enhanced sense of self was perceived as increased wellbeing and attributed to the successful transition. This process followed a common pattern which forms the *dynamic framework of wellbeing*. Three superordinate categories were identified in the coding framework: determinants of current sense of self (the participant's starting point at any given stage of development); influences on transition to enhanced sense of self (the change process involved in improving wellbeing); and indicators of enhanced sense of self (how wellbeing is experienced by participants). Specific factors identified as implicated in the transition – the determinants, influences and indicators – varied across individuals both in quality and in quantity. These factors were linked to personal values, and the values attached to specific factors differed between people and in an individual over time. Different areas of life were associated with a differing sense of self; that is, rather advanced stages in a specific area could coexist with poor sense of self in other areas.

Figure 6.2 shows the dynamic framework of wellbeing, illustrating the direction of change and the relationship between the three superordinate categories. It illustrates the

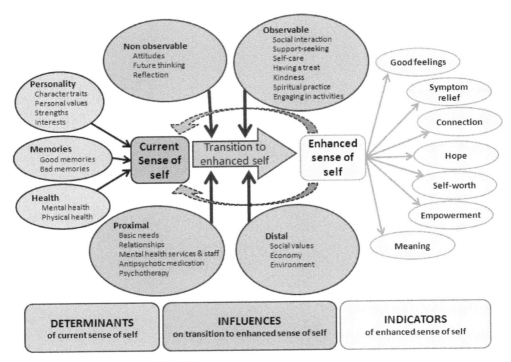

Figure 6.2 Dynamic framework of wellbeing.

interplay of factors on a person's trajectory towards wellbeing and the dynamic nature of the process. As soon as an enhanced sense of self has been achieved, this becomes the new current sense of self allowing further development, such as in other aspects of the self which are perceived as deficient, to start from there. This makes the striving for wellbeing in individuals an iterative and ongoing process, which can also suffer setbacks, through relapse, for example, and may then have to be picked up again at a lower level than before.

A full description of the categories is given in the published report (Schrank, 2014).

Dynamic Framework for Wellbeing

This study found that the process of improving wellbeing in people with psychosis was strongly tied to the sense of self. Current sense of self was determined by three influences: personality, memories and health. Improving wellbeing was an ongoing process in which the current sense of self underwent a transition towards an enhanced sense of self. Influences that impact this transition could be categorised according to the domains of the static framework of wellbeing: observable, nonobservable, proximal and distal (Schrank, 2013). Participants described an enhanced sense of self as equivalent to improved wellbeing. The indicators of enhanced sense of self comprised good feelings, symptom relief, connection, hope, self-worth, empowerment and meaning. The enhanced sense of self may then facilitate transition in other areas in an iterative fashion. Factors involved in the process varied in quality and quantity, both across individuals and over time.

In relation to Objective 3 (validate the static framework), factors influencing transition to an enhanced sense of self were consistent with, and therefore validated, the static framework of wellbeing. The results of the qualitative study also consolidate the findings from the systematic review by placing them in a framework applicable to individuals over time. Specifically, the layers of wellbeing factors identified in the static framework can be viewed as clusters of influences on wellbeing, which may be addressed in an intervention to improve wellbeing. Figure 6.3 shows the transformation of the static into the dynamic framework of wellbeing.

The static framework is based on assessment measures, which often contain items conflating factors that influence wellbeing and wellbeing itself. For example, the latest measure of population wellbeing developed by the Office of National Statistics in the UK considers personal wellbeing, relationships, health, occupation, accommodation, income, education and societal indicators of economic productivity, natural environment and trust in government (Randall, 2014). Other recent concepts of wellbeing have also combined what would be both influences on and indicators of wellbeing according to the results of our study, such as the PERMA model of individual wellbeing, which contains positive emotions, engagement, relationships, meaning and accomplishment (Seligman, 2011).

None of the existing measurement tools or interventions to improve wellbeing described in the literature spans all influences on wellbeing. Interventions to improve wellbeing have been tested in various client groups, with a focus on one of the influences, such as neighbourhood economic status (Ludwig, 2012) or physical exercise (Gademan, 2012), or on specific combinations of some influences such as physical and activity, health behaviour and social engagement (Clare, 2012).

In relation to Objective 4 (dynamic framework), the dynamic framework indicates that context and personal effort can lead to an upward spiral of positive development and continuously increased wellbeing. A similar upward spiral has been found for the

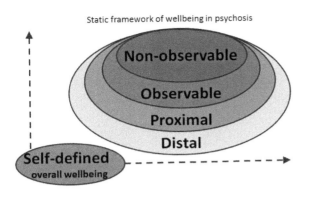

Static framework of wellbeing in psychosis

Figure 6.3 Comparing the static and dynamic frameworks of wellbeing.

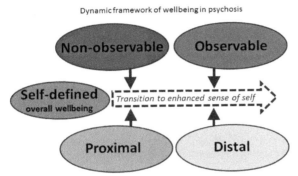

Dynamic framework of wellbeing in psychosis

beneficial effect of positive emotions and a broad repertoire of thought and action which may amplify each other to counteract the detrimental effects of negative emotions and contribute to resilience (Luthans, 2007; Fredrickson, 2002). While an upwards spiral is certainly not without a ceiling, especially given the likelihood of setbacks in the context of severe mental illness and the potential existence of areas resistant to positive change, the conceptualisation of wellbeing in the dynamic framework provides a strengths-oriented supplement to deficit-oriented approaches in mental health care. This places the framework in the context of positive psychology and resource-oriented approaches (Priebe, 2014).

The concepts of wellbeing and recovery do overlap (Amering, 2012). For example, the CHIME framework recovery processes described in Chapter 3 mirror the *indicators* of enhanced self. However, the indicators in the dynamic framework in addition include symptom relief and, most prominently, good feelings. Everyday sources of wellbeing – such as employment, friendship, exercise, sex or prayer – are as important for people experiencing psychosis as for any other group in society. Emphasising commonality in sources of wellbeing between people with and without psychosis may be more helpful than identifying diagnosis-specific sources of wellbeing.

The use of this theory base to develop an intervention to improve wellbeing in psychosis is outlined in Chapter 12.

References

Amering, M. (2012). Recovery, science and human rights. *Epidemiology and Psychiatric Sciences*, 21, 367–369.

Beaumont, J. (2011). Measuring national well-being – Discussion paper on domains and measures. Newport, UK: Office for National Statistics.

Braun, V., & Clarke, V. (2006). Using thematic analysis in psychology. *Qualitative Research in Psychology*, 3, 77–101.

Clare, L., Hindle, J., Jones, I., Thom, J., Nelis, S., Hounsome, B., et al. (2012). The AgeWell study of behavior change to promote health and wellbeing in later life: Study protocol for a randomized controlled trial. *Trials*, 13, 115.

Cummins, R. (1998). The second approximation to an international standard for life satisfaction. *Social Indicators Research*, 43, 307–334.

Diener, E., Robert, E., Randy, L., & Griffin, S. (1985). The Satisfaction With Life Scale. *Journal of Personality Assessment*, 49, 71–75.

Fredrickson, B., & Joiner, T. (2002). Positive emotions trigger upward spirals toward emotional well-being. *Psychological Science*, 13, 172–175.

Gademan, M., Deutekom, M., Hosper, K., & Stronks, K. (2012). The effect of exercise on prescription on physical activity and wellbeing in a multi-ethnic female population: A controlled trial. *BMC Public Health*, 12, 758.

Hanlon, P., & Carlisle, S. (2008). What can the science of well-being tell the discipline of psychiatry – and why might psychiatry listen? *Advances in Psychiatric Treatment*, 14, 312–219.

Hatch, S., Harvey, S., & Maughan, B. (2010). A developmental–contextual approach to understanding mental health and well-being in early adulthood. *Social Science and Medicine*, 70, 261–268.

Hone, L., Jarden, A., Schofield, G., & Duncan, S. (2014). Measuring flourishing: The impact of operational definitions on the prevalence of high levels of wellbeing. *International Journal of Wellbeing*, 4, 62–90.

Ludwig, J., Duncan, G., Gennetian, L., Katz, L., Kessler, R., Kling, J., et al. (2012). Neighborhood effects on the long-term well-being of low-income adults. *Science*, 337, 1505–1510.

Luthans, F., Avolio, B., Avey, J., & Norman, S. (2007). Positive psychological capital: Measurement and relationship with performance and satisfaction. *Personnel Psychology*, 60, 541–572.

Mak, W., Cheung, R., Law, R., Woo, J., Li, P., & Chung, R. (2007). Examining attribution model of self-stigma on social support and psychological well-being among people with HIV+/AIDS. *Social Science and Medicine*, 64, 1549–1559.

Popay, J., Roberts, H., Sowden, A., Petticrew, M., Arai, L., Rodgers, M., et al. (2006). *Guidance on the conduct of narrative synthesis in systematic reviews. Results of an ESRC funded research project.* Lancaster, UK: University of Lancaster.

Priebe, S., Omer, S., Giacco, D., & Slade, M. (2014). Resource-oriented therapeutic models in psychiatry – A conceptual review. *British Journal of Psychiatry*, 204, 256–261.

Randall, C., & Corp, A. (2014). *Measuring national well-being: European comparisons, 2014.* London, UK: Office for National Statistics.

Resnick, S. G., & Rosenheck, R. A. (2006). Recovery and positive psychology: Parallel themes and potential synergies. *Psychiatric Services*, 57, 120–122.

Schrank, B., Bird, V., Tylee, A., Coggins, T., Rashid, T., & Slade, M. (2013). Conceptualising and measuring the well-being of people with psychosis: Systematic review and narrative synthesis. *Social Science and Medicine*, 92, 9–21.

Schrank, B., Riches, S., Bird, V., Murray, J., Tylee, A., & Slade, M. (2014). A conceptual framework for improving well-being in people with a diagnosis of psychosis. *Epidemiology and Psychiatric Sciences*, 23, 377–387.

Schrank, B., Riches, S., Coggins, T., Tylee, A., & Slade, M. (2013). From objectivity to subjectivity: Conceptualisation and measurement of well-being in mental health. *Neuropsychiatry*, 3, 525–534.

Schrank, B., Stanghellini, G., & Slade, M. (2008). Hope in psychiatry: A review of the literature. *Acta Psychiatrica Scandinavica*, 118, 421–33.

Schueller, S. M., & Parks, A. C. (2012). Disseminating self-help: Positive psychology exercises in an online trial. *Journal of Medical Internet Research*, 14, e63.

Schwarzer, R., Luszczynska, A., Boehmer, S., Taubert, S., & Knoll, N. (2006). Changes in finding benefit after cancer surgery and the prediction of well-being one year later. *Social Science and Medicine*, 63, 1614–1624.

Seligman, M. (2011). *Flourish*. London, UK: Nicholas Brealy Publishing.

Slade, M. (2010). Mental illness and well-being: The central importance of positive psychology and recovery approaches. *BMC Health Services Research*, 10, 26.

Spiro, A. I., & Bosse, R. (2000). Relations between health-related quality of life and well-being: The gerontologist's new clothes? *International Journal of Ageing and Human Development*, 50, 297–318.

Willig, C. (2008). *Introducing qualitative research in psychology* (2nd ed.). Maidenhead, UK: Open University Press.

Wissing, M., & Van Eeden, C. (2002). Empirical clarification of the nature of psychological well-being. *South African Journal of Psychology*, 32, 32.

Chapter

7

Meaning in Life and Wellbeing

Michael F. Steger

Much of the effort expended in the medical and social sciences seems to follow an implicit notion that all people desire is a life free from pain, suffering and distress. Our collective effort has identified unending legions of threats, from viruses and bacteria to personal depression and global recession. Without diminishing the importance of identifying and attempting to ameliorate such threats, the past few decades have seen an unprecedented eruption of research that looks less at what people might want to avoid and more at what they might truly desire in life. Perhaps people want not only an absence of sickness but also their share of health. Perhaps people desire not only relief from the sinking pull of psychological suffering but also the buoyancy of psychological wellbeing. And perhaps people not only want to avoid the annihilation of existential emptiness but also strive for lives rich in meaning and purpose. This chapter wholeheartedly embraces these ideas and provides a brief overview of what we know about how finding and pursuing meaning in life may help ameliorate suffering and promote wellbeing.

What Is Meaning in Life?

The title of this chapter is "Meaning in Life and Wellbeing." We shall see that "meaning" is really the umbrella term that spans key concepts, such as "significance" and "purpose." There is the greatest consensus around defining meaning in life as "the extent to which people comprehend, make sense of, or see significance in their lives, accompanied by the degree to which they perceive themselves to have a purpose, mission, or overarching aim in life" (Steger, 2009, p. 682). What this definition really expresses is that the way that social scientists study meaning in life focuses on people's ability to comprehend or understand their life experiences and feel the drive and motivation of some grand, overarching life purpose or mission (or purposes and missions). Most of the past 60 years of research have used a definition of meaning in life that fits well with the one presented here, embracing a cognitive component (making sense of life) and a motivational component (pursuing purpose). More recently, a handful of scholars have made an effort to flesh out a third component of meaning that often seemed implicit in earlier definitions. These new efforts hinge somewhat on the multiple meanings of the word "significance." Significance can be used to refer to the interpretative and communicative qualities of something, as in the way that signs and signals are meant to communicate interpretable information (Steger et al., 2006). This would represent the cognitive component that long has been included in defining meaning in life. Significance also can be used to refer to the value or importance of something, as in the way

Wellbeing, Recovery and Mental Health, ed. Mike Slade, Lindsay Oades and Aaron Jarden.
Published by Cambridge University Press. © Mike Slade, Lindsay Oades and Aaron Jarden 2017

that having a baby can be a significant life event (Martela and Steger, 2015). George and Park (2013) call this component "mattering" and use it to suggest that one's life must be seen to have some value and worthwhileness for it to be meaningful. In other words, a meaningful life must be seen to matter. This new line of inquiry would seek to establish an evaluative component of meaning to join the cognitive and motivational ones (Heintzelman and King, 2014b). As Steger (2012) put it three years after his previous definition, "meaning in life necessarily involves people feeling that their lives matter, making sense of their lives, and determining a broader purpose for their lives" (p. 177). Thus, meaning in life captures the human capacity to make sense of life, to pursue purpose and to lead a life that is worthwhile and important.

What Is the Connection between Meaning in Life and Wellbeing?

Especially when contrasted with feeling that life is pointless, confusing, and worthless, it sounds pretty good to instead be able to find meaning in one's life. It should not be a surprise, then, that hundreds of scientific studies have firmly linked meaning in life to lesser suffering and greater wellbeing, both psychologically and physically (Steger, 2012). On top of that, research has begun to show that people who report greater meaning in life are better relationship partners, neighbors, and citizens. In fact, several of the most prominent theories of wellbeing and human flourishing consider meaning in life to be a fundamental cornerstone of happiness and the best life people can attain (e.g. Diener and Seligman, 2004; Ryan and Deci, 2001; Ryff and Singer, 1998). In this section, I review research connecting meaning in life with psychological, physical and social wellbeing.

Meaning in life is associated with more frequent and intense experiences of positive emotions and vitality (Chamberlain and Zika, 1988; Kennedy et al., 1994; Keyes et al., 2002; King et al., 2006; Ryff, 1989; Steger et al., 2006; Steger et al., 2008c; Steger et al., 2015a; Zika and Chamberlain,1992). Feeling better makes enjoying life easier, and meaning is related to a wide range of broad indicators of happiness and positive adjustment in life in many countries around the world (Bonebright et al., 2000; Debats, 1996; Debats et al., 1993; Fry, 2000, 2001; Garfield, 1973; O'Conner and Vallerand, 1998; Reker, 2002; Reker et al., 1987; Ryff and Keyes, 1995; Scannell et al., 2002; Shek, 1995; Shin et al., 2005; Steger et al., 2008b; Steger et al., 2008d; Thompson et al., 2003; Wong, 1998; Zika and Chamberlain, 1987; Zika and Chamberlain, 1992). In the end, people who feel like their lives are more meaningful also are more satisfied with their lives (Chamberlain and Zika, 1988; Keyes et al., 2002; Ryff, 1989; Steger, 2006; Steger and Frazier, 2005; Steger et al., 2006; Steger and Kashdan, 2006; Steger et al., 2008b).

On a more personal level, those who find their lives to be meaningful express more positive feelings and opinions about themselves, too. They score higher on measures of self-esteem, self-acceptance, and positive self-image (Debats, 1996; Garfield, 1973; Phillips et al., 1974; Ryff, 1989; Shek, 1992; Steger et al., 2008c). These results are not just for lucky people who have grown up in a world of self-congratulation and positive feedback; the link between meaning in life and more positive self-worth appears among people who are living quite outside the mainstream, either by choice as in novice Dominican nuns (Crumbaugh et al., 1970), by necessity as in nursing home residents (O'Conner and Vallerand, 1998) or by adjudication as in prisoners (Reker, 1977).

Although it is wonderful and desirable to feel good about one's life and one's self, meaning does not appear to be just fairy dust, helping people prop up phony smiles and inflated perceptions of self-importance. Instead, meaning also is related to psychological maturity and development, including greater self-actualization, personal growth, ego strength, self-control and responsibility (Ebersole and Quiring, 1991; Furrow et al., 2004; Garfield, 1973; Phillips, 1980; Reker, 1977; Reker and Peacock, 1981; Ryff, 1989; Shek, 1992; Tryon and Radzin, 1972). This psychological maturity may fuel a greater willingness to take charge in one's life. Research shows that meaning is positively related to having an internal locus of control and negatively related to having an external or chance locus of control (Newcomb and Harlow, 1986; Ryff, 1989; Thompson et al., 2003). With this in mind, it is no wonder that people high in meaning report a greater degree of autonomy, ambition and mastery in their lives (Debats et al., 1993; Reid, 1996; Ryff, 1989; Shek, 2001; Steger et al., 2008). There is no evidence, however, that meaning fuels an adversarial or domineering approach to life. Rather, meaning is linked to a positive perception of and approach to the world as well as an optimistic orientation toward the future (Acuff and Allen, 1970; Reker, 1977; Reker and Peacock, 1981; Sharpe and Viney, 1973; Simon et al., 1998; Steger et al., 2008). A meaningful life is a life of hope, optimism, and striving for a better future (Mascaro and Rosen, 2005; Mascaro and Rosen, 2006; Mascaro et al., 2004; Steger, 2006; Steger and Frazier, 2005; Thompson and Pitts, 1993). It may be that successfully overcoming difficulty in the past makes it easier to foresee and pursue a positive future. Indeed, people high in meaning report more effective coping skills and better adjustment following trauma (Debats et al., 1995; Edwards and Holden, 2001; Jim et al., 2006; Steger et al., 2008a; Stevens et al., 1987).

The mind–body connection has been an increasingly influential idea in the science and practice of human health. Due to the extensive and well-documented associations that meaning in life demonstrates with psychological health, we should expect a similar trend for physical health. Indeed, as one recent review determined, there are dozens of studies showing that people who feel their lives are meaningful enjoy better physical health (Roepke et al., 2014). This relationship takes many different forms, including subjective measures of how people rate their own health. Using this approach, research has found positive relations between meaning in life and better subjective health among cancer patients (Brady et al., 1999), cancer survivors (Jim and Anderson, 2007), Alzheimer's disease patients (Boyle et al., 2012) and smoking cessation patients (Steger et al., 2009a). Results concerning subjective measures of health mirror those using more objective, biology-based measures, including physiological indicators of immune system functioning (Krause and Hayward, 2012) and stress response (Ishida and Okada, 2006).

From a psychological point of view, meaning may help support health because those who feel their lives are more meaningful should be more likely to take care of themselves (e.g. Steger et al., 2015a). Research supports this hypothesis, showing that those high in meaning have better nutritional and dietary habits (Piko and Brassai, 2009), engage in more physical activity (Brassai et al., 2015; Holahan et al., 2011), and have healthier attitudes toward sexual prophylactic use (Steger et al., 2015a). Further, they engage in lower levels of substance use (Brassai et al., 2012; Martin et al., 2011). These habits also appear to extend into the ways in which people utilize the health care system itself. A large study of a representative sample of American older adults showed that those higher in meaning and purpose were more likely to engage in recommended preventative health care services, such as getting cholesterol or mammogram tests, and perhaps as a consequence also spent fewer nights in hospitals (Kim et al., 2014). Reduced hospital stays might indicate a profound economic benefit to meaning in life. Using the United States as just one example, in 2011 alone, the total cost of hospital stays was roughly $387 billion (Pfuntner et al., 2012). Finally, and perhaps most importantly, people who feel their lives are meaningful have a lower risk of dying and have longer lives (Boyle et al., 2009; Krause, 2009).

So far, then, this chapter has shown that people living a meaningful life are very likely to be happier, more positive and more psychologically mature, anticipate brighter futures, take care of their health better, feel better physically and enjoy all of these qualities for a longer period of time before death. But meaning is not seen to be a commodity, something to be selfishly hoarded or flaunted. Meaning is supposed to be shared. Most scholars agree that there is an inherent self-transcendence to meaning in life, such that meaning increases as people's concerns expand beyond their own interests to include the stakes of other people, other groups, and perhaps even all of life and the universe around them (e.g. Reker and Chamberlain, 2000). Because of this theoretical emphasis on a meaningful life including others, there should be no surprise that time and again, research has revealed that relationships of one sort or the other are the most commonly nominated source of meaning in people's lives (Steger et al., 2013). This research usually asks people to list, or alternatively to rate an existing list, of things that might make their lives meaningful, yielding a lot of richness and texture on how meaning seems relevant to individuals. At the same time, research specifically focusing on what it is about relationships that seems to benefit meaning in life has been relatively sparse (O'Donnell et al., 2014). There are some important clues, however.

Being rejected or ostracized, or feeling excluded, cause reduce perceived meaning in life (e.g. Williams et al., 2002), whereas meaning in life is higher on days when people feel more close and connected to others (Steger and Kashdan, 2009). Family appears to be an especially important source of connection (Delle Fave et al., 2013), and both perceived family cohesion and family satisfaction are positively related to meaning in life (Lightsey and Sweeney, 2008). Within romantic relationships, meaning in life is positively linked to marital satisfaction and marital adjustment (Shek, 1994), better communication between spouses (Kalantarkousheh and Hassan, 2010) and sexual satisfaction (McCann and Biaggio, 1989) and negatively linked to sexual frustration (Sallee and Casciani, 1976). Outside of one's family, social support and self-reported strength of social bonds are both related to meaning (Dunn and O'Brienn, 2009; Hicks and King, 2009; Krause, 2007), and experiencing meaning in one's workplace is associated with greater trust in managers (Wrzesniewski et al., 1997). From these studies it appears that it not only is important to have people in your life and to feel close to them, but it also seems important to have strong and cohesive bonds. Do people high in meaning do anything to maintain such strong bonds or do they merely harvest the fortuitous benefits of being around others? It seems that people high in meaning do give back to their relationships and communities, through volunteering, providing donations, and relationship-improving activities (Steger et al., 2008b).

What Is the Connection between Meaning in Life and Mental Health Recovery?

Finally, as was noted at the beginning of this chapter, more attention has been paid to whether people are experiencing suffering or distress than to whether they are experiencing wellbeing. Ameliorating suffering is a primary goal of many branches of human services, whether this means working to prevent known causes of suffering, such as poverty, inequality and abuse, or helping people to regain functioning through mental health recovery. In this section, research linking meaning in life with psychological distress, disorders and mental health recovery is reviewed.

Meaning in life seems to play a substantial role in reducing psychological suffering. Meaning in life consistently is negatively related to levels of psychological distress and mental illness, such as symptoms of eating disorders, substance use disorders, post-traumatic stress disorder, depression and anxiety (Park, 2010; Steger et al., 2008a; Steger and Kashdan, 2009; Zika and Chamberlain, 1992). Much of this research has taken place in the context of recovery from tragic or traumatic life events. In most of these models, meaning is a pivotal variable enabling people to move on and often perceive personal growth following trauma (e.g. Linley and Joseph, 2011; Park, 2010; Steger et al., 2015b).

A separate literature has emerged examining the role of meaning in facilitating recovery from mental illness or psychological disorder. At a theoretical level, meaning is one of the key components of models of psychological recovery. For example, meaning and purpose are identified as key processes within a model of psychological recovery that also includes hope, identity, and responsibility (Andresen et al., 2003). Similarly, meaning is a fundamental part of the CHIME model of recovery (Leamy et al., 2011). CHIME stands for Connectedness, Hope and optimism about the future, Identity, Meaning in life and Empowerment. The role of meaning in these models might center on helping people explore their spiritual or religious lives, develop personal goals in their lives or better understand the nature and best use of their strengths (Slade and Wallace, this volume). These models are borne out by evidence that meaning in life predicts better response to treatment for psychological disorders (e.g. Debats, 1996). Thus, meaning in life is linked to better psychological wellbeing, and also to the recovery of psychological functioning following both traumatic events and psychological disorders.

How Is Meaning in Life Measured?

As the review of research presented above shows, meaning in life already has been established as an important facet of wellbeing, and interest has been growing steadily. To continue to advance meaning in life science and practice, particularly in efforts to help people improve their meaning in life, we must be able to reliably measure it. The first measure of meaning in life appeared in the early 1960s, and new measures have been published periodically. The most popular measures often appear to use slightly different understandings and definitions of their target. For example, the first measure of meaning in life included items addressing energy, despair and suicide, and more recent measures appear to prioritize people's abilities to set goals for themselves and maintain active lifestyles (Crumbaugh and Maholick, 1964; Ryff, 1989). Broadening the way in which meaning is measured to include other constructs increases the risk that some of the significant findings yielded by research are due to similarity of the items used rather than to how the variables actually relate to each other. An easy example to use is the relationship between meaning and depression. If the meaning measure asks about despair and suicide, and the depression measure asks about despair and suicide, would it really be earth-shattering if people's scores were related? It is better to use measures that use a more straightforward approach to assessing meaning (e.g. Reker, 1992; Reker and Peacock, 1981). Sometimes meaning-in-life measures are too long to be used frequently – as in clinical settings to measure treatment progress – or in large, representative samples. Some meaning-in-life assessments also have struggled to achieve reasonable psychometric quality, particularly with regard to whether they have a consistent factor structure (e.g. Steger, 2006, 2007).

These issues were the impetus that led me to develop a meaning-in-life measure that could provide simple, straightforward assessment partnered with psychometric properties that met the highest standards. Research so far has been encouraging, but you do not have to take my word for it. According to an independent review, the Meaning in Life Questionnaire (MLQ; Steger et al., 2006) was the only meaning-in-life measure of dozens that warranted a perfect score based on rigor of development and demonstrated psychometric quality (Brandstätter et al., 2012). Others have presented evidence showing that the MLQ has been used to assess more people than other leading meaning-in-life instruments (Heintzelman and King, 2014b). The MLQ is a simple, straightforward tool that assesses both how meaningful people perceive their lives to be and also how intently people feel they are searching for more meaning in their lives (Steger et al., 2008c, 2011). Brief versions, generally consisting of three items assessing the extent of meaning in people's lives, have been used by governmental agencies for public health epidemiological research (e.g. Kobau et al., 2010) and by nongovernmental research institutes conducting health research around the globe, particularly in poorer nations (Samman, 2007). In cross-national research, the psychometric properties of the full MLQ (e.g. Steger et al., 2008d) and the short version (Steger and Samman, 2012) have proven to be very good (Steger and Shin, 2010). The primary drawback of the MLQ is that it trades comprehensiveness and richness for brevity and strong psychometric performance.

Conclusion

There has been a profound shift in how a successful, healthy life is seen, from reactive models that emphasize ridding oneself of threats, maladies, damage and flaws to more progressive and holistic models that are concerned with threats and damage, but are equally concerned with potential, opportunity, strength and wellbeing. Meaning in life is a variable of increasing importance that deftly spans both sides of these new models of health and flourishing. As people develop meaning in their lives, they also seem to develop powerful psychological characteristics, generative social and interpersonal relationships, physical health and happiness. Given the surge of research and the ready availability of measurement tools, the role of meaning in future work seeking to foster human wellbeing seems secure.

References

Acuff, G., & Allen, D. (1970). Hiatus in 'meaning': Disengagement for retired professors. *Journal of Gerontology*, 25, 126–128.

Andresen, R., Oades, L. & Caputi, P. (2003). The experience of recovery from schizophrenia: Towards an empirically-validated stage model. *Australian and New Zealand Journal of Psychiatry*, 37, 586–594.

Battista, J., & Almond, R. (1973). The development of meaning in life. *Psychiatry*, 36, 409–427.

Bonebright, C. A., Clay, D. L., & Ankenmann, R. D. (2000). The relationship of workaholism with work–life conflict, life satisfaction, and purpose in life. *Journal of Counseling Psychology*, 47, 469–477.

Boyle, P. A., Barnes, L. L., Buchman, A. S., & Bennett, D. A. (2009). Purpose in life is associated with mortality among community-dwelling older persons. *Psychosomatic Medicine*, 71, 574–579.

Boyle, P. A., Buchman, A. S., Wilson, R. S., Yu, L., Schneider, J. A., & Bennett, D. A. (2012). Effect of purpose in life on the relation between Alzheimer disease pathologic changes on cognitive function in advanced age. *Archives of General Psychiatry*, 69, 499–504.

Brady, M. J., Peterman, A. H., Fitchett, G., Mo, M., & Cella, D. (1999). A case for including spirituality in quality of life measurement in oncology. *Psycho-oncology*, 8, 417–428.

Brandstätter, M., Baumann, U., Borasio, G. D., & Fegg, M. J. (2012). Systematic review of meaning in life assessment instruments. *Psycho-oncology*, 21, 1034–1052.

Brassai, L., Piko, B. F., & Steger, M. F. (2012). Existential attitudes and eastern European adolescents' problem and health behaviors: Highlighting the role of the search for meaning in life. *Psychological Record*, 62, 719–734.

Brassai, L., Piko, B. F., & Steger, M. F. (2015). A reason to stay healthy: The role of meaning in life in relation to physical activity and healthy eating among adolescents. *Journal of Health Psychology*, 20, 473–482.

Brief, A. P., & Nord, W. R. (1990). *Meanings of occupational work: A collection of essays*. Lexington, MA: Lexington Books.

Chamberlain, K., & Zika, S. (1988). Religiosity, life meaning, and wellbeing: Some relationships in a sample of women. *Journal for the Scientific Study of Religion*, 27, 411–420.

Colby, A., Sippola, L., & Phelps, E. (2001). Social responsibility and paid work in contemporary American life. In A. S. Rossi (Ed.), *Caring and doing for others: Social responsibility in the domains of family, work, and community*. Chicago: University of Chicago Press.

Crumbaugh, J. C., & Maholick, L. T. (1964). An experimental study in existentialism: The psychometric approach to Frankl's concept of noogenic neurosis. *Journal of Clinical Psychology*, 20, 200–207.

Crumbaugh, J. C., Raphael, M., & Shrader, R. R. (1970). Frankl's will to meaning in a religious order. *Journal of Clinical Psychology*, 26, 206–207.

Debats, D. L. (1996). Meaning in life: Clinical relevance and predictive power. *British Journal of Clinical Psychology*, 35, 503–516.

Debats, D. L., Drost, J., & Hansen, P. (1995). Experiences of meaning in life: A combined qualitative and quantitative approach. *British Journal of Psychology*, 86, 359–375.

Debats, D. L., van der Lubbe, P. M., & Wezeman, F. R. A. (1993). On the psychometric properties of the Life Regard Index (LRI): A measure of meaningful life. *Personality and Individual Differences*, 14, 337–345.

Delle Fave, A., Pozzo, M., Bassi, M., & Cetin, I. (2013). A longitudinal study on motherhood and well-being: Developmental and clinical implications. *Terapia Psicologica*, 31, 21–33.

Diener, E., & Seligman, M. E. P. (2004). Beyond money: Toward an economy of well-being. *Psychological Science in the Public Interest*, 5, 1–31.

Dunn, M. G., & O'Brien, K. M. (2009). Psychological health and meaning in life: Stress, social support, and religious coping in Latina/Latino immigrants. *Hispanic Journal of Behavioral Sciences*, 31, 204–227.

Ebersole, P., & Quiring, G. (1991). Meaning in life depth: The MILD. *Journal of Humanistic Psychology*, 31, 113–124.

Edwards, M. J., & Holden, R. R. (2001). Coping, meaning in life, and suicidal manifestations: Examining gender differences. *Journal of Clinical Psychology*, 57, 1517–1534.

Frankl, V. E. (1963). *Man's search for meaning: An introduction to logotherapy*. New York, NY: Washington Square Press.

Fry, P. S. (2000). Religious involvement, spirituality and personal meaning for life: Existential predictors of psychological wellbeing in community-residing and institutional care elders. *Aging and Mental Health*, 4, 375–387.

Fry, P. S. (2001). The unique contribution of key existential factors to the prediction of psychological well-being of older adults following spouse loss. *Gerontologist*, 41, 69–81.

Furrow, J. L., King, P. E., & White, K. (2004). Religion and positive youth development: Identity, meaning, and prosocial concerns. *Applied Developmental Science*, 8(1), 17–26.

Garfield, C. (1973). A psychometric and clinical investigation of Frankl's concept of existential vacuum and anomie. *Psychiatry*, 36, 396–408.

George, L. S., & Park, C. L. (2013). Are meaning and purpose distinct? An examination of correlates and predictors. *Journal of Positive Psychology*, 8(5), 365–375.

Heintzelman, S. J., & King, L. A. (2014a). Life is pretty meaningful. *American Psychologist*, 69, 561–574.

Heintzelman, S. J., & King, L. A. (2014b). (The feeling of) meaning-as-information. *Personality and Social Psychology Review*, 18, 153–167.

Hicks, J. A., & King, L. A. (2009). Positive mood and social relatedness as information about meaning in life. *Journal of Positive Psychology*, 4, 471–482.

Holahan, C. K., Holahan, C. J., Velasquez, K. E., Jung, S., North, R. J., & Pahl, S. A. (2011). Purposiveness and leisure-time physical activity in women in early midlife. *Women and Health*, 51(7), 661–675.

Ishida, R., & Okada, M. (2006). Effects of a firm purpose in life on anxiety and sympathetic nervous activity caused by emotional stress: Assessment by psychophysiological method. *Stress and Health*, 22, 275–281.

Jim, H. S., & Andersen, B. L. (2007). Meaning in life mediates the relationship between social and physical functioning and distress in cancer survivors. *British Journal of Health Psychology*, 12, 363–381.

Jim, H. S., Richardson, S. A., Golden-Kreutz, D. M., & Anderson, B. L. (2006). Strategies used in coping with a cancer diagnosis predict meaning in life for survivors. *Health Psychology*, 25, 763–761.

Kalantarkousheh, S. M., & Hassan, S. A. (2010). Function of life meaning and marital communication among Iranian spouses in Universiti Putra Malaysia. *Procedia-Social and Behavioral Sciences*, 5, 1646–1649.

Kennedy, J. E., Kanthamani, H., & Palmer, J. (1994). Psychic and spiritual experiences, health, well-being, and meaning in life. *Journal of Parapsychology*, 58, 353–383.

Keyes, C. L. M., Shmotkin, D., & Ryff, C. D. (2002). Optimizing well-being: The empirical encounter of two traditions. *Journal of Personality and Social Psychology*, 82, 1007–1022.

Kim, E. S., Strecher, V. J., & Ryff, C. D. (2014). Purpose in life and use of preventive health care services. *PNAS*, 111, 16, 331–16, 336.

King, L. A., Hicks, J. A., Krull, J. L., & Del Gaiso, A. K. (2006). Positive affect and the experience of meaning in life. *Journal of Personality and Social Psychology*, 90, 179–196.

Kobau, R., Sniezek, J., Zack, M. M., Lucas, R. E., & Burns, A. (2010). Well-being assessment: An evaluation of well-being scales for public health and population estimated of well-being among US adults. *Applied Psychology: Health and Well-Being*, 2, 272–297.

Krause, N. (2007). Longitudinal study of social support and meaning in life. *Psychology and Aging*, 22, 456–469.

Krause, N. (2009). Meaning in life and mortality. *Journals of Gerontology Series B: Psychological Sciences and Social Sciences*, 64B, 517–527.

Leamy, M., Bird, V., Le Boutillier, C., Williams, J., & Slade, M. (2011). A conceptual framework for personal recovery in mental health: systematic review and narrative synthesis. *British Journal of Psychiatry*, 199, 445–452.

Lightsey, O., & Sweeney, J. (2008). Meaning in life, emotion oriented coping, generalized self-efficacy, and family cohesion as predictors of family satisfaction among mothers of children with disabilities. *Family Journal*, 16, 212–221.

Linley, P. A., & Joseph, S. (2011). Meaning in life and posttraumatic growth. *Journal of Loss and Trauma*, 16(2), 150–159.

Martin, R. A., MacKinnon, S., Johnson, J., & Rohsenow, D. J. (2011). Purpose in life predicts treatment outcome among adult cocaine abusers in treatment. *Journal of Substance Abuse Treatment*, 40, 183–188.

Mascaro, N., & Rosen, D. H. (2005). Existential meaning's role in the enhancement of hope and prevention of depressive symptoms. *Journal of Personality*, 73, 985–1014.

Mascaro, N., & Rosen, D. H. (2006). The role of existential meaning as a buffer against stress. *Journal of Humanistic Psychology*, 46, 168–190.

Mascaro, N., Rosen, D. H., & Morey, L. C. (2004). The development, construct validity, and clinical utility of the spiritual meaning scale. *Personality and Individual Differences*, 37, 845–860.

McCann, J. T., & Biaggio, M. K. (1989). Sexual satisfaction in marriage as a function of life meaning. *Archives of Sexual Behavior*, 18, 59–72.

Newcomb, M. D., & Harlow, L. L. (1986). Life events and substance use among adolescents: Mediating effects of perceived loss of control and meaningless in life. *Journal of Personality and Social Psychology*, 51, 564–577.

O'Conner, B. P., & Vallerand, R. J. (1998) Psychological adjustment variables as predictors of mortality among nursing home residents. *Psychology and Aging*, 13, 368–374.

O'Donnell, M. B., Shim, Y., Barenz, J. D., & Steger, M. F. (2015). Revisiting the Meaning in Life Questionnaire, Part 2: Intervention research and clinical relevance. *International Forum for Logotherapy*, 38, 41–48.

Park, C. L. (2010). Making sense of the meaning literature: An integrative review of meaning making and its effects on adjustment to stressful life events. *Psychological bulletin*, 136, 257.

Pfuntner, A., Wier, L. M., & Elixhauser, A. (2012). Healthcare Cost and Utilization Project (HCUP) statistical briefs, #144: Overview of hospital stays in the United States, 2011. Rockville, MD: Agency for Health Care Policy and Research.

Phillips, W. M. (1980). Purpose in life, depression, and locus of control. *Journal of Clinical Psychology*, 36, 661–667.

Phillips, W. M., Watkins, J. T., & Noll, G. (1974). Self-actualization, self-transcendence, and personal philosophy. *Journal of Humanistic Psychology*, 14, 53–73.

Piko, B. F., & Brassai, L. (2009). The role of individual and familial protective factors in adolescents' diet control. *Journal of Health Psychology*, 14, 810–819.

Reid, J. K. (1996) Tickets to adulthood? The relationship between life attitudes, death acceptance, and autonomy in adulthood. *Family Therapy*, 23, 135–149.

Reker, G. T. (1977). The purpose-in-life test in an inmate population: An empirical investigation. *Journal of Clinical Psychology*, 33, 688–693.

Reker, G. T. (1992). *Manual: Life Attitude Profile – Revised*. Petersborough, Ontario: Student Psychologists Press.

Reker, G. T. (2002). Prospective predictors of successful aging in community-residing and institutionalized Canadian elderly. *Ageing International*, 27, 42–64.

Reker, G. T., & Chamberlain, K. (2000). *Exploring existential meaning: Optimizing human development across the life span*. Thousand Oaks, CA: Sage Publications.

Reker, G. T., & Peacock, E. J. (1981). The Life Attitude Profile (LAP): A multidimensional instrument for assessing attitudes toward life. *Canadian Journal of Behavioral Science*, 13, 264–273.

Reker, G. T., Peacock, E. J., & Wong, P. T. P. (1987). Meaning and purpose in life and well-being: A life-span perspective. *Journal of Gerontology*, 42, 44–49.

Roepke, A. M., Jayawickreme, E., & Riffle, O. M. (2014). Meaning and health: A systematic review. *Applied Research in Quality of Life*, 9, 1055–1079.

Ryan, R. M., & Deci, E. L. (2001). On happiness and human potentials: A review of research on hedonic and eudaimonic well-being. *Annual Review of Psychology*, 52, 141–166.

Ryff, C. D. (1989). Happiness is everything, or is it? Explorations on the meaning of psychological well-being. *Journal of Personality and Social Psychology*, 57, 1069–1081.

Ryff, C. D., & Keyes, C. L. M. (1995). The structure of well-being revisited. *Journal of Personality and Social Psychology*, 69, 719–727.

Ryff, C. D., & Singer, B. (1998). The contours of positive human health. *Psychological Inquiry*, 9, 1–28.

Sallee, D. T., & Casciani, J. M. (1976). Relationship between sex drive and sexual frustration and purpose in life. *Journal of Clinical Psychology*, 32, 273–275.

Samman, E. (2007), Psychological and subjective wellbeing: A proposal for internationally comparable indicators. *Oxford Development Studies*, 35, 459–486.

Scannell, E. D., Allen, F. C. L., & Burton, J. (2002). Meaning in life and positive and negative well-being. *North American Journal of Psychology*, 4, 93–112.

Sharpe, D., & Viney, L. (1973). Weltanschauung and the Purpose-in-Life Test. *Journal of Clinical Psychology*, 29(4), 489–491.

Shek, D. T. L. (1992). Meaning in life and psychological well-being: An empirical study using the Chinese version of the Purpose in Life Questionnaire. *Journal of Genetic Psychology*, 153, 185–200.

Shek, D. T. (1994). Meaning in life and adjustment amongst midlife parents in Hong Kong. *International Forum for Logotherapy*, 17, 102–107.

Shek, D. T. L. (1995). Marital quality and psychological well-being of married adults in a Chinese context. *Journal of Genetic Psychology*, 156, 45–56.

Shek, D. T. L. (2001). Meanings in life and sense of mastery in Chinese adolescents with economic disadvantage. *Psychological Reports*, 88, 711–712.

Shin, J. Y., Lee, Y. A., & Lee, K.-H. (2005). The effects of life meaning and emotional regulation strategies on psychological well-being. *Korean Journal of Counseling and Psychotherapy*, 17, 1035–1057.

Simon, L., Arndt, J., Greenberg, J., Pyszczynski, T., & Solomon, S. (1998). Terror management and meaning: Evidence that the opportunity to defend the worldview in response to mortality salience increases the meaningfulness of life in the mildly depressed. *Journal of Personality*, 66(3), 359–382.

Steger, M. F. (2006). An illustration of issues in factor extraction and identification of dimensionality in psychological assessment data. *Journal of Personality Assessment*, 86, 263–272.

Steger, M. F. (2007). Structural validity of the Life Regards Index. *Measurement and Evaluation in Counseling and Development*, 40, 97–109.

Steger, M. F. (2009). Meaning in life. In S. J. Lopez (Ed.), *Oxford Handbook of Positive Psychology* (2nd ed.) (pp. 679–687). Oxford, UK: Oxford University Press.

Steger, M. F. (2012). Experiencing meaning in life: Optimal functioning at the nexus of spirituality, psychopathology, and well-being. In P. T. P. Wong (Ed.), *The human quest for meaning* (2nd ed.) (pp. 165–184). New York, NY: Routledge.

Steger, M. F. (2013). Assessing meaning and quality of life. In K. Geissinger (Editor in Chief), B. A. Bracken, J. F. Carlson, J. C. Hansen, N. R. Kuncel, S. P. Reise, & M. C. Rodriguez (Eds.), *APA Handbook of Testing and Assessment in Psychology*, Vol. 2 (pp.489–499). Washington, DC: American Psychological Association.

Steger, M. F., Fitch-Martin, A., Donnelly, J., & Rickard, K. M. (2015a). Meaning in life and health: Proactive health orientation links meaning in life to health variables among American undergraduates. *Journal of Happiness Studies*, 16, 583–597.

Steger, M. F., & Frazier, P. (2005). Meaning in life: One link in the chain from religion to well-being. *Journal of Counseling Psychology*, 52, 574–582.

Steger, M. F., Frazier, P., Oishi, S., & Kaler, M. (2006). The Meaning in Life Questionnaire: Assessing the presence of and search for meaning in life. *Journal of Counseling Psychology*, 53, 80–93.

Steger, M. F., Frazier, P., & Zacchanini, J. L. (2008a). Terrorism in two cultures: Traumatization and existential protective factors following the September 11th attacks and the Madrid train bombings. *Journal of Trauma and Loss*, 13, 511–527.

Steger, M. F., & Kashdan, T. B. (2009). Depression and everyday social activity, intimacy, and well-being. *Journal of Counseling Psychology*, 56, 289–300.

Steger, M. F., Kashdan, T. B., & Oishi, S. (2008b). Being good by doing good: Eudaimonic activity and daily well-being correlates, mediators, and temporal relations. *Journal of Research in Personality*, 42, 22–42.

Steger, M. F., Kashdan, T. B., Sullivan, B. A., & Lorentz, D. (2008c). Understanding the search for meaning in life: Personality, cognitive style, and the dynamic between seeking and experiencing meaning. *Journal of Personality*, 76, 199–228.

Steger, M. F., Kawabata, Y., Shimai, S., & Otake, K. (2008d). The meaningful life in Japan and the United States: Levels and correlates of meaning in life. *Journal of Research in Personality*, 42, 660–678.

Steger, M. F., Mann, J. R., Michels, P., & Cooper, T. C. (2009a). Meaning in life, anxiety, depression, and general health among smoking cessation patients. *Journal of Psychosomatic Research*, 67, 353–358.

Steger, M. F., Oishi, S., & Kashdan, T. B. (2009b). Meaning in life across the life span: Levels and correlates of meaning in life from emerging adulthood to older adulthood. *Journal of Positive Psychology*, 4, 43–52.

Steger, M. F., Oishi, S., & Kesibir, S. (2011). Is a life without meaning satisfying? The moderating role of the search for meaning in satisfaction with life judgments. *Journal of Positive Psychology*, 6, 173–180.

Steger, M. F., Owens, G. P., & Park, C. L. (2015b). Violations of war: Testing the meaning-making model among military veterans. *Journal of Clinical Psychology*, 71, 105–116.

Steger, M. F., & Samman, E. (2012). Assessing meaning in life on an international scale: Psychometric evidence for the Meaning in Life Questionnaire-Short Form among Chilean households. *International Journal of Wellbeing*, 2, 182–195.

Steger, M. F., Shim, Y., Brueske, L., Rush, B., Shin, J. & Merriman, L. (2013). The mind's eye: A photographic method for understanding meaning in people's lives. *Journal of Positive Psychology*, 8, 530–542

Steger, M. F., & Shin, J. Y. (2010). The relevance of the Meaning in Life Questionnaire to therapeutic practice: A look at the initial evidence. *International Forum on Logotherapy*, 33, 95–104.

Stevens, M. J., Pfost, K. S., & Wessels, A. B. (1987). The relationship of purpose in life to coping strategies and time since the death of a significant other. *Journal of Counseling and Development*, 65, 424–426.

Swann, W. B., Jr., Rentfrow, P. J., & Gunn, J. S. (2003). Self-verification: The search for coherence. In Leary, M., & Tangney, J. (Eds.), *Handbook of Self and Identity* (pp. 367–383). New York, NY: Guilford.

Tedeschi, R. G., Park, C. L., & Calhoun, L. G. (1998). Posttraumatic growth: Conceptual issues. In Tedeschi, R. G., Park, C. L., & Calhoun, L. G. (Eds.), *Posttraumatic Growth: Theory and Research on Change in the Aftermath of Crisis* (pp. 1–22). Mahwah, NJ: Lawrence Erlbaum.

Thompson, N. J., Coker, J., Krause, J. S., & Henry, E. (2003). Purpose in life as a mediator of adjustment after spinal cord injury. *Rehabilitative Psychology*, 48, 100–108.

Thompson, S. C., & Pitts, J. (1993). Factors relating to a person's ability to find meaning after a diagnosis of cancer. *Journal of Psychosocial Oncology*, 11, 1–21.

Tryon, W., & Radzin, A. (1972). Purpose-in-life as a function of ego resiliency, dogmatism, and biographical variables. *Journal of Clinical Psychology*, 28, 544–545.

Williams, K. D., Cheung, C. K. T., & Choi, W. (2000). Cyberostracism: Effects of being ignored over the Internet. *Journal of Personality and Social Psychology*, 79, 748–762.

Wong, P. T. P. (1998). Implicit theories of meaningful life and development of Personal Meaning Profile. In Wong, P. T. P., & Fry, P. S. (Eds.), *The Human Quest for Meaning* (pp. 111–140). Mahwah, NJ: Lawrence Erlbaum.

Wrzesniewski, A., McCauley, C., Rozin, P., & Schwartz, B. (1997). Jobs, careers, and callings: People's relations to their work. *Journal of Research in Personality*, 31, 21–33.

Zika, S., & Chamberlain, K. (1987). Relation of hassles and personality to subjective well-being. *Journal of Personality and Social Psychology*, 53, 155–162.

Zika, S., & Chamberlain, K. (1992). On the relation between meaning in life and psychological well-being. *British Journal of Psychology*, 83, 133–145.

Chapter

8

The Complete State Model of Mental Health

Corey L. M. Keyes and Chris C. Martin

The history of public health conventionally begins with John Snow and the cholera outbreak of 1854. This story has become canonical because its central themes are also the themes of public health: surveillance, investigation and prevention of the spread of a pathogen. Although mental health professionals do not typically tackle tangible pathogens, they conceive of their work similarly. Their goal is to track, prevent and cure mental illness.

Despite its intuitive appeal, this *pathogenic* view is incomplete because a person may be free of mental illness without being fully healthy. For a complete perspective, the pathogenic perspective must be complemented with the *salutogenic* perspective. Suffering must be eliminated *and flourishing must be promoted*. The merger of these two perspectives constitutes the complete state model of mental health (Keyes, 2005a).

History

In the modern era, the pathogenic perspective has prevailed, possibly due to the germ theory of disease. Germs are pathogens – their elimination is a pathogenic goal. It was not until the middle of the 20th century that a major health agency recognized that the absence of pathogens (or causes of malaise) did not suffice, and defined health as the presence of a positive state of human capacities and functioning (WHO, 1948). In mental health, Jahoda (1958) drew a similar distinction. Based on a historical and cultural review, Jahoda rejected the idea that freedom from illness constituted mental health and posited six manifestations of mental health. These included autonomy, environmental mastery, accurate self-knowledge and self-actualization.

Problematically, neither the WHO nor Jahoda provided substantial evidence for their views. Indeed, there were no validated measures of positive mental health at the time. Consequently, there was little progress on the salutogenic front. Nevertheless, several developments augured the birth of the complete state model.

First, diverse psychologists, including Gordon Allport, Victor Frankl and Abraham Maslow, recognized the needs for meaning, positive identity and self-actualization. These needs lay outside the scope of Freudian therapy and behaviorist conditioning. Second, the study of quality of life expanded beyond negative indicators to include questions about life satisfaction (Gurin et al., 1960). Third, the study of person–situation interactions evolved to include scenarios where the skill of a person matched the challenge of a situation (Csikszentmihalyi, 1975).

Wellbeing, Recovery and Mental Health, ed. Mike Slade, Lindsay Oades and Aaron Jarden.
Published by Cambridge University Press. © Mike Slade, Lindsay Oades and Aaron Jarden 2017

In the area of individual differences, developments also pointed toward the recognition of positive functioning. Stress models began to incorporate differences in coping (Lazarus and Folkman, 1984), and risk-factor models expanded to include strength and resilience (Werner and Smith, 1977). In addition, gerontologists were confronted with evidence of late generativity and ceased to construe aging as uniform decline (Baltes, 1987).

The 1980s and 1990s witnessed seminal work in wellbeing. In 1984, Diener (1984) reviewed the first generation of research and theory on subjective wellbeing. This generation focused on *hedonic* – or emotional – wellbeing, which comprised low negative affect, high life satisfaction and high positive affect. Complementing Diener's work, Ryff (1989) operationalized *psychological* wellbeing based on humanistic, existential and philosophical sources. Subsequently, Keyes (1998) operationalized *social* wellbeing, drawing from the sociological theories of Karl Marx, Emile Durkheim and others. Both Ryff and Keyes connected their dimensions of wellbeing to functioning well (eudaimonia) as opposed to feeling good (hedonia).

Meanwhile, Martin Seligman and Christopher Peterson catalogued every human strength and virtue that had been espoused in religious or cultural traditions. They found that six broad virtues appeared nearly universally: wisdom, courage, humanity, justice, temperance, and self-transcendence (Peterson and Seligman, 2004). What made this project *positive* was not merely the cataloguing of virtues but also the argument that people should practice their strengths, not eliminate their weaknesses.

Modeling and Measuring Positive Mental Health

The complete state model was developed by merging the pathogenic perspective (informed by clinical psychology) with the salutogenic perspective (informed by the work above). The complete state model specifies that constructs of mental health and mental illness are distinct. Proponents of the model have noted that the latent factors of mental illness and mental health correlate to a moderate degree, but only 28.1% of their variance is shared in Midlife in the United States (MIDUS) data from U.S. adults (Keyes, 2005a; see also Keyes, 2009; Keyes et al., 2008; Westerhof and Keyes, 2010).

The most widely adopted scale for measuring mental health is the Mental Health Continuum – Short Form (MHC–SF; Keyes, 2005b), a form based on a tripartite conception of mental health as emotional wellbeing, psychological wellbeing and social wellbeing. These three types of wellbeing are distinct, but they emanate from a higher-order factor of generalized wellbeing (Gallagher et al., 2009). The MHC–SF derives from the Mental Health Continuum – Long Form (MHC–LF; Keyes, 2002).

Emotional (or Hedonic) Wellbeing

Emotional wellbeing (or hedonic wellbeing) can be conceptualized as satisfaction with life and a surplus of positive emotion. Life satisfaction is typically assessed with a single indicator: respondents rate their "life overall these days" on a 10-point scale (Cantril, 1965; see also Diener, 1984, p. 546). For the assessment of a surplus of positive emotion, respondents report their symptoms of positive affect and negative affect over a time span. For instance, in the Positive Affect and Negative Affect Scale (PANAS; Watson et al., 1988), respondents are asked how much of the time during recent weeks they felt ten kinds of negative affect and positive affect (see also Thompson, 2007).

Affect scales and satisfaction scales evince high levels of internal consistency (Diener, 1994). Satisfaction scales tap into the evaluative dimension of hedonic wellbeing – people translate their life evaluations into affect-laden words. Affect scales, on the other hand, tap into the phenomenological dimension of hedonic wellbeing – people indicate their dispositional emotions.

Psychological Wellbeing

Ryff (1989) posited that happiness is not only about feeling good but also about functioning well. To make this case, Ryff drew from conceptions of happiness that go beyond affect, conceptions including Aristotle's (trans. 1925) view of happiness as proper living, Allport's (1961) treatment of maturation, and Jahoda's (1958) six-dimensional view of positive mental health. In Ryff's model, six dimensions underlie psychological well-being (PWB): self-acceptance, positive relations with others, personal growth, purpose in life, environmental mastery and autonomy.

Self-acceptance is esteem for oneself and satisfaction with one's identity. Healthy individuals accept both positive and negative aspects of themselves. *Environmental mastery* denotes subjective efficacy and mastery in shaping one's surroundings to match one's needs. *Positive relations with others* consists of concern for the welfare of others and the presence of warm, satisfying and trusting relationships. *Autonomy* measures the ability to resist malign social pressures and the capacity to regulate behavior without dependence on others' standards. *Purpose in life* is the belief that one's life has an objective. Last, *personal growth* is the subjective perception that one is fulfilling one's potential and improving one's skills and knowledge. This dimension is most similar to Aristotle's eudaimonia.

Social Wellbeing

Keyes (1998) has attended to the sociological fact that humans belong to social institutions, and that some portion of wellbeing ensues from perceived fit between the self and society. The dimensions in Keyes's model of social wellbeing are social coherence, social actualization, social integration, social acceptance and social contribution.

Social integration is the assessment that one has something in common with fellow citizens and that one feels a sense of belonging and societal inclusion. *Social contribution* is the evaluation that one has something useful to give to the world. *Social coherence* is the perception that society is orderly and functional, and it includes a concern for knowing about the world.

Social growth is the perception that society has a positive trajectory – the overall sense that despite social problems, people have been improving society. *Social acceptance* is the acknowledgment of positive qualities in the average citizen, qualities that include trustworthiness, altruism and industriousness.

From Wellbeing Scores to Mental Health Diagnoses

Wellbeing is assessed with continuous scales, which lack diagnostic thresholds. The Mental Health Continuum – Short Form (MHC–SF) addresses this problem. As noted earlier, it is a "short" form because it derives from a longer form.

The theoretical basis behind the Short Form is the tripartite model of emotional, psychological and social wellbeing, which we discussed earlier. Studies support this tripartite conception among U.S. adults (Gallagher et al., 2009), college students (Robitschek and Keyes, 2009), and adolescents (Keyes, 2005b). In the Short Form, there is one item for each dimension of psychological and social wellbeing. Emotional wellbeing is measured with three items.

The continuum of mental health has three ordered categories: languishing, moderately mentally healthy and flourishing. In questions about frequency of experienced wellbeing, flourishers pick the answers *almost every day* or *every day during the past month* in at least one facet of hedonic wellbeing and six or more facets of positive functioning. Languishers, in contrast, pick the answers *never* or *maybe once or twice during the past month* in at least one facet of hedonic wellbeing and six or more facets of positive functioning. Languishing is the absence of mental health – vitality and engagement are missing. People who are languishing typically feel stuck or trapped. Moderate mental health is the intermediate category between flourishing and languishing.

The measurement invariance, temporally and cross-culturally, of the MHC–SF has been tested. In the temporal case, an analysis of a four-wave survey of 1,932 Dutch adults showed that there were only negligible invariance problems (Lamer et al., 2012). In the cross-cultural case, the MHC–SF was tested in the Netherlands, South Africa and Iran (Joshanloo et al., 2013). Its tripartite factor structure and metric invariance were validated.

Newer Approaches

Figure 8.1 shows the structure of the wellbeing models proposed by Diener (2010), Seligman (2012) and Felicia Huppert (Huppert and So, 2013) with reference to the Mental Health Continuum model of Keyes. In the hedonic cluster (left), there is strong agreement about positive emotions and engagement with life. In the eudaimonic cluster (right), there is strong agreement about self-acceptance (or self-respect or self-esteem); a sense of personal mastery or competence; satisfying relationships; purpose in life; and optimism about the self or society.

Both Diener's and Seligman's models are somewhat parsimonious versions of Keyes' model. Diener and colleagues (Diener et al., 2010) published their flourishing scale (FS) in 2010. This scale excludes the hedonic aspects of flourishing, and includes only positive

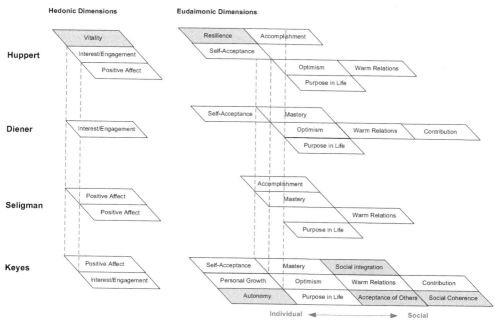

Figure 8.1 Four models of flourishing.

and negative affect. The FS has excellent reliability, but its construct validity is still under scrutiny. The correlation between FS and PWB (averaged across six dimensions) is approximately 0.75 (Diener, 2010).

Seligman's model consists of positive emotions (P), engagement (E), relationships (R), meaning (M) and accomplishment (A). It is therefore abbreviated as PERMA and assessed with the PERMA Profiler (PERMA-P; Butler and Kern, 2013). A factor analysis from an administration of the PERMA-P to 516 male students confirmed the presence of just four factors, with the *meaning* items loading on *relationship*.

The PERA, a variant of the PERMA-P, uses more items per factor than the PERMA (which uses three per factor) and measures only four factors (Kern et al., 2015). For instance, the PERA uses 13 items to assess positive emotions. PERA scores are positively correlated with life satisfaction, hope, gratitude and school engagement. Scores are negatively correlated with depression, anxiety and somatic symptoms. The PERA scale is being developed further.

Huppert (Huppert and So, 2013) created her model by starting with existing models and appending items that measure the antithesis of mental disorder. Vitality is a unique hedonic dimension in Huppert's model, and it connotes energy and composure. Huppert also uniquely includes resilience, or the ability to restore oneself to a normal state after emotional turmoil.

Huppert's 10-item scale was included in the wellbeing module of the European Social Survey (ESS), a survey administered to a representative sample of 43,000 Europeans aged 15 or older. Exploratory factor analysis of ESS responses revealed two latent factors: positive characteristics and positive functions. In a three-factor analysis, where a life-satisfaction item was appended, an additional factor was found: positive emotions.

Prevalence of Mental Health

In the 1995 and 2005 waves of MIDUS, U.S. adults completed the long form of the mental health continuum (MHC–LF), which assesses mental health, and the Composite International Diagnostic Interview Short Form (CIDI-SF) (Kessler et al., 1998), which assesses symptoms of three mental illnesses, namely, major depressive episodes (MDE), panic attacks (PA) and generalized anxiety disorder (GAD).

Mental health appeared to have similar levels of prevalence in 1995 and 2005: differences were 4% or smaller in magnitude. The prevalence of flourishing rose from 19.2% to 22.2%. The prevalence of moderate mental health declined from 64.1% to 60.4%. The prevalence of languishing rose from 16.7% to 17.2%. These levels of stability are comparable to those of mental illness.

However, substantial change occurred at the individual level. Of those languishing in 1995, only 45% were languishing in 2005; 51% improved to moderate mental health and 4% improved to flourishing. Only half of adults flourishing in 1995 were also flourishing in 2005, with a substantial portion (46%) declining to moderate mental health and a trivial portion (3%) declining further (to languishing).

Moderate mental health was similarly unstable at the individual level. Of those who reported moderate mental health in 1995, about 19% improved to flourishing and 14% declined to languishing in 2005. Although these percentages seem small, they are much larger than 4%, which was the maximum prevalence difference. Thus, the prevalence estimates mask two trends. First, the 14% in declines from moderate mental health to languishing is offset by the 55% who improved from languishing to a healthier state. Second, the

19% who improved from moderate mental health to flourishing were offset by the 49% who declined from flourishing to a less healthy state.

Antecedents of Mental Health

Substantial portions of variance in mental health can be explained by both genetic and environmental factors. In recent analyses of data from 670 pairs of MIDUS twins, Keyes and colleagues have found strong support for the heritability of positive mental health. These results also bolster the dual-continua model, which distinguishes health from illness (Keyes et al., 2010b; Kendler et al., 2011).

All three types of subjective wellbeing share a single common source of genetic variance that one might label the latent propensity for good mental health. The three mental illnesses measured in MIDUS – depression, panic and anxiety disorders – also emanated from a shared latent cause. The latent factors of positive mental health and mental illness were heritable at 72% and 61%, respectively. Only 50% of the genetic influences on latent mental health were shared with mental illness. There was an even greater independence at the environmental level – less than 10% of environmental influences were common to the health and illness factors.

Given the nontrivial levels of genetic overlap between mental health and mental illness, a person who inherits a genetic risk factor may find it difficult to flourish, but we caution against a deterministic interpretation. Levels of heritability are sufficiently low and levels of environmental influence are sufficiently high to suggest that genetic risk can be overcome. The independence of the propensities for mental health and mental illness also indicates that the absence of salutary alleles does not indicate malign alleles, and the absence of malign alleles does not indicate salutary alleles.

Consequences of Mental Health

Both personal and societal benefits of mental health are discernible. At the personal level, flourishing is a protective factor against mental illness. The risk of being diagnosed with a mental illness is lowest among those who are consistently flourishing (Keyes et al., 2010a). Among people in the MIDUS dataset who declined from flourishing to moderate mental health, the odds of having a mental illness were approximately three and a half times as high in comparison with those who remained flourishing. Even the maintenance of moderate mental health was a risk factor; respondents who stagnated at this level were over four times as likely to have a 2005 mental illness as those who consistently reported flourishing. The worst outcomes were associated with declines from moderate mental health (or flourishing) to languishing – these individuals had an 86% increase in the odds of a 2005 mental illness.

In contrast, those who improved to flourishing from a less healthy state had a very low risk of future mental illness, and were comparable to those who were consistently flourishing. Even a partial improvement to moderate mental health was associated with a mental-illness risk reduction by nearly half.

Physical illness is another risk among nonflourishing people. Adults and adolescents who are diagnosed as moderately mentally healthy or languishing report poorer physical health outcomes and do worse in terms of healthcare utilization. They also report poorer psychosocial functioning and more missed days of work (Keyes, 2002, 2005a, 2006, 2007, 2009). Medical students who are not flourishing are prone to consider dropping out of school and to attempt suicide (Dyrbye et al., 2012).

Table 8.1 Work Losses and Medical Visits Attributable to Mental Health Condition

		Missed days of work	Days of work cut back	Medical visits: physical health	Medical visits: emotional, mental health
Depressed	N	281	273	276	279
	Days or visits per year	22.8	31	4.7	6.4
	Days or visits due to condition	6,407	8,518	1,297	1,786
	Percentage of total days	42.5%	43.5%	22.4%	45.1%
Not flourishing	N	1,416	1,408	1,420	1,442
	Days or visits per year	5.5	6.8	2.6	1.3
	Days or visits due to condition	7,816	9,631	3,692	1,875
	Percentage of total days	51.9%	49.2%	63.6%	47.3%
Flourishing	N	368	368	369	374
	Days or visits per year	2.3	3.8	2.2	0.81
	Days or visits due to condition	839	1,413	812	303
	Percentage of total days	5.6%	7.2%	14.0%	7.6%
Total days or visits		15,062	19,562	5,801	3,964

Note: Days per year = Mean per month ×12; Days due to condition = N × Days or visits per year; Percentage of total days = Days due to condition ÷ Total days or visits; Total days or visits = Σ(Days or visits due to condition).

Missed days of work are a burden at the societal level. Missed days accrue both because people lag in mental health and because they suffer from mental illness. However, the number of total missed days due to lags in mental health is notably higher because of the larger percentage of the population that is not flourishing. Among adults currently employed in the MIDUS sample, the average depressed individual misses 22.8 days a year and cuts back on another 31 days annually (see Appendix for questions used to measure work losses). In contrast, an adult who is not flourishing misses 5.5 days of work a year and cuts back on another 6.8 days annually. However, when missed and cutback workdays are multiplied by the number of individuals in each mental health condition, adults who not flourishing have slightly more work losses than adults who are depressed. Adults who are not flourishing constitute 52% of total days missed annually compared to about 43% for depressed adults; adults not flourishing constitute 49%, compared to 44% for depressed adults, of days cut back. Individuals flourishing report very few missed days of work and very few cut back workdays. In terms of lost productivity, adults who are not depressed but not flourishing represent as significant of a burden to workplaces as individuals who are depressed.

Medical visits, like lost work productivity, constitute a large part of employers' healthcare costs. Among adults currently employed in the MIDUS sample, the average depressed individual has nearly 5 medical visits for physical health and another 6 visits for mental health (see the Appendix for questions used to measure medical visits). In contrast, an adult who is not flourishing has about 2 visits for physical and 1 visit for mental health annually. However, when medical visits are multiplied by the number of individuals in each mental health condition, adults who not flourishing represent a significantly larger number of medical visits for physical and mental health than adults who are depressed. Adults who are not flourishing constitute about 64%, compared to 22% of depressed adults, of total medical visits for physical health. Adults not flourishing constitute 47%, compared with 45% for depressed adults, of total medical visits for mental health. In terms of medical usage, adults who are not depressed but not flourishing represent as significant if not more of a burden to workplaces as individuals who have depression.

Most importantly, individuals who are not flourishing are more likely to die than those who are flourishing. An analysis of all-cause mortality in the ten-year period between the 1995 and 2005 waves of MIDUS compared the mortality of nonflourishers and flourishers (Keyes and Simoes, 2012). The odds of dying among nonflourishers were 62% higher, after adjusting for known predictors of mortality. Additionally, people with low wellbeing exhibit higher levels of an inflammatory biomarker (Morozink et al., 2010) and an adverse response pattern at the gene transcription level (Fredrickson et al., 2013).

Recovery

The United States Substance Abuse and Mental Health Services Administration (SAMHSA, 2011) recently defined recovery as a "process of change through which individuals improve their health, live a self-directed life, and strive to reach their full potential." SAMHSA posits four dimensions to recovery – health, home, purpose and community – and ten guiding principles of recovery, which include "Recovery is holistic," "Recovery is supported through relationship and social networks" and "Recovery involves individual, family, and community strengths and responsibility." Notably, SAMHSA's corresponding press release excludes two terms: symptoms and illness. The emphasis on the fulfilment of potential and the avoidance of pathogenic terminology hints at a salutogenic approach. As proponents of the two-continua model, we find this heartening, but we propound the complete state model as the best alternative.

What can professionals do to promote positive mental health among recovering patients? In therapeutic settings, clinicians can incorporate techniques such as mindfulness (see Chapter 10), positive psychotherapy (see Chapter 11) and well-being therapy (Ruini and Fava, 2012), which uses Ryff's (1989) model of psychological wellbeing. Clinicians may also differentiate between deficits of emotional wellbeing, psychological wellbeing or social wellbeing.

Sustained increases in emotional wellbeing are elusive because of the "hedonic treadmill" effect. People get habituated to enhancements and revert to their baseline. Overcoming this effect requires mental engagement in continuous appreciation, the practice of variety and the redesign of environments to afford more opportunities for happiness and fewer opportunities for sadness, fear and confusion (Dolan, 2014; Sheldon and Lyubomirsky, 2012).

Money ostensibly promotes hedonic wellbeing, but spending money in a materialist fashion provides ephemeral delight. A better strategy is to spend money on *others*. Such spending elevates positive relations with others, mastery and autonomy, which compose psychological wellbeing (Dunn et al., 2014).

Elevating positive self-regard, another facet of psychological wellbeing, can be challenging. People may feel that their illness has irrevocably contaminated their life story. Yet when people find opportunities for growth, they can reinterpret their illness experience as instructive and build a redemptive life narrative. Such narratives are associated with improvements in mental health (Adler et al., 2015).

Social wellbeing may be the most difficult to enhance. Indeed, some may deem society as dysfunctional because of valid experiences. Taking a top-down approach, governments can also increase social wellbeing by moving beyond treatment and unconditionally sharing resources with homeless people with mental illnesses (e.g. Kirst et al., 2014). Among other classes, there are novel opportunities such as participation in the "sharing economy" whereby people provide an unmediated service that promotes connection rather than alienation. These opportunities provide social integration and social contribution.

Speaking of social contribution, we began this chapter with a reference to John Snow, a doctor who alleviated suffering and bestowed future generations with knowledge. Yet one aspect of Snow's story, often overlooked, is that Snow was just a clinician. He was not officially obliged to tackle an epidemic, but he was intrinsically motivated to investigate the epidemiology of cholera. Thus, the work of John Snow may have been pathogenic, but the person of John Snow was salutogenic. Health professionals may benefit from seeing the salutogenic nature of their own work and from seeing the potential of recovering patients to be generative individuals. Not every person can have the fame of Snow, but people can attain comparable vitality and generativity. Pathogenic models leave no space for these traits, but the complete state model incorporates them.

References

Adler, J. M., Turner, A. F., Brookshier, K. M., Monahan, C., Walder-Biesanz, I., Harmeling, L. H., et al. (2015). Variation in narrative identity is associated with trajectories of mental health over several years. *Journal of Personality and Social Psychology*, 108(3), 476–496.

Allport, G. W. (1961). *Pattern and Growth in Personality*. New York, NY: Holt, Runehart, & Winston.

Aristotle (1925). *The Nicomachean Ethics* (D. Ross, Trans.). New York, NY: Oxford University Press.

Baltes, P. B. (1987). Theoretical propositions of life-span developmental psychology: On the dynamics between growth and decline. *Developmental Psychology*, 23, 611–626.

Butler, J., & Kern, M. L. (2013). *The PERMA-Profiler*. Available at http://margaretkern.org/Questionnaires_files/The%20PERMA-Profiler%20101314.pdf.

Cantril, H. (1965). *The Pattern of Human Concerns*. New Brunswick, NJ: Rutgers University Press.

Csikszentmihalyi, M. (1975). *Beyond Boredom and Anxiety*. San Francisco, CA: Jossey-Bass.

Diener, E. (1984). Subjective well-being. *Psychological Bulletin*, 95, 542–575.

Diener, E. (1994). Assessing subjective well-being: Progress and opportunities. *Social Indicators Research*, 31, 103–157.

Diener, E., Wirtz, D., Tov, W., Kim-Prieto, C., Choi, D. W., Oishi, S., et al. (2010). New well-being measures: Short scales to assess flourishing and positive and negative feelings. *Social Indicators Research*, 97(2), 143–156.

Dolan, P. (2014). *Happiness by Design*. New York, NY: Hudson Street Press.

Dunn, E. W., Aknin, L. B., & Norton, M. I. (2014). Prosocial spending and happiness: Using money to benefit others pays off. *Current Directions in Psychological Science*, 13(2), 347–355.

Dyrbye, L. N., Harper, W., Moutier, C., Durning, S. J., Power, D. V., Massie, F. S., et al. (2012). A multi-institutional study exploring the impact of positive mental health on medical students' professionalism in an era of high burnout. *Academic Medicine*, 87(8), 1024–1031.

Fava, G. A., Rafanelli, C., Grandi, S., Conti, S., & Belluardo, P. (1998). Prevention of recurrent depression with cognitive behavioral therapy: Preliminary findings. *Archives of General Psychiatry*, 55(9), 816–820.

Fredrickson, B. L., Grewen, K. M., Coffey, K. A., Algoe, S. B., Firestine, A. M., Arevalo, J. M., et al. (2013). A functional genomic perspective on human well-being. *Proceedings of the National Academy of Sciences*, 110, 13, 684–13,689.

Gallagher, M. W., Lopez, S. J., & Preacher, K. J. (2009). The hierarchical structure of well-being. *Journal of Personality*, 77, 1025–1049.

Gurin, G., Veroff, J., & Feld, S. (1960). *Americans view their mental health*. New York, NY: Basic Books.

Huppert, F. A., & So, T. T. (2013). Flourishing across Europe: Application of a new conceptual framework for defining well-being. *Social Indicators Research*, 110 (3), 837–861.

Jahoda, M. (1958). *Current Concepts of Positive Mental Health*. New York, NY: Basic Books.

Joshanloo, M., Wissing, M. P., Khumalo, I. P., & Lamers, S. M. A. (2013). Measurement invariance of the Mental Health Continuum – Short Form (MHC-SF) across three cultural groups. *Personality and Individual Differences*, 55, 755–759.

Kendler, K. S., Myers, J. M., Maes, H. H., & Keyes, C. L. M. (2011). The relationship between the genetic and environmental influences on common internalizing psychiatric disorders and mental well-being. *Behavior Genetics*, 41, 641–650.

Kern, M. L., Waters, L. E., Adler, A., & White, M. A. 2015. A multidimensional approach to measuring well-being in students: Application of the PERMA framework. *Journal of Positive Psychology*, 10(3), 262–271.

Kessler, R. C., Andrews, G., Mroczek, D, Ustun, B., & Wittchen, H.-U. (1998). The World Health Organization Composite International Diagnostic Interview Short Form (CIDI–SF). *International Journal of Methods in Psychiatric Research*, 7, 171–185.

Keyes, C. L. M. (1998). Social well-being. *Social Psychology Quarterly*, 61, 121–140.

Keyes, C. L. M. (2002). The mental health continuum: From languishing to flourishing in life. *Journal of Health and Social Behavior*, 43, 207–222.

Keyes, C. L. M. (2005a). Mental illness and/or mental health? Investigating axioms of the complete state model of health. *Journal of Consulting and Clinical Psychology*, 73, 539–548.

Keyes, C. L. M. (2005b). The subjective well-being of America's youth: Toward a comprehensive assessment. *Adolescent and Family Health*, 4, 3–11.

Keyes, C. L. M. (2006). Mental health in adolescence: Is America's youth flourishing? *American Journal of Orthopsychiatry*, 76(3), 395–402.

Keyes, C. L. M. (2007). Promoting and protecting mental health as flourishing: A complementary strategy for improving national mental health. *American Psychologist*, 62(2), 95–108.

Keyes, C. L. M. (2009). The nature and importance of positive mental health in America's adolescents. In R. Gilman, E. S. Huebner, & M. J. Furlong (Eds.), *Handbook of Positive Psychology in Schools* (pp. 9–23). New York, NY: Routledge.

Keyes, C. L. M. (2013). Mental health as a complete state: The salutogenic perspective completes the picture. In G. F. Bauer & O. Hämmig (Eds.), *Bridging Occupational, Organization and Public Health: A Transdisciplinary Approach* (pp. 179–192). Dordrecht, the Netherlands: Springer.

Keyes, C. L. M., Dhingra, S. S., & Simoes, E. J. (2010a). Change in level of positive mental health as a predictor of future risk of mental illness. *American Journal of Public Health*, 100, 2366–2371.

Keyes, C. L. M., Myers, J. M., & Kendler, K. S. (2010b). The structure of the genetic and environmental influences on mental well-being. *American Journal of Public Health*, 100, 2379–2384.

Keyes, C. L. M., & Simoes, E. J. (2012). To flourish or not: Positive mental health and all cause mortality. *American Journal of American Public Health*, 102(11), 2164–2172.

Keyes, C. L. M., Wissing, M., Potgieter, J. P., Temane, M., Kruger, A., & van Rooy, S. (2008). Evaluation of the Mental Health Continuum Short Form (MHC-SF) in Setswana-speaking South Africans. *Clinical Psychology and Psychotherapy*, 15, 181–192.

Kirst, M., Zerger, S., Harris, D. W., Plenert, E., & Stergiopoulos, V. (2014). The promise of recovery: Narratives of hope among homeless individuals with mental illness participating in a Housing First randomised controlled trial in Toronto. *BMJ Open*, 14, e004378.

Lamers, S. M. A., Glas, C. A., Westerhof, G. J., & Bohlmeijer, E. T. (2012). Longitudinal evaluation of the Mental Health Continuum – Short Form (MHC-SF). *European Journal of Psychological Assessment*, 28(4), 290–296.

Lazarus, R. S., & Folkman, S. (1984). *Stress, Appraisal, and Coping*. New York, NY: Springer.

Morozink, J. A., Friedman, E. M., Coe, C. L., & Ryff, C. D. (2010). Socioeconomic and psychosocial predictors of interleukin-6 in the MIDUS national sample. *Health Psychology*, 29(6), 626–635.

NPR (May 4, 2015). People's Republic of Uber: Making friends, chauffeuring people in China. Available at http://www.npr.org/sections/parallels/2015/05/04/403251841/peoples-republic-of-uber-driving-for-connections-in-china.

Peterson, C., & Seligman, M. E. (2004). *Character strengths and virtues: A handbook and classification*. Oxford, UK: Oxford University Press.

Robitschek, C., & Keyes, C. L. M. (2009). The structure of Keyes' model of mental health and the role of personal growth initiative as a parsimonious predictor. *Journal of Counseling Psychology*, 56, 321–329.

Ruini, C., & Fava, G. A. (2012). Role of well-being therapy in achieving a balanced and individualized path to optimal functioning. *Clinical Psychology & Psychotherapy*, 19(4), 291–304.

Ryff, C. D. (1989). Happiness is everything, or is it? Explorations on the meaning of psychological well-being. *Journal of Personality and Social Psychology*, 57, 1069–1081.

Seligman, M. E. P. (2012). *Flourish: A visionary new understanding of happiness and well-being*. New York, NY: Simon and Schuster.

Sheldon, K. M., & Lyubomirsky, S. (2012). The challenge of staying happier: Testing the hedonic adaptation prevention model. *Personality and Social Psychology Bulletin*, 38(5), 670–680.

Thompson, E. R. (2007). Development and validation of an internationally reliable short-form of the positive and negative affect schedule (PANAS). *Journal of Cross-Cultural Psychology*, 38, 227–242.

U.S. Substance Abuse and Mental Health Services Administration (Dec. 22, 2011). SAMHSA announces a working definition of "recovery" from mental disorders and substance use disorders [Press release]. Available at http://www.samhsa.gov/newsroom/press-announcements/201112220300.

Watson, D., Clark, L. A., & Tellegen, A. (1988). Development and validation of brief measures of positive and negative affect: The PANAS scales. *Journal of Personality and Social Psychology*, 54, 1063–1070.

Werner, E. E., & Smith, R. (1977). *Kauai's children come of age*. Honolulu: University of Hawaii Press.

Westerhof, G. J., & Keyes, C. L. M. (2010). Mental illness and mental health: The two continua model across the lifespan. *Journal of Adult Development*, 17, 110–119.

WHO (1948). *Preamble to the Constitution of the World Health Organization as adopted by the International Health Conference, New York, 19–22 June 1946*. Geneva, Switzerland: World Health Organization.

Appendix

Analyses were done on the 1995 Midlife in the United States random digit dialing sample of currently employed adults. The data were weighted. The sample weight poststratifies the sample to match the proportions of adults according to age, gender, education, marital status, race, residence (i.e. metropolitan and nonmetropolitan) and region (Northeast, Midwest, South, and West), based on the October 1995 Current Population Survey.

Currently employed. What about your current employment situation – are you working now for pay, self-employed, looking for work, temporarily laid off, retired, a homemaker, a full-time student, or something else? Analyses were done on respondents who self-reported working now for pay or being self-employed.

Number of missed days of work. In the past 30 days, how many days were you totally unable to go to work or carry out your normal household work activities because of your physical health or mental health? (If necessary, probe: "What's your best estimate?")

Number of work days cut back. Aside from that day/those days when you were totally unable to go to work or carry out your normal household work activities, how many of the other days out of the past 30/how many of the past 30 days did you have to cut back on work or how much you got done, because of your physical health or mental health? (If necessary probe: "What's your best estimate?")

Medical visits for physical health. Please indicate how many times you saw each of the following doctors *in the past 12 months* about your physical health. Include only visits regarding your own physical health, not visits when you took someone else to be examined.

a. A doctor, hospital or clinic for a routine physical check-up or gynecological exam.
b. A doctor, emergency room, or clinic for urgent care treatment (for example, because of new symptoms, an accident or something else unexpected).
c. A doctor, hospital, clinic, dentist or ophthalmologist for scheduled treatment or surgery.

Medical visits for mental, emotional reasons. Please indicate how many times you saw each of the following professionals *in the past 12 months* about a problem with your emotional or mental health or about personal problems, such as problems with marriage, alcohol or drugs or job stress. Include both individual visits and group sessions regarding your own problems, but not visits when you took some one else regarding their problems.

a. A psychiatrist.
b. A general practitioner or other medical doctor.
c. A psychologist, professional counselor, marriage therapist or social worker.
d. A minister, priest, rabbi or other spiritual advisor.

Section 2

What Does a Wellbeing Orientation Mean in Mental Health Services?

Chapter

9

Collaborative Recovery Model
From Mental Health Recovery to Wellbeing

Lindsay G. Oades, Frank P. Deane and Trevor P. Crowe

Traditional mental health care emphasises *living with fewer symptoms*; mental health recovery may be seen as *living well with illness* and wellbeing as simply *living well*. Within this spectrum of aims, this chapter describes the evolution of the Collaborative Recovery Model (CRM) from its origins around the year 1998 until now. The CRM is a conceptual model and training/coaching resource designed to support (a) mental health service provision to become more recovery-oriented and (b) mental health organisational development consistent with mental health recovery values. Through training and coaching, the CRM assists mental health staff and consumers to emphasise hope for recovery, personal meaning and growth in the lives of both people living with mental illness and the staff of the services. Evaluation of this program has been supported by National Health and Medical Research Council and Australian Research Council funding. To maximise quality distribution and sustainability, Neami National, a nongovernmental mental organisation in Australia, was granted a ten-year exclusive license to use the IP from the CRM suite of programs in order to provide training services to other agencies in Australia. Since the license was granted, Neami National has provided training to over 700 practitioners in Australia, on top of the previous 2000 practitioners trained by the University of Wollongong in Australia, China and Canada.

CRM involves two guiding principles and four components. The first guiding principle, 'recovery as an individual process', is underpinned by a model of psychological recovery. In the following chapter psychological recovery is described and contextualised in relation to established theories of wellbeing. The overall CRM is then described, with reference to both the staff training/coaching version referred to as "Coach" and the assisted peer support version referred to as "Flourish". The chapter concludes with reflections upon the challenges of implementation and organisational change within mental health services.

Psychological Recovery

Psychological recovery refers to the establishment of a fulfilling, meaningful life and a positive sense of identity founded on hopefulness and self-determination (Andresen et al., 2003; Slade, 2009; Slade et al., 2008). The model of psychological recovery consists of four psychological component processes and five stages of recovery (Andresen et al., 2003, 2006, 2010, 2011, 2013; Chiba et al., 2010; Copic et al., 2011; Wolstencroft et al., 2010). The four processes are (a) finding and maintaining hope, (b) taking responsibility for life and wellbeing,

Wellbeing, Recovery and Mental Health, ed. Mike Slade, Lindsay Oades and Aaron Jarden.
Published by Cambridge University Press. © Mike Slade, Lindsay Oades and Aaron Jarden 2017

Table 9.1 Five Stages of Psychological Recovery

Stage 1	Moratorium
	Characterised by denial of the 'illness identity', confusion, hopelessness, powerlessness and self-protective withdrawal. It is called moratorium because 'life is on hold'.
Stage 2	Awareness
	The person has a glimmer of hope and the realisation that recovery or change is possible. It involves an awareness of a possible self, other than that of a 'sick person'.
Stage 3	Preparation
	The person resolves to start working on recovering. This stage involves taking stock of the intact self and of one's values, strengths and weaknesses. It involves learning about mental illness and services available, learning recovery skills, becoming involved in groups, connecting with peers and building strengths and confidence.
Stage 4	Rebuilding
	The person works to form a positive identity. This involves setting and working towards personally valued goals, and may require reassessing old goals and values. This stage involves taking responsibility for managing the illness and taking control of one's life. It involves taking risks, suffering setbacks and perseverance.
Stage 5	Growth
	The person is confident in managing the illness and resilient in the face of setbacks and maintains a positive outlook. He or she has a positive sense of self, lives a full and meaningful life and looks forward to the future. Continued striving for personal growth, signifying psychological wellbeing, is a characteristic of this dynamic phase.

(Andresen et al., 2003, 2011).

(c) redefining self and identity and (d) finding meaning and purpose in life. The five conceptual stages of psychological recovery are illustrated in Table 9.1.

A full elaboration of the theoretical and empirical underpinnings of the model of psychological recovery is beyond the scope of this chapter, and the reader is referred to Andresen et al. (2003, 2011). The stages and processes were derived from narratives of people who have lived with enduring mental illness, particularly schizophrenia. Comparisons with other theoretical constructs, including positive psychological constructs, occurred after the analysis of consumer narratives. In the book *Psychological Recovery* (Andresen et al., 2011), the chapter on Psychological Recovery and Positive Psychology details the psychological recovery concepts related to positive psychology research and measurement. It also describes and compares psychological recovery with hope theory, self-determination theory, self-regulation, best possible self, strengths coaching, values clarification and post-traumatic growth (Resnick and Rosenheck, 2006). Table 9.2 further elaborates on these comparisons by contextualising the four component processes of psychological recovery in relation to an analysis of experiences of recovery (Leamy et al., 2011) and established theories.

The first row in Table 9.2 illustrates that positive emotions and future orientation are common across recovery and wellbeing, particularly through the emphasis on hope and goals (Snyder, 2000). Self and identity (Buckley-Walker et al., 2010) feature strongly in mental health recovery processes. These are also elements of Ryff's (2014) well-established theory of psychological wellbeing, which emphasises self-acceptance and complements the self-change element of goals. Meaning and purpose are part of the two recovery models

Table 9.2 Recovery Processes Compared with Established Wellbeing Theories

Andresen et al. (2003) _Lived experience_	Leamy et al. (2011) CHIME _Lived experience_	Ryff (2014) Psychological Wellbeing _General population_	Seligman (2011) Wellbeing Theory (PERMA) _General population_
Hope	Hope & optimism	Meaningful goals and purpose	Positive emotion
Identity	Identity	Self-acceptance	
Meaning & purpose	Meaning	Meaningful goals and purpose	Meaning Engagement
Responsibility	Empowerment	A sense of autonomy Environmental mastery	
	Connectedness	Quality ties Continued growth	Positive relationships Accomplishment

(Andresen et al., 2003; Leamy et al., 2011) and the two wellbeing models (Ryff, 2014; Seligman, 2011). (See Steger, Chapter 7, this volume.)

The CRM conceptualisation of psychological recovery differs from that of Leamy et al. (2011) in that it does not explicitly emphasise social components (i.e. connectedness). However, within the narrative descriptions, there clearly are many references to social relationships, but being 'psychological' recovery, the emphasis was more internal rather than externally derived. That said, it is clear that positive social relationships have a significant impact on psychological processes, and they are central to mental health recovery (Lysaker et al., 2010).

Comparison of responsibility (Andresen et al., 2003) and empowerment (Leamy et al., 2011) suggests a common agency or autonomy theme. The theme of autonomy is also evident in wellbeing theories (e.g. Ryff, 2014). Another well-established wellbeing theory, self determination theory (Deci and Ryan, 2013), also has autonomy as a universal psychological need. Hence, Table 9.2 illustrates that the themes within the lived experience of recovery are very similar to the elements in theories of wellbeing. In both cases it appears that the presence of positive attributes as opposed simply to the removal of negative attributes is central to conceptualisations of both psychological recovery and wellbeing.

The CRM conceptualisation of psychological recovery assisted with framing recovery as an individual process and was strongly informed by individuals' narratives describing their lived experiences of recovery from mental illness. However, what of the services and systems that aim to support people in recovery? How do we deliver recovery-oriented service provision? How do we change and develop organisations so that they can offer recovery consistent services? These are questions that also shaped the development of the Collaborative Recovery Model (CRM) and which we sought to answer through research on the model (Oades et al., 2005, 2013). The two guiding principles and four components of the model summarised in Table 9.3 are now outlined.

Guiding principle 1: Recovery as an individual process. Based on the model of psychological recovery just described, the first principle emphasizes the personal subjective ownership of the recovery process, including hopefulness and personal meaning. It covers issues related to personal identity, particularly the need to move beyond illness and towards one's best possible self. Finally, it encourages individuals to take responsibility for their own well-being (Andresen et al., 2003).

Table 9.3 Architecture of the Collaborative Recovery Model (CRM)

Two guiding principles

(1) Recovery as an individual process
(2) Collaboration and autonomy support

Four components

(1) Change enhancement
(2) Strengths use and values alignment
(3) Collaborative life visioning and goal striving
(4) Collaborative action planning and monitoring

Within the CRM, the *focus of recovery* concept is used to clarify the intervention or approach that is being utilized. The focus of recovery concept can be used to understand the aims of either (a) an individual-recovery-supporting intervention or (b) an overall unit within a mental health service. For example, a person in an acute phase of his or her illness is likely to be focussing in the top left quadrant, as are acute mental health units. As the individuals change, so may their necessary focus of recovery. Likewise, the purpose of a unit may legitimately be in the top left quadrant; however, to have recovery-oriented service provision, some aspects of service provision across a larger system will necessarily need to be in the bottom two quadrants, that is, approaching wellbeing.

Figure 9.1 illustrates the focus of recovery concept. This two-dimensional approach is similar to that of Keyes (2002) in that it recognises that a person can be working towards wellbeing even while still having symptoms. The top two quadrants represent the reduction and prevention of symptoms. The bottom left quadrant represents positive experiences, and the bottom right quadrant represents the use of positive traits (e.g. using strengths to generate positive experiences). The left two columns represent the present. The right two quadrants represent the future.

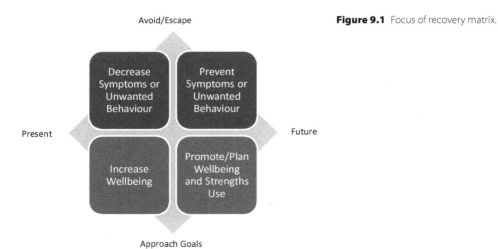

Figure 9.1 Focus of recovery matrix.

The bottom quadrants, which correspond to approach motivation, are comparable to Ben-Shahar's (2007) equation in which happiness = present benefit (pleasure) + future benefit (meaning). The 'recovery as an individual process' guiding principle is used in training and coaching of mental health practitioners and consumers to extend their thinking beyond the top quadrants. One practical implication is the movement away from *avoidance or escape* goal setting (the traditional province of medical care) and towards *approach* goal setting (Elliot, 2006; Elliot and Sheldon, 1997).

While symptom management is important, consumers consistently state that it is only one part of their overall recovery process (Andresen et al., 2003). Furthermore, research also suggests that an avoidance focus is not optimal. For example, Elliot and Sheldon (1997) demonstrated that the pursuit of avoidance goals is related to (1) less satisfaction with goal progress in general and more negative feelings about progress towards personal goals; (2) decreased levels of self-esteem, personal control and vitality; and (3) less life satisfaction and feelings of competence relating to goal pursuit. Having a science of wellbeing to underpin the bottom two approach motivation quadrants provides a fertile base to develop new practices and better equip mental health workers to engage in recovery and wellbeing interventions.

Guiding principle 2: Collaboration and autonomy support. This principle emphasizes important aspects of the working alliance in assisting human growth. As outlined in self-determination theory (Deci and Ryan, 2013), autonomy support refers to environments that support autonomy, in turn impacting upon wellbeing. This is particularly salient in mental health contexts due to the history of paternalism and control that has pervaded so many aspects of health systems and consumer care (Andresen et al., 2003).

There is substantial evidence that supports the link between the working alliance (i.e. the relationship between mental health worker and consumer) and recovery outcomes (Deane and Crowe, 2007; Deane et al., 2010a; Hicks et al., 2012; Sun et al., 2013). However, maintaining a strong working alliance often requires the practitioner to manage interpersonal strains or alliance ruptures, reflect on his/her own reactions to the dynamics of the working relationship (e.g. increased frustration, desire to fix things or rescue the person) and maintain professional boundaries whilst striving to remain present with the person being supported. This is important, as it encourages the practitioner to track and adjust her/his approach as required (e.g. rebuild trust, establish safety, confront, explore feelings), particularly in light of the sometimes subtle changes that can occur in the relationship.

The CRM is growth- and future-focused, conceptualised as a strengths-based coaching model, in which the relationships are coaching relationships rather than counselling or clinical-style relationships (Bianco-Mathis et al., 2002; Oades and Crowe, 2008; Green et al., 2006; Joseph, 2006; Oades et al., 2009; Oades & Passmore, 2014, Martin et al., 2014; Spence and Oades, 2011). To assist with the coaching methods, a protocol referred to as Life Journey Enhancement Tools (LifeJET) (Oades and Crowe, 2008) is employed within CRM. This is made up of four tools using the metaphor of a journey, which is consistent with many recovery metaphors (Mould et al., 2010). The tools are Camera – a coaching resource to clarify strengths and values use; Compass – a coaching resource used to specify and document valued life directions and goals; MAP – a coaching resource used to facilitate action planning and monitoring; and the Good Life Album – a tool to enable life visioning using the metaphor of a photo album. These coaching tools assist the different components of CRM, which are now described.

CRM Component 1: Change Enhancement

This component recognises that many people (including consumers, caregivers and practitioners) within the context of enduring mental illnesses such as schizophrenia, tend to believe that positive change is not possible. Change enhancement draws on skills from motivational interviewing (Miller and Rollnick, 1991) and directly challenges fixed mindsets (Dweck, 2006) regarding the potential for change. This component of the model also highlights the importance of intrinsic motivation and the personal meanings that underpin human change. It aims to shift both attitudes and beliefs about the potential for change. Moreover, it aims to encourage people to learn about the change and personal development process itself (Bridges, 2004; Joseph and Linley, 2008; Prochaska and DiClemente, 1982).

Component 2: Collaborative Strengths and Values

The clarification and use of personal strengths and values is central to the model and is the most popular component for consumers and practitioners alike. Whilst Rapp's (1998) strengths model is well known to mental health practitioners in a case management context, the Bird et al. (2012) systematic review demonstrates limited valid strengths assessments within mental health contexts.

The CRM predominantly draws from contemporary research on character strengths (Petersen and Seligman, 2004), strengths coaching (Linley and Harrington, 2006a, 2006b), values and committed action (Hayes and Strosahl, 2004; Veage et al., 2014). This component enables practitioners and consumers to clarify their personal strengths and values and use them when considering their personal goals and strivings. This is aided by the LifeJET coaching tool called Camera (Oades and Crowe, 2008). This tool enables people to document their personal strengths and/or personal values and consider how frequently or successfully they have been using these strengths or pursuing valued directions in recent times. The discussion of strengths and values is in deliberate contrast to more clinical conversations, which will often focus on illness, deficit and symptoms, usually leading to setting of avoidance/escape goals (i.e. the top two quadrants of the focus of recovery in Figure 9.1). The focus on values is also often highly motivating for participants and identification of intrinsically held values is often a strong resource for sustaining new behaviours.

Component 3: Collaborative Life Visioning and Goal Striving

This third component assumes that despite adversity, a person is still capable of developing a vision for life. The vision involves articulating the person's best possible self and striving towards approach goals that are consistent with his or her personal values and utilize his or her strengths. This work is informed by evidence derived from contexts outside of mental health services. Sheldon and Elliot's (1999) self-concordance model of health goal striving has influenced the development of goal striving training within the CRM. This emphasises the subjective ownership of goals, consistent with self-determination theory (Sheldon and Elliot, 1998).

Collaborative Goal Technology has been coined to describe the approach used in working with goals within CRM (Clarke et al., 2006). This approach uses a range of evidence-based practices in goal setting (e.g. goals being specific and time-limited) to assist mental health practitioners and consumers to collaboratively develop goals (Clarke et al., 2007). In 2008 the Collaborative Goal Technology was adapted and referred to as the Compass in order to better integrate it with the journey metaphor of the LifeJET package (Oades and Crowe, 2008). The Compass provides prompts to identify goals that are linked to values and also provides a structure that allows description, prioritisation and ratings of different levels of goal achievement. This provides a mechanism for formally monitoring progress towards goals.

It was found that training in this goal technology resulted in mental health practitioners developing better-quality goals with their clients and an increased likelihood of using evidence-based approaches to goal planning (Clarke et al., 2009). Subsequent research determined that the goal attainment of people with enduring mental illness mediated the relationship between the distress caused by their symptoms and their perception of personal recovery (Clarke et al., 2009). This finding suggests that goals are central to the recovery process and is consistent with the growth philosophy of the recovery movement.

Finally, amongst clients whose mental health workers had been trained in CRM, it was found that as they progressed along the stages of psychological recovery, approach goals increased in ratio to avoidance goals (Clarke et al., 2012). That is, people set goals more to achieve positive attributes than to remove negative attributes. This is consistent also with the striving processes of the bottom two quadrants of Figure 9.1 within the focus of recovery.

Component 4: Collaborative Action Planning and Monitoring

The fourth component of CRM is informed by research on (a) health behaviour change, (b) therapeutic homework (Kelly et al., 2006) and (c) self-regulation, self-efficacy and monitoring.

The term "action planning" is used in CRM because it does not carry the somewhat negative connotations many people hold with the word "homework" (Kelly et al., 2006, 2007). Meta-analyses have found that therapy outcomes are significantly better for those who receive and complete homework assignments (Kazantzis et al., 2010). Although this research has mostly focused on the treatment of depression and anxiety, there is increasing evidence of its importance in assisting people with enduring mental illnesses such as schizophrenia (Deane et al., 2005; Kelly and Deane, 2009a, 2009b, 2011). Working on agreed actions between meetings is thus an essential ingredient of CRM. Within CRM, the MAP (my action plan) coaching tool assists people with collaborative action planning.

A further important part of this component is the practice of monitoring of behaviours in line with desired goals. Completing the MAP involves a review process that also provides another way for clients to monitor their progress towards a goal. There are many examples of monitoring behaviour, from checking things on a physical calendar to biofeedback measurement of heartrate on one's wrist (e.g. Fitbit). Monitoring may enhance self-regulation and the feedback may lead to corrective actions. Moreover, if there is good behavioural progress it is likely to build self-efficacy. CRM has been designed as a goal striving cycle in which strengths, values, goals and actions are reviewed and adjusted, with the aim of assisting people to be better at value-driven goal striving in general rather than simply achieving one goal.

The Flourish Program – Peer-Assisted Personal Development

The Flourish program is based on CRM principles and uses the same journey metaphor and LifeJET tools (i.e. Compass, MAP. Etc., Oades and Crowe, 2008) as in the staff training/ coaching approaches (Oades et al., 2008). However, the program more explicitly integrates positive psychology constructs (e.g. gratitude) and is run in a group format for consumers by consumers. The program is designed to be facilitated by people with a lived experience of mental illness. This program packages many of the tools already described and is composed of three components: (1) a handbook consisting of eight learning modules (flourishing; using my strengths and values; mapping the journey of change; understanding change; living in the present; staying positive; building a success team; and reviewing my goals); (2) MP3 audios complementing the handbook materials; (3) a consumer peer-led support group (Oades et al., 2008). The program is designed to run over eight sessions and between and during each two sessions participants are encouraged to complete one learning module. This usually involves reading the set topic's material, listening to audio resources and completing set exercises. Semistructured peer-facilitated group discussions are also conducted.

Organisational Development of Mental Health Services and Implementation Issues

Unlike many discrete and individual interventions, the CRM (Oades, 2012; Oades et al., 2013), is a broad systemic framework designed to guide a range of interventions with consumers, caregivers, staff and organizational systems towards recovery-oriented services. The systemic nature of the interventions is imperative given the ingrained culture and history of psychiatric service provision (Davidson et al., 2010). Positive institutions enable people to use their positive traits, such as strengths and values, which in turn yield positive experiences, including positive emotions. In mental health services, organizations require change to enable staff and consumers to utilize strengths and to enable the possibility of the benefits of positive emotions (Park et al., 2004). Without such comprehensive change, recovery-oriented services are unlikely to succeed. The CRM is informed by the principles, evidence and practices of positive psychology and positive organisational scholarship (Cameron et al., 2003; Oades et al., 2013). As detailed below, the use of strengths coaching and parallel process across the organisation rather than only with consumers seeks to build positive organisations.

Le Boutillier et al. (2015) describe the competing priorities of staff when trying to support recovery, which may impact implementation of recovery oriented approaches. During the development and evolution of CRM there have been numerous strategies for improving implementation of the CRM concepts and practices (Deane et al., 2006; Uppal et al., 2010). This began with booster sessions to training programs (Crowe et al., 2006) and the addition of follow-up coaching to increase program implementation (Deane et al., 2010). Within mental health service organisations, parallel process coaching has also been implemented to assist with increased uptake and organisational change (Crowe et al., 2011). In the initial training of staff to use the CRM approach, this includes a focus on values clarification (Deane et al., 2014; Williams et al., 2013). This parallel process has been most strongly elaborated in the coaching processes (Crowe et al., 2011). This involves mental health staff being coached using exactly the same protocols of LifeJET (i.e. Camera for strengths/values clarification and use, Compass for life visioning and goal striving, MAP for action planning and monitoring) in their own lives as are used with service consumers. Coaches utilise these protocols with a focus on general values and goals but also work-specific values and goals. Aspects of parallel process are not limited to the shared structure of the protocols but also carry over to the relational aspects of the coaching process, which have many parallels with the service consumer and mental health worker relationship (Sun et al., 2013). Preliminary research findings indicate that when mental health workers experience shifts towards holding their work values more intrinsically (i.e. more freely and wholeheartedly), there is a decrease in their intentions of leaving their jobs. Further, CRM training and values-based coaching using parallel processes as described above have been associated with greater evidence of recovery-oriented service provision based on pre-/postintervention clinical file audits (Deane et al., 2014). Finally, as with clients who have a mental illness, those mental health workers who were more successful at pursuing valued directions in both work and life in general also had higher ratings of personal wellbeing (Veage et al., 2014). Together, these findings highlight the potential for using parallel processes in both training and coaching of mental health workers that are likely to be mirrored in their work with clients who have mental illnesses. Further, these parallels can be traced back to the substantial overlap in personal recovery as described above and many of the wellbeing theories described by others. The CRM, along with its component tools, offers a framework for working at individual and organisational levels to ultimately support the recovery of people with persistent and recurrent mental illnesses.

References

Andresen, R., Caputi, P., & Oades, L. (2006). The Stages of Recovery instrument: Development of a measure of recovery from serious mental illness. *Australian & New Zealand Journal of Psychiatry*, 40, 972–980.

Andresen, R., Oades, L. G., & Caputi, P. (2003). The experience of recovery from schizophrenia: Towards an empirically validated stage model. *Australian and New Zealand Journal of Psychiatry*, 37, 586–594.

Andresen, R., Oades, L. G., & Caputi, P. (2011). *Psychological recovery from mental illness: A stage model and method*. Chichester, UK: Wiley Blackwell.

Andresen, R., Oades, L., & Caputi, P. (2010). Do clinical outcome measures assess consumer-defined recovery? *Psychiatry Research*, 117, 309–317.

Andresen, R., Caputi, P., & Oades, L. (2013). Development of a short measure of psychological recovery in serious mental illness: The STORI-30. *Australasian Psychiatry*, 21(3), 267–270.

Ben Shahar, T. (2007). *Happier: Learn the secrets to daily joy and lasting fulfilment*. New York, NY: McGraw Hill.

Bianco-Mathis, V. E., Nabors, L. K., & Roman, C. H. (2002). *Leading from the inside out: A coaching model*. Thousand Oaks, CA: Sage.

Bird, V. J., Le Boutillier, C., Leamy, M., Larsen, J., Oades, L. G., Williams, J., et al. (2012, June 18). Assessing the strengths of mental health consumers: A systematic review. Psychological Assessment. Advance online publication. doi:10.1037/a0028983.

Bridges, W. (2004). *Transitions: Making sense of life's changes*. Cambridge, MA: Da Capo Press.

Buckley-Walker, K., Crowe, T. P., & Caputi, P. (2010). Exploring identity within the recovery process of people with serious mental illnesses. *Psychiatric Rehabilitation Journal*, 33(3), 219–227.

Cameron, K., Dutton, J. E., & Quinn, R. E. (Eds.)(2003). *Positive organizational scholarship: Foundations of a new discipline*. San Francisco, CA: Bennett-Koehler Publishers.

Chiba, R., Kawakami, N., Miyamoto, Y., & Andresen, R. (2010). Reliability and validity of the Japanese version of the Self-Identified Stage of Recovery (SISR) for people with long-term mental illness. *International Journal of Mental Health Nursing*, 19(3), 195–202.

Clarke, S. P., Crowe, T. P., Oades, L. G., & Deane, F. P. (2009). Do goal setting interventions improve the quality of goals in mental health services? *Psychiatric Rehabilitation Journal*, 32(4), 292–299.

Clarke, S., Oades, L. G., & Crowe, T. P. (2007) Collaborative goal technology. Theory and practice. *Psychiatric Rehabilitation Journal*, 30, 129–136.

Clarke, S., Oades, L. G., & Crowe, T. P. (2012). Recovery in mental health: A movement towards wellbeing and meaning in contrast with an avoidance of symptoms. *Psychiatric Rehabilitation Journal*, 35(4), 297–304.

Clarke, S., Oades, L., Crowe, T., Caputi, P., & Deane, F. P. (2009). The role of symptom distress and goal attainment in assisting the psychological recovery in consumers with enduring mental illness. *Journal of Mental Health*, 18, 389–397.

Copic, V., Deane, F. P., Crowe, T. P., & Oades, L. G. (2011). Hope, meaning and responsibility across stages of psychological recovery for individuals living with an enduring mental illness. *Australian Journal of Rehabilitation Counselling*, 17(2), 61–73.

Crowe, T. P., Deane, F.P., Oades, L. G., Caputi, P., & Morland, K. G. (2006). Effectiveness of a collaborative recovery training program in Australia in promoting positive views about recovery. *Psychiatric Services*, 57, 1497–1500.

Crowe, T. P., Oades, L. G., Deane, F. P., Ciarrochi, J., & Williams, V. (2011). Parallel processes in clinical supervision: Implications for coaching mental health practitioners. *International Journal of Evidence Based Coaching and Mentoring*, 9(2), 56–66.

Davidson, L. Rakfleldt, J., & Strauss, J. (2010). *The roots of the recovery movement in psychiatry: Lessons learned*. Oxford, UK: Wiley-Blackwell.

Deane, F. P., Andresen, R., Crowe, T. P., Oades, L., Ciarrochi, J., & Williams, V. (2014). A comparison of two coaching approaches to enhance implementation of a recovery-oriented mental health service model. *Administration and Policy in Mental Health and Mental Health Services Research*, 41(5), 660–667. doi:10.1007/s10488-013-0514-4.

Deane, F. P., & Crowe, T. P. (2007). Building and maintaining a recovery focused therapeutic relationship. In King, R., Lloyd C., and Meehan T. (Eds.) (pp. 57–70), *Handbook of Psychosocial Rehabilitation*. Oxford, UK: Blackwell.

Deane, F. P., Crowe, T. P., King, R., Oades, L. G., & Kavanagh, D. J. (2006). Challenges in implementing evidence-based practice in mental health services. *Australian Health Review*, 30, 305–309.

Deane, F. P., Crowe, T. P., & Oades, L. G. (2010a) Therapeutic alliance in vocational rehabilitation. In Lloyd, C. (Ed.) (pp. 95–113), *Vocational Rehabilitation and Mental Health*. Oxford, UK: Wiley-Blackwell.

Deane, F. P., Crowe, T. P., Oades, L. G., Ciarrochi, J., Marshall, S., Williams, V., et al. (2010b). *Facilitating the transfer of collaborative recovery training into clinical practice: Intervention and coaching protocols*. Wollongong, Australia: Illawarra Institute for Mental Health, University of Wollongong.

Deane, F. P., Glaser, N. M., Oades, L. G., & Kazantzis, N. (2005). Psychologists' use of homework assignments with clients who have schizophrenia. *Clinical Psychologist*, 9, 24–30.

Deci, E. L., & Ryan, R. M. (2013). The importance of autonomy for development and well-being. In Sokol, B. W., Grouzet, F. M. E., & Muller, U. (Eds.), *Self-regulation and autonomy: Social and developmental dimensions of human conduct* (pp. 19–46). Cambridge, UK: Cambridge University Press.

Dweck, C. S. (2006). *Mindset: The new psychology of success*. New York, NY: Random House.

Elliot, A. (2006). The hierarchical model of approach–avoidance motivation. *Motivation and Emotion*, 30, 111–116.

Elliot, A. J., & Sheldon, K. M. (1997). Avoidance achievement motivation: A personal goals analysis. *Journal of Personality and Social Psychology*, 73, 171–185.

Green, L. S., Oades, L. G., & Grant, A. M. (2006). Cognitive-behavioural, solution-focused life coaching: Enhancing goal striving, well-being and hope. *Journal of Positive Psychology*, 1, 142–149.

Hayes, S. S., & Strosahl, K. (2004). *A practical guide to acceptance and commitment therapy*. New York, NY: Springer Science, Media & Business.

Hicks, A., Deane, F. P., & Crowe, T. P. (2012). Changes in working alliance and recovery in severe mental illness: An exploratory study. *Journal of Mental Health* 21(2), 127–134. doi:10.3109/09638237.2011.621469

Joseph, S. (2006). Person-centred coaching psychology: A meta-theoretical perspective. *International Coaching Psychology Review*, 1(1), 47–54.

Joseph, S., & Linley, P. A. (Eds.) (2008). *Trauma, recovery and growth: Positive psychological perspectives on post-traumatic stress*. Hoboken, NJ: John Wiley & Sons.

Kazantzis, N., Whittington, C., & Dattilio, F. (2010) Meta-analysis of homework effects in cognitive and behavioral therapy: A replication and extension. *Clinical Psychology: Science and Practice*, 17, 144–156.

Kelly, P. J., Deane, F. P., Kazantzis, N., Crowe, T. P., & Oades, L. G. (2006). Use of homework by mental health case managers in the rehabilitation of persistent and recurring psychiatric disorders. *Journal of Mental Health*, 15(1), 95–102.

Kelly, P. J., Deane, F. P., Kazantzis, N., & Crowe, T. P. (2007). Case managers' attitudes toward the use of homework for people diagnosed with a severe psychiatric disability. *Rehabilitation Counseling Journal*, 51, 34–43.

Kelly, P. J., Deane, F. P., King, R., Kazantzis, N., & Crowe, T. P. (2007). A taxonomy for homework used by mental health case managers when working with individuals with severe and persistent mental disability. *Community Mental Health Journal*, 43, 565–581.

Kelly, P. J., & Deane, F. P. (2009a). Does homework improve outcomes for individuals diagnosed with severe mental illness? *Australian and New Zealand Journal of Psychiatry*, 43, 968–975.

Kelly, P. J., & Deane, F. P. (2009b). (Frontline report). The use of therapeutic homework to support recovery from severe mental illness. *Psychiatric Services*, 60, 1391.

Kelly, P. J., & Deane, F. P. (2011). Do therapeutic homework assignments address areas of need for individuals with serious mental illness? *Community Mental Health Journal*, 47, 124–200.

Keyes, C. L. (2002). The mental health continuum: From languishing to flourishing in life. *Journal of Health and Social Behavior*, 43, 207–222.

Leamy, M., Bird, V., Le Boutillier, C., Williams, J., & Slade, M. (2011). Conceptual framework for personal recovery in mental health: Systematic review and narrative synthesis. *British Journal of Psychiatry* 199, 445–452. doi:10.1192/bjp.bp.110.083733.

Le Boutillier, C., Slade, M., Lawrence, V., Bird, V., Chandler, R., Farkas, M., et al. (2015). Competing priorities: Staff perspectives on supporting recovery. *Administration and Policy in Mental Health and Mental Health Services Research*, 42, 429–438.

Linley, P. A., & Harrington, S. (2006a). Playing to your strengths. *The Psychologist*, 19, 86–89.

Linley, P. A., & Harrington, S. (2006b). Strengths coaching: A potential-guided approach to coaching psychology. *International Coaching Psychology Review*, 1(1), 37–48.

Lysaker, P. H., Ringer, J., Maxwell, C., McGuire, A., & Lecomte, T. (2010). Personal narratives and recovery from schizophrenia. *Schizophrenia Research*, 121, 271–276.

Marshall, S., Oades, L., & Crowe, T. (2009). Mental health consumers' perceptions of receiving recovery-focused services. *Journal of Evaluation in Clinical Practice*, 15, 654–659.

Martin, L. S., Oades, L. G., & Caputi, P. (2014). Intentional personality change coaching: A randomised controlled trial of participant selected personality facet change using the Five-Factor model of personality. *International Coaching Psychology Review*, 9(2), 182–195.

Miller, W. R., & Rollnick, S. (1991). *Motivational interviewing: Preparing people for change*. New York, NY: Guilford Press.

Mould, T. J., Oades, L. G., & Crowe, T. P. (2010). The use of metaphor for understanding and managing psychotic experiences: A systematic review. *Journal of Mental Health*, 19(3), 282–293.

Oades, L. G. (2012) Responding to the challenge of mental health recovery policy. In L'Abate, L. (Ed.) (pp. 391–406), *Mental Illnesses – Evaluation, Treatments and Implications*. Vienna, Austria: InTech.

Oades, L. G., Andresen, R., Crowe, T. P., Malins, G. M., Andresen, R., & Turner, A. (2008). *A handbook to flourish. A self-development programme for people with enduring mental illness*. Wollongong, Australia: Illawarra Institute for Mental Health, University of Wollongong.

Oades, L. G. & Crowe, T. P. (2008). *Life journey enhancement tools (LifeJET)*. Wollongong, Australia: Illawarra Institute for Mental Health, University of Wollongong.

Oades, L. G., Crowe, T. P., & Nguyen, M. (2009). Leadership coaching transforming mental health systems from the inside out: The Collaborative Recovery Model as person-centred strengths based coaching psychology. *International Coaching Psychology Review*, 4, 25–36.

Oades, L. G., Deane, F. P., & Crowe, T. P. (2013). The Collaborative Recovery Model: Positive organisations enabling the use of strengths and values to serve recovery in enduring mental illness. In Boniwell, I., & David, S. (Eds.) (pp. 1050–1066), *Oxford Handbook of Happiness*. Oxford, UK: Oxford University Press.

Oades, L. G., Deane, F. P., Crowe, T. P., Lambert, W. G., Lloyd, C., & Kavanagh, D. (2005). Collaborative recovery: An integrative model for working with individuals that experience chronic or recurring mental illness. *Australasian Psychiatry*, 13(3),279–284.

Oades, L. G., & Passmore, J. (2014). Positive psychology coaching. In Passmore, J. (Ed.) (pp. 15–40), *Mastery in Coaching: A Complete Psychological Toolkit for Advanced Coaching*. London, UK: Kogan Page.

Park, N., Peterson, C., & Seligman, M. E. P. (2004). Strengths of character and well-being. *Journal of Social and Clinical Psychology*, 23, 603–619.

Peterson, C., & Seligman, M. E. P. (2004). *Character strengths and virtues: A handbook and classification*. New York, NY: Oxford University Press/Washington, DC: American Psychological Association.

Prochaska, J. O., & DiClemente, C. C. (1982) Transtheoretical therapy: Toward a more integrative model of change. *Psychotherapy Theory Research and Practice*. 19:276–88.

Rapp, C. A. (1998). *The strengths model: Case management with people suffering from severe and persistent mental illness*. New York, NY: Oxford University Press.

Resnick, S. G., & Rosenheck, R. A. (2006). Recovery and positive psychology: Parallel themes and potential synergies. *Psychiatric Services*, 57, 120–122.

Ryff, C. D. (2014). Psychological well-being revisited: Advances in the science and practice of eudaimonia. *Psychotherapy and Psychomatics*, 83, 10–28.

Seligman, M. E. P. (2011). *Flourish: A new understanding of happiness and wellbeing*. New York, NY: Free Press.

Sheldon, K. M., & Elliot, A. J. (1998). Not all personal goals are personal: Comparing autonomous and controlled reasons as predictors of attainment. *Personality and Social Psychology Bulletin*, 24, 546–547.

Sheldon, K. M., & Elliot, A. J. (1999). Goal striving, need-satisfaction, and longitudinal wellbeing: The Self-Concordance Model. *Journal of Personality and Social Psychology*, 76, 482–497.

Slade, M. (2009). *Personal recovery and mental illness. A guide for mental health professionals*. Cambridge, UK: Cambridge University Press.

Slade, M., Amering, M., & Oades, L. (2008). Recovery: An international perspective. *Epidemiologia e Psichiatria Sociale*, 17(2), 128–137.

Snyder, C. R. (Ed.) (2000). *Handbook of hope: Theory, measures and applications*. San Diego, CA: Academic Press.

Spence, G., & Oades, L. G. (2011). Coaching with self determination in mind. Using theory to advance evidence-based coaching practice. *International Journal of Evidence Based Coaching and Mentoring*, 9 (2), 37–55.

Sun, B., Deane, F. P., Crowe, T. P., Andresen, R., Oades, L., & Ciarrochi, J. (2013). A preliminary exploration of the working alliance and 'real relationship' in two coaching approaches with mental health workers. *International Coaching Psychology Review*, 8(2), 6–17.

Uppal, S., Oades, L., Crowe, T., & Deane, F. P. (2010). Barriers to transfer of collaborative recovery training into Australian mental health services: Implications for the development of evidence-based services. *Journal of Evaluation in Clinical Practice*, 16, 451–455.

Veage, S., Ciarrochi, J., Deane, F. P., Andresen, R., Oades, L., & Crowe, T. P. (2014). Value importance, success and congruence in the workplace: Links with well-being and burnout amongst mental health practitioners. *Journal of Contextual Behavioural Science*, 3, 258–264.

Williams, V., Oades, L. G., Deane, F. P., Crowe, T. P., Ciarrochi, J., & Andresen, R. (2013). Improving implementation of evidence-based practice in mental health service delivery: Protocol for a cluster randomized quasi-experimental investigation of staff focused values interventions. *Implementation Science*, 8, 75–85. doi:10.1186/1748-5908-8-75.

Wolstencroft, K., Oades, L., Caputi, P., & Andresen, R. (2010). Development of a structured interview schedule to assess stage of psychological recovery from enduring mental illness. *International Journal of Psychiatry in Clinical Practice*, 14(3), 182–189

Section 2

What Does a Wellbeing Orientation Mean in Mental Health Services?

Chapter

Positive Psychotherapy

A Wellbeing Approach to Recovery

10

Tayyab Rashid, Ryan N. Howes and Ruth Louden

Positive psychotherapy (PPT) is an emerging clinical approach that systematically and deliberately integrates symptoms with strengths, risks with resources, vulnerabilities with values, deficits with assets and despair with hope to ameliorate symptomatic distress through enhancing various elements of wellbeing. In PPT, clients fully acknowledge and appraise their struggles while simultaneously learning to develop and integrate their cognitive, emotional, social and cultural strengths to promote adaptive actions and habits. The goal is to understand clients in a balanced and coherent manner. This does not reduce them to conglomerates of symptoms nor elevate them to idols of strength. This chapter expands the psychotherapeutic notion of recovery to include nurturing wellbeing through building the client's positive attributes in addition to nursing illness and symptoms. The theoretical and empirical foundations of PPT will be discussed. Practical demonstrations and instruction on how it is to be conducted with be outlined.

Psychotherapy

Psychotherapy is a method of promoting adaptive change in individuals seeking support for life circumstances, behavioural patterns or recurrent cognitions that are felt to be distressing, maladaptive or problematic. The general effectiveness of psychotherapy in removing or at least managing symptoms and disorders is well established (Castonguay, 2013; Seligman, 1995). For symptoms of depression and anxiety, psychotherapy is as effective as psychotropic medication and perhaps better in the long term (Leykin and DuRubeis, 2009; Siddique et al., 2012).

There are many psychotherapeutic paradigms currently in practice (Wedding and Corsini, 2013). PPT is the clinical branch of positive psychology. Although positive psychology has been criticized for not exploring people's troubles deeply enough and steering people quickly to individually based positive notions (Coyne and Tennen, 2010; Ehrenreich, 2009; McNulty and Fincham, 2012), PPT advocates a balanced approach, incorporating authentic consideration of strengths with the traditional focus on symptom alleviation. This chapter advances the position that an explicit incorporation of strengths into psychotherapy can broaden its scope and effectiveness. Psychotherapy tends to place emphasis on problems to be solved, thereby introducing a negatively skewed clinical depiction of clients. Incorporating strengths helps clients expand their perception of psychotherapy beyond a place to disentangle their

Wellbeing, Recovery and Mental Health, ed. Mike Slade, Lindsay Oades and Aaron Jarden.
Published by Cambridge University Press. © Mike Slade, Lindsay Oades and Aaron Jarden 2017

distorted thinking or restore their troubled relationships to a place where they can identify, understand and amplify their strengths, skills, abilities and psychological resources.

Most clients seek therapy because they have come to believe that they are broadly inadequate or inept, incompetent or inexperienced at handling psychological distress. The brain orients towards and responds more potently to negative experiences than it does to positive experiences (Ito et al., 1998; Rozin and Royzman, 2001). Negative impressions and stereotypes are formed quickly and are harder to undo than their positive counterparts (Baumeister et al., 2001). Negative memories stay with us for days, months, or even years while positive memories tend to be transient (Beckwé et al., 2013; Nolen-Hoeksema, 1991). Focusing on events or cognitions that elicit negative emotions is an important, functional adaptation (Ford and Tamir, 2012) but can have negative consequences when indulged chronically. The adaptive value of negative emotions depends on the appropriateness of their expression to contextual needs. When negative emotions become incongruent with the environment proper, psychological symptoms and disorder may result. Throughout therapy, clients and therapists work together in a dynamic process to render intelligible the negative events and experiences that clients share by integrating them into an affectively balanced and coherent explanatory narrative that connects with and makes sense of their current situations. The purpose is to guide clients towards autonomous growth and healing. The personal narratives of clients seeking therapy are often marked by a perception that they are deeply flawed, their psychological immunity is fragile, and the wholesomeness of their selves is fractured. Asking clients to share a narrative, a story of resilience (a positive memory), is the first step towards building their self-efficacy. Research has shown that recall of positive memories plays an important role in mood regulation (Joormann et al., 2007). Moreover, the recall of positive memories often generates positive emotions at the onset of the therapeutic process, which have been argued to powerfully predict therapeutic change (Fitzpatrick and Stalikas, 2008). The balanced incorporation of positives with negatives in the client's personal narrative and self-concept seems to promote therapeutic change and facilitate growth. PPT pays equal attention and effort to strengths and symptoms, offering both therapists and clients a holistic approach to dealing with psychological distress. In doing so, PPT never dismisses, avoids or trivializes negatives or pushes clients to look for positives in a hasty or impromptu manner.

PPT: Theory, Process and Practice

PPT is based on two dominant theories in positive psychology. The first is Seligman's (2002, 2011) PERMA conceptualization of happiness and wellbeing, operationalized into five measurable, manageable, and malleable components: (1) positive emotion, (2) engagement, (3) relationships, (4) meaning and (5) accomplishment (see Table 10.1). The measures derived from this model been shown to be associated with lower rates of depression and higher life satisfaction (Asebedo and Seay, 2014; Bertisch et al., 2014; Headey et al., 2010; Lamont, 2011; Peterson et al., 2005; Sirgy and Wu 2009; Vella-Brodrick et al., 2009). The second is the Virtues in Action Character Strengths model (Peterson and Seligman, 2004). This model identifies 24 strengths that are recognized and valued across cultures (see Table 10.2 for a full list). Clients in PPT use multiple methods to identify their top five strengths, or *signature strengths*. Signature strengths are authentic if clients feel that they own them self-consciously and if they feel invigorated while using them (Seligman, 2002). As will be shown, clients learn to recognize, own and use their strengths throughout PPT to establish and pursue goals and to identify and describe their own behaviour and the behaviour of others in strengths terms.

Table 10.1 PERMA: The Theory of Wellbeing (Seligman, 2011)

Elements	Description
Positive emotions	Experiencing positive emotions such as contentment, pride, serenity, hope, optimism, trust, confidence and gratitude
Engagement	Immersing oneself deeply in activities which utilize one's strengths to experience an optimal state marked with razor-sharp concentration, optimal sate of experience with intense focus and intrinsic motivation to develop further
Relationship	Having positive, secure and trusting relationships
Meaning	Belonging to and serving something with a sense of purpose and belief that it is larger than the self
Accomplishment	Pursuing success, mastery and achievement for their own sake

Assumptions

PPT operates on three assumptions regarding the nature, cause, course and treatment of specific behavioral patterns. These assumptions have preliminary empirical support. We will present each in turn. The first is that psychopathology results from prolonged psychosocial distress that thwarts growth. The second is that positive human qualities are just as real and authentic as negative qualities. The third is that effective therapeutic relationships can be fostered through discussions of client strengths and positive qualities.

Consistent with the humanistic psychology, the first assumption of PPT is that psychopathology ensues when clients' inherent capacities for growth, fulfillment and wellbeing are thwarted by prolonged psychosocial distress. Wellbeing and psychopathology are not entirely endogenous processes; they are the result of a complex interplay between clients' inclinations and environmental factors. People become 'damaged' when this interplay becomes unsupportive, halting their growth. Psychotherapy offers a unique opportunity to initiate or restore human potential through the transformative power of human connection. Remediation makes clients less vulnerable, whereas growth makes them more resilient. Emerging evidence suggests that strengths can be used to promote personal growth, even in the face of significant adversities (Peterson et al., 2008; Bonnano, 2004).

Second, PPT considers *positive emotions and strengths to be authentic and as real as symptoms and disorders, and valuable in their own right*. Strengths are not defenses, illusions or by-products of symptom relief that sit idle on the clinical peripheries. If resentment, deception, competition, jealousy, greed, worry and stress are real, so are attributes such as honesty, cooperation, contentment, gratitude, compassion and serenity. Solid lines of research have demonstrated that absence of symptoms is not presence of mental wellbeing (Bartels et al., 2013; Keyes and Eduardo, 2012). It is therefore imperative that strengths not be considered as simply outcomes of an absence of negative traits but be recognized as independent constructs worthy of research and clinical consideration. Evidence suggests that spending as little as 10 minutes focusing on a client's strengths before each session can improve therapeutic outcomes (Flückiger and Grosse Holtforth, 2008). These findings were reinforced by subsequent research that found that such *capitalization* models (which build upon relative strengths) demonstrate faster therapeutic gains and better outcomes on depression measures than *compensation* models (which reduce relative deficits; Cheavens et al., 2012). These lines

Table 10.2 Character Strengths: Definitions and Usage (Lack/Excess)

Character strengths	Description	Lack/underuse	Excess/overuse
1 **Appreciation of beauty & excellence**	Being moved deeply by beauty in nature, in art (painting, music, theatre, etc.) or in excellence in any field of life	Oblivion	Snobbery
2 **Authenticity & honesty**	Not pretending to be someone one is not; coming across as a genuine and honest person	Shallowness, phoniness	Righteousness
3 **Bravery & valour**	Overcoming fears to do what needs to be done; not giving up in the face of a hardship or challenge	Fears, easily scared	Foolhardiness, risk-taking
4 **Creativity & originality**	Thinking of new and better ways of doing things; not being content with doing things in conventional ways	Conformity	Eccentricity
5 **Curiosity, interest in the world & openness to experience**	Being driven to explore things; asking questions, not tolerating ambiguity easily; being open to different experiences and activities	Uninterest, boredom	Nosiness
6 **Fairness, equity & justice**	Standing up for others when they are treated unfairly, bullied or ridiculed; day-to-day actions show a sense of fairness	Prejudice, partisanship	Detachment
7 **Forgiveness & mercy**	Forgiving easily those who offend; not holding grudges	Mercilessness	Permissiveness
8 **Gratitude**	Expressing thankfulness for good things through words and actions; not taking things for granted	Entitlement	Ingratiation
9 **Hope, optimism & future-mindedness**	Hoping and believing that more good things will happen than bad ones; recovering from setbacks and taking steps to overcome them	Present orientation	Panglossism
10 **Humour & playfulness**	Being playful and funny and using humour to connect with others	Humourlessness	Buffoonery
11 **Kindness & generosity**	Doing kind deeds for others, often without asking; helping others regularly; being known as a kind person	Indifference	Intrusiveness

Table 10.2 *(cont.)*

	Character strengths	Description	Lack/underuse	Excess/overuse
12	**Leadership**	Organizing activities that include others; being someone others like to follow; being chosen often to lead by peers	Compliance	Despotism
13	**Capacity to love and be loved**	Having warm and caring relationships with family and friends; showing genuine love and affection through actions regularly	Isolation, detachment	Emotional promiscuity
14	**Love of learning**	Loving to learn many things, concepts, ideas and facts in school or on one's own	Complacency	"Know-it-all"-ism
15	**Modesty & humility**	Not liking to be the center of attention; not acting as being special; admitting shortcomings readily; knowing what one can and cannot do	Unfounded self-esteem	Self-depreciation
16	**Open-mindedness & critical thinking**	Thinking through and examining all sides before deciding; consulting with others; being flexible enough to change one's mind when necessary	Unreflective	Cynicism, scepticism
17	**Perseverance, diligence & industry**	Finishing most things; being able to refocus when distracted and completing the task without complaining; overcoming challenges to complete the task	Slackness, laziness	Obsessiveness, fixation, pursuit of unattainable goals
18	**Perspective (wisdom)**	Putting things together to understand underlying meanings; settling disputes among friends; learning from mistakes	Superficiality	Ivory tower, arcane & pedantic thinking
19	**Prudence, caution & discretion**	Being careful and cautious; avoid taking undue risks; not easily yielding to external pressures	Recklessness	Prudishness, stuffiness
20	**Religiousness & spirituality**	Believing in God or higher power; liking to participate in religious or spiritual practices, such as prayer, meditation	Anomie	Fanaticism

(cont.)

Table 10.2 (cont.)

Character strengths	Description	Lack/underuse	Excess/ overuse
21 **Self-regulation & self-control**	Managing feelings and behaviour well most of the time; following rules and routines gladly	Self-indulgence	Inhibition
22 **Social intelligence**	Easily understanding others' feelings; managing oneself well in social situations; displaying excellent interpersonal skills	Obtuseness, cluelessness	Psycho-babbling
23 **Teamwork, citizenship & loyalty**	Relating well with teammates or group members; contributing to the success of the group	Selfishness & rebelliousness	Mindless & automatic obedience
24 **Zest, enthusiasm & energy**	Being energetic, cheerful and full of life; being liked by others to hang out with	Passivity, restraint	Hyperactivity

of research demonstrate that strengths have real therapeutic potential. Incorporating strengths with symptoms expands clients' self-perceptions and offers the therapist additional routes of intervening.

The third assumption of PPT is that effective therapeutic relationships can be built on exploration and analysis of positive personal characteristics and experiences (e.g. positive emotions, strengths and virtues). According to the broaden-and-build theory, positive emotions help to change a person's mindset, expanding his or her attention, broadening his or her behavioural repertoire, and enhancing his or her creativity (Fredrickson, 2001, 2004). Although fleeting in nature, positive emotions help clients to broaden their cognitive and behavioral repertoires. Clients become more open and are more likely to think of novel ideas, develop alternative solutions to their problems and reinterpret their current challenges and adopt a fresh problem-solving strategy. Thus, positive emotions build resilience by 'undoing' the effects of negative emotions (Frederickson, 2002; Xu and Robert, 2010). The exercises in PPT aim to cultivate positive emotions in clients. Interestingly, there is emerging evidence that therapist positive emotions can also have beneficial effects on client–therapist relations and treatment outcomes (Scheel et al., 2012; Vandenberghe and Silvestre, 2014), further highlighting the value of positive experiences in the therapeutic relationship. PPT's explicit address of positive emotions is in contrast to the traditional approach in which the psychotherapist analyzes and explains the constellation of symptoms to the client in the form of a diagnosis.

Process and Practice: How Does PPT Work?

There are three phases of PPT. The first phase helps clients to build self-efficacy by recalling and building personalized narratives of resilience. They also identify their salient character strengths. The second phase helps clients learn to reappraise intra- and interpersonal experiences towards the positive to promote a balance perspective. The third phase helps clients pursue meaning and purpose through their strengths. We will outline each phase in turn. Within each phase, we will describe the process and the exercises that are used as practice in session and between sessions. Table 10.3 contains a session-by-session outline of PPT. Although PPT is here demarcated in a concrete, sequential manner, therapists must use their clinical judgment to adaptively apply this process to each client.

Throughout the entire course of therapy, clients are encouraged to keep a *gratitude journal* to describe three good things that happened to them during the course of each day. Most clients find this helpful to direct their attention deliberately towards good experiences, which are often otherwise missed in the hustle and bustle of daily life. By the end of therapy, clients learn habits of journaling everyday positive experiences in written (handwritten scribbles or digital scripts), visual (taking pictures with their mobile devices) or interpersonal sharing formats. This process helps them to sustain the broader experiential awareness they learn to cultivate in sessions and continue to resist our natural penchant for the negativity bias.

Phase 1, process. The first phase of PPT occurs in the first three sessions. From the first session, clients are encouraged to share anecdotes, accounts and stories that show their strengths in tandem with their struggles; that is, to express how they have successfully coped with or overcome some challenges. The therapist empathically listens to presenting concerns of clients to establish and maintain a trusting therapeutic relationship. The discussion of symptomatic distress is deepened with a conversation about simple and unostentatious acts of kindness in everyday life, such as giving a seat on the bus to someone or helping a technologically challenged colleague with a chore that comes naturally to you. These discussions allow clients to bring their attention to small but positive aspects in their lives, which may be obscured by an excessive focus on diagnostic distress. Clients then assess their strengths through multiple resources (described in the next section) and set realistic goals that are relevant to their presenting problems and their wellbeing. The core of the first phase is introducing positives. This process is achieved primarily through writing about resilience, identifying strengths, and exploring one's signature strengths. The therapist actively looks for opportunities to help clients deepen their understanding of how strengths can be used adaptively to handle a challenging situation.

Phase 1, exercises. PPT begins with clients introducing themselves through *positive introduction*, which provides the opportunity for participants to be introduced through a story that depicts them when they believe they are at their best. For homework, participants concretize this into an approximately 300-word written story. For the remainder of the first phase, the focus is on strengths exercises. This begins with a comprehensive strengths assessment. PPT uses a valid and reliable 72-item self-report measure, the *Signature Strength Questionnaire* (Rashid et al., 2013), which is derived from the *Classification of Strengths & Virtues* and its accompanying 240-item questionnaire (Peterson and Seligman, 2004). The strengths assessment also incorporates other self-report measures (identifying strengths based on descriptions and on associated photos) and collateral reports from significant others identifying (*not ranking*) their signature strengths. The collateral reports are acquired between sessions. This comprehensive assessment process enables clients to identify, comprehend and contextualize their strengths in concrete terms. To keep signature strengths in equal prominence with symptoms throughout therapy, therapists are encouraged to gently nudge clients to share memories, experiences, real-life stories, anecdotes, accomplishments and skills that illustrate the use and development of their signature strengths.

Table 10.3 Session-by-Session Overview of PPT

Exercise & homework	Description
1 Orientation to PPT	Presenting problems are discussed in the context of a lack of positive resources such as positive emotions, engagement, positive relationship, meaning, character strengths, positive relationships and meaning.
In-session	Clients complete Positive Psychotherapy Inventory in session, score and reflect upon their scores.
	Clients introduce themselves through a story which shows them at their best.
HW: Positive introduction	Clients write a one-page (about 300 words) "positive introduction" in which they share a concrete and real life story showing them at their best.
2 Character strengths	Character strengths are defined and discussed as important ingredients of therapy; role of character strengths in problem solving and in cultivating engagement is discussed.
In-session	Clients identify their character strengths.
HW: Dynamic strengths assessment	Clients complete an online measure (Signature Strengths Questionnaire; SSQ-72); two significant others (a family member & a friend; *optional*) identify their salient character strengths, to compute their *signature strengths*.
3 Signature strengths	Clients integrate various perspectives to compute their signature strengths; goal setting is discussed.
In-session	Clients and therapist discuss specific, measurable and achievable goals targeting specific problems or to cultivate more engagement.
HW: Signature strength action plan	Clients frame specific goals into a concrete Signature Strengths Action Plan (SSAP).
4 Open & closed memories	The role of open and closed memories in maintaining psychological wellbeing (?) is discussed.
	Clients write about a negative memory and discuss its impact on their emotional wellbeing.
In-session	Positive cognitive reappraisal strategies are discussed to rewrite and repack bad and bitter memories.
HW: Positive appraisal	Clients use one or more positive cognitive reappraisal strategies towards bad memories and feelings of anger and bitterness and their impact in perpetuating emotional distress.
5 Forgiveness	Forgiveness is discussed as a potential option to transform feelings of anger and bitterness associated with a specific transgression into neutrality or even, if possible, into positive emotions.
In-session	Clients complete an exercise on what forgiveness is and what it is not.
HW: Forgiveness letter	Clients write a transgression and its related emotions and consider forgiveness as a viable option. Clients write but do not necessarily deliver the forgiveness letter.

Table 10.3 *(cont.)*

Exercise & homework	Description
6 Gratitude	Gratitude is discussed as enduring thankfulness. The roles of good and bad memories are discussed again, with an emphasis on gratitude.
In-session	Clients recall and write a first draft of a gratitude letter to someone whom they never properly thanked.
HW: Gratitude letter & visit	Clients refine the gratitude letter and deliver it in person to someone they never properly thanked.
7 Mid therapy feedback session	Signature Strengths Action Plan; the forgiveness and gratitude assignments are followed up.
In-session	Therapeutic progress is discussed. Feedback to and from clients is discussed and necessary changes are made.
HW: Exercise completion	Clients complete forgiveness and gratitude letters.
8 Satisficing vs. maximizing	Concepts of satisficing (settling for good enough) and maximizing are discussed.
In-session	Clients reflect and write areas where they maximize.
HW: Satisficing	Clients identify areas where they could benefit from satisficing.
9 Hope, optimism & post-traumatic growth	Optimism and hope are discussed in detail.
In-session	Exercise: One door closed, one door opened: Clients think and write of times when important things were lost but other opportunities opened up. Potential growth from trauma is also explored.
HW: Optimism	Clients use specific strategies to exercise optimism in everyday life.
10 Positive relationships	Role and importance of positive relationships are discussed in wellbeing.
In-session	Clients practice active-constructive responding (ACR) – a strategy to foster positive relationship communication.
HW: ACR practice	Clients self-monitor for active-constructive opportunities.
11 Signature strengths of others	The significance of recognizing and associating through character strengths of family members is discussed.
In-session	Clients complete an exercise to identify signature strengths of their family members.
HW: Family strengths tree	Clients asks family members to take the Signature Strengths Questionnaire (SSQ) online measure, draws a family tree of strengths and arranges an in-person or virtual gathering to discuss family members' signature strengths.
12 Savouring	Ways to savour and strategies to safeguard against adaptation are discussed.
In-session	Clients participate in a savouring exercise which uses various techniques and strategies.
HW: Planned savouring activity	Clients plan a savouring activity using specific techniques.

(cont.)

Table 10.3 *(cont.)*

Exercise & homework	Description
13 Altruism & positive legacy	The therapeutic benefits of helping others are discussed.
In-session	Clients write paragraphs about how they would like to be remembered or what would be their legacies.
HW: Gift of time	Clients plan to give the gift of time doing something that also uses their signature strengths.
14 The full life	Full life is discussed as the integration of positive emotions, engagement, positive relationships, meaning and accomplishment. Therapeutic gains and experiences are discussed and ways to sustain positive changes are devised.

Phase 2, process. The middle phase of PPT constitutes the fourth, fifth, sixth and seventh sessions and focuses on helping clients to apply strengths adaptively through discussions on the nuances of navigating day-to-day hassles effectively and resolving or otherwise constructively addressing more significant adversities, such as grudges, negative memories or traumas. Using the strengths identified in phase 1, therapists support clients in setting specific and attainable goals that adaptively use their signature strengths to address their presenting concerns. While setting goals, clients are also taught to use their strengths in a calibrated and flexible way that could adaptively meet situational challenges (Biswas-Diener et al., 2011). As they do so, specific actions or habits are highlighted that may explain symptoms or troubles as either a lack or an excess of strengths, rather than in deficit terms; for example, worrying excessively construed as a lack of gratitude or narcissism construed as a lack of humility (see Rashid, 2015 for a comprehensive outline). Clients learn to translate abstract concepts of strengths into strategies that foster forgiveness, gratitude and their practical wisdom (as described by Schwartz and Sharpe, 2010). These skills promote competence and autonomy, and thereby facilitate and encourage personal growth through adversity (Ryan and Deci, 2008). Regular discussions on the positive experiences of daily life also promote broader experiential awareness, buttressing against the negativity bias that tends to restrict and commandeer our limited cognitive resources towards negative experiences.

Phase 2, exercises. In the middle phase of PPT, after therapeutic rapport is established and clients are helped to identify their strengths, clients are encouraged to write down grudges, bitter memories or resentments and then discuss the effects of holding onto them. There are a number of exercises that are very important for this process. *Positive appraisal* (Rashid and Seligman, 2013) helps clients to unpack their grudges and resentments and reappraise them through four strategies: (i) psychological space: write a bitter or negative experience from a third person's perspective; (ii) reconsolidation: recall finer and subtler aspects of a bitter or negative experience in a relaxed state of mind; (iii) mindful focus: observe a negative memory rather than reacting; and (iv) diversion: intentionally engage behaviourally in an unrelated or playful task. Relatedly, clients are also invited to consider the process of *forgiveness*, as the goal here is to redirect or reframe clients' negative emotions. The therapist explores scenarios with clients to help them understand what forgiveness is and what it is not. Forgiveness in PPT is conceptualized as a process of change: to willingly forsake one's right (perceived or real) to take revenge (Worthington et al., 2007). Clients are educated that forgiveness is not condoning or pardoning the offender, undermining socially acceptable justice, forgetting the wrong or ignoring the consequences of the offense. They learn that forgiveness is also not simply replacing the negative thoughts or emotions with neutral or positive ones (Enright and Fitzgibbons, 2014). Using this understanding, the client writes about one of his or her own negative experiences with the intention of resolving it through forgiveness.

Gratitude is a state of being thankful for recognized positives in one's life. Gratitude has been reliably found to have strong associations with wellbeing (Wood et al., 2010). Two related exercises are essential to cultivating gratitude in this phase of PPT. The first is the *gratitude letter*. Participants recall a person who did something kind for them for which they never thanked them. In session, participants write a first draft of a letter that clearly and authentically expresses their gratitude, describing the specifics of their acts of kindness and their positive consequences. For homework, participants write another two drafts and then organize a *gratitude visit*. Clients are then encouraged to read the letter to the recipient in person or on the phone. When done in person, this exercise often generates powerful positive emotions on both ends and is often described by clients as a deeply moving experience that they were initially reluctant to engage in.

The final session of the second phase is a review session. In the seventh session, participants spend time reviewing their assignments that were to be pursued outside of session. Therapeutic progress is also discussed. This session is very important because the therapist needs to have a clear idea of what has been working and what has not been working as they approach the final phase of PPT.

Phase 3, process. The final and longest phase of PPT, which spans from session eight to session fourteen, focuses on restoring or fostering positive relationships (both intimate and communal) and encouraging or supporting the search and pursuit of meaning and purpose. While empathically attending to the pain associated with traumatic experiences, PPT gently encourages clients to explore meaning and psychological growth also (Bonanno and Mancini, 2012; Calhoun and Tedeschi, 2006). Meaning has a long tradition in the psychotherapeutic literature (Frankl, 1955) and has garnered many diverse conceptualizations and perspectives as psychological researchers have worked to understand this complex construct (Markman et al., 2013). In PPT, meaning is a sense of purpose or significance that emerges from a subjectively coherent understanding of the world that directs and motivates long-term action and promotes wellbeing when such actions are being pursued. Meaning and purpose can be pursued in a number of ways, such as strengthening close interpersonal and communal relationships; pursuing artistic, intellectual or scientific innovations; or philosophical or religious contemplation (Frankl, 1963; McKnight and Kashdan, 2009; Stillman and Baumeister, 2009; Wrzesniewski et al., 1997). Traumatic events can cause a disruption in meaning because they undermine our beliefs about the world (Janoff-Bulman, 1989). In response to trauma, victims need to develop a new understanding of the world that is able to account for the traumatic event and preserve the possibility of meaning. There is solid evidence that having a sense of meaning and purpose helps individuals to recover or rebound quickly from adversity and buffers against feelings of hopelessness and uncontrollability (Graham et al., 2008; Lightsey, 2006). Individuals who demonstrate greater meaning-making when writing about their lives show higher rates of wellbeing (McLean, 2005; McLean and Pratt, 2006; McLean and Thorne, 2003). PPT aims to support and promote this process through an empathic therapeutic alliance, instruction of relevant concepts and therapeutic exercises that promote conditions conducive to meaning.

Phase 3, exercises. The exercises in the third and final phase of PPT continue to use the client's strengths but focus on using them to belong to and serve something bigger than oneself. Several exercises in the third phase focus on improving interpersonal relationships, which are essential to meaning (Ryan et al., 2008). One exercise, *positive communication*, teaches clients ways to validate and capitalize on precious moments when their partners share good news with them (Gable et al., 2004). Another, the *gift of time*, helps clients experience the importance and effect that explicitly making time for significant others has on the relationship and the individuals within the relationship. Clients also learn to spot strengths in other people and plan interpersonal events around shared or present strengths.

Mindfulness can promote meaning by making us aware of pleasurable moments that would have slipped by unfulfilled if we did not explicitly draw our attention to them. Clinical experience suggests most clients seek therapy to manage the stressors associated with living in fast-paced and highly complex environments. The *savouring* exercise (Bryant, 2007) requires that clients pay close attention to the sensations associated with performing a simple task, such as eating a raisin, touching a feather or smelling a fragrance. Clients tend to find that by simply paying attention to such activities the activities become more pleasurable and interesting. This explicit attentiveness is distinct from mindfulness in that savouring is about engaging with experiences and sensations, not just passively observing them as they occur. The therapist should work to help the client implement savouring in varying aspects of their lives. Another exercise, *satisficing versus maximizing* (Schwartz et al., 2002), helps clients to understand how to be aware of energy and time expenditure towards tasks and to manage this expenditure towards appropriate and beneficial ends. Awareness promotes the setting and maintenance of meaningful long-term goals that are conducive to a sense of purpose and connection with the larger culture or community from which these goals were derived.

Clinical Depictions and Vignettes

Throughout PPT, clients and therapists continue to monitor progress and make necessary changes, continually exploring the nuances of strengths and applying them to resolve challenges. The following case scenarios are from clients seen by the author in individual or group therapy at a university counseling center. These depict goal-directed use of strengths in overcoming presenting problems:

- A single female client in her twenties presented symptoms of emotional dysregulation and a history of unstable relationships. This client was initially highly skeptical of PPT exercises. In the group setting, the client remained quiet for the most part. While most group members shared parts of their positive introduction, the client was asked to share something related to resilience. The client sarcastically said "my introduction includes severe emotional abuse by my family, alcoholism, and untreated mental illness of one of my parents. There is nothing good about it". I felt like committing a faux paus and could feel the weight of the client's distress. After an uncomfortable and long pause, another group member gently asked the client, 'but you are here in this group, every week?' Upon hearing this, a stream of tears flowed from client's eyes. 'This is my only hope ... something I will never let go.' Everyone became silent but was deeply moved.

The client continued individual therapy with the author after the group, attending two sessions every four months on the average, largely maintaining therapeutic gains. In the latest session, client summarized the therapeutic experience in the following way: 'Four years ago, I had very little confidence, I perceived myself as someone who will never get rid of all the terrible things that have happened to me. Today these things do not bother me much. I know that I am not a quitter, despite getting Bs, I love learning, I know my strengths, I love learning, I may not be able to go to graduate school with these grades but somehow, I will find a way to continue my love of learning.'

- A 19-year-old undergraduate university student, despite a solid academic achievement record, expected the worst in the future and believed he would not achieve his goal of getting into a graduate school no matter how hard he tried. This precipitated not only symptoms of depression but also experimentation with illicit drugs. Through individual PPT the client discovered that his signature strengths were love of learning, spirituality, authenticity, persistence, appreciation of beauty and kindness. Over the course of the therapy, he started using his strengths, in particular love of learning and kindness. He read a lot on science of addictive behaviour. After slow progress, he made a breakthrough when he was offered a volunteer position which helped young people to learn healthy coping strategies.

  In an unplanned recent encounter, the client stated that he has been doing well, has not used drugs for the last three years, is about to graduate and will soon be starting a job that involves helping others in a mental health facility.

- The signature strength profile of a single client in her twenties from a conservative cultural background showed that kindness, authenticity, humility, social intelligence and spirituality were core parts of her self-concept. An introvert by disposition, she presented with symptoms consistent with dysthymic depression disorder. Although PPT exercises helped her to improve her mood somewhat, her interpersonal challenges did not improve. Her family responded negatively when she started using strengths in a calibrated manner (e.g. expressing her emotions (social intelligence), asking for more gender-based equality (fairness), standing up for her rights (courage) and not being humble and kind when someone violated her rights). The client felt empowered but friction between her and her family increased. The client dealt with this friction with her kindness, but success was moderate.

  These brief vignettes show ways that clients can use their character strengths to deal adaptively with psychological challenges. Inherent bias towards negativity and symptomatic distress may keep these pathways obscured for clients.

Empirical Evidence

PPT has a growing body of empirical evidence. The exercises in PPT were initially validated individually (Seligman et al., 2005) before being coalesced into the PPT manual (Rashid & Seligman, 2016; Seligman et al., 2006), which has since been used in 14 studies (see Table 10.4 for an overview). These studies have been conducted internationally and have addressed a variety of clinical populations (including depression, anxiety, borderline personality disorder, psychosis and nicotine dependence). Most of these studies have been conducted in a group therapy format. Overall, PPT has been shown to significantly lower symptoms of distress and enhance wellbeing at post-treatment, when compared to control

Table 10.4 Positive Psychotherapy: Summary of Studies

Authors & publication status	Intervention description & sample characteristics	Key findings
1 Seligman et al., 2006, published	Individual PPT ($n = 11$), 12–14 sessions, with clients diagnosed with major depressive disorder (MDD), compared with treatment as usual (TAU; $n = 9$) & treatment as usual plus medication (TAUMED; $n = 12$). Clients were undergraduate and graduate students seeking psychotherapy at a university counselling center in the United States.	Clients completing PPT fared significantly better on measures of depressive, overall psychiatric distress and wellbeing.
2 Seligman et al., 2006, published	Group PPT ($n = 21$) with clients at a university counselling center, experiencing mild to moderate depressive symptoms compared with no-treatment controls ($n = 21$) in six sessions.	PPT did better on measure of depression at post-treatment, 3-, 6- and 12-month follow-up, with a rate of change that was significantly higher than that of the control group.
3 Parks-Schiener, 2009, dissertation	Individuals ($n = 52$) completed six PPT exercises online and were compared with a no-treatment control group ($n = 69$).	Individuals completing PPT exercises reported significantly less depression the post-treatment, three- and six-month follow-ups.
4 Lü et al., 2013	Group PPT ($n = 16$), two hours for 16 weekly sessions with university students in China were compared with a no-treatment control group ($n = 18$). The study explored the impact of positive affect on vagal tone in handling environmental challenges.	Participants completing PPT exercises reported significantly fewer depressive symptoms, fewer negative emotions and more positive emotions.
5 Rashid et al., 2013, published	Group PPT ($n = 9$) was offered in eight sessions to grade six and seven students at a public school in Canada, and compared with no-treatment controls ($n = 9$).	Participants improved on their social skills as rated by their parents and teachers.
6 Reinsch, C., 2012, dissertation	Group PPT ($n = 9$) was compared with a no-treatment control group ($n = 8$) with adults seeking psychotherapy through the Employee Assistance Program in Canada.	Compared with the control group, the treatment group showed a significant decrease in depression at a rate of 45%. Therapeutic gains were maintained one month postintervention.
7 Uliaszek et al., 2016, published	Group PPT ($n = 27$) compared with group dialectical behavior therapy (DBT; $n = 27$), in a randomized clinical trial, with undergraduate students diagnosed with the symptoms of borderline personality disorder who sought treatment at a university counselling centre in Canada.	Participants in both PPT and DBT improved significantly on measures of depression, anxiety, emotional dysregulation, mindfulness, wellbeing and life satisfaction. However, effect sizes for the DBT group ranged from medium to large (Cohen's $d = 0.61$–1.23) and those for the PPT group from small to large ($d = 0.33$–1.29).

Table 10.4 *(cont.)*

Authors & publication status	Intervention description & sample characteristics	Key findings
8 Asgharipoor et al., 2012, published	Group PPT ($n = 9$) was compared with cognitive behavior therapy (CBT) for 12 weeks, each group, with community adults diagnosed with major depressive disorder, seeking treatment at a hospital-affiliated psychological treatment centre in Iran.	At postintervention, PPT group showed significantly higher level of happiness, whereas no differences between two treatments were found on measures of depression.
9 Schrank et al., 2015, published	Group PPT adapted for psychosis, called WELLFOCUS. PPT was completed ($n = 43$) for 11 weeks, vs. treatment as usual (TAU; $n = 41$), with community adults diagnosed with psychosis.	At the postintervention and follow-up, the PPT group, compared with TAU, showed a significant improvement in wellbeing on three different measures as well as for symptoms, depression, hope, self-esteem and sense of coherence.
10 Cuadra-Peralta et al., 2010, published	Group PPT ($n = 8$) in nine sessions, with clients diagnosed with depression, compared with behavioral therapy ($n = 10$) at a community center in Chile.	Compared with behaviour therapy, PPT showed significant increases in happiness and significant decreases in symptoms of depression.
11 Bay and Csillic, 2012, presentation	Group PPT ($n = 10$) compared with group cognitive behavior therapy ($n = 8$) & medication ($n = 8$).	PPT fared better than CBT and medication group on measures of depression, optimism, emotional intelligence and wellbeing.
12 Meyer et al., 2012, published	Group PPT with two cohorts recruited from a hospital and a community mental health centre, diagnosed with a current diagnosis of schizophrenia or schizoaffective disorder, completed ten sessions.	At posttreatment, PPT fared better on measure of depression, happiness, life satisfaction and optimism. In most cases both PPT and CBT fared better than medication group.
13 Kahler et al., 2014, published	Individual PPT ($n = 19$) in eight sessions was integrated with smoking cessation counseling and nicotine patch at a community medical center.	Rate of session attendance and satisfaction with treatment were high with most participants who completed the PPT exercise. Almost one-third (31.6%) of the sample sustained smoking abstinence for six months after their quit date.
14 Goodwin, 2010, dissertation	Group PPT ($n = 11$) in a pre-to-post group design explored relationship satisfaction among anxious and stressed individuals at a community center.	Individuals who experienced a reduction in perceived stress also showed significant improvement in overall relationship functioning. Similarly, participants who experienced a reduction in anxiety also showed significant improvement in relationship satisfaction.

or pretreatment scores, with medium to large effect sizes (for pre-to-post measure score changes on outcome measures and effect sizes, see Rashid, 2015). Four of these studies, including two randomized controlled trials, have compared PPT directly with dialectical behavior therapy and cognitive behavior therapy, two active and well-researched manualized treatments, and found that PPT performed equally well or has exceeded them, notably on wellbeing measures (e.g. Asgharipoor et al., 2012; Cuadra-Peralta et al., 2010).

One study warrants further elaboration because it was the largest study of PPT to date. Schrank et al. (2015) at Kings College, London employed a rigorous research design to evaluate the effectiveness of PPT when adapted for psychosis by comparing participants randomized to PPT groups (n = 43) to a treatment-as-usual control group (n = 41). This adaptation is called WELLFOCUS PPT (Riches et al., 2016). Compared with the control group, the WELLFOCUS PPT group showed significant changes on measures of wellbeing, psychiatric symptoms and depression. In a complementary study that investigated participant perceptions of WELLFOCUS PPT, it was found that participants had very positive views of the program (Brownell et al., 2015), which is important for retention and the therapeutic process. The results of this study and the others discussed above provide auspicious initial data regarding the use of PPT in varying clinical populations.

Caveats

There are a number of caveats that need to be borne in mind when considering the information that has been presented in this chapter. First, many of the empirical studies that have been amassed thus far include studies with small sample sizes. This highlights the need for further research to deepen our understanding of the PPT therapeutic process and its effects. Nevertheless, the auspicious findings outlined above complement research on other positive interventions (for reviews, see Bolier et al., 2013; Sin and Lyubomirsky, 2009), which suggests that the horizons are broad indeed for researchers endeavouring to expand the landscape of wellbeing and recovery through psychotherapeutic practices that are more balanced and humanistic, as well as rigorous and scientific.

Second, although the descriptions of some strengths have a moral leaning, in PPT they are presented as evidence-based attributes. For example, forgiveness and gratitude are favorable traits but solid evidence shows that these are strongly related to life satisfaction.

Third, PPT is not a panacea and will not be appropriate for all clients in all situations. Clinical judgment is needed to determine the suitability of PPT for individual clients. For example, a client with inflated self-perception may use strengths to further support his or her narcissism. Likewise, a client with a deeply entrenched sense of being a victim may feel too comfortable in that role and may not believe in his or her own strengths. The progress of one client should not bias therapist beliefs about the likely progress (or lack of it) of another client. The mechanisms of change in PPT have not been systematically evaluated.

Fourth, it is important to be aware of cultural sensitivities in assessing strengths. An emotive style of communication, interdependence on extended family members or avoiding direct eye contact may all convey zest, love, and respect (Pedrotti, 2011). Modern psychological assessment is largely a product of Western culture. It is important to ensure that assessment does not misconstrue behaviour due to this cultural bias. Discuss assessment results with clients in the context of their cultural backgrounds.

Conclusion

Perhaps more than any other health service, psychotherapy needs to develop with the zeitgeist in which it operates. As Western culture becomes more focused on developing individuals to their greatest potential, psychotherapy needs to expand from its century-old model of remediation to include human development as a central focus. Although PPT still has to answer many sophisticated questions about its viable population, treatment processes, mechanisms of change and outcomes, its approach embodies the humanistic tradition of fostering development, rather than fixing what is wrong. Moving forward, longitudinal and multimethod research designs will be needed to provide empirical answers to the many questions that still linger. As researchers come to approach age-old questions of wellbeing, happiness and human development, psychotherapy will grow ever more towards its ultimate goal of scientifically promoting the human potential for growth and fulfilment.

Further Reading

To help psychotherapists to incorporate positive interventions in their clinical practice, a few books have been published (e.g. Bannink, 2012; Conoley and Conoley, 2009; Joseph and Linley, 2006; Levak et al., 2011; Linley and Joseph, 2004; Magyar-Moe, 2009; Proctor and Linley, 2013). Journal articles exploring theoretical advances in incorporation of strengths into clinical practice have also been published exploring applications of positive psychology and strengths in various applied settings (e.g. Dick-Niederhauser, 2009; Kapur et al., 2013; Lent, 2004; Slade, 2010; Smith, 2006; Wong, 2006). Also, an outcome measure, the Positive Psychotherapy Inventory (PPTI), has been developed and validated to assess the specific active ingredients of PPT, including positive emotions, engagement, meaning and relationships (Bertisch et al., 2014; Guney 2011; Rashid, 2008).

References

American Psychiatric Association (2013). *Diagnostic and Statistical Manual of Mental Disorders*, 5th ed. (DSM-V). Arlington, VA: American Psychiatric Association.

Asebedo, S. D., & Seay, M. C. (2014). Positive psychological attributes and retirement satisfaction. *Journal of Financial Counseling and Planning*, 25(2), 161–173.

Asgharipoor, N., Farid, A. A., Arshadi, H., & Sahebi, A. (2012). A comparative study on the effectiveness of positive psychotherapy and group cognitive-behavioral therapy for the patients suffering from major depressive disorder. *Iranian Journal of Psychiatry and Behavioral Sciences*, 6, 33–41.

Bannink, F. (2012). *Practicing positive CBT: From reducing distress to building success*. New York, NY: Wiley.

Bartels, M., Cacioppo, J. T., van Beijsterveldt, T. C. E. M., & Boomsma, D. I. (2013). Exploring the association between well-being and psychopathology in adolescents. *Behavior Genetics*, 43(3), 177–190.

Baumeister, R. F., Bratslavsky, E., Finkenauer, C., & Vohs, K. D. (2001). Bad is stronger than good. *Review of General Psychology*, 5, 323–370. doi:10.1037/1089–2680.5.4.323.

Bay, M., & Csillic, A. (2012). *Comparing positive psychotherapy with cognitive behavioral therapy in treating depression*. Unpublished manuscript. Paris West University Nanterre La Défense (Université Paris Ouest Nanterre La Défense).

Beckwé, M., Deroost, N., Koster, E. H. W., De Lissnyder, E., & De Raedt, R. (2013). Worrying and rumination are both associated with reduced cognitive control. *Psychological Research*, 78, 651–660. doi:10.1007/s00426-013-0517-5.

Bertisch, H., Rath, J., Long, C., Ashman, T., & Rashid, T. (2014). Positive psychology in rehabilitation medicine: A brief report. *NeuroRehabilitation*. doi:10.3233/NRE-1410.

Biswas-Diener, R., Kashdan, T. K., & Minhas, G. (2011). A dynamic approach to psychological strength development and intervention. *Journal of Positive Psychology*, 6(2), 106–118.

Bolier, L., Haverman, M., Westerhof, G., Riper, H., Smit, F., & Bohlmeijer, E. (2013). Positive psychology interventions: A meta-analysis of randomized controlled studies. *BMC Public Health*, 13(119).

Bonanno, G. A. (2004). Loss, trauma, and human resilience: Have we underestimated the human capacity to thrive after extremely aversive events? *American Psychologist*, 59(1), 20–28. Available at http://resolver.scholarsportal.info/resolve/0003066x/v59i0001/20_ltahrhttaeae.

Bonanno, G. A., & Mancini, A. D. (2012). Beyond resilience and PTSD: Mapping the heterogeneity of responses to potential trauma. *Psychological Trauma: Theory, Research, Practice, and Policy*, 4(1), 74–83. doi:10.1037/a0017829.

Brownell, T., Schrank, B., Jakaite, Z., Larkin, C., & Slade, M. (2015). Mental health service user experience of positive psychotherapy. *Journal of Clinical Psychology*, 71(1), 85–92. doi:10.1002/jclp.22118.

Bryant, F., & Veroff, J. (2007). *Savoring: A new model of positive experience*. Mahwah, N J: Lawrence Erlbaum Associates.

Calhoun, L. G., & Tedeschi, R. G. (Eds.) (2006). *Handbook of posttraumatic growth: Research and practice*. Mahwah, NJ: Erlbaum.

Castonguay, L. G. (2013). Psychotherapy outcome: An issue worth re-revisiting 50 years later. *Psychotherapy (Chicago, Ill.)*, 50(1), 52–67. doi:10.1037/a0030898.

Cheavens, J. S., Strunk, D. S., Lazarus, S. A., & Goldstein, L.A. (2012). The compensation and capitalization models: A test of two approaches to individualizing the treatment of depression. *Behaviour Research and Therapy*, 50, 699–706.

Conoley, C. W., & Conoley, J. C. (2009). *Positive psychology and family therapy: Creative techniques and practical tools for guiding change and enhancing growth*. Hoboken, NJ: Wiley.

Coyne, J. C., & Tennen, H. (2010). Positive psychology in cancer care: Bad science, exaggerated claims, and unproven medicine. *Annals of Behavioral Medicine: A Publication of the Society of Behavioral Medicine*, 39, 16–26. doi:10.1007/s12160–009–9154-z.

Cuadra-Peralta, A., Veloso-Besio, C., Pérez, M., & Zúñiga, M. (2010). Resultados de la psicoterapia positiva en pacientes con depresión [Positive psychotherapy results in patients with depression.]. *Terapia Psicológica*, 28, 127–134. doi:10.4067/S0718–48082010000100012.

Dick-Niederhauser, A. (2009). Therapeutic change and the experience of joy: Toward a theory of curative processes. *Journal of Psychotherapy Integration*, 19, 187–211.

Enright, R. D., & Fitzgibbons, R. P. (2014). *Forgiveness therapy: An empirical guide for resolving anger and restoring hope*. Washington, DC: American Psychological Association.

Ehrenreich, B. (2009). *Bright-sided: How positive thinking is undermining America*. New York, NY: Metropolitan Books.

Fitzpatrick, M. R., & Stalikas, A. (2008). Integrating positive emotions into theory, research, and practice: A new challenge for psychotherapy. *Journal of Psychotherapy Integration*, 18, 248–258.

Flückiger, C., & Grosse Holtforth, M. (2008). Focusing the therapist's attention on the patient's strengths: A preliminary study to foster a mechanism of change in outpatient psychotherapy. *Journal of Clinical Psychology*, 64, 876–890.

Ford, B. Q., & Tamir, M. (2012). When getting angry is smart: Emotional preferences and emotional intelligence. *Emotion*, 12, 685–689. doi:10.1037/a0027149.

Frankl, V. E. (1955). *The doctor and the soul: From psychotherapy to logotherapy*. New York, NY: Random House. [Original work published in 1946.]

Frankl, V. E. (1963). *Man's search for meaning: An introduction to logotherapy*. New York, NY: Washington Square Press.

Fredrickson, B. L. (2001). The role of positive emotions in positive psychology: The broaden-and-build theory of positive emotions. *American Psychologist*, 56(3), 218–226.

Fredrickson, B. L. (2004). The broaden-and-build theory of positive emotions. *Philosophical Transactions of the Royal Society of London, 359,* 1367–1377.

Gable, S. L., Reis, H. T., Impett, E. A., & Asher, E. R. (2004). What do you do when things go right? The intrapersonal and interpersonal benefits of sharing positive events. *Journal of Personality and Social Psychology, 87,* 228–245.

Goodwin, E. M. (2010). Does group positive psychotherapy help improve relationship satisfaction in a stressed and/or anxious population? (Order No. 3428275, Palo Alto University). ProQuest Dissertations and Theses, 166. Available at http://search.proquest.com/docview/822195958?accountid=14707. (822195958).

Graham, J. E., Lobel, M., Glass, P., & Lokshina, I. (2008). Effects of written constructive anger expression in chronic pain patients: Making meaning from pain. *Journal of Behavioral Medicine, 31,* 201–212.

Guney, S. (2011). The Positive Psychotherapy Inventory (PPTI): Reliability and validity study in Turkish population. *Social and Behavioral Sciences, 29,* 81–86.

Headey, B., Schupp, J., Tucci, I., & Wagner, G. G. (2010). Authentic happiness theory supported by impact of religion on life satisfaction: A longitudinal analysis with data for Germany. *Journal of Positive Psychology, 5,* 73–82.

Ito, T. A., Larsen, J. T., Smith, N. K., & Cacioppo, J. T. (1998). Negative information weighs more heavily on the brain: The negativity bias in evaluative categorizations. *Journal of Personality and Social Psychology, 75,* 887–900. doi:10.1037/0022-3514.75.4.887.

Janoff-Bulman, R. (1989). Assumptive worlds and the stress of traumatic events: Applications of the schema construct. In Special Issue: Stress, Coping, and Social Cognition, *Social Cognition, 7,* 113–136.

Joormann, J., Dkane, M., & Gotlib, I. H. (2007). Adaptive and maladaptive components of rumination? Diagnostic specificity and relation to depressive biases. *Behavior Therapy, 37,* 269–280. doi:10.1016/j.beth.2006.01.002.

Joseph, S., & Linley, A. P. (2006). *Positive therapy: A meta-theory for positive psychological practice.* New York, NY: Rutledge.

Kahler, C. W., Spillane, N. S., Day, A., Clerkin, E. M., Parks, A., Leventhal, A. M., et al. (2014). Positive psychotherapy for smoking cessation: Treatment development, feasibility, and preliminary results. *Journal of Positive Psychology, 9*(1), 19–29.

Kapur, N., Cole, J., Manly, T., Viskontas, I., Ninteman, A., Hasher, L., et al. (2013). Positive clinical neuroscience: Explorations in positive neurology. *Neuroscientist, 19,* 354–369. doi:10.1177/1073858412470976.

Keyes, C. L. M., & Eduardo J. S. (2012). To flourish or not: Level of positive mental health predicts ten-year all-cause mortality. *American Journal of Public Health, 102,* 2164–2172.

Lamont, A. (2011). University students' strong experiences of music: Pleasure, engagement, and meaning. *Music and Emotion, 15,* 229–249.

Lent, R. W. (2004). Towards a unifying theoretical and practical perspective on well-being and psychosocial adjustment. *Journal of Counseling Psychology, 5,* 482–509.

Levak, R. W., Siegel, L., & Nichols, D. S. (2011). *Therapeutic feedback with the MMPI-2: A positive psychology approach.* New York, NY: Taylor & Francis.

Leykin, Y., & DeRubeis, R. J. (2009). Allegiance in psychotherapy outcome research: Separating association from bias. *Clinical Psychology: Science and Practice, 16,* 54–65. doi:10.1111/j. 1468-2850.2009.01143.x.

Lightsey, O. (2006). Resilience, meaning, and well-being. *Counseling Psychologist, 34,* 96–107. doi:10.1177/0011000005282369.

Linley, P. A., & Joseph, S. (Eds.) (2004). *Positive psychology in practice.* Hoboken, NJ: Wiley. doi:10.1002/9780470939338.

Lü, W., Wang, Z., & Liu, Y. (2013). A pilot study on changes of cardiac vagal tone in individuals with low trait positive affect: The effect of positive psychotherapy. *International Journal of Psychophysiology, 88,* 213–217. doi:10.1016/j.ijpsycho.2013.04.012.

Magyar-Moe, J. L. (2009). *Therapist's guide to positive psychological interventions.* New York, NY: Elsevier Academic Press.

Markman, K. D., Proulx, T., & Lindberg, M. J. (2013). *The psychology of meaning.* Washington, DC: American Psychological Association.

McKnight, P. E., & Kashdan, T. B. (2009). Purpose in life as a system that creates and sustains health and well-being: An integrative, testable theory. *Review of General Psychology, 13,* 242–251.

McLean, K. C. (2005). Late adolescent identity development: Narrative meaning making and memory telling. *Developmental Psychology, 41,* 683–691.

McLean, K. C., & Pratt, M. W. (2006). Life's little (and big) lessons: Identity statuses and meaning-making in the turning point narratives of emerging adults. *Development Psychology, 42,* 714–722.

McLean, K. C., & Thorne, A. (2003). Late adolescents' self-defining memories about relationships. *Developmental Psychology, 39*(4), 636–645.

McNulty, J. K., & Fincham, F.D. (2012). Beyond positive psychology? Toward a contextual view of psychological processes and well-being. *American Psychologist, 67,* 101–110.

Meyer, P. S., Johnson, D. P., Parks, A., Iwanski, C., & Penn, D. L. (2012). Positive living: A pilot study of group positive psychotherapy for people with schizophrenia. *Journal of Positive Psychology, 7,* 239–248. doi:10.1080/17439760.2012.677467.

Nolen-Hoeksema, S. (1991). Responses to depression and their effects on the duration of depressive episodes. *Journal of Abnormal Psychology, 100,* 569–582.

Pedrotti, J. T. (2011). Broadening perspectives: Strategies to infuse multiculturalism into a positive psychology course. *Journal of Positive Psychology, 6*(6), 506–513. doi:10.1080/17439760. 2011.634817.

Peterson, C., Park, N., Pole, N., D'Andrea, W., & Seligman, M. E. P. (2008). Strengths of character and posttraumatic growth. *Journal of Traumatic Stress, 21*(2), 214–217.

Peterson, C., Park, N., & Seligman M. E. P. (2005). Orientations to happiness and life satisfaction: The full life versus the empty life. *Journal of Happiness Studies, 6,* 25–41.

Peterson, C., & Seligman, M. E. P. (2004). *Character strengths and virtues: A handbook and classification.* New York, NY and Oxford, UK: Oxford University Press/Washington, DC: American Psychological Association.

Proctor, C. & Linley, A. (Eds.) (2013). *Research, applications, and interventions for children and adolescents: A positive psychology perspective.* New York, NY: Springer.

Rashid, T. (2008). Positive psychotherapy. In Lopez, S. J. (Ed.), *Positive Psychology: Exploring the Best in People, Vol 4: Pursuing Human Flourishing* (pp. 188–217). Westport, CT: Praeger.

Rashid, T. (2015). Positive psychotherapy: A strengths-based approach. *Journal of Positive Psychology, 15,* 25–40. doi:10.1080/17439760.2014.920411.

Rashid, T., Anjum, A., Lennex, C., Quinlin, D., Niemiec, R., Mayerson, D., et al. (2013). Assessment of positive traits in children and adolescents. In Proctor, C., & Linley, P. A. (Eds.), *Research, Applications, and Interventions for Children and Adolescents: A Positive Psychology Perspective* (pp. 81–114). New York, NY: Springer.

Rashid, T., & Seligman, M. E. P. (2013). Positive psychotherapy. In Wedding, D., & Corsini, R. J. (Eds.), *Current Psychotherapies* (pp. 461–498). Belmont, CA: Cengage.

Rashid, T., & Seligman, M. E. P. (2016). *Positive psychotherapy: A manual.* Oxford, UK: Oxford University Press.

Reinsch, C. (2012). Adding science to the mix of business and pleasure: An exploratory study of positive psychology interventions with teachers accessing employee assistance counselling. Master's thesis, University of Manitoba, Winnipeg, Manitoba, Canada. Available at http://hdl. handle.net/1993/14436.

Riches, S., Schrank, B., Rashid, T., & Slade, M. (2016). WELLFOCUS PPT: Modifying positive psychotherapy for psychosis. *Psychotherapy, 53*(1), 68–77.

Rozin, P., & Royzman, E. (2001). Negativity bias, negativity dominance, and contagion. *Personality and Social Psychology Review, 5,* 296–320.

Ryan, R. M., & Deci, E. L. (2008). A self-determination theory approach to psychotherapy: The motivational basis for effective change. *Canadian Psychology, 49*(3), 186–193.

Ryan, R. M., Huta, V., & Deci, E. L. (2008). Living well: A self-determination theory perspective on eudaimonia. *Journal of Happiness Studies*, 9, 139–170.

Scheel, M. J., Davis, C. K., & Henderson, J. D. (2012). Therapist use of client strengths: A qualitative study of positive processes. *Counseling Psychologist*, 41, 392–427. doi:10.1177/0011000012439427.

Schrank, B., Brownell, T., Jakaite, Z., Larkin, C., Pesola, F., Riches, S., et al. (2015). Evaluation of a positive psychotherapy group intervention for people with psychosis: Pilot randomized controlled trial. *Epidemiology and Psychiatric Sciences*, doi:10.1017/S2045796015000141.

Schwartz, B., & Sharpe, K. E. (2010). *Practical wisdom: The right way to do the right thing*. New York, NY: Penguin.

Schwartz, R. M., Reynolds, C. F., III, Thase, M. E., Frank, E., Fasiczka, A. L., & Haaga, D. A. F. (2002). Optimal and normal affect balance in psychotherapy of major depression: Evaluation of the balanced states of mind model. *Behavioral and Cognitive Psychotherapy*, 30, 439–450.

Schwartz, B., Ward, A., Monterosso, J., Lyubomirsky, S., White, K., & Lehman, D. R. (2002). Maximizing versus satisficing: Happiness is a matter of choice. *Journal of Personality and Social Psychology*, 83, 1178–1197. doi:10.1037/0022–3514.83.5.1178.

Seligman, M. E. P. (1995). The effectiveness of psychotherapy: The Consumer Reports study. *American Psychologist*, 50, 965–974. doi:10.1037/0003–066X.50.12.965.

Seligman, M. E. P. (2002). *Authentic happiness: Using the new positive psychology to realize your potential for lasting fulfillment*. New York, NY: Free Press.

Seligman, M. E. P. (2011). *Flourish: A visionary new understanding of happiness and well-being*. New York, NY: Simon & Schuster.

Seligman, M. E. P., Rashid, T., & Parks, A. C. (2006). Positive psychotherapy. *American Psychologist*.61, 774–788. doi:10.1037/0003–066X.61.8.774.

Seligman, M. E. P., Steen, T. A., Park, N., & Peterson, C. (2005). Positive psychology progress: Empirical validation of interventions. *American Psychologist*, 60, 410–421. doi:10.1037/0003–066X.60.5.410.

Siddique, J., Chung, J. Y., Brown, H. C., & Miranda, J. (2012). Comparative effectiveness of medication versus cognitive-behavioral therapy in a randomized controlled trial of low-income young minority women with depression. *Journal of Consulting and Clinical Psychology*, 80(6), 995–1006.

Sin, N. L., & Lyubomirsky, S. (2009). Enhancing well-being and alleviating depressive symptoms with positive psychology interventions: A practice-friendly meta-analysis. *Journal of Clinical Psychology*, 65, 467–487. doi:10.1002/jclp.20593.

Sirgy, M. J., & Wu, J. (2009). The pleasant life, the engaged life, and the meaningful life: What about the balanced life? *Journal of Happiness Studies*, 10, 183–196.

Slade, M. (2010). Mental illness and well-being: The central importance of positive psychology and recovery approaches. *BMC Health Services Research*, 10(26).

Smith, E. J. (2006). The strength-based counseling model. *Counseling Psychologist*, 34, 13–79.

Stillman, T. F., & Baumeister, R. F. (2009). Uncertainty, belongingness, and four needs for meaning. *Psychological Inquiry*, 20, 249–251.

Uliaszek, A. A., Rashid, T., Williams, G. E., & Gulamani, T. (2016). Group therapy for university students: A randomized control trial of dialectical behavior therapy and positive psychotherapy. *Behaviour Research and Therapy*, 77, 78–85.

Vandenberghe, L., & Silvestre, R. L. S. (2014). Therapists' positive emotions in-session: Where they come from and what they are good for. *Counselling and Psychotherapy Research. Linking Research with Practice*, 14, 119–127.

Vella-Brodrick, D. A., Park, N., & Peterson, C. (2009). Three ways to be happy: Pleasure, engagement, and meaning: Findings from Australian and U.S. samples. *Social Indicators Research*, 90, 165–179.

Wedding, D., & Corsini, R. J. (Eds.) (2013). *Current Psychotherapies*. Belmont, CA: Cengage.

Wong, W. J. (2006). Strength-centered therapy: A social constructionist, virtue-based psychotherapy. *Psychotherapy*, 43, 133–146.

Wood, A. M., Froh, J. J., & Geraghty, A. W. (2010). Gratitude and well-being: A review and theoretical integration. *Clinical Psychology Review*, 30, 890–905.

Worthington, E. L., Witvliet, C. V. O., Pietrini, P., & Miller, A. J. (2007). Forgiveness, health, and well-being: A review of evidence for emotional versus decisional forgiveness, dispositional forgivingness, and reduced unforgiveness. *Journal of Behavioral Medicine*, 30(4), 291–302. doi:10.1007/s10865–007–9105–8.

Wrzesniewski, A., McCauley, C., Rozin, P., and Schwartz, B. (1997). Jobs, careers, and callings: People's relations to their work. *Journal of Research in Personality*, 31, 21–33.

Xu, J., & Robert, R.E. (2010). The power of positive emotions: It is a matter of life or death – Subjective well-being and longevity over 28 years in a general population. *Health Psychology* 29, 9–19.

Section 2

What Does a Wellbeing Orientation Mean in Mental Health Services?

Chapter

WELLFOCUS PPT for Psychosis

Beate Schrank, Simon Riches and Mike Slade

Positive Psychotherapy

Positive psychotherapy (PPT) is an established psychological therapy that focuses on strengths and positive experiences in order to promote wellbeing (a 'good life'). In contrast to some traditional psychotherapies, PPT is strengths-focused rather than problem-focused. PPT does attend to problems, such as negative memories, but in doing so encourages people to focus on strengths and positive aspects of experience. It attempts to undo problems by building on positives that may be related to specific symptoms; for example, to overcome pessimism and hopelessness, optimism is reinforced. PPT exercises focus on intentionally savouring enjoyable experiences; recording good things; gratitude, forgiveness, identifying and using character strengths, either alone or with others; and focusing on positives in otherwise negative events or memories (Rashid, 2013; Rashid and Seligman, 2013).

PPT was initially validated with people experiencing moderate to severe depressive symptoms. It was based on the assumption that optimal treatment not only targets faulty cognitions, unresolved and suppressed emotions and troubled relationships, but also involves 'directly and primarily building positive emotions, character strengths, and meaning' (p. 775) (Seligman et al., 2006). It is one of a family of 'positive interventions', which are designed to promote wellbeing rather than ameliorate deficits. A meta-analysis of 51 studies of positive interventions demonstrated significantly improved wellbeing and decreased depressive symptoms for people with depression (Sin and Lyubomirsky, 2009). A more recent meta-analysis of 39 randomised studies from positive psychology (the academic discipline of development and evaluation of positive interventions) involving 6,139 participants concluded that positive psychology interventions can be effective in enhancing subjective and psychological wellbeing and reducing depressive symptoms (Bolier et al., 2013). More specifically, randomised controlled trials (RCTs) comparing PPT with no treatment show decreased depressive symptoms in students (Rashid and Anjum, 2008; Seligman et al., 2006; Parks-Sheiner, 2009; Lü et al., 2013) and other nonclinical, community samples (Schueller and Parks, 2012; Seligman et al., 2006; Seligman et al., 2005).

The standard PPT intervention manual (Rashid and Seligman, 2016) describes how to provide PPT to nonclinical (6 sessions) and clinical (14 sessions) samples. The 14-session version is summarised in Table 11.1.

Wellbeing, Recovery and Mental Health, ed. Mike Slade, Lindsay Oades and Aaron Jarden.
Published by Cambridge University Press. © Mike Slade, Lindsay Oades and Aaron Jarden 2017

Table 11.1 Standard 14-Session PPT

Session	Content	Homework
1. **Orientation to PPT**	Group guidelines, importance of homework and presenting problems are discussed	Positive introduction (a story of when you were 'at your best')
2. **Character strengths**	Identify (up to five) character strengths using the Values in Action (VIA) Classification of Character Strengths questionnaire, possibly with family/friends	Blessing journal (identify three good things each night)
3. **Signature strengths**	Identify signature strengths	Signature strength action plan
4. **Good vs. bad memories**	Memories and cognitive reappraisal are discussed	Writing memories (focusing on bad memories and distress)
5. **Forgiveness**	Transforming forgiveness into positive emotions	Forgiveness letter (not necessarily delivered)
6. **Gratitude**	Enduring thankfulness, good/bad memories are discussed	Gratitude letter and visit
7. **Midsession feedback**	Recap signature strengths action plan, forgiveness, gratitude. Discussion of progress	None
8. **Satisficing vs. maximising**	Discuss settling for "good enough" rather than exploring almost all possible options	Plan areas that could benefit from satisficing
9. **Hope, optimism & post-traumatic growth**	Consider unexpected/unintended positives. Optimism, hope and new opportunities are discussed. Growth from trauma is explored	One door closes; one door opens
10. **Positive communication**	Active constructive responding is discussed	Active constructive responding
11. **Signature strengths of others**	Character strengths of family are discussed	Family strengths tree
12. **Savouring**	Take time to notice various elements of an experience. Savouring techniques are discussed	Planned savouring activity
13. **Altruism**	Giving the gift of time to help others is discussed	Gift of time
14. **The full life**	Integration of positive emotions, engagement, positive relationships, meaning and accomplishment. Discuss ways to sustain positive changes	None

Modifying PPT for Other Populations

PPT is now being integrated with other interventions (Cromer, 2013) and used with other client groups; for example, a small sample of smokers found benefits from PPT in combination with smoking cessation counselling and nicotine patch treatment (Kahler et al., 2014).

Brain injury rehabilitation is another area which may benefit from modified PPT (Evans, 2011; Bertisch et al., 2014). PPT has also been adapted for suicidal inpatients (Huffman et al., 2014) and for physical health conditions (Celano et al., 2013; DuBois et al., 2012; Huffman et al., 2011). More generally, positive interventions are being adapted for various populations, such as people with developmental disabilities (Feldman et al., 2002). For a summary of studies using the PPT protocol, see Rashid (2014).

Wellbeing research has not been widely integrated within traditional treatment protocols for people with more severe mental health problems (Slade, 2010), and so a further area that may benefit from modification is psychosis. An uncontrolled feasibility study of 16 people with schizophrenia evaluated a 'positive living' intervention modified from six-session PPT (Meyer et al., 2012). The intervention was shown to be feasible and increased participants' wellbeing, savouring, hope, self-esteem and personal recovery.

In this chapter we describe the development and evaluation of PPT for psychosis, which we call WELLFOCUS. The adaptation is analogous to the modification of standard cognitive behavioural therapy (CBT) to CBT for psychosis (CBTp) and addresses some overlapping issues, including the efficacy of developing meaningful relationships. WELLFOCUS is consistent with 'third wave' cognitive psychotherapy approaches (e.g. acceptance and commitment therapy (ACT), mindfulness-based cognitive therapy (MBCT)) in emphasising strengths and values, and deemphasising thought-challenging (Longmore and Worrell, 2007). It connects to an evolving understanding of wellbeing in psychosis (Schrank et al., 2013) and the importance of a positive identity for recovery (Leamy et al., 2011).

The scientific framework for WELLFOCUS is the Medical Research Council (MRC) Framework for Evaluating Complex Health Interventions (Craig et al., 2008). The three phases of this framework involved establishing the theory, developing a model and intervention manual and testing the intervention in an exploratory trial. The first phase of this framework was described in Chapter 6. In this chapter we describe the development of a testable model and evaluation of the intervention.

Development of WELLFOCUS PPT for Psychosis

We developed a manual for WELLFOCUS PPT by modifying 14-session standard PPT, and then developed an explicit and testable model which identifies the mediating processes and proximal and distal outcomes arising from WELLFOCUS PPT. A full description of the process has been published elsewhere (Riches et al., 2016).

Development of the WELLFOCUS model comprised four stages. Stage 1 involved semi-structured interviews with staff (psychotherapists and care coordinators) and service users (patients with psychosis) to identify candidate modifications to standard PPT. Stage 2 involved consultation with expert therapists to refine the recommendations from Stage 1 and identify target areas of WELLFOCUS PPT. Stage 3 involved development of a manual and model. Stage 4 involved review by clinicians and service users of the WELLFOCUS PPT manual.

Stage 1 (Interviews)

Semistructured interviews employed a topic guide which summarised standard PPT exercises (Rashid, 2008) and sought feedback and suggestions for modification.

A total of 23 service users with a clinical diagnosis of psychosis (mean age: 44.6 years (SD 9.3), 35% female, 15 (65%) with a diagnosis of schizophrenia) and 14 staff (mean age:

Table 11.2 Service User and Staff Generic Views on Standard PPT

Theme	Challenges	Proposed modifications
Attitudes	Positive approach may be rejected as "unrealistic"	Make it realistic, validate negative feelings
Illness	Concentration/motivation may impact exercises	Use clear language; avoid theory, abstraction, didactic style; emphasise structure, flexibility; adapt tasks, use small concrete steps, assess group needs, tailor sessions to individuals
Engagement	Exercises may feel meaningless, negative memories of homework, lack of social/financial opportunities	Explain rationale/session-by-session outline, focus on meaningful life/values, identify realistic, personal goals, such as small tasks, gradually introduce/increase feedback, plan exercises in session, support and be aware of negative memories ("Don't call it homework"), use reminder phone calls/text messages, award certificates, afternoon sessions, breaks with refreshments, provide information to take away
Interaction	Difficulties with social contact, disclosure, self-confidence, group comparison, dominant group members, lack of interest in other people	Warm-up exercises; foster mutual acceptance/equality, trusting environment, honest interest in others; therapist self-disclosure/humour to normalise experiences/integrate group

36.5 years (SD 10.3), 71% female, mean length of relevant experience: 11.6 years (SD 12.4)) were interviewed. Four generic themes emerged as challenges: *attitudes*, *illness*, *engagement* and *interaction*. These four themes are different types of challenges that the interviewees felt might impact the utility of the intervention. This is outlined in Table 11.2.

Thematic analysis also identified PPT exercise-specific challenges and proposed solutions; for example, satisficing vs. maximising and altruism would be challenging and possibly unsuitable for service users with psychosis, so they were removed.

Stage 2 (Consultation)

The standard PPT manual (Rashid and Seligman, 2016) and Stage 1 data analysis were presented to 12 experts in a one-day meeting. Solutions to identified challenges and modifications to standard PPT exercises were proposed and consensus was reached on adaptations to standard PPT.

Stage 3 (Manualisation)

Four key target areas of the WELLFOCUS model were identified from the systematic review (Schrank et al., 2013), dynamic framework (Schrank et al., 2014a) and Stages 1–2 findings: increasing positive experiences, amplifying strengths, fostering positive relationships and creating a more meaningful self-narrative. These components are intended to lead to improved wellbeing, defined as an enhanced sense of self (Schrank et al., 2014a). The resulting WELLFOCUS model is shown in Figure 11.1.

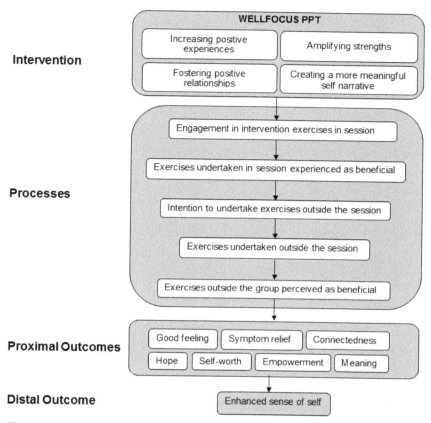

Figure 11.1 The WELLFOCUS model.

The WELLFOCUS manual was then written by developing a generic session structure, identifying number and content of sessions, characterising therapist style and writing session-specific handouts and other session tools.

Stage 4 (Review)

Trial therapists ($n = 9$), a wellbeing expert ($n = 1$) and service users ($n = 6$) reviewed iterative WELLFOCUS manual drafts. The final version is shown in Table 11.3.

Evaluation of WELLFOCUS PPT

The WELLFOCUS intervention was then evaluated in a pilot randomised controlled trial (ISRCTN04199273). The trial protocol was published (Schrank et al., 2014b), and full reports of outcome evaluation (Schrank et al., 2015a) and process evaluation (Brownell, 2015) from the trial were published elsewhere. A target sample size of 30 complete data sets in each trial arm was chosen according to recommendations for pilot trials (Lancaster et al., 2004), with an anticipated 25% dropout. The obtained sample size allowed effectiveness at a medium effect size (Cohen's $d = 0.5$) to be detected with 90% power at a 5% significant level, taking into account 20% attrition.

Table 11.3 WELLFOCUS PPT Sessions

Session	Ongoing exercise	Content	Target area(s)
1. **Welcome to WELLFOCUS PPT**	Positive introduction	Group guidelines, rationale, positive responding	Positive experiences, strengths
2. **Savouring**	Planned savouring activity	Mindful eating, drinking and listening exercises	Positive experiences
3. **Good things**	Identify good things	Identify recent good things using the Good Things Box	Positive experiences
4. **Identifying a personal strength**	Identify a character strength	Identify one character strength using strengths pictures	Strengths
5. **Using personal strengths**	Strength activity	Plan and carry out an activity using your strength	Strengths
6. **Using strengths together**	Strength activity with significant other	Plan and carry out an activity that uses strengths of both individuals	Strengths, positive relationships
7. **Forgiveness 1**	A sea of forgiveness	Focus on letting go of a grudge	Positive relationships, meaningful self-narrative
8. **Forgiveness 2**	Forgiveness letter	Identify a person to forgive and write him or her a letter	Positive relationships, meaningful self-narrative
9. **One door closes another door opens**	One door closes; another door opens	Identify positive conclusions from negative experiences	Meaningful self-narrative
10. **Gratitude**	Writing a gratitude letter	Identifying a person you have never properly thanked and write him or her a letter	Positive relationships
11. **Celebration**	Positive responding	Celebrate achievements	Positive experiences

Inclusion criteria were age 18–65 years; primary clinical diagnosis of psychosis defined as schizophrenia and other psychoses including schizoaffective and delusional disorder but not depressive psychosis or psychosis due to substance misuse; current use of adult mental health services; fluency in English; and ability to give informed consent and participate in group therapy, in the opinion of the key clinician.

Control and intervention group participants received standard care, comprising systematic assessments of health and social needs, formation of a care plan, appointment of a key worker to monitor and coordinate care and regular reviews to adapt the care plan. Care is provided by multidisciplinary mental health teams, and treatments may include medication or social or psychological interventions. Intervention group participants in addition received 11 weekly 90-minute sessions of WELLFOCUS PPT in a closed group format.

The primary outcome measure was the 14-item Warwick–Edinburgh Mental Well-Being Scale (WEMWBS) (Tennant et al., 2007). Two alternative wellbeing measures were also used: the 25-item Positive Psychotherapy Inventory (PPI) measures a PPT-specific concept of wellbeing (Guney, 2011) and the 12-item Manchester Short Assessment (MANSA) measures quality of life framed as satisfaction with life as a whole and with specific life domains (Priebe et al., 1999). Six indicators of wellbeing, as identified in the dynamic framework (Schrank et al., 2014a), were also assessed: the Savoring Beliefs Inventory (SBI) assesses the ability to derive pleasure through anticipating upcoming positive events, savouring positive moments in the present, and reminiscing about past positive experiences (Bryant, 2003); the Integrative Hope Scale (IHS) assesses hope (Schrank et al., 2012); the Rosenberg Self-Esteem Scale (RSES) assesses self-esteem (Schmitt and Allik, 2005); Rogers' Empowerment Scale (RES) assesses empowerment (Rogers et al., 2010); the Sense of Coherence Scale (SCS) assesses orientation to view the environment as comprehensible, manageable and meaningful (Eriksson and Lindstrom, 2006); the Short Depression–Happiness Scale (SDHS) assesses affect on a bipolar continuum between depression and happiness (Joseph and McCollam, 1993). We also used the Health of the Nation Outcome Scale (HoNOS) assessment of social disability (Wing et al., 1998) and the Brief Psychiatric Rating Scale (BPRS) assessment of symptomatology (Overall and Gorham, 1988).

Participants were recruited between April and August 2013 from eight teams in one mental health trust (service provider) in South London, UK. After giving informed consent and completing baseline measures, they were randomised by the independent King's Clinical Trials Unit in groups of 8 to 20 participants (in a block randomization representing multiples of 2 and 4 people). Follow-up interviews took place within two weeks of the intervention finishing.

The flow diagram for the 94 study participants is shown in Figure 11.2.

Baseline participant characteristics are shown in Table 11.4.

WELLFOCUS PPT was provided to six groups, and each group had an average of 8 (range 4 to 10) participants. The median number of sessions attended was seven.

No adverse events were reported. Given the low rate of missing items in questionnaires with only one necessary exclusion of the IHS, reporting of all 84 participants with follow-up assessments is possible for all other scales. Raw data on change for all assessed variables are presented in Table 11.5.

Intention-to-treat (ITT) analysis found no significant effect of the intervention group on the primary outcome of wellbeing (WEMWBS) at followup after adjusting for baseline scores ($p = .37$), and the effect size was small (Cohen's $d = .15$). Table 11.6 summarises ITT analyses for all measures.

Adjusting the model for therapy group minimally increased effect sizes for the BPRS ($F(1,76) = 8.7$, $p = 0.004$, ES = 0.43), and SDHS depression ($F(1,76) = 4.9$, $p = -.03$, ES = 0.41) but did not lead to any more outcomes falling below the $p = 0.05$ significance level. In both models, the highest effect sizes were found for symptom severity (BPRS) and depression (SDHS depression), followed by wellbeing as measured by the PPI.

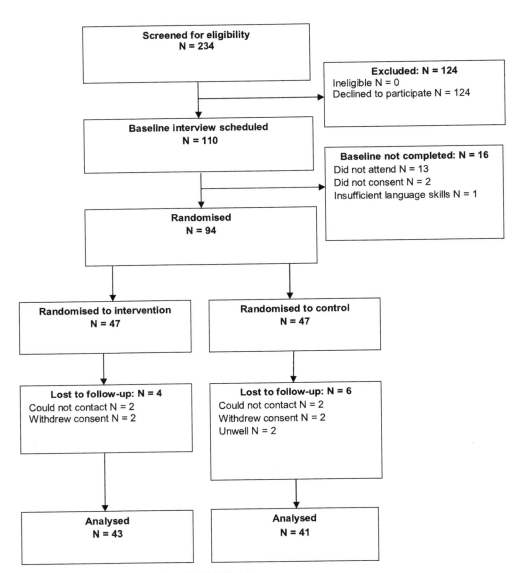

Figure 11.2 Participant flow in the WELLFOCUS trial.

CACE analysis showed a nonsignificant positive association between the intervention and WEMWBS scores at follow-up ($b = .21$, $z = 0.9$, $p = .4$).

Process evaluation indicated that the intervention was experienced positively, with some components identified as specifically helpful: learning to savour experiences, identifying and developing strengths, forgiveness, gratitude and therapist self-disclosure (Brownell et al., 2015).

Table 11.4 Sociodemographic and Baseline Clinical Characteristics ($n = 94$)

		Intervention mean (SD)	Control mean (SD)
Age		43 (11.0)	42 (11.5)
		n (%)	n (%)
Gender	Male	26 (55.3)	30 (63.8)
Ethnicity	White	21 (44.7)	23 (50)
	Nonwhite	26 (55.3)	23 (50)
Birthplace	UK-born	29 (61.7)	27 (57.4)
Accommodation	Owned	8 (17.0)	4 (8.5)
	Rented	27 (57.4)	34 (72.3)
	Other	12 (25.5)	8 (17.0)
Relationship status	Single	39 (83.0)	42 (89.4)
	In partnership	8 (17.0)	5 (10.6)
Qualifications	None	5 (10.9)	2 (4.3)
	Secondary education (11–16 years)	11 (25.6)	16 (34.8)
	Further education (16–18 years)	11 (25.6)	12 (26.1)
	Higher education (18+)	12 (26.1)	10 (23.3)
	Relevant professional training	7 (15.2)	6 (13.0)
Employment	Working or studying	10 (21.3)	10 (21.3)
	Not working	37 (78.7)	37 (78.7)
Years using mental health services		13 (11.0)	14 (11.0)
Warwick-Edinburgh Mental Well-Being Scale (WEMWBS)		3.19 (.76)	3.00 (.89)
Manchester Short Assessment of Quality of Life (MANSA)		4.05 (.85)	4.14 (1.01)
Positive Psychotherapy Inventory (PPI)		3.58 (.73)	3.44 (.80)
Brief Psychiatric Rating Scale (BPRS)		30.70 (8.81)	33.57 (8.42)
Short Depression-Happiness Scale (SDHS)		2.29 (.69)	2.48 (.76)
Integrative Hope Scale (IHS)		4.02 (.79)	3.72 (.85)
Rosenberg Self-Esteem Scale (RSES)		2.24 (.64)	2.09 (.66)
Savoring Beliefs Inventory (SBI)		4.80 (1.22)	4.48 (1.02)
Rogers Empowerment Scale (RES)		2.74 (.32)	2.71 (.32)
Sense of Coherence Scale (SCS)		4.18 (1.05)	3.81 (1.11)
Health of the Nation Outcome Scale (HoNOS)		7.29 (5.05)	9.62 (5.19)

The Future for WELLFOCUS PPT

This is the first study to report a randomized controlled trial of positive psychotherapy specifically adapted for people with psychosis. No significant effect of group was found on wellbeing as the main outcome. However, a significant improvement on the researcher-rated BPRS was found, with a moderate effect size in the ITT analysis comparable to effect sizes

Table 11.5 Changes from Baseline to Follow-Up ($n = 84$, except for IHS $n = 83$)

Measure	Group	Mean difference (CI)	p
WEMWBS	Control	0.15 (−0.10–0.41)	n.s.
	Intervention	0.26 (0.06–0.45)	.010
MANSA	Control	0.11 (−0.07–0.30)	n.s.
	Intervention	0.34 (0.11–0.57)	.004
PPI	Control	−0.02 (−0.15–0.11)	n.s.
	Intervention	0.20 (0.06–0.35)	.000
BPRS	Control	0.78 (−1.16–2.72)	n.s.
	Intervention	−2.51 (−4.70–0.32)	.026
SDHS	Control	−0.07 (−0.22–0.09)	n.s.
	Intervention	−0.24 (−0.45–0.03)	.028
IHS	Control	0.19 (−0.02–0.41)	.080
	Intervention	0.21 (0.00–0.42)	.048
RSES	Control	0.05 (−0.07–0.18)	n.s.
	Intervention	0.19 (0.04–0.34)	.016
SBI	Control	0.05 (−0.16–0.27)	n.s.
	Intervention	0.08 (−0.15–0.32)	n.s.
RES	Control	0.01 (−0.07–0.08)	n.s.
	Intervention	0.07 (−0.01–0.16)	.079
SCS	Control	0.17 (−0.03–0.36)	.088
	Intervention	0.24 (0.01–0.46)	.040
HONOS	Control	−0.37 (−1.91–1.18)	n.s.
	Intervention	0.03 (−1.38–1.44)	n.s.

found for CBT in this client group (Jauhar et al., 2014). Equally strong effects were found on the patient-rated SDHS depression subscale.

This study provides initial evidence on the likely feasibility and acceptability of WELLFOCUS PPT in the client group of people with psychosis. More work is needed to optimize its effectiveness before a definitive RCT can be recommended. The process evaluation identified particularly useful components, allowing further optimisation of the intervention manual. WELLFOCUS PPT may be viable for reducing overall symptom severity and specifically depression. Comorbid depression is a known challenge in the treatment of people with psychosis, affecting about 40% of people at risk of psychosis (Fusar-Poli et al., 2014) and about 50% of people with schizophrenia (Buckley et al., 2009).

The positive impact of WELLFOCUS PPT on depressive symptoms needs to be evaluated further, with specific attention to including research diagnoses and establishing the causal pathway of action. Ways of supplementing the effect on symptoms in general are worth considering in future research, including, for example, a choice or combination of WELLFOCUS PPT and brief CBT intervention (Waller et al., 2014). How to select those participants who are most likely to respond also remains an important question for future research. In addition, a specific measurement challenge remains: how best to assess wellbeing.

Our two wellbeing measures showed very different responsiveness to the intervention: WEMWBS did not change, while the PPI consistently showed improvement. While a wide

Table 11.6 Intention to Treat Analysis ($n = 84$, except for IHS $n = 83$)

Scale	Follow-up mean (s.e.) Control	Follow-up mean (s.e.) Intervention	ANCOVA	Effect size
n	41	43		
WEMWBS	3.24 (0.10)	3.36 (0.10)	$F_{(1,81)} = 0.8, p = .37$	.15
MANSA	4.21 (0.10)	4.42 (0.10)	$F_{(1,81)} = 2.3, p = .13$	.21
PPI	**3.48 (0.07)**	**3.72 (0.07)**	**$F_{(1,81)} = 5.9, p = .02$**	**.30**
BPRS	**33.23 (.98)**	**29.37 (0.96)**	**$F_{(1,81)} = 7.8, p = .006$**	**.42**
SDHS overall	2.34 (0.09)	2.13 (0.08)	$F_{(1,81)} = 3.0, p = .09$	.29
SDHS happiness	2.91 (.10)	3.03 (.10)	$F_{(1,81)} = 0.6, p = .42$	.16
SDHS depression	**2.60 (.10)**	**2.29 (.10)**	**$F_{(1,81)} = 4.7, p = .03$**	**.38**
IHS	4.04 (0.10)	4.11 (0.10)	$F_{(1,81)} = 0.3, p = .62$	.08
RSES	2.21 (0.07)	2.37 (0.07)	$F_{(1,81)} = 2.9, p = .09$	.23
SBI	4.65 (0.11)	4.75 (0.10)	$F_{(1,81)} = 0.4, p = .53$	.09
RES	2.73 (0.04)	2.80 (0.04)	$F_{(1,81)} = 2.0, p = .16$	.22
SCS	4.12 (0.10)	4.26 (0.10)	$F_{(1,81)} = 1.0, p = .32$	.13
HONOS	8.53 (0.68)	8.14 (0.66)	$F_{(1,81)} = 0.2, p = .68$	.07

Note: Bold = significant differences.

range of instruments suggested to measure wellbeing exist, only a few have established sensitivity to change, let alone in samples of people with psychosis (Schrank et al., 2013). Further research is needed to establish whether measuring wellbeing is a technical problem requiring the rigorous development and evaluation of new measures, or a conceptual problem caused by low validity in the construct of wellbeing (Shepherd, 2014). Equivalent challenges are identified in the measurement of health-related quality of life (Connell, 2014). This may include the exploration of sensitivity to change in existing measures of wellbeing or related concepts such as hope.

At a higher level, the challenges of applying positive psychology research to psychosis mirror emerging issues in recovery research. The choice of outcome domains (e.g. wellbeing versus symptoms) reflects assumptions about the purpose of services. Our empirical findings of an impact on BPRS but not on WEMWBS is consistent with the distinction between hedonic wellbeing (maximisation of pleasure) and eudaimonic wellbeing (fulfilment of potential). If – as is argued in Chapter 8 – wellbeing has two dimensions, then it may be that hedonic wellbeing (i.e. reduced affective symptomatology) is more sensitive to change than eudaimonic wellbeing. Similarly, the assessment perspective (clinician versus client) reflects assumptions about where relevant expertise lies. Emerging empirical evidence indicates that clinical and client perspectives on recovery differ (Andresen et al., 2010). This parallels the finding that staff hold differing views about wellbeing for themselves compared with wellbeing for people living with psychosis (Schrank et al., 2015b). Further empirical research is needed to understand the relation between different types of wellbeing and different assessment perspectives in the context of psychosis. Overall, the goal of supporting individuals to live well with psychosis remains.

References

Andresen, R., Caputi, P., & Oades, L. (2010). Do clinical outcome measures assess consumer-defined recovery? *Psychiatry Research*, 177, 309–317.

Bertisch, H., Rath, J., Long, C., Ashman, T., & Rashid, T. (2014). Positive psychology in rehabilitation medicine: A brief report. *NeuroRehabilitation*, 573–585.

Bolier, L., Haverman, M., Westerhof, G. J., Riper, H., Smit, F., & Bohlmeijer, E. (2013). Positive psychology interventions: A meta-analysis of randomized controlled studies. *BMC Public Health*, 13, 119.

Brownell, T., Schrank, B., Jakaite, Z., Larkin, C., & Slade, M. (2015). Mental health service user experience of positive psychotherapy. *Journal of Clinical Psychology*, 71, 85–92.

Bryant, F. (2003). Savoring Beliefs Inventory (SBI): A scale for measuring beliefs about savouring. *Journal of Mental Health*, 12, 175–196.

Buckley, P., Miller, B., Lehrer, D., & Castle, D. (2009). Psychiatric comorbidities and schizophrenia. *Schizophrenia Bulletin*, 35, 383–402.

Celano, C. M., Beale, E. E., Moore, S. V., Wexler, D. J., & Huffman, J. C. (2013). Positive psychological characteristics in diabetes: A review. *Current Diabetes Reports*, 13, 917–929.

Connell, J., O'Cathain, A., & Brazier, J. (2014). Measuring quality of life in mental health: Are we asking the right questions? *Social Science and Medicine*, 120, 12–20.

Craig, P., Dieppe, P., Macintyre, S., Michie, S., Nazareth, I., & Petticrew, M. (2008). Developing and evaluating complex interventions: The new Medical Research Council guidance. *British Medical Journal*, 337, a1655.

Cromer, T. D. (2013). Integrative techniques related to positive processes in psychotherapy. *Psychotherapy*, 50, 307–311.

Dubois, C. M., Beach, S. R., Kashdan, T. B., Nyer, M. B., Park, E. R., Celano, C. M., et al. (2012). Positive psychological attributes and cardiac outcomes: Associations, mechanisms, and interventions. *Psychosomatics*, 53, 303–318.

Eriksson, M., & Lindstrom, B. (2006). Antonovsky's sense of coherence scale and the relation with health: A systematic review. *Journal of Epidemiology and Community Health*, 60, 376–381.

Evans, J. (2011). Positive psychology and brain injury rehabilitation. *Brain Impairment*, 12, 117–127.

Feldman, M. A., Condillac, R. A., Tough, S., Hunt, S. L., & Griffiths, D. (2002). Effectiveness of community positive behavioral intervention for persons with developmental disabilities and severe behavior disorders. *Behavior Therapy*, 33, 377–398.

Fusar-Poli, P., Nelson, B., Valmaggia, L., Yung, A., & Mcguire, P. (2014). Comorbid depressive and anxiety disorders in 509 individuals with an at-risk mental state: Impact on psychopathology and transition to psychosis. *Schizophrenia Bulletin*, 40, 120–131.

Guney, S. (2011). The Positive Psychotherapy Inventory (PPTI): Reliability and validity study in Turkish population. *Social and Behavioral Science*, 29, 81–86.

Huffman, J. C., Dubois, C. M., Healy, B. C., Boehm, J. K., Kashdan, T. B., Celano, C. M., et al. (2014). Feasibility and utility of positive psychology exercises for suicidal inpatients. *General Hospital Psychiatry*, 36, 88–94.

Huffman, J. C., Mastromauro, C. A., Boehm, J. K., Seabrook, R., Fricchione, G. L., Denninger, J. W., et al. (2011). Development of a positive psychology intervention for patients with acute cardiovascular disease. *Heart International*, 6.

Jauhar, S., McKenna, P., Radua, J., Fung, E., Salvador, R., & Laws, K. (2014). Cognitive-behavioural therapy for the symptoms of schizophrenia: Systematic review and meta-analysis with examination of potential bias. *British Journal of Psychiatry*, 204, 20–29.

Joseph, S., & McCollam, P. (1993). A bipolar happiness and depression scale. *Journal of Genetic Psychology*, 154, 127–129.

Kahler, C. W., Spillane, N. S., Day, A., Clerkin, E. M., Parks, A., Leventhal, A. M., et al. (2014). Positive psychotherapy for smoking cessation: Treatment development, feasibility, and preliminary results. *Journal of Positive Psychology*, 9, 19–29.

Lancaster, G. A., Dodd, S., & Williamson, P. R. (2004). Design and analysis of pilot studies: Recommendations for good practice. *Journal of Evaluation in Clinical Practice*, 10, 307–312.

Leamy, M., Bird, V., Le Boutillier, C., Williams, J., & Slade, M. (2011). A conceptual framework for personal recovery in mental health: Systematic review and narrative synthesis. *British Journal of Psychiatry*, 199, 445–452.

Longmore, R. J., & Worrell, M. (2007). Do we need to challenge thoughts in cognitive behavior therapy? *Clinical Psychology Review*, 27, 173–187.

Lü, W., Wang, Z., & Liu, Y. (2013). A pilot study on changes of cardiac vagal tone in individuals with low trait positive affect: The effect of positive psychotherapy. *International Journal of Psychophysiology*, 88, 213–217.

Meyer, P. S., Johnson, D. P., Parks, A., Iwanski, C., & Penn, D. L. (2012). Positive living: A pilot study of group positive psychotherapy for people with schizophrenia. *Journal of Positive Psychology*, 7, 239–248.

Overall, J. E., & Gorham, D. R. (1988). The Brief Psychiatric Rating Scale (BPRS): Recent developments in ascertainment and scaling. *Psychopharmacology Bulletin*, 24 97–99.

Parks-Sheiner, A. C. (2009). Positive psychotherapy: Building a model of empirically supported self-help. *Dissertation Abstracts International: Section B: The Sciences and Engineering*, 70, 3792.

Priebe, S., Huxley, P., Knight, S., & Evans, S. (1999). Application and results of the Manchester Short Assessment of quality of life. *International Journal of Social Psychiatry*, 45, 7–12.

Rashid, T. (2008). Positive psychotherapy. In Abela, J. R. Z., & Hankin, B. L. (Eds.), *Positive Psychology: Exploring the Best in People, Vol. 4: Pursuing Human Flourishing* (pp. 250–287). Westport, CT: Praeger Publishers/Greenwood Publishing Group; US.

Rashid, T. (2013). Positive psychology in practice: Positive psychotherapy. In Boniwell, I., David, S. A., & Ayers, A. C. (Eds.), *The Oxford Handbook of Happiness* (pp. 978–993). New York, NY: Oxford University Press.

Rashid, T. (2014). Positive psychotherapy: A strength-based approach. *Journal of Positive Psychology*, 10, 25–40.

Rashid, T., & Anjum, A. (2008). Positive psychotherapy for young adults and children. In Abela, J. R. Z., & Hankin, B. L. (Eds.), *Handbook of Depression in Children and Adolescents* (pp. 250–287). New York, NY: Guilford Press.

Rashid, T., & Seligman, M. E. (2013). Positive psychotherapy. *In*: Wedding, D. & Corsini, R. J. (Eds.) (pp. 98–110). *Current Psychotherapies*. Belmont, CA: Cengage.

Rashid, T., & Seligman, M. E. (2016). *Positive psychotherapy: A manual*. Oxford, UK: Oxford University Press.

Riches, S., Schrank, B., Rashid, T., & Slade, M. (2016). WELLFOCUS PPT: Modifying positive psychotherapy for psychosis. *Psychotherapy*, 53(1), 68–77. doi:10.1037/pst0000013.

Rogers, E., Ralph, R., & Salzer, M. (2010). Validating the empowerment scale with a multisite sample of consumers of mental health services. *Psychiatric Services*, 61, 933–936.

Schmitt, D., & Allik, J. (2005). Simultaneous administration of the Rosenberg Self-Esteem Scale in 53 nations: Exploring the universal and culture-specific features of global self-esteem. *Journal of Personality and Social Psychology*, 89, 623–642.

Schrank, B., Bird, V., Tylee, A., Coggins, T., Rashid, T., & Slade, M. (2013). Conceptualising and measuring the well-being of people with psychosis: Systematic review and narrative synthesis. *Social Science and Medicine*, 92, 9–21.

Schrank, B., Brownell, T., Jakaite, Z., Larkin, C., Pesola, F., Riches, S., et al. (2015a). Evaluation of a positive psychotherapy group intervention for people with psychosis: Pilot randomized controlled trial. *Epidemiology and Psychiatric Sciences*, doi:10.1017/S2045796015000141.

Schrank, B., Brownell, T., Riches, S., Chevalier, A., Jakaite, Z., Larkin, C., et al. (2015b). Staff views on wellbeing for themselves and for service users. *Journal of Mental Health*, 24, 48–53.

Schrank, B., Riches, S., Bird, V., Murray, J., Tylee, A., & Slade, M. (2014a). A conceptual framework for improving well-being in people with a diagnosis of psychosis. *Epidemiology and Psychiatric Sciences*, 23, 377–387.

Schrank, B., Riches, S., Coggins, T., Rashid, T., Tylee, A., & Slade, M. (2014b). WELLFOCUS PPT – Modified Positive Psychotherapy to improve well-being in psychosis: Study protocol for pilot randomised controlled trial. *Trials*, 15, 202.

Schrank, B., Riches, S., Coggins, T., Tylee, A., & Slade, M. (2013). From objectivity to subjectivity: Conceptualisation and measurement of well-being in mental health. *Neuropsychiatry*, 3, 525–534.

Schrank, B., Woppmann, A., Grant Hay, A., Sibitz, I., Zehetmayer, S., & Lauber, C. (2012). Validation of the Integrative Hope Scale in people with psychosis. *Psychiatry Research*, 198, 395–399.

Schueller, S. M., & Parks, A. C. (2012). Disseminating self-help: Positive psychology exercises in an online trial. *Journal of Medical Internet Research*, 14, e63.

Seligman, M. E., Rashid, T., & Parks, A. C. (2006). Positive psychotherapy. *American Psychologist*, 61, 774–88.

Seligman, M. E., Steen, T. A., Park, N., & Peterson, C. (2005). Positive psychology progress: Empirical validation of interventions. *American Psychologist*, 60, 410–21.

Shepherd, A. (2014). Avoiding surrogate measures and incorporating subjective experience into clinical research. *Psychotherapy and Psychosomatics*, 83, 119.

Sin, N. L., & Lyubomirsky, S. (2009). Enhancing well-being and alleviating depressive symptoms with positive psychology interventions: A practice-friendly meta-analysis. *Journal of Clinical Psychology*, 65, 467–487.

Slade, M. (2010). Mental illness and well-being: The central importance of positive psychology and recovery approaches. *BMC Health Services Research*, 10–26.

Tennant, R., Hiller, L., Fishwick, R., Platt, S., Joseph, S., Weich, S., et al. (2007). The Warwick–Edinburgh Mental Well-Being Scale (WEMWBS): Development and UK validation. *Health and Quality of Life Outcomes*, 5, 63.

Waller, H., Craig, T., Landau, S., Fornells-Ambrojo, M., Hassanali, N., Iredale, C., et al. (2014). The effects of a brief CBT intervention, delivered by frontline mental health staff, to promote recovery in people with psychosis and comorbid anxiety or depression (the GOALS study): Study protocol for a randomized controlled trial. *Trials*, 15, 255.

Wing, J. K., Beevor, A. S., Curtis, R. H., Park, S. B., Hadden, S., & Burns, A. (1998). Health of the Nation Outcome Scales (HoNOS). Research and development. *British Journal of Psychiatry*, 172, 11–18.

Chapter

12

Mobile Health for Illness Management

Dror Ben-Zeev and Nidhi Badiyani

Background

Over the last decade, mobile devices have become ubiquitous. Mobile technology has transformed the way in which we find information, interact with one another and access resources. The United Nations' Telecommunications Agency estimates that there are already 7 billion mobile phone subscriptions worldwide, and mobile-cellular penetration rates stand at 96% globally (International Telecommunication Union, 2013; United Nations Foundation, 2009). Mobile technology has been helpful in bridging the digital information divide between various socioeconomic groups, as several underserved populations who typically could not afford home computers now use smartphones (i.e. mobile phones with computational capacities) as alternative routes to access Internet resources (Smith, 2013). Research has shown that people with serious mental illnesses (SMI) such as schizophrenia and bipolar disorder, including many homeless individuals, own mobile devices (Ben-Zeev et al., 2013a; Eyrich-Garg, 2010; Post et al., 2013). Survey studies conducted in the United States have found that between 72% and 86% of people with SMI own mobile phones and use them regularly (Ben-Zeev et al., 2013a; Carras et al., 2014; Torous et al., 2014b). Similarly, high mobile phone adoption rates have been shown in individuals with mental health conditions in Australia (Proudfoot et al., 2010), the United Kingdom (Ennis et al., 2012) and India (Jain et al., 2015). Approximately 62% of individuals receiving outpatient services at psychiatric clinics in the United States now own smartphones (Torous et al., 2014a).

Mobile devices are being used for a variety of functions. Basic mobile phones serve as a medium for telecommunication in the form of voice calls or bidirectional texting (i.e. SMS). Smartphones have enhanced features such as computational capacity, data storage, Internet connectivity, global positioning systems (GPSs), multiple embedded sensors (e.g. accelerometers, light sensors) and the ability to download tailored software applications ("apps"). These features enable browsing, e-mail communication, social and professional networking, entertainment, shopping, navigation, voice and video calling and text and picture messaging. The functionality of these technologies can be augmented with wearable devices (e.g. bracelets, wristbands, pocket-sized instruments that can be attached to one's waistband) which house sensors to measure movement, location, galvanic skin response, heart rate and other physiological measures (Burns et al., 2011; Patrick et al., 2008). Smartphones can be used to collect, collate, and analyze these sensor data using wireless connectivity, effectively transforming them into multimodal data collection devices (Ben-Zeev et al., 2016).

Wellbeing, Recovery and Mental Health, ed. Mike Slade, Lindsay Oades and Aaron Jarden.
Published by Cambridge University Press. © Mike Slade, Lindsay Oades and Aaron Jarden 2017

The rapid surge in mobile technology and wireless infrastructure, along with the increasing portability, user-friendliness and affordability of mobile devices, has opened new avenues for their application in healthcare (Ben-Zeev, 2012; Proudfoot et al., 2010). Increased interest in harnessing the capabilities and functionality of mobile technology to support healthcare services has led to the evolution of the interdisciplinary field of mobile health (mHealth). Mobile devices in the service of mHealth efforts facilitate something quite revolutionary – they enable us to transport research, assessment and treatment out of the laboratories and clinics and into the real-time/real-world context in which individuals negotiate their daily lives.

mHealth

mHealth approaches are being developed for patients and providers for diagnostics, behavioral prompts, reminders, medication adherence, continuous illness monitoring and self-management programs (Ben-Zeev et al., 2012; Harrison et al., 2011; Luxton et al., 2011). mHealth strategies have been used to manage a variety of health-related conditions (Patrick et al., 2008; Smith & Schatz, 2010). For example, a systematic review and meta-analysis of 22 studies showed that mHealth interventions can promote health awareness and education that produce significant improvements in illness self-management and glycemic control in people diagnosed with diabetes (Liang et al., 2011). Similarly, mHealth approaches have been shown to improve maternal and neonatal health (Lund & Hemed, 2010), reduce transmission of sexually transmitted diseases among inner city youth (Levine et al., 2008), promote smoking cessation (Haug et al., 2008; Riley et al., 2008; Obermayer et al., 2004; Rodgers et al., 2005; Whittaker et al., 2008), increase physical activity (Damen, 2007; Hurling et al., 2007) and promote medication adherence in patients with HIV (Puccio et al., 2006).

Mobile technology can help overcome some of the barriers associated with traditional clinic-based care. This may be particularly relevant to people with psychiatric disabilities who find it challenging to go to a clinic when they experience debilitating symptoms (Ben-Zeev et al., 2012; Depp et al., 2010). If people who are struggling with symptoms do decide to seek in-person treatment, they must contend with the host of challenges that are intrinsic to clinic-based services, including distance from their residence, limited or inconvenient hours of operation, varying quality in clinician training and services and stigma associated with being labeled "mentally ill" or receiving mental health treatments (Ben-Zeev et al., 2012; Corrigan, 2004; Drake, Bond & Essock, 2009; McGuire et al., 2014; Mojtabai et al., 2009). mHealth interventions that use mobile devices to deliver resources directly to the user can augment less than optimal clinic-based care, or in some cases, serve as the main resource for people who would otherwise receive no care at all.

More than 50,000 mHealth applications are available for download on popular online app stores (with more being added daily) (Ben-Zeev et al., 2015a; Tomlinson et al., 2013). However, many of these products have not been developed with careful consideration of the characteristics of their intended user populations, or the settings in which they will be used. The marketers of these products often make bold claims about their utility and helpfulness, but the vast majority of available mHealth tools (e.g. apps, services) have not been rigorously developed or tested in research trials to determine their true clinical effectiveness. Here lies an inherent tension between the rapid pace of commercial technological advancement and the need to develop e-resources in a careful, methodical manner to generate potent tools. On one hand, it may be unrealistic to require that all new mHealth technologies be tested in randomized controlled trials that take several years to complete (perhaps rendering the technology antiquated by the time findings are published). On the other, completely unvetted approaches may have unanticipated iatrogenic effects or prove to be infeasible or unsustainable. Potential consumers of mHealth resources need to be informed about the evidence (or lack of evidence) around a particular tool to make informed decisions. In the following section, we review several innovative examples of mHealth in the service of promoting illness management and wellbeing in people with psychiatric disabilities that have varying levels of reported evidence supporting their use.

mHealth for Mental Health

Mobile devices have been used quite extensively for self-monitoring in the context of mental health research in outpatient and inpatient settings (Ainsworth et al., 2013; Granholm et al., 2008; Trull and Ebner-Priemer, 2013; Kimhy et al., 2014). Surveys and focus groups conducted with individuals with SMI and clinicians show that both patients and providers are interested in using mobile devices for mHealth interventions (Ben-Zeev et al., 2013a, 2013b; Proudfoot et al., 2010; Torous et al., 2014a). This interest has propelled researchers to develop several mHealth tools for individuals with SMI (e.g. Ben-Zeev et al., 2013b, 2014c; Burns et al., 2011; Depp et al., 2010; Myin-Germeys et al., 2011). mHealth interventions vary considerably in terms of their purpose, design and technology used. We provide a brief overview of key developments in this area.

Texting interventions. Text messaging is one of the most commonly used tools in mHealth and has been leveraged to communicate personalized appointment reminders and medication adherence prompts (Montes et al., 2012; Makela et al., 2010; Van Gent and Knoppert Van Der Klein, 2010).

In one study conducted in the Czech Republic, outpatients at high risk for relapse and their family members received weekly text message requests to complete assessments of early warning signs of relapse on their mobile phones, as part of a randomized controlled trial of an information technology–aided relapse prevention in schizophrenia program (ITAREPS) (Spaniel et al., 2012). Over the course of a year, 146 individuals in the study were sent 21,208 autogenerated prompts. When individuals in the intervention arm used texting to report on early signs, automated alerts in the form of an email were sent to their treating psychiatrists with a prompt to follow up with a medication evaluation. Participants in the study responded to 80% of weekly requests over a year, but clinicians' adherence to the protocol in the active arm was low, and in many cases follow-up steps were not taken. When clinicians did respond accordingly, individuals in the active arm did significantly better than controls in terms of hospitalization, number of inpatient days and costs.

In a second study, Granholm et al. (2012) used automated daily mobile phone text messaging as part of the Mobile Assessment and Treatment for Schizophrenia (MATS) intervention. In the MATS intervention, individuals received daily self-assessment texts from a remote server focusing on medication adherence, socialization and auditory hallucinations. Their text replies to the server's prompts would initiate an automated algorithm-based back-and-forth exchange composed of adapted cognitive behavioral techniques and suggestions. During a 12-week pilot trial, individuals in the MATS intervention received up to 840 text messages. Participants' mobile phone self-reports suggested improvement in each of the three target domains; time in the study was associated with improved medication adherence, increased socialization and reduced distress associated with auditory hallucinations (Granholm et al., 2012). However, lab-based pre-/postassessment using valid and reliable measures of symptoms and functioning found no significant changes, and a quarter of the sample did not send valid responses to the automated assessments, or stopped texting within two weeks. The authors of the study concluded that using more advanced smartphone technology would help deliver a more user-friendly (e.g. with the use of touchscreens) and engaging (e.g. with the use of multimedia) intervention which may be more viable with people who struggled with texting (Granholm et al., 2012).

While the two previous examples focused on automated texting, Ben-Zeev et al. (2014c) developed a hybrid clinician/mHealth intervention which involved daily bidirectional text exchanges between a live "Mobile Interventionist" and individuals with SMI and co-occurring substance use. In this model, a community-based provider sends patients daily text assessments and responds to their replies with tailored illness management and recovery/wellness focused exercises and suggestions. This model was found to be highly feasible, acceptable and engaging to patients: In a three-month study of the intervention, 87% of the Mobile Interventionist's daily texts received a reply. Over 90% of participants thought the intervention was useful and rewarding, stating that it helped them be more effective and productive in their lives. Participants' assessments of their relationship with the Mobile Interventionist were very positive; the therapeutic alliance ratings participants provided for their texting clinician, whom they met in person only once, were significantly higher than those they provided for their community-based treatment team clinicians whom they met with regularly (Ben-Zeev et al., 2014c).

Smartphone interventions. Smartphones can be used to deliver text interventions, but also have the capacity to support native intervention software that is downloaded onto the device and treatment models that leverage web resources (e.g. websites, e-mail, and social media), video calling, instant messaging and other smartphone functions.

myCompass is a web-based intervention program that can be delivered via smartphones and/or other computers. It is an automated, self-guided psychological intervention designed for individuals with mild to moderate depression, anxiety and stress. In a recent, randomized controlled study, individuals with these mental health conditions self-monitored their symptoms (i.e. moods, mood triggers and lifestyle behaviors) by scheduling autoreminders and receiving tailored feedback and motivational prompts via text or emails. In addition, they engaged in 12 online evidence-based psychotherapeutic modules designed to support symptom management. The individuals in the intervention group logged in online to use the *myCompass* program an average of 15 times and engaged in self-monitoring an average of 49 times during a seven-week intervention period. With continuous use, the program helped significantly reduce symptoms of depression, anxiety and stress and improved participants' work and social functioning. The results from this study demonstrated that delivery of cognitive behavioral therapy using a combination of mobile phone and web technology is acceptable and effective.

(Proudfoot et al., 2013)

Smartphones can be used as instruments to deliver mHealth interventions that augment in-person treatments. For example, personalized real-time intervention for stabilizing mood (PRISM) is an mHealth approach for self-monitoring of symptoms and planning action steps to address symptoms in bipolar disorders. In a randomized controlled study evaluating PRISM, 82 outpatients diagnosed with bipolar disorder either received PRISM delivered by an Internet-enabled smartphone or engaged in paper-and-pencil mood monitoring for a period of 10 weeks as a part of an augmentation of four-session psychoeducational intervention. Individuals assigned to PRISM received prescheduled text invitations to complete a self-assessment survey at randomly scheduled times within 3–4 hour blocks throughout the day. The messages would include text that automatically opened the web browser on the smartphone, leading the participants to a web page where they could complete the survey using the smartphone touchscreen. Based on their reporting of symptoms or early warning signs on the questionnaires, preprogrammed interactive algorithm-based responses (e.g. suggested coping strategies) were generated and sent. Results showed that compared with the paper-and-pencil group, individuals in the PRISM group were very positive about the intervention and showed significantly greater reduction in depressive symptoms (Depp et al., 2014). Thus, PRISM proved to be a viable mHealth tool that can enhance the efficacy of a brief intervention for bipolar disorder.

Smartphone-based mHealth approaches can be used to facilitate both pretimed and flexible "on demand" resources for illness management and coping. One prominent example for this approach is FOCUS, a comprehensive smartphone system for self-management of schizophrenia (Ben-Zeev et al., 2014a). FOCUS treatment content was adapted from an array of evidence-based interventions (cognitive restructuring, behavioral tailoring, social skills training, anger management, behavioral activation, sleep hygiene) and distilled into brief interactive exchanges that are accompanied by illustrative images (photographs, cartoons) that are displayed on the smartphone touchscreen (see Figure 12.1). Patients can launch self-management assessments and interventions any time they want. To maximize usability, the system was developed in accordance with design principles for electronic resources for people with SMI and cognitive impairment (Rotondi et al., 2007). Iterative cycles of usability

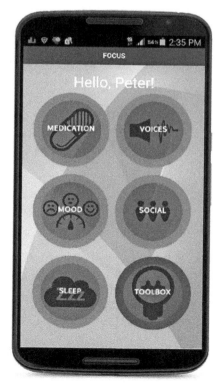

Figure 12.1 FOCUS smartphone intervention prompt and "on-demand" screen.

testing with patients helped inform improvement so that the system would be appropriate for people who may have cognitive deficits, low literacy levels and limited experience with technology.

In one study, FOCUS was given to patients to use over a 30-day period in their own environments. FOCUS feasibility, acceptability and efficacy outcomes were very promising: all participants learned to use the smartphone and the intervention system with ease. On the average, participants used FOCUS 5.6 times a day on 86.5% of the days they had the smartphones. Approximately 62% of FOCUS use was self-initiated by patients. This finding is particularly important, given that participants were not incentivized to engage, and their access to other smartphone resources was not dependent on their use of the intervention – FOCUS use was intrinsically rewarding. Approximately 90% of participants rated the intervention as highly acceptable, usable and engaging. Baseline levels of cognitive functioning, negative symptoms and persecutory ideation did not impede participants' use of the intervention. Moreover, FOCUS was helpful in reducing of positive symptoms of schizophrenia, general symptoms of psychopathology and depression over the course of one month, clinical outcomes that are comparable to or better than many in-person psychosocial interventions that are much more time- and labor-intensive. Because of these promising results, FOCUS is now being tested as part of a large multisite/ multistate services implementation effort in the United States (Ben-Zeev et al., 2014b).

Sensing. Most mHealth approaches for mental health assessment require individuals to respond to overt self-assessment items. However, advances in sensor technology have created novel opportunities for data collection approaches that place little to no burden on the individual. Personal mobile devices can now collect, store and process data that was captured by an array of sensors on the device itself (e.g. smartphone-embedded light sensors) or in one's external (e.g. wearable fitness devices that communicate with a smartphone) or internal (e.g. ingestible) environment.

Behavioral sensing is in its infancy, but findings from early work in this area are very promising. For example, in a study conducted with a nonclinical sample of college students, participants were provided with smartphones with specialized software that could repurpose the smartphone-embedded sensors to continuously collect data about their geospatial activity (using GPS and WiFi), kinesthetic activity (using multiaxial accelerometers), sleep duration (modeled using device use data, accelerometer inferences, ambient sound features and ambient light levels) and time spent proximal to human speech (i.e. speech duration using the microphone and speech detection software) over a 10-week period (Ben-Zeev et al., 2015b). Participants were instructed to carry the devices with them as they went about their daily lives. Data from the smartphones were sent automatically to a remote study server whenever the device was being charged. Participants also completed several measures of mental health (i.e. depression, stress and loneliness) before and after the study period. Results of this study showed that sensor–inferred time spent proximal to human speech, geospatial activity and sleep duration were associated with changes in participants' depression levels over the course of the study. Kinesthetic activity was associated with changes in their subjective ratings of loneliness. This proof-of-concept study demonstrated that smartphones can be harnessed as instruments for unobtrusive monitoring of several behavioral indicators of mental health (Ben-Zeev et al., 2015b).

Several attempts to use mobile behavioral sensing techniques in clinical populations have produced promising findings (Burns et al., 2011; Faurholt-Jepsen et al., 2014). For example, the MONARCA smartphone software combines self-report assessments, device use (e.g. number of incoming and outgoing calls and text messages) and sensor data collection (e.g. cell tower changes) in an attempt to collect subjective and objective measures of symptoms of bipolar disorder. Data collected over the course of a three-month field trial with individuals with bipolar disorder showed that passively collected indicators of how often individuals left their house (operationalized as the number of cell tower changes per day) were related to valid and reliable measures of depressive symptomatology (Faurholt-Jepsen et al., 2014).

Finally, sensors can also transmit information to a mobile device from inside the body. Kane et al. (2013) conducted an observational study in which individuals with schizophrenia or bipolar disorders who were taking oral medications used a digital health feedback system designed to provide objective evaluation of their treatment adherence. The system used microingestible sensors that were placed on tablets that were consumed along with their prescribed medications. After ingestion, the sensor was activated by stomach fluids and sent an identifying signal to an adhesive that sensor participants wore on the torso, which recorded the date and time of each ingestion. The wearable sensor then relayed the information to a smartphone, which stored the data and periodically transmitted them to a remote server where they could be accessed by the participants' providers. The majority of participants in the study found the approach feasible and acceptable, indicating that they would be interested in receiving reminders and notifications on their mobile devices if they forgot to take their medications (Kane et al., 2013).

Summary and Conclusions

People with mental health conditions use widely available mobile technologies in a manner that is similar to the general population. Research findings suggest that even people with severe psychiatric disabilities are willing, able and interested in using these devices for mHealth approaches that can support their illness management efforts. A host of text-based, smartphone and sensor-enabled interventions are emerging to bring innovative interventions out of the physical clinic and into the real-world contexts in which people with mental illnesses negotiate their daily lives. As a community of clinicians, stakeholders and researchers, we must understand that those in need of care are more technologically savvy than ever before. Many already seek information about their psychiatric conditions and treatments online or in the app store. Adapting our clinical models so that they capitalize on the opportunities afforded by contemporary mobile technology will ensure that individuals with psychiatric disabilities reap the rewards of innovative illness management interventions in the years ahead (Ben-Zeev, 2014).

References

Ainsworth, J., Palmier-Claus, J. E., Machin, M., Barrowclough, C., Dunn, G., Rogers, A., et al. (2013). A comparison of two delivery modalities of a mobile phone-based assessment for serious mental illness: Native smartphone application vs text-messaging only implementations. *Journal of Medical Internet Research*, 15, e60.

Ben-Zeev, D. (2012). Mobile technologies in the study, assessment, and treatment of schizophrenia. *Schizophrenia Bulletin*, 38, 384–385.

Ben-Zeev, D. (2014). How I stopped fearing technology-based interventions. *Psychiatric Services*, 65, 1183.

Ben-Zeev, D., Brenner, C. J., Begale, M., Duffecy, J., Mohr, D. C., & Mueser, K. T. (2014a). Feasibility, acceptability, and preliminary efficacy of a smartphone intervention for schizophrenia. *Schizophrenia Bulletin*, 40, 1244–1253.

Ben-Zeev, D., Davis, K. E., Kaiser, S., Krzsos, I., & Drake, R. E. (2013a). Mobile technologies among people with serious mental illness: Opportunities for future services. *Administration and Policy in Mental Health and Mental Health Services Research*, 40, 340–343.

Ben-Zeev, D., Drake, R. E., Corrigan, P. W., Rotondi, A. J., Nilsen, W., & Depp, C. A. (2012). Using contemporary technologies in the assessment and treatment of serious mental illness. *American Journal of Psychiatric Rehabilitation*, 15, 357–376.

Ben-Zeev, D., Drake, R. E., & Marsch, L. (2015a). Clinical technology specialists. *BMJ*, 350, h945.

Ben-Zeev, D., Kaiser, S. M., Brenner, C. J., Begale, M., Duffecy, J., & Mohr, D. C. (2013b). Development and usability testing of FOCUS: A smartphone system for self-management of schizophrenia. *Psychiatric Rehabilitation Journal*, 36, 289–296.

Ben-Zeev, D., Kaiser, S. M., & Krzos, I. (2014c). Remote "hovering" with individuals with psychotic disorders and substance use: Feasibility, engagement, and therapeutic alliance with a text-messaging mobile interventionist. *Journal of Dual Diagnosis*, 10, 197–203.

Ben-Zeev, D., Scherer, E. A., Wang, R., Xie, H., & Campbell, A. T. (2015b). Next-generation psychiatric assessment: Using smartphone sensors to monitor behavior and mental health. *Psychiatric Rehabilitation Journal*, 3.

Ben-Zeev, D., Schueller, S. M., Begale, M., Duffecy, J., Kane, J. M., & Mohr, D. C. (2014b). Strategies for mHealth Research: Lessons from 3 Mobile Intervention Studies. *Administration and Policy in Mental Health and Mental Health Services Research*, 42, 157–167.

Ben-Zeev, D., Wang, R., Abdullah, S., Brian, R., Scherer, E. A., Mistler, L. A., et al. (2016). Mobile behavioral sensing in outpatients and inpatients with schizophrenia. *Psychiatric Services*, 67(5), 558–561.

Berke, E. M., Choudhury, T., Ali, S., & Rabbi, M. (2011). Objective measurement of sociability and activity: mobile sensing in the community. *Annals of Family Medicine*, 9, 344–350.

Burns, M. N., Begale, M., Duffecy, J., Gergle, D., Karr, C. J., Giangrande, E., et al. (2011). Harnessing context sensing to develop a mobile intervention for depression. *Journal of Medical Internet Research*, 13, e55.

Byrne, S., Gay, G., Pollack, J. P., Gonzales, A., Retelny, D., Lee, T., et al. (2011). Caring for mobile phone-based virtual pets can influence youth eating behaviors. *Journal of Children and Media*, 6, 83–99.

Carras, M. C., Mojtabai, R., Furr-holden, C. D., Eaton, W., & Cullen, B. A. (2014). Use of mobile phones, computers and Internet among clients of an inner-city community psychiatric clinic. *Journal of Psychiatric Practice*, 20, 94–103.

Corrigan, P. (2004). How stigma interferes with mental health care. *American Psychologist*, 59, 614–625.

Damen, E. (2007). Simply persuasive: Using mobile technology to boost physical activity. In Fogg, B. J., & Eckles, D. (Eds.), *Mobile Persuasion: 20 Perspectives on the Future of Behavior Change*. Palo Alto, CA: Stanford Captology Media.

Depp, C. A., Ceglowski, J., Wang, V. C., Yaghouti, F., Mausbach, B. T., Thompson, W. K., et al. (2014). Augmenting psychoeducation with a mobile intervention for bipolar disorder: A randomized controlled trial. *Journal of Affective Disorders*, 174, 23–30.

Depp, C. A., Mausbach, B., Granholm, E., Cardenas, V., Ben-Zeev, D., Patterson, T. L., et al. (2010). Mobile interventions for severe mental illness: Design and preliminary data from three approaches. *Journal of Nervous and Mental Disease*, 198, 715–721.

Drake, R. E., Bond, G. R., & Essock, S. M. (2009). Implementing evidence-based practices for people with schizophrenia. *Schizophrenia Bulletin*, 35, 704–713.

Ennis, L., Rose, D., Denis, M., Pandit, N., & Wykes, T. (2012). Can't surf, won't surf: The digital divide in mental health. *Journal of Mental Health*, 21, 395–403.

Eyrich-Garg, K. M. (2010). Mobile phone technology: A new paradigm for the prevention, treatment, and research of the non-sheltered "street" homeless? *Journal of Urban Health*, 87, 365–380.

Faurholt-Jepsen, M., Frost, M., Vinberg, M., Christensen, E. M., Bardram, J. E,. & Kessing, L. V. (2014). Smartphone data as objective measures of bipolar disorder symptoms. *Psychiatry Research*, 217, 124–127.

Granholm, E., Ben-Zeev, D., Link, P. C., Bradshaw, K. R., & Holden, J. L. (2012). Mobile Assessment and Treatment for Schizophrenia (MATS): A pilot trial of an interactive text-messaging intervention for medication adherence, socialization, and auditory hallucinations. *Schizophrenia Bulletin*, 38, 414–425.

Granholm, E., Loh, C., & Swendsen, J. (2008). Feasibility and validity of computerized ecological momentary assessment in schizophrenia. *Schizophrenia Bulletin*, 34, 507–514.

Harrison, V., Proudfoot, J., Wee, P. P., Parker, G., Pavlovic, D. H., & Manicavasagar, V. (2011). Mobile mental health: Review of the emerging field and proof of concept study. *Journal of Mental Health*, 20, 509–524.

Haug, S., Meyer, C., Gross, B., Schorr, G., Thyrian, J. R., Kordy, H., et al. (2008). Continuous individual support of smoking cessation in socially deprived young adults via mobile phones – Results of a pilot study. *Gesundheitswesen*, 70, 364–371.

Hurling, R., Catt, M., Boni, M. D., Fairley, B. W., Hurst, T., Murray, P., et al. (2007). Using Internet and mobile phone technology to deliver an automated physical activity program: Randomized controlled trial. *Journal of Medical Internet Research*, 9, e7.

International Telecommunication Union (2013). *ICT facts and figures: The world in 2013*. Available at www.itu.int/en/ITUD/Statistics/Documents/facts/ICTFactsFigures2013-e.pdf.

Jain, N., Singh, H., Koolwal, G. D., Kumar, S., & Gupta, A. (2015). Opportunities and barriers in service delivery through mobile phones (mHealth) for severe mental illnesses in Rajasthan, India: A multi-site study. *Asian Journal of Psychiatry*, 14, 31–35.

Kane, J. M., Perlis, R. H., Dicarlo, L. A., Au-Yeung, K., Duong, J., & Petrides, G. (2013). First experience with a wireless system incorporating physiologic assessments and direct confirmation of digital tablet ingestions in ambulatory patients with schizophrenia or bipolar disorder. *Journal of Clinical Psychiatry*, 74, e533–540.

Kimhy, D., Vakhrusheva, J., Liu, Y., & Wang, Y. (2014). Use of mobile assessment technologies in inpatient psychiatric settings. *Asian Journal of Psychiatry*, 10, 90–95.

Levine, D., McCright, J., Dobkin, L., Woodruff, A. J., & Klausner, J. D. (2008). SEXINFO: A sexual health text messaging service for San Francisco youth. *American Journal of Public Health*, 98, 393–395.

Liang, X., Wang, Q., Yang, X., Cao, J., Chen, J., Mo, X., et al. (2011). Effect of mobile phone intervention for diabetes on glycaemic control: A meta-analysis. *Diabetic Medicine*, 28, 455–463.

Lund, S., & Hemed, M. (2010). Wired mothers: Use of mobile phones to improve maternal and neonatal health in Zanzibar. Copenhagen: University of Copenhagen. Available at http://www.oresund.org/logistics/content/download/74534/429853/file/Ida%20Marie%20Boas_Wired%20Mothers.pdf.

Luxton, D. D., McCann, R. A., Bush, N. E., Mishkind, M. C., & Reger, G. M. (2011). mHealth for mental health: Integrating smartphone technology in behavioral healthcare. *Professional Psychology: Research and Practice*, 42, 505–512.

Mäkelä, K., Paavola, T., & Stenman, M. (2010). Development of short message service application for patient–provider communication in clinical psychiatry. *Telemedicine and e-Health*, 16, 827–829.

McGuire, A. B., Kukla, M., Green, A., Gilbride, D., Mueser, K. T., & Salyers, M. P. (2014). Illness management and recovery: A review of the literature. *Psychiatric Services*, 65, 171–179.

Mojtabai, R., Fochtmann, L., Chang, S.-W., Kotov, R., Craig, T. J., & Bromet, E. (2009). Unmet need for mental health care in schizophrenia: An overview of literature and new data from a first-admission study. *Schizophrenia Bulletin*, 35, 679–695.

Montes, J. M., Medina, E., Gomez-Beneyto, M., & Maurino, J. (2012). A short message service (SMS)-based strategy for enhancing adherence to antipsychotic medication in schizophrenia. *Psychiatry Research*, 200, 89–95.

Myin-Germeys, I., Birchwood, M., & Kwapil, T. (2011). From environment to therapy in psychosis: A real-world momentary assessment approach. *Schizophrenia Bulletin*, 37, 244–247.

Obermayer, J. L., Riley, W. T., Asif, O., & Jean-Mary, J. (2004). College smoking-cessation using cell phone text messaging. *Journal of American College Health*, 53, 71–78.

Patrick, K., Griswold, W. G., Raab, F., & Intille, S. S. (2008). Health and the mobile phone. *American Journal of Preventive Medicine*, 35, 177–181.

Post, L. A., Vaca, F. E., Doran, K. M., Luco, C., Naftilan, M., Dziura, J., et al. (2013). New media use by patients who are homeless: The potential of mHealth to build connectivity. *Journal of Medical Internet Research*, 15, e195.

Proudfoot, J., Clarke, J., Birch, M. R., Whitton, A. E., Parker, G., Manicavasagar, V., et al. (2013). Impact of a mobile phone and web program on symptom and functional outcomes for people with mild-to-moderate depression, anxiety and stress: A randomised controlled trial. *BMC Psychiatry*, 13, 312.

Proudfoot, J., Parker, G., Hadzi-Pavlovic, D., Manicavasagar, V., Adler, E., & Whitton, A. (2010). Community attitudes to the appropriation of mobile phones for monitoring and managing depression, anxiety, and stress. *Journal of Medical Internet Research*, 12, e64.

Puccio, J. A., Belzer, M., Olson, J., Martinez, M., Salata, C., Tucker, D., et al. (2006). The use of cell phone reminder calls for assisting HIV-infected adolescents and young adults to adhere to highly active antiretroviral therapy: A pilot study. *AIDS Patient Care STDS*, 20, 438–444.

Riley, W., Obermayer, J., & Jean-Mary, J. (2008). Internet and mobile phone text messaging intervention for college smokers. *Journal of American College Health*, 57, 245–248.

Rodgers, A., Corbett, T., Bramley, D., Riddell, T., Wills, M., Lin, R. B., et al. (2005). Do u smoke after txt? Results of a randomised trial of smoking cessation using mobile phone text messaging. *Tobacco Control*, 14, 255–261.

Rotondi, A. J., Sinkule, J., Haas, G. L., Spring, M. B., Litschge, C. M., Newhill, C. E., et al. (2007). Designing websites for persons with cognitive deficits: Design and usability of a psychoeducational intervention for persons with severe mental illness. *Psychological Services*, 4, 202–224.

Sly, J., Miller, S., & Jandorf, L. (2014). The digital divide and health disparities: A pilot study examining the use of short message service (SMS) for colonoscopy reminders. *Journal of Racial and Ethnic Health Disparities*, 1, 231–237.

Smith, A. (2013). Pew Internet and American life project: Smartphone ownership 2013. Available at http://pewinternet.org/Reports/2013/Smartphone-Ownership-2013.aspx.

Smith, J. C., & Schatz, B. R. (2010). Feasibility of mobile phone-based management of chronic illness. *AMIA Annual Symposium Proceedings*, 2010, 757–761.

Smith, J. J., Morgan, P. J., Plotnikoff, R. C., Dally, K. A., Salmon, J., Okely, A. D., et al. (2014). Smartphone obesity prevention trial for adolescent boys in low-income communities: The ATLAS RCT. *Pediatrics*, 134, e723.

Spaniel, F., Hrdlicka, J., Novak, T., Kozeny, J., Hoschl, C., Mohr, P., et al. (2012). Effectiveness of the information technology-aided program of relapse prevention in schizophrenia (ITAREPS): A randomized, controlled, double-blind study. *Journal of Psychiatric Practice*, 18, 269–280.

Tomlinson, M., Rotheram-Borus, M. J., Swartz, L., & Tsai, A. C. (2013). Scaling up mHealth: Where is the evidence? *PLOS Medicine*, 10, e1001382.

Torous, J., Chan, S. R., Tan, S. Y.-M., Behrens, J., Mathew, I., Conrad, E. J., et al. (2014a). Patient smartphone ownership and interest in mobile apps to monitor symptoms of mental health conditions: A survey in four geographically distinct psychiatric cinics. *JMIR Mental Health*, 1, e5.

Torous, J., Friedman, R., & Keshavan, M. (2014b). Smartphone ownership and interest in mobile applications to monitor symptoms of mental health conditions. *JMIR Mhealth Uhealth*, 2, e2.

Trull, T. J., & Ebner-Priemer, U. (2013). Ambulatory assessment. *Annual Review of Clinical Psychology*, 9, 151–176.

United Nations Foundation (2009). *mHealth for development: The opportunity of mobile technology for healthcare in the developing world*. Washington, DC and Berkshire, UK: UN Foundation-Vodafone Foundation Partnership.

Van Gent, E., & Knoppert Van Der Klein, E. (2010). Improving compliance & treatment outcome in bipolar and schizophrenic patients by using Short Message Text Service (SMS). *International Journal of Psychiatry in Clinical Practice*, 14, 39.

Whittaker, R., Maddison, R., McRobbie, H., Bullen, C., Denny, S., Dorey, E., et al. (2008). A multimedia mobile phone-based youth smoking cessation intervention: Findings from content development and piloting studies. *Journal of Medical Internet Research*, 10, e49.

Section 2

What Does a Wellbeing Orientation Mean in Mental Health Services?

13

Wellbeing and Recovery in the Emergency Services

How Do We Care for Those Who Care for Us?

Kristen Hamling and Aaron Jarden

First responders (i.e. operational police officers, firefighters and ambulance officers) perform a critical role in our society, and as such we need them working at their best. In this chapter the authors posit that the wellbeing initiatives in many emergency service organisations are not aimed at first responders achieving their best, but instead, disproportionately, aimed at preventing their worst. That is, there is a greater emphasis on secondary and tertiary interventions that aim to prevent ill health and an incongruous emphasis on primary intervention aimed to promote good health. Applying evidence from the field of positive psychology, the authors propose that there is much to be gained in having a more balanced approach to first responder wellbeing.

The Current State of Health in the Emergency Services

Evidence indicates that emergency service work leads to various adverse consequences for first responders (Regehr and Bober, 2005; Reynolds and Wagner, 2007). First responders are at higher risk of physical (e.g. cardiovascular disease, cancer), social (e.g. divorce, work–family conflict) and psychological problems (e.g. post-traumatic stress disorder, suicide) compared with the general population (Berger et al., 2012; Johnson et al., 2005). Their work also impacts their families, with recent research showing that the spouses of first responders experience secondary traumatic stress and may meet criteria for post-traumatic stress disorder (Alrutz et al., 2015). Although wellbeing programs are commonplace in Western emergency service organisations, many lack evidence of robust effectiveness (e.g. psychological first aid: Shultz and Forbes, 2013), especially long-term effectiveness (e.g. general stress and resilience building programs: Peñalba et al., 2008), or have equivocal effectiveness at best (e.g. psychological debriefing: Devilly et al., 2006). Moreover, most wellbeing programs in emergency service organisations aim to prevent negative health outcomes arising from traumatic operational events, despite evidence that this is not their main source of stress (Stinchcomb, 2004).

International research has shown that stress in first responders is not related to any one factor, but attributable to a complex interplay of multidimensional factors (Reynolds and Wagner, 2007). Factors such as organisational stressors and daily organisational hassles (Stinchcomb, 2004), emotional labour (Blau et al., 2012) and shift work (Blau et al., 2012) all

Wellbeing, Recovery and Mental Health, ed. Mike Slade, Lindsay Oades and Aaron Jarden.
Published by Cambridge University Press. © Mike Slade, Lindsay Oades and Aaron Jarden 2017

uniquely impact the health and wellbeing of first responders. Furthermore, organisational factors have been shown to have stronger associations with traumatic stress reactions than acute critical incidents do (Collins and Gibbs, 2003; Tuckey and Haywood, 2011). According to the job demand–resources model (Bakker and Demerouti, 2007) and the conservation of resources theory (COR) (Hobfoll, 2002), cumulative exposure to high job demands depletes the physical and psychological resources of an individual, leaving fewer resources (e.g. resilience, social support) to cope effectively with subsequent stressors. Having fewer resources increases vulnerability to burnout and psychological strain (Lee and Ashforth, 1996). Such models can explain why constant exposure to organisational stress depletes first responders' personal resources, leaving fewer resources to manage a traumatic operational event when one does occur. Thus, many wellbeing initiatives, which focus on the operational aspects of the job, may not completely meet the needs of first responders.

A further limitation of wellbeing programs in the emergency services is that despite the term 'wellbeing', many of these programs are by and large deficit-based (i.e. they focus on prevention of, and recovery from, illness or injury associated with trauma exposure: Gist and Taylor, 2008). Historically, there has not been the same emphasis on promoting positive health (salutogenesis) in general, or on encouraging growth in recovery. Despite the success of wellbeing programs that specifically aim to promote positive psychological health in first responders (e.g. Priority One, Queensland Ambulance Service: Scully, 2011), promoting salutogenic wellbeing is not the norm across the industry.

In the past few decades there has been a paradigm shift in the way that health, wellbeing and recovery have been conceptualised and understood. Health is no longer conceived merely as the absence of illness or injury but as a state of optimal human functioning and positive wellbeing (Keyes, 2012). Recovery is now considered to involve a process of restoration and optimisation, rather than to be an outcome of reduced negative states (Provencher and Keyes, 2011). As this shift in health perspective has not been uniformly adopted by emergency service organisations (Hughes et al., 2012), the focus of this chapter is on reviewing evidence of the benefits of positive mental health and how this might be achieved within this population.

Completing the Care: Promoting Salutogenic Wellbeing in the Emergency Services

Traditionally health has been defined and measured as the absence of illness, with the alleviation of ill health being thought to result in good mental health (Seligman and Csikszentmihalyi, 2000). However, health and wellbeing are more complex, as recognized in the World Health Organization's definition of health – "a state of complete physical, mental and social wellbeing, and not merely the absence of disease" (1948, p. 1). But what does a complete state of mental wellbeing look like? According to Keyes (2005), health exists along two continua, one indicating the presence or absence of positive mental health and the other indicating the presence or absence of mental illness. Although there is a tendency for mental health to improve as mental illness symptoms decrease, this connection is relatively modest, so mental health cannot be directly inferred from the absence of mental illness (Keyes, 2005; Huppert and Whittington, 2003). To achieve a state of complete mental health, individuals must simultaneously experience symptoms of positive mental health and no symptoms of psychological impairment. Positive mental health includes both (1) hedonic aspects: positive feelings (life satisfaction, positive emotions and the absence of negative emotions) and (2) eudemonic aspects: positive functioning (engagement, fulfilment, sense of meaning, social wellbeing). The focus of this chapter is on positive mental health (also known as flourishing) and salutogenic recovery, due to their associated benefits.

Individuals who flourish in life experience superior psychological (positive emotions, higher resilience, less depression and anxiety), physical (cardiovascular health, stronger immune system) and social (better functioning in families, communities and workplaces) outcomes than those with incomplete health (Boehm and Kubzansky, 2012; Cohen et al., 2003; Llewellyn et al., 2008). People with high wellbeing participate in healthy behaviour more (e.g. eating more healthily, exercising more and smoking less, being involved in positive social relationships), which may explain why they achieve superior health outcomes in life (Blanchflower et al., 2012; Grant et al., 2009; Lyubomirsky et al., 2005). People who flourish in life also experience abundant positive emotions (e.g. happiness, joy, awe), which have been shown to broaden people's cognition and attention. Broadened attention helps people to think more expansively, flexibly and creatively, and this builds a repertoire of coping strategies, enabling resilient responding to stress and trauma (Cohn et al., 2009; Fredrickson, 2002). Positive emotions are particularly relevant to the emergency services, as shown in a recent police study. Galatzer-Levy et al. (2013) demonstrated that lower self-reported negative emotions and higher self-reported positive emotions experienced by police recruits ($n = 234$) predicted resilience outcomes across the first four years of active duty. As positive emotions are associated with lower cortisol (Howell et al., 2007) and improved vagal tone functioning (both shown to regulate heart rate on exposure to stress and trauma, Kok et al., 2013), first responders are likely to benefit from regular doses of positive emotions. Positive emotions may also have a key role to play when dealing with traumatic events. For instance, PTSD is linked with heart rate variability (Tan et al., 2011), and positive emotions have been shown to hasten cardiovascular recovery (Tugade and Fredrickson, 2004), which may help to prevent the onset of PTSD in first responders. Moreover, as PTSD is known to impact the same places in the brain as positive emotions do (i.e. the prefrontal cortex and amygdala, Bryant et al., 2008; Garland et al., 2010), this suggests a further reason to promote flourishing states in all first responders.

When recovery is considered in a salutogenic sense, the focus shifts from restoration to personal growth, strength and transformation. The process of mobilising resources to work through and overcome adversity fosters personal growth for some people, known as post-traumatic growth (PTG) (Tedeschi and Calhoun, 2004). People who experience PTG have a greater appreciation for life, more meaningful relationships, enhanced spiritual beliefs, a new or renewed direction and purpose in life and an increased sense of personal strength (Taku et al., 2008). Fostering the conditions for PTG in the emergency services has merit, with evidence that PTG is linked with lower depression, higher positive wellbeing (i.e. positive affect, self-esteem, life satisfaction) and improved physical health (Helgeson et al., 2006; Triplett et al., 2012).

In summary, due to the superior outcomes arising from positive wellbeing, health agencies and governments internationally (National Institute of Health and Clinical Excellence, 2012; Victorian Government Department of Health, 2011) are increasingly adopting health promotion (salutogenic) models. Moreover, with a recent return on investment (ROI) analysis revealing an average AU$2.30 return in benefits for each dollar spent on staff wellbeing (Beyond Blue and PWC, 2014), staff wellbeing makes good business sense. As such, organisations are increasingly being advised to invest in employee wellbeing because it is the 'Right Thing To Do' (ethically), the 'Legal Thing To Do' (regulatory) and the 'Smart Thing To Do' (fiscally) (Burton, 2010).

Flourishing at All Levels

In considering how to increase positive wellbeing at work, Jarden (2015) argues that workplace wellbeing programs should be addressed at the individual, group and organisational levels (i.e. strategies and tasks that employees do by themselves, with others in their organisations and that impact the whole organisation). Addressing wellbeing at each of these levels is generative, as according to the COR model 'key resources facilitate the development and use of other resources' leading to a more 'solid resource reservoir' (Hobfoll, 2002, p. 318). Individuals with solid resource reservoirs are less susceptible to resource loss and more able to invest resources back into the environment, leading to additional resource gains (Hobfoll and Shirom, 2000). Indeed, highly resourced individuals use more adaptive coping strategies, believing that they have the capacity to improve stressful situations, and low resourced individuals use more avoidant coping strategies, to conserve existing resources and prevent future resource loss (Ito and Brotheridge, 2003). The focus of this section is on resources generated at the individual, group and organisational level linked to wellbeing, resilience and growth.

I. Individual-Level Wellbeing Initiatives

The four psychological resources of hope, resilience, self-efficacy and optimism independently produce significant benefits to employee wellbeing, but when combined produce the higher-order construct known as psychological capital (PsyCap, Avey et al., 2010). PsyCap has been shown to have positive effects on employee health, work and relationships (Luthans et al., 2013) and it has been linked with greater overall wellbeing (Culbertson et al., 2010). The importance of PsyCap to wellbeing was noticeable in a military context, whereby soldiers ($n = 648$) involved in active combat deployment and assessed as having high PsyCap were more likely to appraise a potential traumatic situation as a challenge rather than a threat than individuals low in PsyCap. In turn, high-PsyCap soldiers reported less ill health (i.e. anxiety, somatic complaints and depression; Schaubroeck et al., 2011). Interventions aimed at developing PsyCap at the individual (Luthans et al., 2008) and group levels have been shown to be effective. For example, in a recent police study, Walumbwa et al. (2010) demonstrated that the PsyCap of leaders (lieutenants) significantly predicted their direct followers' (sergeants') PsyCap, which in turn predicted higher performance ratings.

II. Group-Level Wellbeing Initiatives

As each occupation is unique in the demands that are placed upon employees (Bakker and Demerouti, 2007), the resources that protect and promote employee wellbeing will likely differ according to occupational context. Hart et al. (2015) have recently demonstrated that identifying and improving the resources most meaningful to individual employees can improve the general organisational climate within organisations, in turn increasing morale and decreasing psychological distress within individuals and teams. Identifying the resources that are most meaningful to first responders' wellbeing and recovery is difficult, as there are no known studies in this area. Nonetheless, social support and effective leadership are two group-level resources that have been shown to impact wellbeing and recovery positively in diverse occupational groups, including first responders.

Social support has been shown to protect against cardiovascular disease (Kaplan et al., 1988) and against burnout and PTSD symptoms (Brewin et al., 2000) and to enhance

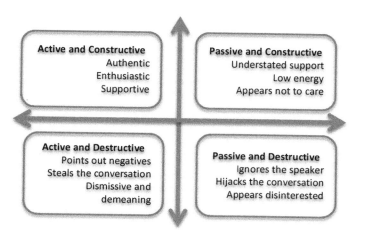

Figure 13.1 Communication styles of responding to good news (Gable et al., 2004).

recovery and post-traumatic growth (Prati and Pietrantoni, 2009). In a study of volunteer firefighters, camaraderie was shown to have the most consistent protective effect against poor psychological health, beyond a number of workplace variables (Tuckey and Hayward, 2011). Social support has also been linked with greater PTG, optimism and adaptive coping in police officers (Prati and Pietrantoni, 2009), paramedics (Shakespeare-Finch et al., 2005) and firefighters (Armstrong, et al., 2014). Given the salience of social support in wellbeing outcomes, there should be greater emphasis on enhancing the quality of supportive relationships available to first responders. A popular psychosocial intervention shown to strengthen relationship is called active constructive responding (Gable et al., 2004). Active constructive responding is a simple exercise that teaches people to respond to good news in an enthusiastic manner, thereby enhancing the feel-good factor of that move; see Figure 13.1.

Responding to others in an active and constructive way has the effect of prolonging conversations and encouraging the sharing of positive events, which in turn promotes relationship satisfaction and increases in wellbeing (Gable et al., 2004; Seligman et al., 2006). Active constructive responding is taught to peer support officers and higher-ranked officers in the US Military's Comprehensive Soldier Fitness Program, with a range of positive outcomes being reported (Reivich et al., 2011). Educating and coaching peer support officers and chain of command in this straightforward technique would be a simple, cost-effective and time-efficient way to yield positive returns (e.g. strengthen relationships and increase positive emotions throughout the organisation).

Leader behaviour has been identified as a direct contributor to stress in first responders (Brough, 2004). Improving the quality of leadership practices within the emergency services may be an effective primary prevention initiative. Indeed, supportive and positive leadership behaviours (e.g. transformational leadership) is associated with increased workplace resources, such as trust, support, teamwork, enhanced job design and organisational climate (Dutton and Spreitzer, 2014), higher wellbeing (Tafvelin et al., 2011), higher resilience (Harland et al., 2005), lower burnout (Corrigan et al., 2002) and less job-related stress (Sosik and Godshalk, 2000).

Transformational leaders have the ability to naturally motivate and appeal to others' emotions, elicit respect from others, support subordinates' unique developmental needs and stimulate subordinates' desire to learn and develop (Bass and Riggio, 2006). Although a number of management programs have shown effectiveness in raising transformational leadership (e.g. Kirkbride, 2006) they are generally expensive and labour-intensive. Given the constraints upon emergency service organisations (budgets, time, cultural considerations) any efforts to encourage a more transformational leadership approach must be made feasible. Lyons and Schneider (2009) demonstrated that simply changing the language (a transformational versus a transactional leadership style of language) in which participants received instructions for a performance-based task improved the performance, perception of social support and efficacy beliefs and reduced the stress associated with the task for each participant. We suggest that educating and coaching managers about the importance of language when communicating with staff may be another simple and cost-effective way to yield significant wellbeing returns. Incorporating transformational leadership into everyday practices within the emergency services might have an incidental flow-on effect to first responder wellbeing. For example, managers could start meetings investigating what has recently gone well, and why it has gone well, as a way of introducing positive emotions into the workplace. The 'what went well' exercise is a powerful positive psychological intervention shown to increase wellbeing (Seligman, 2012). The expression and receipt of gratitude is also strongly linked with positive emotions and wellbeing (Emmons and Mishra, 2011). Encouraging more gratitude within emergency service organisations (e.g. a small but meaningfully sent e-mail or phone call to express gratitude, or taking the time to properly thank someone who is important to you) is likely to have reverberating effects throughout the organisation. Rather than only ever hearing from your boss when something has gone wrong, we suggest that there is much to be gained when first responders hear from their boss when something has gone right.

Job crafting is another simple yet effective process shown to have profound effects on employees' wellbeing and job performance (Wrzesniewski, 2014). Job crafting occurs when employees are empowered to change aspects of their jobs to better meet their psychological needs (e.g. autonomy, strengths, passions, values). In doing so, employees experience more meaning and engagement in their work, which has the effect of generating the resources to better meet their job demands (Tims et al., 2013). The first author believes that there are ample opportunities for job crafting in the emergency services, having witnessed this first-hand over many years. For example, a firefighter who excelled in health and fitness was encouraged to lead the physical training drills for his platoon by his station officer; a police officer who had a passion for helping people was appointed to a community policing role; a paramedic who loved to teach and mentor was directed to an education role. Identifying the strengths, passions and values of first responders and accommodating these through job crafting need not be a difficult endeavour and may yield powerful wellbeing returns.

III. Organisational-Level Wellbeing Initiatives

A positive organisational climate is critical to employee wellbeing and performance. Employees working in positive organisations experience better mental and physical health (Heaphy and Dutton, 2008), higher work engagement (Schaufeli and Bakker, 2004) and lower burnout (Crawford et al., 2010). In a survey of over 1,400 UK soldiers deployed to Afghanistan in 2010, a time of high combat exposure, Jones et al. (2013) found that self-reported high levels of unit cohesion, morale and perceived good leadership were all associated with lower levels of common mental disorders and PTSD. Moreover, positive leadership practices and the quality of an organisational climate have been shown to have a much greater impact on employee wellbeing and organisational performance measures (e.g. absenteeism and compensation premiums) than only reducing or eliminating workplace stressors (for a review see Cotton and Hart, 2003).

In light of the evidence, it seems prudent that organisations also be considered as a source of wellbeing for first responders. The healthy and resilient organisation model (HERO) proposed by Salanova et al. (2012) places equal emphasis on organisational, group and individual factors when considering how to promote the positive health and wellbeing of a workforce. Validation studies of the HERO model have revealed that when organisations have healthy practices and resources at each level (e.g. team autonomy, supportive team climate, transformational leadership), teams report healthier outcomes (e.g. higher self-efficacy, engagement and resilience), which in turn leads to improved organisational outcomes (e.g. team in-role and extra-role performance) and customer loyalty and satisfaction (Salonova et al., 2012). Perhaps emergency service organisations should consider becoming HEROs.

Additionally, as employee wellbeing is affected by the interface between work and non-work, employee wellbeing should also be addressed outside the workplace.

IV. Peripheral-Level Wellbeing Initiatives

Workplace resources (e.g. leadership and workplace support, job control and variety, autonomy and learning opportunities) have been shown to spill over into other life domains (family and friends), enriching the quality and functioning of these roles too (Crain and Hammer, 2013). This spillover effect, labelled work-to-family enrichment, aids in the restoration of energy and resources in nonwork time and leads to a range of positive wellbeing outcomes (Sonnentag et al., 2012). Unfortunately, due to the high demands of emergency service work, first responder resources are often depleted (evidenced as emotional exhaustion) and this also spills over into family life, leading to work–family conflict and further emotional exhaustion (Hall et al., 2010) and secondary traumatic stress in family members (Alrutz, 2015). Nonetheless, first responders in committed relationships fare better in their health than those who are single (Shaffer, 2010).

In order to prevent stress from work spilling over into nonwork time, Sonnentag et al. (2012) have shown that a number of experiences (e.g. sports and exercise) help people to psychologically detach from work, enabling them to connect with family and leisure activities, and restore depleted resources. When people are taught how to psychologically detach from work they experience improvements in a range of wellbeing outcomes (e.g. self-efficacy, sleep quality, perceived stress and affect, Hahn et al., 2011). This is highly relevant to first responders, as their work often travels home with them, in a psychological sense (Regehr and Bober, 2005).

Conclusion

In order to protect and promote first responder wellbeing it is imperative that multidimensional approaches (i.e. primary, secondary and tertiary interventions) guide wellbeing programs (Reynolds and Wagner, 2007). Based on available evidence, we advocate that multidimensional programs focus on a continuum of health, from prevention and treatment to the promotion of good mental health, spanning the careers of first responders. Given evidence that flourishing provides a buffering effect against stress and trauma, we recommend that emergency service organisations increase the rates of flourishing in first responders as a primary prevention initiative. As Cooperrider (2014) suggests, the best way to achieve flourishing states in employees may be indirect, through the dynamic of obliquity (i.e. 'by taking attention away from something, we can actually accomplish even more than if we went directly after it', p. 160). Therefore, the pathway to first responder wellbeing may not be in going after it directly in secondary and tertiary interventions, but in fostering the conditions that naturally promote wellbeing in primary prevention initiatives (e.g. job crafting and improving the quality of social relationships). This may give the much needed intrinsic motivation and energy to effect change across all levels of the organisation.

References

Alrutz, S., Buetow, S., Huggard, P., & Cameron, L. (2015, October). What happens at work goes home. Poster presented at the Australasian Trauma Society Conference, Gold Coast, QLD, Australia.

Armstrong, D., Shakespeare-Finch, J., & Shochet, I. (2014). Predicting post-traumatic growth and post-traumatic stress in firefighters. *Australian Journal of Psychology*, 66(1), 38–46.

Avey, J. B., Luthans, F., Smith, R. M., & Palmer, N. F. (2010). Impact of positive psychological capital on employee well-being over time. *Journal of Occupational Health Psychology*, 15(1), 17–28.

Bakker, A. B., & Demerouti, E. (2007). The job demands-resources model: State of the art. *Journal of Managerial Psychology*, 22(3), 309–328.

Bass, B. M., & Riggio, R. E. (2006). *Transformational leadership*. London, UK: Lawrence Erlbaum Associates Inc.

Berger, W., Coutinho, E. S. F., Figueira, I., Marques-Portella, C., Luz, M. P., Neylan, T. C., et al. (2012). Rescuers at risk: A systematic review and meta-regression analysis of the worldwide current prevalence and correlates of PTSD in rescue workers. *Social Psychiatry and Psychiatric Epidemiology*, 47(6), 1001–1011.

Beyond Blue and Price Waterhouse Coopers (2014). Creating a Mentally Healthy Workplace, an ROI Analysis. [Online] Available at http://www.headsup.org.au/docs/default-source/resources/beyondblue_workplaceroi_finalreport_may-2014.pdf.

Blanchflower, D. G., Oswald, A. J., & Stewart-Brown, S. (2012). Is psychological well-being linked to the consumption of fruit and vegetables? *Social Indicators Research*, 114(3), 785–801.

Blau, G., Bentley, M. A., & Eggerichs-Purcell, J. (2012). Testing the impact of emotional labor on work exhaustion for three distinct emergency medical service (EMS) samples. *Career Development International*, 17(7), 626–645.

Boehm, J. K., & Kubzansky, L. D. (2012). The heart's content: The association between positive psychological well-being and cardiovascular health. *Psychological Bulletin*, 138(4), 655–691.

Bolier, L., Haverman, M., Westerhof, G. J., Riper, H., Smit, F., & Bohlmeijer, E. (2013). Positive psychology interventions: A meta-analysis of randomized controlled studies. *BMC Public Health*, 13(1), 1–20.

Brewin, C. R., Andrews, B., & Valentine, J. D. (2000). Meta-analysis of risk factors for posttraumatic stress disorder in trauma-exposed adults. *Journal of Consulting and Clinical Psychology*, 68(5), 748–759.

Brough, P. (2004). Comparing the influence of traumatic and organizational stressors on the psychological health of police, fire, and ambulance officers. *International Journal of Stress Management*, 11(3), 227–244.

Bryant, R. A., Felmingham, K., Kemp, A., Das, P., Hughes, G., Peduto, A., et al. (2008). Amygdala and ventral anterior cingulate activation predicts treatment response to cognitive behaviour therapy for post-traumatic stress disorder. *Psychological Medicine*, 38(4), 555–561.

Burton, J. (2010). *WHO healthy workplace: Background and supporting literature and practice*. Geneva, Switzerland: World Health Organization.

Cohen, S., Doyle, W. J., Turner, R. B., Alper, C. M., & Skoner, D. P. (2003). Emotional style and susceptibility to the common cold. *Psychosomatic Medicine*, 65(4), 652–657.

Cohn, M. A., Fredrickson, B. L., Brown, S. L., Mikels, J. A., & Conway, A. M. (2009). Happiness unpacked: Positive emotions increase life satisfaction by building resilience. *Emotion*, 9(3), 361–368.

Collins, P. A., & Gibbs, A. C. C. (2003). Stress in police officers: A study of the origins, prevalence and severity of stress-related symptoms within a county police force. *Occupational Medicine*, 53(4), 256–264.

Cooperrider, D. (2014). Afterword. In Laszlo, C., Brown, J., Robson, L., Saillant, R., and Sherman, D. (Eds.), *Flourishing Enterprise: The New Spirit of Business* (pp. 159–178). Palo Alto, CA: Stanford Business Books.

Corrigan, P. W., Diwan, S., Campion, J., & Rashid, F. (2002). Transformational leadership and the mental health team. *Administration and Policy in Mental Health and Mental Health Services Research*, 30(2), 97–108.

Cotton, P., & Hart, P. M. (2003). Occupational wellbeing and performance: A review of organisational health research. *Australian Psychologist*, 38(2), 118–127.

Crain, T. L., & Hammer, L. B. (2013). Work.family enrichment: A systematic review of antecedents, outcomes, and mechanisms. *Advances in Positive Organizational Psychology*, 1, 303–328.

Crawford, E. R., LePine, J. A., & Rich, B. L. (2010). Linking job demands and resources to employee engagement and burnout: A theoretical extension and meta-analytic test. *Journal of Applied Psychology*, 95(5), 834–848.

Culbertson, S. S., Fullagar, C. J., & Mills, M. J. (2010). Feeling good and doing great: The relationship between psychological capital and well-being. *Journal of Occupational Health Psychology*, 15(4), 421–433.

Devilly, G. J., Gist, R., & Cotton, P. (2006). Ready! Fire! Aim! The status of psychological debriefing and therapeutic interventions: In the work place and after disasters. *Review of General Psychology*, 10(4), 318–345.

Dutton, J. E., & Spreitzer, G. M. (2014). *How to be a positive leader: Small actions, big impact.* San Francisco, CA: Berrett-Koehler Publishers.

Emmons, R. A., & Mishra, A. (2011). Why gratitude enhances well-being: What we know, what we need to know. In Sheldon, K. M., Kashdan, T. B., and Steger, M. F. (Eds.) *Designing Positive Psychology: Taking Stock and Moving Forward* (pp. 248–262). New York, NY: Oxford University Press.

Fredrickson, B. L. (2002). The role of positive emotions in positive psychology: The broaden-and-build theory of positive emotions. *American Psychologist*, 56(3), 218–227.

Gable, S. L., Reis, H. T., Impett, E., & Asher, E. R. (2004). What do you do when things go right? The intrapersonal and interpersonal benefits of sharing positive events. *Journal of Personality and Social Psychology*, 87(2), 228–245.

Galatzer-Levy, I. R., Brown, A. D., Henn-Haase, C., Metzler, T. J., Neylan, T. C., & Marmar, C. R. (2013). Positive and negative emotion prospectively predict trajectories of resilience and distress among high-exposure police officers. *Emotion*, 13(3), 545.

Garland, E. L., Fredrickson, B., Kring, A. M., Johnson, D. P., Meyer, P. S., & Penn, D. L. (2010). Upward spirals of positive emotions counter downward spirals of negativity: Insights from the broaden-and-build theory and affective neuroscience on the treatment of emotion dysfunctions and deficits in psychopathology. *Clinical Psychology Review*, 30(7), 849–864.

Gist, R., & Taylor, V. H. (2008). Occupational and organizational issues in emergency medical services behavioral health. *Journal of Workplace Behavioral Health*, 23(3), 309–330.

Grant, N., Wardle, J., & Steptoe, A. (2009). The relationship between life satisfaction and health behavior: A cross-cultural analysis of young adults. *International Journal of Behavioral Medicine*, 16(3), 259–268.

Hahn, V. C., Binnewies, C., Sonnentag, S., & Mojza, E. J. (2011). Learning how to recover from job stress: Effects of a recovery training program on recovery, recovery-related self-efficacy, and well-being. *Journal of Occupational Health Psychology*, 16(2), 202–216.

Hall, G. B., Dollard, M. F., Tuckey, M. R., Winefield, A. H., & Thompson, B. M. (2010). Job demands, work–family conflict, and emotional exhaustion in police officers: A longitudinal test of competing theories. *Journal of Occupational and Organizational Psychology*, 83(1), 237–250.

Harland, L., Harrison, W., Jones, J. R., & Reiter-Palmon, R. (2005). Leadership behaviors and subordinate resilience. *Journal of Leadership and Organizational Studies*, 11(2), 2–14.

Hart, P. M., Cotton, P., & Scollay, C. E. (2015). Flourishing at work: Improving wellbeing and engagement. In Burke, R. M., Page, K. M., and Cooper, C. (Eds.), *Flourishing in Life, Work and Careers: Individual Wellbeing and Career Experiences* (pp. 281–303). Cheltenham, UK: Edward Elgar Publishing.

Heaphy, E. D., & Dutton, J. E. (2008). Positive social interactions and the human body at work: Linking organizations and physiology. *Academy of Management Review*, 33(1), 137–162.

Helgeson, V. S., Reynolds, K. A., & Tomich, P. L. (2006). A meta-analytic review of benefit finding and growth. *Journal of Consulting and Clinical Psychology*, 74(5), 797–816.

Hobfoll, S. E. (2002). Social and psychological resources and adaptation. *Review of General Psychology*, 6(4), 307–324.

Hobfoll, S.E., & Shirom, A. (2000). Conservation of resources theory: Applications to stress and management in the workplace. In Golembiewski, R.T. (Ed*.), Handbook of Organization Behavior* (pp. 57–81). Dekker, New York.

Howell, R. T., Kern, M. L., & Lyubomirsky, S. (2007). Health benefits: Meta-analytically determining the impact of well-being on objective health outcomes. *Health Psychology Review*, 1(1), 83–136.

Hughes, R., Kinder, A., & Cooper, C. (2012). Post-trauma support: Learning from the past to help shape a better future. *International Handbook of Workplace Trauma Support*, 474–485.

Huppert, F. A., & Whittington, J. E. (2003). Evidence for the independence of positive and negative well-being: Implications for quality of life assessment. *British Journal of Health Psychology*, 8(1), 107–122.

Ito, J. K., & Brotheridge, C. M. (2003). Resources, coping strategies, and emotional exhaustion: A conservation of resources perspective. *Journal of Vocational Behavior*, 63(3), 490–509.

Jarden, A., & Jarden, R. (2015). Positive psychological assessment for the workplace. In Oades, L., Steger, M., Della-Fave, A., and Passmore, J. (Eds.), *The Wiley-Blackwell Handbook of the Psychology of Positivity and Strengths-Based Approaches at Work* (in press). John Wiley and Sons.

Johnson, S., Cooper, C., Cartwright, S., Donald, I., Taylor, P., & Millet, C. (2005). The experience of work-related stress across occupations. *Journal of Managerial Psychology*, 20(2), 178–187.

Jones, M., Sundin, J., Goodwin, L., Hull, L., Fear, N. T., Wessely, S., et al. (2013). What explains post-traumatic stress disorder (PTSD) in UK service personnel: Deployment or something else? *Psychological Medicine*, 43(08), 1703–1712.

Kaplan, G. A., Salonen, J. T., Cohen, R. D., Brand, R. J., Syme, S. L., & Puska, P. (1988). Social connections and mortality from all causes and from cardiovascular disease: Prospective evidence from eastern Finland. *American Journal of Epidemiology*, 128(2), 370–380.

Keyes, C. L. (2005). Mental illness and/or mental health? Investigating axioms of the complete state model of health. *Journal of Consulting and Clinical Psychology*, 73(3), 539.

Keyes, C. L. (2012). *Mental well-being: International contributions to the study of positive mental health*. Springer.

Kirkbride, P. (2006). Developing transformational leaders: The full range leadership model in action. *Industrial and Commercial Training*, 38(1), 23–32.

Kok, B. E., Coffey, K. A., Cohn, M. A., Catalino, L. I., Vacharkulksemsuk, T., Algoe, S. B., et al. (2013). How positive emotions build physical health: Perceived positive social connections account for the upward spiral between positive emotions and vagal tone. *Psychological Science*, 24(7), 1123–1132.

Lee, R. T., & Ashforth, B. E. (1996). A meta-analytic examination of the correlates of the three dimensions of job burnout. *Journal of Applied Psychology*, 81(2), 123.

Llewellyn, D. J., Lang, I. A., Langa, K. M., & Huppert, F. A. (2008). Cognitive function and psychological well-being: Findings from a population-based cohort. *Age and Ageing*, 37(6), 685–689.

Luthans, F., Avey, J. B., & Patera, J. L. (2008). Experimental analysis of a web-based training intervention to develop positive psychological capital. *Academy of Management Learning and Education*, 7(2), 209–221.

Luthans, F., Youssef, C. M., Sweetman, D. S., & Harms, P. D. (2013). Meeting the leadership challenge of employee well-being through relationship PsyCap and health PsyCap. *Journal of Leadership and Organizational Studies*, 20(1), 118–133.

Lyons, J. B., & Schneider, T. R. (2009). The effects of leadership style on stress outcomes. *The Leadership Quarterly*, 20(5), 737–748.

Lyubomirsky, S., King, L., & Diener, E. (2005). The benefits of frequent positive affect: Does happiness lead to success? *Psychological Bulletin*, 131(6), 803–855.

National Institute of Health and Clinical Excellence (2012). Methods for the development of NICE public health guidance (third ed.). [Online] Available at https://www.nice.org.uk/article/pmg4.

Peñalba, V., McGuire, H., & Leite, J. R. (2008). Psychosocial interventions for prevention of psychological disorders in law enforcement officers. *Cochrane Database of Systematic Reviews*, 3.

Prati, G., & Pietrantoni, L. (2009). Optimism, social support, and coping strategies as factors contributing to posttraumatic growth: A meta-analysis. *Journal of Loss and Trauma*, 14(5), 364–388.

Provencher, H. L., & Keyes, C. L. (2011). Complete mental health recovery: Bridging mental illness with positive mental health. *Journal of Public Mental Health*, 10(1), 57–69.

Regehr, C., & Bober, T. (2005). *In the line of fire: Trauma in the emergency services*. New York, NY: Oxford University Press.

Reivich, K. J., Seligman, M. E., & McBride, S. (2011). Master resilience training in the US Army. *American Psychologist*, 66(1), 25–34.

Reynolds, C. A., & Wagner, S. L. (2007). Stress and first responders: The need for a multidimensional approach to stress management. *International Journal of Disability Management*, 2(2), 27–36.

Salanova, M., Llorens, S., Cifre, E., & Martínez, I. M. (2012). We need a hero! Toward a validation of the healthy and resilient organization (HERO) model. *Group and Organization Management*, 37(6), 785–822.

Schaubroeck, J. M., Riolli, L. T., Peng, A. C., & Spain, E. S. (2011). Resilience to traumatic exposure among soldiers deployed in combat. *Journal of Occupational Health Psychology*, 16(1), 18–37.

Schaufeli, W. B., & Bakker, A. B. (2004). Job demands, job resources, and their relationship with burnout and engagement: A multi-sample study. *Journal of Organizational Behavior*, 25(3), 293–315.

Scully, P. J. (2011). Taking care of staff: A comprehensive model of support for paramedics and emergency medical dispatchers. *Traumatology*, 17(4), 35.

Seligman, M. E. (2012). *Flourish: A visionary new understanding of happiness and well-being*. Simon and Schuster.

Seligman, M. E., & Csikszentmihalyi, M. (2000). Positive psychology: An introduction. *American Psychologist*, 55(1), 5–14.

Seligman, M. E., Rashid, T., & Parks, A. C. (2006). Positive psychotherapy. *American Psychologist*, 61, 774–788.

Shaffer, T. J. (2010). A comparison of firefighters and police officers: The influence of gender and relationship status. *Adultspan Journal*, 9(1), 36–49.

Shakespeare-Finch, J., Gow, K., & Smith, S. (2005). Personality, coping and posttraumatic growth in emergency ambulance personnel. *Traumatology: An International Journal*, 11(4), 325–334.

Shultz, J. M., & Forbes, D. (2013). Psychological first aid: Rapid proliferation and the search for evidence. *Disaster Health*, 1(2), 1–10.

Sonnentag, S., Niessen, C., & Neff, A. (2012). Recovery: Non-work experiences that promote positive states. In Cameron, K. S., & Spreitzer, G. M. (Eds.), *The Oxford Handbook of Positive Organizational Scholarship*. (pp. 867–881). New York, NY: Oxford University Press.

Sosik, J. J., & Godshalk, V. M. (2000). Leadership styles, mentoring functions received, and job-related stress: A conceptual model and preliminary study. *Journal of Organizational Behavior*, 21(4), 365–390.

Stinchcomb, J. B. (2004). Searching for stress in all the wrong places: Combating chronic organizational stressors in policing. *Police Practice and Research*, 5(3), 259–277.

Tafvelin, S., Armelius, K., & Westerberg, K. (2011). Toward understanding the direct and indirect effects of transformational leadership on well-being: A longitudinal study. *Journal of Leadership and Organizational Studies*, 18(4), 480–492.

Taku, K., Cann, A., Calhoun, L. G., & Tedeschi, R. G. (2008). The factor structure of the Posttraumatic Growth Inventory: A comparison of five models using confirmatory factor analysis. *Journal of Traumatic Stress*, 21(2), 158–164.

Tan, G., Dao, T. K., Farmer, L., Sutherland, R. J., & Gevirtz, R. (2011). Heart rate variability (HRV) and posttraumatic stress disorder (PTSD): A pilot study. *Applied Psychophysiology and Biofeedback*, 36(1), 27–35.

Tedeschi, R. G., & Calhoun, L. G. (2004). Posttraumatic growth: Conceptual foundations and empirical evidence. *Psychological Inquiry*, 15(1), 1–18.

Tims, M., Bakker, A. B., & Derks, D. (2013). The impact of job crafting on job demands, job resources, and well-being. *Journal of Occupational Health Psychology*, 18(2), 230–240.

Triplett, K. N., Tedeschi, R. G., Cann, A., Calhoun, L. G., & Reeve, C. L. (2012). Posttraumatic growth, meaning in life, and life satisfaction in response to trauma. *Psychological Trauma: Theory, Research, Practice, and Policy*, 4(4), 400–410.

Tuckey, M. R., & Hayward, R. (2011). Global and occupation-specific emotional resources as buffers against the emotional demands of fire-fighting. *Applied Psychology*, 60(1), 1–23.

Tugade, M. M., & Fredrickson, B. L. (2004). Resilient individuals use positive emotions to bounce back from negative emotional experiences. *Journal of Personality and Social Psychology*, 86(2), 320–333.

Victorian Government Department of Health (2011). Victorian Public Health and Wellbeing Plan 2011–2015. [Online] Available at http://www.health.vic.gov.au/prevention/vphwplan.htm [accessed 20 June 2014].

Walumbwa, F. O., Peterson, S. J., Avolio, B. J., & Hartnell, C. A. (2010). An investigation of the relationships among leader and follower psychological capital, service climate, and job performance. *Personnel Psychology*, 63(4), 937–963.

Wrzesniewski, A. (2014). Engage in job crafting. In Dutton, J., and Spreitzer, G. (Eds.), *How to Be a Positive Leader: Insights from Leading Thinkers on Positive Organisations*. San Francisco, CA: Berrett-Koehler Publishers.

World Health Organization (1948). *Constitution of the World Health Organization*. Geneva, Switzerland: World Health Organization.

Chapter

14

Recovery Learning Communities and the Road to Wellbeing

Deborah Delman and Jonathan Delman

Like anyone else, people with serious mental health conditions (SMHCs) are interested in being valued members of the community at large. However, people with SMHCs find that the traditional services they encounter are focused mainly on symptom management and stability, and are not designed to help them attain a life beyond "illness" (i.e. recovery). In 2003 the President's New Freedom Commission released its blueprint for transformed mental health services, with "recovery" as the cornerstone (United States Department of Health and Human Services 2003). Since then many recovery-oriented policies and service models have been created and disseminated, but changes in practice have been slow and often unsustainable because of a strong and closed off service culture (Clossey et al., 2011).

In 2005 peer-operated and staffed Recovery Learning Communities (RLCs) emerged in Massachusetts (US) to both develop a statewide peer support network and promote systems transformation through the development of innovative peer services (e.g. respites) (Delman et al. 2014). RLCs train people in being peer support facilitators and then pay them to facilitate peer support groups, educational workshops and public education throughout a designated geographic region. The overall goal is to provide alternatives to traditional mental health services, support self-advocacy and develop collaborations that decrease discrimination and increase mental health recovery-oriented practices in both the service system and the natural community.

The development of the RLC concept in the early 2000s was driven by the Transformation Center (TC), a statewide peer-operated advocacy and training organization that operates two RLCs. While the TC's mission was focused on recovery (from mental illnesses, addictions and/or trauma), the board wanted to bridge the socially created chasm that segregates diagnosed "mental patients" from the community at large. Thus, it developed a *vision* statement promoting "wellbeing," a concept more broadly applicable than "recovery." In addition, RLC activities were made available to both diagnosed and undiagnosed people.

The principles of positive psychology (PP) are well represented in recovery-oriented care and RLC support approaches. PP is a humanistic approach to helping people achieve wellbeing by focusing on a person's strengths, chosen activities and positive outcomes, and is considered applicable to people who are the most troubled or symptomatic (Duckworth et al., 2005).

In this paper, we describe the RLC model, its relationship to PP and how it promoted wellbeing and related positive outcomes. We also discuss the particular challenges people with SMHC face in achieving well-being and how RLCs/recovery diverge from PP in several ways.

Wellbeing, Recovery and Mental Health, ed. Mike Slade, Lindsay Oades and Aaron Jarden.
Published by Cambridge University Press. © Mike Slade, Lindsay Oades and Aaron Jarden 2017

A Conceptual Framework for Recovery Learning Communities

The RLC framework is driven by five key values that delineate the foundation for RLC practices: (1) mutuality, (2) being part of the solution, (3) self-determination, (4) independence, and (5) social justice.

Mutual relationships grow from interchanges that support all involved, not only people who assume a help-recipient role (Mead et al., 2001). Staff and participants realize that supporting another person facilitates one's own recovery.

Being part of the solution. The personal and collective responsibility assumed in this value highlights strengths present in each person that thriving communities depend on. Personal strengths and efficacy are the focus, not symptoms.

Self-determination is having the mind-set and capacity to make decisions about one's life based on one's own motivations, self-knowledge and goals (Corrigan et al. 2012). Thus, participation in any aspect of a RLC's activities is completely voluntary.

Independence. RLC opportunities often build or exercise skills that strengthen self-reliance, such as managing self-care needs and knowing how to advocate for oneself (Repper and Carter 2011).

Social justice protects the rights and privileges of individuals and groups in a community and includes participation in committees that address such concerns (Mead et al., 2001). For example, the RLCs worked collaboratively with others to enact a 2015 law defining a right to fresh air during psychiatric hospitalization.

RLC staff and community member volunteers develop initiatives that promote "recovery," "learning" and "community" throughout the geographic region that the RLC covers. RLCs generate peer support meetings and have an ongoing need for confident peer support facilitators, who receive mentoring and exemplify the five organizational values. Classes and training are typically practical and incorporate experiential exercises. RLCs develop skills through work activities such as peer support volunteerism and paid peer group facilitation. They also support functional growth, including resume development, job search support and computer skill development. Community-building activities include recreation activities and community volunteerism. A common denominator of RLC learning opportunities is the possibility for increased quality of interactions with the public by convening educational and cultural events.

The RLC conceptual model described below (see Figure 14.1) relies on the Donabedian framework for identifying its structure, process and outcomes (Mosadeghrad 2012). Structure refers to the physical and organizational aspects of settings and includes program resources, staff and equipment. Processes are the opportunities and interpersonal interactions among participants and staff. Outcomes are the short- and long-term effects of RLC participation.

Peer-Run and -Staffed Organizations

Peer-run organizations, in which the staff and 51% of the board are people diagnosed with SMHC, are uniquely capable of creating a culture of psychological safety and recovery in which peer support can thrive (Ostrow and Leaf, 2014). Research supports the effectiveness of peer-run programs in improving people's social support, coping skills, vocational status, community tenure and quality of life (U.S. Department of Health and Human Services, Substance Abuse, and Mental Health Services Administration, 2011). Because they are administratively and financially controlled and staffed by peers, non-recovery-focused

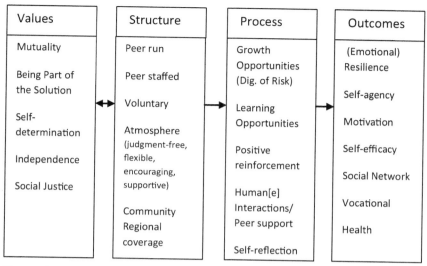

Figure 14.1 Conceptual model for recovery learning communities.

organizational managerial interference is minimized, and there is the potential for organizational growth through training program development and advocacy for recovery-oriented practices.

With peer staffing there is an expectation that participants will be treated with greater empathy, understanding and connectedness (Mead et al., 2001). RLC staff and facilitators are trained to present themselves holistically, thereby minimizing the inevitable power imbalance between staff and participants. RLC staff disclose personal lived experience with mental health problems and information about what helps them in recovery in mutual support contexts that foster genuine connection and friendship. Peer workers recognize that the person is the expert on his/her own life, and that the experience of illness or disability is only one part of the person.

Peer leadership and staff provide the most concrete evidence to participants that recovery and a full life are possible, fostering hopefulness in participants (Ostrow and Leaf, 2014). Many people with SMHCs have been told by clinicians that psychiatric stability is their only goal. Without hope and pathways to explore recovery, people begin to "accept their lot" and settle into an existence that is segregated from the mainstream of life.

RLC Atmosphere/Voluntariness and the Reawakening of Self-Agency

The RLC atmosphere has been described by participants as open, judgment-free, flexible, encouraging and trusting (Delman et al., 2015). Visual arts and music enhance the atmosphere by expanding paths for connection and collaboration. RLCs emphasize creativity through art gallery openings, music lessons and "open mike" events. This atmosphere is derivative of leadership, staff and participants embracing the five core values described above.

RLC participation is completely voluntary. People participate in whatever meetings and activities they choose, in whatever "dosages" they desire. RLCs do not structure participant goal setting; people may articulate a goal in peer support meetings and will receive support and encouragement there, or they may take classes or workshops in which personal goal setting is encouraged. The voluntary nature of the RLC model is founded on the belief that the awakening, sustaining and refining of self-agency are essential to mental health recovery. Thus respect for the choices a person makes is an essential and defining component of RLC organizational culture.

RLC participants choose the activities that make the most sense to them. Participants are not assessed as "needing" a particular activity, and no activity is required, with the exception at some RLCs of orientation to RLC opportunities and responsibilities. Staff and participants are friendly and encourage the person to do what is appealing, eliminating pressure. Staff and participants are trained to welcome involvement, but not to require it. This includes not putting expectations on a person to speak up or be "on the spot" in a support meeting. Trust emerges from this, so that relationships develop with staff and other participants, and leads to a personal openness to try new things. When a person does join an activity or choose to speak up, the action is clearly a personal choice and an initiative the person can recognize as his or her own. These demonstrations of self-agency help launch voluntary learning, self-efficacy and some relief and hope. Participants have often not experienced this kind of "treatment/healing" environment in previous programs, which tend to have more prescribed culture-bound activities.

Participants can appear "awkward" or "strange" and not be concerned with negative judgments. When a person acts in a manner that is disruptive to the atmosphere of relaxation, trust and friendliness, individual support is offered by staff or participants. Staff and participants are trained to facilitate connection and to discuss situations or conflicts from a stance of shared power and support.

Many new RLC participants are isolated and have poor self-images. The RLC atmosphere offers a steady recovery lift-off point for those deeply struggling. Many participants hear the term "recovery" for the first time and observe its reality through peer growth and leadership. Many participants who have been socially isolated except for contact with treatment staff and family begin talking to other people for the first time in a long while. They learn that they cannot depend on the treatment system to improve their quality of life and that their own choices and initiatives drive recovery. The person begins to understand that effort and personal responsibility are not only important, but within his/her grasp.

Improvements for many are incremental, but over time, as they take on new societal responsibilities (e.g. work), their RLC participation may decrease. Skills they learn through RLC participation (including computer, social and vocational) help sustain them beyond the RLC.

Compassionate Human Interaction – Generating Resilience and Health

RLC structures and activities create many opportunities for compassionate human interactions, which we define as caring, sensitive and respectful. Peer support groups exemplify such interactions. Peer support groups take place throughout the day on and off site. With support groups, peers discuss shared concerns and offer emotional support and coping strategies that promote personal wellbeing. Peer support is effective because people dealing with similar issues are more likely to relate to one another with empathy and validation (Mead et al., 2001). With reciprocity all participants benefit through improved self-esteem and personal empowerment (Repper and Carter, 2011).

In RLCs participants have found meaning in their connection to other participants, staff and friends they develop. RLCs bring people who have experienced suffering as well as oppression into contact with each other. This kind of social support acts as a counterbalance to stress, improving overall health and well-being (Delman et al., 2014).

Crisis and wellness planning is based on peer support approaches. This includes regular classes in the Wellness Recovery Action Planning Approach (WRAP). The WRAP program is a peer-led 8–12 week educational skill building class to enhance wellness on a day-to-day basis and to prevent crisis situations. Many RLC participants have reported stress management improvements because of having attended WRAP training (Delman et al., 2015). With increased emotional *resilience*, participants are better able to reduce or weather extreme emotional states. This resilience also prepares them to handle the ups and downs of the recovery process, including significant disappointments along the way.

RLCs maintain a variety of peer support and wellness education activities. For example, those who participate in peer support among voice hearers often find that they learn to reduce distressing and distracting experiences with voice hearing. Participants who try yoga or exercise or another experiential class often report using the activity independently. Additional peer-driven educational opportunities include alternative mindfulness, financial wellness and health self-advocacy.

Opportunities and Communities – Motivation and Self-Efficacy

The "Learning Community" aspect of the RLC model focuses on

- Learning from the peer support context described above
- Learning from classes and workshops
- Learning from engaging with the public across the large geographic span of a RLC region

A core competency for all RLC activity is facilitation skills that bring forth the core value of mutuality. Adult learning is most effective when the learners contribute their knowledge as well as "the teacher." Facilitator training emphasizes supporting a person in taking action to support him/herself, and resisting the temptation to act on behalf of another person. Participants can take a training class when they believe they are ready to do so, not when they are assessed as ready. Classes and workshops reflect participant interests and the skills facilitators have to offer. They tend to focus on three areas: learning to facilitate, learning about recovery in a class and learning through experiential activity (e.g. poetry, yoga, drumming, advocacy, drawing, public speaking).

RLC participants also initiate or participate in a task group to organize a community event, to respond to an RLC need or to address an advocacy issue. Externally the most common opportunities pursued are jobs and education, although people also pursue creative, political, religious and social connections. It is through taking advantage of such opportunities that participants demonstrate to both themselves and others that they "have what it takes" to be full participants in society.

RLCs help participants learn by connecting to the public across the geographic community of the RLC. "Community" is defined by each RLC participant and frequently starts with the RLC itself, but expands to incorporate other people and social groups. RLCs hold open community planning meetings to set short- and long-term priorities through a dynamic process of identifying the community's passion for various initiatives and then assessing available resources. RLCs take stock of the needs and resources within the entire geographic area they are responsible for and develop collaborations to promote local facilitators. For example, if a community homeless shelter lacks peer support options, the RLC will seek and train facilitators who have the lived experience of finding a stable home after homelessness and thus are able to provide peer support in the shelter. If LGBTQI community members lack support and are experiencing extreme emotional distress, the RLC will seek and train LGBTQI facilitators to offer peer support in the local library. If an RLC participant is passionate about promoting exercise as a method he or she uses to improve his or her own mental health, he or she might gather an RLC task group so that the RLC can host a large public exercise event to connect with people in the general public who may be using or may benefit from exercise for mental health.

Social Networks, Health and Vocation

People with SMHC have historically had weak social networks, poor health and low employment rates (Draine et al., 2002). This is largely explained by the social distance that has been created between people with such diagnoses and those without. Mental health clients/patients have historically been segregated for extended periods of time through the delivery of services (e.g. long-term state hospitals) and by being "housed" in large residential "programs" or group homes (Delman et al., 2014). Focusing primarily on clinical stability as they see it, many providers have discouraged social interaction and competitive employment due to a concern that the stress of these activities could cause clients to "relapse." This imposed segregation is internalized as self-stigma, a feeling of not belonging, or even being rejected by the community at large.

In the rich relational RLC context, participants have a chance to ameliorate these challenges to recovery and well-being. At RLCs, staff and participants disclose a broad range of life activity that illustrates the fact that, and the methods by which, people with mental health conditions are able to work, establish stable home environments and nurturing relationships, have a social life and engage in enjoyable activities. Many participants cite making friends with both other participants and others they meet in person or on line as a major accomplishment. Many meet and call each other outside of RLC-sponsored activities. In addition, many RLC participants have successfully established community roles as students, employees, religious/spiritual members, arts society members, advocates, romantic partners and parents. The development of these social networks, as well as wellness action plans, seem to lead to improved wellness for participants, including reduced hospital and emergency room use (Delman et al., 2015).

Practical skills and self-advocacy are part of learning about choices that lead to strengthened social networks and community connection (Draine et al., 2002). People experience success at job searches and learn about electronic social media to communicate with family and to connect with old friends. Financial peace class members successfully achieve their financial goals, which include reducing interest rates on credit card debt, securing affordable car loans, setting up savings accounts and saving for presents for others.

RLCs, Recovery and Positive Psychology

The concepts of recovery and positive psychology (PP) similarly promote a strengths-based, hopeful approach to mental health and service provision.

A recent review identified six core domains for PP: (1) character strengths, (2) happiness, (3) growth, (4) the good life, (5) thriving and (6) resiliency (Schrank et al. 2014). The PP field was formally introduced in the 1990s by Seligman and Csikszentmihalyi as "moving away from studying negative psychological concepts, such as learned helplessness, to investigating what constitutes a good and fulfilling life, such as the study of happiness, learned optimism, and flourishing" (Moran and Nemec, 2013, p. 203).

Recovery is both a process and an outcome for people with SMHC. Deegan and others have delineated it as a process through which the person in his or her chosen manner works to attain a valued social role (Deegan 1996). But while having a serious mental health condition/illness is debilitating and destabilizing, it is not the major barrier to achieving well-being. Not only is recovery a nonlinear, unpredictable process, but also there are multiple barriers, largely externally imposed, that make the recovery process uncertain, very discouraging and very difficult (Cook and Mueser, 2013; Corrigan et al., 2012).

Thus, the U.S. Department of Health and Human Services, Substance Abuse, and Mental Health Services Administration (SAMHSA) has since conceptualized recovery within four dimensions: (1) health, (2) home, (3) community and (4) purpose (U.S. Department of Health and Human Services, 2012). That is, for people with SMHC, home and health are not assumed. People with SMHC often have co-morbid conditions, low life expectancies, and high rates of homelessness or unsafe and unsatisfying housing (Draine et al., 2002). In addition, people with a mental health diagnosis experience discrimination at all levels of community participation. Discrimination represents deep-seated fears of others – not related to reality – frequently resulting in serious social, health access and assessment, civil rights and economic disenfranchisement (Link et al., 2001). Concrete harms include discrimination in employment, housing, parental rights, emergency room triage and court involvement and detention (Draine et al., 2002). For example, people with SMHC find the physicians are less likely to accept their assessments of physical health issues, and are even ignored when reporting physical health emergency, often being placed inappropriately in a psychiatric facility instead. Employment barriers are frequent for people in recovery who often have had periods of time off work, résumé gaps, that make them unappealing to employers. Because many people with SMHC are unable to find or retain work and/or have weak family support, they live in poverty or at subsistence levels with some public assistance (Cook and Mueser, 2013). With lack of access to good treatment and misunderstanding of their behavior, they have high rates of criminal justice involvement, with cascading barriers to housing and employment.

People with SMHC then frequently internalize this discrimination as "stigma," resulting in self-devaluation and a lowered sense of esteem and agency. Many RLC visitors who have been in the traditional system experience shame and self-loathing and are socially isolated. Many RLC participants report losing their friends after receiving a mental illness diagnosis. They are frequently socially marginalized or excluded due to oppression and poverty. Many have been dependent on a narrowly focused service system and have very low expectations bestowed on them by clinicians and family. Thus, along with funding the development of employment and housing supports, SAMHSA has also focused on stigma amelioration and social inclusion, problems not easily impacted, and a major and continuous barrier to well-being that people with SMHC must struggle with.

RLCs that recognize the standard deficit-based approach to healing as ineffective naturally have many of the qualities that PP supports. In Table 14.1, we draw connections between

Table 14.1 RLC Values and Wellbeing Connections

RLC values	Relevance to positive psychology and wellbeing	RLC activity
Mutuality	Positive relationships Positive emotion Meaning	Peer support meetings, individual peer support, recreational/arts/culture events, facilitation style of educational workshops, self-disclosure by staff and participants, personal limit setting by staff and participants
Being part of the solution	Positive emotion Meaning Accomplishment	Volunteer opportunities, decision-making and conflict resolution participation processes, skill development opportunities to strengthen leadership, facilitation, presentation or other skills, RLC leadership activity
Self-determination	Engagement	Self-selection of participation opportunities Self-advocacy skills development Information on resources to support
Independence	Accomplishment	*Skill development opportunities *Leadership development opportunities *Vocational development
Social justice	Meaning	*RLC leadership activity *Collective advocacy for new rights or opportunities

RLC values and their relevance to wellbeing and to related RLC activity, as described in Table 14.1, which draws the link between RLC values and PP.

Below we describe two ways in which we believe that RLCs are not consistent with PP: (1) focus on self-determination and (2) elements of peer support.

Self-determination is more than a value; it is a learned process for reaching desired personal outcomes. The evidence is clear that engaging in a self-determined process and life is significantly associated with improved wellness, motivation and self-efficacy for people with disabilities, including mental illness (Moran et al., 2014; Williams et al., 2011).

Self-determination theory (SDT) has generally not been seen as a key element of PP (Sheldon and Ryan, 2011). As noted by Sheldon and Ryan (2011, p. 33): "SDT goes beyond most PP theories because it also provides a dialectical account of the 'negative' factors and processes which can get in the way of people's optimal functioning." That is, the inducements to "positive" actions of PP can be inconsistent with the focus on intrinsic motivation of SDT. PP practitioners do not necessarily have the requisite self-determination skill-building competencies, which can be difficult to attain. In addition, helpers can be "over-controlling," promoting actions that are most likely to result in what they see as positive outcomes, which is more likely when the client has a mental illness diagnosis (Corrigan et al., 2012). Clients consequently are often reluctant to fully assert themselves within such a relationship (Sheldon and Ryan, 2011). With regard to RLCS and recovery, this would be a poor outcome, since one's "dignity of risk" is essential to a self-determining life.

Speaking personally for the moment, for the first author here, Dr. Jonathan Delman, holding on to this "dignity of risk" was essential to his recovery. When just starting the recovery process, he was told by several practitioners that he should not work with other people. Given the nature of his personality and his own need to work, he ignored what they said. He had to reject these admonishments to attain his current career, relationships and sense of wellbeing.

This "dignity of risk" also has value because people can learn from not taking the "best" path (Corrigan et al., 2012). RLCs meet people whose goal is to become a physician or an accountant, and it does not seem possible given their history and vocational background. Nevertheless we go forward to support them on *their* journeys. Some have learned through reading about job requirements or losing a job that another career direction is a better idea. Other situations are even more personal. One woman wanted support to regain custody of her child through the heartbreaking process of going to meet with social workers and appear in court. For the average person it did not appear that she had a chance, but she won the heart of two RLC women who had experienced custody issues. They helped her prepare and gave her emotional support. With support, the woman came to terms with her grief about not being ready for parenting, yet vigorous engagement in the process convinced the judge to support her son's adoption by a family who were committed to their ongoing relationship.

The nature of peer support also can involve a departure from a positive psychology framework. Peer support meetings offer an opportunity for people to share from their hearts about concerns, hopes, uncertainty, suffering and successes. Facilitators are trained not to intervene by offering solutions or soften the sometimes raw statements of the person who is struggling. Feeling deeply heard by others is often healing in moments of deep sadness, alienation or anger. However, one may share one's experience and then feel that no one "got me." Also, listeners can feel bad because they identify with or reject the person's attitudes. Peer support groups make agreements about how explicit their stories will be. Sharing may be quite explicit in support meetings, where a mutual agreement is made to discuss traumatic experience and healing. While people attend meetings to be heard and to help others, and while facilitators are trained to ensure that each person has time to share and receive acknowledgment, the impact of the meeting may leave people less happy than when they walked in.

Discussion

People who need emotional support are often slow to seek it; situations can become emergencies before help is summoned (Draine et al., 2002). People who have accessed clinical treatment often experience shame and fear. The person may drop from clinical treatment into a silent chasm in the community where there are no stories about pathways to resuming life. Accessing natural support is rare when the person is unwilling to display vulnerabilities.

Systems continue to function around identifying personal deficits, targeting the elimination of symptoms as the goal of treatment, and delivering treatment without the participation of the person, despite national and local policy advising to the contrary (Clossey et al., 2011). It is understandable then that that people with SMHCs experience anger and hopelessness in relation to these persistent sources of suffering. RLCs advocate and engage in strengths and relational-based approaches to positive outcomes.

People with SMHCs along with personal issues must address external barriers to recovery and well-being related to stigma/oppression, discrimination, housing, unemployment and criminal justice involvement. The effects of these coexisting barriers are multifaceted. For example, a person who has not worked recently due to disability is going to have more difficulty finding a job, thus have difficulty with housing and thus feel worse about himself or herself.

RLCs take great pains to address both intrapersonal stigma and societal discrimination. Oppression of people with mental health conditions and people who experience extreme emotional states has been a powerful factor in silencing those who have found recovery – keeping their voices from inspiring others and pointing to solutions (Draine et al., 2002). People who witness someone struggling emotionally may wish to help, but feel frightened or awkward. The RLC model was designed to reduce such social distance and difference, and by doing so to increase the numbers of people and social groups in the community whose resilience is facilitated. While respecting the potentially devastating consequences of disclosure, RLCs are supporting communities in understanding the true range of human experience and the probability that people will be able to experience wellbeing in life. RLCs work to build large communities that are not divided by diagnosis and make clear that people do recover and live well in the community.

"Recovery colleges" (as described in Chapter 16) have an overlapping approach with RLCs. They both challenge more traditional service approaches by significantly involving people with SMHCs in program development and delivery and by offering participants opportunities to develop wellness tools that will allow them to pursue their self-identified recovery goals. RLCs differ from recovery colleges in several ways. While RLCs are run and staffed only by people with SMHCs, recovery colleges are co-produced with valued nonpeer colleagues. In addition, while recovery colleges adopt an educational lens, RLCs focus on wide geographic communities, with support and educational meetings held in the community (e.g. hospitals).

Positive psychology and its focus on wellbeing is an exciting development for the recovery community, in large part because of its emphasis on strengths and hope-inducing actions that promote wellbeing. RLCs and PP have similar methods for providing a pathway to wellbeing for vulnerable people. RLC staff believe each person is capable of attaining a sense of wellbeing and help cultivate the person's capacity and desire to improve his or her life. They, along with peer facilitators, demonstrate and embody recovery, offering hope for wellbeing that the person never previously had. The judgment-free atmosphere and voluntary nature of the RLC promote people's willingness to stay on that pathway, despite challenges and disappointments along the way.

It is important to identify and respect their differences. RLCs support self-determination in ways that can be seen as inconsistent with PP. People with SMHCs have been denied meaningful choices when struggling with disability, so it is important to foster self-determination if they are to truly manage their health and well-being in the community. Making choices that are not the best and risking bad outcomes are part of the recovery path for many. Second, the focus of peer support meetings is not positiveness, but instead what people in the group want to express. Some peer support meetings may address learned helplessness, traumatic experiences or self-inflicted violence, typically not PP topics (Moran and Nemec, 2013, p. 203).

In conclusion, while we see some inconsistencies between RLCs and PP, we see them as compatible and co-supportive. Both approaches take on the established approach to deficit-based treatment and promote wellbeing as the aim for people. We believe that people should be able to make informed choices in their services and support, including whether and how to participate in RLC activities or other treatments and programs. It makes sense that some people with SMHCs may prefer to spend their time with a positive psychologist and/or in PP treatment, but at other points in their recovery want more engagement with RLCs. But the reality is that in the United States, PP has not been integrated into treatment services for people with SMHCs (Galvez et al., 2011). We see the RLC model as one of the closest to a PP approach in the United States and hope that the success of RLCs will support the integration of positive psychology approaches into the treatment system.

References

Clossey, L., Mehnert, K., & Silva, S. (2011). Using appreciative inquiry to facilitate implementation of the recovery model in mental health agencies. *Health & Social work*, 36(4), 259–266.

Cook, J. A., and Mueser, K. T. (2013). Economic security: An essential component of recovery. *Psychiatric Rehabilitation Journal*, 36(1), 1–3.

Corrigan, P. W., Angell, B., Davidson, L., Marcus, S. C., Salzer, M. S., Kottsieper, P., et al. (2012). From adherence to self-determination: Evolution of a treatment paradigm for people with serious mental illnesses. *Psychiatric Services*, 63(2), 169–173.

Deegan, P. (1996). Recovery as a journey of the heart. *Psychiatric Rehabilitation Journal*, 19(3), 91–97.

Delman, J., Delman, D. R., Vezina, B. R., & Piselli, J. (2014). Peer led recovery learning communities: Expanding social integration opportunities for people with the lived experience of psychiatric disability and emotional distress. *Global Journal of Community Psychology Practice*, 5(1). Available at http://www.gjcpp.org/pdfs/2014-SI11-20140519.pdf.

Delman, J., Simon, L., & Albert, K. (2015). Recovery learning community outcomes study. Available at http://www.umassmed.edu/PageFiles/40770/Recovery%20Learning%20Community%20 Outcomes%20Study%2012.2.pdf.

Draine, J., Salzer, M. S., Culhane, D. P., & Hadley, T. R. (2002). Role of social disadvantage in crime, joblessness, and homelessness among persons with serious mental illness. *Psychiatric Services*, 53(5), 565–573.

Duckworth, A. L., Steen, T. A., & Seligman, M. E. (2005). Positive psychology in clinical practice. *Annual Review of Clinical Psychology*, 1, 629–651.

Galvez, J. F., Thommi, S., & Ghaemi, S. N. (2011). Positive aspects of mental illness: A review in bipolar disorder. *Journal of Affective Disorders*, 128(3), 185–190.

Link, B. G., Struening, E. L., Neese-Todd, S., Asmussen, S., & Phelan, J. C. (2001). Stigma as a barrier to recovery: The consequences of stigma for the self-esteem of people with mental illnesses. *Psychiatric Services*, 52(12), 1621–1626.

Mead, S., Hilton, D., & Curtis, L. (2001). Peer support: A theoretical perspective. *Psychiatric Rehabilitation Journal*, 25(2), 134–141.

Moran, G. S., & Nemec, P. B. (2013). Walking on the sunny side: What positive psychology can contribute to psychiatric rehabilitation concepts and practice. *Psychiatric Rehabilitation Journal*, 36(3), 202–208.

Moran, G. S., Russinova, Z., Yim, J. Y., & Sprague, C. (2014). Motivations of persons with psychiatric disabilities to work in mental health peer services: A qualitative study using self-determination theory. *Journal of Occupational Rehabilitation*, 24(1), 32–41.

Mosadeghrad, A. M. (2012). A conceptual framework for quality of care. *Materia Socio-Medica*, 24(4), 251–261.

Ostrow, L., & Leaf, P. J. (2014). Improving capacity to monitor and support sustainability of mental health peer-run organizations. *Psychiatric Services*, 65(2), 239–241.

Repper, J., & Carter, T. (2011). A review of the literature on peer support in mental health services. *Journal of Mental Health*, 20(4), 392–411.

Schrank, B., Brownell, T., Tylee, A., & Slade, M. (2014). Positive psychology: An approach to supporting recovery in mental illness. *East Asian Archives of Psychiatry*, 24, 95–103.

Sheldon, K. M., & Ryan, R. M. (2011). Positive psychology and self-determination theory: A natural interface. In Chirkov, V. I., Ryan, R. M., & Sheldon, K. M. (Eds.), *Human Autonomy in Cross-Cultural Context* (pp. 33–44). New York, NY: Springer.

U.S. Department of Health and Human Services New Freedom Commission on Mental Health (2003). *Achieving the promise: Transforming mental health care in America: Final Report.* Available at https://store.samhsa.gov/shin/content/SMA03-3831/SMA03-3831.pdf.

U.S. Department of Health and Human Services, Substance Abuse, and Mental Health Services Administration (2012). Working definition of recovery. Available at http://www.samhsa.gov/recovery.

Williams, G. C., Teixeira, P. J., Carraça, E. V., & Resnicow, K. (2011). Physical wellness, health care, and personal autonomy. In Chirkov, V. I., Ryan, R. M., & Sheldon, K. M. (Eds.), *Human Autonomy in Cross-Cultural Context* (pp. 133–162). New York, NY: Springer.

Section 2

What Does a Wellbeing Orientation Mean in Mental Health Services?

Chapter

15

Recovery Colleges and Co-production

Geoff Shepherd, Jane McGregor, Sara Meddings and Waldo Roeg

Introduction and Background

'Recovery colleges' (also known as 'recovery education centres') are central to the support of recovery for people with mental health difficulties. They are a relatively new development in the United Kingdom, although they have been present in a similar form in the United States for several years. The first example appeared more than twenty years ago at the Centre for Psychiatric Rehabilitation in Boston (http://cpr.bu.edu/living-well/services), and the concept was then developed by Recovery Innovations in Phoenix, Arizona (Ashcraft and Anthony, 2005).

The model was imported into England in 2010 and has become a central theme in the development of mental health services to support recovery championed by the Implementing Recovery through Organisational Change (ImROC) programme (http://ImROC.org.uk), which was part of the implementation of the Department of Health's No Health without Mental Health strategy (Department of Health, 2011). The first UK recovery college was established by Rachel Perkins and her colleagues from South West London and St George's Mental Health NHS Trust and officially opened by the then Minister for Care Services, Paul Burstow MP, in September 2011. A second college was quickly established in Nottingham, and there are now almost 40 in operation, based on the ImROC model, mainly in England, but also in Scotland, Ireland, Italy, Australia and Japan. What accounts for their apparently strong popularity and rapid growth?

First, recovery colleges offer a different way of thinking about the fundamental processes which underlie mental health care. The traditional approach embodies a set of ideas which may be characterised as the 'therapeutic model' (sometimes erroneously called the '*medical model*'). This involves people (patients) who present problems (symptoms) requiring 'treatment' from professionals who are expert in complex interventions. The educational model used in recovery colleges, while not dismissing traditional symptom/treatment interventions, goes beyond them to focus directly on helping people pursue their preferred life goals based on their existing skills and resources (Zucchelli and Skinner 2013). These differences are summarised in Box 15.1. [The contrast between the two models should not be seen as a simple binary: elements of each approach may co-occur in the other. Nevertheless, it is a useful heuristic].

Recovery colleges therefore have the potential to restore hope by increasing people's sense of control over their lives and supporting them in taking opportunities to pursue their

Box 15.1 An 'educational' vs. a 'therapeutic' model (adapted from Perkins et al., 2012)

Traditional therapeutic/health model	Recovery/educational model
• People seen as patients	• People seen as students
• Focusses on problems, deficits and symptoms	• Helps people recognise and make use of their talents and resources
• Becomes an overarching paradigm, transforming all activities into 'therapies'	• Supports people in exploring their possibilities, developing their skills and achieving their goals and ambitions
• Nature of therapy is chosen and offered by the (expert) therapist after referral and assessment	• Students choose their own courses, become experts in their own self-care
• Maintains power imbalance and reinforces the notion that expertise lies with professionals	• Staff include peers with lived experience and become coaches who help people find their own solutions
	• Training and courses replace therapies

chosen goals. These processes are central to successful recovery (Repper and Perkins, 2003; Shepherd et al., 2008).

There is also one other element in the recovery educational model that is very different from traditional health approaches, and this is the dimension of *power*. In traditional approaches it is usually assumed that most of the knowledge and expertise resides with the professionals. They have specialised information and training in disorders and treatments, and it therefore seems logical that they should be in a position of power in terms of their interactions with 'patients'. (Even if this is not true in every case, this is the stereotype.) In contrast, in the co-produced teaching sessions of the recovery college, the professional and the service user are clearly on a more equal footing, both in terms of facilitating learning and as students. As they learn together, it is obvious that neither has a monopoly on 'truth', and the lived experience of the service user or peer trainer is just as important and valid as the technical competence of the professional.

Of course, every experienced professional – and every experienced service user – already knows this to be the case, but it is seldom explicitly acknowledged. Learning together, in public, thus provides a dramatic demonstration of a very different power relationship. It creates a space where the knowledge and experience of the 'patient' can grow and be explicitly owned. We believe that this demonstrable change in power relationships goes a long way toward accounting for the remarkable consistency of positive results for recovery colleges across cultures.

We will now consider the key defining features of recovery colleges and the process of 'co-production' in more detail. We will then review the outcome evidence and present examples of the experience of a student and a peer trainer. Finally, we will make some suggestions for the future.

Key Defining Features

In the exploration of what characterises recovery colleges, in contrast to other interventions or organisational forms of education, a series of key defining features were drawn up and investigated through interviews with staff and students at eight different colleges. These defining characteristics are shown in Box 15.2. In the future they could be the basis of formal fidelity criteria.

First, there is an explicitly *educational approach* which is structured through a recovery-focussed curriculum and an organisation similar to a further education (FE)

> **Box 15.2** Key defining features of recovery colleges (McGregor et al., 2014)
> 1. *Based on educational principles*– clear structure for lesson plans, courses and terms. Each student has an individual learning plan (ILP).
> 2. *Co-production* – everything is co-produced, with co-facilitation and co-learning.
> 3. *Strengths-based* – for students and staff, not problem-/deficit-based.
> 4. *Person-centred* – students choose the courses they are interested in attending; *not* referral-based. No need for diagnosis or formal risk assessment.
> 5. *Progressive*– students work towards goals beyond the college and graduation.
> 6. *Community facing*– active engagement with agencies in the local community, emphasis on partnership working.
> 7. *Inclusive* – welcomes students of all types, cultures and educational achievement; also staff, relatives, friends and caregivers.

college, with a prospectus, terms/semesters and a strong educational focus in all documentation and language. Rather than 'patients' or 'service users', people attending the college are *students*; and rather than 'therapists', staff are coaches or *tutors* (approximately half the tutors are people with lived experience). Instead of being 'discharged', students *graduate*.

Although the content of the prospectuses does differ from site to site,[1] there are a number of common themes which recur. These include the following:

- *Understanding recovery*, which includes introductory sessions and sessions relating to the understanding of different mental health challenges such as personality disorders or self-harm.
- *Rebuilding your life*, telling your story, taking back control, improving well-being.
- *Developing life skills*, providing the tools and skills to create new opportunities to self-manage (e.g. developing a wellness plan), keeping well, moving towards life goals (e.g. employment).
- *Getting involved*, teaching qualification (for peer trainers), volunteering, becoming a peer worker.

The number of courses offered varies across different colleges. Increasingly sessions are being offered about co-morbidity between physical and mental health problems, acute care and topics such as understanding dementia and palliative care (see Central and North West London Recovery and Wellbeing College, http://www.cnwl.nhs.uk/wp-content/uploads/CNWL_RecoveryCollege_Prospectus_2015.pdf). Every attempt is made to avoid courses which are replicated elsewhere (e.g. in FE colleges or other community facilities), and the emphasis is consistently on learning together about recovery.

As indicated earlier, *co-production*, *co-facilitation* and *co-learning* are fundamental to the operation of recovery colleges in all areas of their work, emphasising reciprocity and changed power relationships. Students and tutors can explore their own experiences in the context of others', and many describe this as leading to transformational changes in their sense of self and what is possible in their lives. More will be said about this process of co-production later.

---

[1] These are generally available through the websites for individual Trusts, e.g. Solent in Hampshire, Central and North West London and Nottinghamshire Healthcare: http://www.highbury.ac.uk/client/content.asp?Contentid=945; http://www.cnwl.nhs.uk/; http://www.nottinghamshirehealthcare.nhs.uk/our-services/local-services/adult-mental-health-services/nottingham-recovery-college/.

The contribution of peer learning advisors and peer trainers who co-facilitate the courses is therefore crucial. They often help students with ILPs and act as role models (see below). They are usually paid for their contributions. On entry to the college, a peer learning advisor usually meets with the new student and helps produce an ILP to identify goals and any special learning needs he or she may have. This uses a *strengths-based* approach. Students *choose* from a prospectus the courses they wish to attend to help them address their personal goals. There is no referral, no requirement to disclose diagnosis and no formal risk assessment. This emphasis on a *person-centred* approach characterises and permeates the context of the learning environment.

It is axiomatic in the colleges that students work towards their own goals and/or to explore and overcome personal challenges; hence there is an intrinsic *progressive function*. They are not 'stopping off places' or bounded by a successful treatment outcome. It is anticipated that students will graduate and move on, for example to 'outside' paid employment, peer support pathways or volunteering. Increasingly, suggestions are made within prospectuses of how students may build on previous courses to structure their experience, although it is emphasised that progression, like recovery itself, is not always linear. Recovery colleges are also '*community facing*', with a variety of partnership relationships with external agencies.

Finally, the *inclusive* nature of the college is reflected by the fact that no educational qualifications are required of students and that all contributions are recognised and valued. If the student has special learning needs – for example, problems with literacy, anxiety about being in a group situation – these will be accommodated through appropriate adjustments to the learning environment, such as provision of handouts or support in class. Courses are also open to staff, relatives and caregivers. Recovery colleges are thereby often experienced as more inclusive, democratic and empowering than traditional educational facilities. This is important given the often negative experiences of many students in formal education.

The overall quality issues in relation to the development and review of courses and the curriculum are usually addressed through the formation of a 'quality/academic board' which consists of college staff, both peer trainers and mental health professionals, managers, senior professionals and students. They approve new courses and ensure that they are co-produced and records kept of process. They also make sure that session planning conforms to recovery educational objectives and activities and that each session is evaluated by students in terms of satisfaction in relation to achievement of the learning objectives. The feedback from each session is then used to inform tutors and to guide ongoing course development. The board may also oversee the broader strategy and governance of the college and ensure that the workings of the college conform to recovery educational principles.

In summary, the transformative power of recovery colleges involves a deep structural shift in people's understanding of themselves, their identity and relationships (Mezirow, 2000). This relates to understandings of power relations, visions of alternative approaches to living and a sense of possibilities/hope for the future. It occurs best where there is an environment in which learners actively communicate through dialogue and collaboration, making new meaning together and taking mutual responsibility for helping each other learn and question accepted frames of reference and assumptions (McGregor, 2012).

Co-production

The importance of 'co-production' in recovery colleges has been referred to repeatedly in this chapter. But what does it really mean? Where does the concept come from, and what is its relation to the development of mental health services?

The term was originally introduced by a political economist (and later Nobel Prize Winner), Elinor Ostrom, in the late 1970s. She had been asked by the Chicago Police Department to account for why crime rates apparently increased when the city's police officers changed their operations from being mainly on the beat to being mainly in cars. Ostrom concluded that the key reason for this was that by moving into cars the police became detached from the communities they were supposed to be protecting. As a result, they lost access to the knowledge, experience, assets and skills of members of the community – including some of the criminals themselves – who also had an interest in controlling crime. This idea was then developed by a Human Rights lawyer, Edgar Cahn, who coined the notion of the 'core economy' to describe the networks of formal and informal relationships that make up local communities (Cahn, 2001). The core economy is thus the platform upon which 'specialist programmes' in society (e.g. public services) are actually built. It is also clearly different from the market economy. This gives us a new way of thinking about the organisation and delivery of public services reflected in the work of two radical, independent, 'think-tanks', concerned with innovation in public services in the UK, the New Economics Foundation (NEF) and Nesta. In a seminal publication they defined co-production as *'delivering public services in an equal and reciprocal relationship between professionals, people using services, their families and their neighbours. Where activities are co-produced in this way, both services and neighbourhoods become effective agents of change'* (Boyle and Harris, 2009, p.11).

According to the NEF (New Economics Foundation, 2011) the main features of co-production are as follows:

1. *Recognising people as assets*: Transforming perceptions of people as passive recipients of care and 'burdens' on the system to equal partners in designing and delivering services.
2. *Building on people's existing capabilities*: Actively supporting people in recognising and using their strengths, rather than conforming to a deficit model.
3. *Reciprocity and mutuality*: Offering service users opportunities to develop reciprocal relationships with professionals (and with each other) and enter into mutual responsibilities and expectations.
4. *Peer support networks*: Enhancing knowledge generation and transfer by engaging personal and peer networks alongside those of professionals.
5. *Breaking down barriers*: Blurring the distinctions between professionals and producers and consumers of services. Reconfiguring the power relations and the way services are developed and provided.
6. *Facilitating rather than delivering*: Enabling professional staff to become catalysts of change, instead of sole providers of services.

Slay and Stephens (2013), in their literature review of co-production in mental health, explicitly highlight changing power relationships between professionals and citizens. Co-production is about doing things *with* people rather than *for* or *to* them. This transformational approach to services has been employed in recovery colleges in a pragmatic and generative fashion. Co-production also goes beyond the planning and delivery of teaching sessions. In Sussex Recovery College (Meddings et al., 2014), all aspects of the college were co-produced, including the curriculum, job descriptions and recruitment of staff, governance, fidelity criteria and the framework for outcome evaluation. For example, potential students and peers defined how they would know if the recovery college was successful, psychologists then sourced questionnaires which appeared to measure these outcomes and a working group of students, peers and mental health professionals chose which questionnaires to use and developed the evaluative process as part of the ILPs.

Fundamental to co-production is that students attending courses experience co-facilitation, with at least two individuals working together – an instantiation of the changed power relationship. 'Working in partnership with people who are experts by experience and those who are experts by training, I have always felt an equal partner with mutual respect, dignity and my enthusiasm appreciated. It is an integral part of Recovery College' (Sussex Recovery College peer trainer). This demonstrates to students that peers, who may have had experiences similar to theirs, can develop strong working relationships and make new lives for themselves. In this way the example of recovery colleges can transform organisations, not just individual care (see Box 15.3).

Box 15.3 My story as a peer trainer in a recovery college (Waldo Roeg, Central and Northwest London)

I worked in the film industry for 25 years and was very successful. I started using hard drugs when I was 17 years old and quickly became heavily addicted. As a result I have been using mental health on and off for 30 years. About 15 years ago I had a complete breakdown: I lost my home, my family, my job, and my career. I was made bankrupt and found myself living on the street for two years. Whilst on the street I was frequently in and out of hospital, as much for my mental health difficulties (I was diagnosed with drug induced psychosis) as for my substance misuse, which had diminished, essentially due to lack of money. This led me to believe that this was now my life and that was how the rest of it would play out. I had lost everything, but most of all I felt I had lost 'me'. I had lost my status as a productive member of the community and was seen as just another 'mad junkie on the streets' with everything that went with that identity. I was therefore very lucky and met someone in my hostel who was able to see me for who I was and not with all the 'baggage' usually associated with my problems. This led to me seeking help through the local mental health services and trying to be proactive in my recovery. After a few years I began to work again through the local mental health service employment program and was given a placement as a Peer Support Volunteer for four months on half a day a week. After that I completed an accredited Peer Support Training and was part of my Trust's bid for ImROC consultancy to look at introducing Recovery education and lived experience into the workforce. This meant I was able to play a key role in starting the local Recovery & Wellbeing College at Central and Northwest London. It is now three years on and it has been the most transformational thing I have ever been involved with or seen, both for me personally and for the local mental health service. It has given staff (as well as service users) a sense of hope and has helped to break down stigma and change the inherent power imbalance that usually exists. 'Co-production' is at the heart of it and is the key to its success. Moving from being purely on the receiving end of help to feeling a part of the solution has been both empowering for myself and most importantly inspiring for the students, staff, service users and their supporters. The Recovery College has done more to raise the expectations I have for myself but, most importantly, it has raised the expectations for all those that attend it and work for it. It has had the effect of being a 'Trojan Horse' in bringing into our Trust a different way of doing things. Being able to model a different way of working has thus been instrumental in disseminating recovery throughout the organization.

Outcomes

We can turn now to the question of outcomes. Recovery colleges are new, and there is little evidence (yet) from controlled trials. However, as we discuss elsewhere (Meddings et al., 2015), there is a strong and consistent body of evidence from several uncontrolled prospective studies in England. To analyse the range of different outcomes reported in these studies, we will use the framework suggested in *Supporting Recovery in Mental Health Services: Quality and Outcomes* (Shepherd et al., 2014). This identified six possible outcome domains, shown below:

1. *Quality of recovery-supporting care.* To what extent do service users feel that staff in services are trying to help them in their recovery?
2. *Achievement of individual recovery goals.* To what extent have goals, as defined by the individual, been attained over time?
3. *Subjective measures of personal recovery.* To what extent do individuals feel that their hopes, sense of control and opportunities for building a life beyond illness have improved as a result of their contact with services?
4. *Achievement of socially valued goals.* Has the person's status on indicators of social roles improved as a result of contact with services?
5. *Quality of life and wellbeing.* Have the person's quality of life and wellbeing improved?
6. *Service use.* As a result of his or her recovery being supported, has the person made an appropriate reduction in the use of formal mental health services?

Quality of Recovery-Supporting Care

There is now very strong evidence showing that recovery colleges are popular and that students are highly satisfied and give very positive course feedback. For example, Rennison et al. (2014) and Meddings et al. (2014) report that over 95% of students said that the course they completed was 'Good' or 'Excellent' and that they would recommend it to others. High quality ratings are confirmed by high attendance rates, which are generally around 60–70%, consistent with mainstream adult education. Students find it helpful to be taught alongside a mixed group of people using services, caregivers and staff and by a peer trainer and mental health professional.

Achievement of Personal Recovery Goals

Perhaps the most important measure of outcome in recovery is whether people feel they have been helped to progress towards their personal life goals, and there is strong evidence that students do feel that this is the case (Rinaldi and Wybourn, 2011; Meddings et al., 2015). These findings are well illustrated by student (service user) narratives (see Box 15.4).

Subjective Measures of Personal Recovery

Sussex Recovery College has demonstrated large and significant improvements in personal recovery using the Process of Recovery Questionnaire and CHOICE, as well as personal goals (Meddings et al., 2015). A number of other colleges report people say they feel more hopeful about the future (e.g. Rinaldi and Wybourn, 2011; Rennison et al., 2014).

Box 15.4– Personal Recovery: A Student Narrative (Hazel Lambe, Sussex Recovery College)

In May 2013, I was in a state of shock from three bombshells in my life: a 'mental health' diagnosis of Bi-Polar Disorder; a three-month acute Hospital stay; and having to adjust to life on medication. I experienced a massive crash in my self-esteem and confidence, my sense of self-worth, and ability to function. At this vulnerable point, I feel lucky to have been introduced to the Recovery College. The prospectus outlined opportunities for learning and put you in control. That is empowering. In my first meeting with Recovery College staff I was warmly greeted by a Peer Trainer, who explained she had suffered with a serious depression herself. This caused a wave of relief and a resonant connection. At an individual learning planning meeting I was supported to focus on personal goals, and knowledge and skills to be gained. Filling in a series of questionnaires could have been daunting, but staff were so positive that it became fun, and relevant. I achieved my goals of improving social skills and confidence. The course learning outcomes measures helped me to chart my progress and I was surprised, and pleased to see how much I had learned. Peer experience ensures a deeply empathic feel to learning, helping professional research theory come alive. Experience from fellow students creates an extra supportive dimension and opportunity for friendships to develop. I was then proud to attend the Graduation Ceremony with fellow students. I was keen to become more involved with the college. I became a Student Representative, ran a student union and fed back opinions to the college. My opinion was valued and my confidence grew. With all this progression, I have been discharged from mental health services. My Recovery College experience led directly to part time employment with a Housing Association, and peer support work with the NHS. A big thank you to the Recovery College that things are looking brighter!

Achievement of Socially Valued Goals

Rinaldi and Wybourn (2011) reported that of the 74 students who responded to a questionnaire regarding the pilot at South West London & St. Georges (83% of the total surveyed), almost 70% had become mainstream students, gained employment or started volunteering. Using the social inclusion web, Rennison et al. (2014) found students reporting significant increases in contact with education, the arts, family and neighbourhood, employment and volunteering, although the relatively small numbers achieved with this measure means that definitive conclusions are hard to draw. Meddings et al. (2015) found increases in social networks, but not work or education. In the Mid-Essex Recovery College they found improved social inclusion, but not at a statistically significant level, perhaps due to small numbers and short follow-up (North Essex Research Network, 2014).

Quality of Life and Wellbeing

In two of the prospective studies, students' quality of life and wellbeing were significantly improved after attending recovery colleges, as measured by the Warwick Edinburgh Wellbeing Scale (WEMWBS) and MANSA (Meddings et al., 2015; North Essex Research Network, 2014). This suggests the possibility of generalised improvements in subjective well-being.

Service Use and Cost Effectiveness

Reductions in service use should not be used on their own as indicators of personal recovery; nevertheless they are important in terms of assessing potential cost effectiveness. There is evidence that attendance at recovery colleges can reduce hospital and community service use, leading to significant cost savings (Rinaldi and Wybourn, 2011; Mid-Essex Recovery College, 2014).[2] In the case of South West London & St. George's, for students attending more than 70% of their chosen courses, this amounted to approximately £800 per student per year.

Impact on Staff

Cost effectiveness may be increased through the benefits to staff who attend and improvements in their wellbeing, leading to reductions in sickness and absences. Recovery colleges are also a resource for training and developing staff skills to support recovery more effectively. One member of staff said, 'attending a recovery college course is the very best introduction to working with people with psychosis' (Sussex Recovery College student). They also have the potential to raise staff expectations of people with mental health challenges (Rinaldi and Suleman, 2012) and thus, as indicated earlier, to transform the organisations in which they are located.

To summarise, there is emerging evidence that recovery colleges are effective and preliminary evidence that they are also cost-effective. From the perspective of students, the key ingredients seem to be the following:

- learning from other students, 'we are all in the same boat';
- co-production and the value of lived experience, 'it was the equality, learning from peer trainers' lived experience and professionals that helped';
- personal qualities of staff, 'empathy, warmth and a welcome';
- learning new knowledge, 'you are gaining coping mechanisms', 'learning something new gave me confidence';
- social opportunities, 'I have met people I will continue to meet up with';
- structure, 'I learned that I need to have a structure to the week';
- choice and control, 'choice is empowering – you choose what course from a prospectus, instead of professionals assessing and referring'.

Future Directions

We have argued that a major reason that recovery colleges are so popular (and effective) is that they challenge the traditional balance of power in mental health services and break down barriers between 'us' and 'them'. They show how staff, caregivers and people with mental health challenges can learn together by valuing lived expertise equally with professional expertise. Of course, this is actually a hypothesis and it needs to be tested. Thus, one of the first priorities for future developments in this area is more detailed qualitative research to investigate the mechanisms of change in recovery colleges from different stakeholder perspectives. Anthropological methods, participant observation, action research and use of narrative accounts are all likely to be useful in these studies and a 'realistic evaluation' approach (Pawson and Tilley, 1997) could provide a convenient overarching framework. If we are now fairly certain that something 'works' in recovery

---

[2] There is also anecdotal evidence that a minority of students (around 20–25%) actually *increase* service use in the first few months of attending, probably due to increased awareness of support options (Sue Barton, Southwest Yorkshire Foundation Trust, personal communication, 2014).

colleges, the next step is to try to be clearer about *what* are the critical elements and *how* they might be enhanced.

Alongside these kinds of qualitative studies, we also need more robust quantitative investigations. As indicated earlier, most of the evidence for the effectiveness of recovery Colleges comes from uncontrolled prospective cohort studies. These are the first steps in health service evaluation, but the design is inherently weak and cannot rule out a number of possible explanations (e.g. 'Hawthorne' effects, passage of time, observer bias) which could account for observed changes in relevant outcome measures. In the case of recovery colleges the results from uncontrolled trials appear to be so consistent and replicable across different countries and cultures that it seems unlikely they are not attributable to the impact of the colleges. Nevertheless, this remains to be conclusively demonstrated and, at some stage, a properly designed, randomised, controlled trial is both necessary and desirable.

Of course, there are problems with randomised controlled trials, particularly the danger that in trying to 'fix' the independent variable – the experience of attending courses – so that it can be replicated, we will overlook important elements in the process. Thus, at this stage in the development of recovery colleges, there is an argument that we should pursue more qualitative studies in order to understand the processes of change better before we move to controlled trial evaluations. When the time is right is a matter of judgement. Certainly, there is a need for both types of investigation.

One aspect of the operation of recovery colleges that particularly needs further investigation is the effects of different locations and organisational links. Thus, is it better that recovery colleges are located inside mental health services because of their potential to change these organisations? Or is it better to be in more community settings where stigma is reduced? What are the key partnership arrangements? Further education? Employment? Community organisations? Can 'hub-and-spoke' models operate effectively while maintaining 'fidelity' to the key defining features? These are important questions for future investigation.

Similarly, there is the question of how recovery colleges may best be maintained over time. We have emerging evidence suggesting good results from these early examples, but does this just reflect the enthusiasm and optimism that often goes with new service developments? Can we collect data that demonstrate continued effectiveness over time which maintains this initial promise? It is therefore clearly important to continue monitoring outcomes and measuring costs, since this is the information required by both sceptical clinicians and hard-pressed managers. The more data we have available where the characteristics of students are carefully described, the process is defined and outcomes are measured using agreed criteria, the better. We do not think that these questions of evaluation are going to be answered by a single, definitive trial. They will depend on the accumulation of 'practice-based evidence' as much as on the demonstration of 'evidence-based practice'.

Finally, we have argued that recovery colleges have the potential to deliver benefits for all the key stakeholder groups: the people receiving the service (students with lived experience, staff, relatives and caregivers), the people delivering the service (peer and staff educators) and the organisations and communities in which they are located. Of course, changing mental health services to become more supportive of recovery will not be achieved simply through the introduction of recovery colleges. It requires a comprehensive programme of organisational change (see http://www.ImROC.org). However, as indicated, we have seen (and heard) very strong evidence for the power of recovery colleges to transform very basic processes in mental health services and change the attitudes of staff and service users alike.

If this proves to be the case – and is replicable – then recovery colleges may turn out to be very important developments indeed.

In terms of the future of 'co-production', this is already beginning to have tangible effects on the development of health and social care services across a wide range of client groups. For example, in England, Nesta and the Innovation Unit recently ran an initiative which they called the 'People Powered Health Programme' (2011–2013) to support innovative services for people with long-term health conditions. They identified co-production as an alternative model of engagement to the dominant model where 'professionals design and deliver services for needy users' and brought together a number of examples from across the health and social care field (see Nesta/Innovation Unit/nef, 2012). These included projects from across the age range (children, teenagers, adults and older people) and with various special populations (offenders, homeless, people with acquired brain damage, learning disabilities, HIV). These programmes demonstrated a range of co-produced interventions including information and advice services, mutual support and self-help, personalisation, pooled budgets, time banks and life coaching. One of the examples was the Nottingham Recovery Education Centre. As an approach to the delivery of public services, co-production is thus growing in strength and variety.

But what are the problems with co-production and how might they be most effectively addressed? First, it is sometimes argued that co-production simply places extra burdens on people – service users and staff – who are already struggling in difficult circumstances. There may be some truth in this, but, as we have seen from the data on recovery colleges, for service user students the benefits that accrue from being able to do something positive and to give something back to others generally far outweigh the additional stresses of co-production. Work *is* stressful, but so is doing nothing. As long as people feel supported and valued, they are generally much happier coping with the stress of meaningful work than coping with the stress of enforced inactivity and a lack of meaning in their lives. Similarly, for staff, although working in a co-productive way may sometimes be a little more time-consuming, the rewards in terms of being able to produce services which much better meet peoples' needs usually more than compensate.

Second, there is a concern, which is often expressed in the current climate of severe financial constraints, that co-production is simply an excuse for reducing services and saving money. This would be the case if the services which are developed through co-production were just watered-down (cheaper) versions of the services they are designed to complement and – in some cases – replace. This should not be the case. Co-produced services are *different*. They demonstrate staff and service users working in a different way, to produce a different kind of experience, which is more empathic, more authentic and more directly relevant to the needs of the people on the receiving end. This is not professional services on the cheap (neither is it services which are simply user-led). It is truly a shared project where both sets of experience are brought together to meet a common aim. It is also not another version of user involvement where the power and control essentially remains with the mental health professionals and service users are 'involved' when the professionals think it is appropriate for them to be.

Of course, co-production is not universally applicable to all health and social care services. It works best where the services are essentially based on *relationships*, rather than *transactions*. Under the pressure of market models, attempts have been made to convert much of health and social care into transactional models, but care is *not* generally a *transaction*. It is not a situation in which an item of service (with a price attached) is exchanged between a provider and consumer: it is an interaction which takes place in the context of an ongoing relationship between people working with common goals and values. Co-production is also most relevant where the interaction is most appropriately seen as involving learning on both sides. Thus, co-production is not very relevant to the work of a heart surgeon, but it is entirely relevant to the work of someone trying to learn how to live better following heart surgery by regular contact with others who have had a similar experience. Co-production therefore has implications for the development of all those health and social care services which are essentially relationship-based.

To conclude, Durose et al. (2013) recently reviewed the evidence on how efficiencies in local public services could be maximised through transformative co-production. They suggested four key conditions:

- ensuring that there are synergies – not conflicts – between co-produced services and traditional, professionally led services;
- incentivising professionals to work in different ways;
- avoiding the trap of simply dropping examples of co-production into existing organisations, rather than aiming for a fundamental review of organisational values and processes;
- building in a credible commitment and effective partnerships between services and communities which are capable of producing local change using methods which can then be scaled up into new forms of national policy.

This seems like a very useful template for using co-production to transform services in the future. We believe that in this way, co-production could provide a new way forward for the development of mental health and other public services which achieves the elusive goal of improving quality while at the same time controlling, and even reducing, costs.

References

Ashcraft, L., & Anthony, W. A. (2005). A story of transformation. An agency fully embraces recovery. *Behavioral Healthcare Tomorrow*, 14, 12–21.

Boyle, D., & Harris, M. (2009). The challenge of co-production: How equal partnerships between professionals and the public are crucial to improving public services. Nesta (online). Available at http://b.3cdn.net/nefoundation/312ac8ce93a00d5973_3im6i6t0e.pdf.

Cahn, E. (2001). *No more throwaway people: The co-production imperative*. Washington, DC: Essential Books.

Department of Health (2011). *No health without mental health: A cross-government mental health outcomes strategy for people of all ages*. London, UK: Department of Health. Available at https://www.gov.uk/government/publications/no-health-without-mental-health-a-cross-government-outcomes-strategy.

Durose, C., Mangan, C., Needham, C., Rees, J., & Hilton, M. (2013). Transforming local public services through co-production. University of Birmingham/Arts and Humanities Research Council. Available at http://www.birmingham.ac.uk/documents/college-social-sciences/government-society/inlogov/briefing-papers/transforming-local-public-services-co-production.pdf.

McGregor, J. (2012). It's not just education, it's about you. Unpublished report. Nottingham, UK: Nottinghamshire Healthcare NHS Trust.

McGregor, J., Repper, J., & Brown, H. (2014). 'The college is so different from anything I have done'. A study of the characteristics of Nottingham Recovery College. *Journal of Mental Health Education Training and Practice*, 9, 3–15.

Meddings, S., Byrne, D., Barnicoat, S., Campbell, E., & Locks, L. (2014). Co-delivered and co-produced: Creating a recovery college in partnership. *Journal of Mental Health Training, Education and Practice*, 9, 16–25.

Meddings, S., Campbell, E., Guglietti, S., Lambe, H., Locks, L., Byrne, D., et al. (2015). From service user to student – The benefits of recovery college. *Clinical Psychology Forum*, 268, 32–37.

Meddings, S., Guglietti, S., Lambe, H., & Byrne, D. (2014). Student perspectives: Recovery college experience. *Mental Health and Social Inclusion*, 18, 142–150.

Meddings, S., McGregor, J., Roeg, W., & Shepherd, G. (2015). Recovery colleges quality and outcomes. *Mental Health and Social Inclusion*, 19 (4).

Mezirow, J. (2000). *Learning as transformation: Critical perspectives on a theory in progress.* San Francisco, CA: Jossey-Bass.

Mid Essex Recovery College (2014). Hope, health, opportunity and purpose for everyone. Evaluation report. Chelmsford, UK: North Essex Partnership University NHS Foundation Trust.

Nesta/Innovation Unit/NEF (2012). People powered health co-production catalogue. Nesta (online). Available at http://www.nesta.org.uk/sites/default/files/co-production_catalogue.pdf.

New Economics Foundation (2011). *In this together. Building knowledge about co-production* London, UK: The New Economics Foundation (NEF).

North Essex Research Network with South Essex Service User Research Group (2014). Evaluation of the Mid Essex Recovery College October–December 2013. Anglia Ruskin University. Available at http://hdl.hand.lenet/10540/347125.

Pawson, R., & Tilley, N. (1997). *Realistic evaluation.* London, UK: Sa.

Perkins, R., Repper, J., Rinaldi, M., & Brown, H. (2012). Recovery colleges, ImROC, Briefing 1. Centre for Mental Health. Available at http://www.centreformentalhealth.org.uk/pdfs/Recovery_Colleges.pdf.

Rennison, J., Skinner, S., & Bailey, A. (2014). CNWL Recovery College Annual Report London, UK: Central and North West London NHS Foundation.

Repper, J., & Perkins, R. (2003). *Social inclusion and recovery.* London, UK: BaillièreTindall.

Rinaldi, M., & Suleman, S. (2012). *Care co-ordinators attitudes to self-management and their experience of the use of South West London Recovery College.* London, UK: South West London and St. Georges Mental Health NHS Trust.

Rinaldi, M., & Wybourn, S. (2011). *The Recovery College Pilot in Merton and Sutton: Longer term individual and service level outcomes.* London, UK: South West London and St. Georges Mental Health NHS Trust.

Shepherd, G., Boardman, J., Rinaldi, M., & Roberts, G. (2014). Supporting recovery in mental health services: Quality and outcomes. ImROC Briefing Paper 8. Centre for Mental Health. Available at http://www.centreformentalhealth.org.uk/pdfs/ImROC_briefing8_quality_and_outcomes.pdf.

Shepherd, G., Boardman, J., & Slade, M. (2008). Making recovery a reality. Centre for Mental Health. Available at http://www.centreformentalhealth.org.uk/pdfs/Making_recovery_a_reality_policy_paper.pdf.

Slay, J., & Stephens, L. (2013). Co-production in mental health: A literature review. New Economics Foundation. Available at http://http://b.3cdn.net/nefoundation/ca0975b7cd88125c3e_ywm6bp3ll.pdf.

Zucchelli, F. A., & Skinner, S. (2013). Central and North West London NHS Foundation Trust's recovery college: The story so far. *Mental Health and Social Inclusion*, 17, 183–189.

Section 2

What Does a Wellbeing Orientation Mean in Mental Health Services?

Chapter

16

Wellbeing in Non-Western Cultures

Samson Tse

Introduction

The earlier chapters have already provided very thorough discussions about the meaning and concept of wellbeing. In this chapter, wellbeing is defined as "more than the absence of illness or pathology; it is subjective (self-assessed) and objective (ascribed) dimensions; it can be measured at the level of individuals or society; it accounts for elements of life satisfaction that cannot be defined, explained or primarily influenced by economic growth" (McAllister, 2005, p. 2). Wellbeing can be regarded as a process where individuals grow and thrive when external living conditions (the so-called liveability of environment) and internal inner life-chances (the so-called life-ability of the person) are favourable (Veenhoven, 2009); alternatively, wellbeing can be seen as the goal or outcome of human existence, which is at least partly in line with Aristotle's perfectionist notion of excellence (Broadie and Rowe, 2002).

Although achieving a satisfying life and feeling good about oneself are likely to be universal goals, Oishi and Diener (2001) argued that culture plays a part in how people define and achieve wellbeing. "Survey researchers often implicitly assume that the concept of well-being is apparent to people in most cultures. Indeed, survey researchers often translate items originally created in English and use them as if they had exactly the same meaning anywhere in the world ... Even when there is a corresponding concept, the way people think about well-being can be very different across cultures" (Diener et al., 2010, pp. 35 and 36). For the purpose of the present discussion, "non-Western cultures" refers to parts of the world that do not share a European culture like that of the countries of Western Europe, North America, the United Kingdom, Australia and New Zealand. Non-Western cultures have unique economic–political and cultural conditions; they often share a history of colonisation such as the European colonisation of Aboriginal and Torres Strait Islander cultures in Australia and the colonisation of the Cape in South Africa by the Dutch and British.

"Non-Western cultures" is not a homogeneous concept. Using Chinese culture as an example, there are different Chinese societies across the globe: the mainland of the People's Republic of China, Taiwan, Hong Kong and Macau, as well as Chinese immigrant communities in host countries – Western and non-Western alike. Furthermore, it is important not to oversimplify and dichotomise Western and non-Western cultures. In many parts of the world, with increasing globalization, a pure form of non-Western culture no longer exists. People are introduced or exposed to aspects of the Western lifestyle such as diet and clothing,

Wellbeing, Recovery and Mental Health, ed. Mike Slade, Lindsay Oades and Aaron Jarden.
Published by Cambridge University Press. © Mike Slade, Lindsay Oades and Aaron Jarden 2017

ideology and political systems. For instance, Hong Kong, Taiwanese and Singaporean societies place emphasis on the traditional Chinese cultural norms (e.g. filial piety and desire for harmonisation) but are also influenced by Western cultural values (e.g. individualism and emotional openness) due to decades of modernisation. University students and young people are disproportionately affected by Western cultures because of their frequent use of information technologies and access to Western media and websites (Sheu et al., 2014). The meaning of wellbeing will be interpreted differently in many different non-Western cultures or communities. For example, a young Thai person in the Mae Sot district, a rural border town between Thailand and Myanmar, where the household income is limited, mental health resources are scarce and the shame associated with mental health problems prevails, is likely to have quite different ideas about wellbeing than another young person residing in downtown Seoul in South Korea. In this chapter, I can only provide tentative suggestions as to how non-Western cultures may influence people's understanding of wellbeing, happiness or life satisfaction. I endeavour to achieve two ends: first, I will briefly review the literature on the issues which are important to our understanding of non-Western cultures and wellbeing; second, I will discuss how mental health services might change if they observed the non-Western perspectives on wellbeing. As I am a native of Hong Kong and have lived in New Zealand for over 20 years, the examples and research data cited in this chapter lean heavily on the Asian and Pacific Rim region.

Non-Western Cultures and Wellbeing: Recent Developments and Challenges

In a lot of respects, systematic and large-scale research in non-Western countries is in the early stage of studies of wellbeing (Camfield and Guillen-Royo, 2010; Ngoo et al., 2014; White et al., 2014; Li et al., 2015). To date, most investigations about wellbeing have been conducted with Western samples from individualist cultures. Without empirical data, gross domestic product has often been used as a proxy measure of wellbeing, with the presumption that a higher level of income will meet people's needs and, in turn, lead to improved subjective wellbeing (SWB, Veenhoven, 1991). It is far beyond the scope of this chapter to review the wellbeing indices or profiles of non-Western cultures. Nevertheless, the Organisation for Economic Co-operation and Development (OECD)'s regional well-being (http://www.oecdregionalwellbeing.org/) provides very powerful data on nine topics important to wellbeing across the globe, including health, safety, housing, access to services, civic engagement, education, jobs, environment and income. This interactive site allows users to measure wellbeing in their regions and compare it with that in 362 other OECD regions based on those nine topics central to the quality of our lives. In this section, I will cover three aspects of recent research on wellbeing in non-Western jurisdictions and the challenges that researchers and scholars are facing in this field of research.

Non-Western Cultures Develop Their Own Concepts and Models of Wellbeing

Wellbeing is not a foreign concept to people from culturally and linguistically diverse backgrounds. In New Zealand, Tangata Whaiora is a term used to describe a person who uses mental health services, which can be literally translated to mean a person who is pursuing health, recovery and a sense of wellbeing. In other words, what a person seeks to achieve is far beyond symptom reduction or illness fixing. To this end, Rose Pere (1991), a Māori educationalist and scholar, has developed a model of Māori health which is based on Te Wheke (the octopus) and the eight tentacles that collectively contribute to waiora or total wellbeing (http://www.health.govt.nz/our-work/populations/maori-health/maori-health-models). The webpage reads as follows:

> The concept of Te Wheke, the octopus, is to define family health. The head of the octopus represents te whānau, the eyes of the octopus as waiora (total wellbeing for the individual and family) and each of the eight tentacles representing a specific dimension of health. The dimensions are interwoven and this represents the close relationship of the tentacles.
> - Te whanau – the family
> - Waiora – total wellbeing for the individual and family
> - Wairuatanga – spirituality
> - Hinengaro – the mind
> - Taha tinana – physical wellbeing
> - Whanaungatanga – extended family
> - Mauri – life force in people and objects
> - Mana ake – unique identity of individuals and family
> - Hā a koro ma, a kui ma – breath of life from forebears
> - Whatumanawa– the open and healthy expression of emotion

Palmer (2004) outlined a brief review of the development of concepts of Māori wellbeing and reported a preliminary study in the development of Hōmai te Waiora ki Ahau, a tool for the measurement of wellbeing, among 31 Māori female participants. Internationally, the Te Wheke model of wellbeing is one of the few indigenous wellbeing models which have been uniquely developed by native people for native people.

For other non-Western native populations, government offices and research centres have developed a resource for people living with a chronic disability. Researchers and policy makers place emphasis on how the wellbeing framework can be translated into practice principles to be applied in primary healthcare services; for example, natives of the First Nations in Canada and Aborigines (Chretien, 2010) and natives of the Torres Strait Islands in Australia (Anonymous, n.d.). The common challenges that population-specific models of wellbeing face include the following: (a) putting the values, principles and dimensions into practice; (b) being supported by empirical data – for instance, how do the population-specific instruments of wellbeing compare with similar but different instruments or the so-called gold standard(s)? (c) unanswered questions surrounding the ethnic-specific models of wellbeing – for example, is the model more applicable to a particular segment of the population (e.g. older people and/or people with a chronic disability) than others? Are there some elements or principles more important or critical than others for initiating changes in one's level of wellbeing? How do different elements work together within the models?

Wellbeing models for indigenous people are needed not only in European or English-speaking countries, but also in non-Western countries such as Thailand and India that have developed their own concepts of wellbeing. The Thai conceptual framework of personal wellbeing is composed of six factors contributing to wellbeing or happiness: health, a warm and loving family, empowerment of communities, a democratic society with good governance, surroundings and ecological system and economic strength and equity (Yiengprugsawan et al., 2010). Conceptually, this framework bears some similarity to the construct of the Personal Wellbeing Index. This Index was subsequently tested by Yiengprugsawan et al. (2010) on 87,134 Thai adults, and it was found that the index would be a useful tool for policy makers to better understand the subjective wellbeing of the Thai population.

Unlike Thailand's experience, scholars and practitioners in India and Zambia felt that the commonly used concept of SWB was inadequate in capturing the lived experience of wellbeing; thus they took up the challenge of conducting extensive fieldwork to articulate the concept of inner wellbeing (IWB) and to validate the psychometric properties of the scale by involving 622 adults at two different times (White et al., 2014). They wrote "while the dominant approaches were originally developed amongst relatively affluent respondents in the West, the theorisation of IWB deliberately prioritised research undertaken in and on countries of the global south, and the scale was developed through research in marginalised rural communities in Zambia and India" (p. 724). They argued that the primary aim of SWB is to produce an abstract summative measure of happiness or life satisfaction, whereas the aim of IWB is "to engage with at least some of the substance of how people are thinking and feeling about different aspects of their lives, so as to understand how their perceptions of different kinds of strength or vulnerability might have a material effect on what they can achieve" (p. 724). The final distinction they made was "where Subjective Wellbeing ultimately positions people as consumers, rating their happiness or satisfaction with their lives, IWB constructs people in active voice, as it seeks to explore the scope of what people think and feel they are able to be and do" (p. 725). There are two aspects of this work worth noting: first, it is one of the rare examples showing that a non-Western country has successfully developed its own culturally sensitive concept of wellbeing in less industrialised, relatively less affluent countries in the global south part of the world. "… the process of developing our quantitative scale to assess IWB was highly qualitative, with a painstaking ongoing process of trying out different questions, listening to how people responded, adjusting and adapting and trying again" (p. 744). Second, the work on IWB was an indirect outcome of a four-country comparative study of wellbeing (Bangladesh, Ethiopia, Peru and Thailand) that was coordinated by the Wellbeing in Developing Countries Research Group (WeD, 2002–2007), based at the University of Bath, UK (http://www.welldev.org.uk). In practical terms, the WeD provided the IWB international research team with distinctive conceptions of wellbeing, and the studies in Bangladesh demonstrated how social, political, religious and spiritual spheres closely intertwine to contribute to one's wellbeing. I feel that cross-country collaboration is the way to go in developing culturally responsive research on wellbeing for non-Western populations in the future.

Expanding Body of Knowledge

I have reviewed research studies on wellbeing that have been carried out over the last 10 years, mainly in the Asian region. For the purposes of this section, the concepts of quality of life and wellbeing are treated as synonymous. There has been a thrust of research on the study of wellbeing covering general Asia (Ngoo et al., 2014); Mainland China – contrasting rural and urban dwelling (Chen and Davey, 2008, 2009; Smyth et al., 2010; Davey and Rato, 2012; Ip and Shek, 2014; Sun et al., 2016); India (White et al., 2014); Japan (Inoguchi and Fujii, 2009); Malaysia (Howell et al., 2012; Mey and Yin, 2014); Singapore students (Sheu et al., 2014); South Korea (Kim et al., 2012; Shin et al., 2003); Hong Kong (Lau et al., 2005; Sing, 2009); Macau (Rato and Davey, 2012); Thailand (Yiengprugsawan et al., 2010); and Algeria (an Arab country in North Africa, Tiliouine et al., 2006). Another trend is the increase in number of studies on psychological measures of wellbeing in non-Western populations (Gough and McGregor, 2007; Diener et al., 2010; Trung et al., 2013).

Although, by far, the evidence suggests that a decent income level and economic growth are necessary but insufficient conditions for wellbeing, it is difficult to draw a direct

Table 16.1 Overall Ranking and Ranking by Dimensions of Children's Wellbeing (adapted from Cho, 2014)

	Material wellbeing	Educational wellbeing	Psychosocial wellbeing	Overall ranking (all dimensions)
Japan	2	3	3	1
Korea	1	2	9	2
Singapore	4	1	7	3
China	3	4	4	4
Hong Kong	6	5	6	5
Taiwan	5	7	2	6
Macau	8	6	8	7
Malaysia	7	10	10	8
Vietnam	10	8	1	9
Thailand	9	9	11	10
Indonesia	11	11	5	11

comparison across these places because different studies not only measured different facets of wellbeing (e.g. SWB, social or personal wellbeing), but also targeted different segments of the populations such as students versus adults. On the other hand, there has been a comparison of children's wellbeing across countries in the Asian region. The results show that Japan, Korea and Singapore perform best, while Malaysia, Vietnam, Thailand and Indonesia do less well in terms of children's wellbeing (Table 16.1, from Cho, 2014).

Using wellbeing in the Chinese adult population as an example, we can identify the following themes (Tang, 2014; Xing and Huang, 2014; Bian et al., 2015; Han, 2015; Sun et al., 2016):

- SWB was evidently associated with income; this finding illustrates the salience of material circumstances (i.e. income and wealth) in Chinese people's perception about wellbeing, although money was not the only determinant.
- Comparisons of urban and rural Chinese further revealed that low income, structural attributions of inequality (e.g. corruption and a sense of injustice about the current system) and negative evaluations of governance (e.g. limited government accountability and ineffective social protection in people's lives) were related to low SWB among both groups.
- Regarding the large income gap between urban and rural areas, especially in the last decade, researchers found that SWB was not higher in the urban counties for the eastern and middle areas. For the eastern area, SWB was even higher in the rural than in the urban counties. There are three possible explanations for this: (a) relatively strong family and community support in the rural compared with the urban counties, (b) urban residents being confronted by more problems (e.g. risk of unemployment, limited access to healthcare services – particularly among individuals and families without city residential status, "Hukou") and (c) the evaluation of relative status – which is assessed by comparing one's current situation over time and/or with other individuals in the local community. "In rural areas, due to limited information and narrow reference groups (people from the same village), residents might have lower

expectations. Meanwhile, income, living and health conditions have increased over time and there is an expectation for improvement in the future as well; therefore, rural residents may have a positive perception of their relative status" (Sun et al., 2016, p. 29).

- Inadequate coverage of the healthcare system and social division (e.g. between social classes and tribal groups) which are part of the social transition of China, were reducing Chinese psychological wellbeing.
- Subjective health status was linked to SWB even after age, sex, region and socioeconomic characteristics were controlled.

Directions for Future Investigations in Non-Western Cultures

Based on the present review of the literature, there are a disproportionate number of studies in relation to geographical area; most research was conducted in Western, high- or middle-income countries, while other places have be subjects of little or no research. Reasons for this pattern are unclear; possibilities include the location of researchers, the number of universities and research institutes in the area and the state of economic development. More research is also needed from a wider range of samples, including children, older people and adults with a physical and mental disability. Furthermore, I propose there are three important directions for future studies about wellbeing in non-Western populations.

Non-Western cultures may undergo sudden and rapid changes. Unstable and diverse political systems, civic unrest (e.g. racial divisions/conflicts, and ethnic violence), epidemics of contagious diseases (e.g. avian influenza, Ebola, severe acute respiratory syndromae; see Lau et al., 2008), terrorist activities (within the country or in neighbouring countries) and rapid economic transformation not only exist in non-Western countries, but also make the countries quite fragile (Shin et al., 2003, Inoguchi and Fujii, 2009, Ip and Shek, 2014). With South Korea as an example, ideologically, its political system has been undergoing a profound and successful transformation from a military regime to a representative democracy (Shin et al., 2003). Since the election of Kim Dae Jung as President in December, 1997, the country has been pursuing better relations with Communist North Korea. Another example is China's social transitions, which have been characterised by the high mortality rate of baby girls and the one-child policy, which have resulted in a serious gender imbalance. This challenges the traditional role of marriage, which has long been seen as a fundamental social institution that maintains and improves psychological wellbeing among Chinese mainlanders (Liu et al., 2014). All of these changes definitely affect people's perception of wellbeing and thus warrant careful and ongoing monitoring of each country's level of wellbeing in the region (Trung et al., 2013).

Influence of information and communication technology on one's wellbeing. In Hong Kong, "access to electronic communication technologies" or digital access was found to be the most important factor in shaping enjoyment, and the second most important factor influencing overall quality of life or sense of wellbeing (Sing, 2009). In an editorial titled "Youth Internet and Wellbeing", the special issue editor wrote powerfully, "(w)ith millions of young people on line and that number growing all the time through increasing use of hand-held mechanisms such as i-phones, this type of research is vital for the welfare and safety of the younger generation … Clearly, the internet is here to stay and it is vital that leaders in the field of government and education take seriously the dangers young people are exposed to online and take steps both to make the internet environment safer for our youth and to teach the younger generation how to protect themselves effectively" (Amichai-Hamburger, 2013, p. 2).

On the other hand, ongoing research and social policy need to be in place to promote the SWB of the entire population by narrowing the digital divide between the rich and poor (who cannot afford to have gadgets and Internet access), the young and old, and the less and the well educated (Sing, 2009).

Impacts of religious and spiritual dimensions on wellbeing in non-Western cultures. Finally, the "spirituality and religion" dimension was found to play an important role in people's sense of wellbeing in Colombia (Wills, 2009), in Thailand (Camfield and Guillen-Royo, 2010) and in a sample of 102 nomads from Tibet (Webb, 2009). Also, in a recent study in China, it was found that believers in Islam (a historically foreign religion to China) or Taoism (a native religion) were happier than believers in any other religion or nonbelievers (Bian et al., 2015). Apart from in these cases, the link between wellbeing and spirituality and religion was not found to be conclusive in other studies. What are the underlying logic and mechanisms whereby ethnic cultures and religious beliefs affect the sense of wellbeing in people from a non-Western cultural background? More research needs to be conducted to look more deeply into the role of religions in non-Western cultures and beyond with regard to wellbeing.

Implications for Recovery-Oriented Mental Health Services

Mental health was found to exert a greater impact than physical health on SWB (Sun et al., 2016). One possible explanation could be that the ability to adapt is different for physical and mental health, with the latter being more difficult to modify. This is exactly the challenge faced by service users and mental health professionals. It is hoped that this section will serve as a primer to encourage mental health practitioners, service planners and researchers to pay more attention to wellbeing, which should be a key goal for mental health promotion interventions and mental health services. There is a need to put wellbeing issues on top of the healthcare agenda, to develop policies and other conditions that enhance and maintain individual and population physical and mental wellbeing (Rato and Davey, 2012; Tang, 2014). I make three specific suggestions about the implications of the present review for recovery-oriented mental health services in non-Western cultures.

Peer Support Services

When reviewing the studies of SWB in non-Western cultures, researchers always checked if a wellbeing rating was within a normative range; this links to the theory of subjective wellbeing homeostasis (Cummins et al., 2002), which asserts that SWB does not vary freely over the 0–100 range. Normative SWB is protected from threats to wellbeing by two mechanisms: (a) resources external to the person (e.g. money and relationships that mediate life's challenges) and (b) internal psychological mechanisms (e.g. processes of adaptation, selective attention and cognitive restructuring), which somehow maintain a balance. Peer support workers (for review on peer support services, see Davidson et al., 2012; Slade et al., 2014) can strengthen external resources and internal psychological processes. Concerning external resources, peer support workers should focus on building up social support, which was found to be a robust protective factor evident in numerous studies. For example, a recent study in China showed that more social integration and social contact were associated with better psychological wellbeing in both rural and urban areas (Liu et al., 2014). Even controlling for its interaction with social transitions in China, the main effect of social support remained significant, especially in urban areas. These findings confirm that social support can improve psychological wellbeing by maintaining positive emotional feelings and mitigating the stress of negative events. Additionally, peer support workers may support individuals in using a variety of practices and non-Western traditions to maintain their wellbeing. These include acupuncture, a balanced diet, tai chi, qi gong and Chinese tea to improve their sleep and bodily vitality, or in other cases taking a specially prepared soup to stay healthy (Tse et al., 2014). Concerning the internal psychological processes, peer support workers can concentrate on a service user's goals, which often represent the salient information that a person uses to steer his/her course of actions and to make judgments of a service user's SWB. Peterson et al. (2005) suggested that the three components which contribute to life goals and satisfaction are pleasure, engagement and meaning. Generally speaking, the survival-of-the-fittest regime, securing a paid job and stable income, remains a prime contributor to wellbeing in non-Western cultures (Sun, 2005).

Wellbeing-Oriented Engagement with Service Users

The essence of wellbeing is "a well-lived life" and "… the concept of well-being should include not only life satisfaction and positive affect, but also purpose in life, a sense of vitality … meaning in life … and meaningful work, or calling" (Diener et al., 2010, p.36). The following items are wellbeing-related useful prompts for mental health workers and peer support workers to use when they engage in therapeutic conversations with service users from non-Western cultures (Shin et al., 2003, Bian et al., 2015).

Individual Level

- What notable changes have taken place in the various objective conditions (e.g. housing arrangement, family situation, work and political system) under which the service users live?
- Which particular conditions of life have become desirable and undesirable?
- How do the service users feel about their own private and public lives (prompts: be aware of the events that have occurred in the community that the service users identify with)?
- Which particular aspects of the service users' life experiences are positive and which are negative (prompts: pay attention to service users' culture-related achievements, such as mastery of cooking skills and craft skills)?
- What kinds of specific life goals and values do the service users cherish most for their own existence and that of their community?
- How do positive and negative life experiences vary across the different segments of the service users' life (prompts: pay attention to the interactions and dynamics between service users and their family)?
- How do service users pursue what they see as wellbeing or a good life (the notion of having "a well-lived life") and what trade-offs are they required to make to attain or preserve it?
- What resources can service users draw on in their pursuit of a good life for themselves, their families and their communities, and what are the political and social barriers?

Societal/Community Level

- How do life priorities vary across the population segments (against the backdrop of the wider sociocultural and political context in non-Western cultures)?

- How have these priorities changed over time?
- How do local people understand wellbeing, and how does this understanding vary according to life phase, gender, socioeconomic status and so forth within the community where the service users reside?

Strengths-Based Intervention

The Personal Wellbeing Index (PWI) has been used by over 100 researchers in 50 countries. Cross-cultural comparisons between Australia and Hong Kong found that the PWI in the former was in the 70–80 range (out of 100), whereas in the latter, scores fell between 65 and 75 (Lau et al., 2005). In Algeria, the PWI and domain scores were relatively low, with a mean of 50 (Tiliouine et al., 2006). The PWI values in Chinese samples (e.g. Hong Kong and mainland China) were generally about 10 points lower than for Western counterparts, partly explained by a response bias caused by modesty in Chinese culture, which is heavily influenced by Confucianism, Taoism and Buddhism (Lu, 2001; Chen and Davey, 2008). "As these three schools of thought advocate spiritual cultivation and mind-work, such as self-retrospection and self-transcendence, they admonish people to eliminate excessive desires, live a simple life and restore a clear mind" (Lai et al., 2013, p. 608). Under this influence, people from non-Western or primarily Asian cultures tend to be more modest and they may not rate themselves readily at the extremes of a positive response scale such as the PWI or strengths assessment (Lau et al., 2005; Tse et al., 2010). Therefore, mental health practitioners need to be creative and culturally sensitive when helping service users explore and identify the strengths and virtues within themselves and the wider environment (e.g. employment opportunity and exercise facilities). In my research and clinical work, I have found it helpful to invite service users to identify what they see as their sources of strength: personal (e.g. knowledge, qualifications, life experience, talents, problem-solving skills, live skills, interests, character and attitude towards life), career/occupation, colleagues at work, family, religious/spiritual sphere, friends, neighbourhoods, social groups (formal or less formal) or the wider community (Tse et al., 2016).

Social Wellbeing: Individualism and Collectivism

How service users define themselves and their relationships with others, which is a key part of social wellbeing, may be different for individuals in different cultural backgrounds (Li et al., 2015). For example, people in Western cultures, such as Americans, often lay stress on individual autonomy and separation from others, viewing themselves as individuals. In comparison, individuals in Eastern cultures, such as Chinese people, often value social connections and interdependence with others, tending to regard themselves as part of a collective (for a review on the applications of the individualistic–collectivistic paradigm in mental healthcare, see Tse and Ng, 2014). In the case of China, mixed results were reported. As part of the social changes and economic transformation in the last three decades, although individuals are encouraged to pursue their own interests in competition with others, the official code or party line continues to foster collectivistic and patriotic values (Wang, 2002). "Thus, the individualist moral code may be trumping the collectivist one in terms of what is most important to individuals in their everyday lives" (Steele and Lynch, 2013, p. 450). In contrast, some studies have revealed that individuals with a high SWB or happy people are those who enjoy good family relationships and are socially integrated into Chinese society (Bian et al., 2015; Sing, 2009). Another illustration is that "Traditional Māori perspectives challenge some treatment goals, such as the focus on developing individuality and self advocacy. Therapies that focus on the individual may be less relevant and less appropriate for Māori, who may place more emphasis on wider relationships. Whānau [family] play an important role in the wellbeing of an individual and in the recovery process. Poor dynamics within the whānau and lack of support can contribute to, or worsen, the illness. There can be a lack of understanding and often a stigma associated with mental health problems. Information can be provided to the patient, their whānau, friends, workplace and community" (Anonymous, 2010, p. 13). The implication for recovery-oriented services is that "[i]nstead of assuming that service users have collectivistic worldviews (again, it greatly depends on the specific social context and individual), practitioners have to discuss the practical meaning of collectivistic (or individualistic) values, their relationships with families, peers and society at large, and the proper way to address the collective needs. The individualistic-collectivistic value orientation could be part of a comprehensive assessment of service users from culturally and linguistically diverse backgrounds" (Tse and Ng, 2014, p. 10).

Conclusion

As the research discussed in this chapter reveals, there have been a number of systematic studies on the relationship between wellbeing and non-Western cultures. Taken as a whole, the emerging results suggest that it might be beneficial to use the topic of wellbeing as the thread that pulls the mental health field together, whether it be related to raising mental health literacy in the community or designing recovery-oriented mental health services for individuals in recovery from severe mental illness. The essence of the proposed implications is to provide a culturally responsive mental health service and to foster an empowering atmosphere that highlights the importance of engaging service users and concerned significant others.

References

Amichai-Hamburger, Y. (2013). Editorial: Youth Internet and wellbeing. *Computers in Human Behavior*, 29, 1–2.

Anonymous (2010). Recognising and managing mental health problems in Maori. *Best Practice Journal*, 8(28), 9–17.

Anonymous (n.d.). A 'wellbeing framework' for Aboriginal and Torres Strait Islander peoples living with chronic disease. Centre of Research Excellence: Intervention Research in Chronic Disease. Available at http://www.kvc.org.au/projects-and-studies/towards-wellbeing-model-aboriginal-torres-strait-islander-peoples-living-chronic-disease/.

Bian, Y., Zhang, L., Yang, J., Guo, X., & Lei, M. (2015). Subjective wellbeing of Chinese people: A multifaceted view. *Social Indicators Research*, 121, 75–92.

Broadie, S., & Rowe, C. (2002). *Aristotle's Nicomachean Ethics: Translation, introduction, and commentary*. Oxford, UK/New York, NY: Oxford University Press.

Camfield, L., & Guillen-Royo, M. (2010). Wants, needs and satisfaction: A comparative study in Thailand and Bangladesh. *Social Indicators Research*, 96, 183–203.

Chen, Z., & Davey, G. (2008). Happiness and subjective wellbeing in Mainland China. *Journal of Happiness Studies*, 9, 589–600.

Chen, Z., & Davey, G. (2009). Subjective quality of life in Zhuhai city, South China: A public survey using the International Wellbeing Index. *Social Indicators Research*, 91, 243–258.

Cho, E.-N. (2014). Children's wellbeing in East and Southeast Asia: A preliminary comparison. *Social Indicators Research*, 123(1), 183–201. doi:10.1007/s11205–014–0731–6.

Chretien, A. (2010). *A resource guide to Aboriginal well-being in Canada*. Toronto, Ontario: Nuclear Waste Management Organization.

Cummins, R. A., Gullone, E., & Lau, A. L. (2002). A model of subjective well-being homeostasis: The role of personality. In Gullone, E., & Cummins, R. A. (Eds.), *The Universality of Subjective Wellbeing Indicators*, Social Indicators Research Series (pp. 7–46). Dordrecht, the Netherlands: Springer.

Davey, G.,& Rato, R. (2012). Subjective wellbeing in China: A review. *Journal of Happiness Studies*, 13, 333–346.

Davidson, L., Bellamy, C., Guy, K., & Miller, R. (2012). Peer support among persons with severe mental illnesses: A review of evidence and experience. *World Psychiatry*, 11, 123–128.

Diener, E., Helliwell, J. F., & Kahneman, D. (2010). *International differences in well-being*. Oxford, UK/ New York, NY: Oxford University Press.

Gough, I., & Mcgregor, J. A. (eds.) (2007). *Wellbeing in developing countries: From theory to research*. Cambridge, UK/New York, NY: Cambridge University Press.

Han, C. (2015). Explaining the subjective well-being of urban and rural Chinese: Income, personal concerns, and societal evaluations. *Social Science Research*, 49, 179–190.

Howell, R. T., Chong, W. T., Howell, C. J., & Schwabe, K. (2012). Happiness and life satisfaction in Malaysia. In Selin, H., & Davey, G. (Eds.), *Happiness across Cultures: Views of Happiness and Quality of Life in Non-Western Cultures* (pp. 43–55). New York, NY: Springer Science + Business Media.

Inoguchi, T., & Fujii, S. (2009). The quality of life in Japan. *Social Indicators Research*, 92, 227–262.

Ip, P.-K., & Shek, D. L. (2014). A tale of three Chinese societies: The quality of life and well-being of Chinese people in a changing world. *Social Indicators Research*, 117, 665–671.

Kim, S., Sargent-Cox, K. A., French, D. J., Kendig, H., & Anstey, K. J. (2012). Cross-national insights into the relationship between wealth and wellbeing: A comparison between Australia, the United States of America and South Korea. *Ageing and Society*, 32, 41–59.

Lai, L. H., Cummins, R., & Lau, A. D. (2013). Cross-cultural difference in subjective wellbeing: Cultural response bias as an explanation. *Social Indicators Research*, 114, 607–619.

Lau, A. D., Cummins, R., & McPherson, W. (2005). An Investigation into the cross-cultural equivalence of the Personal Wellbeing Index. *Social Indicators Research*, 72, 403–430.

Lau, A. L., Chi, I., Cummins, R. A., Lee, T. M., Chou, K.-L., & Chung, L. W. (2008). The SARS (severe acute respiratory syndrome) pandemic in Hong Kong: Effects on the subjective wellbeing of elderly and younger people. *Aging and Mental Health*, 12, 746–760.

Li, M., Yang, D., Ding, C., & Kong, F. (2015). Validation of the social well-being scale in a Chinese sample and invariance across gender. *Social Indicators Research*, 121, 607–618.

Liu, H., Li, S., Xiao, Q., & Feldman, M. W. (2014). Social support and psychological well-being under social change in urban and rural China. *Social Indicators Research*, 119, 979–996.

Lu, L. (2001). Understanding happiness: A look into the Chinese folk psychology. *Journal of Happiness Studies*, 2, 407–432.

McAllister, F. (2005). Wellbeing concepts and challenges: Discussion paper. London, UK: Sustainable Development Research Network.

Mey, S., & Yin, C. (2014). Mental health and wellbeing of the undergraduate students in a research university: A Malaysian experience. *Social Indicators Research*, 122(2), 539–551. doi:10.1007/s11205-014-0704-9.

Ngoo, Y., Tey, N., & Tan, E. (2014). Determinants of life satisfaction in Asia. *Social Indicators Research*, 124(1), 141–156. doi:10.1007/s11205-014-0772-x.

Oishi, S., & Diener, E. (2001). Goals, culture, and subjective well-being. *Personality and Social Psychology Bulletin*, 27(12), 1674–1682.

Palmer, S. (2004). Homai te Waiora ki Ahau: A tool for the measurement of wellbeing among Maori – The evidence of construct validity. *New Zealand Journal of Psychology*, 33, 50–58.

Pere, R. (1991). *Te Wheke: A celebration of infinite wisdom*. Gisborne, New Zealand: AkoGlobal Learning.

Peterson, C., Park, N., & Seligman, M. E. (2005). Orientations to happiness and life satisfaction: The full life versus the empty life. *Journal of Happiness Studies*, 6, 25–41.

Rato, R., & Davey, G. (2012). Quality of life in Macau, China. *Social Indicators Research*, 105, 93–108.

Sheu, H.-B., Chong, S. S., Chen, H.-F., & Lin, W.-C. (2014). Well-being of Taiwanese and Singaporean college students: Cross-cultural validity of a modified social cognitive model. *Journal of Counseling Psychology*, 61, 447.

Shin, D., Rutkowski, C., & Park, C.-M. (2003). The quality of life in Korea: Comparative and dynamic perspectives. *Social Indicators Research*, 62-63, 3-16.

Sing, M. (2009). The quality of life in Hong Kong. *Social Indicators Research*, 92, 295-335.

Slade, M., Amering, M., Farkas, M., Hamilton, B., O'Hagan, M., Panther, G., et al. (2014). Uses and abuses of recovery: Implementing recovery-oriented practices in mental health systems. *World Psychiatry*, 13, 12-20.

Smyth, R., Nielsen, I., & Zhai, Q. (2010). Personal well-being in urban China. *Social Indicators Research*, 95, 231-251.

Steele, L., & Lynch, S. (2013). The pursuit of happiness in China: Individualism, collectivism, and subjective well-being during China's economic and social transformation. *Social Indicators Research*, 114, 441-451.

Sun, J. Y. (2005). The evaluation of China's market economy: The perspective of international dimension (in Chinese). *Journal of Finance and Economics*, 31(10), 108-115.

Sun, S., Chen, J., Johannesson, M., Kind, P., & Burström, K. (2016). Subjective well-being and its association with subjective health status, age, sex, region, and socio-economic characteristics in a Chinese population study. *Journal of Happiness Studies*, 17(2), 833-873. doi:10.1007/s10902-014-9611-7.

Tang, Z. (2014). They are richer but are they happier? Subjective well-being of Chinese citizens across the reform era. *Social Indicators Research*, 117, 145-164.

Tiliouine, H., Cummins, R. A., & Davern, M. (2006). Measuring wellbeing in developing countries: The case of Algeria. *Social Indicators Research*, 75, 1-30.

Trung, N., Cheong, K., Nghi, P., & Kim, W. (2013). Relationship between socio-economic values and wellbeing: An overview research in Asia. *Social Indicators Research*, 111, 453-472.

Tse, S., Divis, M., & Li, Y. B. (2010). Match or mismatch: Use of the strengths model with Chinese migrants experiencing mental illness: Service user and practitioner perspectives. *American Journal of Psychiatric Rehabilitation*, 13, 171-188.

Tse, S., & Ng, R. M. (2014). Applying a mental health recovery approach for people from diverse backgrounds: The case of collectivism and individualism paradigms. *Journal of Psychosocial Rehabilitation and Mental Health*, 1, 7-13.

Tse, S., Tsoi, E. W., Hamilton, B., O'Hagan, M., Shepherd, G., Slade, M., et al. (2016). Uses of strength-based interventions for people with serious mental illness: A critical review. *International Journal of Social Psychiatry*, 62(3), 281-291.

Tse, S., Yuen, Y. M.-Y., & Suto, M. (2014). Expected possible selves and coping skills among young and middle-aged adults with bipolar disorder. *East Asian Archives of Psychiatry*, 24, 117-124.

Veenhoven, R. (1991). Is happiness relative? *Social Indicators Research*, 24, 1-34.

Veenhoven, R. (2009). Well-being in nations and well-being of nations. *Social Indicators Research*, 91, 5-21.

Wang, X. (2002). The post-communist personality: The spectre of China's capitalist market reforms. *China Journal*, 47, 1-17.

Webb, D. (2009). Subjective wellbeing on the Tibetan plateau: An exploratory investigation. *Journal of Happiness Studies*, 10, 753-768.

White, S., Gaines, S., Jr., & Jha, S. (2014). Inner wellbeing: Concept and validation of a new approach to subjective perceptions of wellbeing – India. *Social Indicators Research*, 119, 723-746.

Wills, E. (2009). Spirituality and subjective well-being: Evidences for a new domain in the personal well-being index. *Journal of Happiness Studies*, 10, 49-69.

Xing, Z., & Huang, L. (2014). The relationship between age and subjective well-being: Evidence from five capital cities in Mainland China. *Social Indicators Research*, 117, 743-756.

Yiengprugsawan, V., Seubsman, S., Khamman, S., Lim, L. L. Y., & Sleigh, A. C. (2010). Personal wellbeing index in a national cohort of 87,134 Thai adults. *Social Indicators Research*, 98, 201-215.

Wellbeing Policy in Australia and New Zealand

Rebecca Jarden, Aaron Jarden and Lindsay G. Oades

Introduction

This chapter provides an overview of wellbeing policy in Australia and New Zealand (Aotearoa). We begin by highlighting the challenge that the term 'wellbeing', and its multidimensional nature, provides, particularly for policy makers, researchers and community development stakeholders. An exploration of wellbeing use in policy in New Zealand and Australia is then presented, along with critical comments on similarities and differences between these countries. Examples are provided which demonstrate the usefulness of wellbeing policy. The chapter ends with the shared recognition of the impact of policies on health, wellbeing and equity.

What Is 'Wellbeing'?

The term wellbeing is becoming more popular in media, in general discourse and in academic literature. However, the ability to distinguish meaningfully between types of wellbeing is debatable (see Disabato et al., 2015). A systematic understanding of wellbeing is imperative, as research and policy rely on such conceptualisations. A common framework for wellbeing distinguishes between eudaimonic wellbeing (eudaimonia; Ryan and Deci, 2001) and hedonic wellbeing (hedonia). Hedonia embodies the maximisation of pleasure and minimisation of pain, whereas eudaimonia represents human flourishing, living up to one's full potential (i.e. self-actualization) and working towards personal growth. In plain language, the hedonic approach encapsulates 'feeling good' and the eudaimonic approach encapsulates 'functioning well'; so wellbeing is 'feeling good and functioning well' (see Gordon this volume). Wellbeing is also more than the absence of illness or dysfunction; it incorporates the presence of positive aspects (e.g. positive emotions, strengths use, a sense of meaning in life) that are needed for a good life and for recovery.

Beyond conceptualisation of the multidimensional nature of wellbeing (see Hone et al., 2014b), there is also the tricky issue of measuring 'wellbeing' per se (see Hone et al., 2014a, or OECD, 2013). Consideration of these issues is relevant when the question is how best to apply or consider 'wellbeing' in the policy arena. Such clarity underpins the use of wellbeing in policy. For example, before executives and policy makers allocate resources toward improving wellbeing, they often require a more comprehensive, scientifically based understanding of what exactly humans are striving for. As another example, a cost–benefit analysis

Wellbeing, Recovery and Mental Health, ed. Mike Slade, Lindsay Oades and Aaron Jarden.
Published by Cambridge University Press. © Mike Slade, Lindsay Oades and Aaron Jarden 2017

of policy related to wellbeing and the ensuing political judgements needs to be informed by a common currency measure of wellbeing (Seaford, 2011). Beyond this, the purpose of incorporating wellbeing into policy is, on a larger level, the benefit of society. As McGeorge (2012) mentions, a 'whole of society' policy approach is required for optimal mental health and wellbeing.

Investigating Wellbeing Policy in Australia and New Zealand

For the purposes of this chapter, we conducted two reviews: (1) One to identify government policies in New Zealand and Australia that addressed wellbeing (rather than illbeing), and (2) a second to identify literature reports of wellbeing and policy in legislation or organisations in both countries. The first review of governmental policies searched the two websites https://www.comlaw.gov.au/ (for Australian common legislation; individual Australian states' legislation was not included in this review) and http://www.legislation.govt.nz/ (for New Zealand legislation). Search terms included wellbeing OR well-being OR 'well being'. The second review systematically searched electronic databases (EBSCO Health Databases: MEDLINE, CINHAL Plus with Full Text; Scopus; Proquest; Pubmed) without date limiters up to December 2015 to identify reports of policy and wellbeing in Australia or New Zealand within the literature. Database search terms included wellbeing OR well-being OR "well being" AND polic* AND government OR organi* or work* AND legislat* AND "New Zealand" OR NZ OR Aotearoa OR Australia*.

The results from review one for New Zealand included using the search term wellbeing $n = 25$, well-being $n = 137$, and "well being" $n = 137$. Following removal of duplicates, the total number of policies identified was 162. For Australia, results included using the search term wellbeing $n = 118$, well-being $n = 0$, and well being – search term not valid. Following removal of duplicates, the total number of policies identified was 609. Such a difference in numbers of policies identified should be expected, given the population size difference between Australia (23.97 million) and New Zealand (4.65 million). Titles and abstracts were also screened, and relevant full-text reports were reviewed. Key concepts from this literature search are reported in this chapter.

Wellbeing Policy in New Zealand

The impact of wellbeing policy within New Zealand is evident, for example, in populations related to mental health (McGeorge, 2012; Mental Health Commission, 2012), children and youth (e.g. Maclennan et al., 2011; Public Health Advisory Committee, 2010; Shepherd et al., 2013; Witten et al., 2015), Pacific families living in New Zealand (e.g. Families Commission, 2009), and immigrants (e.g. Horner and Ameratunga, 2012). It is evident because wellbeing in New Zealand is mandated in legislation (e.g. New Zealand Local Government Act, 2002; Mental Health Compulsory Assessment and Treatment Act 1992); Children, Young Persons, and Their Families Act 1989; Vulnerable Children Act 2014; Privacy Act 1993), with indicator-monitoring reports addressing social, economic, environmental and cultural conditions (e.g. Ministry of Social Development's Social Report, Statistics New Zealand's General Social Survey, New Zealand Local Government's Big Cities Quality of Life, Superu's Families and Whānau Status Report), and various projects demonstrating implementation related to this legislation (e.g. New Zealand Mental Health Foundation's 'The Five Ways to Wellbeing' public health promotion campaign, or the Sovereign New Zealand Wellbeing Index longitudinal study: Jarden et al., 2013). For example, the recent Ministry of Social Development publication of Family Wellbeing Guidelines (Ministry of Social Development,

2015a) seeks to guide the Ministry's providers to achieve the two long-term goals of (1) safe and socialised children and young people with a strong sense of identity and wellbeing and (2) family (whānau) equipped to care for and protect their own children and young people. Furthermore, the Ministry of Social Development have also published Towards Wellbeing Service Specifications (Ministry of Social Development, 2015b) with a vision of reducing the numbers of children and young people at risk of suicide and increasing their wellbeing and mental health.

Examples of projects related to mental health within New Zealand include the aforementioned 'Five Ways to Wellbeing' and Toi Te Ora's workplace wellness programme, which focuses on the three levels of organisational, environmental and individual factors to create a sustained approach to workplace wellness (Ruha and Barns, 2012). However, it is notable that within the New Zealand mental health legislation, such as New Zealand's Mental Health (Compulsory Assessment and Treatment) Act 1992, there is predominantly a focus on illbeing rather than wellbeing. For example, within this Act the term 'wellbeing' is mentioned only once, this being in relation to powers being exercised with proper respect for cultural identity and personal beliefs: 'The power must be exercised, or the proceedings conducted, – (b) with proper recognition of the contribution those ties make to the person's wellbeing; ...' (p. 14).

As a backdrop to such initiatives and policies, significant contextual influences include The Treaty of Waitangi (1840), considered a founding constitutional document of New Zealand (Durie, 2005). Further, there has been extensive economic, social and political reform in New Zealand since the mid 1980s. Although the impact of this reform initially focused on the economy, more recently it has been explored from a social perspective (e.g. Crothers et al., 2013). The key resources relating to the social impact of the reforms included the Ministry of Social Development's social report (see http://www.socialreport.msd.govt.nz) and the local government Big Cities Quality of Life project (see http://www.qualityoflifeproject.govt.nz; Cotterell and Crothers, 2011) and more recently the Family Whānau and Wellbeing Project (FWWP; COMPASS). The social report's four key aims are to report on social indicators that complement existing economic and environmental indicators, compare New Zealand with other countries on measures of wellbeing, contribute to better-informed public debate and aid planning and decision making to help identify key areas for action using 43 social wellbeing indicators (Ministry of Social Development, 2010). The Big Cities Quality of Life project was initiated in 1999 due to concern about the impact of urbanisation and its effect on the wellbeing and mental health of residents (also see Morrison, 2011), with the most recent Quality of Life Survey report being 2014. This surveyed six council areas, investigating quality of life, health and wellbeing, crime and safety, community, culture and social networks, council processes, built environment, transport and economic wellbeing (see http://www.qualityoflifeproject.govt.nz/survey.htm). The Family Whānau and Wellbeing Project conducted by COMPASS examined and monitored the social and economic determinants of family (whānau) wellbeing using census data, reporting on the six domains of income, education, work, housing, health and connectedness (Crothers et al., 2013). A subset of census data was also used to explore changes and differences in wellbeing in Samoan, Cook Island, Tongan and Niuean people living in New Zealand (von Randow et al., 2009).

Locking economic wellbeing together with subjective wellbeing, or ensuring that the "social is to properly clothe the economic" (Crothers, 2015, p. 98), had the attention of a special issue of New Zealand Sociology in 2015. Within this issue, Duncan (2015) comments on a framework proposed by Dalziel and Saunders (2014). Whereas Dalziel and Saunders (2014) proposed New Zealand's economic transformation from a 'welfare state' to a 'wellbeing state', putting forth a wellbeing economics framework based on five principles linking economics to personal values, Duncan (2015) suggested that this was little more than rhetoric and it is 'absurd to assume that the "traditional welfare state" was *not* designed to promote (what we now call) "well-being"' (p. 58).

Further authors within the issue explore another example of implementation of wellbeing into policy development, the New Zealand Treasury's Living Standards Framework (see http://www.treasury.govt.nz/abouttreasury/higherlivingstandards) released in 2012. This framework was part of the Treasury's vision of being "a world-class Treasury working for higher living standards for New Zealanders" by considering, in addition to income or GDP, factors which impact wellbeing. Since the release of the framework with its five criteria (economic growth, increasing equity, managing risk, social infrastructure and sustainability for the future), the Treasury has reported its value in ensuring that policy focuses on what matters to people: for example, New Zealand's defence policy and how New Zealand's welfare system contributes to New Zealand's living standards (Au and Karacaoglu, 2015). Easton (2015) has recommended adding a sixth point to the framework, improving quality of life[1].

Embedding wellbeing in policy making is also suggested by Ussher and Walker of Statistics New Zealand (Ussher and Walker, 2015) as the 'next big step', moving from measuring wellbeing to informing decision making. They report that their research related to New Zealanders' social wellbeing demonstrates the application of public policy to single aspects of life. Such work is also on the back of work by the OECD. For example, both New Zealand and Australian mental health services are provided by public and private organisations, located in both the hospital and community settings. These services are influenced by both the OECD framework for measuring wellbeing (OECD, 2013) and the World Health Organisation (WHO) Mental Health action plan 2013–2020 (see http://www.who.int/mental_health/publications/action_plan/en/).

In summary, our review has highlighted many examples of wellbeing policy in New Zealand, and also that this increasing trend of wellbeing focus in policy is a relatively recent phenomenon. We now examine wellbeing policy in Australia.

Wellbeing Policy in Australia

Australia has experienced considerable structural reforms of the health care system with a model of legislative and regulatory power shared between federal, state/territory, and local governments, and as in New Zealand, private health care supplements public health care. As our above review identified, there is much policy development in Australia related to wellbeing ($n = 609$). Again and similar to New Zealand, this is evident in various populations such as Aboriginal and Torres Strait Island residents (see Health Workforce Australia, 2014) and is related to mental health (see Whiteford and Groves, 2009), people living with disabilities (see Layton and Steel, 2015; Tilley et al., 2002), children and adolescents (see Lawrence et al., 2015), and single-mother families (Grahame and Marston, 2012). For example, indigenous Australians reportedly have higher levels of morbidity and mortality from mental illness, assault, self-harm and suicide than other Australians, with significant connections with social, historical and economic disadvantage (Paradies et al., 2008). The Aboriginal and

---

[1] The second author (AJ) also made this suggestion in 2011 to the New Zealand Treasury.

Torres Strait Islander Health Performance Framework (HPF; 2012) was designed to measure the national framework for the health of Aboriginal and Torres Strait Island residents (see http://www.health.gov.au/), in which the health plan sought to build on the United Nations Declaration on the Rights of Indigenous Peoples. The health plan used a strengths-based approach for policies and programs in an effort to improve health, social and emotional wellbeing and resilience and promote positive health behaviour (Commonwealth Government of Australia, 2013). Subsequently, Health Workforce Australia published Leadership of the Sustainability of the Health System (Health Workforce Australia, 2014), with a focus on Aboriginal and Torres Strait Islander health leadership, and proposed key recommendations relating to leadership development.

In relation to mental health, the Australian Department of Health programmes (see http://www.health.gov.au/) have a significant presence of 'wellbeing'; for example, 3,120 documents match for a search on wellbeing, and some of these include Mental Health of Children and Adolescents (2015); Mental Health of Australians 2: Report on the 2007 National Survey of Mental Health and Wellbeing; Supporting Parents and Families: The Mental Health and Wellbeing of Children and Young People; Evaluation of Better Access to Psychiatrists, Psychologists and General Practitioners through the Medicare Benefits Schedule (Better Access) Initiative: Component F: Analysis of the Second National Survey of Mental Health and Wellbeing.

In Australia, each state and territory has mental health legislation, for example, the state of Victoria's Mental Health Act 2014. Within Victoria's Act, a focus on wellbeing is highly prevalent (mentioned more than eight times, for example, 'children, young persons and other dependents of persons receiving mental health services should have their needs, wellbeing and safety recognised and protected', p. 22; 'satisfies the Commissioner that he or she has a genuine interest in the wellbeing of a consumer', p. 174).

What Australia and New Zealand share is a growing interest in considering the impact of policies on health, wellbeing and equity. The Health Impact Assessment (HIA) is one proposed formal tool that assesses the impact of policies on health, wellbeing and equity, for the use of policy makers centrally, regionally and locally. A New Zealand case study analysis using the HIA has highlighted how the tool may be used (Signal et al., 2006). More recently, a review of HIA practice in both New Zealand and Australia demonstrated its increasing prevalence, and possibilities for improvement in the use of the tool (Haigh et al., 2013).

Conclusion

Wellbeing policy provides a great opportunity to have large impacts on wellbeing, mental health and recovery. In order to capitalise on this opportunity, a range of challenges must be faced moving forward. First, different policy users (e.g. policy makers, researchers and community development stakeholders) need to be aware of and learn from each other's experience of conceptualising wellbeing and incorporating wellbeing into policy, or utilising the end results from such policy. Second, there is a significant opportunity for further advances in conceptualising wellbeing in policy development. Last, although there is existing shared interest in considering and measuring the impact of policies on health, wellbeing and equity, there remains a paucity of validated outcome measures for thorough investigation in this area. We hope this chapter, which provides a brief flavour of such wellbeing policy endeavours in the New Zealand and Australian context, provides a foundation for further discussions.

References

Au, J., & Karacaoglu, G. (2015). Using the living standards framework: Update and policy examples. *New Zealand Sociology*, 30(3), 27–40.

Commonwealth Government of Australia (2013). National Aboriginal and Torres Strait Islander Health Plan 2013–2023. Available at http://www.health.gov.au.

Cotterell, G., & Crothers, C. (2011). Social indicators and social reporting in New Zealand, and the potential contribution of the Family Whānau and Wellbeing Project. *Social Policy Journal of New Zealand*, 37, 1–19.

Crothers, C. (2015). Putting social flesh on economic bones: Sociological comments on Dalziel and Saunders. *New Zealand Sociology*, 30(3), 85–98.

Crothers, C., von Randow, M., & Cotterell, G. (2013). Measuring changes in family wellbeing in New Zealand 1981 to 2006. *New Zealand Sociology*, 28(3), 237–254.

Dalziel, P., & Saunders, C. (2014). *Wellbeing economics: Future directions for New Zealand*. Wellington, New Zealand: Bridget Williams Books.

Disabato, D. J., Goodman, F. R., Kashdan, T. B., Short, J. L., & Jarden, A. (2015, September 7). Different types of well-being? A cross-cultural examination of hedonic and eudaimonic well-being. *Psychological Assessment*. doi:10.1037/pas0000209

Duncan, G. (2015). Economy, society and well-being: A response to Dalziel and Saunders. *New Zealand Sociology*, 30(3), 56–67.

Durie, M. (2005). Race and ethnicity in public policy. Does it work? *Social Policy Journal of New Zealand*, 24(1), 1–11.

Easton, B. (2015). Income and wellbeing. *New Zealand Sociology*, 30(3), 99–111.

Families Commission (2009). Pacific families now and in the future: Changing Pacific households. Report No. 1/09. Available at http://www.superu.govt.nz.

Grahame, T., & Marston, G. (2012). Welfare-to-work policies and the experience of employed single mothers on income support in Australia: Where are the benefits? *Australian Social Work*, 65(1), 73–86.

Haigh, F., Harris, E., Chok, H., Baum, F., Harris-Roxas, B., Kemp, L., et al. (2013). Characteristics of health impact assessments reported in Australia and New Zealand 2005–2009. *Australian and New Zealand Journal of Public Health*, 37(6), 534–546.

Health Workforce Australia (2014). Leadership for the sustainability of the health system, Part 4: Aboriginal and Torres Strait Islander health leadership, a key informant interview report. Available at https://www.hwa.gov.au/.

Hone, L., Jarden, A., & Schofield, G. (2014a). Psychometric properties of the Flourishing Scale in a New Zealand sample. *Social Indicators Research*, 119(2), 1031–1042.

Hone, L., Jarden, A., Schofield, G. M., & Duncan, S. (2014b). Measuring flourishing: The impact of operational definitions on the prevalence of high levels of wellbeing. *International Journal of Wellbeing*, 4(1), 62–90. doi:10.5502/ijw.v4i1.1.

Horner, J., & Ameratunga, S. (2012). Monitoring immigrant health and wellbeing in New Zealand: Addressing the tyranny of misleading averages. *Australian Health Review*, 36, 390–393. doi:10.1071/AH11134.

Hudson, S., & Thomson, G. (2011). Policymakers and the example of smoking to children: A qualitative study. *Tobacco Induced Diseases*, 9(1), 1–8.

Hyslop, B., & Tomson, G. (2009). Smoke-free outdoor areas without the smoke-police: The New Zealand local authority experience. *New Zealand Medical Journal*, 122(1303), 67–79.

Jarden, A., MacKay, L., White, K., Schofield, G., Duncan, S., Williden, M., et al. (2013). The Sovereign New Zealand Wellbeing Index. *Psychology Aotearoa*, 5(1), 22–27.

Lawrence, D., Johnson, S., Hafekost, J., Boterhoven De Haan, K., Sawyer, M., Ainley, J., et al. (2015). The mental health of children and adolescents. Report on the second Australian Child and Adolescent Survey of Mental Health and Wellbeing. Canberra, Australia: Department of Health.

Layton, N., & Steel, E. (2015). "An environment built to include rather than exclude me": Creating inclusive environments for human well-being. *International Journal of Environmental Research and Public Health*, 12, 11146–11162. doi:10.3390/ijerph120911146.

Maclennan, B., Kypri, K., Langley, J., & Room, R. (2012). Public sentiment towards alcohol and local governmental alcohol policies in New Zealand. *International Journal of Drug Policy*, 23, 45–53.

McGeorge, P. (2012). The life cycle, achievements and transformation of the New Zealand Mental Health Commission: Opportunities and risks. *Mental Health Review Journal*, 17(4), 187–198.

Mental Health Commission (2012). *Blueprint II: How things need to be.* Wellington, New Zealand: Mental Health Commission.

Ministry of Social Development (2010). *The social report.* Wellington, New Zealand: Ministry of Social Development.

Ministry of Social Development (2015a). *Family wellbeing guidelines.* Wellington, New Zealand: Ministry of Social Development.

Ministry of Social Development (2015b). *Towards wellbeing: Service specifications.* Wellington, New Zealand: Ministry of Social Development.

Morrison, P. (2011). Local expressions of subjective well-being: The New Zealand experience. *Regional Studies*, 45(8), 1039–1058.

OECD (2013). OECD guidelines on measuring subjective well-being. OECD Publishing. doi:10.1787/9789264191655-en.

Paradies, Y., Harris, R., & Anderson, I. (2008). The impact of racism on indigenous health in Australia and Aotearoa: Towards a research agenda. Discussion paper No. 4, Cooperative Research Centre for Aboriginal Health, Darwin.

Public Health Advisory Committee (2010). *The best start in life: Achieving effective action on child health and wellbeing.* Wellington, New Zealand: Ministry of Health.

Rouch, G., Thomson, G., Wilson, N., Hudson, S., Edwards, R., Gifford, H., et al. (2010). Public, private and personal: Qualitative research on policymakers' opinions on smokefree interventions to protect children in 'private' spaces. *BMC Public Health*, 10(797), 1–10.

Ruha, M., & Barns, M. (2012). Working well on employee wellbeing. *Employment Today.* Available at http://www.ttophs.govt.nz.

Ryan, R. M., & Deci, E. L. (2001). On happiness and human potentials: A review of research on hedonic and eudaimonic well-being. *Annual Review of Psychology*, 52, 141–166. doi:10.1146/annurev.psych.52.1.141.

Seaford, C. (2011). Time to legislate for the good life. *Nature*, 477, 532–533.

Shepherd, M., Kool, B., Ameratunga, S., Bland, V., Hassall, I., Chambers, J., et al. (2013). Preventing child unintentional injury deaths: Prioritising the response to the New Zealand child and adolescent injury report card. *Australian and New Zealand Journal of Public Health*, 37(5), 470–474.

Signal, L., Langford, B., Quigley, R., & Ward, M. (2006). Strengthening health, wellbeing and equity: Embedding policy-level HIA in New Zealand. *Social Policy Journal of New Zealand*, 29, 17–31.

Steptoe, A., Deaton, A., & Stone, A. (2015). Subjective wellbeing, health, and ageing. *Lancet*, 385, 640–648.

Tilley, C., Hills, A., Bruce, C., & Meyers, N. (2002). Communication, information and well-being for Australians with physical disabilities. *Disability and Rehabilitation*, 24(9), 503–510. doi:10.1080/09638280110105286.

Trollor, J., & Ching, A. (2014). Accessible mental health services for people with an intellectual disability: A guide for providers. Department of Developmental Disability Neuropsychiatry. Available at http://3dn.unsw.edu.au/the-guide.

Ussher, S., & Walker, P. (2015). Making what matters count: Embedding well-being in public policy and discourse. Paper presented at the 2015 New Zealand Association of Economists (NZAE) Conference, Wellington, New Zealand.

von Randow, M., Cotterell, G., McTaggart, S., Sua'ali'i-Sauni, T., Davis, P., & Patrick, D. (2009). *Pacific families now and in the future: Changing Pacific household composition and wellbeing, 1981–2006.* Wellington, New Zealand: Families Commission.

Whiteford, H., & Groves, A. (2009). Policy implications of the 2007 Australian national survey of mental health and wellbeing. *Australian and New Zealand Journal of Psychiatry*, 43, 644–651.

Witten, K., Kearns, R., & Carroll, P. (2015). Urban inclusion as wellbeing: Exploring children's accounts of confronting diversity on inner city streets. *Social Science and Medicine*, 133, 349–357.

Chapter

18

Population Level
Wellbeing in the General Population

Sarah Stewart-Brown

Wellbeing, Mental Wellbeing and Positive Mental Health

Wellbeing is a term that is in common parlance, but it is sometimes used by different people to mean different things. It has been studied and written about by at least three distinct academic disciplines (philosophy, psychology, social science) and is used with impunity by policy makers, the public and practitioners of a variety of approaches to health and social care, assuming that other people will know what they are talking about.

The Roots of Wellbeing: Philosophy

With respect to writing, philosophers can claim the longest track record. The terms hedonic and eudemonic wellbeing, still in use today (Ryan and Deci, 2001; Adams et al., 1997), stem from the writings of the Greek philosophers Aristotle and Epicurus in particular. Although it has also been translated as 'pleasure,' in current wellbeing debates hedonic wellbeing is often taken as synonymous with happiness and with subjective or affective wellbeing. It is a feeling, a state of mind which comes and goes and is often determined by circumstances beyond the control of the individual. In current debates, eudemonic wellbeing is held to be achieved through the cultivation of character traits and behaviours which are believed to maximise happiness, including good behaviour towards others. The two concepts are therefore related. These traits were the components of Aristotle's good life and are achieved by self-development. Embedded in the concept of eudemonic wellbeing is the recognition that personal wellbeing is related to the wellbeing of others and that the pursuit of the former needs to encompass concern for the latter.

Eastern Traditions

It is likely that the Greek philosophers built on thinking from the East, where philosophers had been writing about wellbeing and how it is attained for four or more centuries. Buddhist philosophy, the Eastern tradition best known in the West, prescribes a path for developing happiness (Ekmund et al., 2005), including meditation, visualisation and the cultivation of acceptance and compassion. These are held to enable the mastery of fear, aggression, envy and pride, which prevent wellbeing and cause problems in relationships. The Upanishads (*Eight Upanishads*, 2004), which include the philosophical theories of Indian traditions, extol the virtues of temperance, self-restraint, truthfulness, charity,

Wellbeing, Recovery and Mental Health, ed. Mike Slade, Lindsay Oades and Aaron Jarden.
Published by Cambridge University Press. © Mike Slade, Lindsay Oades and Aaron Jarden 2017

nonhypocrisy and compassion. They maintain that knowledge is a means to freedom and that truth can be reached only by strictly personal effort which includes meditation. Both these traditions encourage meditation as a way of training the mind. The idea of regular mind exercise through visualisation and meditation is entirely consistent with neuroscientific principles of brain development, which we now know to be a 'develop and use it, or lose it' affair (Begley, 2008).

Modern Times
Psychology

During the last half century the concept of wellbeing has become of interest to psychologists, especially those with an interest in public health (Jahoda, 1958; Albee, 1982). The personal characteristics that tend to be associated with wellbeing are presented as 'psychological' wellbeing (Ryff, 1989; Ryff and Keyes, 1995) and have much in common with those described by Aristotle and the Eastern traditions. They include self-acceptance, environmental mastery or agency, autonomy, purpose in life, personal growth, positive relations with others and engagement with existential challenges of life. Positive psychologists have introduced the concepts of 'flourishing' (Hone et al., 2014), conceived as a composite of hedonic wellbeing, positive psychological functioning and social wellbeing, signature strengths (Seligman, 2002) and emotional intelligence (Salovey and Sluyter, 1997). Signature strengths are the positive character traits that enable happiness. Seligman proposes that people identify and find ways of employing their signature strengths in their day-to-day lives. Emotional intelligence and the closely related concept of emotional literacy are the key skills for positive relationship with others.

Social Science

Social scientists have, on the whole, adopted simpler definitions of wellbeing using measures of life satisfaction and happiness (Diener et al., 1985) in their studies. These tend to focus on the social circumstances and structures which give rise to the greatest levels of what they call subjective wellbeing. Their underlying belief system – that society, rather than individuals themselves, holds all the trump cards when it comes to determining wellbeing – contrasts with that of psychologists and philosophers. For much of modern history, social scientists have espoused the belief that income was the most important determinant of individual wellbeing, and this belief system has profoundly influenced Western governments. A report from the Stiglitz commission (Stiglitz et al., 2009), showing the lack of relationship between gross domestic product (GDP) and life satisfaction (see Figure 18.1), has played a key role in stimulating recent government interest in wellbeing in the United Kingdom and more widely.

Government

The Prime Minister of the United Kingdom proposed in 2010 that wellbeing should be monitored and progress in government and society measured on the basis of changes in wellbeing, as well as the traditional economic indicators such as gross domestic product (GDP). The English Office for National Statistics (ONS) was asked to identify robust measures of wellbeing, so there has been a flurry of interest and research on the topic, and different perspectives have been debated. During a debate on the nature of wellbeing organised by the

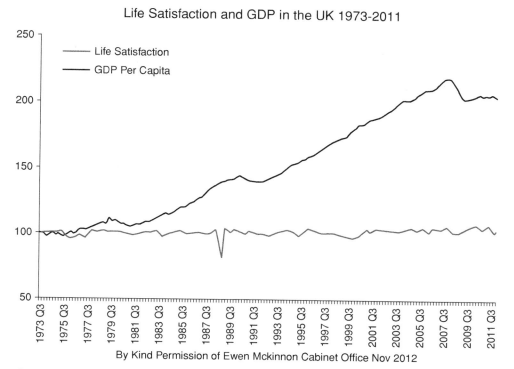

Figure 18.1 GDP and life satisfaction in England.

ONS (Office for National Statistics, 2011), members of the general public were asked to rank specific determinants of wellbeing in order of importance, and they came up with the following: health, good connections with friends and family, job satisfaction, economic security and present and future condition of the environment. Many respondents added to the proffered list; the most frequent contributions were availability of green spaces, work–life balance, cultural and creative activities, fairness and equality, community spirit, trustworthy government and quality of government-provided services.

Emerging Consensus

Although there are different schools of thought about the nature of wellbeing, much is agreed upon. The most important is that wellbeing is more than the absence of 'illbeing' or disease. Another area of agreement is that wellbeing is holistic, covering mental, social and physical components. It will be clear to readers by this stage, however, that dialogue about wellbeing tends to focus on the mental and social aspects rather than the physical. In this way wellbeing can be contrasted with disease, where discussion and teaching focus on the physical. Indeed, in health circles, following the tradition established by Jahoda (1958), wellbeing may be referred to as positive mental health (World Health Organisation, 2004), which is broadly synonymous with mental wellbeing. A third area of agreement is that good relationships with others are fundamental to wellbeing, but there is less consensus about which relationships matter most. Psychologists would put intimate or family relationships as the most important influences, while social scientists tend to focus on societal relationships, for example social support, and trust in government.

Although dissenting voices still claim that mental wellbeing is not sufficiently understood as a concept to be useful for policy or practice (Chief Medical Officer (England), 2014), there is a growing consensus amongst those working in the field of mental wellbeing that it covers both functioning and feeling, including both eudemonic and hedonic concepts, and both psychological wellbeing and 'subjective' wellbeing (Ryan and Deci, 2001). Early definitions of mental wellbeing tended to focus more on functioning than on feeling (e.g. the WHO defining mental health as 'a state of well-being in which the individual realizes his or her own abilities, can cope with the normal stresses of life, can work productively and fruitfully, and is able to make a contribution to his or her community'; World Health Organisation 2004); and the Chief Scientist in the United Kingdom, in his Foresight Report on Mental Health (UK Government Office for Science 2008), as "a dynamic state in which the individual is able to fulfil their personal and social goals and achieve some sense of purpose in society". But both feeling and functioning elements can be observed in more recent definitions, for example in the latest mental health strategy in England (HM Government (England), 2011), wellbeing was defined as 'the ability to cope with life's problems and make the most of life's opportunities';' feeling good and functioning well'; 'resilience'.

Although debates on how to improve wellbeing at a population level are still alive, a consensus is emerging that both supportive social conditions and personal endeavour are necessary. It is very hard for people to change aspects of their thoughts, behaviour and beliefs when feeling frightened, anxious or depressed, so supportive, safe environments are helpful. At the same time, changing social conditions – winning the lottery, getting married, and so forth – have at best short-term effects on wellbeing (Brickman et al., 1978), unless accompanied by personal development.

Models of Mental Health and Wellbeing

Discussion and debate about the nature of wellbeing can be made more challenging by terminology relating to mental health in general (Chief Medical Officer (England), 2014). The stigma surrounding mental illness has led to the adoption of euphemistic terms to describe mental illness and services for the mentally *ill*, which have become known as mental *health* services. The association of the label 'mental health' with mental illness has been partly responsible for the need to identify new labels for the positive end of the spectrum and the emergence of terms such as mental wellbeing. A solution that is compatible with current usage but does not restrict mental health to a dichotomous model (one in which mental health is just the absence of mental illness) is to use *mental health* as the general term covering all components from positive to negative, *mental illness* as covering the negative aspects of mental health and *mental wellbeing* as covering the positive aspects. The latter two can be set against a backdrop of the middle ground, which includes most of the population. Figure 18.2 uses this terminology, depicting mental wellbeing similarly to mental illness as a state from which people tend to come and go. Everyone, including those who have at some stage of their lives been unwell enough to be given a psychiatric diagnosis, could therefore achieve mental wellbeing for some part of their lives, but few are likely to experience mental wellbeing on a permanent basis.

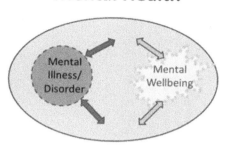

Figure 18.2 A model of mental health.

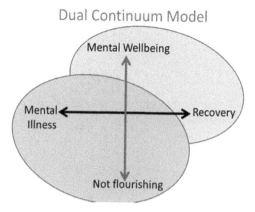

Figure 18.3 The dual continuum model.

For mental illness, this is in line with observation. Somewhere between one-fourth and one-half of us experience mental illness of clinical severity during our lifetimes, but only around 10% of adults have a mental illness of this severity at any one point in time, and fewer still are in the care of psychiatrists (Chief Medical Officer (England), 2014). This means that mental illness severe enough to warrant a psychiatric diagnosis must be able to come and go. Although it is unusual to recover from severe and enduring mental illness completely, it is possible and does happen. And it is fairly normal to recover completely from the common mental disorders such as anxiety and depression.

Psychiatric Illness and Mental Wellbeing: The Dual Continuum Model

Others working on mental wellbeing have come up with different models of mental health. Investigating the concept of flourishing, for example, led Keyes (2002) to agree with earlier writers (Tudor, 1996) that mental wellbeing and mental illness were not necessarily opposite ends of a single continuum. Keyes described one spectrum defined by its two poles of flourishing and languishing, and another orthogonal spectrum with psychiatric illness at one end and lack of illness at the other (see Figure 18.3). This idea has subsequently been validated by Huppert and Whittington (2003).

Keyes provided evidence from population surveys that people with a psychiatric diagnosis could respond to self-report measures of wellbeing with scores in the flourishing range, and people without mental illness could respond in the languishing range (Keyes 2005). This idea has been influential and popular amongst those interested in recovery from mental illness, because a single continuum concept seems to deny those with a diagnosis of mental illness the possibility of enjoying wellbeing at any stage in their lives (Weich et al., 2011). The dual continuum model also lends itself to consideration of whether mental wellbeing might look different amongst people with psychiatric illness than it does amongst the general population. In a similar vein, questions have been asked as to whether interventions shown to promote wellbeing in the well would also be suitable for people with psychiatric illness (Rashid, 2016).

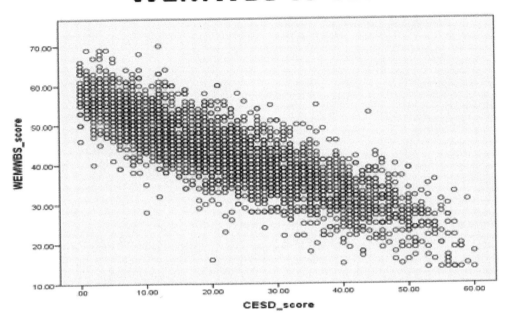

Pearson Correlation Coefficient 0.842

Figure 18.4 Correlation between Warwick–Edinburgh Mental Wellbeing Scale (WEMWBS) scores and scores on the Centre for Epidemiological Studies-Depression Scale (CES-D) in a sample of the general population signing up for an Internet-based CBT programme.

Most studies show measures of mental wellbeing and mental illness to be quite closely correlated (see Figure 18.4, which shows the correlation between mental wellbeing and depression), so the orthogonal picture presented in Figure 18.3 is unlikely to be an accurate representation. This is perhaps to be expected when diagnosis of psychiatric illness is based at some level on 'feeling bad' and 'functioning poorly', and definitions of mental wellbeing on 'feeling good' and 'functioning well'.

The Rose Hypothesis

Professor Geoffrey Rose, one of the founding fathers of modern public health, proposed that where a health issue is continuously distributed in the population, the mean predicts the proportion of the population with a diagnosable illness (see Figure 18.5). The behaviour, thoughts and feelings that are used to make a diagnosis of psychiatric illness are continuously distributed in the population, as can be seen in responses to population-validated mental illness measures, such as the General Health Questionnaire (GHQ)(Goldberg and Williams, 1988) in adults and the Strengths and Difficulties Questionnaire (SDQ) Goodman 1997) in children. Studies using both these measures in different populations have

Distribution of Mental Health

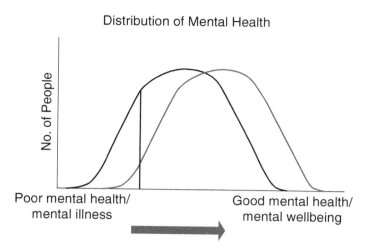

Figure 18.5 The Rose hypothesis: Shifting the mean of a population distribution in a positive direction reduces the proportion of people with a diagnosis.

confirmed that population means do predict the proportion of the population with a diagnosis of psychiatric disorder (Goodman and Goodman, 2011; Veerman et al., 2009). Severe and enduring mental illness (SEMI) is much less common than depression and anxiety in adults and emotional and behavioural problems in children, so these studies have more to say about the relationship between population means and common mental illness than they do about their relationship with SEMIs. The implication of these studies is that if it can be demonstrated that an intervention offered universally improves mean mental health in any population, that intervention will reduce the level of diagnosable illness at least of common mental disorders in that population (Anderson et al., 1993).

The dual continuum model and the Rose model are, in their extreme versions, incompatible. If mental wellbeing and mental illness are orthogonal constructs, then promoting or improving mental wellbeing at a population level would not be expected to have any impact on the prevalence of mental illness or psychiatric disorder. The fact that the Rose hypothesis does seem to hold true, with regard to common mental disorders at least, means that the extreme version of the dual continuum model must be rejected. This argument can prove unpopular with users of mental illness services if it is taken to deny the possibility that people with a psychiatric disorder can experience mental wellbeing, but as argued above, this is not a necessary conclusion. If the two concepts *mental health* and *mental wellbeing* were inversely correlated to a greater or less degree then both models could be true to some extent.

Measurement of Mental Wellbeing

Research and development often depend on accurate measurement, and the creation of instruments which could quantify levels of mental wellbeing has been important in developing our understanding of wellbeing.

Available Scales

As expected from a field in which different disciplines have been involved and definitions debated, a number of different scales have been developed.

Wellbeing scales
Social science
Single item happiness scales
Single item life satisfaction scales
Multiple domain life satisfaction scales

Psychology
Positive and negative affect balance scales (PANAS)
Psychological wellbeing scales

General
WHO-5
Warwick-Edinburgh Mental Well-being Scale (WEMWBS)
Mental Health Continuum Short Form (MHC-SF)
The Flourishing Scale
The Everyday Feeling Questionnaire
Office of National Statistics Questions

Differences between them lie not just in the implicit understanding of wellbeing as hedonic or eudemonic, but also in their length, from single questions (happiness) through to the 54 items of psychological wellbeing scales (Ryff,1989); whether they can be used to derive a single score, such as WHO-5 (Bech, 2004), WEMWBS (Tennant et al. 2007), MHC-SF (Keyes, 2002; Lamers et al., 2011) or the Flourishing Scale (Diener et al., 2010), two scores (PANAS, Watson et al., 1988) or numerous scores (Psychological Wellbeing, Ryff and Keyes 1995). The recent ONS measure of mental wellbeing is based on four separate questions which currently cannot be summed to make a continuous scale (Office for National Statistics, 2011). These scales vary widely in terms of the comprehensibility of the items and the sophistication of the concepts they represent. Many studies of wellbeing have been conducted using reverse scores measures of mental illness, such as the GHQ (Goldberg 1988; Hu et al. 2007). To the extent that these measures are correlated with measures of mental wellbeing, this is a valid approach.

The list does exclude some notable wellbeing indicators, for example that of the OECD (Organisation for Economic Cooperation and Development, 2013) or UNICEF (UNICEF, 2007). These scales were developed in the social science tradition, where the focus is on objective measures of the societal determinants of wellbeing. Although all the determinants are supported by a robust evidence base, the extent to which they actually determine wellbeing (the population-attributable risk in public health terms) is very variable and usually small. Because outcome measures dictate which interventions, projects and programmes are deemed to be effective, such proxy measures have the potential to be profoundly misleading. In this respect, it is therefore of note that they are very seldom used in the context of evaluation, and when they are, they often are deemed not to be the right choice (Spence, 2015).

Measurement Issues

Wellbeing scales vary in the extent to which they represent a balance between the positive and the negative (Psychological Well-Being Scales, PANAS), or focus entirely on the positive (WEMWBS, MHC-SF, WHO-5, the Flourishing Scale). Scales such as the GHQ comprise items covering similar topics, but they are distinguished by their focus on the negative. Balanced scales are considered by some to be ideal because they are thought to be least likely to be subject to block responding (ticking a single level in a Likert scale for all items). On the other hand, wholly positive measures are very popular with those undertaking mental health promotion initiatives. Scales such as WEMWBS implicitly present a positive goal to participants, conveying the belief that practitioners or providers hope to enable participants to develop greater wellbeing. In contrast, negatively oriented scales such as the GHQ implicitly convey the message that practitioners are only really interested in participants if they are mentally ill and aim only to prevent more illness. The difference is subtle but can have an impact on the acceptability of projects and programmes.

Given the possibility that mental wellbeing takes on a slightly different form in psychiatric populations, it is important to test whether wellbeing measures are valid amongst people with mental illness. One qualitative study suggested that wellbeing measures are preferred to measures focusing on the negative in these populations as well as the general population (Crawford et al., 2011). And two scales – WHO-5 (Newnham et al., 2010) and WEMWBS (Trousselard et al., 2015) – have been validated in psychiatric populations.

Distribution of Mental Wellbeing

Multiple surveys have been conducted with measures of mental wellbeing, both at national and local level in the United Kingdom and abroad. The Scots have been monitoring mental wellbeing annually in their Health and Behaviour in the Population Survey (HEPS) since 2007 using WEMWBS, and this measure is now also included in the Health Survey for England. The question is therefore often asked, 'What is the prevalence of mental wellbeing?'

Figure 18.6 shows the almost normal distribution of mental wellbeing scores in the Scottish population and implicitly conveys the fact that there is no clear-cut point between mental wellbeing and lack of mental wellbeing; the distribution is continuous. Although some researchers take the top third or top fifth of the population to represent mental wellbeing, this cut point is arbitrary. It can be used to compare different populations but it cannot be used to estimate prevalence, because cut points made at the level of the top third of the population will provide a prevalence estimate of around 33% and at the level of the top fifth around 20% by the nature of the cut point. Until mental wellbeing has been studied to a greater extent and until programmes and projects have revealed the full extent to which human beings can be mentally well, it may be inappropriate to do this now.

It is possible to compare mental wellbeing in different parts of the population using means and confidence intervals, as in Table 18.1. This shows that there is relatively little variation in mean scores across social groups. The middle-aged tend to have slightly lower scores, and the married slightly higher ones. The unemployed, those with the lowest incomes, those with low levels of education and people who rent their accommodation have slightly lower scores. Only those permanently unable to work because of illness have markedly reduced levels, and a high proportion of these will be unable to work because of mental illness.

A recent analysis of these Health Survey for England data has suggested that these social inequalities may only apply to people with poor mental wellbeing or mental illness (Stewart-Brown et al., 2015). As Figure 18.7 shows, the odds of mental wellbeing are no different amongst people with different levels of education when the group with the highest scores are compared with those with average scores. These data raise questions about causality in well-known studies showing that mental illness is much commoner amongst those

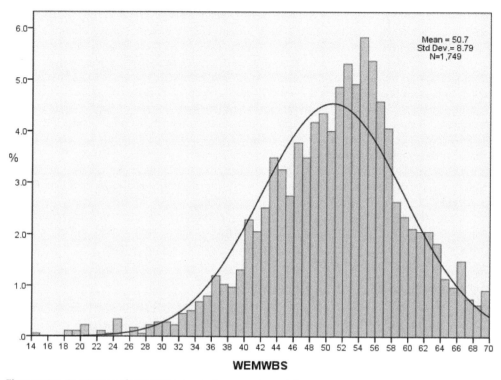

Figure 18.6 Distribution of WEMWBS scores in the general population.

living in social deprivation. If social factors determined levels of mental health in a straight-forward manner, they would be expected to vary across social groups at both ends of the spectrum. If, however, mental illness was a determinant of social deprivation rather than the other way round, this would not necessarily be observed. A recent study of the effects of the banking crisis in Iceland, which had a profound effect on the income of a high proportion of the population, showed relatively little effect on happiness (Gudmunsdottir, 2013).

Promoting Wellbeing

The promotion of wellbeing and the prevention of illness are often referred to as though they were synonymous, but they represent very different ways of working and thinking about the world. Disease prevention is always focused on the negative, on a specific disease or health problem. Interventions are derived from studies of determinants or risk factors for this disease, and the aim of programmes is to reduce the prevalence or incidence of the disease in question. Screening programmes approach mental health from a disease pre-vention point of view. Although seemingly attractive on the face of it, because they help to target scarce resources to people most in need, they have proved ineffective in preventing mental illness. Programmes which are targeted at those most at risk can be valuable and cost-effective. In the context of school health, targeted and universal approaches seem to potentiate each other, working better when they are both included in a programme (Weare and Nind, 2011)

Table 18.1 WEMWBS Scores by Demographic Groups from Health Survey for England 2010 and 2011, Combined

Variable	n	Mean (95% CI)
Total	13,983	51.3 (51.1–51.4)
Sex		
Male	6,145	51.5 (51.2–51.7)
Female	7,838	51.1 (50.9–51.3)
Age in years		
16 – 24	1,453	51.3 (50.9–51.7)
25 – 34	2,086	51.4 (51.1–51.8)
35 – 44	2,525	50.6 (50.2–50.9)
45 – 54	2,523	50.4 (50.0–50.8)
55 – 64	2,332	51.8 (51.5–52.2)
65 – 74	1,752	52.7 (52.3–53.1)
75+	1,312	50.9 (50.4–51.4)
Housing tenure		
Own outright	4,514	52.3 (52.0–52.5)
Own with a mortgage	5,366	51.7 (51.5–51.9)
Rent	3,869	49.4 (49.1–49.7)
Terminal education age		
15 or under	3,125	50.4 (50.0–50.7)
16–18	6,385	50.8 (50.6–51.0)
19 and over	3,745	52.6 (52.3–52.8)
Not finished yet	723	52.2 (51.6–52.8)
Employment status		
In work	8,923	51.8 (51.6–51.9)
Student	256	52.0 (51.0–53.0)
Retired	3,496	51.9 (51.6–52.2)
Looking for paid work	255	48.1 (46.9–49.4)
Permanently unable to work because of long-term sickness	451	41.2 (40.1–42.3)
Looking after home or family	453	48.0 (47.0–49.0)
Marital status		
Single	3,816	50.3 (50.1–50.6)
Married/Living as couple	7,384	52.1 (51.9–52.3)
Divorced	1,326	50.0 (49.5–50.6)
Widowed	1,004	50.7 (50.1–51.3)
Equivalised household income pa Quintiles		
Lowest < = £11,143	1,787	48.2 (47.7–48.7)
Second lowest £11,144 – £19,091	2,228	50.4 (50.0–50.8)
Middle £19,092 – £29,167	2,346	51.4 (51.0–51.7)
Second highest £29,168 – £45,139	2,567	52.2 (51.9–52.5)
Highest > £45,139	2,586	53.1 (52.8–53.4)

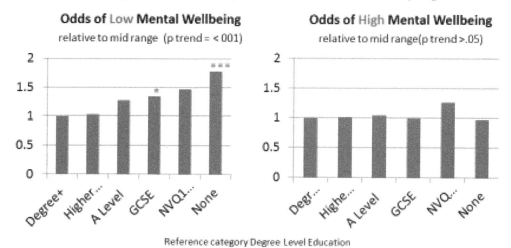

Educational Achievement Mental Wellbeing
adjusted for age, sex, income, employment status, marital status, ethnicity, religion

Odds of Low Mental Wellbeing
relative to mid range (p trend = < 001)

Odds of High Mental Wellbeing
relative to mid range (p trend > .05)

Reference category Degree Level Education

Health Survey for England Adults 16+ 2010 / 2011

Figure 18.7 Mental wellbeing and educational achievement.

The promotion of health and wellbeing is different to disease prevention because of its positive, holistic focus. The great majority of the population stand to gain from programmes to improve their wellbeing, and such programmes impact many different aspects of health. Physical activity programmes, for example, improve mental health, bone health, heart health, diabetes and other health problems (Warburton et al., 2006). According to the Rose hypothesis (as above), improving health across the population will also prevent illness. In contrast, disease prevention programmes, because of the relative sizes of the well and ill populations, can have no more than a minimal impact on population health. Focusing on the positive, on what is wanted rather than what is not wanted, has been found in several areas of study, including positive psychology and parenting programmes, to be an intervention in its own right and makes these programmes more attractive to the public than disease prevention programmes.

Different Perspectives Coming Together

Health promotion involves both making society a healthier place and helping individuals live healthier lives. Social scientists tend to advocate social solutions, measures which reduce poverty and deprivation and make life less stressful for those most at risk of disease. Psychologists tend to focus on interventions which enable personal development. The former seem attractive, at least in the short term, because they require no effort on the part of the group which they are intended to help. The latter are less attractive because they are ineffective unless people engage with them.

However, programmes to support personal development have the benefit of empowering people and giving them skills to enable their happiness which are not dependent on external circumstances. The latter programmes also enable people to interact with others in a more constructive way, enhancing their relationship skills, enabling greater understanding of and trust in others. This phenomenon, not much written about in the mental wellbeing literature, can be likened to the concept of herd immunity in infectious disease control. Here it is well recognised that the level of immunity in a population group determines, to some degree, the extent to which nonimmune people develop infections. In the mental health world, resilience and positive outlook are the equivalents to immunity. The quality of interpersonal and wider community relationships is a recognised determinant of mental illness (Stewart-Brown 2005), and the capacity to form supportive relationships is a recognised component of mental wellbeing (see above), so it follows that promoting the mental wellbeing of those who are not ill is likely to protect the most vulnerable from mental illness. This is a powerful argument for supporting universal approaches to personal development as a way of promoting mental health and preventing mental illness, and studies are now beginning to emerge which demonstrate the theory to be robust (Hill et al., 2015).

In accord with the theme of this chapter, then, there are strong arguments for combining universal and targeted approaches with societal and individual approaches, to deliver the greatest benefits.

Evidence Base for Promoting Wellbeing

In terms of content, some wellbeing promotion programmes have a large and robust evidence base. Amongst these are those that focus on the life course. These include programmes that support parents in developing or enhancing sensitivity to and relationship with their infants and older children (Stewart-Brown and Schrader-McMillan, 2011). Such programmes lay the foundation for the child's relationship skills throughout life and thus have a profound effect on wellbeing. They also include parenting programmes that teach parents behaviour management and help them socialise their children in ways that do not damage them. And they include the very large number of school-based programmes that support the development of children's mental health (Weare and Nind 2011). Both parenting programmes and school-based programmes are optimised if they are both delivered at a population level and more intensively targeted at high-risk groups. The universal elements reduce stigma and also increase the capacity of 'well' parents and children to be compassionate and supportive towards those who are experiencing problems or illness, the herd immunity effect.

In adulthood, the most robustly researched programmes for developing wellbeing are mindfulness programmes (de Vibe et al., 2013) and programmes which promote physical activity (Bock et al., 2014). There is a growing evidence base relating to a range of positive psychology interventions (Parks and Schueller, 2014). At a societal level there is now some evidence for positive benefits from increased provision of green spaces, facilities and programmes to reduce social isolation, libraries and books on prescription schemes, debt counselling programmes and provision of group activities for walking or mindful movement (yoga or tai chi). There is a growing evidence base with regard to the potential for fruit and vegetables to improve mental health (Stranges et al., 2014).

Conclusions

Although for a while a contested area, consensus is emerging on the nature of wellbeing, on its importance for health across the life course and on ways to measure it. The promotion of wellbeing at a population level is both possible and beneficial, but much remains to be done in developing the scientific base for wellbeing at a population level.

References

Adams, T., Bezner, J., & Steinhart, M. (1997). The conceptualisation and measurement of perceived wellness: Integrating balance across and within dimensions. *American Journal of Health Promotion*, 11, 208–218.

Albee, G. W. (1982). Preventing psychopathology and promoting human potential. *American Psychologist*, 37, 1043-1057.

Anderson, J., Huppert, F., & Rose, G. (1993). Normality, deviance and minor psychiatric morbidity in the community: A population-based approach to General Health Questionnaire data in the Health and Lifestyle Survey. *Psychological Medicine*, 23, 475–485.

Bech, P. O. L., Kjoller, M., & Rasmussen, N. K. (2003). Measuring well-being rather than the absence of distress symptoms: A comparison of the SF-36 Mental Health subscale and the WHO-Five Well-Being Scale. *International Journal of Methods in Psychiatric Research*, 2(2), 85–91.

Begley, S. (2008). *Train your mind, change your brain: How a new science reveals our extraordinary potential to transform ourselves*. New York, NY: Random House.

Bock, C., Jarczok, M. N., & Litaker, D. (2014). Community-based efforts to promote physical activity: A systematic review of interventions considering mode of delivery, study quality and population subgroups. *Journal of Science and Medicine in Sport*, 17, 276–282.

Brickman, P., Coates, D., & Janoff-Bulman, R. (1978). Lottery winners and accident victims: Is happiness relative?" *Journal of Personality and Social Psychology*, 36(8), 917–927.

Chief Medical Officer (England) (2014). Annual Report of the Chief Medical Officer 2013. Public Mental Health Priorities: Investing in the evidence [online]. Available at https://www.gov.uk/government/uploads/system/uploads/attachment_data/file/351629/Annual_report_2013_1.pdf.

Crawford, M. J., Robotham, D., Thana, L., Patterson, S., Weaver, T., Barber, R., et al. (2011). Selecting outcome measures in mental health: The views of service users. *Journal of Mental Health*, 20(4), 336–346.

de Vibe, M., Bjørndal, A., Tipton, E., Hammerstrøm, K., & Kowalski, K. (2012). Mindfulness-based stress reduction (MBSR) for improving health, quality of life, and social functioning in adults. *Campbell Systematic Reviews* 3(01). Available at http://www.campbellcollaboration.org/lib/project/117/.

Diener, E., Emmons, R. A., Larsen, R. J., & Griffin, S. (1985). The Satisfaction with Life Scale. *Journal of Personality Assessment*, 49, 71–75.

Diener, E., Wirtz, D., Tov, W., Kim-Prieto, C., Choi, D-W., Oishi, S., et al. (2010). New well-being measures: Short scales to assess flourishing and positive and negative feelings. *Social Indicators Research*, 97, 143–156.

Eight Upanishads, Vols. 1 and 2 (2004). Swami Gambhirananda (Transl.), Commentary by Shankaracharya. Kolkata, India: Advaita Ashrama.

Ekmund, P., Davidson, R. J., Ricard, M., & Callance, B. A. (2005). Buddhist and psychological perspectives on emotions and wellbeing. *Current Directions in Psychological Science*, 14, 59–63.

Goldberg, D., & Williams, P. (1988). *A user's guide to the General Health Questionnaire*. Windsor, UK: NFER-Nelson.

Goodman, R. (1997). The Strengths and Difficulties Questionnaire: A research note. *Journal of Child Psychology and Psychiatry*, 38, 581–586.

Goodman, A., & Goodman, R. (2011). Population mean scores predict child mental disorder rates: Validation SDQ prevalence estimators in Britain. *Journal of Child Psychology and Psychiatry*, 52, 100–108.

Gudmunsdottir, D. (2013). The impact of economic crisis on happiness. *Social Indicators Research*, 110(3), 1083–1101.

Hill, E. M., Griffiths, F. E., & House, T. (2015). Spreading of healthy mood in adolescent social networks. *Proceedings of the Royal Society B*, 282, 1180. doi:10.1098/rspb.2015.1180.

HM Government (England) (2011). No health without mental health: A cross-government mental health outcomes strategy for people of all ages [online]. Available at https://www.gov.uk/government/uploads/system/uploads/attachment_data/file/213761/dh_124058.pdf.

Hone, L., Jarden, A., Schofield, G. M., & Duncan, S. (2014). Measuring flourishing: The impact of operational definitions on the prevalence of high levels of wellbeing. *International Journal of Wellbeing*, 4(1), 62–90. doi:10.5502/ijw.v4i1.1. Available at http://www.internationaljournalofwellbeing.org/index.php/ijow/article/view/391.

Hu, Y., Stewart-Brown, S., Twigg, L., & Weich, S. (2007). Can the 12-item General Health Questionnaire be used to measure positive mental health? *Psychological Medicine*, 37(7), 1005–1014.

Huppert, F. A., & Whittington, J. E. (2003). Evidence for the independence of positive and negative well-being: Implications for quality of life assessment. *British Journal of Health Psychology*, 8(1), 107–122.

Jahoda, M. (1958). *Current concepts of positive mental health*. New York, NY: Basic Books.

Keyes, C. L. M. (2002). The mental health continuum: From languishing to flourishing in life. *Journal of Health and Social Research*, 43(2), 207–222.

Keyes, C. L. M. (2005). Mental illness and/or mental health? Investigating axioms of the complete state model of health. *Journal of Consulting and Clinical Psychology*, 73(3), 539–548.

Lamers, S. M. A., Westerhof, G. J., Bohlmeijer, E. T., ten Kooster, P. M., & Keyes, C. L. M. (2011). Evaluating the psychometric properties of the Mental Health Continuum – Short Form (MHC-SF). *Journal of Clinical Psychology*, 67, 99–110.

Newnham, E. A., Hooke, G. R., & Page, A. C. (2010). Monitoring treatment response and outcomes using the World Health Organization's Wellbeing Index in psychiatric care. *Journal of Affective Disorders*, 122(1), 133–8.

Office for National Statistics (2011). Measuring national well-being: National statistician's reflections on the national debate on measuring national well-being. London ONS. Available at http://www.ons.gov.uk/well-being/wellbeing/understanding-wellbeing/index.html.

Organisation for Economic Co-operation and Development (2013). How's life? Measuring well-being. OECD.

Parks, A. C., & Schueller, S. M. (Eds.) (2014). *The Wiley-Blackwell handbook of positive psychological interventions*. Oxford, UK: Wiley-Blackwell.

Rashid, T. (2016). Positive psychotherapy. In Slade, M., Oades, L., and Jarden, A. (Eds.), *Wellbeing Recovery and Mental Health*. Cambridge, UK: Cambridge University Press.

Ryan, R. M., & Deci, E. (2001). On happiness and human potentials: A review of research on hedonic and eudaimonic well-being. *Annual Review of Psychology*, 52, 141–166. doi:10.1146/annurev.psych.52.1.141.

Ryff, C. D. (1989). Happiness is everything; or is it? Explorations on the meaning of psychological wellbeing. *Journal of Personality and Social Psychology*, 57, 1069–1081.

Ryff, C. D., & Keyes, C. L. M. (1995). The structure of psychological well-being revisited. *Journal of Personality and Social Psychology*, 69, 719–727.

Salovey, P., & Sluyter, J. D. (1997). *Emotional development and emotional intelligence*. New York, NY: Basic Books.

Seligman, M. E. P. (2002). *Authentic happiness: Using the new positive psychology to realise your potential for lasting fulfilment*. New York, NY: The Free Press.

Spence, G. B. (2015). Workplace wellbeing programs: If you build it they may NOT come … because it's not what they really need! *International Journal of Wellbeing*, 5(2), 109–124. doi:10.5502/ijw.v5i2.7.

Stewart-Brown, S. (2005). Interpersonal relationships and the origins of mental health. *Journal of Public Mental Health*, 4(1), 24–28.

Stewart-Brown, S., Samaraweera, P. C., Taggart, F., & Stranges, S. (2015). Socio-economic gradients and mental health: Implications for public health. *British Journal of Psychiatry*, 206, 461–465.

Stewart-Brown, S., & Schrader-McMillan, A. (2011). Parenting for mental health: What does the evidence say we need to do? Report of Workpackage 2 of the DataPrev project. *Health*

Promotion International, 1(26), i10–28. Available at http://heapro.oxfordjournals.org/cgi/reprint/dar056?ijkey=dHL6f6hPM4ByI2u&keytype=ref.

Stiglitz, J. E., Sen, A., & Fitoussi, J. P., (2009). Measurement of economic and social progress revisited. University of Columbia IEC OFCE Working Paper 2009–33. Available at http://archives.cerium.ca/IMG/pdf/1-Measurement.pdf.

Stranges, S., Samaraweera, P. C., Taggart, F., Kandala, N.-B., & Stewart-Brown, S. (2014). Major health-related behaviours and mental well-being in the general population: The Health Survey for England. *BMJ Open* 4:e005878. doi:10.1136/bmjopen-2014–005878.

Tennant, R., Hiller, L., Fishwick, R., Platt, S., Joseph, S., Weich, S., et al. (2007). The Warwick–Edinburgh Mental Well-Being Scale (WEMWBS): Development and UK validation. *Health and Quality of Life Outcomes*, 5(63). doi:10.1186/1477–7525-5-63.

Trousselard, M., Steiler, D., Dutheil, F., Claverie, D., Canini, F., Naughton, G., et al. (2015). Validation of the French Warwick–Edinburgh Mental Well-being Scale (WEMWBS) in both non-clinical and clinical populations. Manuscript submitted for publication.

Tudor, K. (1996). *Mental health promotion: Paradigms and practices*. London, UK: Routledge.

UK Government Office for Science (2008). Mental capital and well-being: Making the most of ourselves in the 21st century [online]. Available at https://www.gov.uk/government/uploads/system/uploads/attachment_data/file/292453/mental-capital-well-being-summary.pdf.

UNICEF (2007). Child poverty in perspective: An overview of child well-being in rich countries. Innocenti Report Card 7, Innocenti Research Centre, Florence, Italy.

Veerman, J. L., Dowrick, C., Ayuso-Mateos, J. L., Dunn, G., & Barendregt, J. J. (2009). Population prevalence of depression and mean Beck Depression Inventory score. *British Journal of Psychiatry*, 195, 516–519.

Warburton, D. E. R., Nicol, C. W., & Bredin, S. S. D. (2006). Health benefits of physical activity: The evidence. *Canadian Medical Association Journal*, 174(6), 801–809. doi:10.1503/cmaj.051351.

Watson, D., Clarke, A., & Tellegen, A. (1988). Development and validation of brief measures of positive and negative affect: The PANAS Scales. *Journal of Personality and Social Psychology*, 54(6), 1063–1079.

Weare, K., & Nind, M. (2011). Mental health promotion and problem prevention in schools: What does the evidence say? *Health Promotion International*, 26(Suppl 1), i29–69. doi:10.1093/heapro/dar075.

Weich, S., Brugha, T. L., King, M., McManus, S., Bebbington, P. L., et al. (2011). Mental well-being and mental illness: Findings from the adult psychiatric morbidity survey for England 2007. *British Journal of Psychiatry*, 199, 23–28.

World Health Organisation (2004). *Promoting mental health concepts, emerging evidence and practice*. Geneva, Switzerland: WHO.

World Health Organisation (2014). Mental health: A state of well-being. Available at http://www.who.int/features/factfiles/mental_health/en/.

Community Level
Translating Wellbeing Policy, Theory and Evidence into Practice

Tony Coggins

Mental health is 'a state of well-being in which an individual realises his or her own abilities, can cope with the normal stresses of life, can work productively and is able to make a contribution to his or her community. In this positive sense, mental health is the foundation for individual well-being and the effective functioning of a community' (WHO, 2014).

Despite this widely accepted definition of mental health, the phrase is often associated with illness and regarded as the domain of mental health services. Yet good mental health requires much more than secondary services treating mental illness. It requires collective, systemwide action by individuals, communities, organisations and decision makers on all levels to protect and promote mental health and wellbeing for ourselves, our families and our communities. This chapter focuses on the translation of wellbeing policy and evidence into practice at a community level. In particular, it suggests approaches to support non-health-service colleagues toward increased community participation, inclusion and sense of belonging and to facilitate mentally healthy workplaces and communities. It takes one intervention, the Mental Well-being Impact Assessment, to provide a practical example of translating theory and evidence into practice at a community level.

Over the past few years, the concept of well-being has gained considerable currency in economic, social and political circles with recognition that wellbeing is vitally important to the healthy functioning of families, communities and society (Foresight Mental Capital and Wellbeing Project, 2008).

There is no doubt that happier people and places are fundamental to achieving success in almost all areas of life and work. Individuals, communities and employees that have positive mental wellbeing are more likely to be motivated, educated (NICE, 2008, 2009b), creative, productive (Boorman, 2009) and healthy (NHS Information Centre, 2011) They contribute to the economy (Lyubomirsky et al., 2005), to communities and to their families (Huppert, 2008). They are more resilient under all types of stress, leading to less of a burden on services (Keyes et al., 2010).

At the individual level, people with positive wellbeing are more likely to be able to stick to lifestyle changes such as being more active, eating more healthily and stopping smoking and less likely to misuse drugs or alcohol or unintentionally get pregnant (Deacon et al., 2009).

At the community level, higher levels of wellbeing lead to neighborhoods where people trust one another, increased democratic participation and volunteering and less antisocial

Wellbeing, Recovery and Mental Health, ed. Mike Slade, Lindsay Oades and Aaron Jarden.
Published by Cambridge University Press. © Mike Slade, Lindsay Oades and Aaron Jarden 2017

and criminal behavior (Coid et al., 2006). This means that there is a strong business case for seeking to maximise mental wellbeing in whatever area of public, voluntary or commercial activity is being considered. So at the current time of global economic recession, when the risk factors for poor mental health increase and our health services struggles to deal with the level of demand, it is no surprise that there is increased interest in and policy support for boosting people's wellbeing and promoting resilient people and communities. In the United Kingdom, as the NHS Five Year Forward Review (DoH, 2014) noted, 'the future health of millions of children, the sustainability of the NHS, and the economic prosperity of Britain all now depend on a radical upgrade in prevention and public health. Twelve years ago, Derek Wanless' health review warned that unless the country took prevention seriously we would be faced with a sharply rising burden of avoidable illness. That warning has not been heeded – and the NHS is on the hook for the consequences' (DoH, 2014).

However, given the complex challenges that shifting the focus of both policy and service development to a more 'upstream' mental health promotion approach will inevitably require, it is hardly surprising that there has been little progress not only in the United Kingdom, but across much of the world. Putting policy into practice is a continuing challenge.

One of the major challenges is that despite the existence of a clear and accepted World Health Organisation definition of mental health as something positive, mental health is still perceived by many as being about illness. Where people do think about good mental health, it tends be associated with an absence of illness rather than a sense of flourishing, of feeling good and doing well. As a result, mental health is still largely perceived as something that needs to be treated, something that is the business of mental health services.

The reality is that most people have their mental wellbeing needs met, or not met, at home, at work, in schools and in communities – not in mental health services. This is because our mental health and wellbeing is determined by a range of factors: genetic factors, individual lifestyle factors, the wider determinants of health such as income, employment and educational achievements and other social and environmental factors. Not only do secondary mental health services not influence many of the determinants of positive mental health, but also they are not in a position to directly affect the mental wellbeing of the whole population, simply because they have contact with 1–2% of the community with serious mental health problems. Therefore, the actions we take as individuals, organisations and communities will have a much greater impact on the mental wellbeing and flourishing of society than secondary mental health services. Mental health needs to be part of everyone's day-to-day business.

So if the solutions lie outside of mental health services, what might an effective approach look like?

The Theory of Effective Mental Health Promotion

The theory of effective mental health promotion requires action at individual, community and structural levels to minimise the risk factors for poor mental health and maximise the protective and promoting factors for positive mental health (see Figure 19.1). Put simply, it is hard for individuals to look after their own wellbeing if they live in an environment where they face discrimination and inequality or do not have a decent place to live or enough to eat. Likewise it is difficult to create an environment or community conducive to wellbeing without a structure and policy framework that supports mental health and wellbeing.

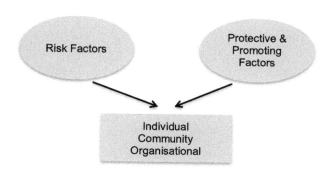

Figure 19.1 Theoretical model of mental health promotion.

Individual Level

Increasing the emotional resilience of individuals by promoting self-esteem and life and coping skills.

Community

Strengthening communities, for example, by increasing community participation, inclusion and sense of belonging and promoting mentally healthy schools and workplaces.

Structural

Create a structural and policy environment that is conducive to positive mental health and wellbeing, such as promoting access to good education, housing, good food and employment and tackling stigma, discrimination and inequality.

Theory into Practice

Applying this model of mental health promotion and translating theory into practice present a number of challenges that need to be addressed to shift the system to a more sustainable upstream approach to mental health and wellbeing.

Challenge One. Shifting individual, community and organisational understanding of mental health to encompass wellbeing, in other words, the view that mental health is something positive that, like physical health, we all have and that, like physical health, is an important resource to be nurtured.

Challenge Two. Given that our mental health is protected and promoted in families, schools, workplaces and communities, how to build the capacity, knowledge and skills of individuals, organisations and communities to understand how they can promote and protect mental health for themselves, their families and their communities?

Challenge Three. How to make available evidence-based, practical tools and approaches to address Challenges One and Two.

Mental Well-Being Impact Assessment is an example of a practical tool (challenge three) that has been developed to build the capacity (challenge two), and understanding of organisations and communities (challenge one) to promote mental health.

Mental Well-being Impact Assessment – A Toolkit for Wellbeing

The Mental Well-being Impact Assessment (MWIA) toolkit was developed in 2003 with Lewisham NRF projects to consider and maximise their impact on mental wellbeing (Cooke

The four protective factors are influenced by population characteristics, wider determinants and the core economy. All of which are influenced by levels equity and social justice.

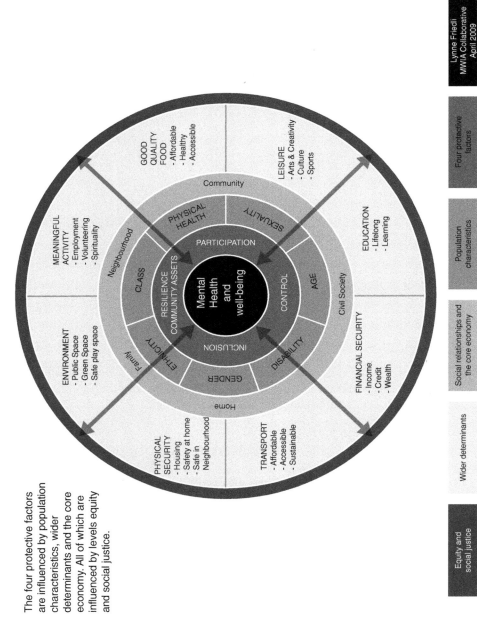

GOOD QUALITY FOOD
- Affordable
- Healthy
- Accessible

LEISURE
- Arts & Creativity
- Culture
- Sports

Community

MEANINGFUL ACTIVITY
- Employment
- Volunteering
- Spirituality

PHYSICAL HEALTH

SEXUALITY

EDUCATION
- Lifelong
- Learning

Neighbourhood

PARTICIPATION

CLASS

RESILIENCE COMMUNITY ASSETS

Mental Health and well-being

ENVIRONMENT
- Public Space
- Green Space
- Safe play space

ETHNICITY

CONTROL

AGE

Civil Society

Family

INCLUSION

DISABILITY

FINANCIAL SECURITY
- Income
- Credit
- Wealth

GENDER

PHYSICAL SECURITY
- Housing
- Safety at home
- Safe in Neighbourhood

Home

TRANSPORT
- Affordable
- Accessible
- Sustainable

Lynne Friedli
MWIA Collaborative
April 2009

Four protective factors

Population characteristics

Social relationships and the core economy

Equity and social justice

Wider determinants

Figure 19.2 A dynamic model of mental wellbeing for assessing mental wellbeing impact.

and Coggins, 2005). The MWIA married the internationally agreed upon Health Impact Assessment (HIA) process with the evidence base for factors that protect and promote mental health. The tool provides an evidence-based framework that enables commissioners, service providers and policy makers to identify, improve and measure impacts of a policy programme or service on mental wellbeing.

The toolkit uses a dynamic model of mental wellbeing (Figure 19.2) to assess and identify the influence of a proposed policy, programme, service or development on wellbeing. At the heart of the toolkit are the four core protective factors for mental wellbeing:

- Enhancing control
- Increasing resilience and community assets
- Facilitating participation
- Promoting inclusion

These protective factors are influenced by the following:

- *Population characteristics* such as age, class, gender and ethnicity; in other words, some population groups are at greater risk of low levels of mental wellbeing or poor mental health
- *Core economy* or social capital, such as friends, family, neighbours and civil society. There is robust evidence that good-quality relationships are associated with a wide range of health benefits including stress buffering.
- The *wider determinants of health* such as financial security, environment, transport and education.
- *Core values* of equity and social justice. An extensive body of research confirms the relationship between inequality and poorer mental health outcomes (Marmot Review, 2010).

The MWIA process asks whether a proposed policy, programme, service or development has positive and/or negative impacts on the core protective factors for mental wellbeing in the context of population characteristics, social capital, wider determinants and inequality.

The toolkit is a step-by-step process that begins with a desk-based screening tool to get an initial assessment of the potential value of undertaking MWIA and refine the focus, followed by a workshop with a cross section of stakeholders to build the stakeholder evidence. A profile of the target is developed and a literature search on the issue or proposal is undertaken. These three sources of evidence are then triangulated to produce a report and a suggestion for action to build on the potential positive impacts and mitigate against the negative ones (see Figure 19.3). This then leads to a co-produced action plan and measures of success.

When the MWIA toolkit is applied to an initiative such as a housing rebuilding programme, a greater focus on how people think and feel emerges than when a standard health impact assessment is conducted. For example, the physical health impacts of replacing damp high-rise blocks that have fallen into disrepair with warm, safe, low-rise housing with access to gardens are fairly obvious, but with a focus on the protective factors for mental wellbeing and how people feel about the proposal, a different picture begins to take shape. For example, people might say things like, 'I have lived in this house all of my life and I really like it, but you are going to knock it down, and I have no choice.' As a result, people talk about feeling out of control. Or people may say, 'this is my community, I know all of my neighbours, my family live close by and my friends drop in and check on me every day, but you are going to "decant" me, move me to a different part of the area and away from my friends and support networks for five years until the new homes are ready.' We know that strong social

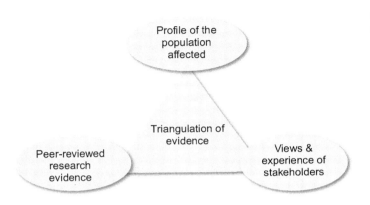

Figure 19.3 Triangulation of evidence.

connections to friends and family have a significant positive impact on health outcomes. So as well as the documented benefits of good quality housing for mental health (Huxley and Rogers, 2001; Blackman and Harvey, 2001), there are aspects to the process of rebuilding houses that are potentially detrimental. Typically such an approach will also identify particular population groups that may be disproportionately affected by the proposal, in this case the decanting process, for example, adolescents for whom attachments to peers, school, family and community are strong protecting factors and can predict the onset and persistence of emotional behavior disorders (Fagg et al., 2006; Fergusson and Horwood 2005).

Here is a sector, regeneration, that has a huge impact on many of the determinants of mental wellbeing for local people at greater risk of poor mental health, but with no way of maximizing benefit or measuring the impact. By using the MWIA to systematically identify and prioritise key impacts on at-risk population groups, organisations are able to develop action plans to mitigate the negatives and maximise the positives to ensure that their programmes have the best wellbeing outcomes possible, enabling regeneration programmes to have improving mental health and wellbeing as an explicit emphasis and outcome, refocusing significant non-health-sector resources on promoting wellbeing and at the same time supporting them in achieving their goals.

Since the development of the original toolkit in 2003, the MWIA has been revised and improved upon. The latest version was published in 2011. It has been used in the United Kingdom on more than 950 different policies, projects and services, from small community youth projects to large programmes such as the Liverpool City of Culture 2009. It is also in use globally with programmes of work running in Europe, New South Wales, Australia and Chile. The MWIA toolkit has been used in a wide variety of settings including housing, education and local communities and has more recently been applied to workplaces.

Application of MWIA in the Workplace: happier@work

Work-related stress, anxiety and depression are the most frequent cause of days off work. The Health and Safety Executive estimate that 9.8 million days were lost due to mental ill health in the United Kingdom in 2009/2010 (Health and Safety Executive, 2010). This costs UK businesses £1,035 a year for every person they employ (NICE, 2009a).

Conversely, higher levels of positive mental health and well-being are associated with improved performance at work (Harvey et al., 2014, Wright and Cropanzano, 2000, Wright, Cropanzano, and Bonett, 2007).

Like regeneration programmes, workplaces have a significant influence on the determinants of wellbeing. Work can provide self-esteem and identity, meaning and purpose and opportunities to develop supportive social networks and relationships. For many people, it also provides their main source of income. As such, the workplace is a key setting for promoting mental health and wellbeing (NICE, 2009a). There is a compelling case for both individuals and organisations to have workplaces that promote and protect mental health.

The Kings Health Partners' happier@work programme has taken this evidence as a starting point to design a workplace mental health programme aimed at improving staff wellbeing within the context of the challenging realities of NHS working life. Kings Health Partners (KHP) is an academic health sciences centre (AHSC). It is a partnership between Kings College London and three Foundation Trusts, Guy's and St. Thomas', Kings College Hospital and the South London and Maudsley. The partners work together to ensure that medical research breakthroughs lead to direct clinical benefits for patients. Between them, the four organisations employ 36,000 staff and have 25,000 students with a turnover of £3.1billion. Based on the Department of Health figures above, the annual cost of poor mental health to an organisation this size is £37,260,000. An effective workplace mental health promotion strategy for an organization of this size has the potential to have a significant impact.

Which Workplace Wellbeing Interventions?

There are a wide range of evidence-based interventions for mental health in the workplace, from support for people with serious mental health problems to retain work to processes for the early detection and treatment of employees with depression, and a growing evidence base for mindfulness in the workplace, but which interventions to choose?

Mental wellbeing at work is determined by the work environment, the nature of the work and the individual (NICE, 2009a). This highlights the importance of taking a whole-system approach to workplace wellbeing that addresses mental health and wellbeing at the individual, team and organisational levels. It is unlikely that one intervention by itself is going to provide the solution.

Therefore, before deciding which workplace mental health interventions to invest in, the happier@work programme sought to understand the wellbeing of staff in the context of their busy working lives in the three NHS Trusts.

The programme used a Double Diamond Design process (Design Council, 2005) to *discover* what was impacting wellbeing for staff, *define* the key issues and *design* and *deliver* a programme of interventions at the individual, team and organisational levels.

Phase One: Discover

Seven teams from across the three hospital Trusts volunteered to take part in the pilot happier@work programme. Each team identified the issue that they felt most impacted their staff's mental health and wellbeing. They also identified if there was a particular staff group that they wanted to focus on. For example, an older adults inpatient unit selected the impact of the nature of the work (i.e. offering care towards the end of people's lives) on the mental health and wellbeing of frontline nurses. A community service picked the impact of a restructure on the whole staff team and a walk-in clinic picked the impact of working across two sites on administration staff.

The teams were asked to undertake three discovery processes: one, complete a health and wellbeing survey; two, have a key member of staff job-shadowed by one of the pilot team; and three, take part in a mental wellbeing impact assessment process as described above.

Each MWIA workshop enabled teams to identify the factors that impact their mental well-being at work, both positively and negatively, and to prioritise them in order of importance. This, combined with a parallel process of job shadowing, a literature search and a staff profile, creates the basis for a service-specific summary report and action plan designed to maximise the positive and minimise the negative impact of the workplace on staff wellbeing. This information was then presented to the team or service for discussion, reflection and ultimately implementation.

Phase Two: Define

The MWIA is based on the three key domains of mental wellbeing: control, resilience and participation and inclusion. Each domain includes ten separate determinants of wellbeing alongside the wider determinants of health. Each pilot service used the three domains and their particular determinants of wellbeing as a framework to prioritise the particular issues they had identified in the screening as affecting their wellbeing. Stakeholders identified the most important factors impacting wellbeing and considered how they might maximise the positive impact and minimise any negatives for the top three priority areas from each domain. This input and a further review of the literature were combined to produce an action plan for each of the teams, which then formed part of the team-level interventions.

The discovery phase provided the pilot team with a wealth of information to identify key themes, drivers and barriers for wellbeing. In addition to the team action plans, the data were used to extrapolate barriers and drivers for mental health and wellbeing for the whole organization. This was achieved through a qualitative thematic analysis. Key themes emerging from the data were identified through an iterative process of categorising different matrices of issues from the MWIAs. This was carried out using the principles of 'thematic charting', where the key impacts on wellbeing, the actions suggested by staff and the report recommendations were categorised into themes through discussion, and a matrix was created on a flip chart with Post-It notes (Ritchie et al., 2003).

Themes Emerging from the Process

The thematic process crystallised a number of themes that appeared to impact wellbeing either positively or negatively across teams and job roles (see Table 19.1).

Table 19.1 Emerging Cross-Cutting Themes

MWIA domain	Increasing control	Resilience	Participation and inclusion	Wider determinants
Priority components	Workplace job control – workload	Emotional well-being- work-life balance	Having a valued role – reward and recognition	The physical environment
		Emotional support – individual and peer-to-peer		Challenging discrimination

A Sense of Control at Work – Workload

Employees in high-demand jobs need to have some control and adequate resources to manage the demands and reduce the risk of mental ill health (Harvey et al., 2014).

All the teams involved felt that wellbeing was being impacted by workload.

Negative impact:

- Teams felt that they had fewer resources, such as money, staff and equipment with which to deal with more complex care needs and a greater quantity of work/caseloads.
- It was important to staff that resources and responsibilities were distributed fairly. Perceptions of unfair distribution had a negative effect on wellbeing.
- Most services gave examples of processes and systems that were not functioning properly, consequently adding to workloads, rather than reducing them as they were designed to do.

Positive impact:

- Opportunities for more learning and development regularly came up as a potential positive impact, although there was often an issue about being released for training (other than mandatory training) due to the pressure of work.

Resilience – Emotional Wellbeing

Appropriate support at work reduced the negative impact of high-pressure jobs on employee wellbeing (Sanne et al., 2005).

Emotional wellbeing and support were a top priority for the pilot teams, with a sense that staff are soaking up the stress and distress of patients, caregivers, colleagues, the organisation and society in general. Staff felt that they were having to care for patients with increasing need using the same or, often, fewer resources.

In addition, changes within the organisations have resulted in over half of the teams involved in the pilot going through restructures and staff facing the threat of redundancy. Reductions in resources were affecting not only the pilot teams but also other services on which the teams depended to provide support, such as IT departments. Economic uncertainly is not limited to the NHS, and staff also described feeling the pressure of wider global insecurity.

Negative impact:

- *Bottling up feelings*: The process highlighted identified both external and internal (staff themselves) expectations that staff should be able to 'keep emotions inside'. Staff felt that partners and friends sometimes did not understand the emotional pressures involved, using responses such as 'you chose to be a nurse'.
- *Work/life balance*: The staff regularly talked about taking work home, being preoccupied with work when they went home, being emotionally exhausted and not having energy or time for friends and families.
- *Lack of time and space for reflection*: A lack of time for reflection and debriefing about what had gone well and what had been difficult was a common theme.
- *Perceptions of occupational health*: Some staff noted the perception of occupational health (OH) as 'punitive', seen as a management tool, rather than a service supporting employees.

Positive impact:

- *Positive peer support*: Informal peer support was identified as the most helpful way of supporting emotional wellbeing. Findings suggest that staff feel generally supportive of each other but feel that recognised organisational systems for support (e.g. OH) are seen as 'only for when things are going wrong'. Findings also suggest that staff recognise that everyone needs emotional support but think that services such as OH are not currently well placed to provide it. People suggested that more team reflection time would be helpful and more thought about how the team and organization enable peer support would be valuable.
- *Importance of good line management and supervision*: Supervision is another potential source of emotional support, but its value is seen very much as dependent on the skills and experience of the particular line manager. Staff acknowledged the high levels of pressure that front-line managers are under themselves.

Participation and Inclusion – Having a Valued Role: Reward and Recognition

The staff appeared to be strongly intrinsically motivated, generally feeling they are doing a worthwhile job and doing it well and feeling competent. However, this is impacted negatively when, for reasons beyond their control, they are unable to do their job to the standard they would like. The reasons often included volume of work, poor systems and reliance on other parts of the system that are not functioning properly.

Negative impacts:

- *Senior management*. There was a perception that senior management (not direct line managers) did not understand or appreciate the work of front-line staff. Suggestions included senior managers occasionally undertaking a shift – getting 'back to the shop floor' – to better understand the challenges facing staff.
- *Not measuring the 'right' things*. Current incentives and systems of measures were sometimes at odds with what staff considered valuable; in other words people had a fairly clear view of what a good job looked like but did not feel that it was always what was being measured.
- *Not feeling 'heard'*. Not feeling heard was another strong theme that impacted wellbeing negatively. Findings from the discovery process suggested that people generally understood the pressures that organisations are under and that there may be little that can be done about some of the stressful aspects of the job. However, having an opportunity to 'have a say' and express these frustrations was seen as important to wellbeing.

Positive impacts:

- Teams involved in the pilot generally trusted their line managers and found them an important source of support. Involvement in the process was voluntary, so it is possible that managers who were willing to put their teams forward were more likely to see staff wellbeing as something they should support.

Wider Determinants of Health – Environment

The quality and condition of the physical environment and the use of space affect emotional and physical wellbeing and productivity. In all but one service, this surfaced as something that impacts staff mental wellbeing and was the most consistent feedback from all of the teams.

Negative impacts:

- *Not valuing staff.* Poor décor and lack of space made staff feel undervalued. In one service all the patient areas had been painted but the staff areas neglected.
- *Limiting performance.* Not feeling able to do a good job due to physical limitations of the space and equipment, from adequate space for meeting patients and relatives to being able to make confidential phone calls.
- *Feelings of safety and control.* In a number of the teams the physical environment made staff feel less safe, due either to how it impacted interactions with patients or to health and safety issues.
- *Reinforces status differences.* In one service it was felt that the organisation of staff space reinforced divisions between clinical and nonclinical staff.

Positive impacts:

- In one service where a lot of thought had been given to the use of space, it was seen as having a positive impact on wellbeing.

Wider Determinants of Health – Discrimination, Equity and Unfairness

When pressure increases, buried or unspoken discrimination often comes to the surface. In some of the assessments, discrimination was identified as a key issue affecting staff wellbeing. There were also some common issues around hierarchy and dignity at work.

- A number of the services identified hierarchies as having an impact on wellbeing, including distinctions between clinical and nonclinical staff.
- Some frontline staff felt unfairly treated.
- In some teams there was a sense that the system supported the organisation over the individual, and therefore a challenge or incident of whistle-blowing became a personal risk.
- There was sometimes a feeling of not being treated with respect.
- Staff felt that where there was an unfair and unequal distribution of work/responsibilities/resources, this had an impact on wellbeing.

Phase 3: Develop and Deliver

A clear message from the assessment process was that much of what was impacting wellbeing positively and negatively was how work was arranged and allocated, whether work processes were effective and supportive, the availability of resources, working relationships and quality of communication. Addressing the causes of stress rather than just delivering training to help staff deal with the resulting negative symptoms was seen as key by staff. Therefore, to tackle the range of issues raised, the project sought to address them at three different levels:

Individual: Actions that staff can take for their own wellbeing, in particular to build individual resources to cope with the impacts of increased workload and stressful situations, such as change, on mental wellbeing and increase people's ability to manage their work/life balance.

Table 19.2 KHP happier@work Interventions and Activities

Individual	Team	Organisational
Stress awareness	Wellbeing action plans co-produced for each of the teams involved in the discovery phase	Establishment of a regular, senior-level employee wellbeing group across organisations
Mindfulness courses	Mental health awareness for line managers	Learning from discovery phase being fed into HR and OH plans
Wellbeing seminars	Physical space and staff wellbeing project	Education and training budgets used to fund staff wellbeing interventions

Team: Actions that the team or team leader can take to improve staff wellbeing – in particular, to encourage informal peer support, ensure that staff feel heard, consider how individual team processes can be improved to support staff wellbeing and increase a sense of reward and recognition for staff.

Organisational: Actions to create an environment that supports wellbeing through positive policies and practices.

Based on information gathered in the discovery phase, the happier@work team developed or commissioned a range of interventions designed to improve staff wellbeing, reduce stress and signpost support for those with mental health problems. Table 19.2 lists the interventions.

Effective workplace mental health promotion programmes seek to enhance workforce mental health and wellbeing by 'minimising the impact of known workplace risk factors and maximising the impact of potential protective factors' (Harvey et al., 2014). In this instance, the application of the MWIA process enabled the organisations to identify the risk, protective and promoting factors for mental health in the workplace at an individual, team and organisational level and develop a tailored programme of activities and interventions to minimise the negative and maximise the positive impacts.

The MWIA has been applied in a wide variety of settings over the last decade. A recent review of the effectiveness of MWIA conducted by the Tavistock Institute of Human Relations concluded that 'there is strong qualitative evidence that MWIA makes a difference to the way initiatives are implemented' and that it orients 'initiatives towards supporting the evidenced protective factors for well-being' (King, 2014). The strength of the tool is that it enables promoting mental health to be part of everyone's day-to-day business.

Conclusion

Our mental health and wellbeing are a dynamic state. It is determined by a mixture of biological, environmental and social factors that can all influence one another. Put simply, it is complex! This is not a cause for despair, but a realisation that good mental health requires more than mental health services treating mental illness. It requires collective, systemwide action by individuals, communities, organisations and decision makers on all levels to protect and promote mental health and wellbeing for ourselves, our families and our communities. The ability to translate evidence and policy into practice at a community level is a vital component of achieving that vision and creating a sustainable future.

References

Blackman, T., and Harvey, J. (2001). Housing renewal and mental health: A case study. *Journal of Mental Health*, 10, 571–583.

Boorman, S. (2009). *NHS health and wellbeing. Final report.* London: Department of Health.

Coid, J., Yang, M., Roberts, A., Ullrich, S., Moran, P., & Bebbington, P. (2006). Violence and psychiatric morbidity in the national household population of Britain: Public health implications. *British Journal of Psychiatry*, 189, 12–19.

Cooke, A., and Coggins, T. (2005). Neighborhood well-being in Lewisham: The development of a mental well-being impact assessment and indicator toolkit. *Journal of Public Mental Health*, 4(2), 23–31.

Cooke, A., Friedli, L., Coggins, T., Edmonds, N., Michaelson, J., et al. (2011). *Mental Well-Being Impact Assessment: A Toolkit for Wellbeing (3rd ed.)*, London: National MWIA Collaborative. Available at http://www.apho.org.uk/resource/view.aspx?RID=70495.

Deacon, L., Carlin, H., Spalding, J., Giles, S., Stansfield, J., & Hughes, S. (2009). *North West mental well-being survey.* Liverpool, UK: North West Public Health Observatory.

Design Council (2005). Eleven lessons for managing design in eleven global brands. Available at http://www.designcouncil.org.uk/sites/default/files/asset/document/ElevenLessons_Design_Council%20(2).pdf.

DoH (2001). Making it happen: A guide to delivering mental health promotion. Available at http://webarchive.nationalarchives.gov.uk/+/www.dh.gov.uk/en/Publicationsandstatistics/Publications/PublicationsPolicyAndGuidance/DH_4007907.

DoH (2014). Five year forward view. Available at http://www.england.nhs.uk/wp-content/uploads/2014/10/5yfv-web.pdf.

Fagg, J., & Curtis, S. et al. (2006). Psychological distress among adolescents and its relationship to individual, family and area characteristics in East London. *Social Science & Medicine*, 63(3).

Fergusson, D., Horwood, J., & Ridder, E. M. (2005). Show me the child at seven: The consequences of conduct problems in childhood psychology for psychosocial functioning in adulthood. *Journal of Child Psychology and Psychiatry*, 46(8), 837–849. [An influential longitudinal study demonstrating the long-term impact of early behavioural problems in young children.]

Foresight Mental Capital and Wellbeing Project (2008). *Final project report.* London: The Government Office for Science.

Harvey, S., Joyce, S., Tan, L., Johnson, A., Nguyen, H., Modini, M., et al. (2014). Developing a mentally healthy workplace: A review of the literature. Australian Government National Mental Health Commission, pp. 1–7.

Health and Safety Executive (2010). Statistics 2009/10. Available at http://www.hse.gov.uk/statistics/overall/hssh0910.pdf.

Huppert, F. A., (2008). Psychological well-being: Evidence regarding its causes and consequences. Foresight State-of-Science Review: SR-X2. Government Office for Science.

Huxley, P., Rogers, A., Thomas, R., Robson, B., Evans, S., & Stordy, J. (2001). Urban regeneration and mental health. *Health Variations*, 7, 8–9.

Huxley, P., Rogers, A., Evans, S., et al. (2001). *Evaluating the impact of a locality based social policy intervention on mental health.* London: ESRCl.

Joint Commissioning Panel for Mental Health (2013). Guidance for commissioning public mental health services. Available at http://www.jcpmh.info.

Keyes, C. L. M., Dhingra, S. S., & Simoes, E. J. (2010). Change in level of positive mental health as a predictor of future risk of mental illness. *American Journal of Public Health*, 100(12), 2366–2371.

King, S., (2014). How effective is mental well-being impact assessment? A Briefing Paper by The Tavistock Institute of Human Relations. In progress.

Lyubomirsky, S., King, L. A., & Diener, E. (2005). The benefits of frequent positive affect: Does happiness lead to success. *Psychological Bulletin*, 131, 803–855.

Marmot Review (2010). *Fair society, healthy lives: Strategic review of health inequalities in England post-2010.* London, UK: The Marmot Review. Available at http://ucl.ac.uk/marmotreview.

NHS Information Centre (2011). Health survey for England – 2010. Well-being, health and work.

NICE (2008). *Promoting children's social and emotional well-being in primary education.* London, UK: NICE.

NICE (2009a). Promoting mental well-being at work: NICE public health guidance 22. Available at https://www.nice.org.uk/guidance/ph2.

NICE (2009b). *Promoting young people's social and emotional wellbeing in secondary education.* London, UK: NICE.

Ritchie, J., Spencer, L., & O'Connor, W. (2003). Carrying out qualitative analysis. In Richie, J., & Lewis, J. (Eds.), *Qualitative Research Practice: A Guide for Social Science Students and Researchers* (231). London, UK: Sage.

Sanne, B., Mykletun, A., Dahl, A. A., Moen, B. E., & Tell, G. S. (2005). Testing the job demand–control–support model with anxiety and depression as outcomes: The Hordaland Health Study. *Occupational Medicine (London),* 55, 463–473.

WHO (2014). Mental health: Strengthening our response. Fact Sheet 220. Available at http://www.who.int/mediacentre/factsheets/fs220/en/.

Wright, T. A., & Cropanzano, R. (2000). Psychological well-being and job satisfaction as predictors of job performance. *Journal of Occupational Health Psychology,* 5, 84–94.

Wright, T. A., Cropanzano, R., & Bonett, D. G. (2007). The moderating role of employee positive well being on the relationship between job satisfaction and job performance. *Journal of Occupational Health Psychology,* 12, 93–104.

Section 3

Beyond Services: What Would a Recovery-Supporting and Wellbeing-Targeted Society Look Like?

Positive Education

Visible Wellbeing and Positive Functioning in Students

Lea Waters, Jessie Sun, Reuben Rusk, Alice Cotton and Alice Arch

Introduction

According to the World Health Organization, "Health is created and lived by people within the settings of their everyday life; where they learn, work, play and love" (WHO, 1986, p. v). Given that schools are institutions in which large numbers of children live out much of their everyday lives, schools are in a powerful position to promote wellbeing at a societal level if they infuse wellbeing principles into school curricula and cultures. The current chapter puts forward a new framework of psychosocial functioning that can be infused into schools to promote student wellbeing.

Schools as Wellbeing-Enhancing Institutions

Are schools the right place to teach wellbeing? From the standpoint of maximising reach and impact, the answer is yes. Schools are a major institution in both Western and Eastern societies that have contact with large numbers of children on a regular basis. From the standpoint of the moral behaviour that positive institutions can inspire in their members, the answer is also yes. Schools work with children across their formative developmental years, when lifelong habits may be established, and thus have the potential to cultivate moral goals that guide students to be caring, responsible and productive people in society.

Over the last two decades, student wellbeing has gained increased attention and focus. For example, student wellbeing has become a focus of international education policy as represented in the interagency initiative between the WHO, UNICEF, UNESCO, Education International, Education Development Center, the Partnership for Child Development and the World Bank, and 'Focusing Resources for Effective School Health' (FRESH). The growth of research on student wellbeing is also evidenced by the number of review papers and meta-analyses on various aspects of wellbeing education that have been published over the last decade (Brunwasser et al., 2009; Durlak et al., 2011; Kavanagh et al., 2009; Kraag et al., 2006, Lovat et al., 2009; Sklad et al., 2012; Waters, 2011; Waters et al., 2015). The growth of research on student wellbeing suggests that it is increasingly being viewed as an important goal of education.

Wellbeing, Recovery and Mental Health, ed. Mike Slade, Lindsay Oades and Aaron Jarden.
Published by Cambridge University Press. © Mike Slade, Lindsay Oades and Aaron Jarden 2017

Why Should Schools Teach Wellbeing? The Learning Case and the Mental Health Case

The increasing emphasis on wellbeing education has arisen for two major reasons: (1) the learning case and (2) the mental health case. With respect to the learning case, the evidence increasingly shows that academic learning is supported by wellbeing (Linnenbrink and Pintrich, 2002; Meyer and Turner, 2006). In particular, the role that emotions play in learning and cognitive functioning has received considerable research interest (Pekrun et al., 2002). Although educationalists have traditionally viewed learning as a cognitive process, advances in neuroscience and psychology now show that learning is profoundly affected by our emotions (Immordino-Yang and Damasio, 2007; Jensen, 2008; Fredrickson, 2001, 2004). Indeed, all the information a student receives in class is routed through both the rational and emotional systems in his/her brain and the emotional climate of a classroom has a significant effect on the degree to which the material taught in class will be committed to memory (Jensen, 2008). As Professor Helen Immordino-Yang eloquently summarises, 'We feel, therefore we learn' (Immordino-Yang and Damasio, 2007).

It is no wonder that research has found a consistent link between wellbeing and academic achievement. For example, a meta-analysis by Durlak and colleagues (2011) of 213 studies involving 270,034 students from kindergarten through high school showed that, on the average, school students enrolled in a social and emotional learning program ranked 11 percentage points higher on achievement tests than school students who did not participate in such a program. In a large-scale study ($N = 4,980$) measuring the impact of a wellbeing intervention on academic performance for students in Australia, Dix et al. (2012) found that the program improved academic performance for students equal to that of six extra months of schooling by year 7 (ages 11–13). In a one-year longitudinal study of middle school students, Suldo et al. (2011) in the United States found that life satisfaction and positive affect significantly predicted objective measures of academic performance (e.g. grade point average) one year later.

As well as the learning case, the focus on wellbeing in schools has also been influenced by public health trends. Specifically, with the rise in youth mental illness,[1] schools now see themselves as being more than just academic institutions and recognise the important role that they can play as wellbeing-enabling institutions. From a health perspective, Seligman et al. (2009) suggest that wellbeing education is needed as an antidote to depression and a vehicle for increasing life satisfaction. Thus, Seligman et al. capture two types of public health approaches: the 'treatment/prevention approach' (treating and preventing depression; removing negative states) and the 'promotion approach' (promoting life satisfaction; increasing positive states).

Similarly, from a promotion approach, Waters (2014) argues that over time, wellbeing education builds a student's emotional intelligence and wellbeing literacy, which act as 'enhancing factors' that promote flourishing. From a prevention approach, Waters also argues that wellbeing education normalises conversations between students and teachers about mental health from a young age. These conversations serve as 'buffering factors' that assist in the prevention of illness and also allow teachers to engage in early detection of illness symptoms so that schools can provide extra support to at-risk students. Thus, schools have the potential to play a positive role in aspects of all areas: student wellbeing, recovery and mental health.

---

[1] World Health Organization statistics show that 20% of children and adolescents worldwide have mental disorders or problems (WHO, 2000).

How Can Schools Support Student Wellbeing?

To build wellbeing, schools must be clear about the definition of wellbeing they are adopting. Definitions of wellbeing abound in the literature, and although it is not within the remit of this chapter to present all of the definitions, there is a consensus that wellbeing is a multidimensional concept that includes both the absence of negative states *and* the presence of positive states (CASEL, 2015; ERO, 2013; Keyes and Lopez, 2002; Noble and McGrath, 2008; Seligman, 2012). In this paper we adopt Huppert and Johnson's (2010) definition of well-being as 'the combination of feeling good and functioning well' (p. 264). To this definition we add the notion of 'doing good for others.' Thus, for the purposes of this chapter, wellbeing is conceptualised as the combination of feeling good, functioning well and doing good.

What do schools need to teach in order to help their students feel good, function well and do good? The opportunity for schools to transform themselves into wellbeing-enabling institutions has given rise to a number of key scholarly movements over the past two decades that have researched various aspects of student wellbeing. These movements include social–emotional learning (SEL; Durlak et al., 2011), emotional intelligence (Hagelskamp et al., 2013), resilience education (Brunwasser et al., 2009), values education (Nielsen, 2005, 2010), character education (Berkowitz and Bier, 2005), civics education (Cogan and Morris, 2001), self-regulated learning (Pintrich and DeGroot, 1990), positive youth development (Lerner et al., 2009), positive education (Seligman et al., 2009) and contemplative education (Broderick and Metz, 2009). Although each of these movements is concerned with student well-being, each has its own emphasis and unique frameworks, with examples shown in Table 20.1 below.

Table 20.1 has been organised from movements that are more focused on intrapersonal strengths to those that focus more on relationships with others and the community at large. These are summarized in Figure 20.1, which places the existing movements along a two-by-two axis with the horizontal axis spanning from movements that have an intrapersonal focus to movements that have an interpersonal focus. Resilience education, emotional intelligence, contemplative education and self-regulated learning tend to focus more on cultivating individual emotional and psychological strengths (i.e. *feeling good* and *functioning well*), whereas character education, values education and civics education take a broader, more interpersonal and values-based perspective towards positive human development (i.e. *doing good*). In between these extremes, social–emotional learning, positive youth development and positive education approaches incorporate both intrapersonal and interpersonal aspects.

The second axis considers the breadth of focus: whereas some movements focus specifically on one area (e.g. emotional intelligence, mindfulness), other movements, such as social–emotional learning, positive education and positive youth development, involve multidimensional components. For example, positive education focuses on cultivating positive states (e.g. gratitude, meaning), teaching positive practices (e.g. savouring, active-constructive responding) and building positive traits (e.g. character strengths and prosocial behaviour). The SEL movement typically includes self-awareness, self-management, social awareness, relationship skills and responsible decision making.

How, then, do educators choose from this proliferation of well-being movements? Given the multidimensional nature of wellbeing and the different needs of particular schools and settings, we argue that it seems unwise to adopt one particular wellbeing education movement exclusively. This is because adopting a single movement means that educators might

Table 20.1 Focus and Dimensions of Student Wellbeing Movements

Movement	Focus	Example programs and competencies of focus
Emotional intelligence	Understanding and regulating own emotions and considering and empathising with how others are feeling	RULER Program (http://ei.yale.edu/ruler/ruler-overview/; Hagelskamp et al., 2013) • Recognising emotions in self and others • Understanding the causes and consequences of emotions • Labeling emotions accurately • Expressing emotions appropriately • Regulating emotions effectively
Resilience education	Cognitive reframing, bouncing back from adversity	Penn Resiliency Program (Brunwasser et al., 2009) • Understanding the link between one's thoughts and feelings and behaviours • Identifying one's explanatory style • Generating alternative interpretations • Evaluating accuracy of one's interpretations using evidence • Putting the implications of negative events into perspective
Contemplative education	Attentional focus, self-awareness and emotion regulation	Learning to Breathe Program (Broderick, 2013) • Emotion regulation (major focus) • Stress management (major focus) • Attention (major focus) • Empathy (minor focus) • Relationship building (minor focus) • Responsible decision making (minor focus)
Self-regulated learning	Requiring students to manage their thoughts, behaviours and emotions and independently plan, monitor and assess their learning	Cyclical Model (Pintrich and Zusho, 2002; Zimmerman, 2000) • Forethought and planning: analyse learning task and set specific goals • Performance monitoring: employ strategies to make progress, monitor the effectiveness of the strategies and monitor motivation for completing the learning task • Reflections on performance: evaluate performance on the learning task and manage emotional responses related to the outcomes of the learning experience
Positive youth development	Building the personal strengths that create positive attributes in young people	Generic Youth Development Framework (Wierenga and Wyn, 2011) • Overarching values: valuing people, doing things of value • Principles: recognising strengths, building the team, looking out for each other, engaging with the real world, being active citizens, becoming reflective, resilient learners • Good practice: acknowledging participation, celebrating achievement, communication,

Table 20.1 *(cont.)*

Movement	Focus	Example programs and competencies of focus
		supporting potential, growing partnerships, recognising diversity, strengthening protective behaviours, serving the community, building character and identity, supporting commitment, growing: resilience, skills, attitudes
Positive education	Increasing positive states and meaning through emotional and cognitive skills	The Positive Education Practices Framework (Noble and McGrath, 2008) • Positive emotions • Positive relationships • Engagement • Social–emotional competency • Meaning and purpose
Social–emotional learning	Emotional and social competency	CASEL Framework (CASEL, 2014a, 2014b) • Self-awareness • Self-management • Social awareness • Relationship skills • Responsible decision making
Character education	Development of positive personal strengths (virtues), good sense and practical wisdom	KIPP Character Approach (http://www.kipp.org/our-approach/character; http://characterlab.org/; Seider et al., 2013) • Focus on seven strengths that predict highly engaged, happy and successful lives: zest, grit, optimism, self-control, gratitude, social intelligence and curiosity
Values education	Understanding and knowledge of values and development of skills and disposition to enact particular values	Curriculum of Giving (Nielsen, 2010) • Self: learning to give to ourselves to have a surplus with which to give to others • Others: giving to those who are closest to us as well as strangers • Communities: expanding our field of generosity to people outside our immediate circle • Environment: giving back to the natural environment • Whole: giving to something "bigger than ourselves"
Civics education	Promoting students' participation in democracy through knowledge, skills, values and dispositions of active and informed citizenship	Australian Curriculum in Victoria (ACARA, 2012) • Civic knowledge and understanding: for example, nature of Australia's democracy, federal parliamentary system, multiculturalism • Community engagement: participation in school celebrations, developing and supporting class rules, understanding roles and responsibilities of leaders and democratic processes when engaging in school and community activities

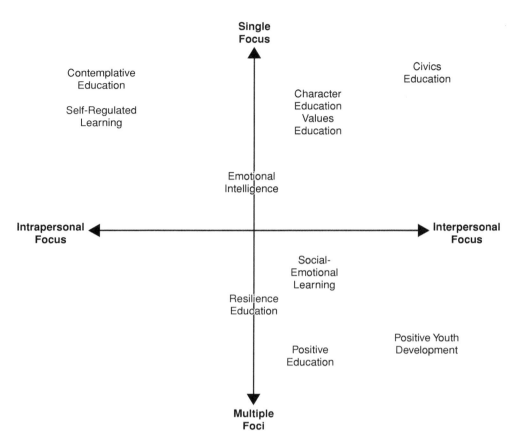

Figure 20.1 Placement of existing wellbeing movements along interpersonal–intrapersonal continuum and single–multiple program foci.

miss out on interventions that fall outside of the focus of that specific movement. For example, adopting the CASEL SEL model without considering other approaches could mean that schools neglect wellbeing interventions that are designed to build meaning and achievement. Similarly, adopting a civics education framework could mean that mindfulness and other meditative and contemplative school-based interventions may not be considered.

Instead of siding with one particular wellbeing movement, we propose the need for a new overarching framework that is broad enough to transcend the boundaries of each of the specific movements. This framework needs to allow schools to choose a specific movement if they wish while giving room for complementary or supplementary interventions from other movements and/or allowing schools to select aspects of various movements while still providing a unifying approach.

The Domains of Positive Functioning Framework

In this chapter we put forward the Domains of Positive Functioning Framework (DPF) as a useful, evidence-based framework for educators to adopt (Rusk and Waters, 2015). The DPF framework identifies the underlying aspects of optimal psychological functioning (e.g. thought processes, explanatory style, emotional understanding) and social functioning (e.g. empathy, social decision making, prosocial behaviour) that lead a person to feel good, function well and do good.

The framework was developed by a metasynthesis of over 18,400 peer-reviewed publications from fields such as psychology, education, public health, neuroscience and social science across an eighteen-year time frame (for further detail about how the framework was developed please refer to the full paper of Rusk and Waters, 2015). We see the fact that the framework was not solely devised within education (although it was informed by findings from education) as an advantage, because it means that the framework has not been restricted by educational ideologies and that the domains of positive functions identified are those that transcend context and are thus universal. Moreover, the fact that the data used to generate the DPF come from both youth and adult samples allows schools to be confident that, in building skills within the psychosocial domains of functioning, they are assisting students to achieve wellbeing now *and* also building the capabilities that will help students grow into well-adjusted, psychologically healthy adults.

The DPF framework identified five overarching domains that contribute to a person's psychosocial functioning: (1) awareness and attention, (2) emotion management, (3) comprehension and coping, (4) goals and habits and (5) virtues and relationships. In the fifth domain, 'virtues and relationships' were statistically clustered together due to the high probability that researchers who studied virtues typically did so in a relational context. While the algorithms in the metasynthesis clustered these two aspects of positive functioning into the one statistical domain, as the researchers who devised the DPF framework, we examined the *practical utility* of this statistical classification. More specifically, we wondered about how those virtues that are not strongly relational in nature, such as wisdom-related virtues (e.g. open-mindedness, critical thinking, problem solving) and some temperance-related virtues (e.g. self-regulation), could be taught if virtues and relationships were taught in a cojoined manner.

After careful deliberation, we decided that when wellbeing is taught in schools, the fifth domain of virtues and relationships has more real-world relevance if it is separated into two domains. The metasynthesis of Rusk and Waters (2015) shows that both virtues and relationships are important aspects of positive functioning in their own right, and education research has well-established ways to teach relationship skills (e.g. SEL), as well as teaching virtues in movements such as character and values education. Hence we propose a six-domain framework for the DPF: (1) awareness and attention, (2) emotion management, (3) comprehension and coping, (4) goals and habits, (5) virtues and (6) relationships (see Figure 20.2).

Domain 1: Attention and Awareness. Broadly speaking, attention has been defined as the ability to focus, either on inner aspects of self, such as emotions and physical sensations, or on external stimuli (e.g. the teacher's lesson in a classroom; Beauchemin et al., 2008; Steiner et al., 2013). According to Steiner et al. (2013), awareness refers to the ability to pay attention to a stimulus as it occurs. Wellbeing is improved when individuals can consciously control their attention and direct it towards particular aspects of sensory or cognitive information.

Domain 2: Emotion Management. Emotions are instinctive feelings that are accompanied by physiological changes. They are influenced by our circumstances, thoughts and physiology (Beck, 1995; Gross, 2002; Schachter and Singer, 1962; Damasio, 1996). Rusk and Waters (2015) showed that being present with one's emotions and being able to identify, understand and manage one's emotions (i.e. reduce negative emotions and increase positive emotions) are a key aspect of psychosocial functioning.

Domain 3: Comprehension and Coping. The DPF domain of comprehension and coping involves individuals being able to grasp the elements of a given situation and understand the attributions they make to their environments (e.g. their own thought processes, explanatory

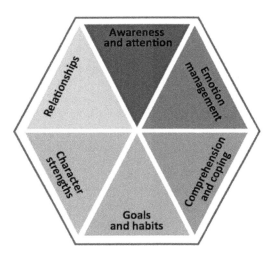

Figure 20.2 The six domains of positive functioning.

style and mindsets). This domain recognises the interplay between the demands placed upon an individual and the resources he/she has to manage those demands. The domain also includes the ways in which people cope with and grow from adversity and stressful life experiences, processes that can aid recovery and thus improve mental health.

Domain 4: Goals and Habits. Goals are the formal objects, achievements and endpoints that people desire and in which they are willing to invest effort (Snyder, 2002). Setting goals is a key component of a well-functioning life and provides children with a sense of purpose, mastery and direction (Madden et al., 2011). Rusk and Waters (2015) showed that this aspect of psychosocial functioning is improved when individuals are able to set goals that match their values and can be used to guide the selection of behaviour in enduring ways and form new skills. This domain also concerns the habits that people develop that allow them to reach their goals as well as to create behavioural change. Habits are patterns of thought and behavior that are acquired through frequent repetition (Costa and Kallick, 2009). People who develop healthy habits of mind and behaviour have higher levels of wellbeing (Costa and Kallick, 2009; Ryan and Deci, 2001; Hassmén et al., 2000). Healthy habits free up our cognitive resources, thus providing more conscious attention for student to focus on learning (Louis and Sutton, 1991)

Domain 5: Virtues. Virtues are defined as moral qualities in a person and are shown through one's thoughts and actions that are guided by moral and ethical principles. States of virtuousness, such as courage and wisdom, represent conditions of ennoblement and personal flourishing. Virtuous behaviour has been found to be associated with happiness, life meaning, physical health and resilience. Research themes that have been studied over the past eighteen years that came forward in the cluster analysis for this domain include honesty, ethics, humility, trust and philanthropy.

Domain 6: Relationships. A child's social skills play an important role in allowing him/her to develop nourishing relationships with others. Schnitzer et al. (2007) argue that strengthening a child's ability to understand, express and manage life's social aspects is critical for wellbeing. The DPF domain of relationships incorporates the skills required to sustain enduring social relationships, as well as capitalise on momentary social interactions.

The DPF framework having been established, Table 20.2 maps existing wellbeing education movements to these six domains to compare the skills that are being developed by

Domain	Description	Links to wellbeing education movements	Example programs
Attention and awareness	The consciously controlled or automatic regulation of attention toward particular aspects of sensory or cognitive information, including novel aspects.	Contemplative Education	Learning to Breathe .b (Mindfulness in Schools Program) MindUp Teaching Happiness and Well-Being in Schools
Emotions	Present-moment experiences of emotion, identification of emotions, understanding emotional associations with stimuli and memories, cultivating positive emotions, reducing negative emotions.	SEL (emotion regulation) Resilience Education (link between thoughts and feelings) Contemplative Education (loving kindness meditation) Positive Education (positive emotions)	Penn Resiliency Program High School Positive Psychology Curriculum Bounce Back! RULER INTEMO MindUp Personal Well-Being Lessons for Secondary Schools Self Science Teaching Happiness and Well-Being in Schools
Comprehending and coping	Comprehend one's situation by using consciously controlled or automatic processes involved with identifying stimuli, determining processes and causal relations within past and present stimuli, and anticipating or predicting future possibilities. This domain includes the application of these comprehension processes to cope effectively with adversity.	Resilience Education Contemplative Education (stress management) Positive Education (positive thinking skills)	Penn Resiliency Program U.K. Resilience Program Optimism and Lifeskills Program Aussie Optimism: Positive Thinking Skills Program beyondblue Schools Intervention Resourceful Adolescent Program Fun FRIENDS Strong Kids High School Positive Psychology Curriculum Bounce Back! You Can Do It! Think Positively: Adolescent Coping MindUp Personal Well-Being Lessons for Secondary Schools Self Science Teaching Happiness and Well-Being in Schools Best of Coping Zippy's Friends

(cont.)

Table 20.2 (cont.)

Domain	Description	Links to wellbeing education movements	Example programs
Goals and habits	Enduring conscious or unconscious values, rules, principles and goals involved in guiding the selection of behaviour and the habits and skills involved in the execution of those behaviours.	Character Education (persistence) Positive Education (goal setting) SEL (organisation and decision-making skills)	Celebrating Strengths Personal Well-Being Lessons for Secondary Schools Going for the Goal Making Hope Happen Self Science Building Happiness, Resilience and Motivation in Adolescents Building Happiness, Resilience and Motivation in Adolescents Feuerstein's Instrumental Enrichment Curriculum Brainology Mental Contrasting with Implementation Intentions
Virtues	Thoughts and actions that are guided by moral and ethical principles	Contemplative Education (empathy and prosocial emotions) Positive Education (character) Civic education Values Education Character Education	Celebrating Strengths Bounce Back! MindUp Personal Well-Being Lessons for Secondary Schools Curriculum of Giving Self Science Teaching Happiness and Well-Being in Schools Building Happiness, Resilience and Motivation in Adolescents Schoolwide Positive Behaviour Support
Relationships	Enduring social relationships and momentary social interactions, including family, friend, romantic, school, societal and spiritual levels	SEL (social awareness and relationship skills) Positive Education (relationships) Civic education Values Education Character Education	Bounce Back! Personal Well-Being Lessons for Secondary Schools Curriculum of Giving Teaching Happiness and Well-Being in Schools Building Happiness, Resilience and Motivation in Adolescents Schoolwide Positive Behaviour Support Nurture Group

different movements. This is a useful way for educators and researchers alike to consider the strengths and gaps left by different approaches to student wellbeing and to aid strategic decisions about developing and implementing new programs.

As seen in Table 20.2, the existing well-being education movements, taken together, address skill development in the six domains of the DPF. However, programs may indirectly affect domains of functioning outside of their main focus, many of the existing movements tend to be situated mainly in one or two domains. For example, contemplative education aligns to the attention and awareness domain, values education appears to be exclusive to the Virtues domain, resilience education fits most strongly in the emotions and the coping and comprehension domains, and positive education focuses on emotions, virtues and relationships. Importantly, as can be seen in Table 20.2, no one movement fully addresses all six domains. Turning to the domains, Table 20.2 also reveals a substantial emphasis on emotions, comprehension and coping, virtues and relationships. This analysis highlights that that there is room for growth in programs that address the domains of attention and awareness and goals and habits.

The Relationship between a Wellbeing Intervention, Psychosocial Functioning and Wellbeing

For schools to prevent illbeing and foster wellbeing in their students, they need to help them to build skills in each of the six domains outlined by the DPF framework. This is because psychosocial functioning is the *pathway* that leads to wellbeing. That is, highly developed attentional skills, emotional capacities, coping skills, goal-setting skills and social skills help students to achieve optimal wellbeing. As shown in Figure 20.3, the relationship between a wellbeing intervention and wellbeing outcomes is influenced by the degree to which the wellbeing intervention improves a student's ability to function psychologically and socially.

This relationship will now be demonstrated using the example of a school-based mindfulness intervention. Mindfulness is a state of present-moment, nonjudgemental attention to one's thoughts, feelings and body sensations and can thus be understood as a type of self-observation (Kabat-Zinn, 1990, 2003; Sedlmeier et al., 2012). Mindfulness is contrasted to other types of attention that are not anchored in the present moment (Kabat-Zinn, 1994). For example, ruminating is a type of attention that is focused in the past and prospection is a type of attention that focuses on the future; both take people away from the present moment and hence do not constitute mindfulness (Brown and Ryan, 2003).

Over the past ten years, youth mindfulness programs have been developed in countries such as England (Mindfulness in Schools Project, DotB), the United States (Mindful Schools and MindUp), Canada (Mindful Education), Israel (The Mindfulness Language) and India (The Alice Project). These programs provide students with mindfulness exercises that help them to build up their 'attentional muscle' and gain awareness of themselves and others. The techniques typically involve a structured mental process where the students are given a target to focus their attention upon (e.g. music, their own breathing) and then asked to notice

Figure 20.3 The relationship between a wellbeing intervention, psychosocial functioning and wellbeing.

when their attention has wandered away from the target and to bring the attention back to the target. Through this structured mental process, students learn how to take more deliberate control over what they pay attention to and how to pay attention for longer periods of time. Mindfulness techniques also build the students' self-awareness about their thought patterns and the physical and emotional sensations they experience.

A recent review of 15 meditation and mindfulness programs in schools provided support for the effectiveness of mindfulness programs in attaining student wellbeing outcomes, with effect sizes ranging from 0.28 to 0.61 (Waters et al., 2015). In other words, mindfulness interventions have been shown to help students feel good, function well and do good.

For example, compared with control groups, students who participate in mindfulness interventions at school report *feeling good* with increases in optimism, self-concept, self-acceptance, calm and general wellbeing (Kuyken et al., 2013; Broderick and Metz, 2009; Schonert-Reichl and Lawlor, 2010).

Mindfulness interventions also help students *function well*. For example, teachers report that students are more settled and focused in class after mindfulness sessions (Campion and Rocco, 2009). In Flook et al.'s (2010) eight-week mindfulness intervention with primary school children, children with poorer initial executive–cognitive functioning also showed improvements in executive–cognitive functioning after the mindfulness training.

Mindfulness also prompts children to *do good*, and in Campion and Rocco's (2009) qualitative exploration of a mindfulness program, students reported that the mindfulness techniques assisted them with anger management, which helped them to have better friendships and more positive interactions with others. This outcome was verified by the teachers, who reported seeing these positive changes in their students' relationships. Similarly, in Rosaen and Benn's (2006) qualitative study, students reported that meditation had helped them to be more socially skilled and to calm their antisocial tendencies. For example, one student commented, 'Like, I'm more nicer and mature … Like I can listen to them.' Another student reported, 'If I meditate, I feel calm and feel like I don't have to argue with anybody.'

The literature suggests that mindfulness interventions help students to feel good, function well and do good. But the question remains of how these mindful practices lead to wellbeing. We suggest that mindful practices enhance wellbeing because they build a student's attentional skills (Domain 1 in the DPF). When the ability to pay attention to the here and now (the psychosocial function) is strengthened, the student becomes relaxed and self-aware (the wellbeing outcome of feeling good) because he or she are not caught in rumination about the past or anxious about the future. Moreover, by teaching students how they can choose what to pay attention to and helping them build their capacity for sustained attention (the psychosocial function), these skills help students to selectively pay attention to the teacher's lesson (the wellbeing outcome of functioning well). In summary, mindfulness interventions foster wellbeing *because* they increase a student's ability to function in the domain of 'attention and awareness', as depicted in Figure 20.4.

The lesson from the mindfulness example above for school leaders and teachers is that when choosing a wellbeing program, they need to examine the degree to which the program is likely to *build underlying skills in psychosocial functioning*, rather than only focusing on the wellbeing outcomes of the program. Thus, effective wellbeing programs should cultivate enduring and generalisable *pathways* to build the many wellbeing outcomes, akin to study skills programs building transferable skills that students can apply to increase their learning across multiple academic disciplines.

Figure 20.4 The relationship between a mindfulness intervention, psychosocial functioning and wellbeing.

Visible Wellbeing: How to Use the Domains of Positive Functioning Framework in Schools

The DPF is not a movement, nor does it suggest a specific program to be used in schools. Instead, the DPF provides educators with a rigorous, evidence-based, overarching framework that allows them to

a. develop a strategic whole-school wellbeing framework that incorporates the six domains of psychosocial functioning;
b. conduct an audit of their existing wellbeing education approach to analyse the degree to which it is building student skills in each of the six domains of psychosocial functioning;
c. evaluate the various wellbeing education movements with regard to the degree to which these movements support the functioning of students in each of the six domains;
d. implement specific programs with a deeper understanding of what aspects of the underlying domains of psychosocial functioning are being impacted within the program;
e. analyse the degree to which the school culture supports staff to develop their functioning in each of the six domains;
f. assist school psychologists and counsellors who are working with students in a more targeted manner to help them overcome mental ill health, relationship conflict or adjustment issues through enhancing students' psychosocial functioning in specific domains identified by the psychologist.

We suggest that Hattie's (2009) Visible Learning approach can be extended to foster 'Visible Wellbeing' and that the DPF provides a framework to make wellbeing visible. The visible learning approach encourages teachers and students to use data in ways that allow student learning to be tracked. Teachers can see if their teaching techniques are improving the learning outcomes in students by analysing the learning data, because the data become the visible marker of the learning process. Data move learning from being a process that takes place inside the student's own mind and make the learning visible (Hattie, 2009). Similarly, collecting data about a student's psychosocial functioning can help to shift wellbeing from being a subjective, internal experience within a student to being a tangible, measurable phenomenon that is visible to teachers and students.

A practitioner-friendly rubric of the six domains of positive psychosocial functioning is currently being developed by the first author of this chapter for use in schools as a way to foster 'Visible Wellbeing'. Teachers will be able to use the rubric on a regular basis for each of their classes to rate the degree to which students are displaying attentional skills, emotional awareness, coping skills, goal-driven behavior, virtuous behavior and relationship skills.

Teachers will also be able to use the rubric to see if and how their teaching practices and curricula are building psychosocial functioning in their students.

In the first author's experience of delivering professional development to teachers on the topic of student and staff wellbeing, many teachers comment that they have an intuitive sense of the wellbeing of their students but do not have a brief, user-friendly, evidence-based tool to assess student wellbeing on a regular, ongoing basis. To address this issue, the Centre for Positive Psychology at the University of Melbourne has recently developed a Wellbeing Profiler for schools (http://www.wbprofiler.com.au). Teachers also remark that they do not have a framework within which to understand what leads to wellbeing, nor a language in which to have wellbeing-related conversations with their students. The DPF provides such a framework to help schools and teachers make student wellbeing visible.

Using the Domains of Positive Functioning Framework to Assist Students in Recovery

The current chapter has focused on schools as wellbeing-enhancing institutions and has concentrated on the idea of wellbeing promotion rather than recovery from illness. However, it is also worth considering how the DPF framework could be used to assist students who are recovering from mental illness or trauma. Indeed, schools play an important role for students in the recovery process, and classrooms can act as a therapeutic environment addressing the effects of adverse childhood experiences and encouraging post-traumatic growth, psychological wellbeing and academic aspirations for these students.

In a recent review of the field of trauma-informed education, Brunzell et al. (2015) identified that the two major educational approaches in working with trauma-affected students are (1) teaching in ways that repair regulatory abilities and (2) teaching in ways that repair disrupted attachments. These two approaches map onto the DPF domains of 'emotion management', 'comprehension and coping' and 'virtues and relationships'.

Adding to the two major approaches of trauma-informed education, Brunzell and colleagues (Brunzell et al., 2016a, 2016b) argue that the recovery journey for students should extend beyond *repair* (e.g. repairing PTSD) to also focus on *growth* (fostering post-traumatic growth where possible and wellbeing). Accordingly, Brunzell et al. (2015) suggest that teaching students about positive emotions is a critical healing ingredient for students in recovery. This can be done by explicitly naming and teaching positive emotions using a 'positivity toolkit' (see Fredrickson, 2009), using visual reminders to capitalise on positive experiences and adopting a 'what went well' routine (see Fox Eades, 2006). A strengths-based approach can also be used to assist students who are in the process of recovery. In particular, within the DPF domain of 'virtues and relationships', teachers can connect students with their character strengths so that students know what inner strengths/resources they can draw upon to help them recover and to also help them to aim for future success.

The DPF framework can also help students who may not necessarily be in recovery from trauma or mental illness, but who struggle with school because of special needs such as learning disorders (e.g. dyslexia, ADHD), disabilities (e.g. visual–hearing impairments, physical disabilities) and/or social–emotional–behavioural disorders (e.g. conduct disorder). The main body of evidence pertaining to wellbeing intervention in special needs students relates to the DPF domain of 'virtues and relationships' and has focused on the potential for peer mentoring programs to promote wellbeing (Cavell et al., 2009; Cavell and Hughes, 2000; Kam et al., 2004; Elledge et al., 2010; Hektner et al., 2003). Research shows that special needs students who go through peer mentoring programs report increases in social–emotional skills, perception and understanding of humour, increases in generating nonconfrontational solutions and reduction in anger (Kam et al., 2004; Jordans et al., 2010; Schnitzer et al., 2007).

It must be noted, however, that the programs are not universally successful (e.g. Cavell and Hughes, 2000) and mixed results have been found with respect to teacher-reported trajectories of social competence and social problem solving (August et al., 2001; Kam et al., 2004). Thus, more research is needed to enhance the effectiveness of the social functioning of students with special needs.

The other DPF domain that has received attention with special needs students is that of 'comprehension and coping.' Interventions designed to improve coping in these student samples include learning problem-solving skills (Cowen et al., 1995), creating and implementing a plan for graduated exposures to fear stimuli (Dadds et al., 1997), teaching cognitive behaviour therapy principles (Firth et al., 2013), activities and games such as dance, drama and drawing to learn stress inoculation techniques (Jordans et al., 2010), doing experiential activities to mobilise social supports (Slone and Shoshani, 2008), learning a coping-enhancing curriculum presented in letters sent by an imaginary character (Wolmer et al., 2011a) and relaxation training using mental imagery (Wolmer et al., 2011b).

Equipping students with skills that enhance their functioning with respect to comprehension and coping (e.g. problem-solving skills, cognitive behaviour skills, relaxation techniques, mobilising social support) has significant benefits for the wellbeing of students with special needs. Research shows that as a result of going through coping programs, students report improvement in hope, self-efficacy, self-control, realistic attributions, school connectedness and happiness, as well as reduction in anxiety and other measures of psychological distress (Cowen et al., 1995; Firth et al., 2013; Jordans et al., 2010; Slone and Shoshani, 2008).

We suggest that students recovering from mental illness or trauma and students who have special needs could benefit from wellbeing interventions that seek to build the psychosocial functioning capacity of students in all six of these domains. Yet, at present, the programs and research do not adequately cover all six domains of the DPF. Not surprisingly, given the healing nature of these programs, the domains that are best covered are emotional management, comprehension and coping and the relationships aspect of virtues and relationships. The domains of attention and awareness and goals and habits have received less focus; yet, given that the relative contributions of each domain are largely unknown, an important future direction is to investigate the extent to which programs that focus on these neglected domains can improve wellbeing for students in recovery or with special needs. Thus, educators and researchers could benefit from using the DPF as a framework with which to design, implement and evaluate wellbeing interventions for students in recovery or with special needs.

Conclusion

Schools serve as important social institutions with a huge potential to build wellbeing in large numbers of youth. The focus on wellbeing education has risen over the last two decades, based on research showing that wellbeing supports academic success (the learning case) and as a reaction to rising levels of youth mental illness, and with the realisation that schools can play a treatment, prevention and/or promotion role in youth mental health (the mental health case).

For teachers to know how to successfully build student wellbeing, they need to be guided by an effective, evidence-based framework, as well as developing teacher effectiveness practices that allow them to collect and analyse real-time and ongoing data so that they know their impact on student wellbeing in a dynamic way across the academic year. The current chapter outlines such a framework, the Domains of Positive Functioning (DPF), and argues that student wellbeing is enhanced when schools teach students ways to improve their functioning across six key domains: (1) awareness and attention, (2) emotion management, (3) comprehension and coping, (4) goals and habits, (5) virtues and (6) relationships. The DPF framework can also be used to promote wellbeing in students who are recovering from illness and trauma, and in students who struggle with school due to learning disorders, disability and social–emotional–behavioural disorders. We offer the DPF framework to schools in the hope that it generates evidence-based approaches which will enhance wellbeing in large numbers of young people.

References

ACARA (2012). The shape of the Australian curriculum: Civics and citizenship. Available at http://www.acara.edu.au/verve/_resources/Shape_of_the_Australian_Curriculum__Civics_and_Citizenship_251012.pdf.

August, G. J., Realmuto, G. M., Hektner, J. M., & Bloomquist, M. L. (2001). An integrated components preventive intervention for aggressive elementary school children: The early risers program. *Journal of Consulting and Clinical Psychology*, 69(4), 614–626. Available at http://www.ncbi.nlm.nih.gov/pubmed/11550728.

Beauchemin, J., Hutchins, T. L., & Patterson, F. (2008). Mindfulness meditation may lessen anxiety, promote social skills, and improve academic performance among adolescents with learning disabilities. *Complementary Health Practice Review*, 13(1), 34–45. doi:10.1177/1533210107311624.

Beck, J. S. (1995). *Cognitive therapy: Basics and beyond*. New York, NY: Guilford.

Berkowitz, M. W., & Bier, M. C. (2005). What works in character education: A research-driven guide for educators. Washington, DC. Available at http://www.rucharacter.org/file/practitioners_518.pdf.

Broderick, P. C. (2013). *Learning to breathe: A mindfulness curriculum for adolescents to coordinate emotion regulation, attention, and performance*. Oakland, CA: New Harbinger.

Broderick, P. C., & Metz, S. (2009). Learning to BREATHE: A pilot trial of a mindfulness curriculum for adolescents. *Advances in School Mental Health Promotion*, 2(1), 35–46.

Brown, K. W., & Ryan, R. M. (2003). The benefits of being present: Mindfulness and its role in psychological well-being. *Journal of Personality and Social Psychology*, 84(4), 822–848. doi:10.1037/0022-3514.84.4.822.

Brunwasser, S. M., Gillham, J. E., & Kim, E. S. (2009). A meta-analytic review of the Penn Resiliency Program's effect on depressive symptoms. *Journal of Consulting and Clinical Psychology*, 77(6), 1042–1054. doi:10.1037/a0017671.

Brunzell, T., Stokes, H., & Waters, L., (2016a). Trauma-informed classrooms and flexible learning: Strengthening regulatory abilities and the readiness to learn. *International Journal of Youth and Family Studies*, 7, 218–239.

Brunzell, T., Stokes, H., & Waters, L. (2016b). Trauma-informed positive education: Using positive psychology to repair and strengthen vulnerable students. *Contemporary School Psychology*, 20, 63–83.

Brunzell, T., Waters, L., & Stokes, H. (2015). Teaching with strengths in trauma-affected students: A new approach to healing and growth in the classroom. *American Journal of Orthopsychiatry: The Community Magazine*, 85, 3–9.

Campion, J., & Rocco, S. (2009). Minding the mind: The effects and potential of a school-based meditation programme for mental health promotion. *Advances in School Mental Health Promotion*, 2(1), 47–55. doi:10.1080/1754730X.2009.9715697.

CASEL (2014a). Outcomes associated with the five competencies. Available at http://www.casel.org/ social-and-emotional-learning/outcomes.

CASEL (2014b). Social and emotional learning core competencies. Available at http://www.casel.org/ social-and-emotional-learning/core-competencies.

CASEL (2015). Social and emotional learning core competencies. Available at http://www.casel.org/ social-and-emotional-learning/core-competencies.

Cavell, T. A., Elledge, L. C., Malcolm, K. T., Faith, M. A., & Hughes, J. N. (2009). Relationship quality and the mentoring of aggressive, high-risk children. *Journal of Clinical Child and Adolescent Psychology*, 38(2), 185–98. doi:10.1080/15374410802698420.

Cavell, T. A., & Hughes, J. N. (2000). Secondary prevention as context for assessing change processes in aggressive children. *Journal of School Psychology*, 38(3), 199–235. doi:10.1016/S0022-4405(99)00040-0.

Cogan, J. J., & Morris, P. (2001). The development of civics values: An overview. *International Journal of Educational Research*, 35(1), 1–9. doi:10.1016/S0883-0355(01)00002-7.

Costa, A. L., & Kallick, B. (2009). *Habits of mind across the curriculum: Practical and creative strategies for teachers*. Alexandria, VA: Association for Supervision and Curriculum Development.

Cowen, E. L., Wyman, P. A., Work, W. C., & Iker, M. R. (1995). A preventive intervention for enhancing resilience among highly stressed urban children. *The Journal of Primary Prevention*, 15(3), 247–60. doi:10.1007/BF02197474.

Dadds, M. R., Spence, S. H., Holland, D. E., Barrett, P. M., & Laurens, K. R. (1997). Prevention and early intervention for anxiety disorders: A controlled trial. *Journal of Consulting and Clinical Psychology*, 65(4), 627–635.

Damasio, A. R. (1996). The somatic marker hypothesis and the possible functions of the prefrontal cortex. *Philosophical Transactions of the Royal Society of London. Series B, Biological Sciences*, 351(1346), 1413–20. doi:10.1098/rstb.1996.0125.

Dix, K. L., Slee, P. T., Lawson, M. J., & Keeves, J. P. (2012). Implementation quality of whole-school mental health promotion and students' academic performance. *Child and Adolescent Mental Health*, 17(1), 45–51. doi:10.1111/j.1475-3588.2011.00608.x.

Duckworth, A. L., Quinn, P. D., & Seligman, M. E. P. (2009). Positive predictors of teacher effectiveness. *Journal of Positive Psychology*, 4(6), 540–547. doi:10.1080/17439760903157232.

Durlak, J. A., Weissberg, R. P., Dymnicki, A. B., Taylor, R. D., & Schellinger, K. B. (2011). The impact of enhancing students' social and emotional learning: A meta-analysis of school-based universal interventions. *Child Development*, 82(1), 405–432.

Education Review Office (2013). Well-being for success: Draft evaluation indicators for student well-being. Available at http://www.ero.govt.nz/content/download/194999/3311315/version/3/file/ ERO_Well-being4Success-final.pdf.

Elledge, L. C., Cavell, T. A., Ogle, N. T., & Newgent, R. A. (2010). School-based mentoring as selective prevention for bullied children: A preliminary test. *Journal of Primary Prevention*, 31(3), 171–87. doi:10.1007/s10935-010-0215-7.

Firth, N., Frydenberg, E., Steeg, C., & Bond, L. (2013). Coping successfully with dyslexia: An initial study of an inclusive school-based resilience programme. *Dyslexia (Chichester, England)*, 19(2), 113–30. doi:10.1002/dys.1453.

Flook, L., Smalley, S. L., Kitil, M. J., Galla, B. M., Kaiser-Greenland, S., Locke, J., et al. (2010). Effects of mindful awareness practices on executive functions in elementary school children. *Journal of Applied School Psychology*, 26(1), 70–95. doi:10.1080/15377900903379125.

Fox Eades, J. (2006). *Classroom tales: Using storytelling to build emotional, social and academic skills across the primary curriculum*. London, UK: Jessica Kingsley Publishers.

Fredrickson, B. L. (2001). The role of positive emotions in positive psychology. The broaden-and-build theory of positive emotions. *American Psychologist*, 56(3), 218–226.

Fredrickson, B. L. (2004). The broaden-and-build theory of positive emotions. *Philosophical Transactions of the Royal Society of London B*, 359(1449), 1367–1378. doi:10.1098/rstb.2004.1512.

Fredrickson, B. L. (2009). *Positivity: Top-notch research reveals the upward spiral that will change your life*. New York, NY: Three Rivers Press.

Gross, J. J. (2002). Emotion regulation: Affective, cognitive, and social consequences. *Psychophysiology*, 39(3), 281–91. doi:10.1017.S0048577201393198.

Hagelskamp, C., Brackett, M. A., Rivers, S. E., & Salovey, P. (2013). Improving classroom quality with the RULER approach to social and emotional learning: Proximal and distal outcomes. *American Journal of Community Psychology*, 51(3–4), 1–14. doi:10.1007/s10464-013-9570-x.

Hassmén, P., Koivula, N., & Uutela, A. (2000). Physical exercise and psychological well-being: A population study in Finland. *Preventive Medicine*, 30(1), 17–25. doi:10.1006/pmed.1999.0597.

Hattie, J. (2009). *Visible learning: A synthesis of over 800 meta-analyses relating to achievement.* Abingdon, UK: Routledge.

Hektner, J. M., August, G. J., & Realmuto, G. M. (2003). Effects of pairing aggressive and nonaggressive children in strategic peer affiliation. *Journal of Abnormal Child Psychology*, 31(4), 399–412. Available at http://www.ncbi.nlm.nih.gov/pubmed/12831229.

Huppert, F. A., & Johnson, D. M. (2010). A controlled trial of mindfulness training in schools: The importance of practice for an impact on well-being. *Journal of Positive Psychology*, 5(4), 264–274. doi:10.1080/17439761003794148.

Immordino-Yang, M. H., & Damasio, A. (2007). We feel, therefore we learn: The relevance of affective and social neuroscience to education. *Mind, Brain, and Education*, 1(1), 3–10. doi:10.1111/j.1751-228X.2007.00004.x.

Jensen, E. (2008). *Brain-based learning: The new paradigm of teaching.* Thousand Oaks, CA: Corwin Press.

Jordans, M. J. D., Komproe, I. H., Tol, W. A., Kohrt, B. A., Luitel, N. P., Macy, R. D., et al. (2010). Evaluation of a classroom-based psychosocial intervention in conflict-affected Nepal: A cluster randomized controlled trial. *Journal of Child Psychology and Psychiatry, and Allied Disciplines*, 51(7), 818–26. doi:10.1111/j.1469-7610.2010.02209.x.

Kabat-Zinn, J. (1990). *Full catastrophe living.* New York, NY: Dell.

Kabat-Zinn, J. (1994). *Wherever you go, there you are.* New York, NY: Hyperion.

Kabat-Zinn, J. (2003). Mindfulness-based interventions in context: Past, present, and future. *Clinical Psychology: Science and Practice*, 10(2), 144–156. doi:10.1093/clipsy/bpg016.

Kam, C.-M., Greenberg, M. T., & Kusche, C. A. (2004). Sustained effects of the PATHS curriculum on the social and psychological adjustment of children in special education. *Journal of Emotional and Behavioral Disorders*, 12(2), 66–78. doi:10.1177/10634266040120020101.

Kavanagh, J., Oliver, S., Lorenc, T., Caird, J., Tucker, H., Harden, A., et al. (2009). School-based cognitive-behavioural interventions: A systematic review of effects and inequalities. *Health Sociology Review*, 18, 61–78. doi:10.5172/hesr.18.1.61.

Kern, M. L., Waters, L., Adler, A., & White, M. (2014). Assessing employee well-being in schools using a multifaceted approach: Associations with physical health, life satisfaction, and professional thriving. *Psychology*, 05(06), 500–513. doi:10.4236/psych.2014.56060.

Keyes, C. L. M., & Lopez, S. J. (2002). Toward a science of mental health: Positive directions in diagnosis and interventions. In C. R. Snyder & S. J. Lopez (Eds.), *Handbook of Positive Psychology* (pp. 45–59). New York: Oxford University Press.

Kraag, G., Zeegers, M. P., Kok, G., Hosman, C., & Abu-Saad, H. H. (2006). School programs targeting stress management in children and adolescents: A meta-analysis. *Journal of School Psychology*, 44(6), 449–472. doi:10.1016/j.jsp.2006.07.001.

Kuyken, W., Weare, K., Ukoumunne, O. C., Vicary, R., Motton, N., Burnett, R., et al. (2013). Effectiveness of the Mindfulness in Schools Programme: Non-randomised controlled feasibility study. *The British Journal of Psychiatry*, 203(2), 126–31. doi:10.1192/bjp.bp.113.126649.

Lerner, J. V, Phelps, E., Forman, Y. E., & Bowers, E. P. (2009). Positive youth development. In *Handbook of Adolescent Psychology*. John Wiley & Sons, Inc. doi:10.1002/9780470479193.adlpsy001016.

Linnenbrink, E. A., & Pintrich, P. R. (2002). Motivation as an enabler for academic success. *School Psychology Review*, 31(3), 313–327.

Louis, M. R., & Sutton, R. I. (1991). Switching cognitive gears: From habits of mind to active thinking. *Human Relations*, 44(1), 55–76. doi:10.1177/001872679104400104.

Lovat, T., Toomey, R., Dally, K., & Clement, N. (2009). Project to test and measure the impact of values education on student effects and school ambience. Canberra, Australia. Available at http://www.curriculum.edu.au/verve/_resources/project_to_test_and_measure_the_impact_of_values_education.pdf.

Madden, W., Green, S., & Grant, A. (2011). A pilot study evaluating strengths-based coaching for primary school students: Enhancing engagement and hope. *International Coaching Psychology Review*, 6(1), 71–83.

Meyer, D. K., & Turner, J. C. (2006). Re-conceptualizing emotion and motivation to learn in classroom contexts. *Educational Psychology Review*, 18(4), 377–390. doi:10.1007/s10648-006-9032-1.

Nielsen, T. W. (2005). Values education through thinking, feeling and doing. *Social Educator*, 23(2), 39–48.

Nielsen, T. W. (2010). Towards pedagogy of giving for well-being and social engagement. In Lovat, T. & Toomey, R. (Eds.), *International Research Handbook on Values Education and Student Well-Being* (pp. 617–630). New York, NY: Springer.

Noble, T., & McGrath, H. (2008). *A scoping study on student well-being*. Canberra, Australia: Department of Education.

Pekrun, R., Goetz, T., Titz, W., & Perry, R. P. (2002). Academic emotions in students' self-regulated learning and achievement: A program of qualitative and quantitative research. *Educational Psychologist*, 37(2), 91–105. doi:10.1207/S15326985EP3702_4.

Pintrich, P. R., & de Groot, E. V. (1990). Motivational and self-regulated learning components of classroom academic performance. *Journal of Educational Psychology*, 82(1), 33–40.

Pintrich, P. R., & Zusho, A. (2002). The development of academic self-regulation: The role of cognitive and motivational factors. In Wigfield, A., & Eccles, J. (Eds.), *Development of Achievement Motivation* (pp. 249–284). San Diego, CA: Academic Press.

Rand, K. L. (2009). Hope and optimism: Latent structures and influences on grade expectancy and academic performance. *Journal of Personality*, 77(1), 231–260. doi:10.1111/j.1467-6494.2008.00544.x.

Rosaen, C., & Benn, R. (2006). The experience of transcendental meditation in middle school students: A qualitative report. *Explore (New York, N.Y.)*, 2(5), 422–425. doi:10.1016/j.explore.2006.06.001.

Rusk, R. D., & Waters, L. (2015). A psycho-social system approach to well-being: Empirically deriving the Five Domains of Positive Functioning. *Journal of Positive Psychology*, 10(2), 141–152. doi:10.1080/17439760.2014.920409.

Rusk, R. D, & Waters, L. E. (2013). Tracing the size, reach, impact, and breadth of positive psychology. *Journal of Positive Psychology*, 8(3), 207–221. doi:10.1080/17439760.2013.777766.

Ryan, R. M., & Deci, E. L. (2001). On happiness and human potentials: A review of research on hedonic and eudaimonic well-being. *Annual Review of Psychology*, 52, 141–166.

Schachter, S., & Singer, J. (1962). Cognitive, social, and physiological determinants of emotional state. *Psychological Review*, 69(5), 379–399.

Schnitzer, G., Andries, C., & Lebeer, J. (2007). Usefulness of cognitive intervention programmes for socio-emotional and behaviour problems in children with learning disabilities. *Journal of Research in Special Educational Needs*, 7(3), 161–171. doi:10.1111/j.1471-3802.2007.00093.x.

Schonert-Reichl, K. A., & Lawlor, M. S. (2010). The effects of a mindfulness-based education program on pre- and early adolescents' well-being and social and emotional competence. *Mindfulness*, 1(3), 137–151. doi:10.1007/s12671-010-0011-8.

Sedlmeier, P., Eberth, J., Schwarz, M., Zimmermann, D., Haarig, F., Jaeger, S., et al. (2012). The psychological effects of meditation: A meta-analysis. *Psychological Bulletin*, 138(6), 1139–1171. doi:10.1037/a0028168.

Seider, S., Gilbert, J. K., Novick, S., & Gomez, J. (2013). The role of moral and performance character strengths in predicting achievement and conduct among urban middle school students. *Teachers College Record*, 115(8), 1–34.

Seligman, M. E. P., Ernst, R. M., Gillham, J., Reivich, K., & Linkins, M. (2009). Positive education: Positive psychology and classroom interventions. *Oxford Review of Education*, 35(3), 293–311. doi:10.1080/03054980902934563.

Sklad, M., Diekstra, R., De Ritter, M., Ben, J., & Gravesteijn, C. (2012). Effectiveness of school-based universal social, emotional, and behavioral programs: Do they enhance students' development in the area of skill, behavior, and adjustment? *Psychology in the Schools*, 49(9), 892–909. doi:10.1002/pits.21641.

Slone, M., & Shoshani, A. (2008). Efficacy of a school-based primary prevention program for coping with exposure to political violence. *International Journal of Behavioral Development*, 32(4), 348–358. doi:10.1177/0165025408090976.

Snyder, C. R. (2002). Hope theory: Rainbows in the mind. *Psychological Inquiry*, 13(4), 249–275.

Steiner, N. E., Sidhu, T. K., Pop, P. G., Frenette, E. C., & Perrin, E. C. (2013). Yoga in an urban school for children with emotional and behavioral disorders: A feasibility study. *Journal of Child & Family Studies*, 22(6), 815–826.

Suldo, S., Thalji, A., & Ferron, J. (2011). Longitudinal academic outcomes predicted by early adolescents' subjective well-being, psychopathology, and mental health status yielded from a dual factor model. *Journal of Positive Psychology*, 6(1), 17–30. doi:10.1080/17439760.2010.536774.

Waters, L. (2011). A review of school-based positive psychology interventions. *Australian Educational and Developmental Psychologist*, 28(2), 75–90. doi:10.1375/aedp.28.2.75.

Waters, L. (2014). Balancing the curriculum: Teaching gratitude, hope and resilience. In *A Love of Ideas* (pp. 117–124). Sydney, Australia: Future Leaders. Available at http://www.futureleaders.com.au/book_chapters/pdf/Love-of-Ideas/Lea-Waters.pdf.

Waters, L, Barsky, A., Ridd, A., & Allen, K. (2015). Contemplative education: A systematic, evidence-based review of the effect of meditation interventions in schools. *Educational Psychology Review*, 27, 103–134. doi:10.1007/s10648-014-9258-2.

Waters, L., & Stokes, H. (2015). Positive education for school leaders: Exploring the effects of emotion-gratitude and action-gratitude. *Australian Educational and Developmental Psychologist*, 32, 1–22. doi:10.1017/edp.2015.1.

WHO (1986). Ottawa Charter for Health Promotion. *Health Promotion International*, 1(4), 405. doi:10.1093/heapro/1.4.405.

WHO (2000). *The world health report 2000: Health systems: Improving performance.* Available at http://www.who.int/whr/2000/en/whr00_en.pdf?ua=1.

Wierenga, A., & Wyn, J. (2011). Generic Youth Development Framework: A discussion document for Department of Defence. Youth Research Centre, Melbourne Graduate School of Education, University of Melbourne.

Wolmer, L., Hamiel, D., Barchas, J. D., Slone, M., & Laor, N. (2011a). Teacher-delivered resilience-focused intervention in schools with traumatized children following the second Lebanon War. *Journal of Traumatic Stress*, 24(3), 309–16. doi:10.1002/jts.20638.

Wolmer, L., Hamiel, D., & Laor, N. (2011b). Preventing children's posttraumatic stress after disaster with teacher-based intervention: A controlled study. *Journal of the American Academy of Child and Adolescent Psychiatry*, 50(4), 340–348. doi:10.1016/j.jaac.2011.01.002.

Zimmerman, B. J. (2000). Attainment of self-regulation: A social cognitive perspective. In Boekaerts, M., Pintrich, P., & Zeidner, M. (Eds.), *Handbook of Self-Regulation, Research, and Applications* (pp. 13–39). Orlando, FL: Academic Press.

Section 3

Beyond Services: What Would a Recovery-Supporting and Wellbeing-Targeted Society Look Like?

Chapter

21

Positive Tertiary Education in a Residential Setting
Kooloobong Village

Lindsay G. Oades and Gordon B. Spence

Introduction

Positive education is the development of educational environments that enable learners to engage in established curricula, while also acquiring knowledge and skills that help to develop their own and others' wellbeing (Oades et al., 2011; Seligman et al., 2009). A key purpose of universities is to educate students. University residences support this process by providing an immersive and hopefully transformative experience in which students can develop as scholars but also as whole people. Positive education makes this latter step more explicit. In this sense, university residential settings potentially can be perfect exemplars of positive education, a proposition this chapter seeks to advance using the case of Kooloobong Village ('KBV' to the residents). The intention is to extend upon Waters et al.'s (this volume) description of positive education to demonstrate how a 'positive residence' like KBV represents an important facet of positive education at the tertiary level.

KBV is a 553-bed student residential community located on the main campus of the University of Wollongong, NSW, Australia. The case study that follows documents the five enablers that have underpinned both program development and organisational development at KBV. These include (1) web- and smartphone-based self-regulation tools; (2) integrated wellbeing social marketing; (3) positive psychology coaching training and culture; (4) wellbeing-informed activity planning; and (5) the enhanced knowledge, use and spotting of personal strengths. The formal program (commonly referred to as the 'Live Out Loud' program) will also be outlined, along with a description of how it is being formally and informally evaluated.

Finally, the chapter will also address the interface between wellbeing and mental health recovery, insofar as it is relevant to KBV (e.g. student mentors as peer support workers). Relatedly, the role of positive tertiary education in mental health prevention and promotion is also explored, and it is argued that the mission of KBV (enabling lifelong wellbeing for self and others) mirrors modern-day population health agendas, albeit delivered at an organisational unit level.

Positive Education and Wellbeing

Although there are vast and well-developed literatures focused on the engagement, satisfaction and achievement of learners in academic settings (e.g. Jungert et al., 2014; Lee and

Wellbeing, Recovery and Mental Health, ed. Mike Slade, Lindsay Oades and Aaron Jarden.
Published by Cambridge University Press. © Mike Slade, Lindsay Oades and Aaron Jarden 2017

Reeve, 2012), research in these areas appears to be ultimately concerned with behavioural (e.g. student dropout) and/or academic (e.g. grade level) outcomes. Although these literatures have no doubt made positive contributions to the way primary, secondary and tertiary education is organised and managed, less attention has been paid to the holistic development of learners in these environments. However, a recent groundswell of interest in the concept of positive education (Brunwasser et al., 2009; Durlack et al., 2011; Waters et al., this volume) has seen the educational research agenda expand to include the cultivation of wellbeing as a key outcome of formal education at all levels (e.g. Oades et al., 2012; Jarden et al., this volume). Whereas past researchers have examined the influence of college residence halls on academic performance (Bliming, 1989, 1993) and on students' lives more widely (Pascarella et al., 1994), Parameswaran and Bowers (2014) recently have argued that although the context for learning is different, residential environments should meet the same pedagogic standards as coursework. Kooloobong Village is now described as a positive residence, where the learning is focussed on wellbeing.

Kooloobong Village as a Positive Residence

KBV is situated on the main campus of the University of Wollongong (UOW), a regional university located approximately 100 km south of Sydney, Australia. The residence currently houses 550 residents, all of whom are students at UOW. After an expansion from 200 beds in 2013, the name 'Kooloobong Village' was adopted and a commitment was made to run the facility as a 'positive residence'. In this chapter, 'positive residence' is considered to be a facet of positive education. It refers to how organisational development and service delivery at KBV are influenced and guided by the science of positive psychology and the principles of positive organisational scholarship. Positive psychology is the science of optimal human functioning, one that is oriented towards understanding the best aspects of human experience and, through the application of this knowledge, the enhancement of wellbeing (i.e. feeling good and functioning well) in a variety of contexts (Rusk and Waters, 2015). Relatedly, a positive organisation is one where leadership and management seek to enhance the use of strengths, positive communication, positive emotions and positive relationships by all those associated with the organisation. To implement these general principles at KBV, five enablers were developed and are now described.

Program and Organisational Development at KBV: The Five Enablers

The five enablers model (shown in Figure 21.1) was developed to capture the underpinning philosophy of KBV and to provide a set of concepts and principles that would assist staff and students to realise its mission and potential. At no stage have the five enablers been used to prescribe programmed activities or impose a 'top down' agenda. Indeed, the enablers were developed through training and support over an eighteen-month period, after which the community leaders were encouraged to use them for the benefit of all people linked to KBV. This co-production of materials has proven very important to the autonomy and sustainability of the program development, and also the ongoing management style and organisational culture.

As can be seen in Figure 21.1, the outer ring of the model captures common features of 'standard' university residents. As the mission of KBV is to improve lifelong wellbeing, the model specifies key initiatives and planning tools that are designed to help approach

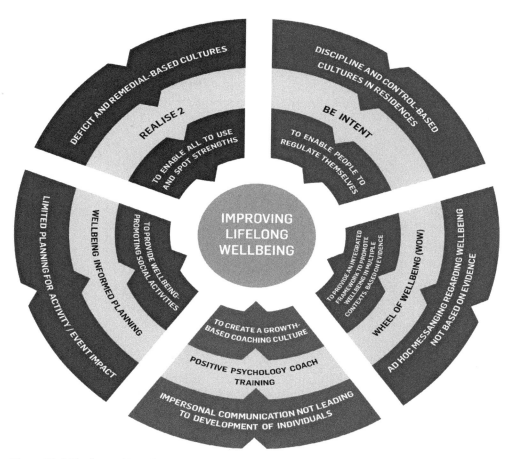

Figure 21.1 The five enablers of program and organisational development at Kooloobong Village.

this target (the inner ring) and actively shape the KBV culture. Each enabler will now be described, starting with the outer ring and moving towards the centre.

Enabler 1: Web- and Smartphone-Based Self-Regulation Tools

The first enabler (between 1 o'clock and 3 o'clock visually) is 'discipline- and control-based cultures in residences'. University residences, colleges, dormitories or housing are predominantly frequented by young adults between 17 and 23 years of age. Popular stereotypes of university students involve their 'running wild' and often attract strict behavioural protocols that aim to minimise unwanted, unhealthy or unlawful behaviours (e.g. binge drinking). To circumvent this dominant paradigm (and remain faithful to a positive psychological approach), KBV encourages residents to take responsibility for their lifestyle decisions via the use of a smartphone-enabled self-regulation tool.

There is significant empirical evidence of the importance of self-regulation skills in day-to-day functioning (e.g. for managing diet, exercise and sleep). At a time when many residents are experiencing significant change (e.g. leaving home and starting university) and coming to terms with increased freedom and responsibilities, the issue of self-regulation becomes paramount.

As with any form of life change, students in residence typically have to deal with a considerable amount of stress and overwhelm. At KBV the aim is to assist students to maintain or adopt coping strategies that will support their intellectual, physical, emotional and social functioning over the long term. To maintain consistency with basic principles of self-regulation (Baumeister and Tierney, 2011), it was important to provide residents with a system that enabled them to develop intentionality (by setting key goals) and maintain awareness (by monitoring and reflecting on progress). In 2014 this enabler was progressed through the piloting of the web-based self-management platform BeIntent.

BeIntent was originally a web-based self-management platform developed for adults in the workplace. Its fundamental aim is to assist individuals to be more intentional about the immediate tasks required for achieving important goals (e.g. remembering to interact with energising people as a step to improving one's mood). In many ways, the technology represents a form of assisted self-regulation. At KBV, BeIntent has been piloted for use with tertiary students, with a key change making it available for smartphone technology and adjusting the words and examples for the tertiary sector. Moreover, at KBV, many of the reminders within the BeIntent platform are adapted to integrate with the other five enablers, particularly the language of the Wheel of Wellbeing.

Enabler 2: Integrated Wellbeing Social Marketing

The second enabler (between 3 o'clock and 5 o'clock visually) refers to 'ad hoc messaging regarding wellbeing, not based on evidence'. Although 'wellbeing' is a frequently used term, it is multifarious in nature and understanding. A lot of the public discourse and social marketing of wellbeing is very piecemeal and often disconnected from wellbeing science (Gordon & Oades, this volume). For this reason, KBV implemented a systematic framework to promote key predictors of wellbeing using established social marketing principles.

The Wheel of Wellbeing (WOW) is a social marketing tool and organisational framework that has been adopted at KBV. The WOW was designed in 2008 and is now part of an ongoing collaboration between the Mental Health Promotion Team at South London and the Maudsley NHS Foundation Trust at Uscreates (for an example of WOW resources visit http://www.wheelofwellbeing.org).

The WOW consists of six domains of mind, body, spirit, people, place and planet, which are visually represented in a wheel to capture the various experiences and conceptions of wellbeing. It was a refinement of the Five Ways to Wellbeing from the New Economics Foundation (NEF, 2011), which was developed to provide a set of evidence-based actions to promote people's wellbeing. The five actions, when ordered to match the first five of the WOW domains, are *Keep Learning, Be Active, Give, Connect and Take Notice*. The WOW added the domain of planet to include the environmental issues linked to wellbeing. These actions were derived from the evidence gathered in the UK government's Foresight Project on Mental Capital and Wellbeing.

The adoption of the WOW as a KBV enabler is related to its utility for framing and organising the Live Out Loud program activities for residents. Where possible, Live Out Loud activities explicitly address the six WOW domains. That is, the range of social and personal activities offered to residents are explicitly categorised into the six domains, with the aim of ensuring that activities are available in all domains. The different colours visually associated with the domains are promoted within the residence. Each of the student leaders is assigned a key domain to promote, and each has different-coloured T-shirts to indicate his or her primary domain of responsibility. Moreover, as part of the broader social marketing of these ideas, KBV also has a 'wellbeing walk'. This walk involves a path to the main university campus buildings with large trees on either side. All students take this walk to go to classes. On the trees on either side of the path are coloured tree bands surrounding the trunks. The bands have repeated WOW domain words (e.g. 'People'), which act as visual reminders of the domains and create intrigue for people less familiar with the positive residence concepts at KBV.

Enabler 3: Positive Psychology Coaching Training and Culture

The third enabler (between 5 o'clock and 7 o'clock visually) refers to 'impersonal communication not leading to development of individuals'. Organisations may communicate to staff and customers through highly impersonal means such as advertising, blanket e-mails, generic training or other nonindividualised means. Although this may lead to information transfer, the nonrelational component may make the message less impactful and certainly less targeted. University residences have a tradition of using tutors, mentors, resident assistants or senior residents, who are often older students who have lived in the residence longer, to provide leadership and mentorship for newer residents. As will be discussed later, this has strong similarities to the use of peer support workers in mental health contexts – except that the lived experience relates to living in residence rather than living with mental illness. As a means to guiding more personalised and tailored growth-based conversations with residents, training in positive psychology coaching has been implemented at KBV, with the ultimate aim of developing a coaching culture.

Oades and Passmore (2014) define positive psychology coaching as an evidence-based approach that seeks to improve short-term wellbeing (i.e. hedonic wellbeing) and sustainable wellbeing (i.e. eudaimonic wellbeing) via the use of knowledge drawn from positive psychology and the science of wellbeing. Importantly, such coaching should also enable a coachee to maintain high levels of wellbeing after it is finished.

At KBV the ultimate aim is to develop a coaching culture, which means that people in the network consistently relate to each other in ways that resemble a coaching style (by using active listening, emphasising strengths, supporting personal goal striving, etc.). At KBV the way that senior student mentors relate to other student residents is a particularly relevant example. Hence, rather than using 'power over' styles, a guiding and Socratic style of relating is encouraged. To date all KBV management and senior student mentors have been trained in coaching skills and continue to be provided with forms of group coaching. As part of the evaluation, more systematic ways to assess the development of a coaching culture are currently being developed.

Enabler 4: Wellbeing-Informed Activity Planning

The fourth enabler (between 7 o'clock and 10 o'clock visually) refers to 'limited planning for activity/event impact'. Activities and events are common to the social and recreational fabric of university residences. These activities may often be driven by tradition or overwhelmingly driven by what is considered fun, which is often focused on alcohol and food consumption. At KBV the aim was to ensure that the important social and recreational activities continued and that their planning was better informed by the science of wellbeing.

Cook et al. (2011) developed the Mental Wellbeing Impact Assessment (MWIA) based on principles and practices of health impact assessment. The essence of the MWIA process can be stated simply in the question, "When a new program, initiative or policy is initiated, what impact is it likely to have on mental wellbeing?" As part of the MWIA toolkit there is a screening instrument which tracks users through the many predictors of mental wellbeing, which range from broader social determinants to individual psychological characteristics. At KBV this tool was adapted to assist residents and staff in planning activities for residents. It is standard practice for university residences to have an array of social and leisure activities for residents. As such activities are so integral to the milieu of the residents, KBV has deliberately and explicitly taken the predictors of wellbeing and built them into activity planning.

Enabler 5: Strengths Knowledge, Use and Spotting

The fifth enabler (between 10 o'clock and 12 o'clock visually) refers to 'deficit- and remedial-based cultures'. Similarly to the critique that positive psychologists have directed towards 'standard' psychology, and the notion that bad is stronger than good (Baumeister et al., 2001), residences also may focus on removing deficits and helping problem students, either academically, behaviourally or emotionally. This is evidenced by increased focus on anti-bullying or anti-harassment campaigns. Although these are important initiatives, they are incomplete. The focus on strengths was seen as an important enabler to assist the development of KBV as a positive residence and has been pursued via the development of strengths knowledge, encouraging strengths use and regular strengths spotting.

Strengths knowledge involves gaining awareness of personal strengths through the use of structured tools such as the Values in Action (VIA) survey (Peterson and Seligman, 2004; Proctor et al., 2011; Madden et al., 2011) or the Realise2 survey. Strengths are defined as personal characteristics that one finds energising and that one is good at (Linley, 2008). For example, people may like writing because it energises them, produces positive emotions and thereby generates a reliable flow of motivation to do it. Moreover, they may also feel that they write to a high standard and experience enhanced competence or effectiveness as a result. *Strengths use* simply refers to the perceived frequency with which one uses a personal strength. *Strengths spotting* involves noticing strengths in self and others when they are being used (Linley et al., 2010). Whereas strengths knowledge is intrapersonal, strengths spotting is interpersonal.

The Realise2 strengths assessment tool has been a key component of developing a strengths-based culture at KBV. Developed in the United Kingdom, Realise2 utilises a three-dimensional model of strengths based on performance, energy and frequency of use. It also organises the assessment results into four areas of reporting (known as the 4M model). Realised strengths, referred to as 'your passions', involve strengths that are high performance, are energising and are currently being used. Learned behaviours, referred to as 'your skillset', involve strengths that can be high performance, are de-energising and are used depending upon need. Weaknesses, referred to as 'your vulnerabilities', generally lead to low performance, being de-energised, and are used at varying levels. Unrealised strengths, referred to as 'your potential', lead to high performance and feeling energised; however, these strengths are currently underused.

The tool is further organised to provide guidance on how one should use the knowledge garnered from completing a Realise2 strengths assessment, including strengths coaching.

The 4M model (as it is known) recommends that individuals Marshal realised strengths for outstanding performance; Moderate learned behaviours for efficiency (and to prevent burn-out); Minimise the impact of weaknesses; and Maximise the use of unrealised strengths for career advancement and personal development.

At KBV strengths assessments have been utilised to assist with improving strengths knowledge, strengths use and strengths spotting amongst the staff, student leaders and residents. In 2014 residents could voluntarily complete a Realise2 assessment to gain a personal strengths profile, and in 2015 all new residents were encouraged to complete an assessment close to their arrival. Several staff members and senior student leaders were also trained in the profile to provide debriefing sessions to help residents understand their personal strengths profiles. The student leader team has also adopted a system of strengths spotting where a person is e-mailed or told directly that one of his or her personal strengths has been spotted. At the time of writing, a new doctoral research program regarding the diffusion of strengths spotting at KBV has also commenced.

In terms of student leader interaction with residents, student leaders have been trained to identify strengths in residents, including during times when the residents' behaviours are outside of required university protocols. For example, rather than simply reporting and seeking further discipline for a misdemeanour, student leaders are encouraged and supported to have strengths-based conversations with residents, including how they can use personal strengths to modify required behaviours to maximise benefits when living in residence. More senior staff responsible for formal disciplinary proceedings on behalf of the University also use this approach.

The Live Out Loud Program

The Live Out Loud Program refers to the covert and observable program components that make up the planned and emergent social and personal activities at KBV. As described, planned activities that emerge from residents are developed in consideration of their likely wellbeing impact. The program is framed around the Wheel of Wellbeing, and all events are promoted in a fashion that links them to the domains of the wheel. For example, a team sporting activity would be promoted under the banner and colour of 'Body' (see Table 21.1). KBV each year employs a resident life coordinator, a resident program coordinator, and a team of student leaders, all of whom are student residents, to coordinate the program of activities.

Figure 21.2 summarises the program logic behind the positive residence programming at KBV. As described in the figure, the goal is a comprehensive and sustainable program that promotes and enables lifelong wellbeing for all people connected to KBV. The program logic outlines the resources that enable the activities, with particular focus on the five enablers described previously. Currently the process evaluation of Year 2 is being completed. As is illustrated in the Year 5 anticipated outcomes, the development of research capacity is also included to enable longer-term rigorous scientific investigation of the trajectories of student wellbeing.

To assist with program development and evaluation, an International Advisory Team has also been appointed, including international experts on wellbeing interventions and practice from Australia, Canada, New Zealand and the United Kingdom. All of the team members have visited KBV.

Table 21.1 Live Out Loud Activities Corresponding to the Wheel of Wellbeing: Evaluation of the Program

Body	Getting Bendy – body balance classes for those who couldn't be bothered waking up on a Monday morning Fit n Fab – personal fitness instructor guides residents through a session Weekend Sports – sports of different sorts run at the University Recreation and Aquatic Centre, basketball/soccer/ultimate frisbee/netball etc.
Mind	We play TED talks that generate interest in a variety of topics and also serve freshly baked cookies/cakes/slice
Spirit	The basement (rec room) is used by students to showcase a country/destination of their choice, for example swapping travel stories and adventures and sampling their favourite dishes
People	Feel the Beat – dance classes with an instructor for salsa and ballroom dance styles The Buzz Zone – the basement (rec room) is used for a party of sorts with different themes every alternate week while promoting safe drinking and "the buzz zone"
Place	Getting Krafty – residents come together to learn knitting, make mason jar lamps, etc. K Adventures – We explore different destinations around Wollongong and the Sydney region
Planet	The students scour the local community (items that people have dumped/left outside for council pickup); upcycling workshops are then run based on the items found, turning them into something useful/pretty with a view to selling these at the fortnightly UOW market stalls, with proceeds yet to be specified
Holistic	Yoga to start the week on a positive and healthy note followed by a healthy breakfast

Wellbeing and Recovery Combined at Kooloobong Village

Thus far the majority of the discussion of KBV has been in terms of wellbeing. Related to the broader question of linking wellbeing ideas with mental health recovery ideas, one could ask, "How might mental health services change if they used the principles of KBV?" The positive psychology principles and the positive organisational principles used are directly relevant to answering this question. However, to explore the issue in further detail, there are three areas to consider.

1. *Mentors are peer support workers.* At KBV, like most university residential facilities, more senior or experienced students are typically employed (often via rent reduction inducements) to provide supportive services to other residents (e.g. mentoring, tutoring). This is because the person has a lived experience of the residence and should have the ability to empathise with and understand the experiences of newer residents. In many ways this is very similar to the consumer–provider model which underpins the peer support approach (Oades et al., 2012).

2. *Residences are built for peer support.* Social support and positive relationships are well established as important predictors and protective factors of wellbeing (Cooke et al., 2011). University residences have a long history (dating back beyond the Oxford and Cambridge model to older monastic traditions) and in many ways are built for their peer support aspects. That is, it is helpful for students to live together because of all of the peer support that they can give each other. Like many residences, KBV actively seeks to promote positive relationships between its residents, who are there for the common

Situation:
- Expanded university residences part of UOW Strategic Plan
- Need for differentiation of positive marketing purposes
- New attractive building facility

Goal:
A comprehensive and sustainable program which promotes and enables lifelong wellbeing for all people connected to KBV.

Inputs

Resources

Strategic Commitment
1) UOW management and ASD commitment to (a) programming and (b) evaluation
2) Statement of Purpose and Mission

Financial Commitment
Student Leader & Staff Training

Industry Expertise
1) 3 year consultancy with Sydney Business School
2) International Advisory Team

Community Engagement

Physical Resources
Building interior decoration and grounds development

Human Resource Commitment
1) Residents
2) Staff/Trainers

Outputs

Activities	Participants
Wheel of Wellbeing framed activities (5D Programming Model)	Student leader training and delivery of activities
	UOW marketing involvement in external and internal messaging
1) Realise 2 strengths profiles	Residents initiating and participating in Realise 2 activities
2) Coaching of student leaders	Residents initiating the coaching of other residents
3) Be-Intent use	
Wellbeing informed planning of activities	Staff involvement in activities
Ongoing Process Evaluation and consultation	UOW Community
Wellbeing informed planning of activities	Participation in focus groups
Utilisation of spaces as part of programming	UOW Community
Live Out Loud Program of resident activities	Staff involvement in activities

Outcomes

Year 1 (2014)	Year 2 (2015)	Year 5 (2018)
Establish baseline of (a) experienced wellbeing and (b) residents' knowledge of wellbeing	Benchmarking of baseline of (a) experienced wellbeing and (b) residents' knowledge of wellbeing	Reputation as world leader in positive student residences
Positive student testimonials of living in a positive residence	Observable wellbeing artefacts when conducting walk through and policy including coaching culture, strengths spotting and unanticipated artefacts	Longitudinal and outcome research commenced to demonstrated empirical benefits
Residents having knowledge of personal strengths	Residents spotting strengths in others	Lifelong impact as evidenced by (a) alumni involvement in program and (b) reports from alumni on programs impact on life
Residents having confidence and knowledge of coaching techniques	Observable Coaching Culture	
Pilot Be-Intent	Students report self-regulation from Be-Intent	Secure additional funding for wellbeing programming
Establish baseline of wellbeing activity participation	Increase in wellbeing activity participation	Influence on UOW programming and environmental factors in expanded residences
Tangible International Advisory Board involvement	Delphi Study completed on "what constitutes a positive residence"	
	Implement signature KBV event	Established and renowned annual signature event
Reinforce relationship between grounds and Goal (Tree Bands)	Design, implement, reinforce additional physical "wellbeing artefacts"	Renowned as location (physical) which fosters and enables wellbeing
Develop and implement Live Out Loud Scale for feedback on activities, social cohesion and environment	Positive Residence Web Presence with explicit information on Positive Residence per se	Secure additional funding for wellbeing programming
	KBV has sustainable capacity to run professional wellbeing centred programming	

Figure 21.2 Program logic for Kooloobong Village program development and evaluation.

purpose of studying at the university. This poses questions for contemporary mental health services that involve residential facilities. What is the common purpose? How well does the organisation promote positive and supportive relationships between residents?

3. *The common objective is to assist people to learn to manage their own wellbeing.* Mental health recovery, mental health promotion and positive education have one unifying theme. They each involve and engender the notion of taking some personal responsibility for one's own health and wellbeing-related behaviours. Hence, the issue of personal agency and autonomy becomes paramount, as do social and environmental factors.

What Is Next for Wellbeing-Enhancing Tertiary Education?

Oades et al. (2011) described various ways to develop a positive university that drew on evidence from positive psychology, positive education and positive organisational scholarship (the idea of positive institutions), as is being done at KBV. Universities and colleges increasingly collect evidence of student performance and graduate outcomes (Bowen et al., 2009). Such data include metrics such as academic performance, student retention, graduate employment and graduate starting salaries. Tertiary institutions have recognised the need for pastoral care for many years; however, only recently has it become more rigorously quantified. One obvious opportunity is to add wellbeing metrics of students and graduates to this suite of measures used to assess the quality of institutions.

In many tertiary and secondary educational institutions, a shift in language is occurring from pastoral care to student wellbeing. However, this is still considered an extracurricular endeavour, not seen as a central or necessary component of the student curriculum. Hence, while tertiary education is linked with better distal economic and health outcomes for individuals involved, there may be even better proximal and distal outcomes if wellbeing literacy is taught explicitly within the curriculum. This is different from teaching students about preventing anxiety and depression. Although an important and worthwhile endeavour, this relates to the absence of ill health as opposed to the presence of positive attributes. With the emerging scientific evidence base from the sciences of wellbeing and positive psychology, there exists a great opportunity to provide future leaders of our communities with explicit education in the literacy of wellbeing.

Conclusion

This chapter has provided a rich organisational case study of Kooloobong Village, a university residence that has been founded on principles derived from positive psychology and positive education, and that aspires to be a positive institution. Arguably KBV serves as a good example of positive education in the tertiary sector, undergirded by a residential community providing immersive and transformative experiences for young people. Given the size and reach of university residential communities, there is great potential for replicating such endeavours and complementing existing approaches, which are primarily focused on preventing illnesses such as anxiety and depression.

References

Baumeister, R. F., Bratslavsky, E., Finkenauer, C., & Vohs, K. D. (2001). Bad is stronger than good. *Review of General Psychology*, 5(4), 323–370.

Baumeister, R., & Tierney, J. (2011). *Willpower: Rediscovering the greatest human strength*. London, UK: Penguin.

Blimling, G. (1989). A meta-analysis of the influence of college residence halls on academic performance. *Journal of College Student Development*, 30(4), 298–308.

Blimling, G. (1993). The influence of college residence halls on students. In Smart, J. (Ed.), *Higher Education: Handbook of Theory and Research 9* (pp. 248–307). New York, NY: AgathonPress.

Brunwasser, S. M., Gillham, J. E., & Kim, E. S. (2009). A meta-analytic review of the Penn Resiliency Program's effect on depressive symptoms. *Journal of Consulting and Clinical Psychology*, 77(6), 1042–1054. doi:10.1037/a0017671.

Bowen, W. G., Chingos, M. W., & Mcpherson, M. S. 2009. *Crossing the finish line: Completing college at America's public universities*. Princeton, NJ: Princeton University Press.

Cameron, K. S. (2008). *Positive leadership: Strategies for extraordinary performance*. San Francisco, CA: Berrett-Koehler Publishers.

Cameron, K., Dutton, J. E., & Quinn, R. E. (Eds.) (2003). *Positive organizational scholarship: Foundations of a new discipline*. San Francisco, CA: Berrett–Koehler Publishers.

Cook, A., Friedli, L., Coggins, T., Edmonds, N., Michaelson, J., O'Hara, K., et al. (2011). *Mental wellbeing impact assessment: A toolkit for well-being*, 3rd ed. London, UK: National MWIA Collaborative.

Durlak, J. A., Weissberg, R. P., Dymnicki, A. B., Taylor, R. D., & Schellinger, K. B. (2011). The impact of enhancing students' social and emotional learning: A meta-analysis of school-based universal interventions. *Child Development*, 82(1), 405–432.

Foresight Mental Capital and Wellbeing Project (2008). Final project report. The Government Office for Science, London.

Govinji, R., & Linley, P. A. (2007). Strengths use, self-concordance, and wellbeing: Implications for strengths coaching and coaching psychologists. *International Coaching Psychology Review*, 2(2), 143–153.

Green, L. S., Robinson, P., & Oades, L. G. (2012). Positive psychology and coaching psychology in schools. In van Nieuwerburgh, C. (Ed.), *Coaching in Education* (pp. 115–132). London, UK: Karnac.

Green, L. S., Oades, L. G., & Grant, A. M. (2006). Cognitive-behavioural, solution-focused life coaching: Enhancing goal striving, well-being and hope. *Journal of Positive Psychology*, 1(3), 142–149. Available at http://www.wheelofwellbeing.org/.

Jungert, T., Alm, F., & Thornberg, R. (2014). Motives for becoming a teacher and their relations to academic engagement and dropout among student teachers. *Journal of Education for Teaching*, 40(2), 173–185.

Lee, W., & Reeve, J. (2012). Teachers' estimates of their students' motivation and engagement: Being in synch with students. *Educational Psychology: An International Journal of Experimental Educational Psychology*, 32(6), 727–747.

Linley, P. A. (2008). *Average to A+: Realising strengths in yourself and others*. Coventry, UK: CAPP Press.

Linley, P. A., Garcea, N., Hill, J., Minhas, G., Trenier, E., & Willars, J. (2010). Strengthspotting in coaching: Conceptualisation and development of the Strengthspotting Scale. *International Coaching Psychology Review*, 5(2), 165–176.

Madden, W., Green, S., & Grant, A. (2011). A pilot study evaluating strengths-based coaching for primary school students: Enhancing engagement and hope. *International Coaching Psychology Review*, 6(1), 71–83.

NEF (2011). *Five ways to wellbeing: New application, new ways of thinking*. London, UK: New Economics Foundation/NHS Confederation.

Oades, L. G., Crowe, T. P., & Nguyen, M. (2009). Leadership coaching transforming mental health systems from the inside out: The Collaborative Recovery Model as person-centred strengths based coaching psychology. *International Coaching Psychology Review*, 4(1), 64–75.

Oades, L. G., Deane, F. P., & Anderson, J. (2012). Peer support in a mental health context. In King, R., Lloyd, C., Meehan, T., Deane, F. P., & Kavanagh, D. (Eds.), *Handbook of Psychosocial Rehabilitation: Practitioner Toolbox*. Oxford, UK: Wiley.

Oades, L. G., & Passmore, J. (2014). Positive psychology coaching, in Passmore, J. (Ed.), *Mastery in Coaching: A Complete Psychological Toolkit for Advanced Coaching* (pp. 15–40). London, UK: KoganPage.

Oades, L. G., Robinson, P., Green, S., & Spence, G. (2011). Towards a positive university. *Journal of Positive Psychology*, 6(6), 432–439.

Parameswaran, A., & Bowers, J. (2014). Student residences: From housing to education, *Journal of Further and Higher Education*, 38(1), 57–74. doi:10.1080/0309877X.2012.699515.

Pascarella, E., Terenzini, P., & Blimling, G. (1994). The impact of residential life on students. In Schroeder, C., & Mable, P. (Eds.), *Realizing the Educational Potential of Residence Halls* (pp. 22–52). San Francisco, CA: Jossey-Bass Publishers.

Peterson, C., & Seligman, M. E. P. (2004). *Character strengths and virtues: A handbook and classification.* Oxford, UK: Oxford University Press.

Proctor, C., Maltby, J., & Linley, P. A. (2011). Strengths use as a predictor of wellbeing and health-related quality of life. *Journal of Happiness Studies*, 12(1), 153–169.

Proctor, C., Tsukayama, E., Wood, A. M., Maltby, J., Fox Eades, J., & Linley, P. A. (2011). Strengths gym: The impact of a character strengths-based intervention on the life satisfaction and wellbeing of adolescents. *Journal of Positive Psychology*, 6(5), 377–388.

Rusk, R. D., & Waters, L. (2015). A psycho-social system approach to well-being: Empirically deriving the five domains of positive functioning. *Journal of Positive Psychology*, 10(2), 141–152. doi:10.1080/17439760.2014.920409.

Salmela-Aro, K., & Upadyaya, K. (2014). School burnout and engagement in the context of demands–resources model. *British Journal of Educational Psychology*, 84, 137–151.

Seligman, M. E. P., Ernst, R. M., Gillham, J., Reivich, K., & Linkins, M. (2009). Positive education: Positive psychology and classroom interventions. *Oxford Review of Education*, 35(3), 293–311. doi:10.1080/03054980902934563.

Williams, V., Oades, L. G., Deane, F. P., Crowe, T. P., & Ciarrochi, J. (2013). Improving implementation of evidence-based practice in mental health service delivery: Protocol for a cluster randomised quasi-experimental investigation of staff-focused values interventions. *Implementation Science*, 8, doi:10.1186/1748-5908-8-75.

Chapter

Living Well in Cities
Towards a Location-Based Model of Perceived Urban Liveability

Pascal Perez and Mohammad-Reza Namazi-Rad

Introduction

How's life? This rather mundane question has become a focus of renewed attention since the first release, in 2011, of the Better Life survey by OECD and its recent updating (OECD, 2013). This survey finds its origin in the famous Stiglitz–Sen–Fitoussi report (2009), which suggests the creation of new indicators to measure social and economic progress, complementary to the traditional GDP marker. Beyond the Easterlin Paradox, justification for such a novel approach lies in the inability of GDP to deal with social inequities and, more fundamentally, with the multidimensional nature of progress. In a recent meeting of the G20 in Australia, the Director of the IMF, Christine Lagarde, made it clear that viable economic development could not be separated from environmental sustainability, social wellbeing and equity.

Another driver of our growing interest in wellbeing is a remarkable and probably irreversible change that happened in 2010. That year, and for the first time in human history, half of the world population lived in cities. At the same time, this proportion had already reached 90% in Australia. There is no questioning the fact that these figures have had and will continue to have a significant impact on the way we plan for and manage our cities. Future cities will have to be liveable and sustainable in order to cope with population growth and resource scarcity.

Liveability Indices

In their Demographic Change and Liveability Panel Report, Hugo and colleagues (MSEWPC, 2010) conclude that 'Three quarters of Australians live in 17 cities with 100,000 or more residents and regardless of any realistic future scenarios more than a majority of the population will continue to live in large cities. However, there is a growing tension between the agglomeration benefits of large city growth and external costs which are compromising the economic, social and/or environmental sustainability of Australia's large cities.' As urban population grows, urban design and infrastructure need to maintain or improve the quality of living environments. Living environments are defined by Detwyler and Marcus (1972) as the external conditions which affect the total population life. The quality of living conditions, also known as 'liveability', is defined by Cox (1972) through eight indicators:

Wellbeing, Recovery and Mental Health, ed. Mike Slade, Lindsay Oades and Aaron Jarden.
Published by Cambridge University Press. © Mike Slade, Lindsay Oades and Aaron Jarden 2017

nuisance-free, healthful, providing proper housing, educational, employment, health and recreational opportunities and modern amenities.

Liveability is a concept closely related to notions such as quality of life and wellbeing. The term 'quality of life' is used to evaluate the general wellbeing of individuals and societies. Standard indicators of the quality of life include not only wealth and employment but also the built environment, physical and mental health, education, recreation and leisure time and social belonging (Gregory et al., 2009). In a nutshell, liveability refers to the environmental conditions that contribute to the quality of life, alongside individual features. It describes the degree to which a place supports quality of life, health and wellbeing. In broad terms, liveable cities are healthy, safe, harmonious, attractive and affordable. They have high amenity, provide good accessibility and are environmentally sustainable (DIT, 2011).

In recent years, the concept of liveability has gained some traction in the media due to the creation of a series of well-publicized quantitative indices used to compare and rank cities around the World (Mercer's Quality of Living index, *The Economist*'s World's Most Livable Cities index or Monocle's Most Liveable Cities index). Initially designed for use by employers assigning hardship allowances as part of job relocation, these indices provide a single rating based on a composite of mostly objective indicators of living conditions. These two characteristics – single ranking and objective indicators – have been subjected to serious criticisms from many experts. Woolcock et al. (2009) remind us that the validity and relevance of composite indicators for developing policy is limited due to the component measures losing their separate meanings through being aggregated. The choice of component measures and form of aggregation reflect the authors' preferences and their perception of the target audience's preferences.

Concerning the single-ranking issue, the Victorian Competition & Efficiency Commission concludes in its State of Liveability report (VCEC, 2008) that while composite measures of liveability offer no benefit for specific policy purposes, disaggregated measures may provide more useful information for policy purposes and decision making, subject to the adequacy of the component indicators. Holloway and Wazjer (2008) note that 'indicators only provide a proxy for performance and are not a perfect or total measure of performance', and establishing the causal relationships between indicators and the real world performance of policy decisions is difficult. We also seek to describe the time-based evolution of liveability, which is not captured in static index values.

The other issue associated with these indices is their reliance on mostly normative criteria of liveability (so-called 'objective' indicators). As a matter of fact, it seems reasonable to assume that safety of a given precinct can be interpreted differently depending on whether the raters use crime rates (objective indicator) or individual perceptions from local residents (subjective indicator). In reaction to the growing dominance of objective indices, Constanza et al. (2008) argue for an integrative framework to evaluate quality of life, drawing from studies on subjective wellbeing (Diener, 2000). In the field of population health, Pacione (2003) comes to the same conclusions, arguing that a fuller understanding of the meaning of objective health status would be facilitated by complementary data covering people's perceptions of their own health, the care they receive or the health services available to them.

Furthermore, empirical evidence generally shows the extent of congruence between objective and subjective indicators of the same phenomenon to vary from a strong relationship to one that is weak or nonexistent, depending on factors such as age, income, education and health status. As reported by Newman et al. (2010) about 'liveable neighbourhood' experiments in Perth (Western Australia), better liveability and its positive externalities are elusive concepts as long as local residents' actual decisions and behaviours are not properly monitored and analysed. A research study led by Marans and Stimson (2011) provides ample evidence of the lack of correlation between so-called objective indicators and subjective perceptions of quality of urban life (QOUL) and suggests that a way forward will need the implementation of coordinated surveys (subjective factors) and monitoring programs (objective factors) associated with modelling frameworks able to digest both types of input data, such as agent-based modelling.

In 2010, the Victorian Competition & Efficiency Commission (VCEC, 2008) proposed a list of liveability indicators to be evaluated individually against objective and subjective criteria: safety, sense of community, cultural diversity, access to services, connectivity (through ICT), transport and housing affordability. More recently, the Property Council of Australia commissioned a national survey ('My City: The People's Verdict') using seventeen indicators to compare major Australian capital cities (Stolper, 2011): urban aesthetics, cleanness, recreational outdoors, cultural venues, public transport, road network, safety, natural environment, sustainability, healthcare services, educational facilities, affordable housing, housing diversity, employment opportunities, standard of living, local climate and social diversity. Participants were asked to rank and value these indicators, providing a rich picture of how people perceived their cities.

Thomas et al. (2011) used interviews to gather information on home, neighbourhood and key demographics in order to demonstrate the importance of neighbourhood density and home location to the perception of liveability in New Zealand. Lupi (2013) discussed the relationships between making room for people in the Dutch housing market and improving affordability and liveability in residential places.

Finally, the Institute for Sustainable Resources, at the Queensland University of Technology (QUT), has recently developed a practical guide to assess the liveability of dwellings in high-density urban areas (QUT Institute for Sustainable Resources, 2010). This guide is informed by local residents' perspectives, based on research undertaken in inner suburbs of Brisbane, Australia. Sense of community is one of the nine key topics identified as important for enhancing the liveability of high-density areas. The practical guide concludes that encouraging a sense of community can bring liveability benefits such as

- psychological benefits for community members from improved social interaction,
- community benefits from an increase in the quality and quantity of social networks and connections (i.e. improved social capital), and
- commercial benefits through improvements in the perceptions of the local area leading to higher demand for local goods and services.

Liveability and Residential Mobility

A household's decision to relocate is influenced by many factors. First of all, work-related circumstances (new jobs or new postings) have a direct influence on relocation. Wong (2002) also identify the following reasons: dissatisfaction with current housing (including both dwelling and location), changes in family situation (income, marital status or family size), attractiveness of alternative properties or market and institutional factors (mortgage rates, Council rates, return on capital and government intervention in housing supply).

In another study, Kim et al. (2005) found that transport-related factors, residential density and quality of schools significantly influence households' intentions to move. These researchers state that increases in travel time to work, travel costs to work and travel costs to supermarkets all increase the probability of a household's decision to move. They further state that higher density and poor quality schools have the same effect.

For many years, economic choice modelling has provided the only conceptually consistent and analytically tractable framework for designing models of residential choice and mobility. In an urban economics context, this willingness-to-pay-driven framework relies on five axioms that provide its consistency: (1) prices adjust to achieve local equilibrium, (2) self-reinforcing effects generate extreme outcomes, (3) externalities cause inefficiency, (4) production is subject to economies of scale and (5) competition generates zero economic profit (O'Sullivan, 2009). Such a framework can convincingly model rational neighbourhood choice based on income-driven demand for public goods or social segregation (racial, religious or cultural). However, many critics of this economically rational choice approach denounce its reductionism, arguing that residential choices encompass factors such as social bonding or sense of place that can hardly fit into a single currency framework.

A newspaper article from Tippet (2005) provides anecdotal evidence of the powerful influence of people's sense of place in shaping the acceptance of their living conditions, regardless of any external evaluation of their quality, based on supposedly objective criteria. In this regard, Louviere and Meyer (2008) have proposed to forge a better alliance between economic theories and behavioural research in order to improve our representation of informal choices within a choice modelling paradigm. But, more fundamentally, one can also argue that price adjustment is merely a consequence of complex social processes rather than the dominant driver of the decisional process itself. From this perspective, willingness to pay is no longer the only prerequisite for formalising a residential choice model.

The advent of agent-based modelling technology has provided an opportunity to relax the conditions imposed by rational choice modelling of residential mobility. In an agent-based model, the decision models that agents use, as well as the information they use (in this case, the liveability of suburbs), can vary through time and is able to accommodate the influence of a complex of interacting factors. The UrbanSim modelling framework (Waddell et al., 2004) uses yearly relocation probabilities based on income and life cycle status. In their ILUTE model, Salvini and Miller (2005) define a 'stress manager' to trigger mobility decisions. The stress manager updates all stressors of a given household at a predefined time interval. Once a household makes the decision to move, the next logical step is to select a new location that meets the household's expectations.

A Conceptual Model of Perceived Liveability

Following Fernandez et al. (2005), we propose to develop a dynamic model of perceived liveability in order to better inform residential choices. The conceptual structure of our liveability model is synthesized in the diagram below (Figure 22.1). From a subjective perspective on liveability, individuals tend to shape their preferences according to six factors describing various aspects of living conditions: (1) home, (2) neighbourhood, (3) transport, (4) entertainment, (5) services and (6) work. Each factor can be described through a series of attributes. The mix of attributes and their associated valence depend on individual perceptions (e.g. an attribute can be perceived negatively or positively).

To implement a decisional process, we propose to adapt the conceptual model proposed by Lindberg et al. (1992) for residential (re)location. The model assumes that a preference is established or a choice is made based on evaluations of the attribute level (Figure 22.2). For each factor, attributes are given even weights and contribute equally to the overall valence of the factor.

Figure 22.1 Conceptual model of perceived liveability.

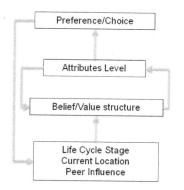

Figure 22.2 Decisional sequence associated with residential choice (adapted from Lindberg et al., 1992).

The factor level can be interpreted as a value/belief structure in which factors can be ranked and given different weights. According to Lindberg et al. (1992), for a given individual, factor ranking and attribute evaluation processes depend on his/her life cycle stage, current location and peer influence. This was confirmed through the empirical work of Li and Walker (2007).

Lindberg et al. (1992) state that individuals hold specific sets of beliefs (or values) about the places they live in. While the belief set remains constant, its structure (e.g. ranking between beliefs) changes according to individual circumstances: stage in life cycle, current location and peer influences. Stage in life cycle relates to age, family situation and professional context. Location-based information is a powerful driver of structural change as individuals try to minimize cognitive dissonance associated with poorly performing beliefs to which they initially gave high priority. For example, urban aesthetics might have been ranked as a high priority by a new resident in a rather dilapidated area who would, after a while, shift his focus on social inclusion or availability of entertainment in the area, as they provide more rewarding outcomes. When the structure of the belief set stabilizes, each belief – equivalent to a liveability driver – is assessed against a set of attributes whose content and significance are entirely subjective. Each belief is assessed against an undetermined number of attributes in order to inform the individual level of satisfaction. For example, a neighbourhood could be assessed against five or more attributes, ranging from friendliness to cleanness. Some attributes will be given high positive values, while others will be given very low values. The way each individual processes this array of values is largely unknown, but the result directly informs individuals' preferences to stay where they are or to move to a 'better' place.

Overall, Lindberg et al. (1992) conclude that 'subjects with children at home prefer to live farther from the city centre, whereas the youngest and oldest subjects are those who prefer most to live centrally. For all subjects, fulfilment of preferences is perceived to depend much on neighbourhood quality. The primary reason for the differences in residential-location preference is that the preferences expressed by subjects who prefer to live father away are more influenced by the psychological values (freedom, well-being, and togetherness), whereas comfort was a more important determinants of the remaining subjects' preferences.'

Location-Based Model of Urban Liveability

In September 2011, we conducted 500 computer-assisted telephone interviews (CATI; response rate 35%)) with people living in southeast Sydney, Australia. Table 22.1 summarizes the questionnaire's domain content; it is worth noting the diachronic nature of the interview (present and past living conditions), which allowed a better understanding of sociodemographic drivers of residential change. Twenty complementary face-to-face interviews were conducted with key interviewees belonging to specific sociodemographic groups in order to clarify some results of the telephonic survey.

We also mapped and extracted locations of various points of interest (*PoIs*) corresponding to the different factors of perceived liveability previously described. For example, we geocoded locations of religious buildings, community centres, shopping centres, recreational precincts, police stations, schools, childcare centres, hospitals, private clinics, sport centres, parks, beaches, bus stops and railway stations. These PoIs were then linked to each interviewee as he or she was asked to provide the closest crossroad to his or her residential place (according to three concentric radii: 500 m, 1 km and 2 km).

Table 22.1 Questionnaire Used in Southeast Sydney (September 2011)

Part I – Population demographics
- Current demographics (household and individual)
- Forecast and modelled future demographics.

Part II – Liveability at the current residential address
- Belief/value ranking (my home, my neighbourhood, my services, my entertainment, my job, my transport)
- Evaluation of attribute level (perception)

Part III – Liveability at the previous residential address
- Updating on demographics at the time
- Belief/value ranking at the time
- Evaluation of attribute level (perception)

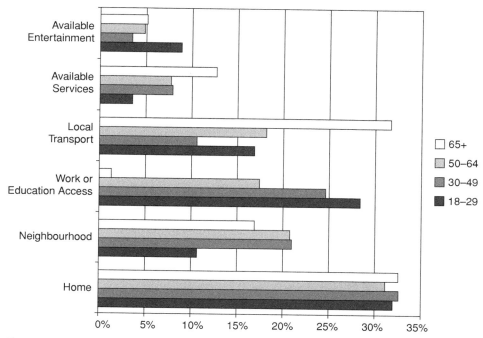

Figure 22.3 Proportion of interviewees considering each liveability factor as 'important' by age group (500 interviews; September 2011, southeast Sydney).

As expected, Figure 22.3 shows that various demographic groups display contrasting priorities in ranking the six liveability factors. While Home is an important factor across all groups, Local Transport and Available Services are particularly relevant to older generations (65+); younger generations are particularly sensitive to Access to Education and Available Entertainment compared with other groups.

Attributes associated with each liveability factor in the survey are then used to assess individual levels of satisfaction attached to each factor. Figure 22.4 shows the overall distribution of satisfaction across seven attributes describing the Transport factor (three attributes for private and four for public transport). While cost of private transport is considered as unsatisfactory by 56% of interviewees, its perceived reliability seems higher than that of public transport, despite chronic traffic congestion in the study area. These results can be analysed further by sociodemographic groups or locations.

A linear additive model was fitted to the survey data in order to calculate perceived liveability (*LI*) based on each interviewee's responses. Then, a linear mixed model was derived to predict the influence of objective indicators (based on PoIs) and sociodemographic characteristics on perceived liveability. This model was then applied to all residents living in the study area, based on Census 2006 information (see the Appendix for more details). We end up with a model allocating individual perceptions of liveability to 110,000 residents in the study area. These perceptions change as personal circumstances evolve (age, family situation and income) as well as location-based information (number of PoIs surrounding the home residence).

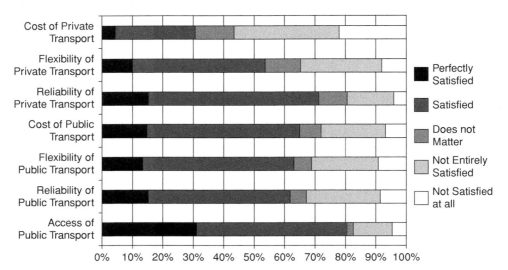

Figure 22.4 Level of satisfaction (%) across seven attributes of the Transport factor (500 interviews; September 2011, southeast Sydney).

Figure 22.5 illustrates outputs from the predictive linear mixed model. Five axes of the radar chart represent liveability factors (Home excluded) as contributing variables, the values correspond to the number of PoIs surrounding the residential location (k) of a given individual (i). The last axis plots the resulting liveability index value ($\times 10$). Left-hand-side graphs present a simple situation where each factor has five PoIs around the residential location; right-hand-side graphs show the influence of doubling the number of PoIs (ten) for the two most important liveability factors associated with a given sociodemographic group. The top pair of graphs correspond to a young (<29 yo) single individual living on $20k per year; the middle pair of graphs correspond to a retiree (>65 yo) living on $50k per year; and the bottom pair of graphs correspond to a young person (<29 yo) living on $80k per year.

In the simple situation where all factors include the same number of PoIs (left-hand-side graphs), the middle case (red polygon) enjoys the highest value of perceived liveability ($L = 1.12$), followed by the bottom case (green polygon; $L = 0.75$) and the top case (blue polygon; $L = 0.20$). These results reflect the interrelated influence of age category and level of income. According to results from the survey, young people in the study area give priority to Access to Education and Available Entertainment, while older groups tend to favour Local Transport and Available Services by comparison with other sociodemographic groups (see Figure 22.3). While doubling the number of PoIs for these individual-specific factors (right-hand-side graphs) does not change the ordering of perceived liveability between the three cases, it has a contrasting impact on the relative improvement for each individual: 130% for the top case, 20% for the middle case, and 30% for the bottom case. These results need to be further validated, but they tend to demonstrate that urban liveability cannot be assumed without looking at the intimate social fabric of our cities and urban precincts. They also suggest that urban planning needs to give more attention to the selective impact of urban renewal options on various sociodemographic groups.

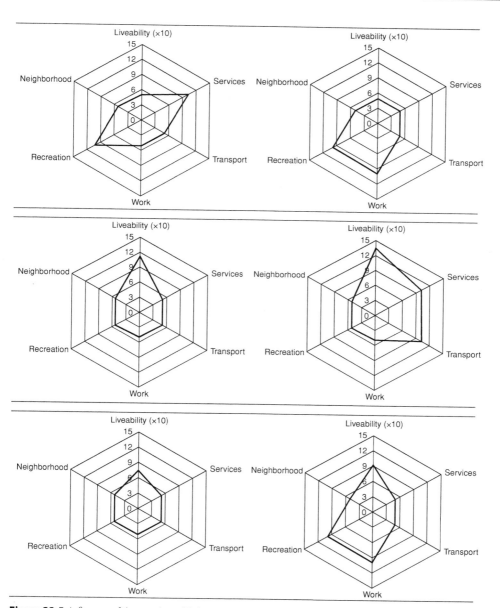

Figure 22.5 Influence of the number of PoIs on perceived liveability (left- and right-hand-side graphs) for three contrasted sociodemographic profiles (top, middle and bottom pairs of graphs).

Conclusion

In this chapter, we have attempted to better define the concept of urban liveability as a way to evaluate the influence of various location-based factors on perceived wellbeing. A semiempirical method was proposed for measuring liveability in South East Sydney as perceived by residents. These perceptions were grouped according to six factors describing various aspects of liveability. A linear additive model was defined in order to calculate a location-based liveability index using computer-assisted telephonic interviews. Then, following Marans and Stimson (2011), we used a linear mixed model to investigate possible relationships between the location-based perception of liveability (subjective factors) and various points of interest (PoIs) available in the study area (objective criteria). The objective was to predict perceived liveability for nonsampled individuals living in the study area.

Our results show that location-based objective indicators associated with sociodemographic information can provide contrasting predictions of individual perceived liveability. Results of this study are particularly applicable to agent-based simulation of residential mobility where reasons for residential mobility (work-related, family-related, education-related etc.) can be disconnected from household-specific criteria for relocation (based on availability, affordability and liveability assessment), providing more realistic mobility patterns than traditional microeconomic models (Perez et al., 2014). The current model represents a first attempt to link individual-specific criteria effectively in a residential choice model, using agent-based technology, to assess the influence of objective environmental indicators. Although we acknowledge the inherent limitations of our empirically driven model, this model has the potential to be refined and expanded to other research domains such as health-related behavior and wellbeing.

There is a need to develop a more integrated research framework where ethnography, epidemiology and modelling interact in a dynamic and iterative way in order to better understand and represent how private factors contribute to personal wellbeing, trigger individual behavior and shape social responses to urban liveability. Moore et al. (2009) have proposed a similar framework for better understanding drug and alcohol abuse and its societal consequences. Following Epstein's proposal, in his book *Generative Social Science* (Epstein, 2006), to use agent-based simulation models to 'grow' social dynamics in silico, our proposed framework would help develop computational metaphors for our urban environments to assess their overall liveability based on heterogeneous and individual wellbeing.

References

Constanza, R., Fisher, B., Ali, S., Beer, C., Bond, L., Boumans, R., et al. (2008). An integrative approach to quality of life measurement, research, and policy. *S.A.P.I.EN.S*, 1.1. Available at http://sapiens.revues.org/169.

Cox, K. R. (1972). *Man, location and behavior: An introduction to human geography*. New York, NY: John Wiley and Sons.

Detwyler, T. R., & Marcus, M. G. (1972). Urbanization and environment in perspective. In Detwyler, T. R., & Marcus, M. G. (Eds.), *Urbanization and Environment*(pp. 3–26). Belmont, CA: Duxbury Press, 3–26.

Diener, E. (2000). Subjective well-being: The science of happiness and a proposal for a national index. *American Psychologist*, 55.(1), 34-43.

DIT (2011). *State of Australian cities 2011*. Canberra, Australia, DIT.

Epstein, J. M. (2006). *Generative social science*. Princeton, NJ: Princeton University Press.

Fernandez, L. E., Brown, D. G., Marans, R. W., & Nassauer, J. I. (2005). Characterizing location preferences in an exurban population: Implications for agent-based modelling. *Environment and Planning B: Planning and Design*, 32, 799–820.

Gregory, D., Johnston, R., & Pratt, G. (2009). Quality of life. In *Dictionary of Human Geography* (5th ed.). Oxford, UK: Wiley-Blackwell.

Holloway, A., & Wajzer, C. (2008). Improving city performance through benchmarking. In Proceedings of the International Cities Town Centres & Communities Society Conference. SGS Economics and Planning/Australia.

Kim, J. H., Pagliara, F., & Preston, J. (2005). The intention to move and residential location choice behaviour. *Urban Studies*, 42, 1621–1636.

Li, J., & Walker, J. L. (2007). Latent lifestyle preferences and household location decisions. *Journal of Geographical Systems*, 9(1), 77–101.

Lindberg, E., Hartig, T., Garvill, J., & Garling, T. (1992). Residential-location preferences across the life span. *Journal of Environmental Psychology*, 12, 187–198.

Louviere, J. J., & Meyer, R. J. (2008). Formal choice models of informal choices: What choice modeling research can (and can't) learn from behavioral theory. In Malhotra, N. K. (Ed.), *Review of Marketing Research*, Vol 4 (pp. 3–32). New York, NY: M. E. Sharpe.

Lupi, T. (2013). Making room for people: Choice, voice and liveability in residential places. *Journal of Housing and the Built Environment*, 28(2), 413–414.

Marans, R. W., & Stimson, R. J. (Eds.) (2011). *Investigating quality of urban life. Theory, methods and empirical research*, Social Indicators Research Series, Vol. 45. Springer.

Moore, D., Dray, A., Green, R., Hudson, R., Jenkinson, R., Siokou, C., et al. (2009). Extending drug ethno-epidemiology using agent-based modelling. *Addiction*, 104(12), 1991–1997.

MSEWPC (2010). Demographic Change and Liveability Panel Report, an appendix to A Sustainable Population for Australia issues paper. Canberra, Australia: MSEWPC.

Newman, P., Giles-Corti, B., & Falconer, R. (2010). Is practice aligned with the principles? Implementing new urbanism in Perth, Western Australia. *Transport Policy*, 17(5), 287–294.

OECD (2013). How's Life? 2013: Measuring Well-Being. doi:10.1787/9789264201392-en.

O'Sullivan, A. (2009). *Urban economics* (seventh ed.). Singapore: McGraw-Hill International Edition.

Pacione, M. (2003). Urban environmental quality and human wellbeing: A social geographical perspective. *Landscape and Urban Planning*, 65, 19–30.

Perez, P., Huynh, N., Cao, V. L., Wickramasuriya, R., & Berryman, M. (2014). TransMob: An agent based simulation of transport demand and residential mobility in South East Sydney. In Miguel Quesada, F. J., Amblard, F., Barceló, J. A., Madella, M., Agirre, C., & Ahrweiler, P. (Eds.), *Advances in Computational Social Science and Social Simulation*. Barcelona: AutònomaUniversity of Barcelona. Available at http://ddd.uab.cat/record/125597.

QUT Institute for Sustainable Resources (2010). High-density liveability guide. Available at http://www.highdensityliveability.org.au/index.php.

Salvini, P., & Miller, E. J. (2005). ILUTE: An operational prototype of a comprehensive microsimulation model of urban systems. *Networks and Spatial Economics*, 5, 217–234.

Stiglitz, J. E., Sen, A., and Fitoussi, J. P. (2009). *Mismeasuring our lives: Why GDP doesn't add up*. Commission on the Measurement of Economic Performance and Social Progress, The New Press.

Stolper, D. (2011). *My city: The people's verdict*. Sydney, Australia: The Property Council of Australia.

Thomas, J. A., Walton, D., & Lamb, S. (2011). The influence of simulated home and neighbourhood densification on perceived liveability. *Social Indicators Research*, 104(2), 253–269.

Tippet, G. (2005). Suburban dreaming. *The Age*, August 20, 2005.

VCEC (2008). *A state of liveability: An inquiry into enhancing Victoria's liveability*. Melbourne, Australia: Victorian Competition and Efficiency Commission.

Waddell, P., & Ulfarsson, G. F. (2004). Introduction to urban simulation: Design and development of operational models. In Button, K. J., Stopher, P., Heynes, K. E., & Hensher, D. A. (Eds.), *Handbook in Transport, Volume 5: Transport Geography and Spatial Systems* (pp. 203–236). Pergamon Press.

Wagner, P., & Wegener, M. (2007). Urban land use, transport and environment models: Experiences with an integrated microscopic approach. *disP*, 170(3), 45–56.

Wong, G. K. M. (2002). A conceptual model of the household's housing decision-making process: The economic perspective. *Review of Urban & Regional Development Studies*, 14, 217–234.

Woolcock, G. (2009). Measuring up? Assessing the liveability of Australian cities. In Manginn, P., & Jones, R. (Eds.), *State of Australian Cities, National Conference*. Canberra, Australia: PromacoConventions.

Appendix – Liveability Model

First, we assume the following notation for our six liveability factors: H for Home, N for Neighbourhood, S for Services, E for Entertainment, WE for Work or Education and T for Transport. Then, we can derive that h_i, n_i, s_i, e_i, we_i and t_i represent the value of satisfaction for each attribute associated with a specific factor (i is the index corresponding to the number of attributes for each factor). We also assume that factors with higher rankings of importance are given a greater weight (W_j with j 1 to 6) for each interviewee. We then end up with the following linear additive model of individual perceived liveability:

$$LI = W_1 \times \sum_{i=1}^{4} \frac{h_i}{4} + W_2 \times \sum_{i=1}^{5} \frac{n_i}{5} + W_3 \times \sum_{i=1}^{4} \frac{s_i}{4} + W_4 \times \sum_{i=1}^{5} \frac{e_i}{5}$$

$$+ W_5 \times \sum_{i=1}^{4} \frac{we_i}{4} + W_6 \times \sum_{i=1}^{7} \frac{t_i}{7}.$$

A second step consists in predicting the value of perceived liveability based on location-based objective indicators (PoIs) and sociodemographic characteristics. We use the following linear mixed model to predict the value of perceived liveability for any individual (i) living in location k within the study area:

$$L_{ik} = \alpha_0 + \langle b \rangle C'_{ik} \beta \langle /b \rangle^* + \langle b \rangle P'_{ik} \delta \langle /b \rangle + \langle b \rangle A'_{ik} \alpha \langle /b \rangle + \langle b \rangle I'_{ik} \alpha \langle /b \rangle^*$$

$$+ \langle b \rangle HT'_{ik} \alpha^{\langle /b \rangle **} + v^*_k + \varepsilon^*_{ik},$$

where α_0 denotes the model intercept and C'_{ik} is a column vector which measures the density of PoIs belonging to each of the six liveability factor categories around a given residential location. We consider concentric 0.5, 1, and 2 km radii around a residential location. The column vector P_{ik} is an approximation for the number of people working and living around the selected individual. The column vector A_{ik} contains variables corresponding to age categories. The column vector I_{ik} contains variables corresponding to household income categories. Finally, the column vector HT_{ik} contains variables corresponding to household type categories. We ascribe v^*_k as a random effect corresponding to location k and ε^*_{ik} as a random error associated with individual i living in location k.

Chapter

23

Wellbeing-Enhancing Workplaces

Kathryn M. Page, Allison J. Milner, Amanda Allisey,
Andrew Noblet and Anthony D. LaMontagne

Introduction

Mental health is a core component of quality of life. Without it, people are likely to experience problems or distress in various aspects of their lives, including their relationships, their work and their physical health (Huppert and So, 2009; WHO, 2005). Improving mental health helps people to function more effectively at work and in society more generally (Dewe and Kompier, 2008). People with higher levels of mental health achieve superior outcomes including better work performance, better social relationships and better physical health (e.g. Huppert, 2009; Lyubomirsky et al., 2005; Richman et al., 2005). Clearly mental health is an important resource that allows people to lead more successful and subjectively enjoyable lives.

Participating in work can significantly improve employee mental health and, importantly, facilitate effective recovery from mental illness. However, while being employed is better for mental health than being unemployed in general, it is important to note that jobs with poor psychosocial quality are worse for mental health than having no job at all (Butterworth et al., 2011). In this chapter, we explore the impact that work can have on mental health outcomes and what workplaces can do to enhance the wellbeing of those already employed. This includes looking at the 'dark side' of work and how workplaces can harm employee mental health, as well as what workplaces can do to enhance employee wellbeing. We argue that wellbeing-enhancing workplaces are those that both prevent the harmful aspects of work by identifying, assessing and managing stressful working conditions and enhance the health-promoting and-protective aspects of work.

Understanding Mental Health

It is well known that depression is predicted to be the main contributor to the burden of disease by 2030 (WHO, 2008). However, minimising depression does not, by itself, guarantee good mental health. Over the last two decades, researchers and mental health experts have significantly advanced their understanding of what it means to have good mental health. Increasingly, experts challenge a *disease-based model of mental health*, which defines mental health as the absence of mental disorder, and focus on a *health-based model of mental health* (Macik-Frey et al., 2009). A health-based model defines mental health as a state of wellbeing or, more specifically, as the presence of positive emotional wellbeing (e.g. joy, happiness,

Wellbeing, Recovery and Mental Health, ed. Mike Slade, Lindsay Oades and Aaron Jarden.
Published by Cambridge University Press. © Mike Slade, Lindsay Oades and Aaron Jarden 2017

contentment), psychological wellbeing (e.g. a sense of purpose, achievement and mastery) and effective social functioning (Diener, 2000; Huppert, 2005; Keyes, 2002, 2005; see also Chapter 8 of this volume).

The distinction between mental health as the absence of disease and mental health as the presence of wellbeing has broadened the array of models used to describe and measure mental health. Keyes' (2002, 2005) concept of good mental health or *flourishing* recognizes that optimal mental health includes both a low level of mental illness, including depression, and a high level of positive wellbeing. Only a small proportion of the population, at least in the United States, meets this criterion (17%), with the majority of people being only moderately mentally healthy (Keyes, 2005). Further, those with optimal mental health report fewer health limitations, missed work days and work cutback days and healthier psychosocial functioning than those with 'incomplete' mental health (i.e. not meeting the criteria for complete mental health), suggesting that mental health is best represented by considering mental health and mental ill health as separate but correlated constructs.

Understanding different approaches to defining and measuring mental health is important for informing the types of interventions that may be successful at enhancing wellbeing. Specifically, a more complete approach to mental health highlights the importance of both preventing the factors that harm mental health and promoting the factors that promote wellbeing or flourishing mental health.

Work and Mental Health

Work has real and demonstrable impacts on employee mental health outcomes. Both unemployment and underemployment are detrimental to mental health. However, while there are health benefits to being employed, being in poor-quality and stressful work is worse for mental health than having no job at all (Butterworth et al., 2011). Therefore, for those employed, work needs to be 'good' work if it is to be health-promoting (Black, 2008; Waddell and Burton, 2006). Importantly, working towards and accessing good work also plays a role in personal recovery from mental health problems, providing access to financial, psychological and social rewards, including a sense of self-worth, supportive relationships, goal attainment and achievement (see Chapter 3 of this volume).

Mental health problems are common amongst working people (Sanderson and Andrews, 2006). In 2007, the prevalence of lifetime-diagnosed depression in the Australian workforce was 12% amongst men and 18% amongst women (14.7% total) (LaMontagne et al., 2010b). This is equivalent to 1.54 million people in the Australian population. Subclinical mental health problems and generalised distress, alongside clinical disorders such as major depression and generalised anxiety, are also prevalent in the working population (Hilton et al., 2008; Sanderson and Andrews, 2006). Therefore, workplaces can play a role in supporting mental health promotion initiatives and the early identification of mental health problems amongst working people, thereby facilitating tertiary prevention efforts.

Work as a Determinant of Mental Health

The relationship between work and health is a matter of great importance to employees and employers alike. In industrialised countries, legislation covers many aspects of the conditions under which people work for pay, covering hours of work, health and safety, equal opportunity and employee and industrial relations. However, despite the presence of legislation, some work environments can be damaging to mental health (Butterworth et al., 2011). Poor-quality jobs are those where a person is exposed to psychosocially hazardous work conditions or job stressors. These are problems with the way work is designed or managed or in its social and organisational context (Leka et al., 2010). Exposure to job stressors is widespread. In Australia, around 25% of working women and 18% of working men (roughly 1 in 4) experience job stress (LaMontagne et al., 2008). Similar rates have been reported in Europe, where work-related stress affects one in three workers (European Agency for Health and Safety at Work, 2002).

Exposure to stressful working conditions, such as excessive job demands combined with little job control, predicts a range of negative employee outcomes, including psychological distress, depressive symptoms, depression, anxiety, suicide and other mental health problems (LaMontagne et al., 2010a; Michie and Williams, 2003; Stansfeld and Candy, 2006). Other established psychosocial work factors known to predict mental health problems include a lack of social support at work, effort–reward imbalance and job insecurity (de Lange et al., 2003; Rugulies et al., 2006; Stansfeld and Candy, 2006).

Importantly, the presence of job demands alone does not necessarily indicate that people are engaged in 'bad' work. High job demands may benefit health when they are balanced by adequate organisational and personal resources. For example, active jobs which involve high demands in combination with high control or decision latitude can promote feelings of mastery (Karasek and Theorell, 1990). Mastery is an important feature of psychological wellbeing (Ryan and Deci, 2000; Ryff, 1989). High job demands can also contribute positively to employee engagement – a positive, active state defined by the characteristics of vigour, absorption and dedication in pursuit of one's work goals – when job resources, such as organisational climate, innovativeness and supervisor support are high (Bakker et al., 2007).

There are many paths through which work can be beneficial to psychological wellbeing, contributing to feelings of self-esteem and self-worth and providing opportunities for employees to pursue goals, experience mastery and develop meaningful relationships (LaMontagne and Keegel, 2009; Waddell and Burton, 2006). The evidence base regarding what constitutes 'good' work, defined as having positive, health-promoting working conditions (Black, 2008), is underdeveloped relative to the evidence base regarding adverse or negative working conditions (LaMontagne et al., 2014). However, research to date has identified a fair organisational climate and commitment to work, the ability of workers to exert control over the task they are doing (Holmgren et al., 2014), good communication in the workplace, high social support and manageable job demands at work as important elements of healthy work (Lowe et al., 2003). Some other potentially important elements include having meaningful work, being able to use one's skills and strengths at work and experiencing growth and development through work (Black, 2008; Waddell and Burton, 2006). Positive and healthy leaders developing supportive and authentic leadership practices in the workplace, for example, are also an important conduit to healthy work (Macik-Frey et al., 2008; Quick et al., 2007; Quick and Quick, 2004; Vella-Brodrick and Page, 2009). Good work has been associated with a range of beneficial individual and organisational outcomes, including high work ability (Arnetz and Blomkvist, 2007; Lindberg et al., 2006) and self-rated health (Lohela et al., 2009). The workplace is also an important setting for mental health promotion and early intervention regardless of cause (LaMontagne et al., 2014).

Creating Wellbeing-Enhancing Workplaces

Given that work can have either a healthy or deleterious effect on mental health, wellbeing-enhancing workplaces are those that strive to prevent the factors that can harm mental health and promote the positive aspects of work and worker strengths and positive capabilities.

Preventing Harm: Managing and Preventing Stressful Working Conditions

Until recently, research on how to prevent stress was dominated by individual-level activities (LaMontagne et al., 2007a): for example, teaching employees how to better manage stress through relaxation training or improving individual help-seeking behaviour for mental health problems. Although individually focused activities can positively impact a person's stress response, and are therefore an important secondary prevention strategy, they have limited effectiveness over the longer term. Primary prevention strategies represent a more sustainable long-term approach to stress (LaMontagne et al., 2007a). Primary strategies involve implementing organizational-level strategies that address stressors at their source, for example, targeting elements of the psychosocial working environment. The systems approach to job stress prevention involves the best of both primary- and secondary-level strategies. Primary preventative strategies typically occur at the organisational level and involve identifying and addressing stressors at their source (e.g. reducing workload or giving workers more control over their work). Secondary strategies are typically individually focused activities that help workers to respond more effectively to stressful working conditions, for example, teaching (LaMontagne et al., 2007a, 2007b). A systems approach also requires active and meaningful employee participation and strategies that are tailored to an organisation's specific context and needs (LaMontagne et al., 2007a, 2007b).

However, while these systematic reviews indicate what to do, questions still remain regarding how to do it. Intervention strategies need to be tailored and context-appropriate (Biron et al., 2012) to stand the best chance for success. This poses a problem in practice: the principles of preventing or managing stressful working conditions are necessarily broad, and considerable effort is needed to tailor solutions to unique work settings (e.g. accounting for how the business is run, worker sociodemographics and occupational skill levels, type of workplace, presence or absence of a union). Although knowledge of context-appropriate solutions for various work settings is growing, there is still a need to apply principles and develop solutions on an organisation-by-organisation basis. This has likely contributed to the slow uptake of effective job stress prevention and control strategies in practice; for example, Human Resources or OH&S staff commonly cite Employee Assistance Programs as their organisation's response to job stress concerns (LaMontagne et al., 2007b). Other barriers to the implementation of evidence-based interventions stem from issues of stigma similar to those concerning mental illness in general, such as a persisting view of job stress as an individual weakness rather than an organisational issue (Page et al., 2013).

Applying a systems approach to stress prevention would likely have a significant impact on both the prevalence and cost of work-related mental illness. LaMontagne et al. (2010b) found that, of the $12.6 billion annual costs accrued to society through major depression amongst working Australians, approximately $730 million was attributable to job strain. Further, the majority of these costs related to employment factors such as lost productivity, absenteeism, turnover and employee replacement costs. Importantly, evidence suggests that job stress – and the associated impacts on individual and organisational health – is preventable through improvements to the psychosocial working environment.

Promoting the Positive: Identifying and Developing the Positive Aspects of Work and Worker Capabilities and Strengths

There is also growing evidence regarding what workplaces can do to promote the positive aspects of work, including developing the positive aspects of work and worker strengths and capabilities. The relevant intervention principles and evidence in this area come predominantly from the fields of positive psychology, positive organisational behaviour and positive organisational scholarship (Macik-Frey et al., 2007; Macik-Frey et al., 2009; Wright and Quick, 2009). Positive psychology focuses on the conditions and processes that contribute to the flourishing or optimal functioning of people, groups and institutions (Gable and Haidt, 2005). Positively focused interventions apply strength-based methods to achieve positive outcomes. Strength-based methods are applied to identify and enhance strengths or what is being done well, rather than trying to identify and fix what is 'wrong' in an individual, group or organisation (Schaufeli, 2004). To date, research in this area has largely focused on individual-level interventions that enhance well-being (Gable and Haidt, 2005). However, there is considerable scope and appetite for more positive-psychology-based organisational-level wellbeing research. While there is not yet a preferred approach to promoting the positive aspects of work, initial research suggests that important gains can be made when organisations invest in the development of positive leaders, provide access to meaningful work and promote a positive organisational climate (Cameron, 2008; Cameron et al., 2003; Cotton and Hart, 2003; Macik-Frey et al., 2008; Quick et al., 2007; Quick and Quick, 2004).

Wellbeing-Enhancing Workplaces in Practice

Recognising that both individual and workplace factors play a role in preventing stress and promoting wellbeing, workplaces need to implement activities at multiple levels within the organisation to be most effective at promoting employee wellbeing. Wellbeing activities also need to integrate wellbeing promotion and stress prevention. This ensures that strategies cover both sides of the illness-to-wellness continuum. Last, to be both sustainable and effective over the longer term, workplaces need to take a strategic approach to managing wellbeing and mental health in the workplace. But what does this look like in practice?

Our team has devoted the majority of our careers to investigating what works to prevent stress and promote wellbeing in the workplace from a practical perspective. Like many practitioners in this space, my (first author) intervention efforts started at the individual level. My doctoral studies involved designing and testing a positive-psychology-based employee wellbeing program. The program, called the Working for Wellness Program, consisted of six one-hour sessions delivered to full-time employees in small groups (Page and Vella-Brodrick, 2010). The sessions covered a number of empirically supported positive psychology strategies including knowing and using strengths, striving for self-concordant goals, getting into flow and cultivating positive relationships. Program participants reported significant increases in wellbeing following the program in comparison to a randomly selected control group (Page and Vella-Brodrick, 2010). From here, I designed and tested a number of other employee wellbeing programs, including a team-based version of the Working for Wellness Program, and later collaborated with a mental health foundation (SuperFriend.com.au) to develop a positive-psychology-based online wellbeing program for teams (http://www.teamtopia.com).

Later, our team was funded by the Victorian Health Promotion (VicHealth) to design a leadership-based stress prevention program, called Creating Healthy Workplaces. Most recently, we expanded the Creating Healthy Workplaces program to include a mental health promotion element in collaboration as part of a broader research team. The latter program, funded by VicHealth and the Victorian WorkCover Authority, is currently being evaluated by a cluster randomised control design, funded by a National Health and Medical Research

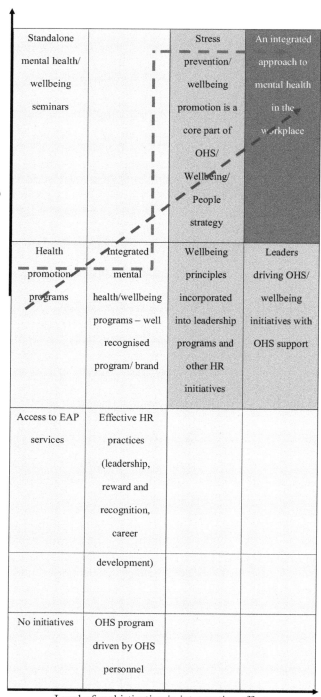

Figure 23.1 Pathways towards an integrated approach to workplace mental health.
Note: dotted lines indicate that there are multiple pathways through which employers can implement an integrated approach to optimal mental health in the workplace.

Table 23.1 Success Factors for Creating Wellbeing-Enhancing Workplaces

Success factors	
• Be strategic: Wellbeing and mental health needs should be a fundamental factor within the company's workforce (e.g. human capital) strategy (alongside or within safety).	• Build credibility with the executive team by demonstrating an understanding of business risks and needs and delivering on objectives.
• Make leaders and managers accountable for driving initiatives, with the support of OH&S and HR. Promote this level of commitment to the broader organisation, for example by displaying leadership commitment statements, signed and dated by a member of the executive team.	• Learn from others who have applied strategies in other organisations; incorporate case stories from other well-respected organisations in your business cases.
• Deliver strategies according to sound business and organisational change principles. This includes effective long-range planning – potentially planning for less but executing well in order to deliver on KPIs and achieve the desired outcomes.	• Integrate workplace mental health messages into existing HR or OH&S initiatives or programs, for example leadership training. Leverage from what has worked in the past.
• Draw on effective marketing and communication principles (and internal resources, where possible) to get clear, consistent messages across and engage all levels of an organisation.	• Innovate. Organise major events that increase the visibility of safety/wellbeing. Use word of mouth well. Refresh and reinvigorate efforts regularly. Ensure systems support rather than thwart innovation.
• Upskill HR or OH&S professionals regarding how to integrate optimal mental health strategies into a workforce strategy.	• Recruit/support/leverage from passionate OHS managers/senior-level staff members.

Note: Refer to superfriend.com.au for more information.

Council Partnership grant. Our collective experience in this area has enabled us to collect a number of evidence-based but practical insights into what workplaces can do to prevent stress and enhance wellbeing. We have found that most workplaces commence their wellbeing journey through the provision of various nonintegrated and ad hoc wellbeing or mental health initiatives and then, over time, move towards more sophisticated and integrated initiatives (see Figure 23.1 for a diagrammatic representation of this). Most commonly, nonintegrated or ad hoc workplace wellbeing strategies include Employee Assistance Programs and lunchtime wellbeing seminars. Ad hoc initiatives are rarely effective and are often viewed by employees as a 'nice to have' or optional extra. Over time, some employers move towards more sophisticated efforts. Such efforts are often championed by a single passionate individual or motivated by a significant workplace event (e.g. a high-profile health and safety event), both of which can help to create organisational readiness to change.

Although, as Figure 23.1 shows, there are multiple possible pathways towards workplace mental health, there are things workplaces can do to improve their chances of building a wellbeing-enhancing workplace.

Table 23.1 summarises a number of enablers for creating wellbeing-enhancing workplaces, which we identified in a recent SuperFriend study (Page et al., 2014). As described here, some of the most successful efforts we have seen are those where wellbeing is integrated into the human capital or people strategy. This ensures that wellbeing is of strategic importance within the organisation and prioritised accordingly. Organisations that make leaders and managers accountable for driving wellbeing initiatives also tend to be more effective. This sends a strong message to the workplace that staff wellbeing is important. Like any business initiative, it is important that wellbeing initiatives are implemented according to sound business and organisational change principles. This includes setting real and measurable targets, tracking progress and coupling projects with well-thought-out communication and change action plans. Another useful idea is to incorporate wellbeing messages and strategies into existing programs, including leadership development and induction programs. This helps to ensure that wellbeing is integrated right across the employee lifecycle rather than being a standalone initiative. We also believe wholeheartedly in the importance of innovation and creative thinking to ensure that wellbeing initiatives are 'front and centre' in people's minds. Organisations must continually refresh wellbeing initiatives if they are to become embedded in the organisation's culture.

Summary and Conclusion

The benefit of work to mental health and recovery from mental ill health has been well noted. However, while in general, employment is better for mental health than being unemployed, it is important to note that jobs of poor psychosocial quality are worse for mental health than having no job at all (Butterworth et al., 2011). In this chapter, we explored the impact that work can have on mental health outcomes and what workplaces can do to enhance the wellbeing of those already employed. First, we outlined the importance of identifying, assessing and managing stressful working conditions in order to prevent harm to worker mental health. Next, we considered how workplaces can promote the positive aspects of work, including employee strengths and positive capabilities. Finally, we highlighted several potential pathways through which workplaces can prevent job stress and promote employee wellbeing.

A key point in this chapter is that there is no one right way to create a wellbeing-enhancing workplace. Workplaces can build momentum towards more enduring and sustainable workplace programs, such as those discussed here, by starting with smaller initiatives. It is critical that senior managers understand why wellbeing is important in order to invest in these larger programs, and sometimes this becomes evident through frequent, smaller initiatives. However, although these smaller efforts are useful in the shorter term, workplaces must work towards more sophisticated efforts. This should involve regularly assessing the psychosocial work environment for risks to mental health, implementing tailored stress prevention and wellbeing promotion programs at both the organisational and individual level, evaluating the success of these efforts and ensuring that workers are meaningfully engaged in the process. Although these initial investments may seem onerous, the value of promoting wellbeing, for individuals, business and society, has been well documented, and wellbeing promotion can have a lasting impact over time.

References

Arnetz, B., & Blomkvist, V. (2007). Leadership, mental health, and organizational efficacy in health care organizations. Psychosocial predictors of healthy organizational development based on prospective data from four different organizations. *Psychotherapy and Psychosomatics*, 76(4), 242–248. doi:10.1159/000101503.

Bakker, A. B., Hakanen, J. J., Demerouti, E., & Xanthopoulou, D. (2007). Job resources boost work engagement, particularly when job demands are high. *Journal of Educational Psychology*, 99(2), 274–284.

Biron, C., Karanika-Murray, M., & Cooper, C. (2012). Organizational interventions for stress and well-being – an overview. In Biron, C., Karanika-Murray, M., & Cooper, C. L. (Eds.), *Improving Organizational Interventions for Stress and Well-Being: Addressing Process and Context* (pp. 21–38). London, UK: Routledge/Psychology Press.

Black, C. (2008). *Working for a healthier tomorrow: Dame Carol Black's review of the health of Britain's working age population.* Norwich, UK: The Stationery Office.

Butterworth, P., Leach, L. S., Strazdins, L., Olesen, S. C., Rodgers, B., & Broom, D. H. (2011). The psychosocial quality of work determines whether employment has benefits for mental health: Results from a longitudinal national household panel survey. *Occupational and Environmental Medicine*, 68(11), 806–812. doi:10.1136/oem.2010.059030.

Cameron, K. S. (2008). *Positive leadership: Strategies for extraordinary performance.* San Francisco, CA: Berrett-Koehler.

Cameron, K. S., Dutton, J., & Quinn, R. (2003). *Positive organizational scholarship.* San Francisco, CA: Berrett-Koehler.

Cotton, P., & Hart, P. M. (2003). Occupational wellbeing and performance: A review of organisational health literature. *Australian Psychologist*, 38(2), 118–127.

de Lange, A. H., Taris, T. W., Kompier, M. A., Houtman, I. L., & Bongers, P. M. (2003). "The very best of the millennium": Longitudinal research and the demand-control-(support) model. *Journal of Occupational Health Psychology*, 8(4), 282–305. doi:10.1037/1076-8998.8.4.282.

Dewe, P., & Kompier, M. (2008). Foresight Mental Capital and Wellbeing Project. Wellbeing and work: Future Challenges. The Government Office for Science, London, UK.

Diener, E. (2000). Subjective well-being. The science of happiness and a proposal for a national index. *American Psychologist*, 55, 34–43.

European Agency for Health and Safety at Work (2002). European Week 2002: Preventing psychosocial risks at work. Accessed 10 March 2010. Available at http://ew2002.osha.europa.eu/.

Gable, S. L., & Haidt, J. (2005). What (and why) is positive psychology? *Review of General Psychology*, 9, 103–110.

Hilton, M., Whiteford, H. A., Sheridan, J., Cleary, C., Chant, D., Wang, P., et al. (2008). The prevalence of psychological distress in employees and associated occupational risk factors. *Journal of Occupational and Environmental Medicine*, 50(7), 746–757.

Holmgren, K., Love, J., Mardby, A. C., & Hensing, G. (2014). Remain in work–What work-related factors are associated with sustainable work attendance: A general population-based study of women and men. *Journal of Occupational and Environmental Medicine*, 56(3), 235–242. doi:10.1097/jom.0000000000000096.

Huppert, F. A. (2005). Positive mental health in individuals and populations. In Huppert, F., Baylis, N., & Keverne, B. (Eds.), *The Science of Well-Being* (pp. 307–340). New York, NY: Oxford University Press.

Huppert, F. A. (2009). Psychological well-being: Evidence regarding its causes and consequences. *Applied Psychology: Health and Well-Being*, 1(2), 137–164.

Huppert, F. A., & So, T. C. (2009). What percentage of people in Europe are flourishing and what characterises them? Prepared for the OECD/ ISQOLS meeting "Measuring subjective well-being: an opportunity for NGSs?" Cambridge University.

Karasek, R., & Theorell, T. (1990). *Stress, productivity and reconstruction of working life.* New York, NY: Basic Books.

Keyes, C. L. M. (2002). The mental health continuum: From languishing to flourishing in life. *Journal of Health and Social Behavior*, 43(2), 207–222.

Keyes, C. L. M. (2005). Mental illness and/or mental health? Investigating axioms of the complete state model of health. *Journal of Consulting and Clinical Psychology*, 73, 539–548.

LaMontagne, A. D., & Keegel, T. (2009). Work environments as a determinant of health. In Keleher, H., & MacDougall, C. (Eds.), *Understanding Health: A Determinants Approach* (2nd ed., pp. 201–217). Oxford, UK: Oxford University Press.

LaMontagne, A. D., Keegel, T., Louie, A. M., & Ostry, A. (2010a). Job stress as a preventable upstream determinant of common mental disorders: A review for practitioners and policy-makers. *Advances in Mental Health*, 9(1), 17–35.

LaMontagne, A. D., Keegel, T., Louie, A. M., Ostry, A., & Landsbergis, P. A. (2007a). A systematic review of the job stress intervention evaluation literature: 1990–2005. *International Journal of Occupational and Environmental Health*, 13(3), 268–280.

LaMontagne, A. D., Keegel, T., & Vallance, D. A. (2007b). Protecting and promoting mental health in the workplace: Developing a systems approach to job stress. *Health Promotion Journal of Australia*, 18(3), 221–228.

LaMontagne, A. D., Keegel, T., Vallance, D. A., Ostry, A., & Wolfe, R. (2008). Job strain – Attributable depression in a sample of working Australians: Assessing the contribution to health inequalities. *BMC Public Health*, 8(181), 1–9.

LaMontagne, A. D., Martin, A., Page, K. M., Reavley, N. J., Noblet, A. J., Milner, A. J., et al. (2014). Workplace mental health: Developing an integrated intervention approach. *BMC Psychiatry*, 14, 131-144.

LaMontagne, A. D., Sanderson, K., & Cocker, F. (2010b). Estimating the Economic Benefits of Eliminating Job Strain as a Risk Factor for Depression (37 pp.). Available at http://www.vichealth.vic.gov.au/jobstrain.

LaMontagne, A. D., Sanderson, K., & Cocker, F. (2010b). Estimating the economic benefits of eliminating job strain as a risk factor for depression (abstract). *Australasian Epidemiologist*, 17(2), 93.

Leka, S., Jain, A., Zwetsloot, G., & Cox, T. (2010). Policy-level interventions and work-related psychosocial risk management in the European Union. *Work and Stress*, 24(3), 298–307.

Lindberg, P., Josephson, M., Alfredsson, L., & Vingard, E. (2006). Promoting excellent work ability and preventing poor work ability: The same determinants? Results from the Swedish HAKuL study. *Occupational and Environmental Medicine*, 63(2), 113–120. doi:10.1136/oem.2005.022129.

Lohela, M., Bjorklund, C., Vingard, E., Hagberg, J., & Jensen, I. (2009). Does a change in psychosocial work factors lead to a change in employee health? *Journal of Occupational and Environmental Medicine*, 51(2), 195–203. doi:10.1097/JOM.0b013e318192bd2c.

Lowe, G. S., Schellenberg, G., & Shannon, H. S. (2003). Correlates of employees' perceptions of a healthy work environment. *American Journal of Health Promotion*, 17(6), 390–399.

Lyubomirsky, S., King, L., & Diener, E. (2005). The benefits of frequent positive effect: Does happiness lead to success? *Psychological Bulletin*, 131, 803–835.

Macik-Frey, M., Quick, J. C., & Cooper, C. L. (2008). Authentic leadership as a pathway to positive health. *Journal of Organizational Behavior*, 29, 1–6.

Macik-Frey, M., Quick, J. C., & Nelson, D. L. (2007). Advances in occupational health: From a stressful beginning to a positive future. *Journal of Management*, 33(6), 809–840.

Macik-Frey, M., Quick, J. D., Quick, J. C., & Nelson, D. L. (2009). Occupational health psychology: From preventative medicine to psychologically healthy workplace. In Antoniou, A. G., Cooper, C. L., Chrousos, G. P., Spielberger, C. D., & Eysenck, M. W. (Eds.), *Handbook of Managerial Behavior and Occupational Health* (pp. 3–19). Cheltenham, UK: Edward Elgar Publishing.

Michie, S., & Williams, S. (2003). Reducing work related psychological ill health and sickness absence: A systematic literature review. *Occupational and Environmental Medicine*, 60, 3–9.

Page, K. M., LaMontagne, A. D., Louie, A. M., Ostry, A. S., Shaw, A, & Shoveller, J. A. (2013). Stakeholder perceptions of job stress in an industrialized country: Implications for policy and practice. *Journal of Public Health Policy*, 13, 1–15. doi:10.1057/jphp.2013.24.

Page, K. M., Milner, A. J., Tchernitskaia, I., & LaMontagne, A. D. (2014). Thriving Workplaces Report. Available at http://www.superfriend.com.au.

Page, K. M., & Vella-Brodrick, D. A. (2010). The Working for Wellness Program: Evaluation of an evidence-based employee well-being program using RCT. Paper presented at the European Academy of Occupational Health Psychology Conference, Rome, Italy.

Quick, J. C., Macik-Frey, M., & Cooper, C. L. (2007). Managerial dimensions of organizational health: The healthy leader at work. *Journal of Management Studies*, 44(2), 189–205.

Quick, J. C., & Quick, J. D. (2004). Healthy, happy, productive work: A leadership challenge. *Organizational Dynamics*, 33(4), 329–337.

Richman, L. S., Kubzansky, L., Maselko, J., Kawachi, I., Choo, P., & Bauer, M. (2005). Positive emotion and health: Going beyond the negative. *Health Pscholology*, 24(4), 422–429.

Rugulies, R., Bultmann, U., Aust, B., & Burr, H. (2006). Psychosocial work environment and incidence of severe depressive symptoms: Prospective findings from a 5-year follow-up of the Danish work environment cohort study. *American Journal of Epidemiology*, 163(10), 877–887. doi:10.1093/aje/kwj119.

Ryan, R. M., & Deci, E. L. (2000). Self-determination theory and the facilitation of intrinsic motivation, social development, and well-being. *American Psychologist*, 55(1), 68–78.

Ryff, C. D. (1989). Happiness is everything, or is it? Explorations on the meaning of psychological well-being. *Journal of Personality and Social Psychology*, 57(6), 1069–1081.

Sanderson, K., & Andrews, G. (2006). Common mental disorders in the workforce: Recent findings from descriptive and social epidemiology. *Canadian Journal of Psychiatry*, 51(2), 63–75.

Schaufeli, W. B. (2004). The future of occupational health psychology. *Applied Psychology: An International Review*, 53(4), 502–517.

Stansfeld, S., & Candy, B. (2006). Psychosocial work environment and mental health – A meta-analytic review. *Scandinavian Journal of Work and Environmental Health*, 32(6), 443–462.

Vella-Brodrick, D. A., & Page, K. M. (2009). Positive leadership: Accentuating and cultivating human resources. In Sarros, J. (Ed.), *Contemporary Perspectives on Leadership: Focus and Meaning for Ambiguous Times.* (pp. 107–140). Prahran, Australia: Tilde University Press.

Waddell, G., & Burton, A. K. (2006). *Is work good for your health and well being?* London, UK: The Stationary Office.

WHO (2005). Promoting mental health: Concepts, emerging evidence, practice. Geneva, Switzerland: World Health Organization, Department of Mental Health and Substance Abuse.

WHO (2008). *The global burden of disease: 2004 update.* Geneva, Switzerland: World Health Organization.

Wright, T. A., & Quick, J. C. (2009). The emerging positive agenda in organizations: Greater than a trickle but not yet a deluge. *Journal of Organizational Behavior*, 30, 147–159.

Section 3

Beyond Services: What Would a Recovery-Supporting
and Wellbeing-Targeted Society Look Like?

Chapter

24

Need-Supportive Parenting and Its Role in the Wellbeing and Recovery of Individuals
A Self-Determination Theory Perspective

Christopher P. Niemiec and Justin C. Coulson

The family might be the single most important unit in society for the wellbeing and full functioning of individuals. Reams of research acknowledge the critical role that parents play in their children's lives, from the antenatal period (Hayes et al., 2013; O'Connor et al., 2002) through infancy and childhood (Bugental and Grusec, 2006; Chorpita and Barlow, 1998; Fletcher et al., 2011; Goldberg and Carlson, 2014; Grolnick et al., 1984), adolescence (Barber, 1996; Gray and Steinberg, 1999; Grolnick, 2003; Padilla-Walker et al., 2012; Pettit et al., 2001; Shek, 2007), late adolescence (Niemiec et al., 2006) and adulthood (Amato, 2010; Feeney and Noller, 1990; Roesler and McKenzie, 1994; Vaillant, 2012). It is well accepted that quality parenting is a central protective factor for children's resilience and wellbeing (Bronfenbrenner, 1986; Rutter, 1987; Werner, 2005). Indeed, parents who effectively fulfill their role as "chief socializing agents" are more likely to raise children with higher wellbeing than parents who are less effective or dysfunctional in that role (Bugental and Grusec, 2006).

The purpose of this chapter is to (1) offer a brief review of research on the importance of parenting for wellbeing; (2) consider the conceptualization of autonomy support within self-determination theory, an empirically derived approach to parenting that is associated with wellbeing; (3) discuss empirical support for the proposition that autonomy support is an optimal approach for children's wellbeing; and (4) reflect on how need-supportive parenting might be useful in a recovery context.

A Brief Review of Research on the Importance of Parenting for Wellbeing

Empirical research is unequivocal: parenting quality is pivotal in children's development (Bugental and Grusec, 2006; Maccoby and Martin, 1983; Masten and Shaffer, 2006; Wald-fogel et al., 2010). Attachment theory (Bowlby, 1969, 1973, 1980) – arguably the most influential theory in child development – asserts that children who are raised with warmth and nurturance from their caregivers are more likely to thrive than children who are raised in harsh, uncaring family contexts. Attachment security refers to the quality of relationship

---

Wellbeing, Recovery and Mental Health, ed. Mike Slade, Lindsay Oades and Aaron Jarden.
Published by Cambridge University Press. © Mike Slade, Lindsay Oades and Aaron Jarden 2017

between parent and child, which is categorized as secure, avoidant, ambivalent, or disorganized (Ainsworth et al., 1978). Optimal (secure) attachment is formed when caregivers are available (both physically and emotionally) and responsive to their offspring, and approximately 60% of children in Western nations are categorized as having a secure attachment to their primary caregiver (Moullin et al., 2014). Importantly, the attachment style that children develop through interaction with caregivers extends into adulthood and impacts their relationships (Feeney and Noller, 1990) and wellbeing (Vaillant, 2012; Werner, 2005) for decades beyond those formative relational experiences in childhood.

Baumrind (1966, 1971, 1991) and those who expanded her research (Aunola and Nurmi, 2005; Gray and Steinberg, 1999) identified two dimensions that are central to optimal parenting and child development, namely, the warmth (vs. hostility) of the parent–child bond and the demandingness (vs. permissiveness) with which limits are set. Neglectful parents are low on both warmth and demandingness, and outcomes for their children tend to be poor. In contrast, permissive parents are high on warmth and low on demandingness, and outcomes for their children tend to be poor, too.

Authoritarian parents (also suboptimal) are high on demandingness and low on warmth. Although children of authoritarian parents tend to be highly compliant (especially when parents are around, or when children might get caught), they also tend to be less resourceful and have fewer social skills and lower wellbeing (Lamborn et al., 1991; Steinberg et al., 1992; Trinkner et al., 2012). Children of authoritarian parents are more likely to engage in risky or delinquent behavior (especially when children are older or will not get caught) (Padilla-Walker et al., 2012) and are at increased risk of depressive symptoms and poor psychological adjustment (Maccoby and Martin, 1983; Milevsky et al., 2007). A significant contributor to these outcomes may be the explicit control that authoritarian parents exert over their children (Grolnick, 2003; Padilla-Walker et al., 2012; Vansteenkiste et al., 2014).

Authoritative parents are highly responsive (warmth) to their children *and* provide clear limits (demandingness) on behavior, and outcomes for their children tend to be optimal. Although authoritative parenting has been established as the "gold standard" for several decades, scholars (Gray and Steinberg, 1999; Kohn, 2014; Lamborn et al., 1991; Lewis, 1981) have suggested that some definitional aspects of this approach are inconsistent with Baumrind's (1971) model. For instance, Lewis (1981) found that outcomes associated with authoritative parenting are not attributable to demandingness per se, as children of permissive parents fared as well as children of authoritative parents. Calafat et al. (2014) reported similar findings, such that children of permissive parents were as likely – or more likely – to avoid alcohol, tobacco, and other drugs, relative to children of authoritative parents. Also, children of permissive parents had fewer personal disturbances, higher self-esteem, and better school performance. It is important, therefore, to consider whether other approaches to parenting may achieve optimal outcomes for children.

To reiterate, parenting style matters for children's wellbeing. Both theory and research over the past several decades (Aunola and Nurmi, 2005; Gray and Steinberg, 1999; Joussemet et al., 2014) have pointed consistently to three factors that are at the core of optimal parenting, namely, affiliation (warmth and nurturance), structure (boundaries and limits), and autonomy support. It is interesting to note that Baumrind's (1971) model reflects both affiliation and structure, but not autonomy support. Nonetheless, research from self-determination theory over the past four decades has highlighted the importance of autonomy support for full functioning and organismic wellness (cf. Niemiec and Ryan, 2013; see also Niemiec et al., 2014). Accordingly, it is important to consider the conceptualization of autonomy support within self-determination theory and to discuss empirical support for the proposition that autonomy support is an optimal approach for children's wellbeing.

The Conceptualization of Autonomy Support within Self-Determination Theory

Self-determination theory (SDT; Deci and Ryan, 2000, 2008; Niemiec et al., 2010; Ryan and Deci, 2000; Vansteenkiste et al., 2010) is an organismic macro-theory of human motivation, emotion and personality in social contexts that recognizes the proactive nature of humans and their tendency toward integration at the intrapersonal and interpersonal levels. At the core of SDT is the specification of three basic psychological needs for autonomy, competence and relatedness. The need for autonomy refers to the experience of behavior as owned, choiceful and reflectively self-endorsed. Notably, autonomy is not defined as independence (Ryan and Deci, 2006). Indeed, individuals can be volitionally independent from or volitionally dependent on close others (Soenens et al., 2009b), which contradicts the claims made by Peterson and Taylor (1980) and Murray et al. (2009) that autonomy is antagonistic to interdependence (see also Niemiec et al., 2014). The need for competence refers to the experience of capability in pursuing and attaining desired outcomes. The need for relatedness refers to the experience of warmth, care, concern and mutual support in connections with important others. From the perspective of SDT, basic psychological needs are defined as "innate psychological nutriments that are essential for ongoing psychological growth, integrity, and well-being" (Deci and Ryan, 2000, p. 229). In other words, support for autonomy, competence and relatedness is theorized to contribute to wellbeing across demographic categories, whereas frustration of the basic psychological needs is theorized to detract from wellbeing and contribute to illbeing. Considerable research has supported these assertions across life domains and cultures (Deci and Ryan, 2008).

Rooted in SDT and based, in part, on the work of Haim Ginott (1965), autonomy-supportive parenting is a prescriptive approach to the relationship between parent and child that is applicable to families at any and every stage of development (Joussemet et al., 2008). With an emphasis on warmth and affiliation, the autonomy-supportive parent works with the child to cultivate an internal, volitional experience from which self-regulation of responsible, appropriate behavior can emerge (see Kohn, 2014). Such an approach is qualitatively different from a traditional parenting model in which the parent acts on the child through coercion, control, force and/or authority to ensure compliance with parental values and norms. As well, it is interesting to note that Joussemet et al. (2014) linked the satisfaction of basic psychological needs derived from autonomy-supportive parenting to the evidence-based triad of optimal parenting strategies (viz., autonomy support, structure and affiliation).

Joussemet et al. (2008) identified four guiding principles for autonomy-supportive parenting, namely, (1) the parent provides a clear rationale for behavioral requests; (2) the parent considers the perspective of the child; (3) the parent offers choice, encourages self-initiation and engages in problem solving with the child; and (4) the parent minimizes use of controlling techniques such as threats, punishments, rewards and bribes. In practice, these principles may or may not be used in a linear way and may or may not be completed in a single interaction with a child, particularly when the issue is complex and/or the child is untrusting toward the parent. It is important to note that autonomy-supportive parenting retains an emphasis on structure and limits (Grolnick and Pomerantz, 2009; Soenens and Vansteenkiste, 2010), which when communicated in an autonomy-supportive way are associated with need satisfaction (Curran et al., 2013) and internalization of parental rules (Soenens et al., 2009a).

Autonomy Support Is an Optimal Approach for Children's Wellbeing

Niemiec et al. (2014) provided a review of research on the importance of autonomy support in different types of social experiences, including the relationship between parent and child, and this literature tells a compelling story. Simply put, support for and satisfaction of the basic psychological needs for autonomy, competence and relatedness are associated with higher psychological wellbeing, physical health and social functioning across the lifespan – from infancy to old age – and across cultures. Here, we briefly describe some more recent findings. For instance, Matte-Gagné et al. (2015) found that autonomy-supportive parenting from mothers toward their 15-month-old children is associated with higher executive function when the child is 3 years old. Outside the realm of parenting dynamics, Nelson et al. (2015) demonstrated that experimentally induced autonomy support around prosocial behavior produces higher wellbeing, relative to no autonomy support. Thus, it is necessary for children's wellbeing that parents (and other authority figures) be child-centered, involved and empathic in their socialization practice.

At the same time, it is critical for children's wellbeing that parents (and other authority figures) refrain from the use of coercion, control, force and/or authority in their socialization practice, as such manipulative tactics are theorized to undermine autonomy and wellness. In fact, empirical evidence points toward an inverse association between psychologically controlling parenting and wellbeing. For instance, Bebes et al. (2015) found that psychological control from mothers is associated with higher psychological symptoms among sexual minority adolescents. In a meta-analysis of 23 studies and nearly 9,000 individuals, Kuppens et al. (2013) observed a positive association between psychological control and relational aggression in children and adolescents. Van Petegem et al. (2015) noted increases in both internalizing and externalizing symptoms as adolescents and young adults reported autonomy frustration due to parental control and pressure. In a longitudinal study, Oudekerk et al. (2015) found that psychological control at age 13 years stymies autonomy and relatedness in children, which in turn predicts lower autonomy and relatedness in friendships between the ages of 13 and 18 years as well as with romantic partners at age 18 years. It is interesting to note, as well, that satisfaction of autonomy and relatedness can be pitted against one another. With parental conditional regard, children must forgo satisfaction of autonomy to gain the attention, affection and approval of their parent(s), and this socialization technique has adverse consequences for children's self-regulation and wellbeing (Assor et al., 2004; Roth et al., 2009).

It is evident from the theory and research reviewed above that the basic psychological needs for autonomy, competence and relatedness are complementary (rather than antagonistic) and necessary nutrients for full functioning and organismic wellness. Accordingly, it is important to reflect on how need-supportive parenting might be useful in a recovery context. (We note our shift in nomenclature from "autonomy support" to "need support," which is done to highlight the importance of providing support for all three basic psychological needs.)

Need-Supportive Parenting in a Recovery Context

Anthony (1993) defined recovery as "a deeply personal, unique process of changing one's attitudes, values, feelings, goals, skills, and/or roles. It is a way of living a satisfying, hopeful, and contributing life even with limitations caused by illness. Recovery involves the development of new meaning and purpose in one's life as one grows beyond the catastrophic effects of mental illness" (p. 527). To be sure, the recovery context often is complex, as individuals work to negotiate the psychosocial challenges that can confound the efforts of those with mental illnesses to live a satisfying life (Warner, 2004). Notably, many scholars view recovery as an individual process and do not focus explicitly on the family context and/or parenting dynamics.

Nonetheless, we make the following proposal. Families that assist the person in recovery to experience satisfaction of the basic psychological needs will facilitate optimal outcomes at both the individual and familial level, relative to families that stifle autonomy, undermine competence and rupture relatedness. Indeed, we anticipate this set of dynamics regardless of whether the person in recovery is an adolescent, young adult or adult, and regardless of whether the recovery context is focused on alcohol or drug abuse, psychopathology or some other incapacity or illness. Theory and research from outside the realms of the family context and parenting dynamics have offered support for this proposal. Raeburn et al. (2015) describe effective recovery processes as those that emphasize voluntary participation in interventions designed to encourage and facilitate attainment of social, education, and employment goals, and that emphasize "coulds" as personal decisions rather than "shoulds" as top-down clinical directives. Empirically, Breitborde et al. (2012) found that satisfaction of the basic psychological needs facilitated recovery and wellbeing in a sample of patients with first-episode psychosis (viz., schizophrenia). In a transdiagnostic eating disorder sample, Carter and Kelly (2015) noted that recovery was facilitated through the use of autonomy-supportive strategies, and that autonomous motivation was more likely to be observed when such strategies were part of the recovery process. Similarly, Darcy et al. (2010) found that collaborative approaches that support autonomy are associated with optimal outcomes in a sample of patients with anorexia nervosa. In the context of vocational rehabilitation, Farholm et al. (2015) observed that autonomy support from the treatment team related positively to change in need satisfaction, which in turn related positively to changes in autonomous motivation and perceived competence for regular physical activity, which in turn related positively to changes in physical activity, wellbeing and – ultimately – return to work.

Although scholars have examined SDT in a recovery context, such research that focuses on the family context and/or parenting dynamics is – to our knowledge – nonexistent. In what follows, therefore, we identify a number of need-supportive parenting strategies that might enhance the wellbeing and recovery of individuals. Table 24.1 provides a summary of need-supportive strategies that parents can use in a recovery context (cf. Niemiec et al., 2014; Williams et al., 2011), and next we offer a vignette (based on true events) that illustrates how parents may use these strategies to facilitate their child's recovery from alcohol abuse, violence and suicidality.

Consider the following individual and his parents for the purpose of illustration. Alexander is a 33-year-old single man with a history of violent alcohol abuse. Recently, Alexander was discharged from an inpatient alcohol-recovery program to which he self-admitted after an alcohol-fueled violent incident that left his aging parents (Peter and Marie) in a hospital with serious injuries. Following the incident, Alexander attempted suicide and was unsuccessful. Alexander felt remorseful and helpless, while Peter and Marie felt betrayed, angry, and heartbroken. Nonetheless, Alexander's parents were working toward forgiveness and wanted to help their son. To that point, Peter and Marie organized

Table 24.1 Summary of Need-Supportive Strategies That Parents Can Use in a Recovery Context

Support for autonomy	1. Elicit, acknowledge, and empathize with the child's thoughts, feelings and perspectives. 2. Explore the child's values and how they relate to the recovery context. 3. Provide support for the child's self-initiation, self-direction and choice around recovery. 4. Provide a clear, meaningful rationale for limits and other behavioral requests. 5. Minimize use of coercion, control, force and/or authority, especially in communication with the child (refrain from language such as "should," "must," "ought" and "have to").
Support for competence	1. Remain positive that the child can succeed. 2. Identify and discuss barriers to success. 3. Work with the child to build skills and solve problems. 4. Offer immediate, accurate and effectance-relevant feedback to the child. 5. Provide structure through clear, consistent and mutually agreed-upon guidelines. 6. Reframe setbacks as short successes.
Support for relatedness	1. Assume a warm, caring and concerned stance toward the child. 2. Communicate empathy. 3. Remain nonjudgmental. 4. Offer unconditional positive regard.

a reconciliation and planning meeting after Alexander's discharge to see how the family might move forward.

After ensuring that safety will not be a concern, Peter and Marie begin to address the issues that have caused pain for their family in a need-supportive way. They start – quite simply – to elicit and acknowledge Alexander's perspective by saying, "We wonder how you make sense of your alcohol use and potential for violence." Indeed, this is a noncoercive, nonconfrontational *invitation* for Alexander to engage in a process of reflection on and dialogue around his experiences. During this time, Peter and Marie remain attentive to and interested in Alexander's thoughts about the situation, and they express nonjudgmental acceptance of his feelings regardless of their valence. Peter and Marie offer unconditional positive regard for Alexander's feeling of being a victim in his struggle with alcohol and his perceived helplessness that led to suicidality. There is a real sense of care, concern, empathy and acceptance.

As the conversation proceeds, Peter and Marie ask Alexander about his values, goals and life aspirations. Although he feels helpless, Alexander is open to an exploration of what matters to him and what he hopes to contribute to the world. Peter and Marie encourage Alexander to take responsibility for his recovery and support his self-initiation, self-direction and choice in the process. Alexander's parents help him to identify barriers to success, build skills, and solve problems while remaining positive that he can succeed in recovery. With warmth and concern, Peter and Marie ask, "How can we support your recovery and help you achieve your goals?" In response, Alexander begins to identify safety nets (e.g. periodic "check-ins" on nights that Alexander plans to drink) that can be put into place to assist him in recovery. Peter, Marie and Alexander build structure through a discussion of clear, consistent and mutually agreed-upon guidelines for behavior that can be achieved, as well as protections against potentially destructive patterns.

It is likely – if not essential – that the conversation will turn toward a consideration of limits and expectations for future behavior, especially around alcohol use and violence. Indeed, Peter and Marie are sure to provide a clear, meaningful rationale for limits and other behavioral requests, and they encourage Alexander to be an active contributor to this conversation. As well, Peter and Marie refrain from controlling language and instead use words such as "prefer," "consider" and "choose".

As life moves forward, Alexander does experience periodic setbacks on his path toward recovery. That being said, Peter and Marie offer immediate, accurate and effectance-relevant feedback and reframe those setbacks as short successes. Alexander works to maintain an open line of communication with his parents, and his parents work to remain warm, caring, empathic and nonjudgmental. Their approach is deeply aligned with need-supportive parenting and is conducive to Alexander's wellbeing and recovery.

Most of the strategies discussed in this vignette have received empirical support from previous research within SDT. However, these strategies have received little or no empirical validation at the interface of recovery, family context and parenting dynamics. We believe that significant progress can be made at this interface in light of the profound influence that parents have on children's wellbeing, and we encourage investigators to examine systematically the impact of need-supportive strategies on wellbeing in a variety of recovery contexts.

Concluding Remarks

Calls have been made for research into the factors that contribute to family flourishing (Coulson et al., 2012) and the beneficial consequences for individuals. Yet few researchers have investigated wellbeing at the interface of recovery, family context and parenting dynamics. In this chapter, we used principles from self-determination theory (SDT) to sketch an application of need-supportive parenting in a recovery context. Although empirical work at this interface is sparse – if even existent – we believe that this may be a fruitful area of inquiry because of the central role that interactions between parents and children have in the human experience (van IJzendoorn, 1995) and because of the voluminous corpus of literature that supports SDT.

Practically speaking, need-supportive parenting is an optimal approach for children's wellbeing in general as well as in a recovery context. To be sure, periodic setbacks are a part of life, especially for children who struggle to recover from alcohol or drug abuse, psychopathology or some other incapacity or illness. In the face of such setbacks, it may be helpful for parents to adopt an attitude of trust in organismic development (Landry et al., 2008), which recognizes that the developmental tendency toward organismic integration will operate most effectively in need-supportive social contexts. Indeed, such "trust" predicts optimal parenting but also optimal outcomes in children. not only

References

Ainsworth, M. D. S., Blehar, M. C., Waters, E., & Wall, S. (1978). *Patterns of attachment: A psychological study of the strange situation*. Hillsdale, NJ: Lawrence Erlbaum Associates.

Amato, P. R. (2010). Research on divorce: Continuing trends and new developments. *Journal of Marriage and Family*, 72, 650–666.

Anthony, W. A. (1993). Recovery from mental illness: The guiding vision of the mental health service system in the 1990s. *Psychosocial Rehabilitation Journal*, 16, 11–23.

Assor, A., Roth, G., & Deci, E. L. (2004). The emotional costs of parents' conditional regard: A self-determination theory analysis. *Journal of Personality*, 72, 47–88.

Aunola, K., & Nurmi, J.-E. (2005). The role of parenting styles in children's problem behavior. *Child Development*, 76, 1144–1159.

Barber, B. K. (1996). Parental psychological control: Revisiting a neglected construct. *Child Development*, 67, 3296–3319.

Baumrind, D. (1966). Effects of authoritative parental control on child behavior. *Child Development*, 37, 887–907.

Baumrind, D. (1971). Current patterns of parental authority. *Developmental Psychology*, 4, 1–103.

Baumrind, D. (1991). Parenting styles and adolescent development. In Brooks-Gunn, J., Lerner, R., & Petersen, A. C. (Eds.), *The Encyclopedia on Adolescence* (pp. 746–758). New York, NY: Garland.

Bebes, A., Samarova, V., Shilo, G., & Diamond, G. M. (2015). Parental acceptance, parental psychological control and psychological symptoms among sexual minority adolescents. *Journal of Child and Family Studies*, 24, 882–890.

Bowlby, J. (1969). *Attachment and loss: Vol. 1. Attachment*. New York, NY: Basic Books.

Bowlby, J. (1973). *Attachment and loss: Vol. 2. Separation: Anxiety and anger*. New York, NY: Basic Books.

Bowlby, J. (1980). *Attachment and loss: Vol. 3. Loss: Sadness and depression*. New York, NY: Basic Books.

Breitborde, N. J. K., Kleinlein, P., & Srihari, V. H. (2012). Self-determination and first-episode psychosis: Associations with symptomatology, social and vocational functioning, and quality of life. *Schizophrenia Research*, 137, 132–136.

Bronfenbrenner, U. (1986). Ecology of the family as a context for human development: Research perspectives. *Developmental Psychology*, 22, 723–742.

Bugental, D. B., & Grusec, J. E. (2006). Socialization processes. In Eisenberg, N. (Vol. Ed.) & Damon, W., & Lerner, R. L. (Series Eds.), *Handbook of Child Psychology: Social, Emotional and Personality Development* (Vol. 3, pp. 366–428). New York, NY: John Wiley & Sons.

Calafat, A., García, F., Juan, M., Becoña, E., & Fernández-Hermida, J. R. (2014). Which parenting style is more protective against adolescent substance use? Evidence within the European context. *Drug and Alcohol Dependence*, 138, 185–192.

Carter, J. C., & Kelly, A. C. (2015). Autonomous and controlled motivation for eating disorders treatment: Baseline predictors and relationship to treatment outcome. *British Journal of Clinical Psychology*, 54, 76–90.

Chorpita, B. F., & Barlow, D. H. (1998). The development of anxiety: The role of control in the early environment. *Psychological Bulletin*, 124, 3–21.

Coulson, J. C., Oades, L. G., & Stoyles, G. J. (2012). Parents' subjective sense of calling in childrearing: Measurement, development and initial findings. *Journal of Positive Psychology*, 7, 83–94.

Curran, T., Hill, A. P., & Niemiec, C. P. (2013). A conditional process model of children's behavioral engagement and behavioral disaffection in sport based on self-determination theory. *Journal of Sport & Exercise Psychology*, 35, 30–43.

Darcy, A. M., Katz, S., Fitzpatrick, K. K., Forsberg, S., Utzinger, L., & Lock, J. (2010). All better? How former anorexia nervosa patients define recovery and engaged in treatment. *European Eating Disorders Review*, 18, 260–270.

Deci, E. L., & Ryan, R. M. (2000). The "what" and "why" of goal pursuits: Human needs and the self-determination of behavior. *Psychological Inquiry*, 11, 227–268.

Deci, E. L., & Ryan, R. M. (2008). Facilitating optimal motivation and psychological well-being across life's domains. *Canadian Psychology*, 49, 14–23.

Farholm, A., Halvari, H., Niemiec, C. P., Williams, G. C., & Deci, E. L. (2015). Changes in return to work among patients in vocational rehabilitation: A self-determination theory perspective. Unpublished manuscript, Buskerud and Vestfold University College, Hønefoss, Norway.

Feeney, J. A., & Noller, P. (1990). Attachment style as a predictor of adult romantic relationships. *Journal of Personality and Social Psychology*, 58, 281–291.

Fletcher, R. J., Feeman, E., Garfield, C., & Vimpani, G. (2011). The effects of early paternal depression on children's development. *Medical Journal of Australia*, 195, 685–689.

Ginott, H. G. (1965). *Between parent and child: New solutions to old problems.* New York, NY: Macmillan.

Goldberg, J. S., & Carlson, M. J. (2014). Parents' relationship quality and children's behavior in stable married and cohabiting families. *Journal of Marriage and Family,* 76, 762–777.

Gray, M. R., & Steinberg, L. (1999). Unpacking authoritative parenting: Reassessing a multidimensional construct. *Journal of Marriage and Family,* 61, 574–587.

Grolnick, W. S. (2003). *The psychology of parental control: How well-meant parenting backfires.* Mahwah, NJ: Lawrence Erlbaum Associates.

Grolnick, W., Frodi, A., & Bridges, L. (1984). Maternal control styles and the mastery motivation of one-year-olds. *Infant Mental Health Journal,* 5, 72–82.

Grolnick, W. S., & Pomerantz, E. M. (2009). Issues and challenges in studying parental control: Toward a new conceptualization. *Child Development Perspectives,* 3, 165–170.

Hayes, L. J., Goodman, S. H., & Carlson, E. (2013). Maternal antenatal depression and infant disorganized attachment at 12 months. *Attachment and Human Development,* 15, 133–153.

Joussemet, M., Landry, R., & Koestner, R. (2008). A self-determination theory perspective on parenting. *Canadian Psychology,* 49, 194–200.

Joussemet, M., Mageau, G. A., & Koestner, R. (2014). Promoting optimal parenting and children's mental health: A preliminary evaluation of the How-to Parenting Program. *Journal of Child and Family Studies,* 23, 949–964.

Kohn, A. (2014). *The myth of the spoiled child: Challenging the conventional wisdom about children and parenting.* Boston, MA: Da Capo Press.

Kuppens, S., Laurent, L., Heyvaert, M., & Onghena, P. (2013). Associations between parental psychological control and relational aggression in children and adolescents: A multilevel and sequential meta-analysis. *Developmental Psychology,* 49, 1697–1712.

Lamborn, S. D., Mounts, N. S., Steinberg, L., & Dornbusch, S. M. (1991). Patterns of competence and adjustment among adolescents from authoritative, authoritarian, indulgent, and neglectful families. *Child Development,* 62, 1049–1065.

Landry, R., Whipple, N., Mageau, G., Joussemet, M., Koestner, R., DiDio, L., et al. (2008). Trust in organismic development, autonomy support, and adaptation among mothers and their children. *Motivation and Emotion,* 32, 173–188.

Lewis, C. C. (1981). The effects of parental firm control: A reinterpretation of findings. *Psychological Bulletin,* 90, 547–563.

Maccoby, E. E., & Martin, J. (1983). Socialization in the context of the family: Parent–child interaction. In Mussen, P. H. (Series Ed.) & Hetherington, E. M. (Vol. Ed.), *Handbook of child psychology: Vol. 4. Socialization, personality, and social development* (pp. 1-101). New York, NY: Wiley.

Masten, A. S., & Shaffer, A. (2006). How families matter in child development: Reflections from research on risk and resilience. In Clarke-Stewart, A., & Dunn, J. (Eds.), *Families Count: Effects on Child and Adolescent Development* (pp. 5–25). Cambridge, UK: Cambridge University Press.

Matte-Gagné, C., Bernier, A., & Lalonde, G. (2015). Stability in maternal autonomy support and child executive functioning. *Journal of Child and Family Studies,* 24, 2610–2619.

Milevsky, A., Schlechter, M., Netter, S., & Keehn, D. (2007). Maternal and paternal parenting styles in adolescents: Associations with self-esteem, depression and life-satisfaction. *Journal of Child and Family Studies,* 16, 39–47.

Moullin, S., Waldfogel, J., & Washbrook, E. (2014). *Baby bonds: Parenting, attachment and a secure base for children.* London, UK: The Sutton Trust. Available at http://www.suttontrust.com/wp-content/uploads/2014/03/baby-bonds-final.pdf.

Murray, S. L., Holmes, J. G., Aloni, M., Pinkus, R. T., Derrick, J. L., & Leder, S. (2009). Commitment insurance: Compensating for the autonomy costs of interdependence in close relationships. *Journal of Personality and Social Psychology,* 97, 256–278.

Nelson, S. K., Della Porta, M. D., Bao, K. J., Lee, H. C., Choi, I., & Lyubomirsky, S. (2015). 'It's up to you': Experimentally manipulated autonomy support for prosocial behavior improves well-being in two cultures over six weeks. *Journal of Positive Psychology.*

Niemiec, C. P., Lynch, M. F., Vansteenkiste, M., Bernstein, J., Deci, E. L., & Ryan, R. M. (2006). The antecedents and consequences of autonomous self-regulation for college: A self-determination theory perspective on socialization. *Journal of Adolescence*, 29, 761–775.

Niemiec, C. P., & Ryan, R. M. (2013). What makes for a life well lived? Autonomy and its relation to full functioning and organismic wellness. In David, S. A., Boniwell, I., & Ayers, A. C. (Eds.), *The Oxford Handbook of Happiness* (pp. 214–226). Oxford, UK: Oxford University Press.

Niemiec, C. P., Ryan, R. M., & Deci, E. L. (2010). Self-determination theory and the relation of autonomy to self-regulatory processes and personality development. In R. H. Hoyle (Ed.), *Handbook of personality and self-regulation* (pp. 169–191). Malden, MA: Blackwell Publishing.

Niemiec, C. P., Soenens, B., & Vansteenkiste, M. (2014). Is relatedness enough? On the importance of need support in different types of social experiences. In Weinstein, N. (Ed.), *Human Motivation and Interpersonal Relationships: Theory, Research and Applications* (pp. 77–96). Dordrecht, the Netherlands: Springer.

O'Connor, T. G., Heron, J., Golding, J., Beveridge, M., & Glover, V. (2002). Maternal antenatal anxiety and children's behavioural/emotional problems at 4 years: Report from the Avon Longitudinal Study of Parents and Children. *British Journal of Psychiatry*, 180, 502–508.

Oudekerk, B. A., Allen, J. P., Hessel, E. T., & Molloy, L. E. (2015). The cascading development of autonomy and relatedness from adolescence to adulthood. *Child Development*, 86, 472–485.

Padilla-Walker, L. M., Fraser, A. M., & Harper, J. M. (2012). Walking the walk: The moderating role of proactive parenting on adolescents' value-congruent behaviors. *Journal of Adolescence*, 35, 1141–1152.

Peterson, A. C., & Taylor, B. (1980). The biological approach to adolescence: Biological change and psychological adaptation. In Adelson, J. (Ed.), *Handbook of Adolescent Psychology* (pp. 117–155). New York, NY: Wiley.

Pettit, G. S., Laird, R. D., Dodge, K. A., Bates, J. E., & Criss, M. M. (2001). Antecedents and behavior-problem outcomes of parental monitoring and psychological control in early adolescence. *Child Development*, 72, 583–598.

Raeburn, T., Schmied, V., Hungerford, C., & Cleary, M. (2015). Self-determination theory: A framework for clubhouse psychosocial rehabilitation research. *Issues in Mental Health Nursing*, 36, 145–151.

Roesler, T. A., & McKenzie, N. (1994). Effects of childhood trauma on psychological functioning in adults sexually abused as children. *Journal of Nervous and Mental Disease*, 182, 145–150.

Roth, G., Assor, A., Niemiec, C. P., Ryan, R. M., & Deci, E. L. (2009). The emotional and academic consequences of parental conditional regard: Comparing conditional positive regard, conditional negative regard, and autonomy support as parenting practices. *Developmental Psychology*, 45, 1119–1142.

Rutter, M. (1987). Psychosocial resilience and protective mechanisms. *American Journal of Orthopsychiatry*, 57, 316–331.

Ryan, R. M., & Deci, E. L. (2000). Self-determination theory and the facilitation of intrinsic motivation, social development, and well-being. *American Psychologist*, 55, 68–78.

Ryan, R. M., & Deci, E. L. (2006). Self-regulation and the problem of human autonomy: Does psychology need choice, self-determination, and will? *Journal of Personality*, 74, 1557–1585.

Shek, D. T. (2007). A longitudinal study of perceived parental psychological control and psychological well-being in Chinese adolescents in Hong Kong. *Journal of Clinical Psychology*, 63, 1–22.

Soenens, B., & Vansteenkiste, M. (2010). A theoretical upgrade of the concept of parental psychological control: Proposing new insights on the basis of self-determination theory. *Developmental Review*, 30, 74–99.

Soenens, B., Vansteenkiste, M., & Niemiec, C. P. (2009a). Should parental prohibition of adolescents' peer relationships be prohibited? *Personal Relationships*, 16, 507–530.

Soenens, B., Vansteenkiste, M., & Sierens, E. (2009b). How are parental psychological control and autonomy-support related? A cluster-analytic approach. *Journal of Marriage and Family*, 71, 187–202.

Steinberg, L., Lamborn, S. D., Dornbusch, S. M., & Darling, N. (1992). Impact of parenting practices on adolescent achievement: Authoritative parenting, school involvement, and encouragement to succeed. *Child Development*, 63, 1266–1281.

Trinkner, R., Cohn, E. S., Rebellon, C. J., & Van Gundy, K. (2012). Don't trust anyone over 30: Parental legitimacy as a mediator between parenting style and changes in delinquent behavior over time. *Journal of Adolescence*, 35, 119–132.

Vaillant, G. E. (2012). *Triumphs of experience: The men of the Harvard Grant Study*. Cambridge, MA: Belknap Press.

van IJzendoorn, M. (1995). Adult attachment representations, parental responsiveness, and infant attachment: A meta-analysis on the predictive validity of the Adult Attachment Interview. *Psychological Bulletin*, 117, 387–403.

Van Petegem, S., Soenens, B., Vansteenkiste, M., & Beyers, W. (2015). Rebels with a cause? Adolescent defiance from the perspective of reactance theory and self-determination theory. *Child Development*, 86, 903–918.

Vansteenkiste, M., Niemiec, C. P., & Soenens, B. (2010). The development of the five mini-theories of self-determination theory: An historical overview, emerging trends, and future directions. In Urdan, T. C., & Karabenick, S. A. (Eds.), *Advances in Motivation and Achievement, v. 16A – The Decade Ahead: Theoretical Perspectives on Motivation and Achievement* (pp. 105–165). London, UK: Emerald Group Publishing Limited.

Vansteenkiste, M., Soenens, B., Van Petegem, S., & Duriez, B. (2014). Longitudinal associations between adolescent perceived degree and style of parental prohibition and internalization and defiance. *Developmental Psychology*, 50, 229–236.

Waldfogel, J., Craigie, T. A., & Brooks-Gunn, J. (2010). Fragile families and child wellbeing. *Future of Children*, 20, 87–112.

Warner, R. (2004). *Recovery from schizophrenia: Psychiatry and political economy*. London, UK: Routledge.

Werner, E. E. (2005). What can we learn about resilience from large-scale longitudinal studies? In Goldstein, S., & Brooks, R. B. (Eds.), *Handbook of resilience in children* (pp. 91–105). New York, NY: Springer.

Williams, G. C., Patrick, H., Niemiec, C. P., Ryan, R. M., Deci, E. L., & Lavigne, H. M. (2011). The Smoker's Health Project: A self-determination theory intervention to facilitate maintenance of tobacco abstinence. *Contemporary Clinical Trials*, 32, 535–543.

Chapter 25

Social Marketing of Wellbeing

Ross Gordon and Lindsay G. Oades

Introduction

This chapter provides an introduction to social marketing and considers applications to wellbeing and conceptual similarities to wellbeing. The chapter begins by identifying that wellbeing is a multifaceted concept that has synergies with social marketing. Key principles and concepts of social marketing are then presented, and examples are provided of how social marketing and wellbeing may overlap. Conceptual similarities between the ethos of social marketing and wellbeing are also highlighted.

What Is Wellbeing?

Wellbeing has become an increasingly used term in popular discourse and academic/scientific literatures over the past twenty years. For this reason, it is important to clarify what is meant by wellbeing.

Historically a key distinction in defining wellbeing has been the debate between two approaches. First, the pleasure or *hedonic* view of wellbeing, drawn from the work of the Greek philosopher Aristippus, views wellbeing as the experience of pleasure and the minimisation of pain. This relates closely to having one's needs satisfied and experiencing positive emotions such as joy or happiness. Alternatively, drawn from the work of Aristotle, wellbeing may be viewed as a state of flourishing, in which one is moving to reach one's potential, in line with personal values. This is known as the *eudaimonic* view of wellbeing (Aristotle, 1980; Kraut, 2007, 2014).

In plain language, some refer to the hedonic approach as 'feeling good' and aspects of the eudaimonic approach as 'functioning well'. Debates continue as to which offers the more elegant or accurate way of defining wellbeing. There is also a view that feeling good is a necessary but not sufficient way to define wellbeing. Combining the hedonic and eudemonic approaches leads to the plainer English definition of *feeling good and functioning well.*

One further important clarification is needed. Wellbeing is more than the absence of illness or dysfunction. Clinical approaches to wellbeing may assume that a person has wellbeing because he or she is symptom-free. Contemporary approaches to wellbeing largely reject this idea.

This definition is at the conceptual level, and needs to be understood across different domains of life (Nussbuam and Glover, 1995). Moreover, many confuse what wellbeing is

Wellbeing, Recovery and Mental Health, ed. Mike Slade, Lindsay Oades and Aaron Jarden.
Published by Cambridge University Press. © Mike Slade, Lindsay Oades and Aaron Jarden 2017

with what may increase or decrease wellbeing. Wellbeing may also be considered at different levels, e.g. personal, family, organisational, community, society. Given the multifaceted nature of wellbeing, the question remains of how to apply social marketing to wellbeing. Social marketing is now described.

What Is Social Marketing?

Social marketing (SM) is the application of marketing principles and practices to advance social good. SM has been applied to a wide range of health and social issues since first being formally defined by Kotler and Zaltman (1971).

In the past 40 years SM has become increasingly prominent both in marketing academe and in the social policy arena. There is increasing evidence that suggests it can be an effective social change approach in its own right (see Gordon et al. 2006; Stead et al. 2007 for reviews of the evidence on social marketing effectiveness) and can make positive contributions to social policy (French, 2011). The field is now proffering new ideas relating to the form and management of the social marketing mix (Tapp and Spotswood, 2013), upstream marketing and public policy (Gordon, 2013), strategic orientation and systems thinking (French and Gordon, 2015), applying service logic (Russell-Bennett et al. 2013), critical thinking (Gordon, 2011), value creation (Zainuddin et al. 2011), sustainability (Smith and O'Sullivan, 2012) and transformative thinking (Lefebvre, 2011). Calls are also being made for a broader, 'systemic' view of SM to be adopted (Hastings and Domegan, 2014; French and Gordon, 2015).

SM in the 21st century is an interdisciplinary, creative, strategic and multifaceted marketing-based approach to facilitating or maintaining social good. It takes a citizen-centred approach in which insight developed with citizens and stakeholders informs the process. This 'participant orientation' is a key pillar of social marketing and differentiates it from many other social intervention approaches, particularly in traditional expert-driven, top-down public health approaches. These developments in social marketing are captured by the recent consensus definition, developed in 2013 by the International Social Marketing Association in collaboration with the European Social Marketing association and the Australian Association of Social Marketing. These organisations defined social marketing as follows:

> Social Marketing seeks to develop and integrate marketing concepts with other approaches to influence behaviours that benefit individuals and communities for the greater social good.
>
> Social Marketing practice is guided by ethical principles. It seeks to integrate research, best practice, theory, audience and partnership insight, to inform the delivery of competition sensitive and segmented social change programmes that are effective, efficient, equitable and sustainable.
>
> (iSMA, ESMA, and AASM, 2013)

To understand social marketing, it is useful to first of all understand what marketing is. The American Marketing Association (AMA, 2013) defines marketing as 'the activity, set of institutions, and processes for creating, communicating, delivering, and exchanging offerings that have value for customers, clients, partners, and society at large'. This definition identifies how all-encompassing the marketing concept is – it is an umbrella under which a host of values, frameworks, models, actors, activities and processes operate. A key focus in commercial marketing is that the marketing process is undertaken with the expectation of fostering commercial gain, driving profits and delivering shareholder value. The most important distinction between social marketing and commercial marketing is that the objective of the former is social good and not commercial gain. However, social marketing is not simply the transfer of commercial marketing ideas to the social arena. At an ideological level social marketing is not, as some may argue, a stalking horse for neoliberalism and for uncontrolled free market economics to be applied to the supply and consumption of social goods and programmes. Nor is it just the application of commercially derived techniques markets to assist with social objectives.

Indeed, social marketing seeks to reclaim the three fundamental human characteristics of *mutuality*, *exchange* and *reciprocity* that have been so successfully used by commercial marketing. These three fundamental human characteristics can and should be used as powerful drivers to promote social good, and for most of human history they have been. The fact that these core human processes are key pillars of marketing often comes as a surprise to people who erroneously believe marketing is merely about advertising and the communication and promotion of goods and services. However, contemporary marketing has been critiqued by leading scholars such as Kotler (2015) for moving away from these traditional values due to corporatisation and diverging from an approach that is focused on mutual benefit and serves firms, consumers and markets. Social marketing, on the other hand, integrates mutuality, exchange and reciprocity to help deliver social good.

In addition to a social good, rather than commercial gain orientation, social marketing differs from commercial marketing in a number of other ways. Given that there is a primary focus on creating social value and fostering social good in social marketing, the conditions in which it operates are often quite different from commercial marketing. For example, commercial marketing firms are most likely to target primary customer segments that will provide them the greatest volume of or the most profitable sales. In social marketing, participants in social programmes are often segmented and engaged based on different criteria, including the significance and prevalence of a given social issue, available resources, the ability to reach and influence certain groups and a group's ability to change behaviours that may result in social good.

Social Marketing Principles, Concepts and Techniques

There are a number of principles, concepts and techniques that form the basis of social marketing (see Lee and Kotler, 2011; Hastings and Domegan, 2014; French and Gordon, 2015).

The Core Social Marketing Principle = Social Good and Wellbeing

As illustrated in Figure 25.1, the core and principal objective of social marketing is to create social good – which results in more equitable, sustainable, healthy, happy and productive societies and individuals. In effect, social marketing is oriented towards facilitating wellbeing in society. However, there are often debates and power relations inherent in how social good is defined. Small groups of powerful elites have always sought to define 'social good'. These elites use what Foucault would describe as the technologies of power, including oratory, law, rituals, religion, communication, entertainment and force to persuade people to behave in ways that are believed to be beneficial for the wider group and for the elite itself (Marr, 2012). However, such elites can be, and have been, challenged by general economic development, literacy, access to information and mass connectivity (e.g. through the Internet and social media) that have created new forms of power relationships and greater engagement in what 'social good' is and identified the need for new forms of social discourse and social development, such as social marketing. Social marketing seeks to put the power to define social good in the hands of citizens and not power elites.

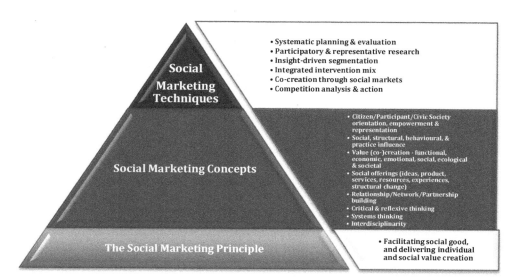

Figure 25.1 Social marketing principles, concepts and techniques model.

Source: Adapted from French and Russell-Bennett, 2015.

Participant Orientation

Participant orientation is a key concept in social marketing. It can be argued that participants need to perceive benefits when purchasing a product or service, performing a behaviour or engaging with an idea. However, with respect to social marketing, there is increasing recognition that participant orientation should focus beyond individual and transactional exchange ideas (what is in it for me?), to delivering individual and social value (what is in it for me, everyone, society and social good?) (French and Gordon, 2015). Essentially the participant orientation fosters a bottom-up, consultative, participatory, collaborative and empowering approach to social marketing and social programmes. As such it requires those involved in social marketing programmes to engage with, conduct research with, consult, collaborate, empower and develop ownership of social change efforts among participants.

For example, a social marketing project in Edinburgh aiming to use a community-led assets-based approach to promote healthy lifestyles and wellbeing was strongly focused on the participant orientation (Stead et al., 2013). The project involved mapping the existing resources, skills and other assets already in the community, engaged a community-led needs assessment process and engaged local people in co-creating and delivering interventions – for example, a local store promoted and invectives healthy food choices, and local school children developed materials promoting healthy lifestyles. The focus on participant orientation is one of the key facets in good social marketing programmes.

Using Research and Insight

Research lies at the heart of social marketing and is strongly linked to participant orientation. The use of research ranges from defining a social issue, scoping knowns and unknowns and engaging participants, stakeholders and institutions to testing social marketing programme components, monitoring implementation and programme evaluation (French and Gordon, 2015). Social marketing research is effectively a form of action research – a process of inquiry conducted by and for those taking action (Lewin, 1946). In social marketing the ultimate goal is to use research insight to help foster social good and wellbeing. For example, research on low-income older people's energy use practices in regional New South Wales identified practices of thrift that could cause health and social harms (see Waitt et al., 2016), and this insight has been used to help develop a comprehensive energy efficiency social marketing programme (see http://www.energyplusillawarra.com.au).

Using Theory Judiciously

Critical to any social marketing programme is that it is informed by and makes judicious use of theory. Traditionally, social marketing has drawn from communications, public health, behavioural and psychological theories such as social cognitive theory, health belief models, stages of change and the theory of planned behaviour (Gordon, 2011). However, more recently, social marketing scholars have encouraged engagement with and identified the relevance of a much broader range of theories, including systems theories and social theories, as well as communications, public health, behavioural and psychology theories. Therefore, ideas such as assemblages and actor-network theories (see Gordon and Gurrieri, 2014), habitus (Spotswood and Tapp, 2013), social practice theory (see French and Gordon, 2015) and the socioecological model (French and Gordon, 2015) have more recently been used in social marketing. Furthermore, a number of planning models and frameworks can be and are used in social marketing, such as PRECEDE-PROCEED (Green and Kreuter, 2005), the WHO COMBI model (WHO, 2012), the P-Process model (O'Sullivan et al., 2003) and STELa (French, 2010). For a more comprehensive discussion on the range of and use of theory in social marketing see French and Gordon (2015, ch. 8).

Theory in social marketing can help conceptualise and understand complex social issues, guide the planning of programmes, make some contribution to effective and efficient programme delivery (Roe et al., 1997; Halpern et al., 2003) and assist with evaluation of programmes. Using theory can result in better planning and targeting, as well as setting out of more explicit aims and objectives. Theory can also help interventions focus more precisely on influencing specific elements of behaviour or social practices, based on a theoretical conception of what has been or is likely to influence people to behave in a certain way.

Schuster et al. (2012) provide an example of using theory relevant to the use of social marketing of m-wellbeing services. They use the model of goal-directed behaviour (MGB) to examine the consumer acceptance of technology-based self-service (TBSS) for a credence service instrumental to a social goal. Their findings generally support using the MGB to enhance understanding of consumers' acceptance of TBSS. Interestingly, they also found evidence of the importance of maintenance self-efficacy, the self-evaluation of the ability to continue using the service and the consumer-level competition that arises between alternatives that achieve the same goal.

There are a range of established theories of wellbeing including self-determination theory, wellbeing theory, broaden and build theory and strengths theory. Each of these theories may provide useful conceptual architecture to build social marketing programs. For example, by adopting a wellbeing theory, the elements of positive emotions, engagement, positive relationships, meaning and accomplishment will be emphasised. Specific behavioural and attitudinal changes can be specified for the appropriate segment, such as secondary school students.

Segmenting and Positioning

Segmentation and positioning of social marketing is a core technique that is used to ensure that social programmes do not take a one-size-fits-all approach. Instead they are delivered using participant orientation and using insight from research. Market segmentation is a well-established business technique that is used to identify and manage diverse customer/participant needs and to target marketing resources (Weinstein, 2004; Dibb and Simkin, 2009). The basic premise of segmentation is that grouping similar groups of people into market segments and then focusing marketing efforts at these different segments as appropriate can manage heterogeneity in preferences (Mahajan and Jain, 1978).

Segmentation can be performed based on a number of different characteristics: for example, demographics, cultures, subcultures attitudes, value perceptions, psychographics and behavioural/social practices (Eagle et al., 2013).

Various packages and toolkits have been developed to aid with segmentation strategy, such as the Values and Lifestyle Survey (VALS) grouping people according to their personal values and lifestyle choices (Della et al., 2009), or the UK Department of Health's 'Healthy Foundations' model, which identifies life stage, environment and attitudes towards health issues as three key dimensions linked with health behaviours (see Department of Health, 2008).

Once participant segments have been identified, social marketers then consider which population segments to target and engage in social programmes. Target groups need to be large enough to warrant attention given the often-limited resources available to deliver social programmes and need to be viable in terms of allocation of resources. For example, running a quit-smoking programme that targets low-income smokers is potentially a viable choice of target, as smoking prevalence is higher in low-income populations. Target groups also need to be reasonably accessible, and channels of communication and engagement with participants need to exist. The target group also needs to be potentially responsive to social marketing efforts – as Hastings and Domegan (2014) identify, there is no point engaging groups that do not need or do not want to be engaged on a given social issue.

Market segmentation is therefore extremely important to increasing awareness of wellbeing and increasing wellbeing-enhancing behaviours or practices at individual and systemic levels. For example, social marketing for school-aged children is very different from that for people in the workplace over the age of fifty years. A key issue here is language related to wellbeing. A further relevant segmentation may be gender. A school-aged male may simply view wellbeing as 'playing sport', whereas a fifty-two-year-old female in the workplace may emphasise quality of social relationships. Without segmentation the attempts may be very crude and untailored. For wellbeing-related initiatives this is likely to be paramount, as wellbeing is abstract and multifaceted and better segmentation is likely to lead to greater tangibility. Psychographic and behavioural segmentation have become increasingly important, moving beyond simple demographic segmentation.

Positioning in social marketing refers to a strategy that is used to foster a perception among participants regarding programme activities that achieve specific goals such as raising awareness, gaining brand recognition or reach of communications. Products, services, issues or ideas are positioned through the use of various marketing mix strategies. Essentially, positioning is a concept in the minds of target segments – how the consumers/participants see the product. In social marketing, it is sometimes necessary to consider repositioning social issues to highlight their importance or to reframe how people might perceive them. Examples include how smoke-free legislation in Scotland was repositioned from a purely public health issue to also be concerned with the civil rights of workers exposed to secondhand smoke (Gordon and Gurrieri, 2014).

This leads to the question of how best to position wellbeing. If the aim is to increase the wellbeing of the general population, what is the best way to position it in people's minds? Many people think of wellbeing simply as happiness or feeling good, positive emotions and a transient state of the individual. This also leaves it open to claims that it is 'soft', 'pollyannaish' or 'subjective' and not deserving of serious policy debate. Similarly, wellbeing is often juxtaposed with 'mental health', leading to many connotations that wellbeing is a euphemism for mental illness. Alternatively, there is an established area of wellbeing economics, and wellbeing could be positioned alongside economic indicators. Hence, the concept of positioning has a great deal to offer the emerging area of social marketing of wellbeing.

Using the Social Marketing Mix

Good social marketing programmes should involve the creative and informed use of a range of social change tools, activities and strategies – known as the social marketing mix. A successful social marketing programme will normally apply a mix of education and engagement, product or service delivery, information provision, environmental and systems change and potentially control methods as well (see French and Gordon, 2015, ch. 4). What is important is that a broad range of intervention tools are available and should be considered and used creatively, strategically, and holistically to deliver social marketing programmes. This means moving beyond the simplistic and limiting 4Ps marketing mix of product, price, place, and promotion that many people are familiar with to using the full range of tools available. A successful selection of the right weighted mix requires using research and if necessary pretesting to determine what intervention mix strategy will be capable of bringing about an affordable and ethical programme capable of delivering the desired social outcomes.

Competition

Competition is also a key differentiator between social marketing and commercial marketing. In commercial marketing, competition comes in the form of different providers of goods and services, or in competition for attention, loyalty and resources from customers, clients and stakeholders. In social marketing, competition can involve biological, social, environmental, economic and systems factors that impact on behaviour and social outcomes. It can also include organisations and individuals that seek to influence target groups and individuals to behave in ways that create social and/or individual harm (for example, the tobacco industry marketing to young people to encourage them to smoke).

Key forces that compete with social marketing programmes and engendering social good that have been identified by French and Gordon (2015) include existing behaviours such as smoking, social, economic and environmental barriers, perceived benefits of existing behaviours and lack of incentives to change.

The nature of the competition that social marketing faces often makes the design and delivery of social marketing programmes more complex and challenging than that of commercial marketing (Lee and Kotler, 2011). Consider the challenges faced when attempting to influence people to stop smoking (give up addictive behaviour that is perceived to relieve stress and/or control weight), reduce thermostat settings to reduce energy consumption (change what is perceived as a comfortable lifestyle choice) or give blood (fear of being uncomfortable and subjected to pain (French and Gordon, 2015)).

It is very useful to ask the question, *What is in competition with promoting wellbeing*?

Baumeister et al. (2001) refer to the negativity bias and the idea that the bad is stronger than the good. In this sense, discussing 'death from cancer' is more likely to gain attention than 'feeling good and functioning well'. This also adds to the motivation to accept individualist and biological approaches to health and illness, reinforcing medical and treatment-based approaches eclipsing both social and preventive approaches, where wellbeing may be most relevant. The adage, 'if it ain't broke, don't fix it', may be the greatest competition to wellbeing approaches.

Critical Thinking

Critical thinking in social marketing is an area that has attracted increasing attention in recent years, as scholars not only have considered issues relating to critique of forces that work in opposition to social marketing, but also have engaged in critical debate about social marketing and encouraged critically reflexive practice in the field. Having already discussed critical analysis of commercial forces and critical competition analysis earlier in this chapter, here we will focus on critical debate within social marketing and on critical reflexivity.

Although most of the focus for critical social marketing has been on competitive analysis and critique of commercial marketing, and corporate institutions and forces (see Gordon, 2011), scholars are increasingly recognising the importance of critical debate in social marketing (Spotswood et al., 2012).

One such criticism of social marketing is that the field is too positivist in nature (Dholakia and Dholakia, 2001), perhaps reflecting the dominant positivist managerialist approach of mainstream marketing (Alvesson, 1994). Other critics have identified that social marketing is a force of neoliberalism (Hackley, 2009) and focuses too much on individual behaviour change while ignoring the broader social and structural environment (Crawshaw, 2012; Langford and Panter-Brick, 2013). These debates have been picked up by social marketers, who have called for greater focus on social and structural forces (Gordon, 2013) and a rejection of neoliberal ideas in the field (see Gordon and Gurrieri, 2014). Critics have also identified a lack of critical reflexivity in social marketing (Tadajewksi and Brownlie, 2008), with social marketers calling for a broadened critical social marketing paradigm that encompasses reflexivity (Spotswood et al., 2012; Gordon and Gurrieri, 2014).

There has also been considerable debate about ethics in social marketing, with questions such as what constitutes social good, what social issues should be tackled, what tactics should be used in social marketing programmes and whether the use of fear appeals to improve public health is ethical and justifiable (see Hastings et al., 2004; Eagle et al., 2013). Other critical debates focus on the nature and use of the social marketing mix (Gordon, 2012; Tapp and Spotswood, 2013) or the use of theory in social marketing (Peattie and Peattie, 2003). These critical debates help develop the discipline and engagement in reflexivity.

Systems Thinking

Systems thinking is the study and gaining of understanding of how systems behave, interact and influence each other. Systems thinking can be applied to solving problems by considering problems as constituent parts of overall systems. Importantly, systems thinking recognises that the usual way of understanding things through a process of analysis involving deconstruction of problems into separate individual components that we then study is often ineffective for understanding complex issues (Bertalanffy, 1968). Systems thinking involves analysis and synthesis. As such, it is just as important to attempt to understand and to synthesise the nature of a system – how things fit together and how a system operates and relates to the environment – in addition to undertaking analysis of the elements of a system and the nature of their interaction. This helps us to understand the how and the why of things.

Systems thinking involves seeing the bigger picture, being strategic and thinking about the short and long term. It also has synergies with identifying and fostering partnerships and engaging in relational thinking to tackle complex social problems. Key ways of thinking that can help people to engage in systems thinking include big picture thinking, non-linear thinking, dynamic thinking, taking a ten-mile view, finding feedback loops and scientific thinking. In taking multiple views of complex issues, it is argued that a better understanding can be formed and issues can be more effectively tackled. Ideas on systems thinking are becoming increasingly relevant in social marketing, given the considerable complexity of the social issues to which it is applied (see French and Gordon, 2015).

Systems thinking applied to wellbeing is very useful. Systems thinking takes into consideration how the characteristics of the system might hold the solution by

- Examining the dynamic interrelationships between the elements of the system
- Engaging with multiple perspectives
- Reflecting on systems boundaries.

For example, wellbeing may be conceptualised at multiple levels from the macro, including economic systems, to the micro, including positive neuroscience. Examples of macro-economic approaches to wellbeing include ongoing debates about the limitations of gross domestic product (GDP) and the need for national accounts of wellbeing. At the organisational level, recent debates regarding integrated capital and the need for accountants to report six types of capital (Gleeson-White, 2014) including financial capital, manufacturing capital, social and relationship capital, intellectual capital, human capital and natural capital. Such approaches are likely to be consistent with broader wellbeing agendas and enable one to examine changes at a broader systemic level.

Creating Value

As identified earlier, exchange, mutuality and reciprocity are key human processes that are important in social marketing. In recent years, a big focus in social marketing has been on the concept of value creation – which draws on these processes and offers a holistic framework for understanding ways to foster social good.

Value can be defined as "the regard that something is held to deserve, the importance, worth, or usefulness of something" (Oxford English Dictionary, 2013). Traditional conceptualisations of value in commercial marketing originate from the value chain framework (Porter, 1985) and emanate from an industrial and supply-chain perspective. This approach views firms as value determinants, creators and deliverers, and consumers as value consumers and destroyers. This concept of *value-in-exchange* is normally goods-oriented – for example, the value in purchasing a washing machine. *Value-in-exchange* can offer extrinsic and intrinsic benefits, though primarily this tends towards extrinsic benefits. In the social marketing context, *value-in-exchange* may be a useful rubric in social programmes that involve distribution of goods, for example, condoms or screening kits in sexual health interventions. However, social marketing often does not involve such tangible or economic exchanges.

More recently, an experiential approach to investigating value, known as the *value-in-use* concept, has emerged. Experiential value considers value to be an interactive and relativistic preference experience related to the total experience of consuming goods and services (Holbrook, 2006). This uses a *value-in-use* approach (Holbrook, 2006) that is process-oriented and has largely emanated from the services marketing paradigm. *Value-in-use* posits that consumer value is realised during the consumption experience, rather than being embedded in goods or services (Sandström et al., 2008). This appears to be of relevance to social marketing by offering a lens through which to understand how people engage with experiences in social marketing programmes – such as using a smoking cessation service or a health clinic.

Recent work by social marketers has focused on whether and how citizens may perceive value in the actual behaviour(s) and practices required in facilitating social good. Zainuddin and Gordon (2014) have proposed moving from a goods orientation housed in economic exchange theory towards not only an experiential orientation, but also a behaviour orientation towards value in social marketing – *value-in-behaviour*. The argument is that if people perceive value in performing behaviours and practices, then this insight can be used to help identify and support the value of doing things that result in social good (Gordon et al., 2015) – an argument that is not new and can be traced back to Aristotle's idea of eudemonic wellbeing, mentioned previously in this chapter.

Value can be perceived by people in buying a product, using a service, or performing behaviours across a number of dimensions. Functional value relates to the performance and functionality that something offers (for example, consistent quality of a breast screening service). Economic value relates to the financial benefit, price and cost–benefit ratio offered by something (e.g. a free smoking cessation service). Emotional value refers to the value derived from the experience of something such as pleasure, confidence or fear (e.g. reduced anxiety from attending a health clinic). Social value relates to value derived from association with others/groups and impact on self-worth through engaging with something (e.g. attending gym classes to fit in with friends who do the same). Ecological value refers to value relating to impact on the environment from engaging with something (using energy efficiently to make a contribution towards reducing climate change). Finally, societal value refers to the value for society at large from engaging with something (e.g. stopping smoking to reduce the potential burden on a national health service from smoking-related illness).

Research by Zainuddin et al. (2013) has shown how important value creation is in social marketing. Their study provides a model of value creation in a preventive health service. Their model focused on how interactions could affect consumer-perceived value and the subsequent impact on key service outcomes of satisfaction and customer behaviour intentions to use a preventive health service again in the future. They demonstrate a key aim of social marketing by showing how the creation and provision of value can lead to the achievement of desirable social behaviour. The practical implications of their results indicate the importance of the resources provided by users in the creation of value, signifying the importance of customer education and management.

In many ways the focus on creating value in social marketing has synergies with creating wellbeing. The creation of value often leads to or is oriented towards fostering wellbeing, and this relates back to the core objective of social marketing, which is to facilitate social good. Therefore, although people working in the social marketing field and the wellbeing field may use different language, theories and concepts, ultimately there are major commonalities in the ultimate objectives in both domains of creating equitable, sustainable, healthy, happy and productive societies and individuals. Approaches in social marketing and wellbeing that focus on value creation, mutualism, social welfare, social justice and social equality demonstrate that the synergies between these domains warrants further exploration.

References

Aked, J., Marks, N., Cordon, C., & Thompson, S. (2011). *Five ways to wellbeing: New applications, new ways of thinking*. Centre for Well-Being, NEF (the New Economic Foundation).

Alvesson, M. (1994). Critical theory and consumer marketing. *Scandinavian Journal of Management*, 10(3), 291–313.

AMA (American Marketing Association) (2013). Definition of marketing. Available at http://www.marketingpower.com/AboutAMA/Pages/DefinitionofMarketing.aspx.

Aristotle (1980). *The Nicomachean Ethics*. Translated with an Introduction by Ross, D. New York, NY: Oxford University Press.

Baumeister, R., Bratslavsky, E., Finkeneauer, C., & Vohs, K. D. (2001). Bad is stronger than good. *Review of General Psychology*, 5(4), 323–370.

Bertalanffy, L. von (1968). *General Systems Theory*. New York, NY: George Braziller.

Crawshaw, P. (2012). Governing at a distance: Social marketing and the (bio) politics of responsibility. *Social Science and Medicine*, 75(1), 200–207.

Church, A. T., Katigbak, M. S., Locke, K. D., Zhang, H., Shen, J., Vargas-Flores, J. de J., et al. (2013). Need satisfaction and well-being: Testing self-determination theory in eight cultures. *Journal of Cross-Cultural Psychology*, 44(4), 507–534.

Della, L. J., DeJoy, D. M., & Lance, C. E. (2009). Explaining fruit and vegetable intake using a consumer marketing tool. *Health Education and Behaviour*, 36(5), 895–914.

Department of Health (2008). *Healthy foundations: A segmentation model*. London, UK: The Stationery Office.

Dholakia, R. R., & Dholakia, N. (2001). Social marketing and development. In Bloom, P., and Gundlach, G. (Eds.), *Handbook of Marketing and Society* (pp. 486–505). Thousand Oaks, CA: Sage.

Dibb, S., & Simkin, L. (2009). Implementation rules to bridge the theory/practice divide in market segmentation. *Journal of Marketing Management*, 25(3), 375–396.

Eagle, L., Dahl, S., Hill, S., Bird, S., Spotswood, F., & Tapp, A. (2013). *Social Marketing*. London, UK: Pearson.

Forgeard, M., Jayawickreme, E., Kern, M., & Seligman, M. (2011). Doing the right thing: Measuring wellbeing for public policy. *International Journal of Wellbeing*, 1(1), 79–106.

Fredrickson, B. L., (2001). The role of positive emotions in positive psychology: The broaden-and-build theory of positive emotions. *American Psychologist*, 56(3), 218–226.

French, J. (2010). STELa Social Marketing Planning Model. Available at http://stelamodel.com/.

French, J. (2011). Business as unusual: The contribution of social marketing to government policy making and strategy development. In Hastings, G., Angus, K., and Bryant, C. (Eds.), *The Sage Handbook of Social Marketing* (pp. 359–374). London, UK: Sage.

French, J., & Gordon, R. (2015). *Strategic social marketing*. London, UK: Sage.

French, J., & Russell-Bennett, R. (2015). A hierarchical model of social marketing. *Journal of Social Marketing*, 5(2), 139–159.

Gaffney, M. (2011). *Flourishing: How to achieve a deeper sense of wellbeing, meaning and purpose – Even when facing adversity*. London, UK: Penguin Books.

Gleeson-White, J. (2014). *Six capitals: The revolution capitalism has to have – Or can accountants save the planet?* Sydney, Australia: Allen & Unwin.

Gordon, R. (2011). Critical social marketing: Definition, application and domain. *Journal of Social Marketing*, 1(2), 82–99.

Gordon, R. (2012). Re-thinking and re-tooling the social marketing mix. *Australasian Marketing Journal*, 20(2), 122–126.

Gordon, R. (2013). Unlocking the potential of upstream social marketing. *European Journal of Marketing*, 47(9), 1525–1547.

Gordon, R., Butler, K., Magee, C., Waitt, G., & Cooper, P. (2015). Using value theory for segmentation in social marketing. World Social Marketing Conference, Sydney.

Gordon, R., & Gurrieri, L. (2014). Towards a reflexive turn: Social marketing assemblages. *Journal of Social Marketing*, 4(3), 261–278.

Gordon, R., McDermott, L., Stead, M., & Angus, K. (2006). The effectiveness of social marketing interventions for health improvement: What's the evidence? *Public Health*, 120(12), 1133–1139.

Green, L., & Kreuter, M. (2005). *Health promotion planning: An educational and ecological approach* (fourth ed.). Mountain View, CA: Mayfield Publishers.

Hackley, C. (2009). Parallel universes and disciplinary space: The bifurcation of managerialism and social science in marketing studies. *Journal of Marketing Management*, 25(7/8), 643–659.

Halpern, D., Bates, C., & Beales, G. (2003). *Personal responsibility and behaviour change*. London, UK: Prime Minister's Strategy Unit, Cabinet Office.

Hastings, G., & Domegan, C. (2014). *Social marketing: From tunes to symphonies* (second ed.). London, UK: Routledge.

Hastings, G., Stead, M., & Webb, J. (2004). Fear appeals in social marketing: Strategic and ethical reasons for concern. *Psychology and Marketing*, 21(11), 961–986.

Holbrook, M. B. (2006). Consumption experience, customer value, and subjective personal introspection: An illustrative photographic essay. *Journal of Business Research*, 59(6), 714–725.

iSMA, ESMA, & AASM (International Social Marketing Association, European Social Marketing Association and Australian Association of Social Marketing) (2013). Consensus definition of social marketing. Available at http://www.i-socialmarketing.org/index.php?option=com_content&view=article&id=84:social-marketing-definition&catid=28:front-page#.VIoD0sKzV2s.

Kraut, Richard (2007). *What is good and why: The ethics of well-being*. Cambridge, MA: Harvard University Press.

Kraut, Richard (2014). Aristotle's ethics. In *Stanford Encyclopaedia of Philosophy*, available at http://plato.stanford.edu/entries/aristotle-ethics/.

Kotler, P., & Zaltman, G. (1971). Social marketing: An approach to planned social change. *Journal of Marketing*, 35(3), 3–12.

Kotler, P. (2015). *Confronting capitalism: Real solutions for a troubled economy*. New York, NY: Amacom.

Langford, R., & Panter-Brick, C. (2013). A health equity critique of social marketing: When interventions have impact but insufficient reach. *Social Science and Medicine*, 83, 133–141.

Lee, N., & Kotler, P. (2011). *Social marketing: Influencing behaviours for good*. New York, NY: Sage.

Lefebvre, R. C. (2012). Transformative social marketing. *Journal of Social Marketing*, 2(2), 118–129.

Lewin, K. (1946). Action research and minority problems. *Journal of Social Issues*, 2(4), 34–46.

Mahajan, V., & Jain, A. K. (1978). An approach to normative segmentation. *Journal of Marketing Research*, 15(3), 338–345.

Marques, S. C., Pais-Ribeiro, J. L., & Lopez, S. J. (2011). The role of positive psychology constructs in predicting mental health and academic achievement in children and adolescents: A two-year longitudinal study. *Journal of Happiness Studies*, 12(6), 1049–1062. doi:10.1007/s10902-010-9244-4.

Marr, A. (2012). *A history of the world*. London, UK: Macmillan.

Nussbaum, M., & Glover, J. (Eds.) (1995). *Women, culture and development: A study of human capabilities*. Oxford, UK: Clarendon Press.

OECD (2013). *OECD guidelines on measuring subjective well-being*. Paris, France: OECD Publishing.

Oxford English Dictionary (2013). Oxford, UK: Oxford University Press.

O'Sullivan, G.A., Yonkler, J.A., Morgan, W., & Merritt, A.P. (2003). *A Field Guide to Designing a Health Communication Strategy*. Baltimore, MD: Johns Hopkins Bloomberg School of Public Health/Centre for Communication Programs.

Peattie, S., & Peattie, K. (2003). Ready to fly solo: Reducing social marketing's dependence on commercial marketing theory. *Marketing Theory*, 3(3), 365–385.

Porter, M. E. (1985). *Competitive Advantage: Creating and Sustaining Superior Performance*. New York, NY: The Free Press.

Roe, L., Hunt, P., Bradshaw, H., & Rayner, M. (1997). *Health Promotion Effectiveness Reviews 6: Health Promotion Interventions to Promote Healthy Eating in the General Population: A Review*. London, UK: Health Education Authority.

Russell-Bennett, R., Wood, M., & Previte, J. (2013). Fresh ideas: Services thinking for social marketing. *Journal of Social Marketing*, 3(3), 223–238.

Ryff, C. D., (1989). Happiness is everything, or is it? Explorations on the meaning of psychological well-being. *Journal of Personality and Social Psychology*, 57(6), 1069–1081.

Sandström, S., Edvardsson, B., Kristensson, P., & Magnusson, P. (2008). Value in use through service experience. *Managing Service Quality*, 18(2), 112–126.

Schuster, L., Drennan, J., & N. Lings, I. (2013). Consumer acceptance of m-wellbeing services: A social marketing perspective. *European Journal of Marketing*, 47(9), 1439–1457.

Seligman, M.E.P. (2011). *Flourish: A visionary understanding of happiness and wellbeing*. New York, NY: Free Press

Smith, A., & O'Sullivan, T. (2012). Environmentally responsible behaviour in the workplace: An internal social marketing approach. *Journal of Marketing Management*, 28(3–4), 469–493.

Spotswood, F., French, J., Tapp, A., & Stead, M. (2012). Some reasonable but uncomfortable questions about social marketing. *Journal of Social Marketing*, 2(3), 163–175.

Spotswood, F., & Tapp, A. (2013). Beyond persuasion: A cultural perspective of behaviour. *Journal of Social Marketing*, 3(3), 275–294.

Stead, M., Arnott, L., & Dempsey, E. (2013). Healthy heroes, magic meals, and a visiting alien: Community-led assets based social marketing. *Social Marketing Quarterly*, 19(1), 26–39.

Stead, M., Gordon, R., Angus, K., & McDermott, L. (2007). A systematic review of social marketing effectiveness. *Health Education*, 107(2), 126–140.

Tadajewski, M., & Brownlie, D. (2008). Critical marketing: A limit attitude. In Tadajewski, M., & Brownlie, D. (Eds.), *Critical Marketing: Issues in Contemporary Marketing* (pp. 1–28). London, UK: John Wiley.

Tapp, A., & Spotswood, F. (2013). From the 4Ps to COM-SM: reconfiguring the social marketing mix. *Journal of Social Marketing*, 3(3), 206–222.

Trout, J., & Rivkin, S. (1996). *The new positioning: The latest on the world's #1 business strategy*. New York, NY: McGraw-Hill.

Weinstein, A. (2004). *Handbook of market segmentation*. New York, NY: The Haworth Press.

WHO (World Health Organization) (2012). *Communication for behavioural impact (COMBI): A toolkit for behavioural and social communication in outbreak response*. Geneva, Switzerland: WHO. Available at http://www.who.int/ihr/publications/combi_toolkit_fieldwkbk_outbreaks/en/.

Zainuddin, N., & Gordon, R. (2014). Social marketing, value, and behaviour: Some important considerations. Paper presented at the International Social Marketing Conference, Frankston.

Zainuddin, N., Previte, J., & Russell-Bennett, R. (2011). A social marketing approach to value creation in a well-women's health service. *Journal of Marketing Management*, 27(3–4), 361–385.

Zainuddin, N., Russell-Bennett, R., & Previte, J. (2013). The value of health and wellbeing: An empirical model of value creation in social marketing. *European Journal of Marketing*, 47(9), 1504–1524.

Wellbeing and Recovery
A Possible Future

Lindsay G. Oades, Mike Slade and Aaron Jarden

Prospection, the representation of possible futures, is a ubiquitous feature of the human mind (Seligman et al., 2013). In this chapter we adopt a subjunctive mood and go beyond evidence within the three sections covered in this book to explore possible futures for both recovery and wellbeing, identifying three emerging themes within each area. Some are well-established themes growing further, such as peer support, whereas others are nascent, such as wellbeing literacy. The chapter concludes with some reflections upon the interaction between wellbeing and recovery in the future – returning the reader to the original intent of this book. Is recovery a transitional discourse? If so, transitioning to what? Will we ever talk of a lived experience of wellbeing? Can wellbeing be conceived of as an emancipatory politics, not in competition with the intent of recovery?

Wellbeing: A Possible Future

We identify overarching themes emerging from wellbeing science and its applications, which have broad implications: wellbeing economics, wellbeing accounting and wellbeing literacy.

Theme 1: Wellbeing Economics

In Chapter 4, Weijers and Jarden discussed the issues surrounding the problems with gross domestic product (GDP) and other traditional economic indicators. We refer to this emerging theme here as wellbeing economics. As Weijers and Jarden argue, the limitations of traditional economic indicators have led researchers to call for scientific measures of wellbeing to augment traditional measures (Diener et al., 2009; Layard, 2005).

As Helliwell (2006) states, a central problem with measures of per capita production, income and wealth is that they do not attribute direct value to many factors widely viewed as essential to high wellbeing, including relationships, health and happiness. Thus, national governments and multinational organisations are investigating new measures of wellbeing to inform policy making (Diener, 2009; Stiglitz et al., 2009).

Diener (2009) reports how many of these new measures have been incorporated into various policy making processes. With the emergence of wellbeing science, and its increased resources and rigor in wellbeing measurement, there is an increased opportunity for wellbeing metrics to sit alongside other established economic indicators, in turn influencing public policy. Such advances will have flow-on effects in the fields of mental health and recovery.

Theme 2: Wellbeing Accounting

In the same way that GDP is criticised in an economic context, it is useful to explore emerging trends within the accounting context – particularly managerial accounting. What exactly does an organisation keep accounts of? We refer to the emerging discussion about the need to augment traditional types of capital (financial and manufacturing) as wellbeing accounting, particularly as it concerns the human, social and relationship capitals which provide opportunities for people to experience wellbeing – for example, environmental mastery, positive relationships.

Gleeson-White (2014) proposes six-capital accounting:

1. Financial capital: the funds available to an organisation to produce goods or provide services
2. Manufactured capital: manufactured physical objects available to an organisation to produce goods or products services, such as buildings, equipment, infrastructure
3. Intellectual capital: knowledge-based intangibles, including patents, copyrights, software and organisational capacity such as systems, protocols and 'tacit knowledge'
4. Human capital: people's skills, abilities, experience, motivation, intelligence, health and productivity
5. Social and relationship capital: institutions and relationships within and between communities, shared norms, common values and behaviour, noting that the carriers of social and relationship capital are networks of humans
6. Natural capital: all renewable and nonrenewable environmental resources and processes that provide goods and services

Importantly, the latter four of the six capitals are referred to as 'living capitals'. We argue that if organisations were indeed required to keep accounts for all types of capital, then discussion and measurement of wellbeing would become more explicit as the fabric of business. Accounting represents an interesting leverage point within more systemic approaches to wellbeing. Based on adages such as 'measure it, treasure it' or 'what gets measured, matters', such trends have a significant potential to create broader changes in the way wellbeing is viewed and accepted as a societal reference point. For example, if relationships are the 'immune system' of society, then a wellbeing accountancy approach allows its measurement. By quantifying various dimensions of a 'healthy society', including dimensions which are currently neglected, wellbeing accountancy has the potential to provide indicators by which the success of policy can be judged.

Theme 3: Wellbeing Literacy

If wellbeing were a foreign language, how best would we teach and learn it? While many may not think of wellbeing as a foreign language, surveying people's vocabulary around wellbeing often leads to lists of illness-bound descriptions, where people view wellbeing as the absence of illness. Many 'mental health and wellbeing' initiatives often revert to illness prevention. Although this is worthwhile in itself, it does not honour recent wellbeing science, which provides further evidence of the antecedents and predictors of wellbeing, beyond what prevents disease. Terms such as mental health literacy, health literacy and emotional literacy already exist (Roffey, 2008). Wellbeing literacy, including physical wellbeing, can be considered as the vocabulary, knowledge and skills that we need to discuss how to improve our wellbeing and the wellbeing of others. If it is a literacy, it can be taught and learnt. Health systems are likely to frame such a discussion within promotion and prevention language, whereas an education system will likely refer to it as learning, particularly social and emotional learning.

In the same way we conceive of national numeracy and literacy, perhaps we can conceive of wellbeing literacy. Which wellbeing words should a ten-year-old school student know? What facts should a ten-year-old student know about what predicts wellbeing? How should this student be able to functionally (i.e. in relation to his or her own situation) use these words by age ten? Could we, for example, identify a set of skills (e.g. ability to demonstrate resilience when faced with challenges; ability to form and maintain relationships with students from different backgrounds; ability to make choices) which wellbeing literacy aims to promote?

As mentioned, emotional literacy is an established area. Assisting people, often school-aged children, to label and identify their emotions and the emotions of others has grown in popularity and evidence. The issue, however, is that emotions are only one part of wellbeing. There are several challenges to enabling greater wellbeing literacy, as described in Table 26.1.

Table 26.1 Challenges in Defining and Understanding Wellbeing

Multidimensionality	Wellbeing is viewed by many as a multidimensional construct – it has multiple parts which may add to confusion when trying to understand, define or measure wellbeing.
Tangibility	Wellbeing as a term is quite abstract and people need to use examples to grasp it. For example, people may say what they are doing when they are experiencing wellbeing, or that wellbeing is being with friends. These are descriptors, not a definition of wellbeing itself.
Conflation of cause/effect	Similarly to the tangibility problem, people will often mix up what causes or predicts wellbeing with a definition of what wellbeing is in itself. For example, improving social inclusion increases wellbeing but in itself is not a definition of wellbeing.
Level of analysis	Wellbeing may be conceptualised at multiple levels of analysis, for example individual, couple, family/team/group, organisation, community, city, region, nation or global. Conceptual confusion is likely to occur if the level of analysis being discussed is not clarified.
Domains	Related to the multidimensionality of wellbeing, the term wellbeing will often be applied to certain domains or aspects of life. For example, people talk about emotional wellbeing, mental wellbeing, physical wellbeing, financial wellbeing, family wellbeing and organisational wellbeing. This further adds to the complexities related to its definition.
Ways of knowing	Different contexts and cultures have different ways of knowing (i.e. differing in epistemology, what we view as acceptable knowledge). Science privileges 'knowing that', generalising across context. However, 'knowing how' to do something, such as driving a car, and 'knowing from' a position or experience, such as having a baby, are other ways of knowing. For these reasons, how people define wellbeing and how well language can be used to describe experiences creates challenges in shared understanding of wellbeing.
Dynamic	If wellbeing is defined as a state, it can be very changeable. Some definitions of wellbeing view it as an emotional state, while others view it as a more stable characteristic. These issues of definition become important when trying to measure wellbeing.

A comprehensive population-based approach to wellbeing literacy represents an interesting possible future, broadening the holders of wellbeing-related knowledge and vocabulary well beyond the province of health systems. The use of social marketing – as discussed in Chapter 25 – is likely to assist with improving wellbeing literacy, in addition to school curricula and workplace initiatives.

Recovery: A Possible Future

We identify overarching themes emerging from recovery-oriented practice and systems and which have wider implications: co-production, peer support and a focus on citizenship.

Theme 1: Co-production

Co-production means 'delivering public services in an equal and reciprocal relationship between professionals, people using services, their families and their neighbours' (Boyle and Harris, 2009). In other words, services "work with rather than do unto others' (Cummins, 2007).

It is an idea which has emerged from a number of sources, and therefore has a number of narratives associated with it. One narrative was described in Chapter 15. Another narrative derives from efforts to conduct top-down and centralised management of human systems. Public sector systems in high-income countries are increasingly inspected, monitored and subject to competitive tendering processes, with the goal of maximising quality. The unintended consequence of these approaches is often reduced efficiency and worker burnout:

> One former member of the Bristol drugs action team complained that he had to keep his eyes on 44 different funding streams, nine different grids and 82 different objectives imposed on him by managers, funders and the government. Before he resigned, he reckoned that he and his colleagues spent less than 40 per cent of their time actually tackling drugs issues. He compared his management regime to a kind of addiction: 'Monitoring has become almost religious in status, as has centralised control', he said. 'The demand for quick hits and early wins is driven by a central desire analogous to the instant gratification demands made by drug users themselves.' The target regime has delivered an illusory control to the centre, based on inaccurate data which, from the perspective of the challenges we now face, is actually hugely inefficient.
>
> (Boyle and Harris, 2009, p. 7)

Other influences include moves towards devolution of power from national to more regional or local levels, pressures on public spending, increasing awareness of new types of knowledge, the increasing emphasis on local democracy and the need for more personalised services (Needham, 2009). These societal changes have moved co-production up the political ladder.

Some key features of co-production are outlined in Chapter 15 and include recognising people as assets, valuing working differently, promoting reciprocity and building social networks (Boyle and Harris, 2009). However, the knowledge base about co-production tends to be based on individual case studies, such as the Villa Family scheme in France (Loubens, 2007), the Local Area Co-ordination scheme in Australia (Bartnik, 2007) and time banks in England (Seyfang, 2004). Perhaps because many of these groundbreaking initiatives have emerged from community development, social care and other nonhealth sectors, there has been less focus on developing and implementing models on a widespread basis.

Co-production has been actively explored in mental health systems. As discussed in relation to recovery learning communities (Chapter 14) and Recovery Colleges (Chapter 15), co-production provides a counterpoint to traditional mental health approaches of there being one expert in a clinician–patient meeting. Co-production is emerging as a useful conceptual vehicle to make expertise by experience more visible, both in individual clinical encounters and through people with lived experience working and leading at many levels of the mental health system. In relation to Recovery Colleges, the role of peer trainer is now well established, with much experiential learning about the need for transparent recruitment processes, active selection, ongoing supervision and support and the need for educational models that support rather than hinder co-production. Mental health systems are good at developing and evaluating models which can then be introduced in other areas and countries. Examples include assertive outreach/assertive community treatment, early psychosis and intensive home treatment approaches. Perhaps because of this culture, Recovery Colleges are being introduced across England and have spread to many other countries such as Australia.

Experiential learning about making co-production a routine part of mental health care has wider relevance beyond mental health systems, as described in relation to positive tertiary education (Chapter 21). The use of co-production in other sectors is now being explored, such as social care (Needham, 2009) and national health systems (Bradley, 2014). If the civil rights mantra 'nothing about us without us' is to become a social reality, then co-production needs to be at the heart of all our social systems.

Theme 2: Peer Support

Peer support is a recurring theme in a number of chapters. This is consistent with its strong evidence base. For example, a synthesis of the evidence from 1,023 studies (including 147 randomised trials and 27 reviews) concluded that 'peer support can help people feel more knowledgeable, confident and happy and less isolated. Peer support may also encourage people to take more care of their health which, in the longer term, could lead to better health outcomes' (The Evidence Centre, 2015). The authors identified cost effectiveness as a knowledge gap.

The role of peer support worker as part of the mental health workforce is now established. In England, a goal of half of the mental health workforce having lived experience is part of the national transformation programme (Shepherd et al., 2010). Peer support is also rapidly expanding in many other countries (Davidson, 2012; Slade, 2014).

The outcomes of peer workers in mental health have been evaluated. With some exceptions (Lloyd-Evans, 2014), reviews by the Cochrane Group (Pitt et al., 2013) and using systematic (Chinman, 2014) and nonsystematic (Miyamoto and Sono, 2012; Davidson, 2012) methodologies all find positive evidence of benefits.

Furthermore, empirically informed understanding of change models (Gillard, 2015) and experiences of peer support working (Walker, 2013) are emerging. Guidelines for the practice and training of peer support have been published (Sunderland, 2013). Cost-effectiveness analyses have been completed (Trachtenberg et al., 2013).

This evidence base has implications for wider society. An understanding of what peer support means, and how it is helpful, will be of relevance to any human system in people in one group ('Group A') working with people in another group ('Group B'). So in a mental health context, peer support comes from people who have used mental health services and now work in them to support other service users. They thus hold a dual identity (as members of both Group A and Group B), which enriches the resources available in Group A. Peer support offers at least two potential benefits. First, if there is a substantial social and cultural separation between Groups A and B, and if Group A holds more power, then stigma is likely to result. In a mental health context, there is a problem with in-system stigma of professionals (Henderson, 2014), and employment of peer support workers as carriers of culture into the system provides an opportunity to reduce the us–them distinction. Currently marginalised groups, such as people living on welfare, migrants and asylum seekers, are vulnerable to experiencing stigmatising attitudes, which may be addressed through the involvement of people from these groups in relevant policy and practice. Second, peer support increases the effectiveness of Group A. The positive experiences of peer support in mental health raises the question of whether there would be benefits, for example, from actively recruiting people with a criminal history to police forces or employing people with experience of homelessness as housing workers or former prisoners as prison officers.

Theme 3: Citizenship

A theme which has emerged repeatedly throughout the discussion of recovery in this book is that it happens in communities and in 'real life', not in hospitals and clinics. It is clear that stigmas and discrimination, both anticipated (Thornicroft et al., 2009) and experienced (Corker et al., 2013), for many people are worse than the illness itself. The implication is that the problem is therefore in part society, and so in line with the civil rights mantra 'Fix society, not people', social solutions should be the first approach (Slade, 2015). For mental health professionals, this means a new emphasis on social and political activism (Slade, 2010). For service users and their allies, it points to the need for solidarity and collective action to challenge human rights violations. For society, this points to the need for the development of healthy societies to be a (perhaps the) primary objective. When, for example, emerging evidence suggests that childhood abuse confers a risk of developing psychosis which is approximately equivalent to the risk of lung cancer caused by smoking (Cooke, 2014), it becomes reasonable to argue that avoidable social determinants such as domestic violence, peer bullying and premature sexualisation of children are public health crises (Read, 2012). Similarly, it is reasonable to view the evidence that people with mental illness die 15–20 years younger than other citizens (Thornicroft, 2011) through the lens of 'human rights violations'.

Citizenship is political, and the hard reality is that power is never given, it is always taken. In England, Parliament gave equal voting rights to women and men in 1928. But it was the suffragette movement, involving activists such as Emily Davison, who was killed when she threw herself under a horse belonging to King George V at the 1913 Epsom Derby, which led to this change. Women were not given the right to vote, they took it – through having a voice, arguing the case, and – sometimes – through direct action in order to get heard. Other alignments with emancipatory politics are outlined by Larry Davidson in his book *The roots of the recovery movement in psychiatry* (Davidson et al., 2010). Overall, it is clear that increasing access by people living with mental illness to the normal entitlements of citizenship will involve political action.

A Possible Future Combining Wellbeing and Recovery

In Chapter 9 of this volume, Oades, Deane and Crowe asserted that traditional mental health care emphasises *living with fewer symptoms*, and that mental health recovery may be seen as *living well with illness* and wellbeing as simply *living well*. These authors also compared processes of recovery from people with lived experience of mental illness with established theories of wellbeing. There are clearly overlaps in the landscapes of mental health recovery and theories of wellbeing – evidenced by mention of constructs such as hope, meaning, purpose, social relationships and autonomy. A further commonality is that of approach motivation, looking to move towards something positive, as opposed to movement away solely from something negative. We would argue that both recovery and wellbeing involve Isaiah Berlin's (1990) 'freedom to' (positive liberty), not only a 'freedom from' (negative liberty). Although a full philosophical coverage is beyond the scope of this chapter, we point to this as a possible future to better elaborate both recovery and wellbeing, and the values and issues of power which underpin them. In both cases of recovery and wellbeing, the presence of positive attributes, not solely the absence of negative attributes, is important to the discussion. In both cases, freedom from pain is an inadequate definition. Likewise, freedom to experience pleasure may also be.

We speculate that future converging recovery and wellbeing research will place a greater emphasis on how we can individually and collectively live lives imbued with meaning (which draws on understandings of spiritual, social and familial relations), what is needed to experience both agency and opportunity (and how the importance placed on these constructs varies across cultures) and what forms of social and political organisation maximise the resilience needed to deal with individual-level and population-level challenges.

Conclusion

To conclude in the subjunctive, imagine a world where the six themes described have gained traction. Nations around the world are consistently and reliably measuring wellbeing and using it to inform public policy making. Organisations around the world are required to account for the living capitals that relate to wellbeing. Wellbeing literacy has become a known term being measured alongside other indicators such as numeracy and literacy. Co-production has become an assumed practice, impacting not only mental health services, but health services and schools more broadly. Peer support has also become an accepted practice, changing relationships not only within mental health service provision, but more broadly in businesses and service systems. People living with mental illness have full citizenship and actively use it within a participatory democracy – as part of a broader emancipatory politics of wellbeing. This chapter represents an attempt to envisage possible futures within wellbeing and recovery – seeing beyond the restraints of the current moment.

References

Bartnik, E., & Chalmers, R. (2007). It's about more than the money: Local area coordination supporting people with disabilities. *Changing Relationships in the Provision of Social Care*, 49, 19–38.

Berlin, I. (1990). *Four essays on liberty*. Oxford, UK: Oxford University Press.

Boyle, D., & Harris, M. (2009). *The challenge of co-production*. London, UK: New Economics Foundation.

Bradley, P., & Willson, A. (2014). *Achieving prudent healthcare in NHS Wales* (revised). Cardiff, UK: Public Health Wales.

Chinman, M., George, P., Dougherty, R., Daniels, A., Ghose, S., Swift, A., et al. (2014). Peer support services for individuals with serious mental illnesses: Assessing the evidence. *Psychiatric Services*, 65, 429–441.

Cooke, A., Basset, T., Bentall, R., Boyle, M., Cupitt, C., Dillon, J., et al. (2014). *Understanding psychosis and schizophrenia*. London, UK: British Psychological Society.

Corker, E., Hamilton, S., Henderson, C., Weeks, C., Pinfold, V., Rose, D., et al. (2013). Experiences of discrimination among people using mental health services in England 2008–2011. *British Journal of Psychiatry*, Suppl. 55, s58–s63.

Cummins, J., & Miller, C. (2007). *Co-production, social capital and service effectiveness*. London, UK: OPM.

Davidson, L., Bellamy, C., Guy, K., & Miller, R. (2012). Peer support among persons with severe mental illnesses: A review of evidence and experience. *World Psychiatry*, 11, 123–128.

Davidson, L., Rakfeldt, J., & Strauss, J. (2010). *The roots of the recovery movement in psychiatry*. Chichester, UK: Wiley-Blackwell.

Diener, E. (2009). *Assessing well-being: The collected works of Ed Diener*. Dordrecht, the Netherlands: Springer.

Diener, E., Lucas, R. E., Schimmack, U., & Helliwell, J. F. (2009). *Well-being for public policy*. Oxford, UK: Oxford University Press.

Gillard, S., Gibson, S., Holley, J., & Lucock, M. (2015). Developing a change model for peer worker interventions in mental health services: A qualitative research study. *Epidemiology and Psychiatric Sciences*, 24, 435–445.

Gleeson-White, J. (2014). *Six capitals; The revolution capitalism has to have – Or can accountants save the planet?* Sydney, Australia: Allen & Unwin.

Helliwell, J. F. (2006). Well-being, social capital and public policy: What's new? *Economic Journal*, 116(510), C34–C45.

Henderson, C., Noblett, J., Parke, H., Clement, S., Caffrey, A., Gale-Grant, O., et al. (2014). Mental health-related stigma in health care and mental health-care settings. *Lancet Psychiatry*, 1, 467–482.

Layard, R. (2005). *Happiness: Lessons from a new science*. London, UK: Penguin.

Lloyd-Evans, B., Mayo-Wilson, E., Harrison, B., Istead, H., Brown, E., Pilling, S., et al. (2014). A systematic review and meta-analysis of randomised controlled trials of peer support for people with severe mental illness. *BMC Psychiatry*, 14, 39.

Loubens, P. (2007). *Villa family: Providing care for the elderly in rural France*. Besançon, France: Ages & Vie.

Miyamoto, Y., & Sono, T. (2012). Lessons from peer support among individuals with mental health difficulties: A review of the literature. *Clinical Practice and Epidemiology in Mental Health*, 8, 22–29.

Needham, C. (2009). *Co-production: An emerging evidence base for adult social care transformation*. London, UK: Social Care Institute for Excellence.

Pitt, V., Lowe, D., Hill, S., Prictor, M., Hetrick, S. E., Ryan, R., et al. (2013). Consumer-providers of care for adult clients of statutory mental health services. *Cochrane Database of Systematic Reviews*, March 28;(3):CD004807.

Read, J., & Bentall, R. (2012). Negative childhood experiences and mental health: Theoretical, clinical and primary prevention implications. *British Journal of Psychiatry*, 200, 89–91.

Roffey, S. (2008). Emotional literacy and the ecology of school wellbeing. *Educational and Child Psychology*, 25, 2, 29–39.

Seligman, M. E. P., Railton, P., Baumeister, R. F., & Sripada, C. (2013). Navigating into the future or driven by the past. *Perspectives on Psychological Science*, 8, 119–141.

Seyfang, G. (2004). Time banks: Rewarding community self-help in the inner city? *Community Development Journal*, 39, 62–71.

Shepherd, G., Boardman, J., & Burns, M. (2010). *Implementing recovery. A methodology for organisation change*. London, UK: Sainsbury Centre for Mental Health.

Slade, M. (2010). Mental illness and well-being: The central importance of positive psychology and recovery approaches. *BMC Health Services Research*, 10, 26.

Slade, M., Amering, M., Farkas, M., Hamilton, B., O'Hagan, M., Panther, G., et al. (2014). Uses and abuses of recovery: Implementing recovery-oriented practices in mental health systems. *World Psychiatry*, 13, 12–20.

Slade, M., & Longden, E. (2015). *The empirical evidence about mental health and recovery: How likely, how long, what helps?* Melbourne, Australia: MI Fellowship.

Stiglitz, J. E., Sen, A., & Fitoussi, J. P. (Eds.) (2009). *Report by the Commission on the Measurement of Economic Performance and Social Progress*. Paris, France: Commission on the Measurement of Economic Performance and Social Progress.

Sunderland, K. (2013). *Guidelines for the practice and training of peer support*. Ottawa, Ontario: Mental Health Commission of Canada.

The Evidence Centre (2015). *Peer support. What is it and does it work?* London, UK: Nesta.

Thornicroft, G. (2011). Physical health disparities and mental illness: The scandal of premature mortality. *British Journal of Psychiatry*, 199, 441–442.

Thornicroft, G., Brohan, E., Rose, D., Sartorius, N., Leese, M., & Group, I. S. (2009). Global pattern of experienced and anticipated discrimination against people with schizophrenia: A cross-sectional survey. *Lancet*, 9661, 408–415.

Trachtenberg, M., Parsonage, M., Shepherd, G., & Boardman, J. (2013). *Peer support in mental health care: Is it good value for money?* London, UK: Centre for Mental Health.

Walker, G., & Bryant, W. (2013). Peer support in adult mental health services: A metasynthesis of qualitative findings. *Psychiatric Rehabilitation Journal*, 36, 28–34.

Index